MORE PRAISE FROM
FOR THE JOBBANK SERIES...

"If you are looking for a job ... before you go to the newspapers and the help-wanted ads, listen to Bob Adams, publisher of *The Metropolitan New York JobBank*."

-Tom Brokaw, *NBC*

"Help on the job hunt ... Anyone who is job hunting in the New York area can find a lot of useful ideas in a new paperback called *The Metropolitan New York JobBank* ..."

-Angela Taylor, *New York Times*

"Because our listing is seen by people across the nation, it generates lots of resumes for us. We encourage unsolicited resumes. We'll always be listed [in *The Chicago JobBank*] as long as I'm in this career."

-Tom Fitzpatrick, Director of Human Resources
Merchandise Mart Properties, Inc.

"Job hunting is never fun, but this book can ease the ordeal ... [*The Los Angeles JobBank*] will help allay fears, build confidence, and avoid wheel-spinning."

-Robert W. Ross, *Los Angeles Times*

"Job hunters can't afford to waste time. *The Minneapolis-St. Paul JobBank* contains information that used to require hours of research in the library."

-Carmella Zagone
Minneapolis-based Human Resources Administrator

"*The Florida JobBank* is an invaluable job-search reference tool. It provides the most up-to-date information and contact names available for companies in Florida. I should know--it worked for me!"

-Rhonda Cody, Human Resources Consultant
Aetna Life and Casualty

"*The Boston JobBank* provides a handy map of employment possibilities in Greater Boston. This book can help in the initial steps of a job search by locating major employers, describing their business activities, and for most firms, by naming the contact person and listing typical professional positions. For recent college graduates, as well as experienced professionals, *The Boston JobBank* is an excellent place to begin a job search."

-Juliet F. Brudney, Career Columnist
Boston Globe

"No longer can jobseekers feel secure about finding employment just through want ads. With the tough competition in the job market, particularly in the Boston area, they need much more help. For this reason, *The Boston JobBank* will have a wide and appreciative audience of new graduates, job changers, and people relocating to Boston. It provides a good place to start a search for entry-level professional positions."

-Journal of College Placement

"*The Phoenix JobBank* is a first-class publication. The information provided is useful and current."

-Lyndon Denton
Director of Human Resources and Materials Management
Apache Nitrogen Products, Inc.

"[*The Ohio JobBank* is] a good resource for the job hunter."

-Virginia Tyler, Human Resources Manager
Battelle Columbus Operations/Ohio

"*The Ohio JobBank* is a very helpful tool for locating and researching potential employers. It's easy to use and even gives advice on winning the job."

-Judith G. Bishop, Manager of Employment
Barberton Citizens Hospital

"*The Seattle JobBank* is an essential resource for job hunters."

-Gil Lopez, Staffing Team Manager
Battelle Pacific Northwest Laboratories

"I read through the "Basics of Job Winning" and "Resumes" sections [in *The Dallas-Ft. Worth JobBank*] and found them to be very informative, with some positive tips for the job searcher. I believe the strategies outlined will bring success to any determined candidate."

-Camilla Norder, Professional Recruiter
Presbyterian Hospital of Dallas

"Through *The Dallas-Ft. Worth JobBank,* we've been able to attract high-quality candidates for several positions."

-Rob Bertino, Southern States Sales Manager
CompuServe

"Packed with helpful contacts, *The Houston JobBank* empowers its reader to launch an effective, strategic job search in the Houston metropolitan area."

-Andrew Ceperley, Director
College of Communication Career Services
The University of Texas at Austin

What makes the JobBank series the nation's premier line of employment guides?

With vital employment information on thousands of employers across the nation, the JobBank series is the most comprehensive and authoritative set of career directories available today.

Each book in the series provides information on **dozens of different industries** in a given city or area, with the primary employer listings providing contact information, telephone numbers, addresses, a summary of the firm's business, and in many cases descriptions of the firm's typical professional job categories, the principal educational backgrounds sought, and the fringe benefits offered.

In addition to the **detailed primary employer listings,** JobBank books give telephone numbers and addresses for **thousands of additional employers.**

All of the reference information in the JobBank series is as up-to-date and accurate as possible. Every year, the entire database is thoroughly researched and verified by mail and by telephone. Adams Media Corporation publishes **more local employment guides more often** than any other publisher of career directories.

In addition, the JobBank series features important information about the local job scene -- **forecasts on which industries are the hottest, overviews of local economic trends,** and **lists of regional professional associations,** so you can get your job hunt started off right.

Hundreds of discussions with job hunters show that they prefer information organized geographically, because most people look for jobs in specific areas. The JobBank series offers **30 regional titles**, from Minneapolis to Houston, and from Boston to San Francisco. Jobseekers moving to a particular area can review the local employment data not only for information on the type of industry most common to that region, but also for names of specific companies.

A condensed, but thorough, review of the entire job search process is presented in the chapter **The Basics of Job Winning**, a feature which has received many compliments from career counselors. In addition, each JobBank directory includes a section on **resumes and cover letters** the *New York Times* has acclaimed as "excellent."

The JobBank series gives job hunters the most comprehensive, timely, and accurate career information, organized and indexed to facilitate the job search. An entire career reference library, JobBank books are the consummate employment guides.

Published by Adams Media Corporation
260 Center Street, Holbrook, MA 02343

Manufactured in the United States of America.

Because addresses and telephone numbers of smaller companies change rapidly, we recommend you call each company and verify the information before mailing to the employers listed in this book. Mass mailings are not recommended.

While the publisher has made every reasonable effort to obtain and verify accurate information, occasional errors are inevitable due to the magnitude of the database. Should you discover an error, or if a company is missing, please write the editors at the above address so that we may update future editions.

ISBN: 1-55850-667-5

This book is available at quantity discounts for bulk purchases.
For information, call 800/872-5627.

Visit our exciting career and employment site at http://www.adamsjobbank.com

THE Virginia JobBank

Managing Editor:	Steven Graber
Series Editor:	Jennifer J. Pfalzgraf
Associate Editors:	Marcie DiPietro Andy Richardson
Editorial Assistants:	Ted Martin Wendy M. Rettman Julie P. Smalley Ashlee K. Stokes
Research Assistant:	Michelle Roy
Editorial Intern:	Kristin Cervero

Adams Media Corporation
HOLBROOK, MASSACHUSETTS

TABLE OF CONTENTS

INTRODUCTION

HOW TO USE THIS BOOK

Right now, you hold in your hands one of the most effective job-hunting tools available anywhere. In *The Virginia JobBank*, you will find a wide array of valuable information to help you launch or continue a rewarding career. But before you open to the book's employer listings and start calling about current job openings, take a few minutes to learn how best to put the resources presented in *The Virginia JobBank* to work for you.

The Virginia JobBank will help you to stand out from other jobseekers. While many people looking for a new job rely solely on newspaper help-wanted ads, this book offers you a much more effective job-search method -- direct contact. The direct contact method has been proven twice as effective as scanning the help-wanted ads. Instead of waiting for employers to come looking for you, you'll be far more effective going to them. While many of your competitors will use trial and error methods in trying to set up interviews, you'll learn not only how to get interviews, but what to expect once you've got them.

In the next few pages, we'll take you through each section of the book so you'll be prepared to get a jump-start on your competition.

The Virginia Job Market: An Overview

To get a feel for the state of the local job scene, read the introductory section called *The Virginia Job Market*. In it, we'll recap the economy's recent performance and the steps that local governments and business leaders are taking to bring new jobs to the area.

Even more importantly, you'll learn where the local economy is headed. What are the prospects for the industries that form the core of the region's economy? Which industries are growing fastest and which ones are laying off? Are there any companies or industries that are especially hot?

To answer these questions for you, we've pored over local business journals and newspapers and interviewed local business leaders and labor analysts. Whether you are new to the area and need a source of regional information, or are a lifelong resident just looking for a fresh start in a new job, you'll find this section to be a concise thumbnail sketch of where the jobs are.

This type of information is potent ammunition to bring into an interview. Showing that you're well versed in current industry trends helps give you an edge over job applicants who haven't done their homework.

Basics of Job Winning

Preparation. Strategy. Time-management. These are three of the most important elements of a successful job search. *Basics of Job Winning* helps you address these and all the other elements needed to find the right job.

One of your first priorities should be to define your personal career objectives. What qualities make a job desirable to you? Creativity? High pay?

Prestige? Use *Basics of Job Winning* to weigh these questions. Then use the rest of the chapter to design a strategy to find a job that matches your criteria.

In *Basics of Job Winning,* you'll learn which job-hunting techniques work, and which don't. We've reviewed the pros and cons of mass mailings, help-wanted ads, and direct contact. We'll show you how to develop and approach contacts in your field; how to research a prospective employer; and how to use that information to get an interview and the job.

Also included in *Basics of Job Winning*: interview dress code and etiquette, the "do's and don'ts" of interviewing, sample interview questions, and the often forgotten art of what to do after the interview. We also deal with some of the unique problems faced by those jobseekers who are currently employed, those who have lost a job, and college students conducting their first job search.

Resumes and Cover Letters

The approach you take to writing your resume and cover letter can often mean the difference between getting an interview and never being noticed. In this section, we discuss different formats, as well as what to put on (and what to leave off) your resume. We review the benefits and drawbacks of professional resume writers, and the importance of a follow-up letter. Also included in this section are sample resumes and cover letters which you can use as models.

The Employer Listings

Employers are listed alphabetically by industry, and within each industry, by company names. When a company does business under a person's name, like "John Smith & Co.", the company is usually listed by the surname's spelling (in this case "S"). Exceptions occur when a company's name is widely recognized, like "JCPenney" or "Howard Johnson Motor Lodge." In those cases, the company's first name is the key ("J" and "H" respectively).

The Virginia JobBank covers a very wide range of industries. Each company profile is assigned to one of the industry chapters listed below.

Accounting and Management Consulting
Advertising, Marketing, and Public Relations
Aerospace
Apparel and Textiles
Architecture, Construction, and Engineering
Arts and Entertainment/Recreation
Automotive
Banking/Savings and Loans
Biotechnology, Pharmaceuticals, and Scientific R&D
Business Services and Non-Scientific Research
Charities and Social Services
Chemicals/Rubber and Plastics
Communications: Telecommunications and Broadcasting
Computer Hardware, Software, and Services
Educational Services
Electronic/Industrial Electrical Equipment
Environmental and Waste Management Services
Fabricated/Primary Metals and Products
Financial Services
Food and Beverage/Agriculture

Government
Health Care: Services, Equipment, and Products
Hotels and Restaurants
Insurance
Legal Services
Manufacturing: Miscellaneous Consumer
Manufacturing: Miscellaneous Industrial
Mining/Gas/Petroleum/Energy Related
Miscellaneous Wholesaling
Paper and Wood Products
Printing and Publishing
Real Estate
Retail
Stone, Clay, Glass, and Concrete Products
Transportation
Utilities: Electric/Gas/Water

Many of the company listings offer detailed company profiles. In addition to company names, addresses, and phone numbers, these listings also include contact names or hiring departments, and descriptions of each company's products and/or services. Many of these listings also feature a variety of additional information including:

Common positions - A list of job titles that the company commonly fills when it is hiring, organized in alphabetical order from Accountant to X-ray Technician. Note: Keep in mind that *The Virginia JobBank* is a directory of major employers in the area, not a directory of openings currently available. Many of the companies listed will be hiring, others will not. However, since most professional job openings are filled without the placement of help-wanted ads, contacting the employers in this book directly is still a more effective method than browsing the Sunday papers.

Educational backgrounds sought - A list of educational backgrounds that companies seek when hiring.

Benefits - What kind of benefits packages are available from these employers? Here you'll find a broad range of benefits, from the relatively common (medical insurance) to those that are much more rare (health club membership; child daycare assistance).

Special programs - Does the company offer training programs, internships, or apprenticeships? These programs can be important to first time jobseekers and college students looking for practical work experience. Many employer profiles will include information on these programs.

Parent company - If an employer is a subsidiary of a larger company, the name of that parent company will often be listed here. Use this information to supplement your company research before contacting the employer.

Number of employees - The number of workers a company employs.

Companies may also include information on other U.S. locations and any stock exchange the firm may be listed on.

Because so many job openings are with small and mid-sized employers, we've also included the addresses and phone numbers of such employers. While none of these listings include any additional hiring information, many of them do offer rewarding career opportunities. These companies are found under each industry heading. Within each industry, they are organized by the type of product or service offered.

A note on all employer listings that appear in *The Virginia JobBank*: This book is intended as a starting point. It is not intended to replace any effort that you, the jobseeker, should devote to your job hunt. Keep in mind that while a great deal of effort has been put into collecting and verifying the company profiles provided in this book, addresses and contact names change regularly. Inevitably, some contact names listed herein have changed even before you read this. We recommend you contact a company before mailing your resume to ensure nothing has changed.

At the end of each industry section, we have included a directory of other industry-specific resources to help you in your job search. These include: professional and industrial associations, many of which can provide employment advice and job search help; magazines that cover the industry; and additional directories that may supplement the employer listings in this book.

Employment Services

Immediately following the employer listings section of this book are listings of local employment services firms. Many jobseekers supplement their own efforts by contracting "temp" services, headhunters, and other employment search firms to generate potential job opportunities.

This section is a comprehensive listing of such firms, arranged alphabetically under the headings Employment Agencies, Temporary Agencies, and Executive Search Firms. Each listing includes the firm's name, address, telephone number and contact person. Most listings also include the industries the firm specializes in, the type of positions commonly filled, and the number of jobs filled annually.

Index

The Virginia JobBank index is a straight alphabetical listing.

THE VIRGINIA JOB MARKET: AN OVERVIEW

Virginia has a great deal to offer prospective employees and entrepreneurs alike. While its moderate climate, rich historical background, and hundreds of miles of scenic coastline make the prospect of relocating to Virginia appealing, even more persuasive to business people are the commonwealth's economic history and impressive labor trends.

In many respects, Virginia is truly booming. Its population growth through the year 2000 is expected to be nearly twice the national rate, while its unemployment rate has been, and is expected to remain, somewhere between two-thirds and three-quarters of the national jobless rate. Thirteen *Fortune* 500 companies are headquartered here, placing Virginia second only to Georgia as the Southeast's leading *Fortune* 500 headquarters state. The bulk of employment growth has been centered around Virginia's three largest metropolitan areas: Northern Virginia, Norfolk-Virginia Beach-Newport News, and Richmond-Petersburg. Most major industries, with the exception of manufacturing and mining, have experienced continued growth over the last ten years, and as seems to be the trend nationwide, the service-providing sector has paved the way.

Retail Trade

As the number of dual-income families in Virginia continues to increase, retail trade should see a marked rise in employment. Families will have more money, but less time to provide services for themselves, increasing the need to eat outside the home, bring home prepared foods, and visit the automobile repair shop. Retail sales are expected to provide more openings than any other occupation, employing a projected 132,470 Virginians by the year 2000 -- up from 1988's 103,190 employees. Leading retailers are projected to be: eating and drinking establishments, accounting for 27.5 percent of employment growth; food stores (16.5 percent); general stores (14 percent); and automobile dealers and service stations (11.8 percent). One leading retailer is *Fortune* 500 company **Circuit City Stores** (headquartered in Richmond), which currently employs 3,400 people in Virginia.

Business Services

Business services, between 1988 and 2000, are expected to account for a projected 40.4 percent of all employment growth in the services division. Employment opportunities are projected for secretaries, office clerks, and bookkeeping and accounting clerks, among others. Demand for business services is fueled by the increasing push for corporate productivity, leading companies to contract out work formerly done in-house, including advertising, photocopying, payroll processing, commercial equipment rental, building maintenance, security, and data processing. One Virginia company that is filling that need is **DYNCORP**, one of the nation's leading providers of management and technical services to industry and government organizations. Headquartered in Reston, DYNCORP currently employs an estimated 23,600 people nationwide.

Health Services

Second only to business services, health services are expected to make up 24.5 percent of the entire service division's employment growth between the years 1988 and 2000. In Richmond alone, five of the area's 50 largest employers are hospitals, accounting for over 6,500 jobs. Leading the way are **St. Mary's Hospital**, **Henrico Doctor's Hospital**, and **Richmond Memorial Hospital**, employing 1,723, 1,383, and 1,350 respectively. Add to this the fact that by the year 2000, Virginia's elderly (65+) are expected to account for 11.1 percent of the state's population, up from 9.5 percent in 1980. This rise in older citizens has, and will continue to, create a need for more health care workers, primarily home health aides (HHAs). HHAs are projected to have a 138 percent increase in employment between 1992 and 2005, giving them the highest growth rate of all service occupations. According to the Bureau of Labor Statistics, other hot sectors of the health care industry include: physical and corrective therapy assistants, radiologic technologists and technicians, medical records technicians, and medical assistants.

Manufacturing

Virginia's manufacturing employment growth, although declining, is still well above the national level. The industry's future in Virginia, however, does not look promising. By the year 2000, the number of people employed in manufacturing is projected to fall to 425,500, down from 427,400 in 1988. In keeping with what seems to be a national trend, this is due in part to the increase in automation designed to improve productivity and eliminate the need for manual labor at manufacturing facilities. *One bright spot:* Virginia's manufacturing employment has not fallen below its 1970 level, despite downturns in the nation's economy since that time. In fact, Virginia posted a 10.1 percent increase in manufacturing employment from 1970 to 1994, during a time when national manufacturing employment fell 6.9 percent.

Mining

In a situation similar to that of the manufacturing industry, automation has taken its toll on Virginia's mining work force, enabling mine owners to increase productivity while decreasing their number of employees. Despite the fact that in 1993, over 40 million tons of bituminous coal (one of Virginia's most important natural commodities) valued at $1.23 billion were produced from the Southwest Virginia Coal Field, industry employment levels are slipping. Between 1992 and 1994, mining employment dropped by about 1,300 jobs, or 10 percent. *The silver lining:* Although employment levels are decreasing, the mining industry paid the highest weekly wages in Virginia in 1994, an average of $700 per week.

Construction

By the year 2000, the construction industry is projected to employ an estimated 216,300 people in Virginia -- up from the 1988 figure of 181,600. Close to two-thirds of that growth should be for special trade contractors (plumbing, electrical, and masonry). Heavy construction, including the building of bridges, tunnels, pipelines, and power lines, along with the construction of buildings, highways, and streets, is also expected to increase, but at a much slower pace. Virginia's construction companies include **NVR, Inc.**, one of the nation's leading home builders, and its subsidiaries, **NV Homes** and **Ryan Homes, Inc.**

WEST VIRGINIA

West Virginia's economic outlook has long been dependent on its geographical location in the heart of the Appalachian Region. Mineral wealth, with an abundance of natural resources, including coal, oil, natural gas, salt, limestone, and clay, helped form the basis of West Virginia's economic development. However, the mining industry has not been as quick as other, more broad-based industries to mature economically, and has been subject to rather wild fluctuations. Within recent decades, technological improvements in the extraction process have drastically minimized the labor required, thus creating a surplus of workers that have been snapped up by other West Virginia industries.

The Software Valley

With the mining industry, once the mainstay of the state's economy, becoming less lucrative, the time is ripe for new industry growth in West Virginia. Along Route I-79, spanning Harrison, Marion, and Monongalia Counties, a large-scale project known as the Software Valley has been formed. Initiated by state government and business, academic, and community groups, the Software Valley is aimed at stimulating growth in computer services, making the high-tech industry a leading state employer. The area is already home to a number of high-tech companies, including the **Federal Bureau of Investigation**'s identification facility located in Clarksburg, and is still experiencing rapid growth.

Manufacturing

Despite its relatively stale performance over the past couple of years, West Virginia's manufacturing industry has recovered and is beginning to show steady growth. Leading the way is the lumber, wood products, and furniture industry in eastern and southern West Virginia. Fabricated metals, electrical, and nonelectrical machinery have also recorded increases in employment in this decade. While the production of durable goods has been steadily increasing, nondurable goods employment has continued to decline. Once a colossal statewide employer, the chemical industry, instituting corporate downsizing to improve plant productivity, has been largely responsible for the overall decrease in the nondurable goods industry.

Services

West Virginia's service-producing sector has shown rapid growth in the 1990s, and is expected to grow by another 20,000 jobs between July 1996 and July 1998. Business services (with the advent of telemarketing) and health services (with West Virginia's sizable elderly population) have experienced the most substantial growth, due in part to large employers such as **St. Joseph Hospital** in Parkersburg, with a staff of 1,500. Jobs in retail, including eating and drinking places, general merchandise stores, auto dealers and service stations, and food stores, have also swelled.

Other sources of information for jobseekers:

Commonwealth of Virginia, Governor's Office, Department of Economic Development, 901 East Byrd Street, P.O. Box 798, Richmond VA 23206-0798. 804/371-8100.

Virginia Employment Commission, Economic Information Services Division, 703 East Main Street, Richmond VA 23219-3307. 804/786-8223.

Greater Richmond Partnership of Virginia, 901 East Byrd Street, Suite 801, Richmond VA 23219-4070. 804/643-3227.

West Virginia Bureau of Employment Programs, Office of Labor and Economic Research, 112 California Avenue, Charleston WV 25305-0112. 304/558-2660.

THE JOB SEARCH

THE BASICS OF JOB WINNING: A CONDENSED REVIEW

This chapter is divided into four sections. The first section explains the fundamentals that every jobseeker should know, especially first-time jobseekers. The following three sections deal with special situations faced by specific types of jobseekers: those who are currently employed, those who have lost a job, and college students.

THE BASICS:

Things Everyone Needs to Know

Career Planning

The first step to finding your ideal job is to clearly define your objectives. This is better known as career planning (or life planning if you wish to emphasize the importance of combining the two). Career planning has become a field of study in and of itself.

If you are thinking of choosing or switching careers, we particularly emphasize two things. First, choose a career where you will enjoy most of the day-to-day tasks. This sounds obvious, but most of us have at one point or another been attracted by a glamour industry or a prestigious job title without thinking of the most important consideration: Would we enjoy performing the everyday tasks the position entails?

The second key consideration is that you are not merely choosing a career, but also a lifestyle. Career counselors indicate that one of the most common problems people encounter in job-seeking is that they fail to consider how well-suited they are for a particular position or career. For example, some people, attracted to management consulting by good salaries, early responsibility, and high-level corporate exposure, do not adapt well to the long hours, heavy travel demands, and constant pressure to produce. Be sure to ask yourself how you might adapt to not only the day-to-day duties and working environment that a specific position entails, but also how you might adapt to the demands of that career or industry choice as a whole.

Choosing Your Strategy

Assuming that you've established your career objectives, the next step of the job search is to develop a strategy. If you don't take the time to develop a strategy and lay out a plan, you may find yourself going in circles after several weeks of randomly searching for opportunities that always seem just beyond your reach.

The most common job-seeking techniques are:

- following up on help-wanted advertisements
- using employment services
- relying on personal contacts
- contacting employers directly (the Direct Contact method)

Many professionals have been successful in finding better jobs using each one of these approaches. However, the Direct Contact method boasts twice the success rate of the others. So unless you have specific reasons to believe that other strategies would work best for you, Direct Contact should form the foundation of your job search.

If you prefer to use other methods as well, try to expend at least half your effort on Direct Contact, spending the rest on all of the other methods combined. Millions of other jobseekers have already proven that Direct Contact has been twice as effective in obtaining employment, so why not benefit from their experience?

Setting Your Schedule

With your strategy in mind, the next step is to work out the details of your search. The most important detail is setting up a schedule. Of course, since job searches aren't something most people do regularly, it may be hard to estimate how long each step will take. Nonetheless, it is important to have a plan so that you can monitor your progress.

When outlining your job search schedule, have a realistic time frame in mind. If you will be job-searching full-time, your search could take at least two months or more. If you can only devote part-time effort, it will probably take at least four months.

You probably know a few currently employed people who seem to spend their whole lives searching for a better job in their spare time. Don't be one of them. If you are presently working and don't feel like devoting a lot of energy to job-seeking right now, then wait. Focus on enjoying your present position, performing your best on the job, and storing up energy for when you are really ready to begin your job search.

The first step in beginning your job search is to clearly define your objectives.

Those of you who are currently unemployed should remember that job-hunting is tough work physically and emotionally. It is also intellectually demanding work that requires you to be at your best. So don't tire yourself out by working on your job campaign around the clock. At the same time, be sure to discipline yourself. The most logical way to manage your time while looking for a job is to keep your regular working hours.

If you are searching full-time and have decided to choose several different contact methods, we recommend that you divide up each week, designating some time for each method. By trying several approaches at once, you can evaluate how promising each seems and alter your schedule accordingly. But be careful -- don't judge the success of a particular technique just by the sheer number of interviews you obtain. Positions advertised in the newspaper, for instance, are likely to generate many more interviews per opening than positions that are filled without being advertised.

If you are searching part-time and decide to try several different contact methods, we recommend that you try them sequentially. You simply won't have enough time to put a meaningful amount of effort into more than one method at once. Estimate the length of your job search, and then allocate so many weeks or months for each contact method, beginning with Direct Contact.

And remember that all schedules are meant to be broken. The purpose of setting a schedule is not to rush you to your goal but to help you periodically evaluate how you're progressing.

The Direct Contact Method

Once you have scheduled your time, you are ready to begin your search in earnest. If you decide to begin with the Direct Contact method, the first step is to develop a checklist for categorizing the types of firms for which you'd like to work. You might categorize firms by product line, size, customer type (such as industrial or consumer), growth prospects, or geographical location. Your list of important criteria might be very short. If it is, good! The shorter it is, the easier it will be to locate a company that is right for you.

Now you will want to use this *JobBank* book to assemble your list of potential employers. Choose firms where *you* are most likely to be able to find a job. Try matching your skills with those that a specific job demands. Consider where your skills might be in demand, the degree of competition for employment, and the employment outlook at each company.

Separate your prospect list into three groups. The first 25 percent will be your primary target group, the next 25 percent will be your secondary group, and the remaining names you can keep in reserve.

After you form your prospect list, begin work on your resume. Refer to the Resumes and Cover Letters section following this chapter to get ideas.

Once your resume is complete, begin researching your first batch of prospective employers. You will want to determine whether you would be happy working at the firms you are researching and to get a better idea of what their employment needs might be. You also need to obtain enough information to sound highly informed about the company during phone conversations and in mail correspondence. But don't go all out on your research yet! You probably won't be able to arrange interviews with some of these firms, so save your big research effort until you start to arrange interviews. Nevertheless, you should plan to spend several hours researching each firm. Do your research in batches to save time and energy. Start with this book, and find out what you can about each of the firms in your primary target group. Contact any pertinent professional associations that may be able to help you learn more about an employer. Read industry

> **The more you know about a company, the more likely you are to catch an interviewer's eye. (You'll also face fewer surprises once you get the job!)**

publications looking for articles on the firm. (Addresses of associations and names of important publications are listed after each industrial section of employer listings in this book.) Then try additional resources at your local library. Keep organized, and maintain a folder on each firm.

If you discover something that really disturbs you about the firm (they are about to close their only local office), or if you discover that your chances of getting a job there are practically nil (they have just instituted a hiring freeze), then cross them off your prospect list. If possible, supplement your research efforts by contacting individuals who know the firm well. Ideally you should make an informal contact with someone at that particular firm, but often a direct competitor, or a major supplier or customer, will be able to supply you with just as much information. At the very least, try to obtain whatever printed information the company has available -- not just annual reports, but product brochures and any other printed materials that the firm may have to offer, either about its operations or about career opportunities.

DEVELOPING YOUR CONTACTS: NETWORKING

Some career counselors feel that the best route to a better job is through somebody you already know or through somebody to whom you can be introduced. These counselors recommend that you build your contact base beyond your current acquaintances by asking each one to introduce you, or refer you, to additional people in your field of interest.

The theory goes like this: You might start with 15 personal contacts, each of whom introduces you to three additional people, for a total of 45 additional contacts. Then each of these people introduces you to three additional people, which adds 135 additional contacts. Theoretically, you will soon know every person in the industry.

Of course, developing your personal contacts does not work quite as smoothly as the theory suggests because some people will not be able to introduce you to anyone. The further you stray from your initial contact base, the weaker your references may be. So, if you do try developing your own contacts, try to begin with as many people that you know personally as you can. Dig into your personal phone book and your holiday greeting card list and locate old classmates from school. Be particularly sure to approach people who perform your personal business such as your lawyer, accountant, banker, doctor, stockbroker, and insurance agent. These people develop a very broad contact base due to the nature of their professions.

Getting the Interview

Now it is time to arrange an interview, time to make the Direct Contact. If you have read many books on job-searching, you may have noticed that most of these books tell you to avoid the personnel office like the plague. It is said that the personnel office never hires people; they screen candidates. Unfortunately, this is often the case. If you can identify the appropriate manager with the authority to hire you, you should try to contact that person directly. However, this will take a lot of time in each case, and often you'll be bounced back to personnel despite your efforts. So we suggest that initially you begin your Direct Contact campaign through personnel offices. If it seems that the firms on your prospect list do little hiring through personnel, you might consider some alternative courses of action.

The three obvious means of initiating Direct Contact are:

- Showing up unannounced
- Mail
- Phone calls

Cross out the first one right away. You should never show up to seek a professional position without an appointment. Even if you are somehow lucky enough to obtain an interview, you will appear so unprofessional that you will not be seriously considered.

Mail contact seems to be a good choice if you have not been in the job market for a while. You can take your time to prepare a letter, say exactly what you want, and of course include your resume. Remember that employers receive many resumes every day. Don't be surprised if you do not get a response to your inquiry, and don't spend weeks waiting for responses that may never come. If you do send a letter, follow it up (or precede it) with a phone call. This will increase your impact, and because of the initial research you did, will underscore both your familiarity with and your interest in the firm.

Another alternative is to make a "Cover Call." Your Cover Call should be just like your cover letter: concise. Your first statement should interest the employer in you. Then try to subtly mention your familiarity with the firm. Don't be overbearing; keep your introduction to three sentences or less. Be pleasant, self-confident, and relaxed. This will greatly increase the chances of the person at the other end of the line developing the conversation. But don't press. If you are asked to follow up with "something in the mail," this signals the conversation's natural end. Don't try to prolong the conversation once it has ended, and don't ask what they want to receive in the mail. Always send your resume and a highly personalized follow-up letter, reminding the addressee of the phone conversation. *Always* include a cover letter if you are asked to send a resume.

Always include a cover letter if you are asked to send a resume.

Unless you are in telephone sales, making smooth and relaxed cover calls will probably not come easily. Practice them on your own, and then with your friends or relatives.

If you obtain an interview as a result of a telephone conversation, be sure to send a thank-you note reiterating the points you made during the

DON'T BOTHER WITH MASS MAILINGS OR BARRAGES OF PHONE CALLS

Direct Contact does not mean burying every firm within a hundred miles with mail and phone calls. Mass mailings rarely work in the job hunt. This also applies to those letters that are personalized -- but dehumanized -- on an automatic typewriter or computer. Don't waste your time or money on such a project; you will fool no one but yourself.

The worst part of sending out mass mailings, or making unplanned phone calls to companies you have not researched, is that you are likely to be remembered as someone with little genuine interest in the firm, who lacks sincerity -- somebody that nobody wants to hire.

HELP WANTED ADVERTISEMENTS

Only a small fraction of professional job openings are advertised. Yet the majority of jobseekers -- and quite a few people not in the job market -- spend a lot of time studying the help wanted ads. As a result, the competition for advertised openings is often very severe.

A moderate-sized employer told us about their experience advertising in the help wanted section of a major Sunday newspaper:

It was a disaster. We had over 500 responses from this relatively small ad in just one week. We have only two phone lines in this office and one was totally knocked out. We'll never advertise for professional help again.

If you insist on following up on help wanted ads, then research a firm before you reply to an ad. Preliminary research might help to separate you from all of the other professionals responding to that ad, many of whom will have only a passing interest in the opportunity. It will also give you insight about a particular firm, to help you determine if it is potentially a good match. That said, your chances of obtaining a job through the want ads are still much smaller than they are with the Direct Contact method.

conversation. You will appear more professional and increase your impact. However, unless specifically requested, don't mail your resume once an interview has been arranged. Take it with you to the interview instead.

Preparing for the Interview

Once the interview has been arranged, begin your in-depth research. You should arrive at an interview knowing the company upside-down and inside-out. You need to know the company's products, types of customers, subsidiaries, parent company, principal locations, rank in the industry, sales and profit trends, type of ownership, size, current plans, and much more. By this time you have probably narrowed your job search to one industry. Even if you haven't, you should still be familiar with the trends in the firm's industry, the firm's principal competitors and their relative performance, and the direction in which the industry leaders are headed.

Dig into every resource you can! Read the company literature, the trade press, the business press, and if the company is public, call your stockbroker (if you have one) and ask for additional information. If possible, speak to someone at the firm before the interview, or if not, speak to someone at a competing firm. The more time you spend, the better. Even if you feel extremely pressed for time, you should set aside several hours for pre-interview research.

You should arrive at an interview knowing the company upside-down and inside-out.

If you have been out of the job market for some time, don't be surprised if you find yourself tense during your first few interviews. It will probably happen every time you re-enter the market, not just when you seek your first job after getting out of school.

Tension is natural during an interview, but knowing you have done a thorough research job should put you more at ease. Make a list of questions that you think might be asked in each interview. Think out your answers carefully and practice them with a friend. Tape record your responses to the problem questions. If you feel particularly unsure of your interviewing skills, arrange your first interviews at firms you are not as interested in. (But remember it is common courtesy to seem enthusiastic about the possibility of working for any firm at which you interview.) Practice again on your own after these first few interviews. Go over the difficult questions that you were asked.

Interview Attire

How important is the proper dress for a job interview? Buying a complete wardrobe of Brooks Brothers pinstripes or Donna Karan suits, donning new wing tips or pumps, and having your hair styled every morning are not enough to guarantee you a career position as an investment banker. But on the other hand, if you can't find a clean, conservative suit or won't take the time to wash your hair, then you are just wasting your time by interviewing at all.

Top personal grooming is as important as finding appropriate clothes for a job interview. Careful grooming indicates both a sense of thoroughness and self-confidence. This is not the time to make a statement -- take out the extra earrings and avoid any garish hair colors not found in nature. Women should not wear excessive makeup, and both men and women should refrain from wearing any perfume or cologne (it only takes a small spritz to leave an allergic interviewer with a fit of sneezing and a bad impression of your meeting). Men should be freshly shaven, even if the interview is late in the day, and men with long hair should have it pulled back and neat.

Men applying for any professional position should wear a suit, preferably in a conservative color such as navy or charcoal gray. It is easy to get away with wearing the same dark suit to consecutive interviews at the same company; just be sure to wear a different shirt and tie for each interview.

Women should also wear a businesslike suit. Professionalism still dictates a suit with a skirt, rather than slacks, as proper interview garb for women. This is usually true even at companies where pants are acceptable attire for female employees. As much as you may disagree with this guideline, the more prudent time to fight this standard is after you land the job.

SKIRT VS. PANTS:
An Interview Dilemma

For those women who are still convinced that pants are acceptable interview attire, listen to the words of one career counselor from a prestigious New England college:

I had a student who told me that since she knew women in her industry often wore pants to work, she was going to wear pants to her interviews. Almost every recruiter commented that her pants were "too casual," and even referred to her as "the one with the pants." The funny thing was that one of the recruiters who commented on her pants had been wearing jeans!

The final selection of candidates for a job opening won't be determined by dress, of course. However, inappropriate dress can quickly eliminate a first-round candidate. So while you shouldn't spend a fortune on a new wardrobe, you should be sure that your clothes are adequate. The key is to dress at least as formally or slightly more formally and more conservatively than the position would suggest.

What to Bring

Be complete. Everyone needs a watch, a pen, and a notepad. Finally, a briefcase or a leather-bound folder (containing extra, *unfolded*, copies of your resume) will help complete the look of professionalism.

Sometimes the interviewer will be running behind schedule. Don't be upset, be sympathetic. There is often pressure to interview a lot of candidates and to quickly fill a demanding position. So be sure to come to your interview with good reading material to keep yourself occupied and relaxed.

The Interview

The very beginning of the interview is the most important part because it determines the tone for the rest of it. Those first few moments are especially crucial. Do you smile when you meet? Do you establish enough eye contact, but not too much? Do you walk into the office with a self-assured and confident stride? Do you shake hands firmly? Do you

BE PREPARED:
Some Common Interview Questions

Tell me about yourself...

Why did you leave your last job?

What excites you in your current job?

Where would you like to be in five years?

How much overtime are you willing to work?

What would your previous/present employer tell me about you?

Tell me about a difficult situation that you faced at your previous/present job.

What are your greatest strengths?

What are your greatest weaknesses?

Describe a work situation where you took initiative and went beyond your normal responsibilities.

Why do you wish to work for this firm?

Why should we hire you?

make small talk easily without being garrulous? It is human nature to judge people by that first impression, so make sure it is a good one. But most of all, try to be yourself.

Often the interviewer will begin, after the small talk, by telling you about the company, the division, the department, or perhaps, the position. Because of your detailed research, the information about the company should be repetitive for you, and the interviewer would probably like nothing better than to avoid this regurgitation of the company biography. So if you can do so tactfully, indicate to the interviewer that you are very familiar with the firm. If he or she seems intent on providing you with background information, despite your hints, then acquiesce.

But be sure to remain attentive. If you can manage to generate a brief discussion of the company or the industry at this point, without being forceful, great. It will help to further build rapport, underscore your interest, and increase your impact.

Soon (if it didn't begin that way) the interviewer will begin the questions, many of which you will have already practiced. This period of the interview usually falls into one of two categories (or somewhere in between): either a structured interview, where the interviewer has a prescribed set of questions to ask; or an unstructured interview, where the interviewer will ask only leading questions to get you to talk about yourself, your experiences, and your goals. Try to sense as quickly as possible in which direction the interviewer wishes to proceed. This will make the interviewer feel more relaxed and in control of the situation.

> **The interviewer's job is to find a reason to turn you down; your job is to not provide that reason.**
>
> -John L. LaFevre, author,
> *How You Really Get Hired*
>
> Reprinted from the 1989/90 *CPC Annual,* with permission of the National Association of Colleges and Employers (formerly College Placement Council, Inc.), copyright holder.

Remember to keep attuned to the interviewer and make the length of your answers appropriate to the situation. If you are really unsure as to how detailed a response the interviewer is seeking, then ask.

As the interview progresses, the interviewer will probably mention some of the most important responsibilities of the position. If applicable, draw parallels between your experience and the demands of the position as detailed by the interviewer. Describe your past experience in the same manner that you do on your resume: emphasizing results and achievements and not merely describing activities. But don't exaggerate. Be on the level about your abilities.

The first interview is often the toughest, where many candidates are screened out. If you are interviewing for a very competitive position, you will have to make an impression that will last. Focus on a few of your greatest strengths that are relevant to the position. Develop these points carefully, state them again in different words, and then try to summarize them briefly at the end of the interview.

Often the interviewer will pause toward the end and ask if you have any questions. Particularly in a structured interview, this might be the one chance to really show your knowledge of and interest in the firm. Have a list prepared of specific questions that are of real interest to you. Let your questions subtly show your research and your knowledge of the firm's activities. It is wise to have an extensive list of questions, as several of them may be answered during the interview.

> **Getting a job offer is a lot like getting a marriage proposal. Someone is not going to offer it unless they're pretty sure you're going to accept it.**
>
> -Marilyn Hill, Associate Director, Career Center, Carleton College

Do not turn your opportunity to ask questions into an interrogation. Avoid reading directly from your list of questions, and ask questions that you are fairly certain the interviewer can answer (remember how you feel when you cannot answer a question during an interview).

Even if you are unable to determine the salary range beforehand, do not ask about it during the first interview. You can always ask about it later. Above all, don't ask about fringe benefits until you have been offered a position. (Then be sure to get all the details.)

Try not to be negative about anything during the interview (particularly any past employer or any previous job). Be cheerful. Everyone likes to work with someone who seems to be happy.

Don't let a tough question throw you off base. If you don't know the answer to a question, simply say so -- do not apologize. Just smile. Nobody can answer every question -- particularly some of the questions that are asked in job interviews.

Before your first interview, you may be able to determine how many rounds of interviews there usually are for positions at your level. (Of course it may differ quite a bit even within the different levels of one firm.) Usually you can count on attending at least two or three interviews, although some firms are known to give a minimum of six interviews for all professional positions. While you should be more relaxed as you return for subsequent interviews, the pressure will be on. The more prepared you are, the better.

Depending on what information you are able to obtain, you might want to vary your strategy quite a bit from interview to interview. For instance, if the first interview is a screening interview, then be sure a few of your strengths really stand out. On the other hand, if later interviews are primarily with people who are in a position to veto your hiring, but not to push it forward, then you should primarily focus on building rapport as opposed to reiterating and developing your key strengths.

If it looks as though your skills and background do not match the position the interviewer was hoping to fill, ask him or her if there is another division or subsidiary that perhaps could profit from your talents.

After the Interview

Write a follow-up letter immediately after the interview, while it is still fresh in the interviewer's mind (see the sample follow-up letter format found in the Resumes and Cover Letters chapter). Then, if you haven't heard from the interviewer within a week, call to stress your continued interest in the firm, and the position, and request a second interview.

THE BALANCING ACT:

Looking for a New Job While Currently Employed

For those of you who are still employed, job-searching will be particularly tiring because it must be done in addition to your normal work responsibilities. So don't overwork yourself to the point where you show up to interviews looking exhausted and start to slip behind at your current job. On the other hand, don't be tempted to quit your present job! The long hours are worth it. Searching for a job while you have one puts you in a position of strength.

Making Contact

If you're expected to be in your office during the business day, then you have additional problems to deal with. How can you work interviews into the business day? And if you work in an open office, how can you even call to set up interviews? As much as possible you should keep up the effort and the appearances on your present job. So maximize your use of the lunch hour, early mornings, and late afternoons for calling. If you keep trying, you'll be surprised how often you will be able to reach the executive you are trying to contact during your out-of-office hours. You can catch people as early as 8 a.m. and as late as 6 p.m. on frequent occasions.

Scheduling Interviews

Your inability to interview at any time other than lunch just might work to your advantage. If you can, try to set up as many interviews as possible for your lunch hour. This will go a long way to creating a relaxed atmosphere. (Who isn't happy when eating?) But be sure the interviews don't stray too far from the agenda on hand.

Lunchtime interviews are much easier to obtain if you have substantial career experience. People with less experience will often find no alternative to taking time off for interviews. If you have to take time off, you have to take time off. But try to do this as little as possible. Try to take the whole day off in order to avoid being blatantly obvious about your job search, and try to schedule two to three interviews for the same day. (It is very difficult to maintain an optimum level of energy at more than three interviews in one day.) Explain to the interviewer why you might have to juggle your interview schedule -- he/she should honor the respect you're

Try calling as early as 8 a.m. and as late as 6 p.m. You'll be surprised how often you will be able to reach the executive you want during these times of the day.

showing your current employer by minimizing your days off and will probably appreciate the fact that another prospective employer is interested in you.

References What do you tell an interviewer who asks for references? Just say that while you are happy to have your former employers contacted, you are trying to keep your job search confidential and would rather that your current employer not be contacted until you have been given a firm offer.

IF YOU'RE FIRED OR LAID OFF:
Picking Yourself Up and Dusting Yourself Off

If you've been fired or laid off, you are not the first and will not be the last to go through this traumatic experience. In today's changing economy, thousands of professionals lose their jobs every year. Even if you were terminated with just cause, do not lose heart. Remember, being fired is not a reflection on you as a person. It is usually a reflection of your company's staffing needs and its perception of your recent job performance and attitude. And if you were not performing up to par or enjoying your work, then you will probably be better off at another company anyway.

Be prepared for the question "Why were you fired?" during job interviews.

A thorough job search could take months, so be sure to negotiate a reasonable severance package, if possible, and determine what benefits, such as health insurance, you are still legally entitled to. Also, register for unemployment compensation immediately. Don't be surprised to find other professionals collecting unemployment compensation -- it is for everyone who has lost their job.

Don't start your job search with a flurry of unplanned activity. Start by choosing a strategy and working out a plan. Now is not the time for major changes in your life. If possible, remain in the same career and in the same geographical location, at least until you have been working again for a while. On the other hand, if the only industry for which you are trained is leaving, or is severely depressed in your area, then you should give prompt consideration to moving or switching careers.

Avoid mentioning you were fired when arranging interviews, but be prepared for the question "Why were you fired?" during an interview. If you were laid off as a result of downsizing, briefly explain, being sure to reinforce that your job loss was not due to performance. If you were in fact fired, be honest, but try to detail the reason as favorably as possible and portray what you have learned from your mistakes. If you are confident one of your past managers will give you a good reference, tell the interviewer to contact that person. Do not to speak negatively of your past employer and try not to sound particularly worried about your status of being temporarily unemployed.

Finally, don't spend too much time reflecting on why you were let go or how you might have avoided it. Think positively, look to the future, and be sure to follow a careful plan during your job search.

THE COLLEGE STUDENT:
How to Conduct Your First Job Search

While you will be able to apply many of the basics covered earlier in this chapter to your job search, there are some situations unique to the college student's job search.

Gaining Experience

Perhaps the biggest problem college students face is lack of experience. Many schools have internship programs designed to give students exposure to the field of their choice, as well as the opportunity to make valuable contacts. Check out your school's career services department to see what internships are available. If your school does not have a formal internship program, or if there are no available internships that appeal to you, try contacting local businesses and offering your services -- often, businesses will be more than willing to have any extra pair of hands (especially if those hands are unpaid!) for a day or two each week. Or try contacting school alumni to see if you can "shadow" them for a few days, and see what their day-to-day duties are like. Either way, try to begin building experience as early as possible in your college career.

What do you do if, for whatever reason, you weren't able to get experience directly related to your desired career? First, look at your previous jobs and see if there's anything you can highlight. Did you supervise or train other employees? Did you reorganize the accounting system, or boost productivity in some way? Accomplishments like these demonstrate leadership, responsibility, and innovation -- qualities that most companies look for in employees. And don't forget volunteer activities and school clubs, which can also showcase these traits.

> **THE GPA QUESTION**
>
> You are interviewing for the job of your dreams. Everything is going well: You've established a good rapport, the interviewer seems impressed with your qualifications, and you're almost positive the job is yours. Then you're asked about your GPA, which is pitifully low. Do you tell the truth and watch your dream job fly out the window?
>
> *Never* lie about your GPA (they may request your transcript, and no company will hire a liar). You can, however, explain if there is a reason you don't feel your grades reflect your abilities, and mention any other impressive statistics. For example, if you have a high GPA in your major, or in the last few semesters (as opposed to your cumulative college career), you can use that fact to your advantage.

On-Campus Recruiting

Companies will often send recruiters to interview on-site at various colleges. This gives students a chance to get interviews at companies that may not have interviewed them otherwise, particularly if the company schedules "open" interviews, in which the only screening process is who is first in line at the sign-ups. Of course, since many more applicants gain interviews in this format, this also means that many more people are rejected. The on-campus interview is generally a screening interview, to see if it is worth the company's time to invite you in for a second interview. So do everything possible to make yourself stand out from the crowd.

The first step, of course, is to check out any and all information your school's career center has on the company. If the information seems out of date, call the company's headquarters and ask to be sent the latest annual report, or any other printed information.

Many companies will host an informational meeting for interviewees, often the evening before interviews are scheduled to take place. DO NOT MISS THIS MEETING. The recruiter will almost certainly ask if you attended. Make an effort to stay after the meeting and talk with the company's representatives. Not only does this give you an opportunity to find out more information about both the company and the position, it also makes you stand out in the recruiter's mind. If there's a particular company that you had your heart set on, but you weren't able to get an interview with them, attend the information session anyway. You may be able to convince the recruiter to squeeze you into the schedule. (Or you may discover that the company really isn't suited for you after all.)

Try to check out the interview site beforehand. Some colleges may conduct "mock" interviews that take place in one of the standard interview rooms. Or you may be able to convince a career counselor (or even a custodian) to let you sneak a peek during off-hours. Either way, having an idea of the room's setup will help you to mentally prepare.

Be sure to be at least 15 minutes early to the interview. The recruiter may be running ahead of schedule, and might like to take you early. But don't be surprised if previous interviews have run over, resulting in your 30-minute slot being reduced to 20 minutes (or less). Don't complain; just use whatever time you do have as efficiently as possible to showcase the reasons *you* are the ideal candidate.

LAST WORDS

A parting word of advice. Again and again during your job search you will be rejected. You will be rejected when you apply for interviews. You will be rejected after interviews. For every job offer you finally receive, you probably will have been rejected a multitude of times. Don't let rejections slow you down. Keep reminding yourself that the sooner you go out and get started on your job search, and get those rejections flowing in, the closer you will be to obtaining the job you want.

RESUMES AND COVER LETTERS

When filling a position, a recruiter will often have 100-plus applicants, but time to interview only a handful of the most promising ones. As a result, he or she will reject most applicants after only briefly skimming their resumes.

Unless you have phoned and talked to the recruiter -- which you should do whenever you can -- you will be chosen or rejected for an interview entirely on the basis of your resume and cover letter. Your cover letter must catch the recruiter's attention, and your resume must hold it. (But remember -- a resume is no substitute for a job search campaign. *You* must seek a job. Your resume is only one tool.)

RESUME FORMAT:
Mechanics of a First Impression

The Basics

Recruiters dislike long resumes, so unless you have an unusually strong background with many years of experience and a diversity of outstanding achievements, keep your resume length to one page. If you must squeeze in more information than would otherwise fit, try using a smaller typeface or changing the margins.

Keep your resume on standard 8-1/2" x 11" paper. Since recruiters often get resumes in batches of hundreds, a smaller-sized resume may get lost in the pile. Oversized resumes are likely to get crumpled at the edges, and won't fit easily in their files.

First impressions matter, so make sure the recruiter's first impression of your resume is a good one. Print your resume on quality paper that has weight and texture, in a conservative color such as white, ivory, or pale gray. Use matching paper and envelopes for both your resume and cover letter.

Getting it on Paper

Modern photocomposition typesetting gives you the clearest, sharpest image, a wide variety of type styles, and effects such as italics, bold-facing, and book-like justified margins. It is also much too expensive for many jobseekers. And improvements in laser printers mean that a computer-generated resume can look just as impressive as one that has been professionally typeset.

A computer or word processor is the most flexible way to type your resume. This will allow you to make changes almost instantly and to store different drafts on disk. Word processing and desktop publishing systems also offer many different fonts to choose from, each taking up different amounts of space. (It is generally best to stay between 9-point and 12-point font size.) Many other options are also available, such as bold-facing for emphasis, justified margins, and the ability to change and manipulate spacing.

The end result, however, will be largely determined by the quality of the printer you use. You need at least "letter quality" type for your resume. Do not use a "near letter quality" or dot matrix printer. Laser printers will generally provide the best quality.

Household typewriters and office typewriters with nylon or other cloth ribbons are *not* good enough for typing your resume. If you don't have access to a quality word processor, hire a professional who can prepare your resume with a word processor or typesetting machine.

Don't make your copies on an office photocopier. Only the personnel office may see the resume you mail. Everyone else may see only a copy of it, and copies of copies quickly become unreadable. Either print out each copy individually, or take your resume to a professional copy shop, which will generally offer professionally-maintained, extra-high-quality photocopiers and charge fairly reasonable prices.

Proof with Care

Whether you typed it yourself or paid to have it produced professionally, mistakes on resumes are not only embarrassing, but will usually remove you from further consideration (particularly if something obvious such as your name is misspelled). No matter how much you paid someone else to type, write, or typeset your resume, *you* lose if there is a mistake. So proofread it as carefully as possible. Get a friend to help you. Read your draft aloud as your friend checks the proof copy. Then have your friend read aloud while you check. Next, read it letter by letter to check spelling and punctuation.

If you are having it typed or typeset by a resume service or a printer, and you can't bring a friend or take the time during the day to proof it, pay for it and take it home. Proof it there and bring it back later to get it corrected and printed.

> **The one piece of advice I give to everyone about their resume is: Show it to people, show it to people, show it to people. Before you ever send out a resume, show it to at least a dozen people.**
>
> -Cate Talbot Ashton,
> Associate Director,
> Career Services,
> Colby College

If you wrote your resume on a word processing program, also use that program's built-in spell checker to double-check for spelling errors. But keep in mind that a spell checker will not find errors such as "to" for "two" or "wok" for "work." It's important that you still proofread your resume, even after it has been spell-checked.

Types of Resumes

The two most common resume formats are the functional resume and the chronological resume (examples of both types can be found at the end of this chapter). A functional resume focuses on skills and de-emphasizes job titles, employers, etc. A functional resume is best if you have been out of the work force for a long time and/or if you want to highlight specific skills and strengths that your most recent jobs don't necessarily reflect.

Choose a chronological format if you are currently working or were working recently, and if your most recent experiences relate to your desired field. Use reverse chronological order. To a recruiter your last job and your latest schooling are the most important, so put the last first and list the rest going back in time.

Organization

Your name, phone number, and a complete address should be at the top of your resume. Try to make your name stand out by using a slightly larger font size or all capital letters. Be sure to spell out everything -- never abbreviate St. for Street or Rd. for Road. If you are a college student, you should also put your home address and phone number at the top.

Next, list your experience, then your education. If you are a recent graduate, list your education first, unless your experience is more important than your education. (For example, if you have just graduated from a teaching school, have some business experience, and are applying for a job in business, you would list your business experience first.)

Keep everything easy to find. Put the dates of your employment and education on the left of the page. Put the names of the companies you worked for and the schools you attended a few spaces to the right of the dates. Put the city and state, or the city and country, where you studied or worked to the right of the page.

This is just one suggestion that may work for you. The important thing is simply to break up the text in some way that makes your resume visually attractive and easy to scan, so experiment to see which layout works best for your resume. However you set it up, stay consistent. Inconsistencies in fonts, spacing, or tenses will make your resume look sloppy. Also, be sure to use tabs to keep your information vertically lined up, rather than the less precise space bar.

RESUME CONTENT:
Say it with Style

Sell Yourself

You are selling your skills and accomplishments in your resume, so it is important to inventory yourself and know yourself. If you have achieved something, say so. Put it in the best possible light. But avoid subjective statements, such as "I am a hard worker" or "I get along well with my coworkers." Just stick to the facts.

While you shouldn't hold back or be modest, don't exaggerate your achievements to the point of misrepresentation. Be honest. Many companies will immediately drop an applicant from consideration (or fire a current employee) if inaccurate information is discovered on a resume or other application material.

Keep it Brief Write down the important (and pertinent) things you have done, but do it in as few words as possible. Your resume will be scanned, not read, and short, concise phrases are much more effective than long-winded sentences. Avoid the use of "I" when emphasizing your accomplishments. Instead, use brief phrases beginning with action verbs.

While some technical terms will be unavoidable, you should try to avoid excessive "technicalese." Keep in mind that the first person to see your resume may be a human resources person who won't necessarily know all the jargon -- and how can they be impressed by something they don't understand?

Also, try to keep your paragraphs at six lines or shorter. If you have more than six lines of information about one job or school, put it in two or more paragraphs. The shorter your resume is, the more carefully it will be examined. Remember: Your resume usually has between eight and 45 seconds to catch an employer's eye. So make every second count.

Job Objective A functional resume may require a job objective to give it focus. One or two sentences describing the job you are seeking can clarify in what capacity your skills will be best put to use.

Examples: An entry-level position in the publishing industry.
A challenging position requiring analytical thought and excellent writing skills.

Don't include a job objective in a chronological resume. Even if you are certain of exactly what type of job you desire, the presence of a job objective might eliminate you from consideration for other positions that a recruiter feels are a better match for your qualifications. But even though you may not put an objective on paper, having a career goal in mind as you write can help give your resume a sense of direction.

Work Experience Some jobseekers may choose to include both "Relevant Experience" and "Additional Experience" sections. This can be useful, as it allows the jobseeker to place more emphasis on certain experiences and to de-emphasize others.

Emphasize continued experience in a particular job area or continued interest in a particular industry. De-emphasize irrelevant positions. Delete positions that you held for less than four months (unless you are a very recent college grad or still in school). Stress your results, elaborating on how you contributed in your previous jobs. Did you increase sales, reduce costs, improve a product, implement a new program? Were you promoted? Use specific numbers (i.e., quantities, percentages, dollar amounts) whenever possible.

Mention all relevant responsibilities. Be specific, and slant your past accomplishments toward the position that you hope to obtain. For example, do you hope to supervise people? If so, then state how many people, performing what function, you have supervised.

Education

Keep it brief if you have more than two years of career experience. Elaborate more if you have less experience. If you are a recent grad with two or more years of college, you may choose to include any high school activities that are directly relevant to your career. If you've been out of school for awhile, list post-secondary education only.

Mention degrees received and any honors or special awards. Note individual courses or research projects you participated in that might be relevant for employers. For example, if you are an English major applying for a position as a business writer, be sure to mention any business or economics courses.

USE ACTION VERBS

How you write your resume is just as important as *what* you write. The strongest resumes use short phrases beginning with action verbs. Below are a few action verbs you may want to use. (This list is not all-inclusive.)

achieved
administered
advised
analyzed
arranged
assembled
assisted
attained
budgeted
built
calculated
collaborated
collected
compiled
completed
computed
conducted
consolidated
constructed
consulted
controlled
coordinated
created
designed
determined
developed
devised
directed
discovered
distributed
eliminated
established
evaluated
examined
executed
expanded
expedited
facilitated
formulated
founded
generated
headed
identified
implemented
improved
increased
initiated
installed
instituted
instructed
integrated
interpreted
interviewed
invented
launched
maintained
managed
marketed
mediated
monitored
negotiated
obtained
operated
ordered
organized
participated
performed
planned
prepared
presented
processed
produced
proposed
provided
published
purchased
reduced
regulated
reorganized
represented
researched
resolved
restored
restructured
revised
scheduled
selected
served
sold
solved
streamlined
studied
supervised
supplied
supported
tested
trained
updated
upgraded
wrote

Highlight Impressive Skills

Be sure to mention any computer skills you may have. You may wish to include a section entitled "Additional Skills" or "Computer Skills," in which you list any software programs you know. An additional skills section is also an ideal place to mention fluency in a foreign language.

Personal Data

This section is optional, but if you choose to include it, keep it very brief (two lines maximum). A one-word mention of hobbies such as fishing, chess, baseball, cooking, etc., can give the person who will interview you a good way to open up the conversation. It doesn't hurt to include activities that are unusual (fencing, bungee jumping, snake-charming) or that somehow relate to the position or the company you're applying to (for instance, if you are a member of a professional organization in your industry). Never include information about your age, health, physical characteristics, marital status, or religious affiliation.

References

The most that is needed is the sentence, "References available upon request," at the bottom of your resume. If you choose to leave it out, that's fine.

HIRING A RESUME WRITER:
Is it the Right Choice for You?

If you write reasonably well, it is to your advantage to write your own resume. Writing your resume forces you to review your experience and figure out how to explain your accomplishments in clear, brief phrases. This will help you when you explain your work to interviewers.

> **Those things [marital status, church affiliations, etc.] have no place on a resume. Those are illegal questions, so why even put that information on your resume?**
>
> -Becky Hayes, Career Counselor
> Career Services, Rice University

If you write your resume, everything will be in your own words -- it will sound like you. It will say what you want it to say. If you are a good writer, know yourself well, and have a good idea of which parts of your background employers are looking for, you should be able to write your own resume better than anyone else can. If you decide to write your resume yourself, have as many people review and proofread it as possible. Welcome objective opinions and other perspectives.

When to Get Help

If you have difficulty writing in "resume style" (which is quite unlike normal written language), if you are unsure of which parts of your background you should emphasize, or if you think your resume would make your case better if it did not follow one of the standard forms outlined either here or in a book on resumes, then you should consider having it professionally written.

There are two reasons even some professional resume writers we know have had their resumes written with the help of fellow professionals. First, they may need the help of someone who can be objective about their background, and second, they may want an experienced sounding board to help focus their thoughts.

If You Hire a Pro

The best way to choose a writer is by reputation -- the recommendation of a friend, a personnel director, your school placement officer, or someone else knowledgeable in the field.

Important questions:

- "How long have you been writing resumes?"
- "If I'm not satisfied with what you write, will you go over it with me and change it?"
- "Do you charge by the hour or a flat rate?"

There is no sure relation between price and quality, except that you are unlikely to get a good writer for less than $50 for an uncomplicated resume and you shouldn't have to pay more than $300 unless your experience is very extensive or complicated. There will be additional charges for printing.

Few resume services will give you a firm price over the phone, simply because some resumes are too complicated and take too long to do for a predetermined price. Some services will quote you a price that applies to almost all of their customers. Once you decide to use a specific writer, you should insist on a firm price quote before engaging their services. Also, find out how expensive minor changes will be.

COVER LETTERS:
Quick, Clear, and Concise

Always mail a cover letter with your resume. In a cover letter you can show an interest in the company that you can't show in a resume. You can also point out one or two skills or accomplishments the company can put to good use.

Make it Personal

The more personal you can get, the better. If someone known to the person you are writing has recommended that you contact the company, get permission to include his/her name in the letter. If you have the name of a person to send the letter to, address it directly to that person (after first calling the company to verify the spelling of the person's name, correct title, and mailing address). Be sure to put the person's name and title on both the letter and the envelope. This will ensure that your letter will get through to the proper person, even if a new person now occupies this position. But even if you don't have a contact name and are simply addressing it to the "Personnel Director" or the "Hiring Partner," definitely send a letter.

Type cover letters in full. Don't try the cheap and easy ways, like using a computer mail merge program, or photocopying the body of your letter and typing in the inside address and salutation. You will give the impression that you are mailing to a host of companies and have no particular interest in any one.

Cover letter do's and don'ts

- *Do* keep your cover letter brief and to the point.
- *Do* be sure it is error-free.
- *Don't* just repeat information verbatim from your resume.
- *Don't* overuse the personal pronoun "I."
- *Don't* send a generic cover letter -- show your personal knowledge of and interest in that particular company.
- *Do* accentuate what you can offer the company, not what you hope to gain from them.

FUNCTIONAL RESUME

(Prepared on a word processor and laser printed.)

PENELOPE FRANCES PANZ
430 Miller's Crossing
Essex Junction VT 05452
802/555-9354

Objective

A position as a graphic designer commensurate with my acquired skills and expertise.

Summary

Extensive experience in plate making, separations, color matching, background definition, printing, mechanicals, color corrections, and personnel supervision. A highly motivated manager and effective communicator. Proven ability to:

- **Create Commercial Graphics**
- **Produce Embossed Drawings**
- **Color Separate**
- **Control Quality**
- **Resolve Printing Problems**
- **Analyze Customer Satisfaction**

Qualifications

Printing:
Knowledgeable in black and white as well as color printing. Excellent judgment in determining acceptability of color reproduction through comparison with original. Proficient at producing four- or five-color corrections on all media, as well as restyling previously reproduced four-color artwork.

Customer Relations:
Routinely work closely with customers to ensure specifications are met. Capable of striking a balance between technical printing capabilities and need for customer satisfaction through entire production process.

Specialties:
Practiced at creating silk screen overlays for a multitude of processes including velo bind, GBC bind, and perfect bind. Creative design and timely preparation of posters, flyers, and personalized stationery.

Personnel Supervision:
Skillful at fostering atmosphere that encourages highly talented artists to balance high-level creativity with maximum production. Consistently meet or beat production deadlines. Instruct new employees, apprentices, and students in both artistry and technical operations.

Experience

Graphic Arts Professor, University of Vermont, Burlington VT (1987-1993).
Manager, Design Graphics, Barre VT (1993-present).

Education

Massachusetts Conservatory of Art, Ph.D. 1987
University of Massachusetts, B.A. 1984

CHRONOLOGICAL RESUME

(Prepared on a word processor
and laser printed.)

MAURICE DUPETREAUX
412 Maple Court
Seattle, WA 98404
(206) 555-6584

EXPERIENCE

THE CENTER COMPANY — Seattle, WA
Systems Programmer — 1993-present

- Develop and maintain over 100 assembler modules.
- Create screen manager programs, using Assembler and Natural languages, to trace input and output to the VTAM buffer.
- Install and customize Omegamon 695 and 700 on IBM mainframes.
- Develop programs to monitor complete security control blocks, using Assembler and Natural.
- Produce stand-alone IPLs and create backrests on IBM 3380 DASD.

INFO TECH, INC. — Seattle, WA
Technical Manager — 1991-1993

- Designed and managed the implementation of a network providing the legal community with a direct line to Supreme Court cases, using Clipper on IBM 386s.
- Developed a system which catalogued entire library inventory, using Turbo Pascal on IBM AT.
- Used C to create a registration system for university registrar on IBM AT.

EDUCATION

SALEM STATE UNIVERSITY — Salem, OR
B.S. in Computer Science. — 1989
M.S. in Computer Science. — 1991

COMPUTER SKILLS

- Programming Languages: C, C++, Assembler, COBOL, Natural, Turbo Pascal, dBASE III+, and Clipper.
- Software: VTAM, Complete, TSO, JES 2, ACF 2, Omegamon 695 and 700, and Adabas.
- Operating Systems: MVS/XA, MVS/SP, MS-DOS, and VMS.

FUNCTIONAL RESUME

(Prepared on an office-quality typewriter)

LORRAINE AVAKIAN
70 Monback Avenue
Oshkosh, WI 54901
(608) 586-1243

OBJECTIVE:
To contribute over eight years of experience in promotion, communications, and administration to an entry-level position in advertising.

SUMMARY OF QUALIFICATIONS:

- Performed advertising duties for small business.
- Experience in business writing and communications skills.
- General knowledge of office management.
- Demonstrated ability to work well with others, in both supervisory and support staff roles.
- Type 75 words per minute.

SELECTED ACHIEVEMENTS AND RESULTS:
Promotion:
Composing, editing, and proofreading correspondence and PR materials for own catering service. Large-scale mailings.

Communication:
Instruction; curriculum and lesson planning; student evaluation; parent-teacher conferences; development of educational materials. Training and supervising clerks.

Computer Skills:
Proficient in MS Word, Lotus 1-2-3, Excel, and Filemaker Pro.

Administration:
Record-keeping and file maintenance. Data processing and computer operations, accounts receivable, accounts payable, inventory control, and customer relations. Scheduling, office management, and telephone reception.

WORK HISTORY:
Teacher; Self-Employed (owner of catering service); Floor Manager; Administrative Assistant; Accounting Clerk.

EDUCATION:
Beloit College, Beloit, WI, BA in Education, 1987

CHRONOLOGICAL RESUME

(Prepared on a word processor and laser printed)

T. WILLIAM MAGUIRE
16 Charles Street
Marlborough CT 06447
203/555-9641

EDUCATION

Keene State College, Keene NH
Bachelor of Arts in Elementary Education, 1995
- Graduated *magna cum laude*
- English minor
- Kappa Delta Pi member, inducted 1993

EXPERIENCE

September 1995-Present

Elmer T. Thienes Elementary School, Marlborough CT
Part-time Kindergarten Teacher
- Instruct kindergartners in reading, spelling, language arts, and music.
- Participate in the selection of textbooks and learning aids.
- Organize and supervise class field trips and coordinate in-class presentations.

Summers 1993-1995

Keene YMCA, Youth Division, Keene NH
Child-care Counselor
- Oversaw summer program for low-income youth.
- Budgeted and coordinated special events and field trips, working with Program Director to initiate variations in the program.
- Served as Youth Advocate in cooperation with social worker to address the social needs and problems of participants.

Spring 1995

Wheelock Elementary School, Keene NH
Student Teacher
- Taught third-grade class in all elementary subjects.
- Designed and implemented a two-week unit on Native Americans.
- Assisted in revision of third-grade curriculum.

Fall 1994

Child Development Center, Keene NH
Daycare Worker
- Supervised preschool children on the playground and during art activities.
- Created a "Peter Rabbit Corner," where children could quietly look at books or take a voluntary "time-out."

ADDITIONAL INTERESTS

Martial arts, skiing, politics, reading, writing.

GENERAL MODEL FOR A COVER LETTER

Your mailing address
Date

Contact's name
Contact's title
Company
Company's mailing address

Dear Mr./Ms. _________:

Immediately explain why your background makes you the best candidate for the position that you are applying for. Describe what prompted you to write (want ad, article you read about the company, networking contact, etc.). Keep the first paragraph short and hard-hitting.

Detail what you could contribute to this company. Show how your qualifications will benefit this firm. Describe your interest in the corporation. Subtly emphasizing your knowledge about this firm and your familiarity with the industry will set you apart from other candidates. Remember to keep this letter short; few recruiters will read a cover letter longer than half a page.

If possible, your closing paragraph should request specific action on the part of the reader. Include your phone number and the hours when you can be reached. Mention that if you do not hear from the reader by a specific date, you will follow up with a phone call. Lastly, thank the reader for their time, consideration, etc.

Sincerely,

(signature)

Your full name (typed)

Enclosure (use this if there are other materials, such as your resume, that are included in the same envelope)

SAMPLE COVER LETTER

16 Charles Street
Marlborough CT 06447
March 16, 1996

Ms. Lia Marcusson
Assistant Principal
Jonathon Daniels Elementary School
43 Mayflower Drive
Keene NH 03431

Dear Ms. Marcusson:

Janet Newell recently informed me of a possible opening for a third grade teacher at Jonathon Daniels Elementary School. With my experience instructing third-graders, both in schools and in summer programs, I feel I would be an ideal candidate for the position. Please accept this letter and the enclosed resume as my application.

Jonathon Daniels' educational philosophy that every child can learn and succeed interests me, since it mirrors my own. My current position at Elmer T. Thienes Elementary has reinforced this philosophy, heightening my awareness of the different styles and paces of learning and increasing my sensitivity toward special needs children. Furthermore, as a direct result of my student teaching experience at Wheelock Elementary School, I am comfortable, confident, and knowledgeable working with third-graders.

I look forward to discussing the position and my qualifications for it in more detail. I can be reached at 203/555-9641 evenings or 203/555-0248 weekdays. If I do not hear from you before Tuesday of next week, I will call to see if we can schedule a time to meet. Thank you for your time and consideration.

Sincerely,

Bill Maguire

T. William Maguire

Enclosure

GENERAL MODEL FOR A FOLLOW-UP LETTER

Your mailing address
Date

Contact's name
Contact's title
Company
Company's mailing address

Dear Mr./Ms.________:

Remind the interviewer of the reason (i.e., a specific opening, an informational interview, etc.) you were interviewed, as well as the date. Thank him/her for the interview, and try to personalize your thanks by mentioning some specific aspect of the interview.

Confirm your interest in the organization (and in the opening, if you were interviewing for a particular position). Use specifics to re-emphasize that you have researched the firm in detail and have considered how you would fit into the company and the position. This is a good time to say anything you wish you had said in the initial meeting. Be sure to keep this letter brief; a half-page is plenty.

If appropriate, close with a suggestion for further action, such as a desire to have an additional interview, if possible. Mention your phone number and the hours that you can be reached. Alternatively, you may prefer to mention that you will follow up with a phone call in several days. Once again, thank the person for meeting with you, and state that you would be happy to provide any additional information about your qualifications.

Sincerely,

(signature)

Your full name (typed)

PRIMARY EMPLOYERS

ACCOUNTING AND MANAGEMENT CONSULTING

As the number of accounting graduates drops and the economy strengthens, all types of accounting professionals will benefit. According to the Bureau of Labor Statistics, the number of accounting jobs may grow by as much as 40 percent by the year 2005. A recent survey conducted by Robert Half International found that the best opportunities for accountants were in the financial, insurance, and real estate sector, followed by the retail and wholesale industries.

Even faster growth is projected for the management consulting industry, where the number of jobs is expected to grow almost three times faster than the rate for all industries. The increasing complexity of business will contribute to industry growth. Among other things, today's managers must worry about rapid technological innovations, changes in government regulations, growing environmental concerns, continuing reduction of trade barriers, and globalization of markets. Because it has become difficult to keep abreast of these changing conditions, corporations, institutions, and governments will increasingly need the aid of well-trained, well-informed management consulting professionals.

BOOZ-ALLEN & HAMILTON, INC.
8283 Greensboro Drive, McLean VA 22102. 703/902-5000. **Fax:** 703/902-3620. **Recorded Jobline:** 703/902-5400. **Contact:** Sheila Carney, Recruiting Services Manager. **Description:** Booz-Allen's Technology Center provides systems development and technology services in the areas of defense, space, computing, communications, transportation, environment, and management sciences to government and industry. **Common positions include:** Budget Analyst; Computer Programmer; Computer Systems Analyst; Electrical/Electronics Engineer; Operations Research Analyst; Secretary; Software Engineer; Systems Analyst; Transportation/Traffic Specialist. **Educational backgrounds include:** Computer Science; Engineering; Finance. **Benefits:** Dental Insurance; Disability Coverage; Life Insurance; Medical Insurance; Pension Plan; Savings Plan; Tuition Assistance. **Corporate headquarters location:** This Location. **Operations at this facility include:** Service.

DELOITTE & TOUCHE
500 Lee Street, 1215 Laidley Tower, Charleston WV 25301. 304/342-5300. **Contact:** Jeffrey Potts, Managing Partner. **Description:** Deloitte & Touche is an international firm of certified public accountants, providing professional accounting, auditing, tax, and management consulting services to widely diversified clients. With more than 500 offices throughout the world, the company has a specialized program consisting of some 25 national industry groups and 50 functional (technical) groups that cross industry lines. Groups are involved in various disciplines, including accounting, auditing, taxation management advisory services, small and growing businesses, mergers and acquisitions, and computer applications. Deloitte & Touche has international facilities.

A. FOSTER HIGGINS & COMPANY
Riverfront Plaza, West Tower, 901 East Byrd Street, Suite 800, Richmond VA 23219-4070. 804/344-3700. **Contact:** Human Resources. **Description:**

Foster Higgins helps employers develop and manage employee benefit programs and discover ways to further corporate objectives through the effective use of human resources. With more than 60 years of experience, the company employs a diverse range of consultants in systems and information, in a strong network of offices across the country and affiliates in Canada and abroad. Areas of service include: Information and Research Services; Retirement Income; Retiree Health Care; Group Health and Welfare Plans; Health Care Delivery Systems; Flexible Compensation; Human Resource Administration; and Communications. Foster Higgins draws on its sister firm Sibson & Company, a nationally-recognized leader in compensation consulting, to complete the range of human resource consulting services the firm provides its clients. **NOTE:** Interested jobseekers should address inquiries to Laura Smith, Human Resources, A. Foster Higgins & Company, One Lafayette Center, 1120 20th Street NW, Suite 800, Washington DC 20036-3406.

JACKSON HEWITT INC.
4575 Bonney Road, Virginia Beach VA 23462. 804/473-3300. **Fax:** 804/473-8409. **World Wide Web:** http://www.infi.net/~jhewitt. **Contact:** Human Resources. **Description:** A full-service, year-round tax preparation company specializing in computerized tax preparation and electric filing. The foundation of Jackson Hewitt's tax service is Hewtax, a proprietary software program. The company offers a number of filing options, including: SuperFast Refund, through which customers receive a refund anticipation loan within one to two days of filing; Accelerated Check Refund, which allows Jackson Hewitt to set up a bank account for the IRS to deposit the taxpayer's refund; or a standard electronically filed return. Jackson Hewitt has locations in 212 Montgomery Ward stores, as well as other locations that are company-owned or franchised. The company also operates an in-house travel agency open to the public, Campbell Travel. **Corporate headquarters location:** This Location. **Listed on:** NASDAQ. **Number of employees nationwide:** 200.

ROBBINS-GIOIA, INC.
209 Madison Street, Third Floor, Alexandria VA 22310. 703/548-7006. **Fax:** 703/684-5189. **Contact:** Donna Winsor, Human Resources Manager. **Description:** Founded in 1980. Services include program/project management, configuration management, cost-estimating, acquisition management, software development, systems design, technical support, life cycle management, and risk management. Robbins-Gioia functions as a prime contractor, team member, or subcontractor in various industries including the automotive industry, and state, local, and federal government. Experience managing large projects in logistics, mergers, personnel, finance, automated data processing, information resource management, systems integration, and new product development. **Common positions include:** Computer Programmer; Computer Systems Analyst; Cost Estimator; Industrial Engineer; Management Analyst/Consultant; Management Trainee; Program Manager. **Educational backgrounds include:** Business Administration; Computer Science. **Benefits:** 401K; Dental Insurance; Disability Coverage; Life Insurance; Medical Insurance; Tuition Assistance. **Corporate headquarters location:** This Location. **Other U.S. locations:** Nationwide. **Operations at this facility include:** Administration; Sales; Service. **Listed on:** Privately held. **Number of employees nationwide:** 360.

Note: *Because addresses and telephone numbers of smaller companies change rapidly, we recommend you call each company to verify the information below before inquiring about job opportunities. Mass mailings are not recommended.*

Additional small employers:

ACCOUNTING, AUDITING, AND BOOKKEEPING SERVICES

Grant Thornton
2070 Chain Bridge Rd, Ste 375, Vienna VA 22182-2500. 703/749-2900.

Price Waterhouse
3110 Fairview Park Dr, Falls Church VA 22042-4503. 703/538-7982.

Healthcare Financial Service Inc.
1204 Kanawha Blvd E, Charleston WV 25301-2900. 304/345-4371.

Coopers & Lybrand
1530 Wilson Blvd, Ste 800, Arlington VA 22209-2447. 703/908-1500.

MANAGEMENT SERVICES

Access America Services Corp.
6600 W Broad St, Richmond VA 23230-1702. 804/285-3300.

JL Associates Inc.
22 Enterprise Pky, Ste 310, Hampton VA 23666-5844. 804/838-8400.

RCG/Hagler Bailly Inc.
1530 Wilson Blvd, Ste 900, Arlington VA 22209-2447. 703/351-0300.

CTB MacMillan-McGraw Hill
1618 East Ave, Mc Lean VA 22101-4144. 703/760-0813.

David Orr Associates
8629 Sudley Rd, Ste 202, Manassas VA 22110-4590. 703/335-5497.

Hanscomb Associates
1600 Duke St, Alexandria VA 22314-3421. 703/684-6550.

Brantley Enterprises
3887 Plaza Dr, Fairfax VA 22030-2512. 703/385-3603.

Victor Management Company
11832 Rock Landing Rd, Ste 304, Newport News VA 23606-4278. 804/873-1000.

Lewis Management Co.
Rt 29 North, Madison Hts VA 24572. 804/845-0181.

Health Management Strategies International
1725 Duke St, Alexandria VA 22314-3457. 703/706 4100.

BUSINESS CONSULTING SERVICES

Development Associates
1730 N Lynn St, Arlington VA 22209-2004. 703/276-0677.

Development Management Systems
1700 N Moore St, Ste 720, Arlington VA 22209-1903. 703/525-1489.

EDS
13600 EDS Dr, Herndon VA 22071-3225. 703/742-1500.

Governmental Entities Management Service
7231 Forest Ave, Ste 206, Richmond VA 23226-3793. 804/273-0038.

Hay Management Consultants
4301 Fairfax Dr, Arlington VA 22203-1627. 703/841-0079.

Information Spectrum
1235 Jefferson Davis Hwy, Arlington VA 22202-3283. 703/892-5500.

Information Spectrum
5107 Leesburg Pike, Falls Church VA 22041-3234. 703/845-3000.

KPMG Peat Marwick
17010 Dahlgren Rd, King George VA 22485-5836. 540/663-9223.

LSA Inc.
1215 Jefferson Davis Hwy, Ste 1, Arlington VA 22202-4302. 703/979-4600.

Maximums Inc.
1356 Beverly Rd, Mc Lean VA 22101-3625. 703/734-4200.

National Systems Management
4600 H Pinecrest Ofc Pk Dr, Alexandria VA 22312. 703/941-9021.

Phamis Inc.
4601 Fairfax Dr, Arlington VA 22203-1500. 703/841-1008.

The Three Sigma Group
9302 Lee Hwy, Fairfax VA 22031-1214. 703/385-9815.

SRS Technologies
1500 Wilson Blvd, Arlington VA 22209-2404. 703/522-5588.

For more information on career opportunities in accounting and management consulting:

Associations

AMERICAN ACCOUNTING ASSOCIATION
5717 Bessie Drive, Sarasota FL 34233. 813/921-7747. An academically-oriented accounting association that offers two quarterly journals, a semi-annual journal, a newsletter, and a wide variety of continuing education programs.

AMERICAN INSTITUTE OF CERTIFIED PUBLIC ACCOUNTANTS
1211 Avenue of the Americas, New York NY 10036. 212/596-6200. A national professional organization for all CPAs. AICPA offers a comprehensive career package to students.

AMERICAN MANAGEMENT ASSOCIATION
Management Information Service, 135 West 50th Street, New York NY 10020. 212/586-8100. Provides a variety of publications, training videos, and courses, as well as an Information Resource Center, which provides management information, and a library service.

ASSOCIATION OF GOVERNMENT ACCOUNTANTS
2200 Mount Vernon Avenue, Alexandria VA 22301. 703/684-6931.

ASSOCIATION OF MANAGEMENT CONSULTING FIRMS
521 Fifth Avenue, 35th Floor, New York NY 10175. 212/697-9693. Offers certification programs.

INSTITUTE OF INTERNAL AUDITORS
49 Maitland Avenue, Altamont Springs FL 32701. 407/830-7600. Publishes magazines and newsletters. Provides information on current issues, a network of more than 50,000 members in 100 countries, and professional development and research services.

INSTITUTE OF MANAGEMENT ACCOUNTANTS
10 Paragon Drive, Box 433, Montvale NJ 07645-1760. 201/573-9000. Offers a Certified Management Accountant Program, periodicals, seminars, educational programs, a research program, a financial management network, and networking services.

INSTITUTE OF MANAGEMENT CONSULTANTS
521 Fifth Avenue, 35th Floor, New York NY 10175. 212/697-8262. Offers certification and professional development and a directory of members.

NATIONAL ASSOCIATION OF TAX PRACTITIONERS
720 Association Drive, Appleton WI 54914. 414/749-1040. Offers seminars, research, newsletters, preparer worksheets, state chapters, insurance, and other tax-related services.

NATIONAL BUSINESSWOMEN'S LEADERSHIP ASSOCIATION
6901 West 63rd Street, P.O. Box 2949, Shawnee Mission KS 66201. World Wide Web address: http://www.natsem.com. A professional organization dedicated to advancing the careers of women in management.

NATIONAL SOCIETY OF PUBLIC ACCOUNTANTS
1010 North Fairfax Street, Alexandria VA 22314. 703/549-6400. Offers professional development services, government representation, a variety of publications, practice aids, low-cost group insurance, and annual seminars.

Directories

AICPA DIRECTORY OF ACCOUNTING EDUCATION
American Institute of Certified Public Accountants, 1211 Avenue of the Americas, New York NY 10036. 212/596-6200. $150.00. Only available to AICPA members.

ACCOUNTING FIRMS AND PRACTITIONERS
American Institute of Certified Public Accountants, 1211 Avenue of the Americas, New York NY 10036. 212/596-6200. $150.00. Only available to AICPA members.

Magazines

CPA JOURNAL
530 Fifth Avenue, New York NY 10136. 212/719-8300. Published monthly by The New York State Society.

CPA LETTER
American Institute of Certified Public Accountants, 1211 Avenue of the Americas, New York NY 10036. 212/596-6200.

JOURNAL OF ACCOUNTANCY
American Institute of Certified Public Accountants, 1211 Avenue of the Americas, New York NY 10036. 212/596-6200.

MANAGEMENT ACCOUNTING
Institute of Management Accounting, 10 Paragon Drive, Montvale NJ 07645. 201/573-9000.

WENDELL'S REPORT FOR CONTROLLERS
Warren, Gorham, and Lamont, Inc., 210 South Street, Boston MA 02111. 617/423-2020.

ADVERTISING, MARKETING, AND PUBLIC RELATIONS

Due to several trends shaping the industry, finding a job in advertising is as tough today as it has ever been. To remain competitive, the industry's largest firms have been downsizing to save money for larger campaigns. On the other hand, smaller agencies are increasingly specializing in fields such as direct marketing and public relations in order to gain a stronger presence in the market. Meanwhile, the growing cable industry has opened the door to new business opportunities, as has the Internet. Increasingly, advertisers are using the information highway to conduct business, as well as to target specific "digital" audiences.

In the public relations field, there has been an explosion in the number and range of consultants in the marketplace. Partially as a result of the recession of the early '90s, many senior executives who were released from their contracts at major firms have launched companies of their own.

EARLE PALMER BROWN
1710 East Franklin Street, Richmond VA 23223. 804/775-0700. **Contact:** Mary McMurtrey, Office Manager. **Description:** An agency offering the following services: advertising; public relations; marketing research; Yellow Pages advertising; direct marketing; and sales promotion. **Corporate headquarters location:** Bethesda MD. **Other U.S. locations:** St. Petersburg FL; New York NY; Philadelphia PA.

THE MARTIN AGENCY
500 North Allen Avenue, Richmond VA 23220. 804/254-3400. **Contact:** Tom Hoffman, Director of Human Resources. **Description:** An advertising agency.

CHARLES RYAN ASSOCIATES
1021 Kanawha Boulevard East, Box 2464, Charleston WV 25329. 304/342-0161. **Contact:** Charlotte Fields, Human Resources Director. **Description:** A public relations agency.

Note: *Because addresses and telephone numbers of smaller companies change rapidly, we recommend you call each company to verify the information below before inquiring about job opportunities. Mass mailings are not recommended.*

Additional small employers:

MISC. ADVERTISING SERVICES

Fahlgren Martin Inc.
Rosemar Rd & Seminary Rd, Parkersburg WV 26102. 304/424-3591.

Martin Retail
1711 E Main St, Richmond VA 23223-6959. 804/648-4754.

Black, Manafort, Stone & Kelly
211 North Union Street, Suite 300, Alexandria VA 22314-2643. 703/683-6612.

Chesapeake Directory Sales Co.
340 MacCorkle Ave SE, Suite 300, Charleston WV 25314. 304/357-6800.

Telmark Yellow Pages International
707 E Main St, Ste 490,

Richmond VA 23219-2802. 804/344-7740.

The Thomas Company
4604 Village Run Ct, Glen Allen VA 23060-3346. 804/270-7539.

Hicks Outdoor Advertising
811 Grand Central Ave, Vienna WV 26105-2145. 304/295-3345.

Advision
209 Broad St, Charleston WV 25301-2408. 304/345-8510.

Northeast TV Advertising
Professional Bldg, Williamstown WV 26187. 304/375-5829.

Daily Press-Southside Bureau
1617 S Church St, Smithfield VA 23430-1831. 804/357-4137.

PUBLIC RELATIONS SERVICES

Martin Public Relations
707 E Main St, Ste 400, Richmond VA 23219-2802. 804/648-8609.

DIRECT MAIL ADVERTISING SERVICES

The Best Lists Inc.
2070 Chain Bridge Rd, Vienna VA 22182-2500. 703/442-9030.

Diversified Mailing Service
4333 Davenport Rd, Fredericksbrg VA 22408-8716. 540/898-6245.

Eggleston Services
402 W 22nd St, Norfolk VA 23517-2119. 804/640-0588.

For more information on career opportunities in advertising, marketing, and public relations:

Associations

ADVERTISING RESEARCH FOUNDATION
641 Lexington Avenue, New York NY 10022. 212/751-5656. Fax: 212/319-5265. World Wide Web address: http://www.arfsite.org/arf. A nonprofit organization comprised of advertising, marketing, and media research companies. For institutions only.

AMERICAN ASSOCIATION OF ADVERTISING AGENCIES
666 Third Avenue, New York NY 10017. 212/682-2500. Offers educational and enrichment benefits such as publications, videos, and conferences.

AMERICAN MARKETING ASSOCIATION
250 South Wacker Drive, Suite 200, Chicago IL 60606-5819. 312/831-2764. Fax: 312/648-5625. World Wide Web address: http://www.ama.org. An association with nearly 50,000 members worldwide. Offers 25 annual conferences, library and research services, and 25 annual issues of *Marketing News.*

DIRECT MARKETING ASSOCIATION
1120 Avenue of Americas, New York NY 10036-6700. 212/768-7277. Offers monthly newsletters, seminars, and conferences.

INTERNATIONAL ADVERTISING ASSOCIATION
521 Fifth Avenue, Suite 1807, New York NY 10175. 212/557-1133. Fax: 212/983-0455. E-mail address: IAA@ibnet.com. Over 3,600 members in 89 countries. Membership includes: publications; professional development; congresses, symposia, and conferences; annual report and membership directory; and worldwide involvement with governments and other associations. Overall, the organization looks to promote free speech and the self-regulation of advertising.

LEAGUE OF ADVERTISING AGENCIES
2 South End Avenue #4C, New York NY 10280. 212/945-4991. Seminars available.

MARKETING RESEARCH ASSOCIATION
2189 Silas Deane Highway, Suite #5, Rocky Hill CT 06067. 860/257-4008. Publishes several magazines and newsletters.

PUBLIC RELATIONS SOCIETY OF AMERICA
33 Irving Place, New York NY 10003. 212/995-2230. Publishes three magazines for public relations professionals.

Directories

AAAA ROSTER AND ORGANIZATION
American Association of Advertising Agencies, 666 Third Avenue, 13th Floor, New York NY 10017. 212/682-2500.

DIRECTORY OF MINORITY PUBLIC RELATIONS PROFESSIONALS
Public Relations Society of America, 33 Irving Place, New York NY 10003. 212/995-2230.

O'DWYER'S DIRECTORY OF PUBLIC RELATIONS FIRMS
J. R. O'Dwyer Company, 271

Madison Avenue, Room 600, New York NY 10016. 212/679-2471.

PUBLIC RELATIONS CONSULTANTS DIRECTORY
American Business Directories, Division of American Business Lists, 5711 South 86th Circle, Omaha NE 68127. 402/593-4500.

PUBLIC RELATIONS JOURNAL / REGISTER ISSUE
Public Relations Society of America, 33 Irving Place, New York NY 10003. 212/995-2230.

STANDARD DIRECTORY OF ADVERTISING AGENCIES
Reed Reference Publishing Company, P.O. Box 31, New Providence NJ 07974. 800/521-8110.

<u>**Magazines**</u>

ADVERTISING AGE
Crain Communications, 740 North Rush Street, Chicago IL 60611. 312/649-5316.

ADWEEK
BPI, 1515 Broadway, 12th Floor, New York NY 10036-8986. 212/536-5336.

BUSINESS MARKETING
Crain Communications, 740 North Rush Street, Chicago IL 60611. 312/649-5260.

JOURNAL OF MARKETING
American Marketing Association, 250 South Wacker Drive, Suite 200, Chicago IL 60606. 312/648-0536.

THE MARKETING NEWS
American Marketing Association, 250 South Wacker Drive, Suite 200, Chicago IL 60606. 312/648-0536.

PR REPORTER
PR Publishing Company, P.O. Box 600, Exeter NH 03833. 603/778-0514.

PUBLIC RELATIONS JOURNAL
Public Relations Society of America, 33 Irving Place, New York NY 10003. 212/995-2230.

PUBLIC RELATIONS NEWS
Phillips Publishing Inc., 1202 Seven Locks Road, Suite 300, Potomac MD 20854. 301/340-1520.

AEROSPACE

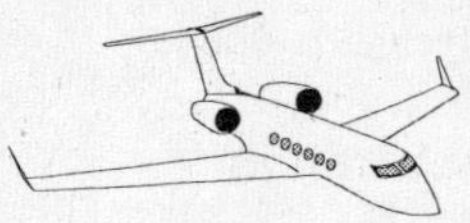

The aerospace industry, wracked by layoffs throughout the early '90s, has yet to pull out of its tailspin. As ever, the slump is being fueled by declining commercial aircraft orders and further defense cuts. As a result, research and development dollars have been trimmed, and many of the biggest firms in the industry have now merged. As of early 1996, the industry was continuing to shrink -- and is now dominated by fewer, larger companies.

While this consolidation has led to a surge in profits, it also means that rapid downsizing will continue. Some analysts believe that even though the defense industry has cut well over 1 million jobs since the late '80s, the industry still needs to cut its workforce by another 30 percent.

Many companies are trying to shift to commercial production, reducing their dependence on dwindling defense contracts. Even so, defense purchases still support a significant number of aerospace workers. Over the long haul, the industry's focus on advanced technology will mean more professional and technical positions -- with engineers leading the way.

ATLANTIC RESEARCH CORPORATION
5945 Wellington Road, Gainsville VA 22065. 703/754-5300. **Contact:** Patrick Davis, Vice President, Human Resources. **Description:** Designs, develops, and manufactures solid propellant rocket motors for missile systems and other uses. Atlantic Research also manufactures electromagnetic security systems and offers professional services. **Common positions include:** Accountant/Auditor; Aerospace Engineer; Chemical Engineer; Chemist; Computer Programmer; Department Engineer; Electrical/Electronics Engineer; General Manager; Industrial Engineer; Mechanical Engineer; Metallurgical Engineer; Operations/Production Manager; Purchasing Agent and Manager; Quality Control Supervisor; Systems Analyst; Technical Writer/Editor. **Educational backgrounds include:** Accounting; Business Administration; Chemistry; Computer Science; Engineering. **Benefits:** Dental Insurance; Disability Coverage; Life Insurance; Medical Insurance; Pension Plan; Savings Plan; Tuition Assistance. **Corporate headquarters location:** This Location. **Operations at this facility include:** Administration; Divisional Headquarters; Manufacturing; Research and Development; Sales; Service.

BELL HELICOPTER
2101 Executive Drive, Hampton VA 23666-2404. 804/827-7222. **Contact:** Human Resources. **Description:** A sales office. Bell Helicopter manufactures a variety of commercial and civilian helicopters, and also conducts extensive research and development activities.

BFGOODRICH/AEROSPACE
HC 75, Box One, Union WV 24983. 304/772-3062. **Contact:** Joe Naizer, Human Resources Director. **Description:** This location is an aircraft de-icer manufacturing facility. Parent company, The BFGoodrich Company, provides aircraft systems, components, and services and manufactures a wide range of specialty chemicals. The business units comprising the aerospace division of BFGoodrich consist of Landing Systems, Sensors and Integrated Systems, Safety Systems, and Maintenance, Repair, and Overhaul. Specialty chemical business units include Specialty Plastics, Specialty Additives, Sealants, Coatings, and Adhesives, and Water Systems and Services.

BRITISH AEROSPACE INC.
22070 Broderick Drive, Sterling VA 20166. 703/406-2000. **Fax:** 703/406-1330. **Contact:** Frank Sterrett, Director of Human Resources. **Description:** This location provides marketing and customer support for British Aerospace, an aircraft manufacturer. **Common positions include:** Accountant/Auditor; Attorney; Budget Analyst; Buyer; Computer Programmer; Computer Systems Analyst; Construction and Building Inspector; Customer Service Representative; Financial Analyst; Public Relations Specialist; Purchasing Agent and Manager; Quality Control Supervisor. **Educational backgrounds include:** Accounting; Business Administration; Computer Science; Finance; Marketing. **Benefits:** 401K; Dental Insurance; Disability Coverage; Life Insurance; Medical Insurance; Pension Plan; Tuition Assistance. **Special Programs:** Internships. **Corporate headquarters location:** This Location. **Parent company:** British Aerospace (England). **Operations at this facility include:** Administration; Sales; Service. **Number of employees at this location:** 350.

THE FLIGHT INTERNATIONAL GROUP, INC.
Newport News/Williamsburg International Airport, Newport News VA 23602. 804/886-5500. **Contact:** Human Resources. **Description:** An aviation services company that performs military training services using specially-modified commercial aircraft, principally under contracts with the U.S. Department of Defense, other government agencies, and foreign countries. In addition, The Flight International Group has established a market for training and testing in the aerospace industry. The company also operates a fixed base operation and owns a flight school at the Newport News/Williamsburg International Airport. **Subsidiaries include:** Flight International, Inc.; Flight International of Florida, Inc.; and Flight International Aviation, Inc. **Corporate headquarters location:** This Location. **Number of employees nationwide:** 136.

ORBITAL SCIENCES CORPORATION
21700 Atlantic Boulevard, Dulles VA 20166-3729. 703/406-5000. **Contact:** Kathy Jones, Manager of Employment and Compensation. **Description:** Designs, manufactures, operates, and markets a broad range of space products. Products include: space transportation systems (space and suborbital launch vehicles and orbit transfer vehicles); spacecraft systems and payloads (spacecraft systems and subsystems, and space sensors and instruments); and satellite-based services and space support products (satellite-based data communications services and environmental and remote sensing services). **Number of employees at this location:** 350. **Number of employees nationwide:** 1,165.

Note: *Because addresses and telephone numbers of smaller companies change rapidly, we recommend you call each company to verify the information below before inquiring about job opportunities. Mass mailings are not recommended.*

Additional small employers:

AIRCRAFT EQUIPMENT AND PARTS

Alliant Techsystems Inc.
St Rte 956, P.O. Box 210, Keyser WV 26726. 304/726-5000.

P&WC Aircraft Services Inc.
Rural Route #3, Box 16, Bridgeport WV 26330-9506. 304/842-5421.

BFGoodrich Aircraft Evacuation
RR 1, Box 7, Grantsville WV 26147-9707. 304/354-6126.

Naval Aviation Depot
PO Box 11094, Norfolk VA 23517-0094. 804/445-4136.

De-Ice Systems International Inc.
1377 N Liberty St, Harrisonburg VA 22801-4510. 540/432-0101.

Lockheed Aeronautical Systems Co.
PO Box 1566, Clarksburg WV 26302-1566. 304/624-6562.

AIRCRAFT

Boeing Company
1700 North Moore Street Floor 20, Arlington VA

22209-1903. 703/558-9600.

Hughes Aircraft Company
1100 Wilson Blvd, Arlington VA 22209-2297. 703/525-1550.

Grumman Space Station
10700 Parkridge Boulevard, 6th Fl, Reston VA 22091-5429. 703/438-5000.

For more information on career opportunities in aerospace:

__Associations__

AIR TRANSPORT ASSOCIATION OF AMERICA
1301 Pennsylvania Avenue NW, Suite 1100, Washington DC 20004. 202/626-4000. A trade association for the major U.S. airlines.

AMERICAN INSTITUTE OF AERONAUTICS AND ASTRONAUTICS
85 John Street, 4th Floor, New York NY 10038. 212/349-1120. Membership required. Publishes six journals and books.

FUTURE AVIATION PROFESSIONALS OF AMERICA
4959 Massachusetts Boulevard, Atlanta GA 30337. 770/997-8097. Publishes a monthly newsletter which monitors the job market for flying jobs; a pilot employment guide, outlining what is required to become a pilot; and a directory of aviation employers.

NATIONAL AERONAUTIC ASSOCIATION OF USA
1815 North Fort Meyer Drive, Suite 700, Arlington VA 22209. 703/527-0226. Publishes a magazine. Membership required.

PROFESSIONAL AVIATION MAINTENANCE ASSOCIATION
500 NW Plaza, Suite 1016, St. Ann MO 63074. 314/739-2580. Members' resumes are distributed to companies who advise the organization of employment opportunities. Many local chapters also provide job referrals. Members have access to the Worldwide Membership Directory.

APPAREL AND TEXTILES

The apparel industry is facing an uncertain future. Women's apparel prices dropped 4.4 percent in 1994, and many experts expect continued deflation through 1996. Consumers have remained disinterested in new fashions and refuse to pay higher prices. Textile and apparel mills are under pressure from the other end of the supply chain as well -- the cost of cotton and other raw materials has remained at close to record highs, with raw cotton prices jumping 35 percent in 1994. As a result, many textile producers have recently reported significant drops in earnings. However, improved consumer confidence, more attractive fashions, and lower prices may prod consumers to buy. This will eventually increase business for mills. Especially hot: sales of men's suits. This trend is expected to continue as men look for upscale casual wear to accommodate more relaxed dress codes. The highest consumer demand in apparel will probably be for lower-priced clothing produced for discount stores.

AJD CAP CORPORATION
3301 Castlewood Road, Richmond VA 23234. 804/231-0211. **Contact:** Human Resources. **Description:** A manufacturer of baseball caps.

ALPHA INDUSTRIES INC.
1600 Spring Hill Road, Suite 220, Vienna VA 22182. 703/506-2482. **Fax:** 703/506-2487. **Contact:** Linda Dunlap, Office Manager. **Description:** Founded in 1959 in a leased building with 40 employees, Alpha Industries Inc. has grown to become one of the largest military clothing manufacturers in the United States. More than 37 years ago Alpha Industries received it first U.S. Department of Defense contract for field jackets and has produced them continuously since then. In 1961 Alpha Industries landed its first U.S. government contract for MA-1 flight jackets and since that time, Alpha has supplied virtually all of the MA-1's to the U.S. Military. Alpha Industries' manufacturing facilities in Knoxville, TN, utilize modern equipment and manufacturing techniques to produce the technical, specialized military clothing required by the world's sophisticated military forces, as well as civilians seeking cold weather clothing.

BASSETT-WALKER, INC.
P.O. Box 606, Brookneal VA 24528. 804/376-3543. **Contact:** Charlotte Moorefield, Human Resources Director. **Description:** A manufacturer of men's, women's, and children's fleecewear.

BASSETT-WALKER, INC.
Route Two, Box 120, Chatham VA 24531. 804/432-0444. **Contact:** Rosalin Davidson, Human Resources Director. **Description:** A manufacturer of men's, women's, and children's fleecewear.

BASSETT-WALKER, INC.
Route Five, Box 1560, Stuart VA 24171-9088. 540/694-3118. **Contact:** Human Resources. **Description:** Primary activity at this facility involves the dyeing and cutting of fabrics used to manufacture fleecewear.

BIBB CO.
813 Lynchburg Avenue, Brookneal VA 24528. 804/376-2311. **Contact:** Janice Raley, Human Resources Director. **Description:** A manufacturer of a broad range of textiles, including sheets, pillowcases, and draperies. **NOTE:**

Interested candidates may contact Human Resources for application procedure. This firm does not accept unsolicited resumes. Please only respond to advertised openings.

BRISTOL LINGERIE
203 Bob Morrison Boulevard, Bristol VA 24201-3899. 540/669-7188. **Contact:** Belinda Venable, Human Resources Manager. **Description:** Bristol Lingerie manufactures women's lingerie.

BRODNAX MILLS INC.
P.O. Box A, Brodnax VA 23920. 804/729-2325. **Contact:** Mabel Pulley, Human Resources. **Description:** A yarn manufacturer.

BURLINGTON INDUSTRIES, INC.
P.O. Box 1410, Clarksville VA 23927. 804/374-8111. **Contact:** Mr. Shuford, Human Resources Manager. **Description:** A finishing plant. Burlington Industries, Inc. is a manufacturer of men's and women's clothing.

BURLINGTON INDUSTRIES, INC.
P.O. Box 669, Halifax VA 24558. 804/476-6501. **Contact:** Human Resources Manager. **Description:** A manufacturing facility. Burlington Industries, Inc. is a manufacturer of men's and women's clothing.

BURLINGTON INDUSTRIES, INC.
P.O. Box 2000, Hurt VA 24563. 804/324-4211. **Contact:** Carol McCrickard, Human Resources Manager. **Description:** A dyeing and finishing plant. Burlington Industries, Inc. is a manufacturer of men's and women's clothing.

BUSTER BROWN APPAREL INC.
P.O. Box 558, Chilhowie VA 24319. 540/646-3116. **Contact:** Charlotte Goff, Office Coordinator. **Description:** Manufactures children's clothing.

BUSTER BROWN APPAREL INC.
P.O. Box 1798, Coeburn VA 24230. 703/395-3304. **Contact:** Catherine Bevins, Office Coordinator. **Description:** A manufacturer of children's clothing.

CAMAC CORPORATION
P.O. Box 8930, Bristol VA 24203-1004. 540/669-1161. **Contact:** Gary Wolfe, Human Resources Manager. **Description:** A manufacturer of synthetic fibers for use primarily in carpets and furniture upholstery.

CLOVER YARNS INC.
P.O. Box Eight, Clover VA 24534. 804/454-7151. **Contact:** Human Resources. **Description:** A textile plant that manufactures yarn.

CRADDOCK-TERRY INC.
Route Two, Box 160, Farmville VA 23901. 804/392-3783. **Contact:** Robert Orange, Personnel Director. **Description:** Craddock-Terry Inc. manufactures men's and women's dress shoes and military shoes. The company consists of a catalog division as well as a retail store, and its military shoes are contracted to the armed services.

CRADDOCK-TERRY INC.
601 12th Street, Lynchburg VA 24504-3000. 804/392-3783. **Contact:** Brantley Blair, Human Resources Manager. **Description:** Craddock-Terry Inc. manufactures men's and women's dress shoes and military shoes. The company consists of a catalog division as well as a retail store, and its military shoes are contracted to the armed services. **Corporate headquarters location:** This Location.

CROSS CREEK APPAREL INC.
P.O. Box 726, Hillsville VA 24343. 540/728-2134. **Contact:** Michelle Dalton, Human Resources Representative. **Description:** A sewing plant. Cross Creek Apparel Inc. manufactures men's and women's knit shirts.

CROSS CREEK APPAREL INC.
1020 Stafford Umberger Drive, Wytheville VA 24382. 540/228-3511. **Contact:** Human Resources. **Description:** A manufacturer of men's and women's knit shirts.

DAN RIVER, INC.
2291 Memorial Drive, Danville VA 24541. 804/799-7000. **Contact:** Edward Carroll, Vice President, Human Resources. **Description:** A manufacturer and marketer of textile products for the home fashions and apparel fabrics markets. Dan River manufactures a coordinated line of home fashions products consisting of packaged bedroom furnishings such as comforters, sheets, pillowcases, shams, bed skirts, decorative pillows, and draperies. The company also manufactures a broad range of woven and knit cotton and cotton-blend apparel fabrics and is a leading domestic supplier of men's dress shirt fabrics, primarily oxford and pinpoint oxford cloth. Dan River distributes home fashions products through a full range of domestic distribution channels, including department stores, specialty home fashion stores, direct marketers, national chains, mass merchants, and regional discounters. **Subsidiaries include:** Dan River Factory Stores, Inc., which operates 12 factory outlet stores in the Midwest and Southeast. **Benefits:** Retirement Plan. **Corporate headquarters location:** This Location. **Parent company:** Braelan Corporation. **Listed on:** Privately held. **Number of employees nationwide:** 4,900.

DIVERSIFIED APPAREL RESOURCES
1201 East Main Street, Pulaski VA 24301-5316. 703/980-5601. **Contact:** Mary Shelor, Human Resources. **Description:** A manufacturer of Sparkle brand children's apparel.

E.I. DuPONT deNEMOURS & CO.
400 Dupont Boulevard, Waynesboro VA 22980. 540/949-2000. **Contact:** Human Resources. **Description:** Manufactures lycra and nylon. E.I. DuPont de Nemours & Company is a corporation whose diverse activities include the manufacturing of biomedical, industrial, and consumer products (such as photographic, data-recording, and video devices); the production of man-made fiber products (with applications in a variety of consumer and commercial industries); polymer products (such as plastic resins, elastomers, and films); agricultural and industrial chemicals (such as herbicides and insecticides, pigments, fluorochemicals, petroleum additives, and mineral acids); the exploration and production of crude oil and natural gas; the refining, marketing, and downstream transportation of petroleum; and the mining and distribution of steam and metallurgical coals. Industries served range from aerospace, agriculture, and apparel to transportation, health care, and printing and publishing.

LEVI STRAUSS & COMPANY
P.O. Box 580, Warsaw VA 22572. 804/333-4007. **Contact:** Alice Mundie, Human Resources Assistant. **Description:** Designs, manufactures, and markets worldwide a diversified line of apparel, primarily jeans and jeans-related products under the brand names Levi's and Britannia. The company also makes the Dockers line of clothing for U.S. markets. Operates 44 manufacturing and warehouse facilities and eight distribution centers in the U.S., and 22 and 19, respectively, overseas.

LIBERTY FABRICS INC.
One Cleveland Street, P.O. Box 308, Gordonsville VA 22942. 703/832-2261. **Fax:** 703/832-7145. **Contact:** Laura M. Byrnes, Personnel Manager/Training Administrator. **Description:** One of the largest producers of

lace in the country. Liberty Fabrics also produces knit fabrics. This facility is responsible for dyeing and finishing the products. **Common positions include:** Accountant/Auditor; Budget Analyst; Buyer; Customer Service Representative; Human Resources Specialist; Industrial Engineer; Industrial Production Manager; Operations/Production Manager; Services Sales Representative; Textile Manager. **Educational backgrounds include:** Chemistry; Textiles. **Benefits:** 401K; Disability Coverage; Life Insurance; Medical Insurance; Profit Sharing; Spending Account; Tuition Assistance. **Corporate headquarters location:** New York NY. **Other U.S. locations:** Janesville NC; North Bergen NJ; Woolwine VA. **Parent company:** Courtaulds Textiles. **Operations at this facility include:** Administration; Manufacturing; Research and Development; Sales. **Number of employees at this location:** 250. **Number of employees nationwide:** 1,200.

LOGAN MANUFACTURING CO.
110 Phico Street, Chapmanville WV 25508. 304/752-7200. **Contact:** Jim Ferguson, Plant Manager. **Description:** A manufacturer of men's and women's outerwear.

NATALIE KNITTING MILLS
Hwy 11 East, Chilhowie VA 24319. 540/646-8941. **Contact:** Wanda Morgan, Human Resource Manager. **Description:** Established in 1973, Natalie Knitting Mills manufactures and distributes fashion knit sweaters both nationally and internationally to such companies as Lands End. **Number of employees at this location:** 250.

NEW RIVER INDUSTRIES, INC.
P.O. 1132, Radford VA 24141. 703/639-2486. **Contact:** Bill Bryant, Director of Human Resources. **Description:** Established in 1988, New River Industries, Inc. is a textile manufacturing company that weaves fabrics and sells these to converters nationally. **Number of employees at this location:** 525.

PRECISION FABRICS GROUP, INC.
P.O. Box 337, Vinton VA 24179. 703/343-4448. **Contact:** Greg Adams, Human Resource Manager. **Description:** A textile manufacturer. Established in 1988. Precision Fabrics Group, Inc. sends their product to another company to be distributed. **Number of employees at this location:** 600.

RUSSELL MANUFACTURING
650 Haber Drive, Lebanon VA 24266. 703/889-1437. **Contact:** Personnel Office. **Description:** Manufacturer of ladies loungewear and sleepwear.

SARA LEE KNIT PRODUCTS
RR 1 623-S, Hillsville VA 24343. 540/728-1400. **Contact:** Jim Cobb, Human Resource Manager. **Description:** A sewing facility. Sara Lee Knit Products manufactures casual wear.

SARA LEE KNIT PRODUCTS
P.O. Box 4626, Martinsville VA 24115. 540/956-7100. **Contact:** Human Resources. **Description:** A textiles and apparel company. **NOTE:** This firm does not accept unsolicited resumes. Please only respond to advertised openings.

TULTEX CORPORATION
101 Commonwealth Boulevard, P.O. Box 5191, Martinsville VA 24115. 703/632-2961. **Contact:** Human Resources Department. **Description:** Manufactures fleece and jersey-knit activewear and leisure apparel. **Number of employees at this location:** 7,500.

H. WARSHOW & SONS INC.
P.O. Box 488, Tappahannock VA 22560. 804/443-3391. **Contact:** Richard Carlton, Director of Human Resources. **Description:** A textile mill.

Note: *Because addresses and telephone numbers of smaller companies change rapidly, we recommend you call each company to verify the information below before inquiring about job opportunities. Mass mailings are not recommended.*

Additional small employers:

APPAREL WHOLESALE

Spring Ford Knitting Co.
51 Lee Hwy, Chilhowie VA 24319. 540/646-2185.

Aileen Inc.
Flint Hill, Flint Hill VA 22627. 540/675-3311.

Ammar's Inc.
710 S College Ave, Bluefield VA 24605-1639. 703/322-4686.

Trade Winds Import Co.
PO Box 10549, Lynchburg VA 24506-0549. 804/239-0391.

BROADWOVEN FABRIC MILLS

Fieldcrest Cannon Inc.
Field Ave, Fieldale VA 24089. 540/673-6771.

Stillwater Inc.
S R 42, Augusta Sprgs VA 24411. 540/997-9221.

The Velvet Textile Co. Inc.
300 Church St, Blackstone VA 23824-1602. 804/292-7211.

Firestone Fibers & Textiles Company
105 Winston Churchill Dr, Hopewell VA 23860-5235. 804/541-2000.

JPS Converter & Industrial
203 Pell Ave, Rocky Mount VA 24151-1114. 540/483-5116.

JPS Converter & Industrial
2305 Vaughan St, South Boston VA 24592-3522. 804/572-2921.

CARPETS AND RUGS

Lees Carpet
404 Anderson St, Glasgow VA 24555-2802. 540/258-2811.

Shaw Industries Inc.
9351 Northeast Dr, Fredericksbrg VA 22408-8722. 540/899-5590.

Troy Mills Inc.
625 N Pennsylvania Ave, Harrisville WV 26362. 304/643-2972.

NARROW FABRIC AND OTHER SMALLWARES MILLS

Alkahn Labels Inc.
PO Box 1288, Weston WV 26452-1288. 304/269-2332.

Franklin Braid Manufacturing
620 Davis St, Emporia VA 23847-1405. 804/634-4142.

Paxar Corp.
400 Virginia Ave, Hillsville VA 24343-1625. 540/728-2121.

Labels East Inc.
920 Business Park Dr, Chesapeake VA 23320-2445. 804/420-5036.

KNITTING MILLS

Superior Mills Inc.
Hwy 11 E, Chilhowie VA 24319. 540/646-8972.

Durham Hosiery Mills
525 Lynn St, Danville VA 24541-1451. 804/792-5011.

Renfro Corp.
4100 Bob White Blvd, Pulaski VA 24301. 540/980-1900.

Royce Hosiery Mills Inc.
750 Baltimore St, Martinsburg WV 25401-2822. 304/263-8961.

Quality Sweats
840 W 2nd St, Weston WV 26452-1764. 304/269-7497.

Tultex Corp.
216 Mineral St, South Boston VA 24592-3712. 804/572-2914.

Virginia Garment Co. Inc.
501 N 17th St, Richmond VA 23219-2003. 804/648-1222.

Elastic Corp. Of America
Rt 8 N, Woolwine VA 24185. 540/930-3031.

TEXTILE FINISHING

Southampton Textile Co.
520 Reese St, Emporia VA 23847-1435. 804/634-2159.

Star Children's Dress Company
9120 Pridesville Rd, Amelia Ct House VA 23002-4862. 804/561-5060.

Stillwater Inc.
Rt 39, Goshen VA 24439. 540/997-9231.

Virginia Mills Cotton Products
505 6th St SW, Roanoke VA 24016-3523. 540/343-4495.

Revolution Processors
859 Jefferson St, Danville VA 24541-2419. 804/792-5553.

Ronile Inc.
510 Orchard Ave, Rocky Mount VA 24151-1810. 540/483-0261.

YARN AND THREAD MILLS

Jefferson Mills Inc.
Valley St, Pulaski VA 24301. 540/980-1530.

JPS Elastomerics Corp.
Hwy 58 E, Stuart VA 24171. 540/694-3131.

NONWOVEN FABRICS

Liberty Fabrics Inc.
S R 618, Woolwine VA 24185. 540/930-2323.

United Elastic Corp.
PO Box 519, Stuart VA 24171-0519. 540/694-7171.

TEXTILE GOODS

Fred Whitaker Co.
941 Industry Ave SE, Roanoke VA 24013-2927. 540/427-4343.

Unifi Inc.
Morris Mill Rd, Staunton VA 24402. 540/885-1211.

WNI Fiber Processing
2000 S Delphine Ave, Waynesboro VA 22980. 540/946-3700.

MEN'S AND BOYS' CLOTHING

Buena Vista Manufacturing Co.
324 E 32nd St, Buena Vista VA 24416-1275. 540/261-7425.

Dublin Garment Co. Inc.
RR 2 Box 128A, Castlewood VA 24224-9760. 540/794-9141.

Jafree Shirt Co. Inc.
1200 W Main St, Wytheville VA 24382-2110. 540/228-2116.

Lee Textile Inc.
Sand Cave Rd, Ewing VA 24248. 703/445-5171.

Springford Knitting Co/Plant 2
Hwy 11, Chilhowie VA 24319. 540/646-8951.

St. Paul Apparel Inc.
RR 1 Box 570, Saint Paul VA 24283-9514. 540/762-0082.

Clintwood Garment Co.
Factory Dr, Clintwood VA 24228. 540/926-4633.

Hartz-Broadway Inc.
101 Hartz Blvd, Broadway VA 22815-9476. 540/896-2200.

Jonbil Inc.
PO Box 37, Chase City VA 23924-0037. 804/372-3181.

Mr. Casuals
Mr. Casuals Ln, Trout Dale VA 24378. 540/677-3611.

Wrangler Inc.
Washington St, Madison VA 22727. 540/948-4504.

Wrangler Inc.
113 Indian Spring Rd, Woodstock VA 22664-1601. 540/459-2181.

Wrangler Inc.
323 Pulaski Ave, Shenandoah VA 22849-1731. 540/652-8149.

Wrangler Inc.
101 Blue Bell Ave, Luray VA 22835-1656. 540/743-5147.

Britches Of Georgetowne
544 Herndon Pky, Herndon VA 22070-5297. 703/471-7900.

Corbin Ltd
1040 Vernon St, Huntington WV 25704-2053. 304/429-1388.

Lars Hanssons Big and Tall
1507 Hershberger Rd NW, Roanoke VA 24012-7319. 540/366-4669.

Reidbord Bros Co.
Wilson Ln, Elkins WV 26241. 304/636-1946.

Rugged Sportswear
201 Sharp St, Lawrenceville VA 23868-1615. 804/848-3306.

Tultex Corp.
Hwy 11 E, Chilhowie VA 24319. 540/646-8927.

Tultex Corp.
PO Box 40, Bastian VA 24314-0040. 540/688-3335.

WOMEN'S AND MISSES' CLOTHING

Dublin Garment Co. Inc.
320 Newbern Rd, Dublin VA 24084-3317. 540/674-4651.

Economy Industries
412 S Cross St, Harrisville WV 26362-1372. 304/643-2907.

Halmode Apparel Inc.
728 Wertz Rd NE, Roanoke VA 24012-4544. 540/563-2801.

Lebanon Apparel Corp.
RR 2, Box 498, Lebanon VA 24266-9515. 540/889-3656.

Oxford Industries
Mountain View Industrial Pk, Pearisburg VA 24134. 540/921-3813.

Parksley Apparel Co.
18554 Bennett St, Parksley VA 23421. 804/665-5114.

Rural Retreat Garment Co.
Mount View Dr, Rural Retreat VA 24368. 540/686-4124.

Carolyn Manufacturing Co.
21 Washington St, Bristol VA 24201-4540. 540/466-3231.

Craig Manufacturing Co.
RR 3, Box 440, New Castle VA 24127-9515. 540/864-5141.

Halmode Apparel Inc.
920 S Lexington Ave, Covington VA 24426-1919. 703/965-0489.

Lee County Garment Co.
PO Box 9, Dryden VA 24243-0009. 540/546-2603.

Aileen Inc.
Tidewater Ave, Victoria VA 23974. 804/696-2118.

Aileen Inc.
Old Brandy Rd, Culpeper VA 22701. 540/825-8363.

Fabric Cutters Inc.
326 Oxford Street, Floyd VA 24091. 540/745-4141.

Gordon Garment Co.
1001 Rhode Island Ave, Bristol VA 24201-4648. 540/669-1125.

Maid Bess Corp.
865 Cleveland Ave, Salem VA 24153-2920. 540/389-8113.

Perry Manufacturing Co.
Comers Rock Rd, Elk Creek VA 24326. 540/655-4110.

Russell Apparel Corp.
219 Norwood St, Radford VA 24141-3922. 540/639-5761.

Skyline Sportswear Inc.
302 S Locust St, Floyd VA 24091-2320. 540/745-2281.

Virginia Apparel Corp.
721 N Main St, Rocky Mount VA 24151-2202. 540/483-0231.

Woolfolk Manufacturing Corp.
401 E Main St, Louisa VA 23093-9758. 540/967-1313.

Elkton Garment
RR 1, Elkton VA 22827-9801. 540/298-1288.

Jacqueline Manufacturing Corp.
Clinch St, Richlands VA 24641. 540/964-9614.

HEAD WEAR

M&B Headwear Co. Inc.
2323 E Main St, Richmond VA 23223-7843. 804/648-1603.

Nomad Manufacturing
3209 Washington Ave, Newport News VA 23607-3330. 804/380-6020.

CHILDREN'S AND INFANTS' CLOTHING

Amelia Dress Co. Inc.
RR 2, Box 24, Appomattox VA 24522-9359. 804/352-7145.

Amelia Dress Co. Inc.
U S Hwy 460 E, Farmville VA 23901. 804/392-4573.

Courtland Manufacturing Co. Inc.
PO Box 266, Boydton VA 23917-0266. 804/352-7154.

Healthtex Inc.
2499 N Main St, Danville VA 24540-2396. 804/836-0543.

Spencer's Inc.
Indl Pk, Stuart VA 24171. 540/694-4775.

Strasburg Manufacturing
Aileen Ave, Strasburg VA 22657. 540/465-5144.

Louisa Manufacturing Corp.
213 Fredericksburg Ave, Louisa VA 23093-9767. 540/967-0474.

Lovingston Manufacturing/Plant 2
28 W Rock St, Harrisonburg VA 22801-3804. 540/434-9971.

Petersburg Garment Co.
PO Box 99, Petersburg WV 26847-0099. 304/257-1977.

ROBES AND DRESSING GOWNS

Hampco Apparel Inc.
220 Cabell St, Martinsville VA 24112-3256. 540/632-9733.

CURTAINS AND DRAPERIES

VQC Inc/Commercial Industries Division
1 North Side Industrial Pk, South Hill VA 23970. 804/447-5091.

TRIMMINGS, APPAREL FINDINGS, AND RELATED PRODUCTS

Collegiate Pacific Co.
1302 Rockland Ave NW, Roanoke VA 24012-3838. 540/366-2451.

T-Shirt International Inc.
2101 Grace St, Culloden WV 25510-9033. 304/743-7905.

T-Shirt International Inc.
2660 Main St, Hurricane WV 25526-1419. 304/562-2401.

Waverly Textile Process
8401 Fort Darling Rd, Richmond VA 23237-1368. 804/275-0400.

EMBROIDERY

D&P Embroidery Co.
Rt 198, Cobbs Creek VA 23035. 804/725-2153.

FABRICATED TEXTILE PRODUCTS

Narricot Industries Inc.
1556 Montgomery Street, South Hill VA 23970-3919. 804/447-7629.

BOOT AND SHOE CUT STOCK AND FINDINGS

Hanover Shoe Co.
300 2nd Ave, Marlinton WV 24954-1130. 304/799-6856.

MISC. APPAREL AND ACCESSORIES

Morgan Shirt Corporation
PO Box 867, Morgantown WV 26507-0867. 304/292-8451.

FOOTWEAR

Boot & Shoemaker Shop
104 W Duke Of Gloucester St, Williamsburg VA 23185-4258. 804/229-1000.

Hanover Shoe Co.
PO Box 310, Franklin WV 26807-0310. 304/358-2335.

Pro-Track Of VA
1116 Court Street, Victoria VA 23974-9477. 804/696-2179.

Virginia Shoe Manufacturing
120 East Second Street, Farmville VA 23901-1321. 804/392-9947.

For more information on career opportunities in the apparel and textiles industries:

Associations

AMERICAN APPAREL MANUFACTURERS ASSOCIATION
2500 Wilson Boulevard, Suite 301, Arlington VA 22201. 703/524-1864. Publishes numerous magazines, newsletters, and bulletins for the benefit of employees in the apparel manufacturing industry.

AMERICAN TEXTILE MANUFACTURERS INSTITUTE
Office of the Chief Economist, 1801 K Street NW, Suite 900, Washington DC 20006-1301. 202/862-0500. Fax: 202/862-0570. The national trade association for the domestic textile industry. Members are corporations only.

THE FASHION GROUP
597 5th Avenue, 8th Floor, New York NY 10017. 212/593-1715. A nonprofit organization for professional women in the fashion industries (apparel, accessories, beauty, and home). Offers career counseling workshops 18 times per year.

INTERNATIONAL ASSOCIATION OF CLOTHING DESIGNERS
475 Park Avenue South, 17th Floor, New York NY 10016. 212/685-6602. Fax: 212/545-1709.

Directories

AAMA DIRECTORY
American Apparel Manufacturers Association, 2500 Wilson Boulevard, Suite 301, Arlington VA 22201. 703/524-1864. A directory of publications distributed by the American Apparel Manufacturers Association.

APPAREL TRADES BOOK
Dun & Bradstreet Inc., 430 Mountain Avenue, New Providence NJ 07974. 908/665-5000.

FAIRCHILD'S MARKET DIRECTORY OF WOMEN'S AND CHILDREN'S APPAREL
Fairchild Publications, 7 West 34th Street, New York NY 10001. 212/630-4000.

Magazines

ACCESSORIES
Business Journals, 50 Day Street, P.O. Box 5550, Norwalk CT 06856. 203/853-6015.

AMERICA'S TEXTILES
Billiam Publishing, 37 Villa Road, Suite 111, P.O. Box 103, Greenville SC 29615. 864/242-5300.

APPAREL INDUSTRY MAGAZINE
Shore Communications Inc., 6255 Barfield Road, Suite 200, Atlanta GA 30328-4893. 404/252-8831.

BOBBIN
Bobbin Publications, P.O. Box 1986, 1110 Shop Road, Columbia SC 29202. 803/771-7500.

TEXTILE HILIGHTS
American Textile Manufacturers Institute, Office of the Chief Economist, 1801 K Street NW, Suite 900, Washington DC 20006.

WOMEN'S WEAR DAILY (WWD)
Fairchild Publications, 7 West 34th Street, New York NY 10001. 212/630-4000.

ARCHITECTURE, CONSTRUCTION, AND ENGINEERING

The U.S. Department of Labor has estimated 1.2 million new construction jobs from 1992 through 2005, due to the need to replace aging experienced workers. Residential construction will grow slowly, as a result of the expected decline in population growth. Industrial construction, however, will be stronger because of an increase in exports by manufacturers. Heavy construction is growing faster than the industry average, with much activity in highway, bridge, and street construction.

Job prospects for engineers have been good for a number of years, and will continue to improve into the next century. Employers will need more engineers as they increase investment in equipment in order to expand output. In addition, engineers will find work improving the nation's deteriorating infrastructure.

ALCOA BUILDING PRODUCTS
P.O. Box 538, Stuarts Draft VA 24477-0538. 540/943-0802. **Contact:** Human Resources. **Description:** Manufactures vinyl siding for sale to distributors.

MICHAEL BAKER CORPORATION
CIVIL AND WATER RESOURCES DIVISION
3601 Eisenhower Avenue, Suite 600, Alexandria VA 22304. 703/960-8800. **Fax:** 703/960-9125. **Contact:** Human Resources. **Description:** Michael Baker Corporation is a professional services company that provides engineering consulting and design services, construction services, and operations and maintenance services. Established in 1940 as the company's core business, the engineering group encompasses a broad range of disciplines required to plan, design, and inspect the construction of architectural and engineering projects and other facilities. Baker's construction group consists of: construction management and design, heavy and highway construction, and general construction.

BARBER & ROSS COMPANY
110 Catoctin Circle, P.O. Box 1294, Leesburg VA 22075. 703/478-1970. **Contact:** Dan Reeves, Assistant Controller. **Description:** Manufactures window units, interior and exterior door units, door entrance features, and other door and sash products. **Corporate headquarters location:** This Location.

BURGESS & NIPLE, LTD.
Suite 1203, 707 Virginia Street East, Charleston WV 25301. 304/342-0000. **Contact:** Tom Hibbard, Recruiting Specialist. **Description:** An engineering and architecture firm engaged in study, analysis, and design services. Programs include waterworks, waste water, industrial services, hydropower, energy conservation, transportation, HVAC, systems analysis, and geotechnical. **Common positions include:** Architect; Civil Engineer. **Corporate headquarters location:** Columbus OH.

DEWBERRY & DAVIS
8401 Arlington Boulevard, Fairfax VA 22031-4666. 703/849-0525. **Fax:** 703/849-0185. **Contact:** Department of Human Resources. **Description:** A

full-service architectural and engineering firm. Dewberry & Davis has been included in the top 50 of *Engineering News-Record*'s Top 500 Design Firms for the past several years. Operations of the company include water resources, environmental engineering, transportation engineering, mechanical/electrical and structural engineering, planning, landscape architecture, architecture, program management, and digitized mapping services, as well as land development engineering and surveying. **Common positions include:** Architect; Civil Engineer; Construction Contractor and Manager; Designer; Draftsperson; Electrical/Electronics Engineer; Environmental Engineer; Geographer; Landscape Architect; Mechanical Engineer; Structural Engineer; Surveyor; Urban/Regional Planner. **Educational backgrounds include:** Architecture; Engineering; Geography; Urban Planning. **Benefits:** 401K; Credit Union; Dental Insurance; Disability Coverage; Employee Discounts; Life Insurance; Medical Insurance; Savings Plan; Tuition Assistance. **Corporate headquarters location:** This Location. **Other U.S. locations:** Annapolis MD; Gaithersburg MD; Lanham MD; Raleigh NC; Danville VA; Leesburg VA; Manassas VA; Marion VA; Richmond VA. **Subsidiaries include:** Goodkind & O'Dea, Inc., in New York NY, Rutherford NJ, North Haven CT, Boston MA, and Dillsburg PA; TOLK, Inc.; Dewberry & Davis Service Operations, Inc.; Dewberry & Davis Risk Management, Inc.; and American Digital Systems. **Operations at this facility include:** Regional Headquarters. **Listed on:** Privately held. **Number of employees at this location:** 400. **Number of employees nationwide:** 1,000.

DIXON LUMBER COMPANY, INC.
152 Boyer Road, P.O. Box 907, Galax VA 24333. 540/236-9963. **Fax:** 540/236-9490. **Contact:** Kathy Anderson, Personnel Assistant. **Description:** A manufacturer of unfinished and finished hardwood flooring, unfinished dimensions, stairs, and accessories. **Common positions include:** Accountant/Auditor; Automotive Mechanic/Body Repairer; Blue-Collar Worker Supervisor; Buyer; Clerical Supervisor; Credit Manager; Customer Service Representative; Electrician; General Manager; Human Resources Specialist; Manufacturer's/Wholesaler's Sales Rep.; Operations/Production Manager; Purchasing Agent and Manager; Quality Control Supervisor; Wholesale and Retail Buyer. **Benefits:** 401K; Life Insurance; Medical Insurance. **Corporate headquarters location:** This Location. **Operations at this facility include:** Administration; Manufacturing; Sales; Service. **Number of employees at this location:** 325.

FAILURE ANALYSIS ASSOCIATES
310 Montgomery Street, Alexandria VA 22314. 703/549-9565. **Contact:** Human Resources. **Description:** Founded in 1967, Failure Analysis Associates has performed the scientific analysis of thousands of cases, from headline-making multi-million dollar disasters to small accident investigations and routine risk assessments. The company's expertise is used in areas such as accident reconstruction, biomechanics, construction/structural engineering, aviation and marine investigations, environmental assessment, materials and product testing, warnings and labeling issues, accident statistic data analysis, and risk prevention/mitigation. **NOTE:** Employment inquiries may be addressed to human resources at 149 Commonwealth Drive, Menlo Park CA 94025. **Parent company:** The Failure Group, Inc.

R.E. LEE & SON, INC.
P.O. Box 7226, Charlottesville VA 22906. 804/973-1321. **Contact:** Human Resources. **Description:** A general contractor.

NVR
7601 Lewinsville Road, McLean VA 22102. 703/761-2000. **Contact:** Laurel Leslie, Human Resource Manager. **Description:** Home builder and mortgage banking company. NVR serves people in 13 metropolitan areas, primarily on the East Coast. **Subsidiaries include:** Ryan Homes and NV Homes (both of which are also at this location).

NATIONWIDE HOMES, INC.
1100 Rives Road, Martinsville VA 24112. 703/632-7100. **Contact:** John Adams, Personnel Director. **Description:** Nationwide Homes constructs modular homes.

PIERCE ASSOCIATES
4216 Wheeler Avenue, Alexandria VA 22304. 703/751-2400. **Fax:** 703/751-2479. **Contact:** Robert N. Keyser, Senior Vice President. **Description:** Pierce Associates is a special trades contractor in mechanical construction, including such concentrations as HVAC, plumbing, and fire protection. **Common positions include:** Mechanical Engineer. **Benefits:** 401K; Dental Insurance; Life Insurance; Medical Insurance. **Corporate headquarters location:** This Location. **Listed on:** Privately held. **Number of employees at this location:** 40.

RYAN HOMES, INC.
7601 Lewinsville Road, Suite 300, McLean VA 22102. 703/761-2255. **Fax:** 703/761-2259. **Contact:** Joseph Madigan, Director, Human Resources. **Description:** A home builder and financial services company. Ryan Homes and sister company NV Homes are both wholly-owned subsidiaries of NVR, Inc. (also at this location). **Common positions include:** Accountant/Auditor; Construction Contractor and Manager; Customer Service Representative; Economist/Market Research Analyst; Financial Analyst; Services Sales Representative. **Educational backgrounds include:** Accounting; Business Administration; Communications; Economics; Finance; Liberal Arts; Marketing; Mathematics. **Benefits:** 401K; Dental Insurance; Disability Coverage; Employee Discounts; Life Insurance; Medical Insurance; Profit Sharing. **Other U.S. locations:** DE; MD; NC; NY; PA; VA. **Parent company:** NVR, Inc. **Operations at this facility include:** Divisional Headquarters; Regional Headquarters; Sales; Service. **Listed on:** American Stock Exchange. **Number of employees at this location:** 500. **Number of employees nationwide:** 2,000.

TIDEWATER CONSTRUCTION CORPORATION
P.O. Box 57, Norfolk VA 23501. 804/420-4140. **Fax:** 804/420-3551. **Contact:** Paul Rose, Labor Relations Manager. **Description:** Tidewater Construction is an *ENR* 200 heavy and industrial contractor with operations primarily in the Southeast. **Common positions include:** Civil Engineer; Secretary; Stationary Engineer; Welder. **Educational backgrounds include:** Engineering. **Benefits:** Dental Insurance; Disability Coverage; Life Insurance; Medical Insurance; Pension Plan; Tuition Assistance. **Corporate headquarters location:** This Location. **Parent company:** Hanson, PLC. **Number of employees nationwide:** 150.

VECELLIO & GROGAN, INC.
P.O. Box V, Beckley WV 25802. 304/252-6575. **Contact:** Penny Jones, Human Resources. **Description:** A construction company specializing in highways and bridges.

WILLIAMS INDUSTRIES INC.
2849 Meadow View Road, Falls Church VA 22042. **Contact:** Human Resources. **Description:** A construction company. **Common positions include:** Accountant/Auditor; Adjuster; Attorney; Civil Engineer; Computer Programmer; Construction and Building Inspector; Construction Contractor and Manager; Cost Estimator; Industrial Engineer. **Educational backgrounds include:** Accounting; Energy. **Benefits:** 401K; Dental Insurance; Life Insurance; Medical Insurance. **Corporate headquarters location:** This Location. **Operations at this facility include:** Administration; Sales. **Listed on:** NASDAQ.

***Note:** Because addresses and telephone numbers of smaller companies change rapidly, we recommend you call each company to verify the information below before inquiring about job opportunities. Mass mailings are not recommended.*

Additional small employers:

CONSTRUCTION MATERIALS WHOLESALE

Construction Materials Company
820 W Chestnut, Covington VA 24426. 703/962-2139.

PLUMBING, HEATING, AND A/C EQUIPMENT WHOLESALE

Barnett Brass & Copper Company
5600 Charles City Cir, Richmond VA 23231-4539. 804/236-0025.

Hajoca
1 Boulevard St SW, Roanoke VA 24016-2501. 540/345-3824.

Frischkorn Inc.
1801 Roseneath Rd, Richmond VA 23230-4330. 804/353-0181.

ENGINEERING SERVICES

Advanced Communication Systems
1900 N Beauregard St, Ste 300, Alexandria VA 22311-1716. 703/553-4389.

C-Cubed Corporation
5252 Cherokee Ave, Ste 400, Alexandria VA 22312-2000. 703/658-9685.

CH2M Hill-Northeast Regional Office
PO Box 4400, Reston VA 22090-1483. 703/471-1441.

Comsearch
2002 Edmund Halley Dr, Reston VA 22091-3436. 703/620-6300.

Hayes, Seay, Mattern & Mattern
1315 Franklin Road Southwest, Roanoke VA 24016-4607. 540/857-3100.

Henkels & McCoy
PO Box 1507, Newington VA 22122-1507. 703/550-0450.

Entek Inc.
333 N Fairfax St, # 301, Alexandria VA 22314-2632. 703/578-5900.

Industrial Resources Inc.
PO Box 2648, Fairmont WV 26555-2648. 304/363-4100.

Jaycor Advanced Technology Management
1608 Spring Hill Rd, Vienna VA 22182-2224. 703/847-4000.

JJH Inc.
5400 Shawnee Rd, Alexandria VA 22312-2300. 703/642-3152.

MMM Design Group
229 W Bute St, Norfolk VA 23510-1405. 804/623-1641.

Person-System Integration Ltd
2401 Huntington Ave, Alexandria VA 22303-1531. 703/960-5555.

Sentel Corp.
1735 Jefferson Davis Hwy, Arlington VA 22202-3401. 703/413-1100.

Techmatics Inc.
12450 Fair Lakes Cir, Ste 800, Fairfax VA 22033-3832. 703/802-8300.

Techmatics Inc.
2231 Crystal Dr, Arlington VA 22202-3711. 703/521-3818.

Titan Systems Group
1900 Campus Commons Dr, Reston VA 22091-1535. 703/883-9200.

TRW/Systems Integration Group
12900 Federal Sys Park Dr, Fairfax VA 22033. 703/968-1000.

Vitro Corporation
2611 Jefferson Davis Hwy, Arlington VA 22202-4016. 703/418-8300.

Wiley & Wilson
2310 Langhorne Rd, Lynchburg VA 24501-1547. 804/947-1901.

Harding Lawson Associates
3175 21st St N, Arlington VA 22201-5107. 703/528-5809.

Roy F. Weston Inc.
315 70th St SE, Charleston WV 25304-2909. 304/926-2900.

Day & Zimmermann International Inc.
10800 Midlothian Tpke, Richmond VA 23235-4700. 804/379-9300.

Greeley & Hansen Engineers
2116 W Laburnum Ave, Richmond VA 23227-4359. 804/355-9993.

Johnson Mirmiram & Thompson
9011 Arboretum Pky, Richmond VA 23236-3476. 804/323-9900.

Schnabel Engineering Associates
114 North Railroad Avenue, Ashland VA 23005-1517. 804/798-0081.

Wilbur Smith Associates
2921 Telestar Ct, Falls Church VA 22042-1205. 703/698-9780.

Bartholomew Harland & Associates
1001 Boulders Parkway, Richmond VA 23225-5522. 804/320-0447.

HNTB Corporation
99 Canal Center Plaza, Alexandria VA 22314-1588. 703/684-2700.

Integrated Systems Analysts Inc.
1717 S Park Ct, Chesapeake VA 23320-8911. 804/424-2400.

Louis Berger & Associates
1001 E Broad St, Ste 220, Richmond VA 23219-1928. 804/225-0348.

Rust Environmental & Infrastructure
11240 Waples Mill Rd, Fairfax VA 22030-6078. 703/385-3566.

Schnabel Engineering Associates Inc.
2601 S Main St, Blacksburg VA 24060-6627. 540/953-1239.

John Brown Engineers
417 39th St, Parkersburg WV 26101-1049. 304/422-6040.

ARCHITECTURAL SERVICES

Henningson, Durham & Richardson
103 Oronoco St, Alexandria VA 22314-2015. 703/683-3400.

John J. McMullen Associates Inc.
11771 Rock Landing Rd, Ste A, Newport News VA 23606-4205. 804/873-6500.

Rosenblatt & Son Inc.
2341 Jefferson Davis Hwy, Arlington VA 22202. 703/415-7800.

Semcor Inc.
4471 James Madison Pkwy, Dahlgren VA 22448. 540/663-0652.

SURVEYING SERVICES

Greenhorne & O'Mara
5444 Jefferson Davis Hwy, Fredericksbrg VA 22407-2627. 540/891-1600.

GENERAL CONTRACTORS

Blueridge General Inc.
3422 Strathmore Ave, Norfolk VA 23504-4613. 804/627-9914.

Brown & Root Inc.
20935 Belmont Ridge Rd, Ashburn VA 22011-4311. 703/729-5195.

Centex Simpson Constrction Co.
10300 Eaton Pl, Ste 300, Fairfax VA 22030-2239. 703/273-3311.

Centex-Simpson Construction Co.
PO Box 427, Merrifield VA 22116-0427. 703/273-3311.

Charles H Thompkins Co.
1225 E Marshall St, Richmond VA 23219-2045. 804/644-4827.

EL Collins Co.
2313 Aiken Dr, Richmond VA 23294-4438. 804/747-7408.

Fralin and Waldron Inc.
PO Box 20069, Roanoke VA 24018-0503. 540/774-4415.

Hitt Contracting Inc.
2704 Dorr Ave, Fairfax VA 22031-4901. 703/849-9000.

Industrial Contractors
806 Avery St, Parkersburg WV 26101-4723. 304/422-1216.

K&M Builders Inc.
517 C St, Charleston WV 25303-1251. 304/744-0531.

Long Enterprises Inc.
8253-J Backlick Rd, Lorton VA 22079. 703/339-0330.

Nielsen Construction Co.
3588 Early Rd, Harrisonburg VA 22801-9724. 540/434-7376.

NV Homes
11440 Commerce Park Dr, Ste 220, Reston VA 22091-1544. 703/734-1056.

Reinsch Construction Corp.
2040 Columbia Pike, Arlington VA 22204-4605. 703/920-3600.

Stafford & Sons Builders
1357 N Great Neck Rd, Virginia Beach VA 23454-2237. 804/496-9535.

Toll Brothers Inc.
15090 Stillfield Pl, Centreville VA 22020-1100. 703/450-0461.

Turner Construction Co.
7204 Glen Forest Dr, Richmond VA 23226-3778. 804/288-8300.

WM Schlosser Co. Inc.
8000 Jefferson Davis Hwy, Richmond VA 23297. 804/743-7532.

William Prince Construction Company
9599 Hawkins Dr, Manassas VA 22110-3907. 703/361-1005.

Ace Home Improvement Company
1013 Campbell Ave SE, Roanoke VA 24013-1115. 540/345-5457.

A1 Contractors
533 N Pinetta Dr, Richmond VA 23235-4921. 804/272-5559.

Partners In Carpentry
906 S Main St, Blacksburg VA 24060-5302. 540/552-6926.

Poff Construction Inc.
360 Reading Rd, Christiansbrg VA 24073-5364. 540/382-3722.

Centex Homes
2006 Old Greenbrier Rd, Ste 5, Chesapeake VA 23320-2648. 804/366-5500.

NV Homes
4352 Glastonbury Ct, Dumfries VA 22026-3138. 703/680-1259.

OPERATIVE BUILDERS

Miller & Smith Inc.
1568 Spring Hill Rd, Mc Lean VA 22102-3016. 703/821-2500.

Stanley-Martin Companies
8000 Towers Crescent Dr, Fl 8, Vienna VA 22182-2700. 703/760-8100.

GENERAL INDUSTRIAL CONTRACTORS

Barlows Inc.
2801 Dorr Ave, Fairfax VA 22031-1504. 703/641-1500.

American Buildings Co.
501 Golden Eagle Dr, La Crosse VA 23950. 804/757-2220.

Morton Buildings Inc.
18478 Industrial Rd, Culpeper VA 22701-4148. 540/825-3633.

CBC Enterprises Inc.
4535 E Princess Anne Rd, Norfolk VA 23502-1613. 804/855-6100.

Falls Church Construction Corp. VA
11244 Waples Mill Rd, Fairfax VA 22030-6040. 703/591-0600.

Scott-Long Construction
14170 Newbrook Dr, Ste 200, Chantilly VA 22021-2231. 703/802-1300.

ROAD CONSTRUCTION

Basic Construction Company
538 Oyster Point Rd, Newport News VA 23602-6920. 804/249-3789.

RL Rider and Co.
PO Box 73, Warrenton VA 22186-0073. 540/347-1611.

Shirley Contracting Corp.
8435 Backlick Rd, Lorton VA 22079-1498. 703/550-8100.

WF Magann Corp.
3220 Mariner Ave, Portsmouth VA 23703-2420. 804/484-2820.

Williams Corporation
PO Box 938, Norfolk VA 23501-0938. 804/420-1140.

Asphalt Pave & Seal Coating
13077 Beech Creek Ln, Ashland VA 23005-7120. 804/798-4622.

Day Paving Inc.
Hwy 58-E, South Boston VA 24592. 804/572-3307.

F&H Paving Inc.
7464 Zachary Taylor Hwy, Unionville VA 22567-2030. 540/854-4515.

Slurry Pavers Inc.
8738 Vulcan Ln, Manassas VA 22110-3951. 703/369-1326.

HEAVY CONSTRUCTION

CW Wright Construction
11500 Iron Bridge Rd, Chester VA 23831-1449. 804/768-1054.

Carl E. Smith Inc.
Junction Rtes 21 & 56, Sandyville WV 25275. 304/273-9313.

Danella Southeast Inc.
11170 Lee Hwy, Fairfax VA 22030-5016. 703/691-9157.

Flowmole Corp.
5847 Hargrove St, Norfolk VA 23502-4636. 804/427-5320.

Rockingham Construction
220 Spring St, Herndon VA 22070-5209. 703/435-0028.

Suburban Grading and Utilities
1190 Harmony Rd, Norfolk VA 23502-2357. 804/461-1800.

PLUMBING, HEATING, AND A/C

Warwick Plumbing & Heating Co.
11048 Warwick Blvd, Newport News VA 23601-3229. 804/599-6111.

Breeden Mechanical Inc.
12329 Braddock Rd, Fairfax VA 22030-6308. 703/631-2711.

Gregory & Graham Heating, Cooling & Plumbing
1300 Semmes Ave, Richmond VA 23224-2162. 804/231-5700.

James Vito Inc.
14004 Willard Rd, Chantilly VA 22021-2929. 703/802-2268.

Raub Supply Company
1325 Alum Spring Rd, Fredericksbrg VA 22401-7001. 540/373-5914.

Smith & Keene Electric Service Inc.
807 Blue Crab Rd, Newport News VA 23606-4220. 804/873-0459.

Jesco M-E Division
309 McLaws Cir, Williamsburg VA 23185-5675. 804/872-6993.

Calvert-Jones Co. Inc.
5703 Edsall Rd, Alexandria VA 22304-4720. 703/370-5850.

Ellington Energy
1812 W 3rd St, Farmville VA 23901-2696. 804/392-3176.

GJ Hopkins Inc.
6737 Thirlane Rd NW, Roanoke VA 24019-2907. 540/362-1864.

Kerstein Heating
613 Tennessee Ave, Charleston WV 25302-2327. 304/342-5118.

Quality Fuels Of VA
2403 Commerce Rd, Richmond VA 23234-1804. 804/233-0669.

York International Corp.
3605 Saunders Ave, Richmond VA 23227-4354. 804/359-2600.

ELECTRICAL WORK

Pritchard Electric Company
PO Box 2503, Huntington WV 25725-2503. 304/529-2566.

Truland Corp.
3330 Washington Blvd,

Arlington VA 22201-4502. 703/524-4900.

LC Allen Enterprise
2102 Lirio Ct, Reston VA 22091-1308. 703/758-9209.

LT Bowden Inc.
13944F Willard Rd, Chantilly VA 22021-2965. 703/631-1100.

Newcomb Electric Co
2708 Shenandoah Ave NW, Roanoke VA 24017-5250. 540/342-5498.

S Rock Eastabrook Corp.
Hwy 50, Arcola VA 22010. 703/327-2020.

MASONRY, STONEWORK, AND PLASTERING

Bratti Associates Inc.
4 Herbert St , #19B, Alexandria VA 22305-2628. 703/549-9699.

Sprinkle Masonry Inc.
1030 Ruritan Blvd, Chesapeake VA 23324-3646. 804/545-8435.

Drummond Construction
2101 E Franklin St, Richmond VA 23223-7044. 804/649-9460.

PAINTING AND PAPER HANGING

The House Doctor
2022 Kilgore Rd, Falls Church VA 22043-1353. 703/893-7811.

CARPENTRY AND FLOOR WORK

Builders Floor Service
7904 Yarnwood Ct, Springfield VA 22153-2826. 703/569-6000.

ROOFING, SIDING, AND SHEET METAL WORK

Blackburns General Contractor
2942 Brentwood Cir, Richmond VA 23237-1165. 804/271-7553.

States Roofing Corp.
1215 Saint Julian Ave, Norfolk VA 23504-2630. 804/627-1412.

RH Smith Roofing Co.
5516 E Virginia Beach Blvd, Norfolk VA 23502-2418. 804/461-4234.

MISC. SPECIAL TRADE CONTRACTORS

Haley, Chisholm & Morris
Rt 743 Earlysville Rd, Charlottesvle VA 22901. 804/978-1000.

Shoosmith Brothers Inc.
11800 Lewis Rd, Chester VA 23831-3735. 804/748-5823.

Wrecking Corp. America
3680 Wheeler Ave, Alexandria VA 22304-6403. 703/823-3850.

Montgomery Elevator Co.
7427 Whitepine Rd, Richmond VA 23237-2255. 804/271-6519.

Schindler Elevator Corp.
37 Oak Circle Dr, Wheeling WV 26003-4877. 304/233-4600.

Furmanite America Inc.
2645 International Pky, Virginia Beach VA 23452-7802. 804/427-1991.

Meador's Distribution Co.
4140 Washington St W, Charleston WV 25313-2438. 304/744-7790.

Centennial Contractors Enterprises Inc.
1801 Alexander Bell Dr, Ste 100, Reston VA 22091-4344. 703/264-0235.

Open Plan Systems Inc.
4299 Carolina Ave, Richmond VA 23222-1403. 804/321-0006.

MOBILE HOMES

Fleetwood Homes Of Virginia
Hwy 40 W, Rfd 4, Rocky Mount VA 24151. 540/483-5171.

Virginia Homes Manufacturing
Hwy 58 E, Boydton VA 23917. 804/738-6107.

PREFABRICATED WOOD BUILDINGS AND COMPONENTS

American Standard Building Systems
700 Commerce Ct, Martinsville VA 24112-1219. 540/638-3991.

Cardinal Homes Inc.
Hwy 15, Wylliesburg VA 23976. 804/735-8111.

Mod-U-Kraf Homes Inc.
822 Pell Ave, Rocky Mount VA 24151-2803. 540/483-0291.

North American Housing Corp.
S R 684, Boones Mill VA 24065. 540/334-5000.

North American Housing Corp.
Rt 55 W, Front Royal VA 22630. 540/636-2991.

For more information on career opportunities in architecture, construction, and engineering:

<u>**Associations**</u>

AACE INTERNATIONAL: THE ASSOCIATION FOR TOTAL COST MANAGEMENT
209 Prairie Avenue, Suite 100, P.O. Box 1557, Morgantown WV 26507-1557. 304/296-8444. 800/858-2678. Toll-free number provides information on scholarships for undergraduates. Fax: 304/291-5728. A membership organization which offers *Cost Engineering,* a monthly magazine; employment referral services; technical reference

information and assistance; insurance; and a certification program accredited by the Council of Engineering Specialty Boards.

AMERICAN ASSOCIATION OF ENGINEERING SOCIETIES
1111 19th Street NW, Suite 608, Washington DC 20036-3690. 202/296-2237. A multi-disciplinary organization of professional engineering societies. Publishes reference works, including *Who's Who in Engineering Directory of Engineering Societies and Related Organizations,* and the *Thesaurus of Engineering and Scientific Terms,* as well as statistical reports from studies conducted by the Engineering Workforce Commission.

AMERICAN SOCIETY OF MECHANICAL ENGINEERS
8996 Burke Lake Rd, Burke VA 22015-1607. 703/978-5000.

AMERICAN CONSULTING ENGINEERS COUNCIL
1015 15th Street NW, Suite 802, Washington DC 20005. 202/347-7474. Fax: 202/898-0068. A national organization of more than 5,000 member firms. Offers *Last Word,* a weekly newsletter; *American Consulting Engineer* magazine; life and health insurance programs; books, manuals, video and audiotapes, and contract documents; conferences and seminars; and voluntary peer reviews.

AMERICAN INSTITUTE OF ARCHITECTS
1735 New York Avenue NW, Washington DC 20006. 202/626-7300. 800/365-2724. Contact toll-free number for brochures.

AMERICAN SOCIETY OF CIVIL ENGINEERS
345 East 47th Street, New York NY 10017. 212/705-7496. Toll-free number: 800/548-2723. A membership organization which offers subscriptions to *Civil Engineering* magazine and *ASCE News,* discounts on various other publications, seminars, audio and videotapes, specialty conferences, an annual convention, group insurance programs, and pension plans.

AMERICAN SOCIETY OF HEATING, REFRIGERATING AND AIR CONDITIONING ENGINEERS
1791 Tullie Circle NE, Atlanta GA 30329. 404/636-8400. Fax: 404/321-5478. A society of 50,000 members which offers handbooks, a monthly journal, a monthly newspaper, discounts on other publications, group insurance, continuing education, and registration discounts for meetings, conferences, seminars, and expositions.

AMERICAN SOCIETY OF LANDSCAPE ARCHITECTS
4401 Connecticut Avenue NW, Washington DC 20008. 202/686-2752. World Wide Web address: http://www.asla.org. Look for Joblink for employment listings.

AMERICAN SOCIETY FOR ENGINEERING EDUCATION
1818 N Street NW, Suite 600, Washington DC 20036. 202/331-3500. Promotes engineering education. Publishes monthly magazines.

AMERICAN SOCIETY OF MECHANICAL ENGINEERS
345 East 47th Street, New York NY 10017. 212/705-7722. Handles educational materials for certified engineers, as well as scholarships.

AMERICAN SOCIETY OF NAVAL ENGINEERS
1452 Duke Street, Alexandria VA 22314. 703/836-6727. Holds symposiums based on technical papers. Publishes a journal and newsletter bimonthly.

AMERICAN SOCIETY OF PLUMBING ENGINEERS
3617 Thousand Oaks Boulevard, Suite 210, Westlake CA 91362-3694. 805/495-7120. Provides technical and educational information.

AMERICAN SOCIETY OF SAFETY ENGINEERS
1800 East Oakton Street, Des Plaines IL 60018-2187. 847/692-4121. Jobline service available at ext. 243. Fax: 847/296-3769. A membership organization offering *Professional Safety,* a monthly journal; educational seminars; an annual professional development conference and exposition; technical publications; certification preparation programs; career placement services; and group and liability insurance programs.

ASSOCIATED BUILDERS AND CONTRACTORS
1300 North 17th Street, Rosslyn VA 22209. 703/812-2000. Sponsors annual career fair. Currently in the process of creating a service to find workers for construction companies.

ASSOCIATED GENERAL CONTRACTORS OF AMERICA, INC.
1957 E Street NW, Washington DC 20006. 202/393-2040. A full-service construction association of

subcontractors, specialty contractors, suppliers, equipment manufacturers, and professional firms. Services include government relations, education and training, jobsite services, legal services, and information services.

ILLUMINATING ENGINEERING SOCIETY OF NORTH AMERICA
120 Wall Street, 17th Floor, New York NY 10005-4001. 212/248-5000. An organization for industry professionals involved in the manufacturing, design, specification, and maintenance of lighting systems. Conference held annually. Offers a Technical Knowledge Examination.

JUNIOR ENGINEERING TECHNICAL SOCIETY
1420 King Street, Suite 405, Alexandria VA 22314-2794. 703/548-JETS. Fax: 703/548-0769. E-mail address: jets@nas.edu. A nonprofit, educational society promoting interest in engineering, technology, mathematics, and science. Provides information to high school students and teachers regarding careers in engineering and technology.

NATIONAL ACTION COUNCIL FOR MINORITIES IN ENGINEERING
3 West 35th Street, New York NY 10001. 212/279-2626. Offers scholarship programs for students.

NATIONAL ASSOCIATION OF HOME BUILDERS
1201 15th Street NW, Washington DC 20005. 202/822-0200. A trade association promoting safe and affordable housing. Provides management services and education for members.

NATIONAL ASSOCIATION OF MINORITY ENGINEERING
1133 West Morse Boulevard, Suite 201, Winter Park FL 32789. 407/647-8839.

NATIONAL SOCIETY OF BLACK ENGINEERS
1454 Duke Street, Alexandria VA 22314. 703/549-2207. A nonprofit organization run by college students. Offers scholarships, editorials, and magazines.

NATIONAL SOCIETY OF PROFESSIONAL ENGINEERS
1420 King Street, Alexandria VA 22314-2794. 703/684-2800. Call 703/684-2830 for scholarship information for students. Fax: 703/836-4875. A society of over 73,000 engineers. Membership includes the monthly magazine *Engineering Times;* continuing education; scholarships and fellowships; discounts on publications; health and life insurance programs; and employment service programs.

SOCIETY OF FIRE PROTECTION ENGINEERS
One Liberty Square, Boston MA 02109-4825. 617/482-0686. Fax: 617/482-8184. A professional society which offers members reports, newsletters, *Journal of Fire Protecting Engineering,* insurance programs, short courses, symposiums, tutorials, an annual meeting, and engineering seminars.

Directories

DIRECTORY OF ENGINEERING SOCIETIES
American Association of Engineering Societies, 1111 19th Street NW, Suite 608, Washington DC 20036. 202/296-2237. $185.00. Lists other engineering association members, publications, and convention exhibits.

DIRECTORY OF ENGINEERS IN PRIVATE PRACTICE
National Society of Professional Engineers, 1420 King Street, Alexandria VA 22314. 703/684-2800. $50.00. Lists members and companies.

Magazines

THE CAREER ENGINEER
National Society of Black Engineers, 1454 Duke Street, Alexandria VA 22314. 703/549-2207.

CAREERS AND THE ENGINEER
Adams Media Corporation, 260 Center Street, Holbrook MA 02343. 617/767-8100.

CHEMICAL & ENGINEERING NEWS
American Chemical Society 1155 16th Street NW, Washington DC 20036. 202/872-4600.

COMPUTER-AIDED ENGINEERING
Penton Publishing, 1100 Superior Avenue, Cleveland OH 44114. 216/696-7000.

EDN CAREER NEWS
Cahners Publishing Company, 275 Washington Street, Newton MA 02158. 617/964-3030.

ENGINEERING TIMES
National Society of Professional Engineers, 1420 King Street, Alexandria VA 22314. 703/684-2800.

NAVAL ENGINEERS JOURNAL
American Society of Naval Engineers, 1452 Duke Street, Alexandria VA 22314. 703/836-6727. Subscription: $48.

ARTS AND ENTERTAINMENT/RECREATION

Job opportunities in the entertainment and recreation industries are projected to increase 39 percent through the year 2005, faster than the average for all industries. Higher incomes, growth of leisure time due to a growing population of retirees, and increasing awareness of the health benefits of physical fitness will affect employment growth.

The market for leisure activities is changing. In the past, amusement and recreation services catered to those in their '20s and '30s who had steadily growing incomes. Now that those baby boomers have grown up, companies are targeting adults between 50 and 75 years old.

In Hollywood, the past several years have been marked by mergers: Disney and ABC/Capital Cities, Westinghouse and CBS, Turner Broadcasting and Time Warner, and Seagram and MCA, to name a few of the biggest headline-stealers. And then there's the growing alliance between Hollywood and Silicon Valley. Microsoft, for example, has joined forces with NBC to create an online news station.

ATLANTIC VIDEO INC.
150 South Gordon Street, Alexandria VA 22304. 703/823-2800. **Fax:** 703/370-3708. **Contact:** Tom Kitner, Master Control Supervisor. **Description:** A provider of videotape distribution and production services. **NOTE:** Resumes should be sent to Personnel, 650 Massachusetts Avenue, Washington DC 20001.

BOWL AMERICA INC.
6446 Edsall Road, Alexandria VA 22312. 703/941-6300. **Contact:** Human Resources. **Description:** Engaged in the operation of 25 bowling centers, with food and beverages service in each center. Fourteen centers are located in metropolitan Washington DC; three in metro Baltimore, Maryland; two in the Orlando, Florida area; three in metro Richmond, Virginia; and three in the Jacksonville, Florida area. The company is actively seeking new bowling locations. **NOTE:** Interested jobseekers should contact the individual locations for employment. **Benefits:** ESOP; Profit Sharing. **Corporate headquarters location:** This Location. **Listed on:** American Stock Exchange. **Number of employees nationwide:** 800.

BUSCH GARDENS/WATER COUNTRY USA
One Busch Gardens Boulevard, Williamsburg VA 23185. 804/253-3020. **Contact:** Personnel. **Description:** A theme park. Parent company, Anheuser-Busch is a diverse company which is involved in the entertainment, brewing, baking, and manufacturing industries. The company is one of the largest domestic brewers, operating 13 breweries throughout the U.S. and distributing through over 900 independent wholesalers. Beer brands include Budweiser, Michelob, Busch, King Cobra, and O'Doul's non-alcoholic beverages. Related businesses include can manufacturing, paper printing, and barley malting. Anheuser-Busch is also one of the largest operators of amusement parks in the U.S., with other locations in Florida, Texas, Ohio, and California. Through subsidiary Campbell Taggart Inc., Anheuser-Busch is also one of the largest commercial baking companies in the United States, producing foods under the Eagle Snacks, Cape Cod, and Colonial brand names, among others. Anheuser-Busch also has real estate interests.

COLONIAL NATIONAL HISTORICAL PARK
P.O. Box 210, Yorktown VA 23690. 804/898-3400. **Contact:** Annette Spragan, Personnel Assistant. **Description:** A national historical park that preserves, protects, and interprets the site of the first permanent English settlement in the New World (Jamestown) and the site of the last major battle of the American Revolutionary War. Established in 1916.

THE COLONIAL WILLIAMSBURG FOUNDATION
P.O. Box 1776, Williamsburg VA 23187-1776. 804/220-7713. **Fax:** 804/220-7259. **Recorded Jobline:** 804/220-7129. **Contact:** Perry Matthews, Human Resources Representative. **Description:** The Colonial Williamsburg Foundation is a nonprofit, educational organization. It consists of education and research operations, administrative support groups, property management, and business operations. **Common positions include:** Accountant/Auditor; Architect; Automotive Mechanic/Body Repairer; Blue-Collar Worker Supervisor; Budget Analyst; Buyer; Civil Engineer; Clerical Supervisor; Computer Systems Analyst; Construction Contractor and Manager; Counselor; Customer Service Representative; Designer; Draftsperson; Economist/Market Research Analyst; Editor; Education Administrator; Electrician; Financial Analyst; Food Scientist/Technologist; General Manager; Hotel Manager/Assistant Manager; Human Resources Specialist; Human Service Worker; Landscape Architect; Librarian; Library Technician; Management Analyst/Consultant; Mechanical Engineer; Occupational Therapist; Preschool Worker; Public Relations Specialist; Purchasing Agent and Manager; Quality Control Supervisor; Reporter; Restaurant/Food Service Manager; Services Sales Representative; Structural Engineer; Teacher; Wholesale and Retail Buyer. **Educational backgrounds include:** Accounting; Art/Design; Business Administration; Communications; Computer Science; Engineering; Finance; Liberal Arts; Marketing; Museum Studies; Restaurant Management. **Benefits:** 401K; 403B; Daycare Assistance; Dental Insurance; Disability Coverage; Employee Discounts; Home Loan Assistance; Life Insurance; Medical Insurance; Pension Plan; Savings Plan; Tuition Assistance. **Special Programs:** Internships. **Corporate headquarters location:** This Location. **Operations at this facility include:** Administration; Divisional Headquarters; Research and Development; Sales; Service. **Number of employees at this location:** 3,500.

JAMESTOWN-YORKTOWN FOUNDATION
P.O. Drawer JF, Williamsburg VA 23187. 804/253-4939. **Contact:** Debbie Jarvis, Human Resources. **Description:** Institution that operates Jamestown Settlement and the Yorktown Victory Center, museums that preserve and interpret the first English settlement in the New World and the story of the American Revolution. Established in 1956.

RINGLING BROTHERS
BARNUM & BAILEY COMBINED SHOWS, INC.
8607 Westwood Center Drive, Vienna VA 22182. 703/448-4000. **Fax:** 703/448-4100. **Contact:** Gary Baron, Office Manager. **Description:** Operates circuses, television productions and ice shows. **Corporate headquarters location:** This Location.

SCOPE
201 East Brambleton Avenue, Norfolk VA 23501. 804/664-6464. **Contact:** Human Resources. **Description:** A cultural center.

SHEPHERD STADIUM
P.O. Box 3401, Colonial Heights VA 22834. 804/520-9390. **Contact:** Shawn Gleason, Director of Human Resources. **Description:** Shepherd Stadium has 1,300 seats and is home to the Boys Invitational Baseball Tournament.

SUMMER FESTIVAL, ASH LAWN-HIGHLAND
Route Six, P.O. Box 37, Charlottesville VA 22902. 804/293-4500. **Fax:** 804/293-8000. **Contact:** Judith Walker, Human Resources Director. **Description:** Summer festival producing opera and musical theater and bringing in additional musical and theatrical productions for all ages. A nonprofit organization owned by the College of William and Mary. Established in 1976.

WHEELING DOWNS RACING ASSOCIATION
One South Stone Street, Wheeling WV 26003. 304/232-5050. **Contact:** Controller's Office. **Description:** A greyhound racing track.

Note: *Because addresses and telephone numbers of smaller companies change rapidly, we recommend you call each company to verify the information below before inquiring about job opportunities. Mass mailings are not recommended.*

Additional small employers:

MOTION PICTURE AND VIDEO TAPE PRODUCTION AND DISTRIBUTION

Henninger Richmond Inc.
2306 E Main St, Richmond VA 23223-7844. 804/644-5006.

International Tape Place
9304 Old Keene Mill Rd, Ste A, Springfield VA 22015-4279. 703/569-6967.

MOTION PICTURE THEATERS

Neighborhood Entertainment Inc.
1510 E Ridge Rd, Richmond VA 23229-5740. 804/282-0303.

Theatre IV
114 W Broad St, Richmond VA 23220-4270. 804/344-8040.

PROFESSIONAL SPORTS CLUBS AND PROMOTERS

Richmond Braves Baseball Club
3001 N Boulevard, Richmond VA 23230-4331. 804/359-4444.

RACING AND TRACK OPERATION

Charles Town Races Inc.
PO Box 551, Charles Town WV 25414-0551. 304/725-2021.

PHYSICAL FITNESS FACILITIES

US Tae Kwon Do
3825-G S George Mason Dr, Falls Church VA 22041. 703/820-4459.

Bally's Holiday Fitness Centers
7281 Arlington Blvd, Falls Church VA 22042-3200. 703/573-0660.

AMUSEMENT PARKS AND RECREATION CENTERS

Paramount's Kings Dominion
PO Box 2000, Doswell VA 23047-2000. 804/876-5000.

Huntington Park Tennis Center
361 Hornet Cir, Newport News VA 23607-1503. 804/247-8451.

Fun-N-Games
Charleston Town Center, Charleston WV 25301. 304/342-1573.

New Kent Paint Ball Games
14375 Marine Corp. Dr, Lanexa VA 23089-5448. 804/966-5104.

MEMBERSHIP SPORTS AND RECREATION CLUBS

Burke Indoor Racquet
6001 Burke Commons Road, Burke VA 22015-2806. 703/425-7270.

Sport & Health Clubs
1800 Old Meadow Road, McLean VA 22102-1819. 703/556-6550.

Washington Tennis Center
1524 Springhill Road, McLean VA 22102. 703/356-0335.

Annandale Sport & Health Center
4317 Ravensworth Road, Annandale VA 22003-5654. 703/256-6600.

AMUSEMENT AND RECREATION SERVICES

Calvary Ridge Stables
42953 Croson Ln, Ashburn VA 22011-7101. 703/729-3557.

Baldwin Oaks Pool
12500 Racquet Circle, Manassas VA 22111. 703/361-9382.

MUSEUMS AND ART GALLERIES

Reuel B. Pritchett Museum
E College St, Bridgewater VA 22812. 540/828-2501.

The Doll House Museum
211 S High St, Blackstone VA 23824-1837. 804/292-3487.

For more information on career opportunities in arts, entertainment, and recreation:

Associations

AMERICAN ASSOCIATION OF MUSEUMS
1225 I Street NW, Suite 200, Washington DC 20005. 202/289-1818. Fax: 202/289-6578. Publishes *AVISO,* a monthly newsletter containing employment listings for the entire country.

AMERICAN COUNCIL FOR THE ARTS
1 East 53rd Street, New York NY 10022. 212/223-2787. Fax: 212/980-4857. Visual Artist Information Hotline: 800/232-2789. A nonprofit organization for the literary, visual, and performing arts. Supports K-12 education and promotes public policy through meetings, forums, and seminars.

AMERICAN CRAFTS COUNCIL
72 Spring Street, New York NY 10012. 212/274-0630. Operates a research library. Publishes *American Crafts* magazine.

AMERICAN DANCE GUILD
31 West 21st Street, New York NY 10010. 212/627-3790. Holds an annual conference with panels, performances, and workshops. Operates a job listings service (available at a discount to members.)

AMERICAN FEDERATION OF MUSICIANS
1501 Broadway, Suite 600, New York NY 10036. 212/869-1330. Membership required.

AMERICAN FEDERATION OF TELEVISION AND RADIO ARTISTS
260 Madison Avenue, New York NY 10016. 212/532-0800. Membership required.

AMERICAN FILM INSTITUTE
2021 North Western Avenue, Los Angeles CA 90027. 213/856-7706. Toll-free phone: 800/774-4AFI. Membership is required, and includes: a newsletter; members-only discounts on events, seminars, workshops, and exhibits; and two free tickets and discounts at the AFI Theater in Washington, DC.

AMERICAN MUSIC CENTER
30 West 26th Street, Suite 1001, New York NY 10010-2011. 212/366-5260. Fax: 212/366-5265. A nonprofit research and information center for contemporary music and jazz. Provides information services and grant programs. World Wide Web address: http://www.amc.net/amc/.

AMERICAN SOCIETY OF COMPOSERS, AUTHORS, AND PUBLISHERS (ASCAP)
One Lincoln Plaza, New York NY 10023. 212/621-6000. Fax: 212/724-9064. A membership association which licenses members' work and pays members royalties. Offers showcases and educational seminars and workshops.

AMERICAN SYMPHONY ORCHESTRA LEAGUE
1156 15th Street NW, Suite 4800, Washington DC 20005. 202/628-0099.

AMERICAN ZOO AND AQUARIUM ASSOCIATION
Oglebay Park, Wheeling WV 26003. 304/242-2160. Produces a monthly newspaper.

ASSOCIATION OF INDEPENDENT VIDEO AND FILMMAKERS
625 Broadway, 9th Floor, New York NY 10012. 212/807-1400.

NATIONAL ARTISTS' EQUITY ASSOCIATION
P.O. Box 28068, Central Station, Washington DC 20038-8068. 202/628-9633. A national, nonprofit organization dedicated to improving economic, health, and legal conditions for visual artists.

NATIONAL DANCE ASSOCIATION
1900 Association Drive, Reston VA 22091. 703/476-3436. Fax: 703/476-9527. Promotes the development and implementation of philosophies and policies in all forms of dance and in dance education at all levels.

NATIONAL ENDOWMENT FOR THE ARTS
1100 Pennsylvania Avenue NW, Washington DC 20506. 202/682-5400.

NATIONAL RECREATION AND PARK ASSOCIATION
2775 South Quincy Street, Suite 300, Arlington VA 22206. 703/820-4940. Fax: 703/671-6772. A national, nonprofit service organization. Offers professional development and training opportunities in recreation, parks, and leisure services. Publishes a newsletter and magazine.

PRODUCERS GUILD OF AMERICA
400 South Beverly Drive, Suite 211, Beverly Hills CA 90212. 310/557-0807. Membership is required, and

includes: credit union access; subscription to *P.O.V. Magazine* and the association newsletter; attendance at the organization's annual Golden Laurel Awards and other events; and special screenings of motion pictures at the time of the Academy Awards.

THEATRE COMMUNICATIONS GROUP
355 Lexington Avenue, New York NY 10017. 212/697-5230.

WOMEN'S CAUCUS FOR ART
Moore College of Art, 20th & The Parkway, Philadelphia PA 19103. 215/854-0922. Fax: 215/854-0915. A national organization of professionals in the visual arts. Over 3,700 members. Membership includes an annual conference; participation in juried shows; local chapter meetings and regional conferences; publications including an annual exhibition catalog of honors awards and a quarterly newsletter; and insurance programs.

Directories

ARTIST'S MARKET
Writer's Digest Books, 1507 Dana Avenue, Cincinnati OH 45207. 513/531-2222.

CREATIVE BLACK BOOK
866 3rd Avenue, 3rd Floor, New York NY 10022. 212/254-1330.

PLAYERS GUIDE
165 West 46th Street, New York NY 10036. 212/869-3570.

ROSS REPORTS TELEVISION
Television Index, Inc., 40-29 27th Street, Long Island City NY 11101. 718/937-3990.

Magazines

AMERICAN ARTIST
One Astor Place, 1515 Broadway, New York NY 10036. 212/764-7300. 800/346-0085, ext. 477.

AMERICAN CINEMATOGRAPHER
American Society of Cinematographers, P.O. Box 2230, Hollywood CA 90028. 213/969-4333.

ART BUSINESS NEWS
Myers Publishing Company, 19 Old Kings Highway South, Darien CT 06820. 203/656-3402.

ART DIRECTION
10 East 39th Street, 6th Floor, New York NY 10016. 212/889-6500.

ARTFORUM
65 Bleecker Street, New York NY 10012. 212/475-4000.

ARTWEEK
12 South First Street, Suite 520, San Jose CA 95113. 408/279-2293.

AVISO
American Association of Museums, 1225 I Street NW, Suite 200, Washington DC 20005. 202/289-1818.

BACK STAGE
1515 Broadway, New York NY 10036. 212/764-7300.

BILLBOARD
Billboard Publications, Inc., 1515 Broadway, New York NY 10036. 212/764-7300.

CASHBOX
157 West 57th Street, Suite 503, New York NY 10019. 212/245-4224.

CRAFTS REPORT
300 Water Street, Wilmington DE 19801. 302/656-2209.

DRAMA-LOGUE
P.O. Box 38771, Los Angeles CA 90038. 213/464-5079.

HOLLYWOOD REPORTER
5055 Wilshire Boulevard, 6th Floor, Los Angeles CA 90036. 213/525-2000.

VARIETY
249 West 17th Street, New York NY 10011. 212/779-1100. 800/323-4345.

WOMEN ARTIST NEWS
300 Riverside Drive, New York NY 10025. 212/666-6990.

AUTOMOTIVE

The automotive industry saw a big turnaround in 1994, with sales of new cars and trucks reaching a six-year high. Unfortunately, the boom didn't last. Rising interest rates in early 1995 put the brakes on auto sales. Although the year can't be classified as truly weak, 1995 sales dropped 2.6 percent off 1994's pace. Rising steel prices have also put pressure on the Big Three automakers to cut costs and boost productivity, so don't look for job opportunities to grow very rapidly in '96. Even so, analysts are predicting a 2 percent sales gain in 1996, spurred in part by dropping interest rates.

Jobseekers should look to auto parts suppliers in addition to the Big Three. While Detroit is using fewer suppliers than in the past, the suppliers that are under contract are being asked to provide more of the finished product. Look for large employers with financial backing and superior skills.

ABEX FRICTION PRODUCTS
2410 Papermill Road, Winchester VA 22601-3621. 703/662-3871. **Contact:** Kaye Carter, Human Resources Manager. **Description:** One of the world's largest full-line manufacturers of friction materials for brakes. All brake linings are 100 percent non-asbestos.

CARBONE OF AMERICA
P.O. Box M, Farmville VA 23901. 804/392-4111. **Contact:** Personnel Department. **Description:** This location is the Commutation Components Division and manufactures brushes for automobile parts, such as starters, alternators, and fan belts.

EAGLE-PICHER AUTOMOTIVE GROUP
201 Industrial Park Road SE, Blacksburg VA 24060. 703/552-7674. **Contact:** Richard Holbrook, Superintendent of Human Relations. **Description:** Manufactures gaskets. Overall, Eagle-Picher Automotive Group develops, markets, and manufactures automotive components worldwide.

FLEETWOOD TRAVEL TRAILERS
380 Battaile Drive, Winchester VA 22601-4261. 703/662-3436. **Contact:** Bill Look, General Manager. **Description:** Manufactures travel trailers. Parent company, Fleetwood Enterprises Inc., is a producer of recreational vehicles and manufactured housing with operations in the U.S., Canada, and Germany. The company's recreational vehicles are primarily motor homes sold under brand names including American Eagle, Coronado, Bounder, Flair, and PaceArrow. Fleetwood also owns subsidiaries which offer financial services and supplies. The company has an 80 percent interest in Niesmann & Bischoff, a motor home manufacturer in Germany. **Parent company:** Fleetwood Enterprises.

FORD MOTOR COMPANY
NORFOLK ASSEMBLY
2424 Springfield Avenue, Norfolk VA 23523-2495. 804/494-2000. **Contact:** Human Resources. **Description:** A truck manufacturing facility. Parent company is engaged in the design, development, manufacture, and sale of cars, trucks, tractors, and related components and accessories. Ford is also one of the largest providers of financial services in the United States. The company has manufacturing, assembly, and sales affiliates in 29 countries outside the United States. In 1993, Ford companies employed approximately 322,200 people worldwide. The company's two core businesses are the

Automotive Group and the Financial Services Group (Ford Credit, The Associates, USL Capital, and First Nationwide). Ford also is engaged in a number of other businesses, including electronics, glass, electrical and fuel-handling products, plastics, climate-control systems, automotive service and replacement parts, vehicle leasing and rental, and land development.

GENERAL MOTORS CORPORATION
1000 Warm Springs Avenue, P.O. Box 1248, Martinsburg WV 25401. 304/267-5600. **Contact:** Personnel Director. **Description:** This facility serves as a warehousing location and distribution center for motor vehicle parts. Also engaged in coating, engraving, and related services. Overall, General Motors Corporation, founded in 1908, is one of the world's largest full-line vehicle manufacturers, and also has substantial interests in information technology, electronics, and finance. GM conducts business through the following sectors: North American Automotive Operations, Delphi Automotive Systems, International Operations, General Motors Acceptance Corporation (GMAC), Electronic Data Systems Corporation (EDS), and GM Hughes Electronics Corporation. North American Automotive Operations includes Sales/Service Groups (Buick, Cadillac, Chevrolet, GMC Truck, Oldsmobile, Pontiac, and Saturn) and Vehicle Development Groups (Power train, Truck Group, Small Car Group, and Midsize/Luxury Car Group). Delphi Automotive Systems, formerly known as Automotive Components Group, consists of Delphi Chassis Systems, Delphi Packard Electric Systems, Delphi Energy & Engine Management Systems, Delphi Saginaw Steering Systems, Delphi Harrison Thermal Systems, Delphi Interior & Lighting Systems, Delphi Automotive Systems European Region, Delphi Automotive Systems Asia/Pacific Region, and Delphi Automotive Systems South America. International Operations include GM Europe (GME); Asia Pacific Operations (APO); and Latin America, Africa, Middle East Operations (LAAMO). GMAC, which provides financing and insurance to GM customers and dealers, consists of North American Operations, International Operations, Motors Insurance Corporation, and GMAC Mortgage Group. EDS applies information technologies to more than 8,000 customers globally in the communications, energy/chemical, insurance, public sector, travel and transportation, financial services, manufacturing, and retail industries. GM Hughes Electronics Corporation is involved in automotive electronics, telecommunications and space electronics, and defense electronics. **Corporate headquarters location:** Detroit MI.

INTERMET CORPORATION
ARCHER CREEK PLANT
P.O. Box 11589, Lynchburg VA 24506. 804/528-8702. **Fax:** 804/528-8486. **Contact:** Walter Vrobel, Human Resources Manager. **Description:** A cast metals manufacturing operation supplying ductile iron castings to the automobile industry. **Common positions include:** Blue-Collar Worker Supervisor; Industrial Engineer; Management Trainee; Materials Engineer; Mechanical Engineer. **Educational backgrounds include:** Business Administration; Engineering; Liberal Arts; Physics. **Benefits:** 401K; Dental Insurance; Disability Coverage; Life Insurance; Medical Insurance; Tuition Assistance. **Corporate headquarters location:** Atlanta GA. **Other U.S. locations:** Columbus GA; Ironton OH; Radford VA. **Operations at this facility include:** Manufacturing. **Listed on:** NASDAQ. **Number of employees at this location:** 700.

LEAR CORPORATION
806 East Queen Street, P.O. Box 181, Strasburg VA 22657. 540/465-3741. **Contact:** Betty Stelzl, Manager of Personnel. **Description:** Manufactures and distributes automotive trim and accessories. **Common positions include:** Industrial Engineer; Process Engineer; Quality Control Supervisor.

NEW RIVER CASTINGS COMPANY
1701 First Street, Radford VA 24141. 703/731-0500. **Contact:** Wes Kavanaugh, Human Resource Manager. **Description:** Manufactures castings for the automotive industry.

SIEMENS AUTOMOTIVE
615 Bland Boulevard, Newport News VA 23602. 804/875-7000. **Contact:** Brenda Lively, Staffing Administrator. **Description:** Manufactures fuel injectors.

***Note:** Because addresses and telephone numbers of smaller companies change rapidly, we recommend you call each company to verify the information below before inquiring about job opportunities. Mass mailings are not recommended.*

Additional small employers:

INDUSTRIAL VEHICLES AND MOVING EQUIPMENT

Multiton
4200 Oakleys Lane, Richmond VA 23223-5938. 804/737-7400.

Utility Trailer Manufacturing
Mt Empire Industrial Park, Atkins VA 24311. 540/783-8800.

INTERNAL COMBUSTION ENGINES

Volvo Penta Of The Americas
1300 Volvo Penta Drive, Chesapeake VA 23320-4691. 804/436-2800.

MOTOR VEHICLES AND EQUIPMENT

Chrysler Technologies Corp.
1725 Jefferson Davis Hwy, Arlington VA 22202. 703/521-8540.

Panda Motors Corp.
8000 Towers Crescent Dr, Vienna VA 22182-2700. 703/761-7000.

JGB Industries Inc.
1700 Summit Ave, Richmond VA 23230-4516. 804/358-0481.

Volvo G M Heavy Truck Corp.
Rt 643, Dublin VA 24084. 540/674-4181.

Automotive Industries
31 Stoney Brook Ln, Luray VA 22835-9066. 540/743-7123.

Automotive Industries
308 W Thacker Ave, Covington VA 24426-2263. 540/965-6500.

Bridgeport Piedmont Manufacturing Co.
205 Frazier Rd, Altavista VA 24517-1020. 804/369-4741.

Dana Corp.
3200 Green Forest Ave, Buena Vista VA 24416-3907. 540/261-8300.

Dana Corp.
S R 788, Atkins VA 24311. 540/782-6600.

Friction Inc.
1000 Falls Run Dr, Fredericksbrg VA 22406-1107. 540/371-8010.

ITT Automotive Inc.
111 W Lovers Ln, Culpeper VA 22701. 540/825-4100.

Quality Automotive Co.
Airport Rd, Tappahannock VA 22560. 804/443-5356.

AUTOMOTIVE STAMPINGS

Mascotech Industrial Components
PO Box 387, Duffield VA 24244-0387. 540/431-2641.

South Charleston Stamping & Manufacturing
3100 MacCorkle Ave SW, S Charleston WV 25303-1440. 304/744-4601.

TD Wheel Co.
227 Allison Gap Road Saltville VA 24370-3311. 540/496-5121.

MOTOR VEHICLE EQUIPMENT WHOLESALE

Harrisonburg Auto Auction
Exit 62 & Interstate 81, Harrisonburg VA 22801. 540/434-5991.

Fischer Auto Parts Inc.
512 Greenville Ave, Staunton VA 24401-4755. 540/885-8905.

Fisher Auto Parts Inc.
523 Edmunds St, South Boston VA 24592-2415. 804/572-3978.

Goode Omega Inc.
3280 Formex Rd, #24159, Richmond VA 23224-6370. 804/231-0669.

Hofmann Mondial Export
PO Box 10369, Lynchburg VA 24506-0369. 804/846-8411.

Chesapeake Rim & Wheel Distribution
3901 Castlewood Rd, Richmond VA 23234-2613. 804/743-1011.

Morgan Auto Parts
3109 University Ave, Morgantown WV 26505-3238. 304/598-1050.

Standard Motor Products
7070 Golf Course Dr, Disputanta VA 23842-6054. 804/862-1500.

The Automotive Parts Co.
5314 MacCorkle Ave SE, Charleston WV 25304-2222. 304/925-1101.

American Dealer Accessories
927 Barlow Dr, Charleston WV 25311-1207. 304/345-1565.

Capital Freightliner
3617 Nine Mile Rd, Richmond VA 23223-4811. 804/222-5600.

Leonard Building & Truck
8520 Timberlake Rd, Lynchburg VA 24502-3131. 804/237-5301.

Mountain International Trucks
Exit 47 I-64, Cross Lanes WV 25313. 304/776-5600.

Standard Parts Corp.
2345 Tyler Rd, Christiansbrg VA 24073-6325. 540/731-0002.

Truck City Parts Inc.
Rt 50 E, Clarksburg WV 26301. 304/622-2003.

Appalachian Tire Products
2907 4th Ave, Charleston WV 25312-1721. 304/744-9473.

Appalachian Tire Products
400 Broad Street, Charleston WV 25301-1713. 304/343-9541.

Goodyear Commerical Tire & Service
5421 Brook Rd, Richmond VA 23227-2263. 804/266-8733.

Merchants Tire Inc.
9073 Euclid Ave, Manassas VA 22110-5306. 703/368-3171.

Wholesale Tire Inc.
PO Box 1660, Clarksburg WV 26302-1660. 304/624-8465.

AUTOMOTIVE REPAIR SHOPS

Engine Xpress
1600 S Military Hwy, Chesapeake VA 23320-2655. 804/420-6401.

Sudley Car Care Center
10540 Lomond Dr, Manassas VA 22110-2817. 703/361-6208.

Monro Muffler Brake
2870 Market St, Christiansbrg VA 24073-6505. 540/381-1037.

For more information on career opportunities in the automotive industry:

__Associations__

AMERICAN AUTOMOBILE MANUFACTURERS ASSOCIATION
1401 H Street NW, Suite 900, Washington DC 20005. 202/326-5500. Fax: 202/326-5567. A trade association whose members consist of the Big Three U.S. automakers: Chrysler, Ford, and General Motors. Sponsors research projects, distributes publications, and reviews social and public policies pertaining to both the motor vehicle industry and its customers.

AUTOMOTIVE SERVICE INDUSTRY ASSOCIATION
25 Northwest Point Boulevard, Suite 425, Elk Grove Village IL 60007-1035. 847/228-1310. Members are manufacturers and distributors of automobile replacement parts. Sponsors a trade show, and also publishes educational guidebooks and manuals.

ASSOCIATION OF INTERNATIONAL AUTOMOBILE MANUFACTURERS
1001 19th Street North, Suite 1200, Arlington VA 22209. 703/525-7788.

AUTOMOTIVE SERVICE ASSOCIATION
1901 Airport Freeway, Suite 100, P.O. Box 929, Bedford TX 76095. 817/283-6205. Automotive Service Association works with shops to find workers. Publishes a monthly magazine with classified advertisements.

__Directories__

AUTOMOTIVE NEWS MARKET DATA BOOK
Crain Communications, Automotive News, 1400 Woodbridge Avenue, Detroit MI 48207-3187. 313/446-6000.

WARD'S AUTOMOTIVE YEARBOOK
Ward's Communications, 3000 Town Center, Suite 2750, Southville MI 48075. 810/357-0800.

__Magazines__

AUTOMOTIVE INDUSTRIES
Chilton Book Company, 201 King of Prussia Road, Radnor PA 19089. 800/695-1214.

AUTOMOTIVE NEWS
1400 Woodbridge Avenue, Detroit MI 48207. 313/446-6000.

WARD'S AUTO WORLD
Ward's Communications, Inc., 3000 Town Center, Suite 2750, Southville MI 48075. 810/357-0800.

WARD'S AUTOMOTIVE REPORTS
Ward's Communications, Inc., 3000 Town Center, Suite 2750, Southville MI 48075. 810/357-0800.

BANKING/SAVINGS AND LOANS

The banking industry has fared well over the past few years. Banks reported record earnings from 1992 to 1995. Low interest rates have decreased the number of bad loans and have increased investment profits. The early '90s were also a good time for banking professionals, who, despite numerous mergers and consolidations throughout the industry, avoided the large layoffs that hit workers in other industries. As a result of rising interest rates in early 1995, times have begun to change. Analysts argue that there are simply too many banks clogging the market. This glut of banks (over 10,000 in the United States as compared to 60 in Canada), the emphasis on multi-branch banking, and the decline in traditional transactions, has forced banks to consolidate and close branches. This has led to shrinking employment with dramatic layoffs of tellers, bank office workers, and managers. This trend will continue to take place into the next century.

AMERICAN BANCORPORATION
1025 Main Street, Wheeling WV 26003. 304/233-5006. **Contact:** Human Resources. **Description:** American Bancorporation is a bank holding company, organized in 1966 to develop a network of community banks and related companies. The company does business through its two affiliate banks. The Wheeling National Bank serves its customers through seven full service offices located in Ohio County, Hancock County, and Wetzel County, West Virginia. Columbus National Bank serves its customers through 11 full service offices located in Belmont County, Harrison County, Guernsey County, Jefferson County, and Franklin County, Ohio.

AMERICAN NATIONAL BANKSHARES INC.
P.O. Box 191, Danville VA 24543. 804/792-5111. **Contact:** Mr. Cameron Clement, Assistant Vice President. **Description:** A bank holding company whose only subsidiary is American National Bank and Trust Company. The bank offers a wide variety of retail, commercial, and trust banking services throughout its six offices located in Danville. **Corporate headquarters location:** This Location.

BANK OF CLARKE COUNTY
EAGLE FINANCIAL SERVICES, INC.
Two East Main Street, P.O. Box 391, Berryville VA 22611. 703/955-2510. **Contact:** Daisy McDonald, Vice President, Human Resources. **Description:** The Bank of Clarke County provides general banking services. Eagle Financial Services, a bank holding company for Bank of Clarke County, grants commercial, financial, agricultural, residential, and consumer loans to customers in Virginia and eastern West Virginia. **Benefits:** Pension Plan; Retirement Plan. **Corporate headquarters location:** This Location. **Number of employees nationwide:** 64.

BENCHMARK COMMUNITY BANK
BENCHMARK BANKSHARES, INC.
P.O. Box 569, Kenbridge VA 23944. 804/676-8444. **Contact:** Susan Parrish, Operations Manager. **Description:** Benchmark Community Bank is a savings and loan institution with five branch offices located in southern Virginia: Kenbridge (this location), Farmville (two offices), Victoria, and South Hill. Benchmark Bankshares is the holding company for Benchmark Community Bank. **Corporate headquarters location:** This Location.

CENIT BANK, FSB
CENIT BANCORP, INC.
225 West Olney Road, Norfolk VA 23510-1586. 804/446-6600. **Contact:** Mary Anderson, Human Resources Manager. **Description:** CENIT Bank operates 12 retail banking offices in the cities of Norfolk, Portsmouth, Virginia Beach, Chesapeake, Hampton, and York County, Virginia. The bank also operates a mortgage origination office in Chesapeake. Through its branches, the bank attracts retail deposits from the general public in its market area through a variety of deposit services. CENIT Bank also offers permanent and construction residential loans, consumer loans, and commercial real estate and business loans. In 1995, CENIT Bancorp merged with Princess Anne Bank, a Virginia commercial bank. Princess Anne Bank became a wholly-owned subsidiary of CENIT Bancorp, and continues to operate several locations in Virginia Beach under the name Princess Anne Bank. This location houses both the holding company, CENIT Bancorp, Inc., and a branch of the bank. **Benefits:** 401K; ESOP; Retirement Plan; Stock Option. **Corporate headquarters location:** This Location. **Listed on:** NASDAQ. **Number of employees nationwide:** 169.

CENTRAL FIDELITY NATIONAL BANK
1311 Dolly Madison Boulevard, McLean VA 22101. 703/556-7785. **Contact:** Caryl Mitchell, Human Resources. **Description:** A full-service savings bank. This location formerly operated under the name Household Bank. **Common positions include:** Accountant/Auditor; Bank Officer/Manager; Branch Manager; Computer Programmer; Customer Service Representative; Financial Analyst; Insurance Agent/Broker; Loan Officer; Management Trainee; Manufacturer's/Wholesaler's Sales Rep.; Secretary; Underwriter/Assistant Underwriter. **Educational backgrounds include:** Accounting; Business Administration; Communications; Finance; Liberal Arts; Marketing; Mathematics. **Benefits:** Dental Insurance; Life Insurance; Medical Insurance; Paid Vacation; Profit Sharing; Tuition Assistance. **Corporate headquarters location:** Richmond VA.

CENTRAL FIDELITY NATIONAL BANK
P.O. Box 27602, Richmond VA 23261. 804/782-4000. **Recorded Jobline:** 804/782-4253. **Contact:** William H. Leedom, Vice President, Human Resources. **Description:** Central Fidelity is a bank holding company. Through its subsidiaries, the company conducts business through 230 branches across Virginia. Services include commercial banking operations, credit card services, international banking activities, and mortgages. Most loans consist of commercial and residential real estate. Central Fidelity's principal subsidiary is also located at this address. **Common positions include:** Accountant/Auditor; Bank Officer/Manager; Branch Manager; Credit Manager; Customer Service Representative; Department Manager; Financial Manager; Human Resources Specialist; Management Trainee; Marketing Specialist; Operations/Production Manager. **Educational backgrounds include:** Accounting; Business Administration; Economics; Finance; Liberal Arts. **Benefits:** Dental Insurance; Disability Coverage; Employee Discounts; Life Insurance; Medical Insurance; Pension Plan; Profit Sharing; Savings Plan; Tuition Assistance. **Corporate headquarters location:** This Location. **Operations at this facility include:** Administration; Divisional Headquarters; Regional Headquarters. **Listed on:** NASDAQ.

CENTRAL VIRGINIA BANK
CENTRAL VIRGINIA BANKSHARES, INC.
2501 Anderson Highway, P.O. Box 39, Powhatan VA 23139. 804/598-4216. **Contact:** Diana Schaefer, Assistant Vice President, Human Resources. **Description:** Engaged in a general community and commercial banking business, emphasizing the banking needs of individuals and small- to medium-sized businesses in its principle service area, Powhatan County and extending into Chesterfield and Cumberland Counties. Central Virginia Bank offers a wide range of services, including checking accounts, savings accounts, and certificates of deposit, as well as installment, construction,

and permanent residential mortgage loans and other consumer lending services. The bank also offers other related services, such as travelers checks, safe deposit, deposit transfer, customer note payment, collections, notary public, and escrow. Central Virginia Bankshares, Inc., the holding company for Central Virginia Bank, is located here, as well as a branch of the bank. **Benefits:** Profit Sharing; Stock Option. **Corporate headquarters location:** This Location. **Other U.S. locations:** Brandermill VA; Cartersville VA; Midlothian VA; Powhatan VA. **Listed on:** NASDAQ. **Number of employees nationwide:** 50.

CITIZENS AND FARMERS BANK
C&F FINANCIAL CORPORATION
Eighth and Main Streets, P.O. Box 391, West Point VA 23181. 804/843-2360. **Contact:** Susan Newsome, Personnel. **Description:** Citizens and Farmers Bank is a savings and loan institution with 10 branch locations in Virginia. C&F Financial Corporation was founded in 1994 to be the bank holding company for Citizens and Farmers Bank. Other subsidiaries of C&F Financial Corporation include C&F Title Agency, Inc., which was organized in 1992 as a title insurance agent. This location houses both the holding company and a branch of the bank. **Benefits:** Incentive Plan; Pension Plan; Profit Sharing; Stock Option. **Corporate headquarters location:** This Location. **Number of employees nationwide:** 95.

CITIZENS FINANCIAL CORPORATION
213 Third Street, Elkins WV 26241-3832. 304/636-4095. **Contact:** Human Resources. **Description:** A bank holding company with a subsidiary that performs commercial banking operations and other related financial activities. **Number of employees at this location:** 67.

CITY HOLDING COMPANY
3601 MacCorkle Avenue SE, Charleston WV 25304-1421. 304/925-6611. **Contact:** Human Resources. **Description:** A holding company, which through a number of banking-related subsidiaries, performs commercial banking operations, mortgage banking, brokerage services, and related activities.

CO-OPERATIVE SAVINGS BANK, F.S.B.
CSB FINANCIAL CORPORATION
2120 Langhorne Road, P.O. Box 340, Lynchburg VA 24505. 804/847-3800. **Fax:** 804/847-3818. **Contact:** Ann Hicks, Human Resources. **Description:** CSB Financial Corporation is the bank holding company for Co-operative Savings Bank, F.S.B. The bank originates nonresidential and multi-family real estate loans, construction loans, and commercial and consumer loans. The investment portfolio of Co-operative Savings Bank includes U.S. government and federal agency securities, mortgage-backed securities, and high-grade corporate debt issues. The bank has 10 branch offices in Virginia, located in Lynchburg (six), Madison Heights, Amherst, Forest, and Danville. **Benefits:** 401K; ESOP; Incentive Plan; Pension Plan. **Corporate headquarters location:** This Location. **Subsidiaries include:** CSB Financial Services, Inc. This location houses both the holding company and a branch of the bank. **Listed on:** NASDAQ. **Number of employees nationwide:** 91.

COMMERCIAL BANCSHARES INC.
415 Market Street, Parkersburg WV 26101-5338. 304/424-0300. **Contact:** Human Resources. **Description:** A commercial banking company. **Number of employees nationwide:** 215.

CRESTAR FINANCIAL CORPORATION
919 East Main Street, Richmond VA 23219. 804/782-5867. **Contact:** Human Resources. **Description:** Crestar Financial is a bank holding company with 332 subsidiary banking offices, most of which are in Virginia. **Corporate headquarters location:** This Location. **Subsidiaries include:** Crestar Bank of Virginia, Crestar Bank, N.A. of Washington D.C., and Crestar Bank of Maryland. Non-banking subsidiaries conduct a variety of financial operations

including discount brokerage, insurance, mortgage banking, and investment advisory services. **Listed on:** New York Stock Exchange.

EAGLE BANCORP, INC.
227 Capitol Street, Charleston WV 25301-2209. 304/340-4600. **Contact:** Human Resources. **Description:** A savings and loan banking company.

FCFT, INC.
1001 Mercer Street, Princeton WV 27740-5909. 304/487-9000. **Contact:** Human Resources. **Description:** A holding company whose subsidiaries include commercial banks and savings and loan banks.

F&M BANK CORPORATION
FARMERS & MERCHANTS BANK
P.O. Box F, Timberville VA 22853. 703/896-8941. **Contact:** Human Resources. **Description:** F&M Bank Corporation is a bank holding company with subsidiaries which offer such services as trusts, checking accounts, savings accounts, IRAs, and annuities. The company consists of one main office (this location) and four branch offices located throughout the county. **Corporate headquarters location:** This Location. **Number of employees nationwide:** 56.

F&M NATIONAL CORPORATION
F&M BANK CORPORATION
38 Rouss Avenue, P.O. Box 2800, Winchester VA 22604. 703/665-4200. **Contact:** Colleen Bly, Human Resources. **Description:** Organized primarily as a financial holding company which operates through subsidiary organizations or establishments which are engaged in banking and in bank and finance related businesses. F&M National Corporation operates 11 commercial banks located in Springfield, Harrisonburg, Warrenton, Richmond, and Winchester (this location), Virginia; and Ranson, Keyser, and Martinsburg, West Virginia. **Benefits:** Incentive Plan; Retirement Plan; Stock Option. **Corporate headquarters location:** This Location. **Listed on:** New York Stock Exchange. **Number of employees nationwide:** 1,053.

FAIRFAX BANK & TRUST
FB&T FINANCIAL CORPORATION
4117 Chain Bridge Road, Fairfax VA 22030. 703/359-9090. **Contact:** Cindy Fisher, Human Resources. **Description:** FB&T Financial Corporation became the holding company for Fairfax Bank & Trust Company and its subsidiary, Bank Title Company, in 1994. Fairfax Bank & Trust is a community-oriented bank providing customer service and a full range of banking services to businesses and individuals through 11 branch offices in Fairfax and Prince William Counties, Virginia. Bank Title Company was incorporated in 1988 to engage in the land title insurance business. **Benefits:** 401K; Stock Option. **Corporate headquarters location:** This Location. **Listed on:** NASDAQ. **Number of employees nationwide:** 107.

FED ONE BANCORP
21 Twelfth Street, Wheeling WV 26003-3295. 304/234-1100. **Contact:** Human Resources. **Description:** A holding company for a savings and loan bank.

FEDERAL RESERVE BANK OF RICHMOND
P.O. Box 27622, Richmond VA 23261. 804/697-8000. **Contact:** Personnel Department. **Description:** A branch bank of the Federal Reserve System, which consists of 12 regional Federal Reserve banks that, along with the Federal Reserve Board of Governors in Washington, DC, and the Federal Open Market Committee (FOMC), comprise the Federal Reserve System, the nation's central bank. As the nation's central bank, the Federal Reserve is charged with three major responsibilities: monetary policy, banking supervision and regulation, and processing payments. **Other U.S. locations:** Denver CO; Miami FL; Atlanta GA; Chicago IL; Boston MA; Minneapolis MN;

St. Louis MO; Charlotte NC; New York NY; Philadelphia PA; Dallas TX; Houston TX; Salt Lake City UT.

FIDELITY FEDERAL SAVINGS BANK
P.O. Box 85050, Richmond VA 23261-5050. 804/756-0200. **Contact:** Mr. Cary Morris, Vice President, Human Resources. **Description:** Fidelity Federal Savings Bank began its operations in 1986 as a federally-chartered stock savings bank. The bank is primarily engaged in the business of obtaining funds in the form of deposits, and investing funds in mortgage loans on residential and commercial real estate and, to a lesser extent, commercial business and consumer loans. The bank is a member of the Federal Home Loan Bank system, and its deposits are insured by the FDIC. Fidelity Federal Savings Bank has seven retail banking offices, and two mortgage lending offices. **Benefits:** 401K; Stock Option. **Corporate headquarters location:** This Location. **Listed on:** NASDAQ.

FIRST MERCHANTS BANCORP, INC.
Fourth Avenue and Washington Street, Montgomery WV 25136-1109. 304/442-2475. **Contact:** Human Resources. **Description:** A commercial banking company.

FIRST PATRIOT BANKSHARES CORPORATION
12120 Sunset Hills Road, Reston VA 22090. 703/471-0900. **Fax:** 703/708-7242. **Contact:** Ms. Sandy Zareski, Human Resources Director. **Description:** A bank holding company founded in 1989. **Corporate headquarters location:** This Location. **Subsidiaries include:** Patriot National Bank, and 2071 Chain Bridge Road, L.L.C. (75 percent owned), which owns and maintains an office building in Tysons Corner, Virginia that will house the First Patriot Bankshares Corporation's corporate and operations offices. Patriot National Bank operates five full service banking offices which provide services to individuals and corporate customers located in the Washington DC metropolitan area. **Listed on:** NASDAQ.

FIRST UNION NATIONAL BANK OF VIRGINIA
1560 Wilson Boulevard, Arlington VA 22209. **Recorded Jobline:** 703/903-7777. **Contact:** Human Resources. **Description:** A large banking and financial services organization. This location formerly operated as a branch of Columbia First Bank. **Corporate headquarters location:** Roanoke VA. **Other U.S. locations:** DC; FL; GA; MD; NC; SC; TN; VA. **Parent company:** First Union Corporation (Charlotte, NC). **Listed on:** New York Stock Exchange. **Number of employees nationwide:** 31,858.

FIRST UNION NATIONAL BANK OF VIRGINIA
1970 Chain Bridge Road, McLean VA 22102. 703/821-7777. **World Wide Web:** http://www.firstunion.com. **Contact:** Human Resources. **E-Mail Address:** comments@firstunion.com. **Description:** A full-service commercial bank providing corporate and consumer services. First Union National Bank of Virginia operates 177 offices. The parent company, First Union Corporation, is one of the nation's largest bank holding companies with subsidiaries which operate over 1,330 full-service bank branches in the South Atlantic states. These subsidiaries provide retail banking, retail investment, and commercial banking services. The corporation provides other financial services including mortgage banking, home equity lending, leasing, insurance, and securities brokerage services from 222 branch locations. The corporation also operates one of the nation's largest ATM networks. **Corporate headquarters location:** Roanoke VA. **Other U.S. locations:** DC; FL; GA; MD; NC; SC; TN; VA. **Parent company:** First Union Corporation (Charlotte, NC). **Listed on:** New York Stock Exchange. **Number of employees nationwide:** 31,858.

FIRST UNION NATIONAL BANK OF VIRGINIA
P.O. Box 13327, Roanoke VA 24040-7366. 540/563-6393. **Recorded Jobline:** 540/563-7907. **World Wide Web:** http://www.firstunion.com.

Contact: Gwen Whitley, Senior Vice President/Personnel. **E-Mail Address:** comments@firstunion.com. **Description:** A full-service bank providing corporate and consumer services. First Union National Bank of Virginia operates 177 offices. The parent company, First Union Corporation, is one of the nation's largest bank holding companies with subsidiaries which operate over 1,330 full-service bank branches in the South Atlantic states. These subsidiaries provide retail banking, retail investment, and commercial banking services. The corporation provides other financial services including mortgage banking, home equity lending, leasing, insurance and securities brokerage services from 222 branch locations. The corporation also operates one of the nation's largest ATM networks. **Common positions include:** Account Manager; Accountant/Auditor; Bank Officer/Manager; Branch Manager; Customer Service Representative; Financial Analyst; Human Resources Specialist; Instructor/Trainer. **Educational backgrounds include:** Accounting; Business Administration; Economics; Finance; Liberal Arts. **Benefits:** 401K; Daycare Assistance; Disability Coverage; Employee Discounts; Life Insurance; Medical Insurance; Pension Plan; Savings Plan; Stock Option; Tuition Assistance. **Corporate headquarters location:** This Location. **Other U.S. locations:** DC; FL; GA; MD; NC; SC; TN; VA **Parent company:** First Union Corporation (Charlotte, NC). **Operations at this facility include:** Administration; Regional Headquarters; Sales. **Listed on:** New York Stock Exchange. **Number of employees at this location:** 2,200. **Number of employees nationwide:** 31,858.

FIRST VIRGINIA BANKS INC.
One First Virginia Plaza, 6400 Arlington Boulevard, Falls Church VA 22042-2336. 703/241-3657. **Contact:** Terrence Bayly, Assistant Vice President, Human Resources. **Description:** A bank holding company. First Virginia Banks, Inc., with assets of $7.8 billion, is one of the oldest banks headquartered in Virginia. The company has a network of 14 Virginia member banks with 269 offices; five banks in Maryland operating 57 offices in 13 counties; and four banks in Tennessee that operate 23 offices in seven counties. The company also owns several firms that are engaged in financially-related activities such as mortgage banking and insurance in seven states. **Corporate headquarters location:** This Location. **Subsidiaries include:** First Virginia Bank (306 offices); Atlantic Bank (four offices); The Caroline County Bank (one office); Farmers Bank of Maryland (15 offices); Bank of Madisonville (five offices); First Knoxville Bank (three offices); Tri-City Bank and Trust Company (12 offices); and United Southern Bank (three offices). Non-banking subsidiaries include: First Virginia Mortgage Company; First General Mortgage Company; First Virginia Life Insurance Company; First Virginia Insurance Services, Inc.; First Virginia Credit Services, Inc.; First Virginia Services, Inc.; and Springdale Advertising Agency, Inc. **Listed on:** New York Stock Exchange; Philadelphia Exchange. **Number of employees nationwide:** 5,575.

FIRST WEST VIRGINIA BANCORP, INC.
1701 Warwood Avenue, Wheeling WV 26003. 304/277-1100. **Contact:** Human Resources. **Description:** A commercial bank.

GUARANTY SAVINGS AND LOAN, F.A.
1700 Seminole Trail, P.O. Box 7206, Charlottesville VA 22906-7206. 804/974-1100. **Contact:** Rita Lynch, Vice President, Human Resources. **Description:** A federally chartered savings association. The principle business of Guaranty Savings and Loan is attracting funds in the form of deposits and originating, servicing, investing in, and selling loans secured by first mortgage liens on single family dwellings. Guaranty also lends funds to retail customers by means of home equity and installment loans, and to a lesser extent, originates loans secured by commercial property. The bank is a member of the Federal Home Loan Bank system, and its deposits are insured by the FDIC. **Corporate headquarters location:** This Location. **Subsidiaries include:** GMSC, Inc., a financing company; and Guaranty Investments Corporation. **Listed on:** NASDAQ.

HIGHLANDS BANKSHARES, INC.
P.O. Box 929, Petersburg WV 26847-0929. 304/257-4111. **Contact:** Human Resources. **Description:** A multi-bank holding company engaged in commercial banking, insurance services, and other related financial activities.

HORIZON BANCORP, INC.
One Park Avenue, Beckley WV 25802-2803. 304/255-7000. **Contact:** Human Resources. **Description:** A commercial banking company.

HUNTINGTON NATIONAL BANK
P.O. Box 2490, 23 West Pike, Clarksburg WV 26302-2490. 304/623-7280. **Contact:** Sally Hardman, Personnel Director. **Description:** A full-service bank. **Common positions include:** Accountant/Auditor; Bank Officer/Manager; Branch Manager; Credit Manager; Customer Service Representative; Department Manager; Financial Analyst; General Manager; Human Resources Specialist; Management Trainee. **Educational backgrounds include:** Accounting; Business Administration; Economics; Finance. **Benefits:** Dental Insurance; Disability Coverage; Employee Discounts; Life Insurance; Medical Insurance; Pension Plan; Profit Sharing; Savings Plan; Tuition Assistance. **Corporate headquarters location:** This Location.

LIFE SAVINGS BANK, FSB
LIFE BANCORP, INC.
109 East Main Street, Norfolk VA 23510. 804/858-1000. **Contact:** Human Resources. **Description:** A bank holding company for Life Savings Bank, FSB, a federal stock savings bank. Life Bancorp services more than 115,000 accounts through its 20 retail banking offices in Chesapeake, Norfolk, Portsmouth, Suffolk, Virginia Beach, Hampton, and Newport News. The company delivers a wide range of banking products and services to meet the needs of individuals, businesses, and organizations. Lending activities include permanent and construction residential loans, second mortgages and equity lines of credit, consumer loans, commercial real estate and business loans, and lines of credit to businesses and individuals. This location houses both the headquarters of the parent company as well as a branch of the bank. **NOTE:** Interested jobseekers should address inquiries to the attention of Mary Alice Dalton, Vice President of Human Resources, Life Savings Bank, 4530 East Virginia Beach Boulevard, Norfolk VA 23502. **Benefits:** 401K; ESOP; Pension Plan. **Corporate headquarters location:** This Location. **Listed on:** NASDAQ.

MATEWAN BANCSHARES, INC.
Box 100, Williamson WV 25661. 304/235-1544. **Contact:** Human Resources. **Description:** A bank holding company headquartered in Williamson, West Virginia. The company's subsidiaries include 1) Matewan National Bank, a commercial bank; 2) Matewan Bank, FSB, a federally chartered savings bank; and 3) a venture capital company. The commercial bank subsidiary has eight full-service offices and one loan office providing services to customers in southern West Virginia and eastern Kentucky. The savings bank, which is located in Kentucky, has two offices in eastern Kentucky. The venture capital company was formed to develop new business, rehabilitate and expand existing businesses, and to expand economic growth in southern West Virginia.

NATIONSBANK OF VIRGINIA
P.O. Box 27025, Richmond VA 23261-1000. 804/553-5000. **Recorded Jobline:** 804/788-2611. **Contact:** Mike Clement, Senior Vice President. **Description:** A full-service banking institution. In addition to a complete selection of financial accounts, NationsBank offers a variety of services that are designed to make banking as easy and convenient as possible. NationsBank also offers direct deposit and an automatic savings transfer program, allowing regular transfer of money from checking to savings.

NATIONSBANK OF VIRGINIA
Three Commercial Place, Norfolk VA 23510. 804/446-3726. **Recorded Jobline:** 800/587-5627. **Contact:** Employment Office. **Description:** In addition to a complete selection of financial accounts, NationsBank offers a variety of services that are designed to make banking as easy and convenient as possible. NationsBank also offers direct deposit and an automatic savings transfer program, allowing regular transfer of money from checking to savings.

ONE VALLEY BANCORP OF WEST VIRGINIA, INC.
P.O. Box 1793, Charleston WV 25326. 304/348-7028. **Contact:** Human Resources. **Description:** A multi-bank holding company headquartered in Charleston, West Virginia. One Valley owns 11 bank subsidiaries with assets that range between $103 million to $1.6 billion. Through these banks, the company operates in 50 cities and towns with full-service banking operations in 79 locations located throughout West Virginia. One Valley is also the parent of a real estate management corporation that owns and operates the fifteen-floor office building that serves as the company's headquarters in Charleston. **Common positions include:** Accountant/Auditor; Administrator; Bank Officer/Manager; Branch Manager; Credit Manager; Customer Service Representative; Department Manager; Financial Analyst; General Manager; Human Resources Specialist; Management Trainee; Marketing Specialist; Operations/Production Manager; Public Relations Specialist; Systems Analyst. **Educational backgrounds include:** Accounting; Business Administration; Finance. **Benefits:** Dental Insurance; Disability Coverage; Life Insurance; Medical Insurance; Pension Plan; Savings Plan; Tuition Assistance. **Corporate headquarters location:** This Location.

PIEDMONT BANKGROUP INC.
P.O. Box 4751, Martinsville VA 24115. 703/632-2971. **Contact:** Human Resources Department. **Description:** A multi-bank holding company. Piedmont BankGroup, through its affiliate banks, engages in general banking business and provides a broad spectrum of full-service banking to consumers, businesses, institutions, and governments, including accepting demand, savings, and time deposits; making commercial, personal, installment, mortgage, and construction loans; issuing letters of credit; discount brokerage; trust services; bank-card services; mortgage banking; and investment services. The bank operates a total of 28 offices located primarily in south central Virginia. **Corporate headquarters location:** This Location. **Subsidiaries include:** First National Bank of Saltville (3); First National Bank of Ferrum (3); First Community Bank (7); Bank of Carroll (3); First National Bank of Stuart (6); and Piedmont Trust Bank (6). **Number of employees nationwide:** 485.

POCAHONTAS BANKSHARES CORPORATION
500 Federal Street, Bluefield WV 24701-3010. 304/325-8181. **Contact:** Human Resources. **Description:** A bank holding company which, through its subsidiaries, provides commercial banking operations, credit card services and related activities.

POTOMAC BANCSHARES, INC.
111 East Washington Street, Charlestown WV 25414-0906. 304/725-8431. **Contact:** Human Resources. **Description:** A commercial bank.

SIGNET BANK/VIRGINIA
7799 Leesburg Pike, Fourth Floor, Falls Church VA 22043. 703/714-5073. **Contact:** Carol Robinette, Assistant Vice President. **Description:** A full service commercial bank with nine area banking locations. **Parent company:** Signet Banking Corporation (Richmond VA).

SIGNET BANK/VIRGINIA
P.O. Box 25339, Richmond VA 23260. 804/747-2000. **Contact:** Human Resources. **Description:** A full-service commercial bank with nine area

banking locations. **NOTE:** Send all resumes to Management Recruitment, P.O. Box 25970, Richmond, VA 23260. **Parent company:** Signet Banking Corporation (Richmond VA).

SIGNET BANKING CORPORATION
Seven North Eighth Street, Richmond VA 23219. 804/747-2000. **Contact:** Management Recruitment. **Description:** A bank holding company with $11.5 billion in assets, Signet Banking Corporation is engaged in consumer and small-company lending through 239 branches and a credit card business. Non-banking subsidiaries conduct operations such as trust services, commercial and consumer finance, and discount brokerage services. **NOTE:** All resumes should be addressed Management Recruitment, P.O. Box 25970, Richmond, VA 23260. **Corporate headquarters location:** This Location. **Listed on:** New York Stock Exchange. **Number of employees nationwide:** 7,339.

SOUTH BRANCH VALLEY BANCORP, INC.
310 North Main Street, Moorefield WV 26836. 304/538-2353. **Contact:** Human Resources. **Description:** A commercial banking company. **Number of employees at this location:** 55.

UNITED BANCSHARES INC.
300 United Center, 500 Virginia Street East, Charleston WV 25301. 304/424-8761. **Contact:** Human Resources. **Description:** A commercial bank.

VIRGINIA FIRST SAVINGS BANK
P.O. Box 2009, Petersburg VA 23804. 804/733-0333. **Contact:** MaryAnn Harris, Human Resources. **Description:** Incorporated in 1888, Virginia First Savings Bank is one of the oldest financial institutions in Virginia. The bank's services include checking and savings deposits, which are offered to the general public through retail banking offices, as well as the origination, service, investment in and sale of loans secured by first mortgage liens on single family dwellings, including condominiums. The company also provides home equity and installment loans, and, to a lesser extent, originates loans secured by commercial property, multi-family dwellings, and manufactured housing units. The company invests in some U.S. government and agency obligations and other investments. The company's operations depend heavily on net interest income. Virginia First operates 23 full-service retail facilities throughout southside, central, and southwestern Virginia, as well as in southern Maryland. **Parent company:** Virginia First Financial Corporation.

WESBANCO
One Bank Plaza, Wheeling WV 26003-3564. 304/234-9000. **Contact:** Human Resources. **Description:** A commercial banking company.

Note: *Because addresses and telephone numbers of smaller companies change rapidly, we recommend you call each company to verify the information below before inquiring about job opportunities. Mass mailings are not recommended.*

Additional small employers:

COMMERCIAL BANKS

Crestar Bank
424 East Grace Street, Richmond VA 23219-1838. 804/782-5531.

First National Bank Of Stuart
PO Box 352, Stuart VA 24171-0352. 540/694-3135.

Flat Top National Bank
211 Federal Street, Bluefield WV 24701-3099. 304/325-7151.

Fredericksburg Savings & Loan
3600 Plank Rd, Fredericksbrg VA 22407-6833. 540/899-5503.

Huntington Bank
1 Commerce Sq, Charleston WV 25301-1726. 304/348-5000.

Jefferson National Bank
123 E Main St, Charlottesvle VA 22902-5283. 804/972-1100.

Tazewell Farm Bureau
PO Box 217, N Tazewell

VA 24630-0217. 540/988-4131.

United National Bank
500 Virginia St E, Charleston WV 25301-2199. 304/348-8400.

Virginia Beach Federal Savings Bank
2101 Parks Ave, Ste 400, Virginia Beach VA 23451-4160. 804/428-9331.

1st American Bank Of VA
1751 Pinnacle Dr, Mc Lean VA 22102-3833. 703/760-6735.

Bank Of Carroll
145 N Main St, Hillsville VA 24343-1430. 540/728-3111.

Chevy Chase Bank, FSB
2952 Chain Bridge Rd, Ste H, Oakton VA 22124-3024. 703/938-7423.

Columbia First Bank
1560 Wilson Blvd, Arlington VA 22209-2409. 703/247-5000.

Crestar Bank
4020 University Dr, Fairfax VA 22030-6802. 703/691-8023.

First Community Bank
PO Box 195, Forest VA 24551-0195. 804/525-1617.

First Community Bank
PO Box 5939, Princeton WV 24740-5939. 304/487-9000.

First National Bank Saltville
PO Box B, Saltville VA 24370-1116. 540/496-7716.

First Virginia Bank Tidewater
PO Box 3097, Norfolk VA 23514-3097. 804/628-6600.

Huntington National Bank-WV
126 Second Street, Saint Marys WV 26170-1002. 304/684-2427.

Marshall National Bank & Trust
8372 E Main St, Marshall VA 22115-3228. 540/364-1555.

National Bank Fredericksburg
10430 Courthouse Road, Spotsylvania VA 22553-1746. 540/899-3200.

Shore Savings Bank, FSB
RR 13 Box 920 Vd, Onley VA 23418. 804/787-1335.

South Boston Bank
1002 Virginia Ave, Clarksville VA 23927-9035. 804/374-0018.

Southern Financial FSB
101 W Washington St, Middleburg VA 22117. 540/687-3500.

Twentieth Street Bank
1900 3rd Ave, Huntington WV 25703-1107. 304/526-6200.

United National Bank
Rt 34 & Poplar Fork Rd, Scott Depot WV 25560. 304/757-7575.

Wesbanco Bank Wheeling
2003 Eldersville Rd, Follansbee WV 26037-1127. 304/527-3603.

SAVINGS INSTITUTIONS

Fredericksburg Savings & Loan Association
400 George St, Fredericksbrg VA 22401-5818. 540/899-5503.

Providence Savings & Loan
515 Maple Ave E, Vienna VA 22180-4713. 703/938-5900.

Washington Federal Savings Bank of Virginia
570 Herndon Pkwy, Herndon VA 22070-5239. 703/478-9100.

United National Bank-North
1501 Market St, Wheeling WV 26003-3569. 304/233-4500.

CREDIT UNIONS

Home Shopping Network Federal Credit Union
115 Brand Road, Salem VA 24153. 540/389-8121.

Long Reach Empoyees Federal Credit Union
PO Box 180, Sistersville WV 26175-0180. 304/652-3211.

Monsanto Nitro Employees Federal Credit Union
One Monsanto Road, Nitro WV 25143-2526. 304/759-4244.

N&W Federal Credit Union
5660 Indian River Rd, Ste 107, Virginia Beach VA 23464-5240. 804/424-9163.

Naval Air Federal Credit Union
160 Newtown Rd, Virginia Beach VA 23462-2408. 804/552-1000.

Naval Air Federal Credit Union
100 Fairview Dr, Franklin VA 23851-1238. 804/562-5161.

Naval Federal Credit Union
820 Follin Ln, Merrifield VA 22119. 703/255-8000.

Pentagon Federal Credit Union
PO Box 19308, Alexandria VA 22320-0308. 703/838-1375.

Pentagon Federal Credit Union
1001 N Fairfax St, Alexandria VA 22314-1539. 703/838-1000.

Richmond Transit
PO Box 27323, Richmond VA 23261-7323. 804/358-3871.

Clinch River Plant Employees Credit Union
PO Box 157, Cleveland VA 24225-0157. 540/889-1540.

Dixiecon Credit Union
2000 Jefferson Davis Hwy, Richmond VA 23224. 804/232-1292.

Honaker Mills Employee Credit Union
RR 2, Box 19, Honaker VA 24260-9608. 540/873-6821.

Lipton Suffolk Employee Credit Union
1046 W Washington St, Suffolk VA 23434-6244. 804/539-3403.

Nabisco Employees Credit Union
6002 S Laburnum Ave, Richmond VA 23231-5002. 804/222-1307.

Raleigh Co. Educators Credit Union
105 Adair St, Beckley WV 25801-3733. 304/256-4600.

S&S Machinery Credit Union
RR 3, Box 70, Cedar Bluff VA 24609-9409. 703/963-0841.

UBCP Richmond Credit Union
2801 Cofer Rd, Richmond VA 23224-7101. 804/232-5681.

OFFICES OF BANK HOLDING COMPANIES

Allegheny Bankshares Corp.
109 South Jefferson Street, Lewisburg WV 24901-1314. 304/645-2500.

First Fidelity Bancorp Inc.
301 Adams St, #1152, Fairmont WV 26554-3168. 304/363-1300.

Freedom Bankshares Inc.
315 Crim Ave, Belington WV 26250-9469. 304/823-1531.

George Mason Bankshares
11185 Main St, Fairfax VA 22030-5008. 703/352-1100.

Huntington Bancshares West Virginia Inc.
201 High St, Morgantown WV 26505-5414. 304/291-7700.

Old Point Financial Corp.
1 W Mellen St, Hampton VA 23663-2305. 804/722-7451.

For more information on career opportunities in the banking/savings and loans industry:

__Associations__

AMERICA'S COMMUNITY BANKERS
900 19th Street NW, Suite 400, Washington DC 20006. 202/857-3100. A trade association representing the expanded thrift industry. Members are institutions (not individuals).

AMERICAN BANKERS ASSOCIATION
1120 Connecticut Avenue NW, Washington DC 20036. 202/663-5221. Provides banking education and training services, sponsors industry programs and conventions, and publishes articles, newsletters, and the ABA Service Member Directory.

__Directories__

AMERICAN SAVINGS DIRECTORY
McFadden Business Publications, 6195 Crooked Creek Road, Norcross GA 30092. 770/448-1011.

POLK'S BANK DIRECTORY
R.L. Polk & Co., P.O. Box 305100, Nashville TN 37320-5100. 615/889-3350.

BUSINESS WEEK/TOP 200 BANKING INSTITUTIONS ISSUE
McGraw-Hill, Inc., 1221 Avenue of the Americas, 39th Floor, New York NY 10020. 212/512-4776.

AMERICAN BANK DIRECTORY
Thomson Financial Publications, 6195 Crooked Creek Road, Norcross GA 30092. 770/448-1011.

MOODY'S BANK AND FINANCE MANUAL
Moody's Investors Service, Inc., 99 Church Street, First Floor, New York NY 10007. 212/553-0300.

RANKING THE BANKS/THE TOP NUMBERS
American Banker, Inc., 1 State Street Plaza, New York NY 10004. 212/943-6700.

__Magazines__

ABA BANKING JOURNAL
American Bankers Association, 1120 Connecticut Avenue NW, Washington DC 20036. 202/663-5221.

BANK ADMINISTRATION
1 North Franklin, Chicago IL 60606. 800/323-8552.

BANKERS MAGAZINE
Warren, Gorham & Lamont, Park Square Building, 31 St. James Avenue, Boston MA 02116-4112. 617/423-2020.

JOURNAL OF COMMERCIAL BANK LENDING
Robert Morris Associates, P.O. Box 8500 S-1140, Philadelphia PA 19178. 215/851-9100.

BIOTECHNOLOGY, PHARMACEUTICALS, AND SCIENTIFIC R&D

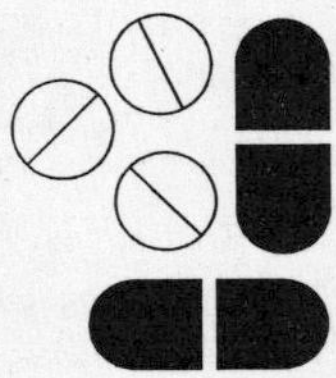

During the early '90s, the pharmaceutical industry was characterized by a mass of mergers and acquisitions, with drug companies concentrating on cutting costs to boost profit margins.

While more mergers may be on the way, most of the big staff cuts are history, and profitability is up. Even so, industry watchers don't expect the arrival of many big-selling new products in the near future, and many companies have slashed research and development budgets. According to the Pharmaceutical Research and Manufacturers of America, the 8 percent growth in R&D spending was the lowest in 20 years.

As more drug patents continue to expire, the impact will be felt by the larger pharmaceutical companies. There will be a negative impact on their sales growth. Conversely, the expired patents mean more opportunities for generic drug manufacturers, who should continue to gain market share through 1996.

ALLIEDSIGNAL, INC.
RESEARCH AND DEVELOPMENT
P.O. Box 31, Petersburg VA 23804. 804/520-3000. **Contact:** Personnel Department. **Description:** A technical and research center. Overall, AlliedSignal serves a broad spectrum of industries through its more than 40 strategic businesses, which are grouped into three sectors: Aerospace, Automotive, and Engineered Materials. AlliedSignal is one of the nation's largest industrial organizations. **Parent company:** AlliedSignal Corporation. **Number of employees at this location:** 600.

ANSER (ANALYTIC SERVICES INC.)
1215 Jefferson Davis Highway, Suite 800, Arlington VA 22202. 703/416-3093. **Contact:** Devette L. Lancon, Senior Employment Administrator. **Description:** An independent, non-profit scientific research corporation engaged in program analysis, systems analysis, and operations research for the U.S. Air Force and other government agencies. **Common positions include:** Accountant/Auditor; Aerospace Engineer; Biological Scientist/Biochemist; Budget Analyst; Chemical Engineer; Chemist; Civil Engineer; Computer Programmer; Computer Systems Analyst; Cost Estimator; Economist/Market Research Analyst; Electrical/Electronics Engineer; Environmental Engineer; Financial Analyst; Geologist/Geophysicist; Human Resources Specialist; Industrial Engineer; Mathematician; Mechanical Engineer; Metallurgical Engineer; Physicist/Astronomer; Science Technologist; Software Engineer; Statistician; Systems Analyst; Technical Writer/Editor. **Educational backgrounds include:** Accounting; Computer Science; Economics; Engineering; Mathematics; Physics. **Benefits:** 401K; Dental Insurance; Disability Coverage; Life Insurance; Medical Insurance; Pension Plan; Tuition Assistance. **Special Programs:** Internships. **Corporate headquarters location:** This Location. **Other U.S. locations:** Torrance CA; Colorado Springs CO; Tampa FL; Dayton OH; Hampton VA; Newport News VA. **Operations at this facility include:** Research and Development. **Number of employees at this location:** 481.

APPLIED BIOSCIENCE INTERNATIONAL INC.
ENVIRON CORPORATION
4350 North Fairfax Drive, Suite 300, Arlington VA 22203-1627. 703/516-2490. **Fax:** 703/516-2462. **Contact:** Human Resources. **Description:** Provides a broad range of research and consulting services in the life and environmental sciences. Services provided by Applied Bioscience International include biological safety testing of pharmaceuticals, biologicals, and chemicals (including agrochemical products); clinical research and development of pharmaceutical products, biologicals, and medical devices; biostatistical analysis; chemical risk assessment and risk management; and analytical laboratory services. Such services are provided under contract to clients in the pharmaceutical, general chemical, agrochemical, biotechnology, and other industries throughout the world. The company operates through two groups, the Life Sciences Group and the Environmental Sciences Group. Life Sciences provides life science-related services through Pharmaco LSR International Inc. and Pharmaco LSR Ltd. Pharmaco LSR International provides contract toxicological testing through two laboratories in the United Kingdom and the United States. Environmental Sciences provides environmental science-related services through APBI Environmental Sciences Group, Inc., which is a multi-disciplinary environmental and health sciences consulting firm that provides a broad range of services relating to the presence of hazardous substances in the environment, consumer products, and the workplace. Another subsidiary of the Environmental Sciences Group, Astrix Software Technology, develops and markets data analysis software systems for use in analytical laboratory settings. **NOTE:** All hiring for APBI is done out of Austin TX. Only financial positions are available. **Corporate headquarters location:** This Location. **Parent company:** APBI (this location). **Listed on:** NASDAQ. **Number of employees at this location:** 1,912.

CEL-SCI CORPORATION
66 Canal Center Plaza, Suite 510, Alexandria VA 22314. 703/549-5293. **Fax:** 703/549-6269. **Contact:** Human Resources. **Description:** A biotechnology company developing products for the treatment of diseases which affect the immune system. CEL-SCI Corporation is involved with the research and development of natural human interleukin-2 and cytokine-related products and processes using the company's proprietary cell culture technologies. The compounds, compositions, and processes of CEL-SCI are being tested to determine if they are effective in improving the immune response of advanced cancer patients. CEL-SCI owns 50 percent of Viral Technologies, Inc., a privately-held company engaged in the development of a possible vaccine for AIDS. **Benefits:** 401K; Incentive Plan; Stock Option. **Corporate headquarters location:** This Location.

COLUMBIA RESEARCH CORPORATION
2531 Jefferson Davis Highway, Suite 100, Arlington VA 22202. 703/841-1445. **Contact:** Mary Ann Matsko, Human Resources. **Description:** A government contractor which is involved in naval and naval logistics research.

CORNING HAZLETON, INC.
9200 Leesburg Turnpike, Vienna VA 22182. 703/893-5400. **Contact:** Priscilla Altmann, Human Resources Manager. **Description:** A life sciences firm, providing biological and chemical research services. Corning Hazleton is also a supplier of laboratory animals and biological products. Clients include research institutes, industrial companies, government agencies, and manufacturers of pharmaceuticals, chemicals, food, and cosmetics. **Common positions include:** Biological Scientist/Biochemist; Chemist. **Educational backgrounds include:** Biology; Chemistry. **Benefits:** 401K; Dental Insurance; Disability Coverage; Employee Discounts; Life Insurance; Medical Insurance; Pension Plan; Profit Sharing; Savings Plan; Tuition Assistance. **Corporate headquarters location:** Herndon VA. **Parent company:** Corning Inc. (Corning,

NY). **Operations at this facility include:** Administration; Research and Development. **Listed on:** New York Stock Exchange.

CYTECH
One Dugger Drive, Willow Island WV 26134-9711. 304/665-2422. **Contact:** Jim Seay, Director of Human Resources. **Description:** Processes raw materials for the production of biochemicals. **Common positions include:** Accountant/Auditor; Agricultural Scientist; Biological Scientist/Biochemist; Biomedical Engineer; Blue-Collar Worker Supervisor; Clinical Lab Technician; Computer Programmer; Computer Systems Analyst; Construction Contractor and Manager; Electrical/Electronics Engineer; Electrician; Human Resources Specialist; Industrial Engineer; Industrial Production Manager; Mechanical Engineer. **Educational backgrounds include:** Accounting; Biology; Chemistry; Engineering; Liberal Arts. **Benefits:** 401K; Dental Insurance; Disability Coverage; Employee Discounts; Life Insurance; Medical Insurance; Pension Plan; Savings Plan; Tuition Assistance. **Corporate headquarters location:** Wayne NJ. **Parent company:** American Cyanamid Company produces the antibiotic aureomycin. **Operations at this facility include:** Administration; Manufacturing. **Listed on:** American Stock Exchange; NASDAQ; New York Stock Exchange. **Number of employees at this location:** 100.

MERCK AND COMPANY, INC.
Highway 340 South, Elkton VA 22827. 703/298-1211. **Contact:** Human Resources. **Description:** Manufactures chemicals and pharmaceuticals.

OGDEN PROFESSIONIAL SERVICES
3211 Jermantown Road, Fairfax VA 22030. 703/246-0200. **Contact:** Ruth Campbell, Manager of Human Resources. **Description:** A research and development corporation specializing in defense contracting. **Common positions include:** Accountant/Auditor; Computer Programmer; Electrical/Electronics Engineer; Mechanical Engineer; Systems Analyst; Technical Writer/Editor. **Educational backgrounds include:** Accounting; Business Administration; Computer Science; Engineering; Finance; Mathematics; Physics. **Benefits:** Dental Insurance; Disability Coverage; Life Insurance; Medical Insurance; Pension Plan; Savings Plan; Tuition Assistance. **Corporate headquarters location:** This Location. **Operations at this facility include:** Research and Development. **Listed on:** New York Stock Exchange.

PHARMACO LSR INTERNATIONAL INC.
2244 Dabney Road, Richmond VA 23230. 804/359-1900. **Fax:** 804/353-1860. **Contact:** Sandra Devaun, Human Resources Director. **Description:** Provides contract biological safety (toxicological) testing services on a worldwide basis through two laboratories in the United States and the United Kingdom. The toxicology divisions of Pharmaco LSR conduct studies designed to test pharmaceutical products, biologicals, chemical compounds, and other substances in order to produce the data required to identify, quantify, and evaluate the risks to humans and the environment resulting from the manufacture or use of these substances. These divisions also perform analytical and metabolic chemistry services. Pharmaco LSR also performs clinical trials of new and existing pharmaceutical and biotechnology products and medical devices in humans. The company is engaged in the clinical development process, including analytical chemistry, evaluation of clinical data, data processing, biostatistical analysis, and the preparation of supporting documentation for compliance with regulatory requirements. **Corporate headquarters location:** Austin TX. **Other U.S. locations:** Columbia MD; East Millstone NJ. **Parent company:** Applied Bioscience International Inc. (Arlington VA).

RESEARCH TRIANGLE INSTITUTE
One Enterprise Parkway, Hampton VA 23666-1564. 804/766-3825. **Contact:** Human Resources Department. **Description:** A non-profit independent research organization involved in many scientific fields, under

contract to business, industry, federal, state, and local governments, industrial associations, and public service agencies. The institute was created as a separately-operated entity by the joint action of North Carolina State University, Duke University, and the University of North Carolina at Chapel Hill, however, close ties are maintained with the universities' scientists, both through the active research community of the Research Triangle region in North Carolina and through collaborative research for government and industry clients. RTI responds to national priorities in health, the environment, advanced technology, and social policy with contract research for the U.S. government including applications in statistics, social sciences, chemistry, life sciences, environmental sciences, engineering, and electronics. Applied research for industry was the fastest growing segment of RTI's activities in 1994. In conducting this R&D, the institute applies the knowledge, experience, and technology created in its government funded research. The institute operates a 180-acre campus in the center of Research Triangle Park, North Carolina which includes laboratory and office facilities for all technical programs. In addition, fully staffed research facilities are maintained at this site and in Florida and Washington, DC. **Corporate headquarters location:** Research Triangle Park NC. **Other U.S. locations:** Washington DC; Cocoa Beach FL. **Number of employees nationwide:** 1,500.

SCIENCE & TECHNOLOGY CORPORATION
101 Research Drive, Hampton VA. 23666 804/865-1894. **Fax:** 804/865-1294. **Contact:** Wayne L. Ewing, Director of Human Resources. **E-Mail Address:** ewing@stcnet.com. **Description:** A defense contractor doing atmospheric research for the government. **Common positions include:** Aerospace Engineer; Biological Scientist/Biochemist; Biomedical Engineer; Clinical Lab Technician; Computer Programmer; Computer Systems Analyst; Environmental Engineer; Geologist/Geophysicist; Mathematician; Mechanical Engineer; Meteorologist; Physicist/Astronomer. **Educational backgrounds include:** Engineering. **Benefits:** 401K; Dental Insurance; Disability Coverage; Life Insurance; Medical Insurance; Pension Plan; Profit Sharing; Tuition Assistance. **Corporate headquarters location:** This Location. **Other U.S. locations:** Nationwide. **Operations at this facility include:** Administration; Divisional Headquarters. **Listed on:** Privately held. **Number of employees at this location:** 75. **Number of employees nationwide:** 350.

SCIENCE APPLICATIONS INTERNATIONAL CORPORATION
1710 Goodridge Drive, Room 1408, McLean VA 22102. 703/821-4300. **Contact:** Human Resources Department. **Description:** A commercial physical and biological research institute.

WHITEHALL-ROBINS COMPANY, INC.
1407 Cummings Drive, Richmond VA 23220. 804/257-2000. **Contact:** Bill King, Director of EEO. **Description:** A pharmaceuticals and health and beauty aids company.

Note: *Because addresses and telephone numbers of smaller companies change rapidly, we recommend you call each company to verify the information below before inquiring about job opportunities. Mass mailings are not recommended.*

Additional small employers:

MEDICAL AND DENTAL LABORATORIES

American Medical Laboratories
14225 Newbrook Dr, Chantilly VA 22021-2228. 703/802-6900.

Chippenham Clinical Laboratory
7101 Jahnke Rd, Richmond VA 23225-4017. 804/323-8820.

Genetics & IVF Institute
3020 Javier Rd, Fairfax VA 22031-4627. 703/698-7355.

Henrico Doctors' Hospital
8002 Discovery Dr, Ste 217, Richmond VA 23229-8601. 804/285-5121.

National Health Laboratories
2000 Bremo Rd, Ste 101, Richmond VA 23226-2440. 804/288-8125.

Riverside Laboratories
8600 Quioccasin Rd, Richmond VA 23229-5514. 804/741-0872.

Roche Analytics Lab
4530 Professional Cir, Ste 1A, Virginia Beach VA 23455-6141. 804/456-9773.

Roche Biomedical Laboratories
850 Greenbrier Cir, Chesapeake VA 23320-2644. 804/420-2883.

Roche Biomedical Laboratories
1732 Sir William Osler Dr, Virginia Beach VA 23454-3003. 804/496-0322.

Roche Biomedical Laboratories
611 Jefferson Davis Hwy, Fredericksbrg VA 22401-4436. 540/373-9673.

Strategic Health Services
511 Brooks St, Charleston WV 25301-1321. 304/343-8542.

SVI Laboratory Services
830 Pennsylvania Ave, Ste 101, Charleston WV 25302-3389. 304/345-5215.

Virginia Radiology Associates
1701 N George Mason Dr, Arlington VA 22205-3671. 703/558-6151.

PHARMACEUTICAL PREPARATIONS

Mylan Pharmaceuticals
781 Chestnut Ridge Rd, Morgantown WV 26505-2730. 304/599-2595.

For more information on career opportunities in biotechnology, pharmaceuticals, and scientific R&D:

Associations

AMERICAN ASSOCIATION FOR CLINICAL CHEMISTRY
2101 L Street NW, Suite 202, Washington DC 20037-1526. 202/857-0717 or 800/892-1400. International scientific/medical society of individuals involved with clinical chemistry and other clinical lab science-related disciplines.

AMERICAN ASSOCIATION OF COLLEGES OF PHARMACY
1426 Prince Street, Alexandria VA 22314-2841. 703/739-2330. An organization composed of all U.S. pharmacy colleges and over 2,000 school administrators and faculty members. Career publications include: *Shall I Study Pharmacy?*, *Pharmacy: A Caring Profession*, and *A Graduate Degree in the Pharmaceutical Sciences: An Option For You?*

AMERICAN COLLEGE OF CLINICAL PHARMACY (ACCP)
3101 Broadway, Suite 380, Kansas City MO 64111. 816/531-2177. Operates ClinNet jobline at 412/648-7893 for both members and nonmembers, for a fee.

AMERICAN SOCIETY FOR BIOCHEMISTRY AND MOLECULAR BIOLOGY
9650 Rockville Pike, Bethesda MD 20814-3996. 301/530-7145. A non-profit scientific and educational organization whose primary scientific activities are in the publication of the *Journal of Biological Chemistry* and holding an annual scientific meeting. Also publishes a career brochure entitled *Unlocking Life's Secrets: Biochemistry and Molecular Biology.*

AMERICAN SOCIETY OF HEALTH SYSTEM PHARMACISTS
7272 Wisconsin Avenue, Bethesda MD 20814. 301/657-3000. Provides pharmaceutical education. Updates pharmacies on current medical developments. Offers a service for jobseekers for a fee.

BIOMEDICAL RESEARCH INSTITUTE
355 K Street, Chula Vista CA 91911-1209. 619/427-9940. Fax: 619/427-2634. A non-profit organization which promotes scientific research and education and provides annual scholarships to students. Maintains a national Institutional Review Board.

BIOTECHNOLOGY INDUSTRY ORGANIZATION
1625 K Street NW, Suite 1100, Washington DC 20006-1604. 202/857-0244. Fax: 202/857-0237. Represents agriculture, biomedical, diagnostic, food, energy, and environmental companies.

AMERICAN PHARMACEUTICAL ASSOCIATION
2215 Constitution Avenue NW, Washington DC 20037. 202/628-4410. Operates a resume referral service for all members.

NATIONAL PHARMACEUTICAL COUNCIL
1894 Preston White Drive, Reston VA 22091. 703/620-6390. Fax: 703/476-0904. An organization of

research-based pharmaceutical companies. Fax requests to the attention of Pat Adams, Vice President of Finance and Administration.

Directories

DRUG TOPICS RED BOOK
Medical Economics Company, 5 Paragon Drive, Montvale, NJ 07645. 201/358-7200.

Magazines

DRUG TOPICS
Medical Economics Company, 5 Paragon Drive, Montvale NJ 07645. 201/358-7200.

PHARMACEUTICAL ENGINEERING
International Society of Pharmaceutical Engineers, 3816 West Linebaugh Avenue, Suite 412, Tampa FL 33624. 813/960-2105.

BUSINESS SERVICES AND NON-SCIENTIFIC RESEARCH

The business services sector, which includes 16 of the 20 fastest growing industries, covers a broad spectrum of careers, including everything from adjustment and collection services to data processing companies. While the job outlook varies upon which service is being discussed, in general, the business services sector is among the fastest-growing in the nation. Increasingly, American companies are "outsourcing" functions like data processing to outside firms. Often large organizations will go so far as to hand over the management of their entire data center to an outside service provider. This trend is expected to boost opportunities for those who work for data processing services.

Other types of services that benefit from this trend include security firms and personnel services firms. Many businesses are using temporary workers instead of hiring new permanent staffers, thus avoiding the much higher overhead costs such as health insurance. Companies that supply these temporary workers, as well as those that place permanent workers, are among the fastest-growing in the nation. While one-third of the jobs available are administrative support occupations, there is a growing trend toward specialization which will open up more positions for highly skilled workers, such as engineers or managers.

ABSTRACT JANITORIAL SERVICES
403 Green Drive #12, Sterling VA 20164. 703/406-4401. **Contact:** Human Resources. **Description:** Provides building cleaning and maintenance services. **Number of employees at this location:** 250.

ALFATECH CORPORATION
2300 Clarendon Boulevard, Suite 302, Arlington VA 22201. 703/243-8700. **Contact:** Anita Brooks, Human Resources Administrator. **Description:** Provides professional, contracting, and information technology services. **Corporate headquarters location:** This Location.

BOAT AMERICA CORPORATION
880 South Pickett Street, Alexandria VA 22304. 703/823-9550. **Fax:** 703/461-4395. **Contact:** Evelyn Matey, Director of Human Resources. **Description:** Provides boating services, including marine insurance and representation in Congress to members of Boat/US, the national association of recreational boat owners. **Common positions include:** Adjuster; Management Trainee; Technical Writer/Editor; Underwriter/Assistant Underwriter. **Educational backgrounds include:** Business Administration; Liberal Arts; Marketing. **Benefits:** 401K; Dental Insurance; Employee Discounts; ESOP; Life Insurance; Medical Insurance; Tuition Assistance. **Corporate headquarters location:** This Location. **Other U.S. locations:** 33 locations. **Operations at this facility include:** Administration; Sales; Service. **Number of employees at this location:** 500. **Number of employees nationwide:** 1,000.

CORT BUSINESS SERVICES CORPORATION
4401 Fair Lakes Court, Suite 300, Fairfax VA 22033. 703/968-8500. **Fax:** 703/968-8503. **Contact:** Ed Baer, Director of Human Resources. **Description:**

A leading national provider of rental furniture, accessories, and related services in the rent-to-rent segment of the furniture rental industry. The segment serves both corporate and individual customers who desire flexibility to meet their temporary and transitional needs. CORT Business Services Corporation focuses on corporate customers by offering office and residential furniture and related accessories through a direct sales force of approximately 450 salespeople and a network of 94 showrooms in 26 states and the District of Columbia. Corporate customers include *Fortune* 500 companies, small businesses and professionals, and owners and operators of apartment communities. The company operates under two names: CORT Furniture Rental, which attracts more corporate customers and upper-income individuals; and General Furniture Leasing, which focuses on middle-income individuals and residential customers. **Benefits:** 401K; Incentive Plan; Retirement Plan; Stock Option. **Corporate headquarters location:** This Location. **Number of employees at this location:** 50. **Number of employees nationwide:** 1,500.

DYNCORP
2000 Edmund Halley Drive, Reston VA 22091-3436. 703/264-0330. **Contact:** Manager of Personnel. **Description:** Provides management and technical services to industry and government organizations, including aviation services; facilities management services; security and telecommunications services; range operations; test and evaluation services; computer and information services; health and information technological services; biomedical technology support; and energy, environmental, and management consulting services. **Corporate headquarters location:** This Location. **Number of employees nationwide:** 23,600.

NATIONAL RIFLE ASSOCIATION OF AMERICA
11250 Waples Mill Road, Fairfax VA 22030. 703/267-1260. **Fax:** 703/267-3938. **Contact:** Neil Sawyer, Recruitment Specialist. **Description:** Founded in 1871, the NRA promotes marksmanship skills, firearm safety, and firearm educational programs. The NRA sponsors yearly seminars, clinics, training courses, and competitions designed to promote safe and responsible firearms ownership and to improve marksmanship skills. **Common positions include:** Accountant/Auditor; Chef/Cook/Kitchen Worker; Computer Operator; Computer Programmer; Market Research Analyst; Public Relations Specialist; Receptionist; Secretary; Telephone Service Representative. **Educational backgrounds include:** Business Administration; English; Marketing; Political Science; Public Administration. **Benefits:** Cafeteria; Dental Insurance; Disability Coverage; Employee Discounts; Fitness Program; Life Insurance; Medical Insurance; Pension Plan; Tuition Assistance. **Special Programs:** Internships. **Corporate headquarters location:** This Location. **Number of employees nationwide:** 530.

OMNI SERVICES, INC.
14115 Lovers Lane, Culpeper VA 22701. 703/825-6800. **Fax:** 703/825-2365. **Contact:** Beth Neuberger, Human Resources Director. **Description:** Provides uniform rental services, industrial laundering, and restroom services. Omni Services has locations nationwide. **Common positions include:** Accountant/Auditor; Blue-Collar Worker Supervisor; Computer Programmer; Computer Systems Analyst; General Manager; Human Resources Specialist; Industrial Engineer; Industrial Production Manager; Management Trainee; Manufacturer's/Wholesaler's Sales Rep.; Mechanical Engineer; Quality Control Supervisor; Services Sales Representative. **Educational backgrounds include:** Accounting; Business Administration; Computer Science; Economics; Engineering; Finance; Liberal Arts; Marketing; Mathematics; Physics. **Benefits:** Dental Insurance; Disability Coverage; Employee Discounts; Life Insurance; Medical Insurance; Pension Plan; Savings Plan; Tuition Assistance. **Corporate headquarters location:** This Location. **Subsidiaries include:** Rus; Sanis. **Operations at this facility include:** Administration; Divisional Headquarters; Manufacturing; Regional

Headquarters; Sales; Service. **Listed on:** Privately held. **Number of employees at this location:** 140. **Number of employees nationwide:** 2,600.

RESOURCE CONSULTANTS, INC. (RCI)
1960 Gallows Road, Vienna VA 22182. 703/893-6120. **Fax:** 703/893-0917. **Contact:** Robert J. Duarte, Employment Director. **Description:** A diversified defense contractor supporting many U.S. Navy life cycle management and communications equipment contracts. RCI also provides job placement counseling to the U.S. Army at over 50 locations worldwide. **Common positions include:** Counselor; Electrical/Electronics Engineer; Management Analyst/Consultant; Software Engineer; Technical Writer/Editor; Technician. **Educational backgrounds include:** Computer Science; Economics; Engineering. **Corporate headquarters location:** This Location. **Other U.S. locations:** Vallejo CA; Panama City FL; Charleston SC. **Parent company:** Gilbert Associates. **Listed on:** NASDAQ. **Number of employees at this location:** 100. **Number of employees nationwide:** 1,200.

VSE CORPORATION
2550 Huntington Avenue, Alexandria VA 22303. 703/329-4220. **Fax:** 703/329-4623. **Recorded Jobline:** 703/329-4784. **Contact:** Jim McFarland, Personnel Administrator. **Description:** Offers engineering services, logistical support services, and data processing services. **Common positions include:** Administrative Services Manager; Aerospace Engineer; Chemical Engineer; Civil Engineer; Computer Programmer; Computer Systems Analyst; Designer; Draftsperson; Economist/Market Research Analyst; Editor; Electrical/Electronics Engineer; Electrician; Financial Analyst; Industrial Engineer; Management Trainee; Mechanical Engineer; Purchasing Agent and Manager; Technical Writer/Editor. **Benefits:** 401K; Dental Insurance; Disability Coverage; Medical Insurance; Pension Plan; Savings Plan; Tuition Assistance. **Other U.S. locations:** Nationwide. **Number of employees at this location:** 200. **Number of employees nationwide:** 1,800.

THE WACKENHUT CORPORATION
4303 MacCorkle Avenue, South Charleston WV 25309. 304/768-7862. **Contact:** Lisa Garrett, Human Resources Director. **Description:** Wackenhut provides physical security services, correction services, and products to businesses, governments, and individuals from more than 150 domestic and foreign offices. Specific services include security guard services; corrections staffing; private investigative services; the assembly and sale of electronic security equipment and systems; the training of security guards and fire and crash rescue personnel; providing fire protection and emergency ambulance service to municipalities; security consulting; planning, designing, and implementing integrated security systems; and providing specialized services to the nuclear power industry. Wackenhut has 90 offices located in most major United States cities. International opportunities exist in foreign countries. **Subsidiaries include:** Wackenhut Corrections, Inc. and Wackenhut International.

Note: *Because addresses and telephone numbers of smaller companies change rapidly, we recommend you call each company to verify the information below before inquiring about job opportunities. Mass mailings are not recommended.*

Additional small employers:

LINEN SUPPLY

National Linen Service
725 South Pickett Street, Alexandria VA 22304-4603. 703/751-5783.

Bardusch Rental Uniform Service
1801 Commerce Rd, Richmond VA 23224-7801. 804/634-2785.

ADJUSTMENT AND COLLECTION SERVICES

Modern Collect Systems VA
4912 W Broad St,

Richmond VA 23230-3123. 804/358-6726.

Syndicated Collection Agency Ltd
710 W Ridge Rd, Wytheville VA 24382-1061. 540/228-8227.

CREDIT REPORTING SERVICES

The Credit Bureau Inc.
227 Chestnut St, Morgantown WV 26505-5409. 304/292-7381.

Trans Union Corporation
7814 Carousel Ln, Ste 45, Richmond VA 23294-4211. 804/747-3633.

PHOTOCOPYING AND DUPLICATING SERVICES

Copy Cat
658A J Clyde Morris Blvd, Newport News VA 23601-1833. 804/874-2228.

SECRETARIAL AND COURT REPORTING SERVICES

Dataprint
2302 Colonial Ave SW, Roanoke VA 24015-3100. 540/345-9040.

Keyboard Communications
9300 Forest Point Cir #131, Manassas VA 22110. 703/631-9356.

Word Wizard
10296 Cedar Ridge Dr, Manassas VA 22110-6629. 703/368-9567.

CLEANING AND MAINTENANCE SERVICES

Dodson Brothers Exterminating
3712 Campbell Ave, Lynchburg VA 24501-4504. 804/847-9051.

Connors Pest Control
7219 Poplar St, Annandale VA 22003-3081. 703/658-8824.

Orkin Exterminating Co.
1001 W Baltimore St, McMechen WV 26040-1503. 304/233-5088.

Paramount Pest Control
406E Hudgins Rd, Fredericksbrg VA 22408-4171. 540/373-1234.

International Building Service LP
5681 Columbia Pike, Falls Church VA 22041-2870. 703/931-1000.

Mason & Hanger Service
P O Box 668 Langley Air Force, Hampton VA 23665. 804/864-1327.

Parsons Brinckerjoff Facilities
475 Springpark Pl, Ste 500, Herndon VA 22070. 703/318-1380.

Raven Services Corp.
6204B Old Franconia Rd, Alexandria VA 22310-2529. 703/922-8201.

Continental Building Maintenance Inc.
4265 Brookfield Corporate Dr, Chantilly VA 22021-1696. 703/631-7300.

Dotties Custom Clean
9 Redbud Ln, Newport News VA 23602-5411. 804/872-9338.

General Maintenance Service Co.
2800 S Shirlington Rd, Arlington VA 22206-3601. 703/578-6440.

Miracle Cleaning Services
12201 Sunrise Valley Dr, Reston VA 22091-3401. 703/620-2591.

Morton G Thalhimer Service Corp.
1534 High St, Richmond VA 23220-2314. 804/643-1984.

Pritchard Industries
1621 N Kent St, Arlington VA 22209-2131. 703/522-1326.

Servicemaster By Gamb
5030 Cedarbend Ln, Richmond VA 23237-3264. 804/751-0748.

Triangle Services Of VA
2428 Almeda Ave, Ste 168, Norfolk VA 23513-2448. 804/855-2646.

Morris Speciality Cleaning
111 S 6th St, Richmond VA 23219-3839. 804/648-8150.

MISC. EQUIPMENT RENTAL AND LEASING

McLean Rentals Inc.
PO Box 579, Newington VA 22122-0579. 703/550-8966.

COMPUTER PROCESSING AND DATA PREPARATION SERVICES

Automatic Data Processing
Laconia Bldg, Wheeling WV 26003. 304/232-1109.

Financial Tech Inc.
14300 Sullyfield Cir, Chantilly VA 22021-1621. 703/631-4400.

International Business Service
8150 Leesburg Pike, Ste 500, Vienna VA 22182-2714. 703/892-0660.

ARA Computers
5055 Seminary Rd Apt 307, Alexandria VA 22311-2004. 540/344-1987.

Calcomp
4900 Seminary Rd, Alexandria VA 22311-1811. 703/931-4784.

Bisys Inc.
8827 Staples Mill Rd, Richmond VA 23228-2014. 804/264-7300.

CGW Data
3060 Williams Dr, Fairfax VA 22031-4648. 703/207-3088.

Logicon Inc.
1815 N Lynn St, Arlington VA 22209-2003. 703/243-6606.

Maintech
3800 Concorde Pky, Ste 500, Chantilly VA

22021-1127. 703/818-1280.

Pinkerton Computer Consultants Inc.
1900 N Beauregard St, Ste 200, Alexandria VA 22311-1716. 703/820-5571.

Rexnord Data Systems
1817 Leslie Ave, Alexandria VA 22301-1223. 703/683-8410.

Structured Management Systems Inc.
4224 Cox Rd, Glen Allen VA 23060-6742. 804/273-0033.

DETECTIVE, GUARD, AND ARMORED CAR SERVICES

Allied Security Inc.
1222 Leone Ln, Dunbar WV 25064-3000. 304/768-1064.

Allied Security Inc.
901 S Highland St, Arlington VA 22204-2459. 703/521-3600.

MVM Inc.
5113 Leesburg Pike, Falls Church VA 22041-3204. 703/671-8710.

Vance International Inc.
10467 White Granite Dr, Oakton VA 22124-2763. 703/385-6754.

Wackenhut Corp.
5652 Parliament Dr, Virginia Beach VA 23462-3319. 804/499-6891.

Burns International Security Services
8229 Boone Blvd, Vienna VA 22182-2604. 703/448-3306.

Admiral Security Services
2807 N Parham Rd, Richmond VA 23294-4410. 804/270-1392.

Advance Security Inc.
500 Hawley Bldg, Wheeling WV 26003. 304/233-3744.

Advance Security Inc.
380 Maple Ave W, Vienna VA 22180-5616. 703/242-1851.

Advance Security Inc.
325 6th Ave SW, Charleston WV 25303-1200. 304/744-4391.

Barton Protective Services
3141 Fairview Park Dr, Ste 740, Falls Church VA 22042-4507. 703/849-1960.

Barton Protective Services
3130 Fairview Park Dr, Falls Church VA 22042-4509. 703/849-1961.

Key Security Services
806 Norview Ave, Norfolk VA 23509-1541. 804/855-6666.

Pinkerton Security Services
6601 Irongate Sq, Richmond VA 23234-6076. 804/743-0703.

Pinkerton Security Services
1032 12th St W, Huntington WV 25704-2408. 304/697-4502.

Security America Inc.
5407 MacCorkle Ave SE, Charleston WV 25304-2223. 304/925-4747.

The Wackenhut Corp.
1200 Electric Rd, Salem VA 24153-6434. 540/389-9861.

Commonwealth Training Academy
2807 N Parham Rd, Richmond VA 23294-4410. 804/762-9244.

Marston Agency Inc.
2807 N Parham Rd, Richmond VA 23294-4410. 804/346-3111.

Vintage Resources
1445 Montague Dr, Mc Lean VA 22102. 703/759-5912.

ADT Security Systems
2019 Cunningham Dr, Ste 310, Hampton VA 23666-3318. 804/838-0681.

MISC. BUSINESS SERVICES

American Workshop Inc.
5608 Virginia Beach Blvd, Ste 5, Virginia Beach VA 23462-5631. 804/557-0005.

Community Benefit Corp.
3805 Cutshaw Ave, Richmond VA 23230-3943. 804/358-4991.

National Card Control Inc.
1700 Cardwell Rd, Crozier VA 23039-2305. 804/784-5868.

PCI Of Virginia
5300 Klockner Dr, Richmond VA 23231-4337. 804/222-3444.

Transamerica Marketing Service
8130 Boone Blvd, Ste 350, Vienna VA 22182-2640. 703/903-9500.

Wolff-Fording & Co.
2220 E Main St, Richmond VA 23223-7053. 804/643-2600.

Equifax Commercial Specialists
8100 Three Chopt Rd, Ste 149, Richmond VA 23229-4833. 804/285-4509.

Corderman Interior Design
5317 Leavells Crossing Dr, Fredericksbrg VA 22407-7709. 540/898-8480.

Snyder Szantner & Peters
1011 E Main St, Richmond VA 23219-3503. 804/643-7644.

ICT Group
Cypress Point Shopping Center, Virginia Beach VA 23454. 804/490-6901.

ICT Group Inc.
863 Glenrock Rd, Norfolk VA 23502-3701. 804/461-8700.

Cox Cable Hampton Roads
5200 Cleveland St, Virginia Beach VA

23462-6504. 804/497-1071.

Techlaw Inc.
3675 Concorde Pky, Chantilly VA 22021-1130. 703/803-0366.

RGIS Inventory Specialists
8003 Franklin Farms Dr, Ste 110, Richmond VA 23229-5107. 804/282-7511.

Eric Document Reproduction Service
7420 Fullerton Rd, Ste 110, Springfield VA 22153-2836. 703/440-1400.

National Micrographics Systems Inc.
9710 Farrar Court, Suite M, Richmond VA 23236-3666. 804/272-8600.

Ozonia North America Inc.
2924 Emerywood Pky, Richmond VA 23294-3746. 804/756-0500.

FACILITIES SUPPORT SERVICES

Diversified Tech and Service Of VA
PO Box 12988, Newport News VA 23612-2988. 804/873-0725.

For more information on career opportunities in miscellaneous business services and non-scientific research:

<u>Associations</u>

EQUIPMENT LEASING ASSOCIATION OF AMERICA
1300 17th Street, Suite 1010, North Arlington VA 22209. 703/527-8655.

AMERICAN SOCIETY OF APPRAISERS
P.O. Box 17265, Washington DC 20041. 703/478-2228. Toll-free number: 800/ASA-VALU. Fax: 703/742-8471. An international, non-profit, independent appraisal organization. ASA teaches, tests, and awards designations.

NATIONAL ASSOCIATION OF PERSONNEL SERVICES
3133 Mt. Vernon Avenue, Alexandria VA 22305. 703/684-0180. Fax: 703/684-0071. Provides federal legislative protection, education, certification, and business products and services to its member employment service agencies.

CHARITIES AND SOCIAL SERVICES

The outlook for social service workers is better than average. In fact, opportunities for qualified applicants are expected to be excellent, partly due to the rapid turnover in the industry as a result of lower wages offered.

Note: Because of the high turnover rate and the continuous need for social services, the outlook for this industry has remained constant over the past few years.

NATIONAL ALLIANCE FOR THE MENTALLY ILL (NAMI)
200 North Glebe Road, Suite 1015, Arlington VA 22203-3754. 703/524-7600. **Contact:** Human Resources. **Description:** NAMI provides a wide range of services to families living with mental illness: support, which offers support groups and special interest networks; education, which provides up-to-date, scientific information through publications, a toll-free help line, and annual Mental Illness Awareness Week campaigns; advocacy for services; and support for research.

SALVATION ARMY
P.O. Box 269, Alexandria VA 22313. 703/684-5500. **World Wide Web address:** http://www.winkcomm.com/saweb/home.htm. **Contact:** Human Resources Department. **Description:** Nationwide, the Salvation Army offers services such as food, medical attention, and daycare for the homeless. **Corporate headquarters location:** This Location. **Other U.S. locations:** Nationwide.

UNITED WAY OF AMERICA
701 North Fairfax Street, Alexandria VA 22314-2045. 703/836-7100. **Contact:** Michael Liacaw, Human Resources Director. **Description:** Through a vast network of volunteers and local charities, local United Way organizations throughout America help meet the health and human-care needs of millions of people. United Way's 107-year history is built on local organizations helping people in their own communities. The United Way system includes approximately 1,900 community-based organizations. United Way of America is the national service and training center, supporting its members with national services that include advertising, training, corporate relations, research, networks, and government relations. **Corporate headquarters location:** This Location.

UNITED WAY OF KANAWHA VALLEY
One United Way Square, Charleston WV 25301-1098. 304/340-3500. **Contact:** Kim Good, Office Manager. **Description:** Through a vast network of volunteers and local charities, local United Way organizations throughout America help meet the health and human-care needs of millions of people. United Way's 107-year history is built on local organizations helping people in their own communities. The United Way system includes approximately 1,900 community-based organizations. United Way of America is the national service and training center, supporting its members with national services that include advertising, training, corporate relations, research, networks, and government relations.

Note: *Because addresses and telephone numbers of smaller companies change rapidly, we recommend you call each company to verify the information below before inquiring about job opportunities. Mass mailings are not recommended.*

Additional small employers:

MISC. SOCIAL SERVICES

CARES Of Kanawha Valley
1716 7th Ave, Charleston WV 25312-1931. 304/341-0337.

Boys & Girls Club
2653 Decatur St, Richmond VA 23224-3600. 804/230-0757.

Braley & Thompson
906 A 3rd Grand Central Ave, Vienna WV 26105. 304/295-5175.

Capture Life
First Ave, Alberta VA 23821. 804/949-6000.

Children's Home Society Of WV
Cherry St, Daniels WV 25832. 304/255-0408.

LDS Social Services
8110 Virginia Pine Ct, Richmond VA 23237-2203. 804/743-0727.

Putnam County Community Action
Winfield, Charleston WV 25313. 304/755-4920.

JOB TRAINING AND VOCATIONAL REHABILITATION SERVICES

Education & Training Corp.
108 N Wayne Ave, Waynesboro VA 22980-4524. 540/943-8420.

Lynchburg Sheltered Industries
3120 Odd Fellows Road, Lynchburg VA 24501-5010. 804/847-4488.

For more information on career opportunities in charities and social services:

<u>Associations</u>

AMERICAN COUNCIL OF THE BLIND
1155 15th Street NW, Suite 720, Washington DC 20005. 202/467-5081. Membership. Offers an annual conference, a monthly magazine, and scholarships.

CATHOLIC CHARITIES USA
1731 King Street, Suite 200, Alexandria VA 22314. 703/549-1390. Membership.

FAMILY SERVICE ASSOCIATION OF AMERICA
11700 West Lake Park Drive, Park Place, Milwaukee WI 53224. 414/359-1040. Membership.

NATIONAL COUNCIL ON FAMILY RELATIONS
3989 Central Avenue NE, Suite 550, Minneapolis MN 55421. 612/781-9331. Fax: 612/781-9348. Membership. Publishes two quarterly journals. Offers an annual conference and newsletters.

NATIONAL FEDERATION OF SOCIETIES FOR CLINICAL SOCIAL WORK, INC.
P.O. Box 3740, Arlington VA 22203. 703/522-3866. A lobbying organization. Offers newsletters and a conference every two years to membership organizations.

NATIONAL FEDERATION OF THE BLIND
1800 Johnson Street, Baltimore MD 21230. 410/659-9314. Membership of 50,000 in 600 local chapters. Publishes a monthly magazine.

NATIONAL MULTIPLE SCLEROSIS SOCIETY
733 Third Avenue, New York NY 10017. 212/986-3240. Toll-free: 800/344-4867. Publishes a quarterly magazine.

NATIONAL ORGANIZATION FOR HUMAN SERVICE EDUCATION
Brookdale Community College, Newman Springs Road, Lyncroft NJ 07738. 908/842-1900, ext. 546.

CHEMICALS/RUBBER AND PLASTICS

First the good news: Overall growth in the chemical industry is on the upswing. Chemical products and services are currently in high demand, thus creating a need for more workers, and recent price increases are holding steady.

Now the bad news: Costs for pollution reduction are rising. Factories are running at 85 percent capacity, and if companies increase spending on plant and equipment, an oversupply could result if economic growth slows too quickly.

Growth prospects for the domestic synthetic rubber industry remain mixed, reflecting the industry's dependence on tire manufacturing. The tire industry shows signs of stabilizing after undergoing a period characterized by massive restructuring, the effects of recession in the domestic market, and consistently high levels of imports.

In the plastics industry, greater reliance on computer-aided design and manufacturing is expected in the last half of the 1990s, as production is streamlined. These measures will be aimed at strengthening the industry's competitiveness in the areas of quality control and improved client relations.

ABLEMARLE CORPORATION
330 South Fourth Street, P.O. Box 1335, Richmond VA 23210. 804/788-6000. **Contact:** Human Resources. **Description:** Ablemarle Corporation is a global supplier of specialty and performance chemicals that enhance consumer products. The company serves markets for petroleum and agricultural chemicals, detergents, polymers, electronics, and pharmaceuticals. The company entered the marketplace with an established line of performance chemicals critical to the manufacture of numerous finished products. The company is the number one or two producer in most segments of its three core business units and one of the world's leading producers of alpha olefins, bromine chemicals, ibuprofen, and a host of other specialty chemicals. **NOTE:** Interested jobseekers should contact human resources at 451 Florida Boulevard, Baton Rouge LA 70801. **Number of employees worldwide:** 3,700.

ALLIED COLLOIDS, INC.
2301 Wilroy Road, Suffolk VA 23434-2021. 804/538-3700. **Contact:** Sean Chagray, Human Resources. **Description:** A manufacturer of specialty chemicals used in agriculture.

ALLIEDSIGNAL, INC.
P.O. Box 831, Hopewell VA 23860. 804/530-6000. **Contact:** Personnel Department. **Description:** This location produces a variety of chemicals. Overall, AlliedSignal serves a broad spectrum of industries through its more than 40 strategic businesses, which are grouped into three sectors: Aerospace, Automotive, and Engineered Materials. AlliedSignal is one of the nation's largest industrial organizations. **Parent company:** AlliedSignal Corporation.

AQUALON COMPANY
1111 Hercules Road, Hopewell VA 23860-5245. 804/541-4505. **Contact:** Joe Fleming, Human Resources Representative. **Description:** Manufactures water-soluble polymers.

BEAR CORPORATION
P.O. Box 500, New Martinsville WV 26155. 304/455-4400. **Contact:** Mrs. M.M. Wilcox, Supervisor/Employment. **Description:** Produces pigments and synthetic resins. **Common positions include:** Chemical Engineer; Chemist. **Educational backgrounds include:** Chemistry; Engineering. **Benefits:** Dental Insurance; Disability Coverage; Life Insurance; Medical Insurance; Pension Plan; Savings Plan; Tuition Assistance. **Corporate headquarters location:** Pittsburgh PA. **Parent company:** Bayer USA. **Operations at this facility include:** Manufacturing.

BLUE RIDGE INDUSTRIAL, INC.
266 Arbor Court, Winchester VA 22602. 703/662-3383. **Contact:** Claudia Nusu, Human Resources Manager. **Description:** An injection molding manufacturing company.

CARPENTER COMPANY, INC.
P.O. Box 27205, Richmond VA 23261. 804/359-0800. **Contact:** Inga Warner, Employment Manager. **Description:** An international manufacturer of foams and related materials for consumer and industrial applications. **NOTE:** Although the company is based in Richmond, positions are available throughout the United States and Canada. **Common positions include:** Accountant/Auditor; Chemical Engineer; Chemist; Computer Programmer; Computer Systems Analyst; Electrical/Electronics Engineer; Environmental Engineer; Industrial Engineer; Mechanical Engineer; Software Engineer; Technical Writer/Editor. **Educational backgrounds include:** Accounting; Business Administration; Chemistry; Computer Science; Engineering. **Benefits:** Disability Coverage; Life Insurance; Medical Insurance; Profit Sharing; Tuition Assistance. **Corporate headquarters location:** This Location. **Other U.S. locations:** Nationwide. **Operations at this facility include:** Administration; Divisional Headquarters; Research and Development. **Listed on:** Privately held. **Number of employees nationwide:** 5,400.

E.I. DuPONT deNEMOURS & COMPANY
901 West DuPont Avenue, Belle WV 25015. 304/357-1000. **Contact:** Elbert Price, Personnel Director. **Description:** Produces synthetics, inorganic industrial chemicals, and agricultural chemicals. E.I. DuPont de Nemours & Company is a corporation whose diverse activities include the manufacturing of biomedical, industrial, and consumer products (such as photographic, data-recording, and video devices); the production of man-made fiber products (with applications in a variety of consumer and commercial industries); polymer products (such as plastic resins, elastomers, and films); agricultural and industrial chemicals (such as herbicides and insecticides, pigments, fluorochemicals, petroleum additives, and mineral acids); the exploration and production of crude oil and natural gas; the refining, marketing, and downstream transportation of petroleum; and the mining and distribution of steam and metallurgical coals. Industries served range from aerospace, agriculture, and apparel to transportation, health care, and printing and publishing. **Corporate headquarters location:** Wilmington DE.

GENERAL FOAM PLASTICS CORP.
3321 East Princess Anne Road, Norfolk VA 23502. 804/857-0153. **Contact:** Laura Williams, Personnel Director. **Description:** Manufactures a variety of plastic products, including holiday decorations and swimming pools.

GOODYEAR TIRE & RUBBER CO.
1901 Goodyear Boulevard, Danville VA 24541-6607. 804/791-9200. **Contact:** Personnel. **Description:** Manufactures truck and airplane tires.

Goodyear Tire & Rubber Co.'s principal business is the development, manufacture, distribution, and sale of tires for a number of applications worldwide. Goodyear also manufactures and sells a broad spectrum of rubber products and rubber-related chemicals for various industrial and consumer markets and provides auto repair services. The company operates 32 plants in the United States, 42 plants in 29 other countries, and more than 1,800 retail tire and service centers and other distribution facilities around the globe. Strategic business units of Goodyear Tire & Rubber include: North American Tire; Kelly-Springfield, Goodyear Europe; Goodyear Latin America; Goodyear Asia; Engineered Products; Chemicals; Celeron; and Goodyear Racing.

HUNTSMAN CHEMICAL CORPORATION
5100 Bainbridge Boulevard, Chesapeake VA 23320. 804/494-2500. **Contact:** Ms. Dina Beimler, Human Resources Manager. **Description:** Manufactures plastics materials and synthetic resins. **Common positions include:** Accountant/Auditor; Chemist; Electrical/Electronics Engineer; Human Resources Specialist; Mechanical Engineer; Petroleum Engineer; Transportation/Traffic Specialist. **Educational backgrounds include:** Business Administration; Chemistry; Computer Science; Engineering; Finance; Marketing.

O'SULLIVAN CORPORATION
P.O. Box 3510, Winchester VA 22604. 703/667-6666. **Contact:** Human Resources. **Description:** Operates in two business segments: 1) calendered and molded plastic products, which involves the manufacture of calendered plastics for the automotive and specialty plastics manufacturing industries and 2) lawn and garden consumer products.

PPG INDUSTRIES, INC.
P.O. Box 191, New Martinsville WV 26155. 304/455-2200. **Contact:** Tim Lovesky, Human Resources Manager. **Description:** A diversified global manufacturer, PPG Industries is a supplier of products for manufacturing, building, automotive, processing, and numerous other world industries. Established in 1883, the Pittsburgh-based company makes decorative and protective coatings, flat glass and fabricated glass products, continuous-strand fiber glass, and industrial and specialty chemicals. PPG operates 68 major manufacturing facilities in Canada, China, France, Germany, Ireland, Italy, Mexico, the Netherlands, Portugal, Spain, Taiwan, the United Kingdom, and the United States. **Common positions include:** Chemical Engineer; Mechanical Engineer. **Educational backgrounds include:** Chemistry; Computer Science; Engineering. **Benefits:** Dental Insurance; Disability Coverage; Employee Discounts; Life Insurance; Medical Insurance; Pension Plan; Profit Sharing; Savings Plan; Tuition Assistance. **Corporate headquarters location:** Pittsburgh PA. **Operations at this facility include:** Manufacturing. **Listed on:** New York Stock Exchange.

PRESTO PRODUCTS COMPANY
P.O. Box 527, South Boston VA 24592. 804/572-6961. **Contact:** Wayne Connor, Human Resource Manager. **Description:** Presto Products manufactures and nationally distributes plastic bags. **Number of employees at this location:** 300.

RADVA CORPORATION
P.O. Box 2900, Radford VA 24143. 540/639-2458. **Contact:** Alva Phipps, Human Resources Director. **Description:** Produces and sells molded and fabricated expanded polystyrene foam products such as packaging materials and containers. Radva Corporation has also developed and patented housing construction panels utilizing expanded polystyrene foam reinforced with steel. In addition, the company builds and sells machinery used to manufacture the panels along with the licensing rights to market the panels. Foreign licenses are held by companies in Guam, Australia, and Mexico, and a joint venture agreement exists between Radva and a company in Russia.

Corporate headquarters location: This Location. **Subsidiaries include:** Thermastructure, Ltd.; and Radva RU, Inc. **Other U.S. locations:** Portsmouth VA. **Operations at this facility include:** Engineering and Design; Manufacturing; Marketing. **Listed on:** NASDAQ. **Number of employees nationwide:** 120.

RAT CARR TIRE, INC.
P.O. Box RCTI, Harrisonburg VA 22801. 540/434-5900. **Contact:** Tim Nicely, Human Resource Manager. **Description:** Manufactures tires.

RUBBERMAID COMMERCIAL PRODUCTS, INC.
3124 Valley Avenue, Winchester VA 22601. 703/667-8700. **Fax:** 703/542-8770. **Contact:** Sean Gillespie, Human Resources Manager. **Description:** Manufactures plastic products for the maintenance, refuse, food service, and agriculture markets. **Common positions include:** Accountant/Auditor; Designer; Financial Analyst; General Manager; Industrial Engineer; Manufacturer's/Wholesaler's Sales Rep.; Materials Engineer; Mechanical Engineer; Operations/Production Manager; Purchasing Agent and Manager; Quality Control Supervisor. **Educational backgrounds include:** Business Administration; Economics; Engineering; Finance; Marketing. **Benefits:** 401K; Dental Insurance; Disability Coverage; Employee Discounts; Life Insurance; Medical Insurance; Pension Plan; Profit Sharing; Tuition Assistance. **Corporate headquarters location:** Wooster OH. **Parent company:** Rubbermaid, Inc. **Operations at this facility include:** Administration; Divisional Headquarters; Manufacturing; Research and Development; Sales. **Listed on:** New York Stock Exchange. **Number of employees at this location:** 900.

SHELL CHEMICAL COMPANY
State Route 2, Apple Grove WV 25502. 304/576-2041. **Contact:** Mike Harrington, Employment Manager. **Description:** Produces polyester resins. **Corporate headquarters location:** Akron OH.

TRINITY PACKAGING CORPORATION
P.O. Box 367, Remington VA 22734. 703/439-3226. **Contact:** Mr. Pat Roe, Human Resources Manager. **Description:** Trinity Packaging Corp. manufactures plastic bags.

UNION CARBIDE CORPORATION
437 McCorkle Avenue SW, South Charleston WV 25303. 304/747-5955. **Contact:** Don Gatewood, Placement Manager. **Description:** Union Carbide Corporation is a worldwide, basic chemicals company with advanced process technologies and large-scale chemical production facilities. Union Carbide is among the largest manufacturers of polyethylene, the world's most widely used plastic, and the technology leader in this industry; one of the world's largest producers of ethylene glycol, used for polyester fiber, resin and film, automotive antifreeze, and other products; a leading North American supplier of solvents and intermediates to the paint and coatings industry; and a leading manufacturer and supplier of specialty chemicals and services used in the personal care products, pharmaceuticals, automotive, oil and gas, and industrial lubricant industries. **Common positions include:** Chemical Engineer; Chemist; Computer Systems Analyst. **Educational backgrounds include:** Chemistry; Engineering. **Benefits:** 401K; Dental Insurance; Disability Coverage; Life Insurance; Medical Insurance; Pension Plan; Profit Sharing; Savings Plan; Tuition Assistance. **Special Programs:** Internships. **Corporate headquarters location:** Danbury CT. **Other U.S. locations:** LA; NJ; TX. **Operations at this facility include:** Manufacturing; Research and Development; Sales. **Listed on:** New York Stock Exchange. **Number of employees nationwide:** 13,000.

***Note:** Because addresses and telephone numbers of smaller companies change rapidly, we recommend you call each company to verify the information below before inquiring about job opportunities. Mass mailings are not recommended.*

Additional small employers:

INDUSTRIAL GASES

BOC Gases Inc.
RR 2 F-6, PO Box 247, Chester WV 26034. 304/387-0889.

INDUSTRIAL INORGANIC CHEMICALS

Magnox Pulaski Inc.
4 Magnox Dr, Pulaski VA 24301-4943. 703/980-3500.

Akzo Nobel
St Rte 2, PO Box 1721, Galipolis Fry WV 25515. 304/675-1150.

Albright & Wilson Amer Inc. Industries
PO Box 26229, Richmond VA 23260-6229. 804/752-6100.

GE Specialty Chemicals
1000 Dupont Rd Bldg 816, Morgantown WV 26505-9624. 304/296-2554.

Goldschmidt Chemical Corp.
914 E Randolph Rd, Hopewell VA 23860-2458. 804/541-8658.

Hercules Inc.
Hwy 671, Franklin VA 23851. 804/562-3121.

Hickson Danchem Corp.
1975 Richmond Blvd, Danville VA 24540-3961. 804/797-8100.

Kingsford Products Co.
Rt 219 S, Parsons WV 26287. 304/478-2911.

Koppers Industries Inc.
100 Koppers Rd, Follansbee WV 26037-1247. 304/527-0110.

Olin Corp.
95 MacCorkle Ave SW, South Charleston WV 25303-1411. 304/746-3000.

PLASTICS MATERIALS, SYNTHETICS, AND ELASTOMERS

Alloy Polymers Inc.
3310 Deepwater Terminal Rd, Richmond VA 23234-1828. 804/232-8000.

Aristech Chemical Corp.
2334 Big Sandy Rd, Kenova WV 25530-9663. 304/453-1371.

GE Plastics
P.O. Box 68, Washington, WV 26181. 304/424-5411.

Hoechst Celanese Corp.
3340 W Norfolk Rd, Portsmouth VA 23703-2433. 804/483-7000.

ICI Films
Discovery Dr, Hopewell VA 23860. 804/530-9300.

Reiss Corp.
1 Polymer Pl, Blackstone VA 23824. 804/292-1600.

INDUSTRIAL ORGANIC CHEMICALS

BASF Corp.
PO Box 2166, Huntington WV 25722-2166. 304/528-2300.

TIRES AND INNER TUBES

Yokohama Tire Corp.
1500 Indiana St, Salem VA 24153-7058. 540/389-5426.

MISC. RUBBER AND PLASTICS PRODUCTS

Parsons Footwear
222 Davis St, Parsons WV 26287-1298. 304/478-2864.

Ashworth Brothers Inc.
450 Armourdale, Winchester VA 22601-3459. 540/662-3494.

MANMADE FIBERS

Fibair
Route 92, PO Box 478, Reedsville WV 26547. 304/864-3321.

Fred Whitaker Co.
PO Box 12886, Roanoke VA 24029-2886. 540/344-4343.

AGRICULTURAL CHEMICALS

Rhone-Poulenc Co.
PO Box 2831, Charleston WV 25330-2831. 304/767-6000.

ADHESIVES AND SEALANTS

Sandvik Rock Tools Inc.
PO Box 639, Bristol VA 24203-0639. 540/669-8311.

PRINTING INK

Sicpa Securink Corp.
8000 Research Way, Springfield VA 22153-3131. 703/455-8050.

CHEMICALS AND CHEMICAL PREPARATIONS

Chemtreat Inc.
500 Lickinghole Rd, Ashland VA 23005-3224. 804/798-3231.

Chemtreat Inc.
4301 Dominion Blvd, Ste 200, Glen Allen VA 23060-6744. 804/965-0505.

RUBBER PRODUCTS

Acadia
Rt 1705 Tannery Rd, Iron Gate VA 24448. 540/863-2100.

Bellofram Corp.
State Rte 2, Newell WV 26050. 304/387-1200.

American National Rubber Company
PO Box 7338, Huntington WV 25776-7338. 304/453-1311.

American National Rubber Company
Main & High Sts, Ceredo WV 25507. 304/453-1311.

Groendyk Manufacturing
S Main St, Buchanan VA 24066. 540/254-1010.

Longwood Elastomers
655 Fairview Rd, Wytheville VA 24382-4503. 540/228-5406.

Rex Hide Industries Inc.
PO Box 370, Grafton WV 26354-0370. 304/265-5100.

Rubatex Corporation
5221 Valleypark Dr, Roanoke VA 24019-3004. 540/561-6000.

SMR Technologies Inc.
Rte 39, PO Box 200, Fenwick WV 26202. 304/846-2554.

Wirt Inflatable Specialists
PO Box 520, Elizabeth WV 26143-0520. 304/275-3306.

UNSUPPORTED PLASTICS PRODUCTS

Midwesco Filter Resources
400 Battaile Dr, Winchester VA 22601-4263. 540/667-8500.

Teno Films Inc.
600 Hays Ave, Staunton VA 24401-3830. 540/886-2301.

Polymer Corp.
2530 N 4th St, Wytheville VA 24382-4420. 540/228-0100.

PLASTICS PRODUCTS

Southeastern Container Inc.
265 Brooke Rd, Fredericksbrg VA 22405-1868. 540/722-2600.

Amoco Corp.
PO Box 3178, Winchester VA 22604-2378. 540/667-9740.

Aker Plastics Martinsburg
2011 Mid Atlantic Pky, Martinsburg WV 25401-3857. 304/263-2525.

Aeroquip Corp.
Rosemont Rd, Bassett VA 24055. 540/629-5318.

Bacova Ltd
1 Main St, Bacova VA 24412. 540/839-5313.

Hartley Manufacturing Co.
PO Box 398, Ravenswood WV 26164. 304/273-5931.

Marley Mouldings Inc.
Bear Creek Rd, Marion VA 24354. 540/783-8161.

Plastics One Inc.
6591 Merriman Rd, Roanoke VA 24018-6664. 540/772-7950.

Polymerland Inc.
501 Avery St, Parkersburg WV 26101-5123. 304/424-5411.

Shelcore Toys Inc.
4489 Carolina Ave, Richmond VA 23222-1416. 804/321-3500.

Southern VA Plastics Inc.
300 Court St, Victoria VA 23974-9468. 804/696-2111.

Variform Inc.
1403 Charles Town Rd, Martinsburg WV 25401-9359. 304/263-7766.

Virginia Design Packaging
1401 Progress Rd, Suffolk VA 23434-2147. 804/538-2000.

Automotive Industries Inc.
Plant 1, Strasburg VA 22657. 540/465-3741.

CARBON AND GRAPHITE PRODUCTS

UCAR Carbon Co. Inc.
PO Box 2170, Clarksburg WV 26302-2170. 304/624-7651.

CHEMICALS AND ALLIED PRODUCTS WHOLESALE

Albright & Wilson Americas
100 Lakeridge Pkwy, Ashland VA 23005. 804/550-4300.

Choes China Town
70 Colony Rd # B, Newport News VA 23602-5656. 804/988-1516.

Westvaco Corp. Chemical Division
205 E Hawthorne St, Covington VA 24426-1620. 703/962-1121.

PAINTS, VARNISHES, AND SUPPLIES WHOLESALE

Duron Paints and Wallcoverings
4806 Jefferson Davis Hwy #A, Fredericksbrg VA 22408-4258. 540/898-0208.

Duron Paints and Wallcoverings
11311 Midlothian Tpke, Richmond VA 23235-4715. 804/379-3004.

For more information on career opportunities in the chemicals/rubber and plastics industries:

__Associations__

AMERICAN ASSOCIATION FOR CLINICAL CHEMISTRY
2101 L Street NW, Suite 202, Washington DC 20037-1526. 202/857-0717 or 800/892-1400. International scientific/medical society of individuals involved with clinical

chemistry and other clinical labscience-related disciplines.

AMERICAN CHEMICAL SOCIETY
Career Services, 1155 16th Street NW, Washington DC 20036. 202/872-4600.

AMERICAN INSTITUTE OF CHEMICAL ENGINEERS
345 East 47th Street, New York NY 10017. 212/705-7338 or 800/242-4363. Provides leadership in advancing the chemical engineering profession as it meets the needs of society.

AMERICAN INSTITUTE OF CHEMISTS, INC.
7315 Wisconsin Avenue, Suite 502 E, Bethesda MD 20814. 301/652-2447. A professional organization supporting the social, economic, and career objectives of the individual scientist.

CHEMICAL MANAGEMENT & RESOURCES ASSOCIATION
60 Bay Street, Suite 702, Staten Island NY 10301. 718/876-8800. Fax: 718/720-4666. Engaged in marketing, marketing research, business development, and planning for the chemical and allied process industries. Provides technical meetings, educational programs, and publications to members.

CHEMICAL MANUFACTURERS ASSOCIATION
2501 M Street NW, Washington DC 20037. 202/887-1100. A trade association that develops and implements programs and services and advocates public policy that benefits the industry and society.

THE ELECTROCHEMICAL SOCIETY
10 South Main Street, Pennington NJ 08534-2896. An international educational society dealing with electrochemical issues. Also publishes monthly journals.

SOAP AND DETERGENT ASSOCIATION
475 Park Avenue South, 27th Floor, New York NY 10016. 212/725-1262. A trade association and research center.

SOCIETY OF PLASTICS ENGINEERS
14 Fairfield Drive, P.O. Box 403, Brookfield CT 06804-0403. 203/775-0471. Dedicated to helping members attain higher professional status through increased scientific, engineering, and technical knowledge.

THE SOCIETY OF THE PLASTICS INDUSTRY, INC.
1275 K Street NW, Suite 400, Washington DC 20005. 202/371-5200. Promotes the development of the plastics industry and enhances public understanding of its contributions while meeting the needs of society.

Directories

CHEMICAL INDUSTRY DIRECTORY
State Mutual Book and Periodical Service, Order Department, 17th Floor, 521 5th Avenue, New York NY 10175. 516/537-1104.

CHEMICALS DIRECTORY
Cahners Publishing, 275 Washington Street, Newton MA 02158. 617/964-3030.

DIRECTORY OF CHEMICAL ENGINEERING CONSULTANTS
American Institute of Chemical Engineering, 345 East 47th Street, New York NY 10017. 212/705-7338.

DIRECTORY OF CHEMICAL PRODUCERS
SRI International, 333 Ravenswood Avenue, Menlo Park CA 94025. 415/326-6200.

Magazines

CHEMICAL & ENGINEERING NEWS
American Chemical Society 1155 16th Street NW, Washington DC 20036. 202/872-4600.

CHEMICAL MARKETING REPORTER
Schnell Publishing Company, 80 Brot Street, 23rd Floor, New York NY 10004. 212/248-4177.

CHEMICAL PROCESSING
Putnam Publishing Company, 301 East Erie Street, Chicago IL 60611. 312/644-2020.

CHEMICAL WEEK
888 7th Avenue, 26th Floor, New York NY 10106. 212/621-4900.

COMMUNICATIONS: TELECOMMUNICATIONS AND BROADCASTING

The telecommunications and broadcasting industries are poised on the edge of a revolution. At long last, Congress has deregulated the telecommunications industry, allowing long-distance carriers, local phone companies, and cable TV operators to get into each other's businesses. For the first time, consumers will be able to choose their local phone company, and that company will probably also provide them with their cable hookups.

Business in the telecommunications industry has been booming even without deregulation. The industry continues to break new ground and reach more customers, especially in wireless phone service. However, the industry has been shaken by recent layoffs at AT&T.

In broadcasting, competition is high, especially for high-profile positions such as newscasters and DJs. In television, the hottest industry is cable. Cable companies are rapidly expanding, and opportunities for technical workers are growing. In radio, syndicated radio shows are tearing up the airwaves. Larger stations with more money, more experience, and bigger names are producing shows which smaller stations are picking up to save money. This increase in syndication will lead to continued competition in the radio industry.

AT&T (AMERICAN TELEPHONE & TELEGRAPH COMPANY)
3033 Chain Bridge Road, Oakton VA 22185. 703/691-5000. **World Wide Web Address:** http://www.att.com. **Contact:** Human Resources. **Description:** AT&T is a major long-distance telephone company which provides domestic and international voice and data communications and management services, telecommunications products, and leasing and financial services. The company manufactures data communications products, computer products, switching and transmission equipment, and components. **Corporate headquarters location:** Basking Ridge NJ. **Subsidiaries include:** AT&T Capital Corporation, offering financing, leasing and provides consumer credit through its AT&T Universal credit card. In 1993, AT&T acquired McCaw Cellular Communications, the largest cellular carrier in the U.S. **Other U.S. locations:** Nationwide.

AMERICA ONLINE INC.
8619 Westwood Center Drive, Vienna VA 22182-2285. 703/448-8700. **Contact:** Mark Stavish, Vice President of Human Resources. **Description:** America Online is a global leader in the market for interactive services. AOL offers its more than 3.5 million members a wide variety of services via personal computer and other intelligent devices. These include electronic mail, conferencing, software, computing support, interactive magazines and newspapers, and online classes, as well as access to the Internet. AOL is also a provider of data network services, new media and interactive marketing services, and multimedia and CD-ROM production services. The company has alliances with Time Warner, Capital Cities/ABC, Knight-Ridder, Tribune, Hachette, IBM, and American Express. AOL has plans to expand its operations to Europe. **Benefits:** 401K; ESOP; Incentive Plan. **Corporate headquarters location:** This Location. **Listed on:** American Stock Exchange; Chicago Stock Exchange; NASDAQ; Pacific Exchange. **Number of employees at this location:** 527. **Number of employees nationwide:** 2,500.

AMERICAN MOBILE SATELLITE CORPORATION
10802 Parkridge Boulevard, Reston VA 22091. 703/758-6000. **Fax:** 703/758-6111. **Contact:** Susan Byrd Lubert, Vice President, Human Resources. **Description:** AMSC is a mobile satellite communications provider offering a variety of voice and data products to the wireless communications industry. The company, established in 1988 by a consortium of industry leaders, holds the FCC-issued license to provide the first nationwide seamless voice and data mobile communications services. Products of American Mobile Satellite Corporation include: SKYCELL Satellite Telephone Service, which makes satellite-only mobile telephone communications available to a broad array of markets, including maritime, public safety, transportation, aeronautical, and rural residences; and Fleet Communication Products, which provide two-way mobile messaging and position location services to commercial markets. **Corporate headquarters location:** This Location. **Number of employees nationwide:** 192.

BELL ATLANTIC-VIRGINIA, INC.
1320 North Court House Road, 6th Floor, Arlington VA 22201. 703/974-3000. **World Wide Web Address:** http://www.bel-atl.com. **Contact:** Mr. Gene Weidemoyer, Human Resources. **Description:** Serving 18.9 million customer lines in seven eastern states, Bell Atlantic is a major exchange telephone services provider. The company provides advanced voice and data services in the Mid-Atlantic region, and wireless communications throughout East Coast markets and parts of the Southeast and Southwest. Bell Atlantic also publishes telephone directories and is a major cellular telephone service provider with nearly 1.3 million customers. Bell Atlantic offers a paging service, computer services, CPE equity sales, training programs, and various financial and real estate services. The company has investments in Grupo Iusacell, S.A. de C.V. (Mexico); Telecom Corporation of New Zealand Limited; and Bell Communications Research, Inc. **Corporate headquarters location:** Philadelphia PA. **Other U.S. locations:** Washington DC; Baltimore MD; Newark NJ; Richmond VA; Charleston WV. **Number of employees nationwide:** 80,950.

BELL ATLANTIC-VIRGINIA, INC.
600 East Main Street, Richmond VA 23219. **World Wide Web Address:** http://www.bel-atl.com. **Contact:** Human Resources. **Description:** Serving 18.9 million customer lines in seven eastern states, Bell Atlantic is a major exchange telephone services provider. The company provides advanced voice and data services in the Mid-Atlantic region, and wireless communications throughout East Coast markets and parts of the Southeast and Southwest. Bell Atlantic also publishes telephone directories and is a major cellular telephone service provider with nearly 1.3 million customers. Bell Atlantic offers a paging service, computer services, CPE equity sales, training programs, and various financial and real estate services. The company has investments in Grupo Iusacell, S.A. de C.V. (Mexico); Telecom Corporation of New Zealand Limited; and Bell Communications Research, Inc. **Corporate headquarters location:** Philadelphia PA. **Other U.S. locations:** Washington DC; Baltimore MD; Newark NJ; Arlington VA; Charleston WV. **Number of employees nationwide:** 80,950.

BELL ATLANTIC-WEST VIRGINIA, INC.
1500 MacCorkle Avenue SE, Charleston WV 25314. 304/343-9911. **Recorded Jobline:** 800/642-9220. **World Wide Web Address:** http://www.bel-atl.com. **Contact:** Human Resources. **Description:** Serving 18.9 million customer lines in seven eastern states, Bell Atlantic is a major exchange telephone services provider. The company provides advanced voice and data services in the Mid-Atlantic region, and wireless communications throughout East Coast markets and parts of the Southeast and Southwest. Bell Atlantic also publishes telephone directories and is a major cellular telephone service provider with nearly 1.3 million customers. Bell Atlantic offers a paging service, computer services, CPE equity sales, training programs, and various financial and real estate services. The company has

investments in Grupo Iusacell, S.A. de C.V. (Mexico); Telecom Corporation of New Zealand Limited; and Bell Communications Research, Inc. **NOTE:** This firm does not accept unsolicited resumes. Please only respond to advertised openings. **Corporate headquarters location:** Philadelphia PA. **Other U.S. locations:** Washington DC; Baltimore MD; Newark NJ; Arlington VA; Richmond VA; Charleston WV. **Number of employees nationwide:** 80,950.

CFW COMMUNICATIONS COMPANY
401 Spring Lane, Suite 300, P.O. Box 1990, Waynesboro VA 22980. 540/946-3500. **Contact:** Steve Carpenter, Director of Human Resources/Government Relations. **Description:** A holding company providing a full range of telecommunications products and services through its six operating subsidiaries. CFW Telephone Company provides telephone service in the cities of Waynesboro, Clifton Forge, and Covington, Virginia and surrounding communities. CFW Network Inc. leases transmission capacity on an advanced 350 mile fiber optic network throughout the Shenandoah Valley. CFW Cellular Inc. provides cellular telephone service for Harrisonburg, Staunton, Waynesboro, and surrounding communities. CFW Communications Services Inc. offers regional customers a single point-of-contact for business phone systems, paging, voice mail, network access, long distance, prepaid calling cards, security systems, and alarm monitoring. CFW Cable Inc. operates wireless cable TV systems in the Charlottesville area and the Shenandoah Valley. CFW Information Services provides long distance directory assistance services for interexchange and local exchange carriers in a multi-state region. **Corporate headquarters location:** This Location. **Number of employees nationwide:** 232.

CABLE & WIRELESS COMMUNICATIONS, INC.
8219 Leesburg Pike, Vienna VA 22182. 703/790-5300. **Fax:** 703/760-1758. **Contact:** Human Resources. **Description:** Offers domestic and international voice and data services to businesses. Cable & Wireless Communications has locations in 40 major cities around the U.S. **Common positions include:** Accountant/Auditor; Adjuster; Attorney; Budget Analyst; Buyer; Computer Operator; Computer Programmer; Computer Systems Analyst; Credit Clerk and Authorizer; Customer Service Representative; Draftsperson; Electrical/Electronics Engineer; Employment Interviewer; Financial Analyst; Manufacturer's/Wholesaler's Sales Rep.; Market Research Analyst; Paralegal; Payroll Clerk; Receptionist; Secretary; Software Engineer; Systems Analyst; Technical Writer/Editor; Typist/Word Processor. **Educational backgrounds include:** Accounting; Business Administration; Communications; Computer Science; Engineering; Finance; Liberal Arts; Marketing; Mathematics. **Benefits:** Dental Insurance; Disability Coverage; Employee Discounts; Life Insurance; Medical Insurance; Pension Plan; Savings Plan; Stock Option; Tuition Assistance. **Other U.S. locations:** Denver CO; St. Louis MO. **Parent company:** Cable & Wireless plc. **Operations at this facility include:** Administration; Manufacturing; Research and Development; Sales; Service. **Listed on:** New York Stock Exchange. **Number of employees at this location:** 800. **Number of employees nationwide:** 2,000.

COHERENT COMMUNICATIONS SYSTEMS CORPORATION
44084 Riverside Parkway, Leesburg VA 22075-5102. 703/729-6400. **Toll-free phone:** 800/443-0726. **Fax:** 703/729-6152. **World Wide Web Address:** http://www.coherent.com. **Contact:** Mike Shepelak, Director of Human Resources. **Description:** Develops, manufactures, and markets voice enhancement products for wireless (including digital cellular), satellite-based, and wireline telecommunications systems throughout the world. Principle products of Coherent Communications Systems Corporation are echo canceller products and teleconference products. In 1995, the company made *Business Week*'s list of 100 Hot Growth Companies, as well as *Forbes*' list of the World's Best Small Companies. Regional offices providing sales and service support are located in the United Kingdom (handling Europe, the Middle East, and Africa) and Australia, as well as district sales offices located throughout the world. **Number of employees worldwide:** 140.

Corporate headquarters location: This Location. **Other U.S. locations:** Hauppauge NY.

COMDIAL CORPORATION
1180 Seminole Trail, Charlottesville VA 22906. 804/978-2200. **Fax:** 804/978-2293. **Contact:** Joe Ford, Vice President, Human Resources. **Description:** Founded in 1977, Comdial began as a residential telephone manufacturer. Following the breakup of the Bell System in 1984, Comdial redirected its resources toward the design, manufacture, and marketing of small- to medium-sized business telephone systems as well as a broad range of advanced telecommunications products and systems solutions based on computer telephone integration, primarily for the hospitality industry. **Corporate headquarters location:** This Location. **Subsidiaries include:** American Phone Centers, Inc.; American Telecommunications Corporation; Comdial Business Communications Corporation; Comdial Consumer Communications Corporation; Comdial Enterprise Systems, Inc.; Comdial Telecommunications, Inc.; Comdial Telecommunications International, Inc.; and Scott Technologies Corporation. **Listed on:** NASDAQ. **Number of employees nationwide:** 788.

ERICSSON INC.
One Mountainview Road, Lynchburg VA 24502. 804/948-6618. **Fax:** 804/948-6543. **Contact:** Natalie Martin, Recruiter. **Description:** Designs and manufactures advanced telecommunications equipment for wired and mobile communications in public and private networks worldwide. **Common positions include:** Aerospace Engineer; Computer Programmer; Computer Systems Analyst; Economist/Market Research Analyst; Electrical/Electronics Engineer; Financial Analyst; Industrial Engineer; Industrial Production Manager; Management Analyst/Consultant; Mechanical Engineer; Purchasing Agent and Manager; Quality Control Supervisor; Science Technologist; Software Engineer. **Educational backgrounds include:** Business Administration; Communications; Computer Science; Economics; Engineering; Finance; Marketing. **Corporate headquarters location:** Sweden. **Other U.S. locations:** New York NY; Richardson TX. **Number of employees nationwide:** 5,000.

FAIRCHILD COMMUNICATIONS SERVICES COMPANY
300 West Service Road, P.O. Box 10804, Chantilly VA 22021. 703/478-5980. **Contact:** Personnel. **Description:** One of the largest providers of comprehensive centralized telecommunications services for tenants in commercial office buildings. Fairchild Communications Services Company offers a full range of telecommunications services, including advanced digital switching and telephone features; local, long distance, and international voice service; data circuits; voice mail; telephone calling cards; 800 service; local area networks; and telephone calling installation. The company serves in excess of 10,000 commercial and governmental customers located throughout the United States. **Parent company:** The Fairchild Corporation (this location).

GTE GOVERNMENT SYSTEMS CORPORATION
INFORMATION SYSTEMS DIVISION
15000 Conference Center Drive, P.O. Box 10814, Chantilly VA 22021. 703/818-4000. **Contact:** Charles Virtue, Human Resources Department. **Description:** GTE Government Systems Corporation is a leader in the advancement of communications, command, control, and intelligence systems; tactical and strategic communication systems; communication switching; information systems for defense, government, and industry worldwide; systems integration; and electronic defense systems. The corporation operates research, engineering, and manufacturing units in California, Massachusetts, North Carolina, and the Washington DC area. **Common positions include:** Accountant/Auditor; Administrator; Electrical/Electronics Engineer; Technician. **Educational backgrounds include:** Computer Science; Engineering; Finance; Mathematics. **Benefits:** Dental

Insurance; Disability Coverage; Life Insurance; Medical Insurance; Pension Plan; Savings Plan; Tuition Assistance. **Corporate headquarters location:** Stamford CT. **Operations at this facility include:** Administration; Regional Headquarters. **Listed on:** New York Stock Exchange.

GLOBAL ONE
12490 Sunrise Valley Drive, Reston VA 22096. 703/689-6000. **Contact:** Human Resources Department. **Description:** Global One is a diversified telecommunications company.

INTERNATIONAL FAMILY ENTERTAINMENT, INC.
2877 Guardian Lane, Virginia Beach VA 23452. 804/459-6000. **Fax:** 804/459-6486. **Recorded Jobline:** 804/459-6140. **Contact:** Lisa Garrett, Senior Personnel Assistant. **Description:** Produces, exhibits, and distributes entertainment and informational programming as well as related products targeted at families worldwide. International Family Entertainment's principal business is The Family Channel, an advertiser-supported cable television network that provides family-oriented entertainment programming in the United States. The company also owns MTM Entertainment, Inc., a producer and worldwide distributor of television series and made-for-television movies, and is the owner of a significant library of television programming. **Common positions include:** Accountant/Auditor; Attorney; Budget Analyst; Buyer; Clerical Supervisor; Computer Programmer; Computer Systems Analyst; Credit Manager; Editor; Financial Analyst; Human Resources Specialist; Paralegal; Public Relations Specialist. **Educational backgrounds include:** Accounting; Art/Design; Business Administration; Communications; Engineering; Finance; Marketing. **Benefits:** 401K; Dental Insurance; Disability Coverage; Employee Discounts; Life Insurance; Medical Insurance; Tuition Assistance. **Corporate headquarters location:** This Location. **Subsidiaries include:** The Family Channel (UK), an advertiser-supported health and fitness cable network which operates in the United Kingdom; Cable Health Club, an advertiser-supported health and fitness cable network which operates principally in the United States; Great American Entertainment Company, a producer of live musical variety shows; and the Ice Capades, an ice touring show. **Other U.S. locations:** Nationwide. **Operations at this facility include:** Administration; Research and Development; Service. **Listed on:** American Stock Exchange; New York Stock Exchange. **Number of employees at this location:** 300. **Number of employees nationwide:** 737.

LCI INTERNATIONAL, INC.
8180 Greensboro Drive, McLean VA 22102. **Toll-free phone:** 800/296-0220. **Contact:** Amy Comcowich, Human Resources. **Description:** A long distance telecommunications carrier that provides a broad array of domestic and international voice and data services to commercial and residential customers. LCI provides service to its customers through its network of digital fiber optic facilities. **Corporate headquarters location:** This Location. **Listed on:** New York Stock Exchange. **Number of employees nationwide:** 1,136.

LANDMARK COMMUNICATIONS, INC.
150 West Brambleton Avenue, Norfolk VA 23510. 804/446-2010. **Contact:** Charlie Hill, Vice President, Human Resources. **Description:** A broadcasting and publishing company.

MEDIA GENERAL CABLE OF FAIRFAX
14650 Old Lee Road, Chantilly VA 22021. 703/378-8411. **Contact:** Linda Clark, Vice President of Human Resources. **Description:** A local general cable distributor of the Fairfax County. Media General Cable of Fairfax offers all basic channels, as well as a separate subscription for HBO, Cinemax, The Movie Channel, Home Team Sports and the Arabic Network of America (ANA).

MEDIA GENERAL, INC.
333 East Grace Street, P.O. Box 85333, Richmond VA 23293-0001. 804/649-6000. **Contact:** Frank McDonald, Vice President of Human Resources. **Description:** A diversified communications company with major interests in newspapers, broadcast television, cable television, newsprint production, commercial printing, and publications. Wholly owned newspaper operations of Media General include morning and Sunday newspapers in Richmond VA, Tampa FL, and Winston-Salem NC, with a combined average daily circulation of 570,000. The television division operates three network-affiliated television stations in Tampa and Jacksonville FL, and Charleston SC; two growing cable networks in northern Virginia with over 229,000 subscribers; and a cable advertising agency. The company's newsprint division is a major producer of 100 percent recycled newsprint. **Corporate headquarters location:** This Location. **Listed on:** American Stock Exchange. **Number of employees nationwide:** 7,300.

METROCALL, INC.
6677 Richmond Highway, Alexandria VA 22306. 703/660-6677. **Contact:** Human Resources Department. **Description:** A leading provider of local and regional paging services in the Northeast, Mid-Atlantic, and Southeast regions of the United States, as well as California, Nevada, and Arizona. Metrocall also provides nationwide wireless communications to pagers, data terminals, personal computers, and personal digital assistants in approximately 850 cities. In 1994, Metrocall acquired FirstPAGE USA, Inc. and MetroPaging, Inc. **Corporate headquarters location:** This Location. **Listed on:** NASDAQ. **Number of employees nationwide:** 776.

MITEL, INC.
MITEL TELECOMMUNICATIONS SYSTEMS
205 Van Buren Street, Suite 400, Herndon VA 22070. 703/318-7020. **Fax:** 703/318-0591. **Contact:** Human Resources. **Description:** Canadian-based Mitel supplies telecommunications solutions to 83 countries worldwide, with its primary markets being supplier North America and the United Kingdom. In total, the company has sold over 180,000 business telephone systems. Specific products sold include PBX systems, consoles and telephone sets. Mitel also makes semiconductors, hybrid circuits and custom wafer products for sale to world markets. In addition, the company sells telecommunications products such as dialers used in route voice and fax traffic to a specific carrier, the GX5000 rural end office switch, and the RADICALL Set Handler that makes telephone companies' Centrex applications easier to use. The company is pursuing opportunities in wireless applications, Computer Telephony Integration, and emerging technology systems. **Other U.S. locations:** Calgary, Alberta ; Halifax, Nova Scotia; Mississauga, Ontario; St.-Laurent, Quebec; Winnipeg, Manitoba; Guadalajara, Mexico; Mexico City, Mexico; Monterey, Mexico; Gwent, Wales; Aberdeen, Scotland; Birmingham, England; E.Kilbride, Scotland; Haycock Park, England; London, England; Slough, England; Wanchi, Hong Kong; Tianjin, China; Kanata, Ontario; Bromont, Quebec; Filderstadt, Germany; Kasuga City, Japan; Portskewett, Wales; Singapore, Malaysia; Encino CA; Irvine CA; Sacramento CA; San Diego CA; Meriden CT; Fort Lauderdale FL; Orlando FL; Mt. Dora FL; Atlanta GA; Marietta GA; Naperville IL; Stoneham MA; Mendota Heights MN; Charlotte NC; Raleigh NC; Clifton NJ; East Syracuse NY; Latham NY; New Hartford NY; New York NY; Ogdensburg NY; Plainview NY; Vestal NY; Dayton OH; Rocky River OH; Dallas TX; Houston TX; Fairfax VA; Richmond VA; Little Chute WI; Milwaukee WI; Stevens Point WI. **Number of employees nationwide:** 3,600.

NEC AMERICA INC.
14040 Park Center Road, Herndon VA 22071. 703/834-4000. **Contact:** James Eddy, Director of Human Resources. **Description:** A telecommunications corporation. NEC America manufactures communications systems and equipment, computers, industrial electronic systems, electronic devices, and home electronic products.

NETRIX CORPORATION
13595 Dulles Technology Drive, Herndon VA 22071. 703/742-6000. **Fax:** 703/742-4048. **World Wide Web Address:** http://www.netrix.com. **Contact:** Judy Neff, Vice President of Human Resources. **Description:** Manufactures and markets products that are used to build cost-effective, international wide area networks by combining and compressing data, voice, and image traffic over the same telephone lines. Applications implemented on these networks include voice and fax communications, electronic mail, point-of-sale, LAN internetworking, and interbank transactions. Netrix Corporation focuses on multinational companies, and sells to government and industry, providing sales and service in over 50 countries. International headquarters are located in the United Kingdom. **Corporate headquarters location:** This Location. **Subsidiaries include:** Netrix International Corporation; and Netrix Telcom Systems Corporation (formerly Republic Telcom Systems Corporation). **Other U.S. locations:** Los Angeles CA; San Francisco CA; Atlanta GA; Chicago IL; Boston MA; New York NY; Pittsburgh PA; Houston TX. **Listed on:** NASDAQ. **Number of employees worldwide:** 294.

PSI (PERFORMANCE SYSTEMS INTERNATIONAL, INC.)
510 Huntmar Park Drive, Herndon VA 22070. 703/904-4100. **Fax:** 703/904-8733. **World Wide Web Address:** http://www.psi.net. **Contact:** David Mann, Human Resources Director. **E-Mail Address:** info@psi.com. **Description:** An Internet service provider offering a wide range of Internet access services to organizations and individuals by means of its high performance computer network, PSINet. PSINet is comprised of points of presence located in 225 U.S. cities and 13 international cities. PSI offers a broad spectrum of Internet access services designed to meet the varied needs of its customers, ranging from low-cost network dial-up services to high performance continuous access services using dedicated high speed telephone circuits. The company had close to 30,000 individual subscribers as of May 1995. Founded in 1990. **Corporate headquarters location:** This Location. **Listed on:** NASDAQ. **Number of employees nationwide:** 215.

PULSECOM
2900 Towerview Road, Herndon VA 22071. 703/471-2900. **Contact:** Gary Andrews, Human Resources Director. **Description:** Produces telecommunications products and remote-control supervisory systems for industrial processes. **Common positions include:** Electrical/Electronics Engineer. **Educational backgrounds include:** Engineering. **Benefits:** Dental Insurance; Disability Coverage; Life Insurance; Medical Insurance; Pension Plan; Savings Plan; Tuition Assistance. **Corporate headquarters location:** Orange CT. **Parent company:** Hubbell, Inc. **Operations at this facility include:** Administration; Divisional Headquarters; Manufacturing; Research and Development; Sales; Service.

RACAL-GUARDATA, INC.
480 Spring Park Place, Suite 900, Herndon VA 22070. 703/471-0892. **Fax:** 703/437-9333. **Contact:** Human Resources Department. **Description:** Manufactures data communications equipment including WANs, LANs, and access products. The company also offers related services including project management, installation, consultation, network integration, maintenance, disaster recovery, and training. Racal-Guardata has foreign locations in Asia, Europe, Canada, Australia, and France. **Parent company:** The Racal Corporation.

RESOURCE CONSULTANTS, INC. (RCI)
1960 Gallows Road, Vienna VA 22182. 703/893-6120. **Fax:** 703/893-0917. **Contact:** Robert J. Duarte, Employment Director. **Description:** A diversified defense contractor supporting many U.S. Navy life cycle management and communications equipment contracts. RCI also provides job placement counseling to the U.S. Army at over 50 locations worldwide. **Common positions include:** Counselor; Electrical/Electronics Engineer; Management Analyst/Consultant; Software Engineer; Technical Writer/Editor;

Technician. **Educational backgrounds include:** Computer Science; Economics; Engineering. **Corporate headquarters location:** This Location. **Other U.S. locations:** Vallejo CA; Panama City FL; Charleston SC. **Parent company:** Gilbert Associates. **Listed on:** NASDAQ. **Number of employees at this location:** 100. **Number of employees nationwide:** 1,200.

SPRINT-CENTEL VIRGINIA
2211 Hydraulic Road, Charlottesville VA 22901-2706. 804/971-2243. **Contact:** Employment. **Description:** A local and long-distance telecommunications carrier. **NOTE:** All employment inquiries should be forwarded to Sprint Mid-Atlantic Telecommunications, Corporate Headquarters, 1411 Capital Boulevard, Wake Forest NC 27587.

TRANSACTION NETWORK SERVICES, INC.
13873 Park Center Road, Suite 405, Herndon VA 22071. 703/742-0500. **Contact:** Robyne Husky, Human Resources. **Description:** Transaction Network Services, Inc. (TNS) is a national communications network firm providing transaction-oriented data services. TNS's communications network uses '950' call routing technology and has been designed to provide low cost, high speed, widely accessible network services for the point-of-sale transaction processing industry. The company uses '950' service obtained from local exchange carriers and '800' service obtained from an interexchange carrier to provide access to its services. TNS was the first provider of '950' service to third-party point-of-sale transaction processors. The company services 120 local access transport areas, covering about 90 percent of the U.S.

Note: *Because addresses and telephone numbers of smaller companies change rapidly, we recommend you call each company to verify the information below before inquiring about job opportunities. Mass mailings are not recommended.*

Additional small employers:

COMMUNICATIONS EQUIPMENT

Fibercom Inc.
3353 Orange Avenue Northeast, Roanoke VA 24012-6335. 540/342-6700.

International Telesystems Corp.
555 Herndon Parkway, Herndon VA 22070-5226. 703/478-9808.

Texcom Inc.
801 Water St, #500, Portsmouth VA 23704-3839. 804/397-0035.

Technology Service Group
315 Byrd St, Orange VA 22960-1837. 540/672-5017.

Continental Cablevision
1520 West Main Street, Richmond VA 23220-4687. 804/355-6565.

LCC Inc.
2300 Clarendon Blvd, Ste 800, Arlington VA 22201-3367. 703/351-6666.

Dynatech Communications
12650 Darby Brook Court, Woodbridge VA 22192-2457. 703/550-0011.

Tracor Applied Sciences
821 Live Oak Dr, Chesapeake VA 23320-2601. 804/424-4640.

TELEPHONE COMMUNICATIONS

Map Mobile Communication
840 Greenbrier Cir, Ste 202, Chesapeake VA 23320-2645. 804/424-1191.

C&P Telephone Co.
1135 6th Ave, Huntington WV 25701-2309. 304/351-4971.

C&P Telephone Co. Of VA
52 Richneck Rd, Newport News VA 23608-3008. 804/875-2765.

Chesapeake & Potomac Phone Co.
221 Dorset Ave, Virginia Beach VA 23462-5305. 804/667-6020.

Chesapeake & Potomac Phone Co.
921 Market St, Parkersburg WV 26101-4736. 304/485-7926.

Chesapeake & Potomac Phone Co.
425 S Holden St, Clarksburg WV 26301-3736. 304/626-9911.

Shenandoah Telecom Co.
124 S Main St, Edinburg VA 22824. 703/984-4141.

ATX Telecommunications Service
4001 Fairfax Dr, Arlington VA 22203-1614. 703/522-2400.

C&P Telephone Co.
5701 Cleveland St, Virginia Beach VA 23462-1751. 804/667-5921.

International Teleconnect Corp.
115 N 1st St, Richmond VA 23219-2125. 804/783-1970.

Kahar Telecommunications Corp.
801 N Fillmore St, Arlington VA 22201-2030. 703/525-6845.

Sprint
127 E Church St, Martinsville VA 24112-2805. 540/666-4000.

Sprint
192 Ballard Ct, Virginia Beach VA 23462-6538. 804/877-8076.

Citizens Telecom
300 Bland St, Bluefield WV 24701-3020. 304/325-1400.

Universal Network Services
100 W Plume St, Norfolk VA 23510-1612. 804/623-8230.

Applied Quality Communications Inc.
2875 Towerview Dr, Herndon VA 22071-3205. 703/318-9481.

BTI
5555 Greenwich Rd, Virginia Beach VA 23462-6542. 804/497-9200.

Corporate Communications Consultants Inc.
5476 Virginia Beach Blvd # 127, Virginia Beach VA 23462-1724. 804/496-6550.

Faxguard Systems Corp.
8230 Old Courthouse Rd, Vienna VA 22182-3853. 703/448-6100.

Henkels & McCoy Inc.
RR 1 Box 44, Aldie VA 22001-9500. 703/471-5085.

Keystone Corp.
1850 Centennial Pk Dr, Ste 530, Reston VA 22091-1517. 703/715-7900.

MCC Phone Center
Oceana Naval Air Station, Virginia Beach VA 23460. 804/425-6577.

MLD-ITT
700 Monticello Ave, Norfolk VA 23510-2523. 804/627-3511.

Telstar Communications
600 Technology Dr, S Charleston WV 25309-8540. 304/744-4558.

TELEGRAPH AND OTHER MESSAGE COMMUNICATIONS

Western Union
201 Progress St NE, Blacksburg VA 24060-7319. 540/552-3251.

Infoquest
2461 Freetown Dr, Reston VA 22091-2527. 703/715-2402.

RADIO BROADCASTING STATIONS

EZ Communications Inc.
10800 Main St, Fairfax VA 22030-4702. 703/591-1000.

Jones Satellite Networks
832 Le Cove Dr, Virginia Beach VA 23464-1656. 804/420-8382.

Metro Traffic Control Inc.
5701 Princess Anne Rd, Ste G, Virginia Beach VA 23462-3253. 804/499-8885.

Metro Traffic Control Inc.
1001 E Main St, Ste 425, Richmond VA 23219-3536. 804/644-0300.

Mutual Broadcasting System Inc.
1755 Jefferson Davis Hwy, Arlington VA 22202-3509. 703/413-8300.

Sconnix Broadcasting Co.
1921 Gallows Rd, Ste 850, Vienna VA 22182-3900. 703/356-6000.

WZBB Radio Station
Rt 40, Ferrum VA 24088. 540/365-1988.

TELEVISION BROADCASTING STATIONS

WAVY Television Inc.
300 Wavy St, Portsmouth VA 23704-5200. 804/393-1010.

WDBJ
2001 Colonial Ave SW, Roanoke VA 24015-3210. 540/344-7000.

WGNT
1318 Spratley St, Portsmouth VA 23704-1829. 804/393-2501.

WTKR TV
720 Boush St, Norfolk VA 23510-1502. 804/446-1000.

WVEC TV Inc.
613 Woodis Ave, Norfolk VA 23510-1017. 804/628-6287.

Nostalgia Television
4217 Wheeler Ave, Alexandria VA 22304-6414. 703/212-9000.

Prestige Channel 3
10843 Houser Dr, Fredericksbrg VA 22408-2451. 540/891-0176.

WOWK TV Huntington
1601 Kanawha Blvd W, Charleston WV 25312-2500. 304/343-1313.

CABLE/PAY TELEVISION SERVICES

Adelphia Cable Communications
Rt 29 N, Monroe VA 24574. 804/929-3400.

Telecable Corp.
999 Waterside Drive, Suite 900, Norfolk VA 23510-3300. 804/624-5000.

MISC. COMMUNICATIONS SERVICES

Allnewsco Inc.
7600-D Boston Boulevard, Springfield VA 22153-3136. 703/912-5300.

MCI Consumer Markets
1200 S Hayes St, Arlington VA 22202-5005. 703/415-6000.

Source Telecomputing Corp.
1616 Anderson Road, McLean VA 22102-1602. 703/734-7500.

For more information on career opportunities in the communications industries:

Associations

ACADEMY OF TELEVISION ARTS & SCIENCES
5220 Lankershim Boulevard, North Hollywood CA 91601. 818/754-2800.

AMERICAN WOMEN IN RADIO AND TELEVISION, INC.
1650 Tysons Boulevard, Suite 200, McLean VA 22102. 703/506-3290. A national, nonprofit professional organization of women and men who work in electronic media and related fields. Services include *News and Views,* a fax newsletter transmitted biweekly to members; Careerline, a national listing of job openings available to members only; and the AWRT Foundation, which supports charitable and educational programs and annual awards.

INTERACTIVE SERVICES ASSOCIATION
8403 Colesville Road, Suite 865, Silver Springs MD 20910. 301/495-4955. World Wide Web address: http://www.isa.net.

INTERNATIONAL TELEVISION ASSOCIATION
6311 North O'Connor Road, Suite 230, Irving TX 75309. 214/869-1112. Membership required.

NATIONAL ASSOCIATION OF BROADCASTERS
1771 N Street NW, Washington DC 20036. 202/429-5300, ext. 5490. Fax: 202/429-5343. Provides employment information.

NATIONAL CABLE TELEVISION ASSOCIATION
1724 Massachusetts Avenue NW, Washington DC 20036-1969. 202/775-3651. Fax: 202/775-3695. A trade association. Publications include *Cable Television Developments, Secure Signals, Kids and Cable, Linking Up, Only on Cable,* and *Producers' Sourcebook: A Guide to Program Buyers.*

PROMAX INTERNATIONAL
2029 Century Park East, Suite 555, Los Angeles CA 90028. 310/788-7600. Fax: 310/788-7616. Ask for the jobline.

U.S. TELEPHONE ASSOCIATION
1401 H Street NW, Suite 600, Washington DC 20005-2136. 202/326-7300. A trade association for local telephone companies.

Magazines

BROADCASTING AND CABLE
Broadcasting Publications Inc., 1705 DeSales Street NW, Washington DC 20036. 202/659-2340.

ELECTRONIC MEDIA
Crain Communications, 220 East 42nd Street, New York NY 10017. 212/210-0100.

COMPUTER HARDWARE, SOFTWARE, AND SERVICES

Hardware and software: Companies are starting to invest more in corporate technology after several years of lean spending. Network servers have been the hot business product recently, and that trend will continue through 1996. Expect the boom in big machines -- parallel computers, mainframes, and minicomputers -- to support a growing interest in online databases, accessing the Internet, and e-mail. PCs will remain the strongest part of the hardware market. The composition of the software industry is shrinking with many firms merging or acquiring others. Despite consolidation in the industry, and despite the crisis at Apple Computer, the overall number of software jobs is still rising.

What's hot on the market? Although it still accounts for a tiny percentage of software sales, Internet-related software -- and World Wide Web browsing software in particular -- is quickly transforming the industry. Analysts predict that sales of Internet software will double every year through at least 2000, and by then sales could hit $4 billion a year.

Services: Computer services professionals perform three activities: systems integration, custom programming, and consulting/training. Consulting and integration are the fastest-growing segments in computing due to the demand for networking. With more computer power available, more computer support will be needed.

AMERICAN MANAGEMENT SYSTEMS INC.
12601 Fair Lakes Circle, Fairfax VA 22033. 703/227-6000. **Contact:** Human Resources. **Description:** American Management Systems is engaged in helping large organizations solve complex management problems by applying information technology and systems engineering. Its marketing and development resources are targeted at large organizations that have a crucial need for these services. The company combines specific industry experience, business function expertise, proven systems development practices, and technical competence to help clients achieve their business goals. Industries and markets served include financial service institutions; insurance companies; federal agencies; defense, state, and local government; colleges and universities; telecommunications firms; health care providers; and energy companies. **NOTE:** Interested jobseekers should contact Human Resources at 4050 Legato Road, Fairfax VA 22033. **Common positions include:** Computer Engineer; Computer Programmer; Computer Scientist; Manager of Information Systems; Software Engineer. **Corporate headquarters location:** Fairfax VA. **Number of employees nationwide:** 4,250.

AMERICAN MANAGEMENT SYSTEMS INC.
4050 Legato Road, Fairfax VA 22033. 703/267-8000. **Contact:** Judy Blair, Vice President, Human Resources. **Description:** American Management Systems is engaged in helping large organizations solve complex management problems by applying information technology and systems engineering. Its marketing and development resources are targeted at large organizations that have a crucial need for these services. The company combines specific industry experience, business function expertise, proven

systems development practices, and technical competence to help clients achieve their business goals. Industries and markets served include financial service institutions; insurance companies; federal agencies; defense, state, and local government; colleges and universities; telecommunications firms; health care providers; and energy companies. **Corporate headquarters location:** This Location. **Number of employees nationwide:** 4,250.

ANSTEC, INC.
10530 Rosehaven Street, Suite 600, Fairfax VA 22030-2840. 703/591-4000. **Contact:** Curt White, Staffing Manager. **Description:** Provides computer systems integration and design services. **Common positions include:** Computer Engineer; Computer Programmer; Customer Service Representative; Production Coordinator.

BDM INTERNATIONAL, INC.
1501 BDM Way, McLean VA 22102. 703/848-5000. **Fax:** 703/848-5006. **Contact:** Mr. Ronnie Kinsley, Vice President, Human Resources. **E-Mail Address:** collrela@lan.mcl.bdm.com. **Description:** BDM International, Inc. is a global provider of information technology and other technology solutions, systems, and support for governmental and commercial clients. The largest BDM company, BDM Federal, Inc., provides advanced information technology and other technology services and systems to the federal government. BDM Technologies, Inc. brings highly-focused information technology expertise and solutions to industry, commercial enterprises, and state and local governments. The companies of BDM operate in the U.S., Europe, the Middle East, and elsewhere; and employ 7,000 people in over 60 locations worldwide. **Common positions include:** Computer Programmer; Computer Systems Analyst; Electrical/Electronics Engineer; Environmental Engineer; Financial Analyst; Industrial Engineer; Management Analyst/Consultant; Science Technologist; Software Engineer; Statistician. **Educational backgrounds include:** Computer Science; Engineering; Mathematics; Technology. **Benefits:** 401K; Daycare Assistance; Dental Insurance; Disability Coverage; Employee Discounts; Life Insurance; Medical Insurance; Savings Plan; Stock Option; Tuition Assistance. **Special Programs:** Internships. **Corporate headquarters location:** This Location. **Other U.S. locations:** Huntsville AL; Boulder CO; Denver CO; Albuquerque NM; Dayton OH. **Operations at this facility include:** Administration; Divisional Headquarters; Regional Headquarters; Research and Development; Service. **Listed on:** NASDAQ. **Number of employees nationwide:** 7,000.

BTG, INC.
1945 Old Gallows Road, Vienna VA 22182. 703/556-6518. **Fax:** 703/761-3245. **World Wide Web Address:** http://www.btg.com. **Contact:** Karen Wall, Director of Human Resources. **Description:** An information technology company providing complete solutions to specific system and product needs of the United States government, its agencies and departments, and other customers, combining systems development, integration, and engineering with the value-added reselling of hardware, software, and integrated systems. Founded in 1982. **Common positions include:** Software Engineer. **Corporate headquarters location:** This Location. **Other U.S. locations:** San Diego CA; Annapolis Junction MD; San Antonio TX. **Subsidiaries include:** BDS, Inc. (a value-added reseller of computer software and hardware and a provider of integrated information systems) located in McLean, VA and Brussels, Belgium; Advanced Computer Technology, Inc. (a value-added reseller of software and hardware and a seller of high-performance computers) with two locations in Arlington, VA; and Delta Research Corporation (a software developer and systems integrator focusing on project planning, cost controls, and environmental engineering, primarily for the government) which has facilities in Arlington, VA, Niceville, FL (two), Colorado Springs, CO, and Santa Maria, CA. **Listed on:** NASDAQ. **Number of employees worldwide:** 650.

CACI, INC.
1100 North Glebe Road, Arlington VA 22201. 703/841-7800. **Contact:** Carol Harvey, Human Resources. **Description:** An international high-technology and professional services corporation. CACI is a leader in advanced information systems, systems engineering, logistics sciences, proprietary analytical software products, market analysis consulting services, and information products and systems. **Common positions include:** Accountant/Auditor; Computer Programmer; Department Manager; Electrical/Electronics Engineer; Financial Analyst; Marketing Specialist; Purchasing Agent and Manager; Quality Control Supervisor; Systems Analyst; Technical Writer/Editor. **Educational backgrounds include:** Accounting; Business Administration; Computer Science; Engineering; Finance; Marketing; Mathematics. **Benefits:** Dental Insurance; Disability Coverage; Life Insurance; Medical Insurance; Pension Plan; Tuition Assistance. **Corporate headquarters location:** This Location. **Operations at this facility include:** Administration. **Number of employees nationwide:** 1,463.

CERNER CORPORATION
2201 Cooperative Way, Suite 301, Herndon VA 22071-3024. 703/904-1871. **Contact:** Marilyn Cassara, Branch Administrator. **Description:** Cerner designs, installs, and supports information systems for the health care industry worldwide, including hospitals, HMOs, clinics, physicians' offices, and integrated health organizations. All Cerner applications are structured around a single architectural design, called Health Network Architecture (HNA), which allows information to be shared among clinical disciplines and across multiple facilities. Health professionals using Cerner systems are able to make more effective decisions, deliver care more effectively, and ultimately streamline their processes. Cerner's information systems are focused in four areas: Clinical Management, Care Management, Repositories, and Knowledge. Clinical management systems include: PathNet, which automates the processes of the clinical laboratory; MedNet, which supports pulmonary medicine, respiratory care, and other internal medicine departments; RadNet, which focuses on automating radiology department operations; PharmNet, which automates the processes of the pharmacy; SurgiNet, which addresses the information management needs of the operating room team; and MSMEDS, which provides information management for the pharmacy. Care management systems include ProNet, which automates the processes of patient management and registration, order communication, scheduling, and tracking. Repositories include the Open Clinical Foundation, an enterprise-wide, relational database that contains information captured by various clinical systems to form the computer-based patient record; Open Management Foundation, a repository of process-related information to support management analysis and decision making; MRNet, which automates the chart management process for the medical records department; and Open Engine, an interface engine that collates interfaces, linking systems at a single point. Cerner's knowledge system is Discern, a family of applications that provides support for improving the quality and effectiveness of care. **Corporate headquarters location:** Kansas City MO.

COMPUCARE COMPANY
12110 Sunset Hills Road, Suite 600, Reston VA 22090. 703/709-2300. **Fax:** 703/709-2490. **Contact:** Human Resources Specialist. **Description:** A developer of both hardware and software information systems for hospitals and other health care facilities. **Common positions include:** Computer Programmer; Computer Systems Analyst; Software Engineer. **Educational backgrounds include:** Business Administration; Computer Science. **Benefits:** 401K; Dental Insurance; Disability Coverage; Life Insurance; Medical Insurance; Tuition Assistance. **Corporate headquarters location:** This Location. **Other U.S. locations:** Fountain Valley CA. **Operations at this facility include:** Administration; Research and Development; Sales; Service. **Listed**

on: Privately held. **Number of employees at this location:** 150. **Number of employees nationwide:** 250.

COMPUTER ASSOCIATES
575 Herndon Parkway, Herndon VA 22070. 703/708-3000. **Contact:** Sean Friedman, Human Resources Representative. **Description:** A software development and consulting firm. This location was formerly Legent Corporation, which was bought out by Computer Associates in 1995. **Special Programs:** Internships. **Number of employees at this location:** 400.

COMPUTER SCIENCES CORPORATION
3160 Fairview Park Drive, Falls Church VA 22042. 703/876-1000. **Fax:** 703/573-9311. **Contact:** Jack Farrell, Director. **Description:** Provides corporate customers with a variety of computer-related services, including consulting, reengineering, and outsourcing. Another company sector, the Systems Group division, designs, engineers, and integrates computer-based systems and communications systems, providing all the hardware, software, training, and related elements necessary to operate a system. The Consulting division includes consulting and technical services in the development of computer and communication systems to non-federal organizations in the U.S. and Europe. The Industry Services Group provides services to health care, insurance, and financial services, as well as providing large-scale claim processing and other insurance-related services. CSC Health Care markets business systems and services to the managed health care industry, clinics, and physicians. CSC Enterprise provides consumer credit reports and account management services to credit grantors.

DELEX SYSTEMS INC.
1953 Gallows Road, Suite 700, Vienna VA 22182. 703/734-8300. **Fax:** 703/893-5338. **Contact:** Director of Human Resources. **Description:** Offers operationally-oriented systems engineering and analyses. Delex Systems provides computer-based training systems and intelligence analysis to the defense community. **Common positions include:** Accountant/Auditor; Aerospace Engineer; Computer Programmer; Computer Systems Analyst; Economist/Market Research Analyst; Electrical/Electronics Engineer; Financial Analyst; Human Resources Specialist; Purchasing Agent and Manager; Software Engineer; Technical Writer/Editor. **Educational backgrounds include:** Computer Science; Engineering; Mathematics; Physics. **Benefits:** 401K; Dental Insurance; Disability Coverage; Life Insurance; Medical Insurance; Tuition Assistance. **Corporate headquarters location:** This Location. **Other U.S. locations:** CA; OH. **Operations at this facility include:** Administration; Sales. **Listed on:** Privately held. **Number of employees at this location:** 140. **Number of employees nationwide:** 250.

GRC INTERNATIONAL INC.
1900 Gallows Road, Vienna VA 22182. 703/506-5000. **Fax:** 703/448-6890. **Contact:** Arlene Rimson, Director of Human Resources. **Description:** An international provider of knowledge-based professional services and technology-based product solutions to government and commercial customers. GRC International's activities encompass sophisticated telecommunications products, network systems analysis, and network software development operations for the commercial market. The company is involved in creating large-scale decision-support systems and software engineering environments; applying operations research and mathematical modeling to business and management systems; and implementing advanced database technology. GRC International also provides studies and analysis capabilities for policy development and planning; modeling and simulation of hardware and software used in real-time testing of sensor, weapon, and battlefield management command, control, and communication systems; and testing and evaluation. **Corporate headquarters location:** This Location. **Other U.S. locations:** Nationwide . **Listed on:** New York Stock Exchange. **Number of employees worldwide:** 1,245.

GRC INTERNATIONAL INC.
2121 Eisenhower Avenue, Suite 200, Alexandria VA 22314. 703/548-8168. **Fax:** 703/689-3620. **Contact:** Human Resources. **Description:** An international provider of knowledge-based professional services and technology-based product solutions to government and commercial customers. GRC International's activities encompass sophisticated telecommunications products, network systems analysis, and network software development operations for the commercial market. The company is involved in creating large-scale decision-support systems and software engineering environments; applying operations research and mathematical modeling to business and management systems; and implementing advanced database technology. GRC International also provides studies and analysis capabilities for policy development and planning; modeling and simulation of hardware and software used in real-time testing of sensor, weapon, and battlefield management command, control, and communication systems; and testing and evaluation. **NOTE:** Please direct all employment inquiries to Arlene Rimson, Director of Human Resources, GRC International, Inc., 1900 Gallows Road, Vienna VA 22182. **Corporate headquarters location:** Vienna VA. **Other U.S. locations:** Nationwide. **Listed on:** New York Stock Exchange. **Number of employees worldwide:** 1,245.

GRC INTERNATIONAL INC.
Crystal Gateway Two, 1225 Jefferson Davis Highway, Suite 200, Arlington VA 22202. 703/414-5000. **Contact:** Human Resources. **Description:** An international provider of knowledge-based professional services and technology-based product solutions to government and commercial customers. GRC International's activities encompass sophisticated telecommunications products, network systems analysis, and network software development operations for the commercial market. The company is involved in creating large-scale decision-support systems and software engineering environments; applying operations research and mathematical modeling to business and management systems; and implementing advanced database technology. GRC International also provides studies and analysis capabilities for policy development and planning; modeling and simulation of hardware and software used in real-time testing of sensor, weapon, and battlefield management command, control, and communication systems; and testing and evaluation. **NOTE:** Please direct all employment inquiries to Arlene Rimson, Director of Human Resources, GRC International, Inc., 1900 Gallows Road, Vienna VA 22182. **Corporate headquarters location:** Vienna VA. **Other U.S. locations:** Nationwide. **Listed on:** New York Stock Exchange. **Number of employees worldwide:** 1,245.

GRC INTERNATIONAL INC.
Crystal Gateway One, 1235 Jefferson Davis Highway, Suite 501, Arlington VA 22202. 703/416-0020. **Fax:** 703/416-0034. **Contact:** Human Resources. **Description:** An international provider of knowledge-based professional services and technology-based product solutions to government and commercial customers. GRC International's activities encompass sophisticated telecommunications products, network systems analysis, and network software development operations for the commercial market. The company is involved in creating large-scale decision-support systems and software engineering environments; applying operations research and mathematical modeling to business and management systems; and implementing advanced database technology. GRC International also provides studies and analysis capabilities for policy development and planning; modeling and simulation of hardware and software used in real-time testing of sensor, weapon, and battlefield management command, control, and communication systems; and testing and evaluation. **NOTE:** Please direct all employment inquiries to Arlene Rimson, Director of Human Resources, GRC International, Inc., 1900 Gallows Road, Vienna VA 22182. **Corporate headquarters location:** Vienna VA. **Other U.S. locations:** Nationwide. **Listed on:** New York Stock Exchange. **Number of employees worldwide:** 1,245.

GRC INTERNATIONAL INC.
14120 Parke Long Court, Suite 101, Chantilly VA 22021. 703/803-1304. **Fax:** 703/803-8797. **Contact:** Human Resources. **Description:** An international provider of knowledge-based professional services and technology-based product solutions to government and commercial customers. GRC International's activities encompass sophisticated telecommunications products, network systems analysis, and network software development operations for the commercial market. The company is involved in creating large-scale decision-support systems and software engineering environments; applying operations research and mathematical modeling to business and management systems; and implementing advanced database technology. GRC International also provides studies and analysis capabilities for policy development and planning; modeling and simulation of hardware and software used in real-time testing of sensor, weapon, and battlefield management command, control, and communication systems; and testing and evaluation. **NOTE:** Please direct all employment inquiries to Arlene Rimson, Director of Human Resources, GRC International, Inc., 1900 Gallows Road, Vienna VA 22182. **Corporate headquarters location:** Vienna VA. **Other U.S. locations:** Nationwide. **Listed on:** New York Stock Exchange. **Number of employees worldwide:** 1,245.

GRC INTERNATIONAL INC.
621 Lynnhaven Parkway, Suite 360, Virginia Beach VA 23452. 804/463-0683. **Fax:** 804/463-2996. **Contact:** Human Resources. **Description:** An international provider of knowledge-based professional services and technology-based product solutions to government and commercial customers. GRC International's activities encompass sophisticated telecommunications products, network systems analysis, and network software development operations for the commercial market. The company is involved in creating large-scale decision-support systems and software engineering environments; applying operations research and mathematical modeling to business and management systems; and implementing advanced database technology. GRC International also provides studies and analysis capabilities for policy development and planning; modeling and simulation of hardware and software used in real-time testing of sensor, weapon, and battlefield management command, control, and communication systems; and testing and evaluation. **NOTE:** Please direct all employment inquiries to Arlene Rimson, Director of Human Resources, GRC International, Inc., 1900 Gallows Road, Vienna VA 22182. **Corporate headquarters location:** Vienna VA. **Other U.S. locations:** Nationwide. **Listed on:** New York Stock Exchange. **Number of employees worldwide:** 1,245.

GTSI
GOVERNMENT TECHNOLOGY SERVICES, INC.
4100 Lafayette Center Drive, Chantilly VA 22021. 703/631-3333. **Fax:** 703/222-5240. **Contact:** Bob Boehm, Manager, Human Resource Services. **Description:** Government Technology Services, Inc. specializes in providing government customers with the broadest selection of brand name computer hardware, software, and peripheral products. GTSI sells directly to all departments and agencies of the federal government, many state and local governments, and indirectly to the government market through hundreds of system integrators and prime contractors. GTSI's selection of desktop, mobile, and engineering workstation computing products continues to expand along with its ability to provide technical expertise in systems integration and network configuration to an ever-expanding government market. Recent acquisitions include Falcon Microsystems, Inc. **Common positions include:** Accountant/Auditor; Budget Analyst; Computer Systems Analyst; Customer Service Representative; Financial Analyst; Software Engineer. **Educational backgrounds include:** Business Administration; Marketing. **Benefits:** 401K; Dental Insurance; Disability Coverage; Life Insurance; Medical Insurance. **Special Programs:** Internships. **Corporate headquarters location:** This Location. **Operations at this facility include:**

Administration; Sales; Service. **Listed on:** NASDAQ. **Number of employees at this location:** 433.

GENICOM CORPORATION
One Genicom Drive, Waynesboro VA 22980. 540/949-1000. **Contact:** Dick Gooch, Manager of Human Resources. **Description:** An international supplier of network system, service, and printer solutions. Through its Harris Adacom Network Service Solutions business unit, GENICOM provides integrated network system solutions including a broad portfolio of hardware and software products, technology consulting, and diagnostic and monitoring services. The company's Enterprising Service Solutions business unit provides logo and multi-vendor product field support and depot repair, express parts, and professional services. GENICOM's Impact and Laser Printing Solutions business unit designs, manufactures, and markets a wide range of computer printer technologies for general purpose applications. **Common positions include:** Accountant/Auditor; Buyer; Computer Programmer; Electrical/Electronics Engineer; Financial Analyst; Industrial Engineer; Marketing Specialist; Mechanical Engineer; Software Engineer. **Educational backgrounds include:** Accounting; Business Administration; Computer Science; Engineering; Finance; Physics. **Benefits:** 401K; Dental Insurance; Disability Coverage; Life Insurance; Medical Insurance; Savings Plan; Tuition Assistance. **Corporate headquarters location:** Chantilly VA. **Other U.S. locations:** Nationwide. **Subsidiaries include:** GENICOM Pty. Ltd. (Australia); GENICOM Canada, Inc. (Canada); GENICOM S.A. (France); GENICOM GmbH (Germany); GENICOM SpA (Italy); GENICOM Limited (UK); and Harris Adacom Inc. (Canada). **Operations at this facility include:** Administration; Manufacturing; Research and Development; Service. **Listed on:** NASDAQ. **Number of employees nationwide:** 2,147.

GENICOM CORPORATION
14800 Conference Center Drive, Suite 400, Westfields, Chantilly VA 22021-3806. 703/802-9200. **Fax:** 703/802-9039. **Contact:** Human Resources. **Description:** An international supplier of network system, service, and printer solutions. Through its Harris Adacom Network Service Solutions business unit, GENICOM Corporation provides integrated network system solutions including a broad portfolio of hardware and software products, technology consulting, and diagnostic and monitoring services. The company's Enterprising Service Solutions business unit provides logo and multi-vendor product field support and depot repair, express parts, and professional services. GENICOM's Impact and Laser Printing Solutions business unit designs, manufactures, and markets a wide range of computer printer technologies for general purpose applications. **Common positions include:** Accountant/Auditor; Services Sales Representative. **Educational backgrounds include:** Business Administration; Computer Science; Marketing. **Benefits:** 401K; Dental Insurance; Disability Coverage; Life Insurance; Medical Insurance. **Corporate headquarters location:** This Location. **Other U.S. locations:** Nationwide. **Subsidiaries include:** GENICOM Pty. Ltd. (Australia); GENICOM Canada, Inc. (Canada); GENICOM S.A. (France); GENICOM GmbH (Germany); GENICOM SpA (Italy); GENICOM Limited (UK); and Harris Adacom Inc. (Canada). **Operations at this facility include:** Administration; Divisional Headquarters; Sales. **Listed on:** NASDAQ. **Number of employees at this location:** 30. **Number of employees nationwide:** 2,147.

GLOBALINK, INC.
9302 Lee Highway, Fairfax VA 22031. 703/273-5600. **Fax:** 703/273-3866. **World Wide Web Address:** http://www.globalink.com. **Contact:** Jean Ellen Wood, Director of Human Resources. **Description:** Designs, develops, markets, and supports foreign language translation software for business and professional use, including language and applications, books, and other products for the microcomputer marketplace. In addition, the company provides professional language services through its multilingual staff and through contract arrangements with independent linguists and translators. Globalink offers a wide array of bilingual translation tools for French,

German, Italian, and Spanish. The software enables users to automatically translate text at their computer. The company is currently working on a software package which translates Portuguese, to be released in mid-1996. **Corporate headquarters location:** This Location. **Other U.S. locations:** San Diego CA. **Listed on:** American Stock Exchange. **Number of employees nationwide:** 93.

HADRON INC.
9990 Lee Highway, Fifth Floor, Fairfax VA 22030. 703/359-6404. **Contact:** Human Resources. **Description:** Offers computer engineering services.

IBM (INTERNATIONAL BUSINESS MACHINE CORPORATION)
145 Summers Street, Charleston WV 25301. 304/347-7300. **Contact:** Human Resources. **Description:** International Business Machines (IBM) is a developer, manufacturer, and marketer of advanced information processing products, including computers and microelectronic technology, software, networking systems and information technology-related services. The company strives to offer value worldwide, through its United States, Canada, Europe, Middle East, Africa, Latin America and Asia Pacific business units, by providing comprehensive and complete product choices.

ITC (INDUSTRIAL TRAINING CORPORATION)
13515 Dulles Technology Drive, Herndon VA 22071-3416. 703/713-3335. **Toll-free phone:** 800/638-3757. **Fax:** 703/713-0065. **Contact:** Leslye Schrank, Human Resources Director. **Description:** A full-service training company specializing in the development, production, marketing, and sale of both off-the-shelf and custom multimedia training courseware for corporate, educational, and governmental organizations. The vast majority of ITC's products and services are multimedia programs, but the company also markets, sells, and distributes certain linear training products (primarily videotape and text-based) through its USA Training division. Standard multimedia platforms for ITC products include both laserdisc and CD-ROM. **Corporate headquarters location:** This Location. **Subsidiaries include:** CI Acquisition Corporation **Listed on:** NASDAQ. **Number of employees nationwide:** 75.

INFODATA SYSTEMS INC.
12150 Monument Drive, Suite 400, Fairfax VA 22033. 703/934-5205. **Fax:** 703/934-7154. **Contact:** Aimee Schwartz, Human Resources Generalist. **Description:** Provides mainframe-based software products and services which help business, government, and educational institutions to automate collections of documents consisting of large amounts of text. Infodata Systems also provides complete Electronic Document Management System solutions to address developing client/server technologies, through the sale of products and software integration services. In support of its proprietary software products, the company offers a range of ongoing product support services, including training, a telephone hotline service, product enhancements, and maintenance releases. **Corporate headquarters location:** This Location. **Subsidiaries include:** Infodata Systems International Inc.; and Infodata Research and Development Corporation. **Listed on:** NASDAQ. **Number of employees at this location:** 56.

INFORMATION ANALYSIS INC.
2222 Gallows Road, Suite 300, Dunn Loring VA 22027. 703/641-0955. **Contact:** Leslie Reed, Human Resources Director. **Description:** Engaged in various facets of the computer and information field. Information Analysis Inc. performs activities primarily related to software applications development, hardware and software consulting services, and software sales and support services. These services include systems re-engineering, feasibility and requirements analysis, systems planning analysis and design, data base design and management, software development, and project management. In 1991, the company formed subsidiary Allied Health and Information Systems, Inc., to provide medical personnel to penal institutions

to provide physical examinations and patient management, and perform primary care and minor surgery. **Corporate headquarters location:** This Location. **Subsidiaries include:** DHD Systems, Inc., which operates as a single business unit with Information Analysis Inc. **Number of employees nationwide:** 162.

INFORMATION MANAGEMENT CONSULTANTS INC.
7915 Westpark Drive, McLean VA 22102. 703/893-3100. **Contact:** John Marlette, Director of Human Resources. **Description:** A computer consulting company.

INTERNATIONAL RESEARCH INSTITUTE
12200 Sunrise Valley Drive, Suite 300, Reston VA 22091. 703/715-9605. **Contact:** Don Zerbe, Human Resources Director. **Description:** A software research company.

MRJ INC.
10560 Arrowhead Drive, Fairfax VA 22030. 703/385-0700. **Contact:** Elaine White, Director of Human Resources. **Description:** A computer engineering company.

JAMES MARTIN & COMPANY INC.
3050 Chain Bridge Road, Suite 600, Fairfax VA 22030. 703/620-9504. **Contact:** Ms. Kim Wilkins, Human Resources Recruiter. **Description:** A computer consulting firm.

MICRODYNE CORPORATION
3601 Eisenhower Avenue, Suite 300, Alexandria VA 22304. 703/739-0500. **Contact:** Paul Sinclair, Director of Human Resources. **Description:** Designs, manufactures, markets, and supports a broad line of data communications hardware products that enable local area network and remote network access communications. Microdyne is a leading supplier of LAN adapter cards which provide the essential connection between computers (including personal computers, file servers, minicomputers, and mainframe computers) and the network. The company's products support all established computer bus structures, wiring systems, and network topologies, including Ethernet, Fast Ethernet, and Token Ring. Microdyne is divided into three businesses: networking products, which support inter-computer network communications; aerospace telemetry, which manufacture receivers used in a variety of applications involving missiles, aircraft, satellites, and other space vehicles; and manufacturer support services. Foreign locations include: Berkshire, England; Munich, Germany. **Corporate headquarters location:** This Location. **Other U.S. locations:** Carson CA; San Jose CA; Ocala FL; Indianapolis IN. **Listed on:** NASDAQ. **Number of employees worldwide:** 470.

NETWORK IMAGING CORPORATION
500 Huntmar Park Drive, Herndon VA 22070. 703/478-2260. **Contact:** Human Resources. **Description:** Designs and markets open systems document imaging and optical disk storage software geared to businesses and government agencies that are looking to substantially reduce their enormous volume of paper documents, cut down on storage space and improve work efficiency. The company's systems also accommodate blueprints, x-rays and data in video and audio format. The company's software manages the storage of scanned data and allows users to quickly retrieve and access documents. Network Imaging systems can also serve as a key component for video and audio-on-demand. **Corporate headquarters location:** This Location. **Listed on:** NASDAQ. **Number of employees nationwide:** 505.

ORACLE COMPLEX SYSTEMS CORPORATION
196 Van Buren Street, Herndon VA 22070. 703/904-8200. **Contact:** Michelle Rouse, Human Resources Director. **Description:** A computer

systems integration company providing solutions and services to federal and commercial clients.

PRC, INC.
1500 PRC Drive, McLean VA 22102. 703/556-1000. **Fax:** 703/556-2269. **Contact:** Peggy R. Caine, Human Resources Representative. **Description:** PRC is a global provider of scientific and technology-based systems and services to government and commercial clients. Founded in 1954, PRC provides computer systems integration, systems engineering, software development, environmental engineering, and consulting services to government and commercial clients worldwide. **Common positions include:** Accountant/Auditor; Aerospace Engineer; Attorney; Budget Analyst; Chemical Engineer; Computer Operator; Computer Programmer; Computer Systems Analyst; Editor; Electrical/Electronics Engineer; Employment Interviewer; Financial Analyst; Graphic Artist; Industrial Engineer; Mechanical Engineer; Meteorologist; Nuclear Engineer; Receptionist; Secretary; Software Engineer; Technical Support Representative; Typist/Word Processor. **Educational backgrounds include:** Accounting; Computer Science; Economics; Engineering; Finance; Geology; Liberal Arts. **Benefits:** 401K; Dental Insurance; Disability Coverage; Employee Discounts; Life Insurance; Medical Insurance; Pension Plan; Savings Plan; Tuition Assistance. **Corporate headquarters location:** This Location. **Parent company:** Black & Decker. **Operations at this facility include:** Administration; Regional Headquarters. **Listed on:** New York Stock Exchange. **Number of employees at this location:** 3,500. **Number of employees nationwide:** 7,000.

QUESTECH, INC.
7600 West Leesburg Pike, Falls Church VA 22043. 703/760-1000. **Fax:** 703/760-1062. **Contact:** Mark Hartung, Manager of Personnel. **Description:** A diversified high-technology company that provides scientific, engineering, and management services in electronics, computer science, and other advanced technologies to government and industry. These services encompass the entire life cycle of fielded hardware. This process includes research and development, system design, engineering, technical and program management support, test and evaluation, and system installation and maintenance. **Common positions include:** Accountant/Auditor; Aerospace Engineer; Buyer; Draftsperson; Electrical/Electronics Engineer; Physicist/Astronomer; Software Engineer; Statistician; Systems Analyst; Technical Writer/Editor. **Educational backgrounds include:** Accounting; Communications; Computer Science; Engineering; Mathematics; Physics. **Benefits:** Dental Insurance; Disability Coverage; Life Insurance; Medical Insurance; Pension Plan; Profit Sharing; Savings Plan; Tuition Assistance; Vision Insurance. **Corporate headquarters location:** This Location. **Operations at this facility include:** Administration; Divisional Headquarters; Research and Development. **Listed on:** NASDAQ. **Number of employees nationwide:** 400.

SOFTWARE AG OF NORTH AMERICA
11190 Sunrise Valley Drive, Reston VA 22091. 703/860-5050. **Contact:** Human Resources Department. **Description:** A supplier of advanced information system development software. The company's products include: ADABAS, COM-PLETE, and NATURAL. **NOTE:** Software AG of North America does not accept unsolicited resumes. Jobseekers should apply only for advertised openings.

STAR TECHNOLOGIES
515 Shaw Road, Sterling VA 20166. 703/689-4400. **Contact:** Human Resources. **Description:** Star Technologies, founded in 1981, delivers high-performance computing solutions for medical diagnostic imaging, defense signal processing, defense simulation training, advanced scientific research, and oil exploration. Over the past ten years, much of Star's focus has been on supplying image reconstruction processors for medical imaging CT scanners. Star is currently expanding upon its imaging and technical

experience to deliver a range of solutions for the digital imaging and information systems markets.

TELOS CORPORATION
460 Herndon Parkway, Herndon VA 22070. 703/471-6000. **Fax:** 703/318-1895. **Contact:** Human Resources Department. **Description:** Telos Corporation is a leader in providing complete computer information management solutions. The company offers hardware production and creation, extensive software and system engineering and software support, as well as hardware and system maintenance and training. **Common positions include:** Accountant/Auditor; Buyer; Draftsperson; Electrical/Electronics Engineer; Financial Analyst; Industrial Engineer; Mechanical Engineer; Operations/Production Manager; Quality Control Supervisor; Receptionist; Secretary; Software Engineer; Stock Clerk; Systems Analyst; Technical Writer/Editor. **Educational backgrounds include:** Accounting; Business Administration; Economics; Finance; Marketing. **Benefits:** Daycare Assistance; Dental Insurance; Disability Coverage; Life Insurance; Medical Insurance; Pension Plan; Tuition Assistance. **Corporate headquarters location:** This Location. **Parent company:** C3 Inc. **Operations at this facility include:** Administration; Manufacturing; Research and Development; Sales; Service. **Listed on:** NASDAQ. **Number of employees at this location:** 280. **Number of employees nationwide:** 2,100.

TRESP ASSOCIATES, INC.
4900 Seminary Road, Suite 700, Alexandria VA 22311. 703/845-9400. **Contact:** Gary Frenn, Human Resources Director. **Description:** TRESP Associates, Inc. is a diversified, high technology company specializing in the applications of information systems technologies in solving complex technical problems for government and commercial clients. Areas of specialization include: network engineering and LAN technology, including support and network administration; applied information technology, including research and analysis, information engineering, maintenance, and administration, and program support; logistics, including inventory and distribution, logistic systems management, and maintenance operations; and training. TRESP Associates' major projects include research, MIS, and administrative support for the U.S. Department of Transportation Federal Highway Administration; integrated management and technical support for the Defense Information Systems Agency, Center for Information Management's Office of Technical Integration; facilities management for the Office of the Secretary of Defense; logistics support for the U.S. Army Strategic Logistics Agency; conference and meeting planning for the U.S. Department of Transportation Urban Mass Transit Administration; LAN/office automation for the U.S. Army; network engineering/LAN technology for the U.S. Department of Justice National Institute of Corrections; and program coordination and evaluation for the NASA Office of Education.

Note: *Because addresses and telephone numbers of smaller companies change rapidly, we recommend you call each company to verify the information below before inquiring about job opportunities. Mass mailings are not recommended.*

Additional small employers:

COMPUTERS AND COMPUTER EQUIPMENT WHOLESALE

Project Design Systems Corp.
2711 Jefferson Davis Hwy 200, Arlington VA 22202-4015. 703/415-1660.

Hitachi Data Systems
951 E Byrd St, Ste 950, Richmond VA 23219-4075. 804/644-7200.

NCube
1760 Business Center Dr, Reston VA 22090-5310. 703/438-3994.

Tandem Computers Incorporated
10700 Parkridge Blvd, Reston VA 22091-5429. 703/476-0550.

Telco
4219 Lafayette Center Dr, Chantilly VA 22021-1209. 703/803-0330.

Thomas-Conrad Corporation
6103 Winnepeg Dr, Burke VA 22015-3846. 703/321-8053.

COMPUTER SOFTWARE, PROGRAMMING, AND SYSTEMS DESIGN

Anadac Inc.
2200 Clarendon Blvd, Ste 900, Arlington VA 22201-3331. 703/685-0021.

GTE Vantage Solutions
15000 Conference Center Dr, Chantilly VA 22021-3819. 703/818-5742.

HFSI
7900 Westpark Dr, #1209, McLean VA 22102-4203. 703/827-3000.

Imix Corp.
950 Herndon Pky, Ste 440, Herndon VA 22070-5531. 703/318-1034.

Infonet
3040 Williams Dr, Fairfax VA 22031-4618. 703/538-7200.

Lucas Management Systems
3702 Pender Dr, Ste 300, Fairfax VA 22030-6066. 703/222-1111.

MCI Communications
1650 Tysons Blvd, Mc Lean VA 22102-3915. 703/506-6000.

MPR Associates Inc.
320 King St, Alexandria VA 22314-3230. 703/519-0250.

Nimbus Information Systems
PO Box 7427, Charlottesvle VA 22906-7427. 804/985-4300.

Systems Engineering Division
3160 Fairview Park Dr, Falls Church VA 22042-4509. 703/876-1000.

Titan Applications Inc.
1950 Old Gallows Road, Vienna VA 22182-3933. 703/883-9200.

Unisys Government Systems Inc.
8008 Westpark Dr Fl 6, McLean VA 22102-3106. 703/556-5000.

Arms Inc.
808 Moorefield Park Dr, Ste 111, Richmond VA 23236-3672. 804/560-0500.

Business Computer Consultants
2801 S Main St, Blacksburg VA 24060-6649. 540/951-2294.

Comeau & Associates
8260 Greensboro Dr, McLean VA 22102-3806. 703/760-7650.

Cornell Technical Services
1964 Gallows Rd, Ste 200, Vienna VA 22182-3814. 703/734-8599.

Mantech Services Corp.
5360 Robin Hood Rd, Norfolk VA 23513-2422. 804/858-5600.

Claritas Corp.
201 N Union St, Alexandria VA 22314-2642. 703/683-8300.

Datatel Inc.
4375 Fair Lakes Ct, Fairfax VA 22033-4234. 703/968-9000.

Dektek Systems Inc.
8280 Greensboro Dr, McLean VA 22102-3807. 703/734-8606.

Edunetics Corp.
1600 Wilson Blvd, Ste 710, Arlington VA 22209-2505. 703/243-2602.

Landmark Systems Corp.
8000 Towers Cres Dr 150, Vienna VA 22182-2700. 703/902-8000.

NCI Information Systems
8260 Greensboro Dr, Ste 400, Mc Lean VA 22102-3806. 703/903-0325.

Software Productivity Consort.
2214 Rock Hill Rd, Herndon VA 22070-4214. 703/742-8877.

Verdix Corp.
205 Van Buren St Fl 4, Herndon VA 22070-5336. 703/318-5800.

Base 32 Inc.
1810 Michael Faraday Dr, Reston VA 22090-5313. 703/471-0032.

Edge Systems Inc.
3805 Cutshaw Ave, Ste 212, Richmond VA 23230-3937. 804/355-7040.

Metro Information Services
7202 Glen Forest Dr, Ste 105, Richmond VA 23226-3770. 804/285-7800.

Newtrend Company
516 Herndon Pky, Herndon VA 22070-5225. 703/478-2290.

Sabtech Industries
6037 Providence Rd, Virginia Beach VA 23464-3817. 804/420-5834.

SDRC
12007 Sunrise Valley Dr, Reston VA 22091-3446. 703/620-6222.

Strategic Software Systems
3800 Deepwater Terminal Rd, Richmond VA 23234-2227. 804/231-6633.

American Technical Resources
7353 McWhorter Pl, Annandale VA 22003-5648. 703/658-0066.

Cexec Inc.
8618 Westwood Center Dr, #100, Vienna VA 22182-2222. 703/893-3220.

Keydata Systems Inc.
10342 Battleview Pky, Manassas VA 22110-2338. 703/330-4500.

Quality Systems Inc.
4000 Legato Rd, Ste 1100, Fairfax VA 22033-4055. 703/352-9200.

RGI Inc.
5203 Leesburg Pike, Ste 1300, Falls Church VA 22041-3401. 703/820-4900.

Universal Systems Inc.
4350 Fair Lakes Ct, Ste 300, Fairfax VA 22033-4253. 703/222-2840.

COMPUTER MAINTENANCE AND REPAIR

Professional Software & Engineering Inc.
11838 Rock Landing Rd, Ste 150, Newport News VA 23606-4232. 804/873-1100.

Data Support Systems
7318 Impala Dr, Richmond VA 23228-4204. 804/261-7852.

EDS
1600 N Beauregard St, Alexandria VA 22311-1704. 703/820-0200.

COMPUTERS AND RELATED EQUIPMENT

New Visions Electronics
198 Semple Farm Rd, Hampton VA 23666-1453. 804/865-7173.

Newbridge Networks Inc.
593 Herndon Pky, Herndon VA 22070-5242. 703/834-3600.

Accel
4810 Beauregard St, Ste 323, Alexandria VA 22312. 703/354-1111.

Erni Components Inc.
520 Southlake Blvd, Richmond VA 23236-3043. 804/794-6367.

GTE Spacenet Corp.
1700 Old Meadow Rd, McLean VA 22102-4302. 703/848-1000.

Micromax Distribution Inc.
2700 Avenger Dr, Virginia Beach VA 23452-7302. 804/431-4500.

Northern Telecom Inc.
2010 Corporate Rdg, McLean VA 22102-7838. 703/712-8000.

Ost Inc.
14225 Sullyfield Circle, Ste F, Chantilly VA 22021. 703/817-0400.

For more information on career opportunities in the computer industry:

Magazines

COMPUTER-AIDED ENGINEERING
Penton Publishing, 1100 Superior Avenue, Cleveland OH 44114. 216/696-7000.

COMPUTERWORLD
IDG, 375 Cochituate Road, P.O. Box 9171, Framingham MA 01701-9171. 508/879-0700.

DATA COMMUNICATIONS
McGraw-Hill, 1221 Avenue of the Americas, New York NY 10020. 212/512-2000.

DATAMATION
Cahners Publishing, 275 Washington Street, Newton MA 02158. 617/964-3030.

IDC REPORT
International Data Corporation, Five Speen Street, Framingham MA 01701. 508/872-8200.

Associations

ASSOCIATION FOR COMPUTING MACHINERY
1515 Broadway, 17th Floor, New York NY 10036. 212/869-7440. Membership required.

INFORMATION TECHNOLOGY ASSOCIATION OF AMERICA
1616 North Fort Myer Drive, Suite 1300, Arlington VA 22209. 703/522-5055.

MULTIMEDIA DEVELOPMENT GROUP
2601 Mariposa Street, San Francisco CA 94110. 415/553-2300. Fax: 415/553-2403. Internet: info@mdg.org. A non-profit trade association dedicated to the business and market development of multimedia companies.

EDUCATIONAL SERVICES

Job prospects for college and university faculty, elementary school teachers, counselors, and education administrators should show moderate improvement throughout the '90s, although most of the openings will result from retirements. Among kindergarten and elementary school teachers, the best opportunities await those with training in special education. The employment outlook is also good for teacher aides, as many assist special education teachers, as school reforms call for more individual attention to students, and as the number of students who speak English as a second language rises. Adult education and secondary school teachers, and sports and physical fitness instructors and coaches are other occupations expected to grow faster than average.

AVERETT COLLEGE
420 West Main Street, Danville VA 24541. 804/791-5600. **Contact:** Rachel Meal, Human Resources Representative. **Description:** A private, four-year, co-ed, liberal arts college. Averett offers a Bachelor of Arts and a Bachelor of Science degree in 46 undergraduate programs, as well as a Master of Business Administration, a Master of Arts and Teaching, and a Master of Education at the graduate level.

BLUEFIELD STATE COLLEGE
219 Rock Street, Bluefield WV 24701. 304/327-4049. **Fax:** 304/325-7747. **Contact:** Elizabeth M. Belcher, Director of Human Resources. **Description:** A state-supported commuter college with a primary focus on career and technical two- and four-year programs. The college offers baccalaureate and associate degrees and certificate programs. **Common positions include:** Accountant/Auditor; Civil Engineer; Computer Programmer; Counselor; Electrical/Electronics Engineer; Librarian; Library Technician; Mechanical Engineer; Public Relations Specialist; Radiological Technologist; Registered Nurse; Teacher; Technical Writer/Editor. **Educational backgrounds include:** Accounting; Art/Design; Biology; Business Administration; Chemistry; Computer Science; Economics; Engineering; Finance; Health Care; Liberal Arts; Marketing; Mathematics; Physics. **Benefits:** Dental Insurance; Disability Coverage; Life Insurance; Medical Insurance; Pension Plan; Tuition Assistance. **Operations at this facility include:** Administration. **Number of employees at this location:** 227.

CHRISTOPHER NEWPORT UNIVERSITY
50 Shoe Lane, Newport News VA 23606. 804/594-7000. **Contact:** Human Resources. **Description:** A four-year comprehensive, coeducational, state-supported institution within Virginia's public university system. The university has an enrollment of approximately 5,000 students, and offers 23 undergraduate degree programs and eight graduate degree programs. The academic areas of the university are divided into the College of Arts and Humanities, the College of Business and Economics, the College of Social Science and Professional Studies, and the College of Science and Technology. CNU is accredited by the Commission on Colleges of the Southern Association of Colleges and Schools to award degrees at the baccalaureate level and is a candidate for accreditation to award degrees at the master's level.

COLLEGE OF WILLIAM AND MARY
P.O. Box 8795, Williamsburg VA 23187-8795. 804/221-3169. **Contact:** Personnel Department. **Description:** A four-year college offering bachelor's, master's (including MBA's), first professional, and doctoral degrees.

Approximately 5,250 undergraduate and 2,400 graduate students attend the College of William and Mary.

CONCORD COLLEGE
P.O. Box 1000, Athens WV 24712. 304/384-5235. **Contact:** Deborah Stutler, Director of Human Resources. **Description:** A state college. **Common positions include:** Computer Systems Analyst; Teacher. **Educational backgrounds include:** Accounting; Art/Design; Biology; Business Administration; Chemistry; Computer Science; Economics; Finance; Liberal Arts; Physics. **Benefits:** Daycare Assistance; Disability Coverage; Life Insurance; Medical Insurance; Pension Plan; Tuition Assistance. **Number of employees at this location:** 300.

GEORGE MASON UNIVERSITY
4087 University Drive, Fairfax VA 22030-4000. 703/993-2600. **Contact:** Keith Bushey, Vice President, Human Resources. **Description:** A four-year university offering bachelor's, master's (including MBA), professional, and doctoral degrees. Approximately 21,300 students attend George Mason University.

HAMPTON UNIVERSITY
Personnel Department, Armstrong Slater Building, Hampton VA 23668. 804/727-5250. **Contact:** Charlotte Pearson, Director of Personnel. **Description:** A four-year university offering bachelor's and master's degrees, including an MBA. Approximately 4,600 undergraduate and 400 graduate students attend Hampton University.

JAMES MADISON UNIVERSITY
Employee Relations and Training, Harrisonburg VA 22807. 703/568-6144. **Fax:** 703/568-7916. **Contact:** Kathy Shuler, Employment Representative. **Description:** A four-year university offering bachelor's and master's degrees, including a Master of Business Administration. Approximately 10,000 undergraduate and 700 graduate students attend James Madison University. **Common positions include:** Accountant/Auditor; Administrator; Blue-Collar Worker Supervisor; Buyer; Computer Programmer; Editor; Human Resources Specialist; Public Relations Specialist; Purchasing Agent and Manager; Reporter; Systems Analyst; Teacher. **Benefits:** Dental Insurance; Disability Coverage; Employee Discounts; Life Insurance; Medical Insurance; Pension Plan; Tuition Assistance. **Corporate headquarters location:** This Location.

LIBERTY UNIVERSITY
3765 Candlers Mountain Road, Lynchburg VA 24506. 804/582-7330. **Contact:** Laura Wallace, Director of Human Resources. **Description:** A four-year liberal arts university.

MARSHALL UNIVERSITY
400 Hal Greer Boulevard, Huntington WV 25755. 304/696-6455. **Fax:** 304/696-6453. **Contact:** Bill Burdett, Acting Director of Human Resources. **Description:** A university. **Common positions include:** Electrician; Human Resources Specialist; Librarian; Physician; Teacher. **Educational backgrounds include:** Accounting; Art/Design; Biology; Business Administration; Chemistry; Communications; Economics; Engineering; Finance; Geology; Liberal Arts; Marketing; Mathematics; Physics. **Benefits:** Dental Insurance; Disability Coverage; Employee Discounts; Life Insurance; Medical Insurance; Pension Plan; Tuition Assistance. **Operations at this facility include:** Administration.

MARY WASHINGTON COLLEGE
1301 College Avenue, Fredricksburg VA 22401. 703/899-4100. **Contact:** Personnel Office. **Description:** Four year, co-educational, state-supported, residential college of the liberal arts and sciences. Mary Washington College has a full-time enrollment of 3,000. Majors include: American Studies, Art History, Biology, Business Administration, Chemistry, Classics, Computer

Science, Dramatic Arts, Economics, English, Environmental Science, French, Geography, German, Historic Preservations, History, International Affairs, Mathematics, Music, Performing Arts, Philosophy, Physics, Political Science, Psychology, Religion, Sociology, Spanish, Studio Art, Pre-Dental, Pre-Law and Pre-Med.

MARYMOUNT UNIVERSITY
2807 North Glebe Road, Arlington VA 22207. 703/522-5600. **Contact:** Norman Minter, Director of Personnel Services. **Description:** An independent and coeducational establishment related to the Catholic Church, enrolling 2,000 students in undergraduate studies and 2,100 students in graduate studies in the liberal arts tradition. Marymount University offers three degree levels: associates degree, bachelors degree and masters degree. This college offers various degrees in majors in the following schools: Arts and Sciences, Business Administration, Education and Human Services and Nursing.

NORFOLK STATE UNIVERSITY
2401 Corprew Avenue, Norfolk VA 23504. 804/683-8600. **Contact:** Jimmy Wilson, Human Resource Manager. **Description:** Established in 1979 as Norfolk State University. This college is home to 8,700 on-campus students and offers four years of education and a graduate program. Majors include: English, Foreign Language, Fine Arts, Music, Accounting, Business, Social Work, Nursing, Chemistry, Biology, Special Education and Fashion Design.

NORTHERN VIRGINIA COMMUNITY COLLEGE
4001 Wakefield Chapel Road, Annandale VA 22003. 703/323-3000. **Contact:** James VanDyke, Human Resources Director. **Description:** A community college.

OLD DOMINION UNIVERSITY
1510 West 48th Street, Norfolk VA 23529. 804/683-3042. **Contact:** Personnel. **Description:** A university.

J.S. REYNOLDS COMMUNITY COLLEGE
P.O. Box 85622, Richmond VA 23285-5622. 804/371-3249. **Fax:** 804/371-3386. **Contact:** Sandra Kirk, Personnel Analyst. **Description:** A community college. Employs 360 full-time, 600 part-time. **Common positions include:** Blue-Collar Worker Supervisor; Counselor; Education Administrator; Librarian; Library Technician; Teacher. **Educational backgrounds include:** Business Administration; Finance; Liberal Arts; Teaching. **Benefits:** 401K; Dental Insurance; Employee Discounts; Life Insurance; Medical Insurance; Pension Plan; Savings Plan; Tuition Assistance. **Corporate headquarters location:** This Location. **Operations at this facility include:** Administration.

ROANOKE COLLEGE
221 College Lane, Salem VA 24153. 703/375-2500. **Contact:** Kathy Page, Human Resource Manager. **Description:** Founded in 1842, this is the second oldest Lutheran college in the nation. This four year liberal arts undergraduate college offers 29 majors, 28 minors and 13 concentrations. Roanoke College has 1,750 students and 100 full-time teacher-scholars, 90 percent hold Ph.D.s or the highest degree in their area of expertise. The campus includes 52 buildings on 146 acres.

SHENANDOAH UNIVERSITY
1460 University Drive, Winchester VA 22601. 703/665-4500. **Contact:** Marie Laudes, Personnel Director. **Description:** Founded in 1875, Shenandoah is a private, coeducational school offering both a liberal arts program and career preparation. Baccalaureate and associate degree programs are available in Health Professions, Arts and Sciences, Harry F. Byrd, Jr. School of Business, and the Shenandoah Conservatory. Along with the academic programs, Shenandoah honors the traditions of the United Methodist Church. There are about 1,700 students and 214 part- and full-time faculty members at the university. The student/faculty ratio is 10:1.

UNIVERSITY OF CHARLESTON
2300 MacCorkle Avenue SE, Charleston WV 25304-1099. 304/357-4736. **Fax:** 304/357-4715. **Contact:** Kathy Roten, Director of Human Resources. **Description:** A university. **Common positions include:** Blue-Collar Worker Supervisor; Computer Programmer; Computer Systems Analyst; Education Administrator; Electrician; Human Resources Specialist; Librarian; Library Technician; Purchasing Agent and Manager; Restaurant/Food Service Manager; Teacher. **Educational backgrounds include:** Accounting; Art/Design; Biology; Business Administration; Chemistry; Communications; Computer Science; Economics; Engineering; Finance; Geology; Liberal Arts; Marketing; Mathematics; Physics. **Benefits:** 403B; Dental Insurance; Disability Coverage; Employee Discounts; Life Insurance; Medical Insurance; Tuition Assistance. **Corporate headquarters location:** This Location. **Operations at this facility include:** Administration; Service. **Number of employees at this location:** 215.

UNIVERSITY OF VIRGINIA
914 Emmett Street, Charlottesville VA 22906. 804/924-4444. **Fax:** 804/924-4486. **Contact:** Human Resources Department. **Description:** A state university with a comprehensive health sciences center. **Common positions include:** Accountant/Auditor; Administrator; Architect; Architectural Engineer; Biological Scientist/Biochemist; Biomedical Engineer; Buyer; Chemist; Civil Engineer; Computer Programmer; Dietician/Nutritionist; Electrical/Electronics Engineer; Financial Analyst; Mechanical Engineer; Purchasing Agent and Manager; Systems Analyst. **Educational backgrounds include:** Accounting; Biology; Business Administration; Chemistry; Computer Science; Finance; Health Care; Liberal Arts. **Benefits:** Dental Insurance; Life Insurance; Medical Insurance; Pension Plan. **Special Programs:** Internships. **Operations at this facility include:** Administration; Research and Development; Service.

VIRGINIA COMMONWEALTH UNIVERSITY
1000 East Marshall Street, P.O. Box 980066, Richmond VA 23298-0066. 804/828-9433. **Contact:** Employee Relations. **Description:** A state university.

VIRGINIA TECH
Southgate Center, First Floor, Blacksburg VA 24061-0318. 703/231-5301. **Fax:** 703/231-3830. **Contact:** Personnel Services, Employment Manager. **Description:** A land grant university, providing high quality advanced instruction, research and outreach programs. Continuing education is also offered at Roanoke Graduate Center, Northern Virginia Graduate Center, and Tidewater Graduate Center. **Common positions include:** Accountant/Auditor; Administrative Services Manager; Agricultural Engineer; Agricultural Scientist; Architect; Budget Analyst; Clerical Supervisor; Computer Programmer; Computer Systems Analyst; Counselor; Education Administrator; Electrician; Food Scientist/Technologist; Forester/Conservation Scientist; Human Resources Specialist; Landscape Architect; Librarian; Library Technician; Mechanical Engineer; Pharmacist; Physicist/Astronomer; Property and Real Estate Manager; Public Relations Specialist; Purchasing Agent and Manager; Radio/TV Announcer/Broadcaster; Registered Nurse; Restaurant/Food Service Manager; Science Technologist; Sociologist; Software Engineer. **Educational backgrounds include:** Accounting; Art/Design; Biology; Business Administration; Chemistry; Communications; Computer Science; Economics; Engineering; Finance; Geology; Health Care; Liberal Arts; M.D./Medicine; Marketing; Mathematics; Physics. **Benefits:** Dental Insurance; Leave Time; Life Insurance; Medical Insurance; Pension Plan; Sabbatical Leave; Savings Plan. **Corporate headquarters location:** This Location. **Operations at this facility include:** Administration; Education; Research and Development. **Number of employees at this location:** 6,000.

WEST VIRGINIA UNIVERSITY
P.O. Box 6640, Morgantown WV 26506-3405. 304/293-0111. **Contact:** Wilson White, Manager of Human Resources. **Description:** A state university.

Note: *Because addresses and telephone numbers of smaller companies change rapidly, we recommend you call each company to verify the information below before inquiring about job opportunities. Mass mailings are not recommended.*

Additional small employers:

ELEMENTARY AND SECONDARY SCHOOLS

Collegiate School
201 N Mooreland Rd, Richmond VA 23229-7101. 804/740-7077.

Islamic Saudi Academy
8333 Richmond Hwy, Alexandria VA 22309-2329. 703/780-0606.

Norfolk Academy
1585 Wesleyan Dr, Norfolk VA 23502-5512. 804/461-6236.

St. Anne's Belfield School
2132 Ivy Rd, Charlottesvle VA 22903-1785. 804/296-5106.

St. Catherine's School
6001 Grove Ave, Richmond VA 23226-2600. 804/288-2804.

Covenant School
1000 Birdwood Rd, Charlottesvle VA 22903-5300. 804/979-2389.

Grafton School
PO Box 112, Berryville VA 22611-0112. 540/955-2400.

Norfolk Psychiatric Center
100 Kingsley Ln, Norfolk VA 23505-4679. 804/489-1072.

Birdneck Elementary School
957 S Birdneck Rd, Virginia Beach VA 23451-4801. 804/437-4819.

Glenwood Elementary School
2213 Round Hill Dr, Virginia Beach VA 23464. 804/471-5858.

Brandon Middle School
1700 Pope St, Virginia Beach VA 23464-6630. 804/366-4545.

Grace Metz Junior High School
9700 Fairview Ave, Manassas VA 22111-5106. 703/257-8600.

Hammond Junior High School
4646 Seminary Rd, Alexandria VA 22304-1424. 703/461-4100.

Salem Middle School
2380 Lynnhaven Pky, Virginia Beach VA 23464-8522. 804/474-8411.

Swift Creek Middle School
3700 Old Hundred Road, Midlothian VA 23112-4744. 804/739-6315.

Albemarle High School
2775 Hydraulic Rd, Charlottesville VA 22901-8916. 804/974-4319.

Annandale High School
4700 Medford Dr, Annandale VA 22003-5497. 703/256-4600.

Bayside High School
4960 Haygood Rd, Virginia Beach VA 23455-5299. 804/473-5050.

Bethel High School
1067 Big Bethel Road, Hampton VA 23666-1946. 804/825-4400.

Bird High School
10301 Courthouse Road, Chesterfield VA 23832-6699. 804/768-6110.

Brooke High School
RR 3 Box 610, Wellsburg WV 26070-9748. 304/527-1410.

Cabell Midland High School
2300 Route 60, Ona WV 25545-9712. 304/743-7400.

Cave Spring High School
3712 Chaparral Dr, Roanoke VA 24018-4899. 540/772-7550.

Chantilly High School
4201 Stringfellow Rd, Chantilly VA 22021-2600. 703/222-8100.

Clover Hill High School
13900 Hull Street Rd, Midlothian VA 23112-2013. 804/739-6230.

Cox High School
2425 Shorehaven Dr, Virginia Beach VA 23454-1749. 804/496-6767.

Denbigh High School
259 Denbigh Blvd, Newport News VA 23608-3327. 804/886-7700.

Edison High School
5801 Franconia Rd, Alexandria VA 22310-2722. 703/971-6850.

Fairfax High School
3500 Old Lee Hwy, Fairfax VA 22030-1888. 703/591-8350.

Fauquier High School
705 Waterloo Rd, Warrenton VA 22186-3093. 540/347-6100.

Ferguson Senior High School
11 Shoe Ln, Newport News VA 23606-2911. 804/591-4600.

First Colonial High School
1272 Mill Dam Rd, Virginia Beach VA 23454-2322. 804/496-6711.

Franklin County Sr High School
506 Pell Ave, Rocky Mount VA 24151-1141. 540/483-0221.

Garfield High School
14000 Smoketown Rd,

Woodbridge VA 22192-4704. 703/670-2131.

Gloucester High School
6680 Short Ln, Gloucester VA 23061. 804/693-2526.

Granby Senior High School
7101 Granby St, Norfolk VA 23505-4013. 804/441-1265.

Great Bridge High School
301 Hanbury Rd W, Chesapeake VA 23320-4228. 804/482-5191.

Green Run High School
1700 Dahlia Dr, Virginia Beach VA 23456-2199. 804/431-4040.

Halifax County High School
PO Box 310, South Boston VA 24592-0310. 804/572-4977.

Hampton Senior High School
1491 W Queen St, Hampton VA 23669-3769. 804/825-4430.

Hayfield Secondary School
7630 Telegraph Rd, Alexandria VA 22315-3898. 703/922-5020.

Hermitage High School
8301 Hungary Spring Rd, Richmond VA 23228-1984. 804/756-3000.

Herndon High School
700 Bennett St, Herndon VA 22070-3199. 703/810-2200.

Jefferson Sci-Tech High School
6560 Braddock Rd, Alexandria VA 22312-2206. 703/750-8300.

John Marshall High School
1300 Wheeling Ave, Glen Dale WV 26038-1729. 304/843-4444.

Kecoughtan Senior High School
522 Woodland Rd, Hampton VA 23669-1762. 804/850-5000.

Kellam High School
2323 Holland Rd, Virginia Beach VA 23456-3530. 804/427-3232.

Kempsville High School
5194 Chiefs Ln, Virginia Beach VA 23464-2796. 804/474-8400.

Lafayette High School
4460 Longhill Rd, Williamsburg VA 23188-1535. 804/565-0373.

Lake Braddock Secondary School
9200 Burke Lake Rd, Burke VA 22015-1682. 703/323-9000.

Lake Taylor High School
1384 Kempsville Rd, Norfolk VA 23502-2299. 804/441-5650.

Lakeland High School
214 Kenyon Rd, Suffolk VA 23434-7452. 804/925-5530.

Lee High School
6540 Franconia Rd, Springfield VA 22150-1499. 703/971-6000.

Lee-Davis Senior High School
7052 Mechanicsville Tpke, Mechanicsville VA 23111-3629. 804/746-5261.

Madison High School
2500 James Madison Dr, Vienna VA 22181-5536. 703/938-2225.

Manchester High School
12601 Bailey Bridge Rd, Midlothian VA 23112-1805. 804/739-6275.

Maury High School
322 Shirley Ave, Norfolk VA 23517-2175. 804/441-2611.

McLean High School
1633 Davidson Rd, McLean VA 22101-4399. 703/356-0700.

Menchville High School
275 Menchville Rd, Newport News VA 23602-6805. 804/886-7722.

Monacan High School
11501 Smoketree Dr, Richmond VA 23236-2598. 804/378-2480.

Mount Vernon High School
8515 Old Mount Vernon Rd, Alexandria VA 22309-2015. 703/360-5900.

Nansemond River High School
3301 Nansemond Pky, Suffolk VA 23434-2046. 804/538-5420.

North Stafford High School
839 Garrisonville Rd, Stafford VA 22554-3900. 540/659-4176.

Oakton High School
2900 Sutton Rd, Vienna VA 22181-6199. 703/281-4900.

Open Campus High School
4400 Virginia Beach Blvd, Virginia Beach VA 23462-3107. 804/473-5200.

Osbourn Park High School
8909 Euclid Ave, Manassas VA 22111-2498. 703/361-1101.

Oscar Smith High School
1994 Tiger Dr, Chesapeake VA 23320-6855. 804/548-0696.

Parkersburg High School
2101 Dudley Ave, Parkersburg WV 26101-3492. 304/420-9595.

Parkersburg South High School
1511 Blizzard Dr, Parkersburg WV 26101-6424. 304/420-9610.

Petersburg Senior High School
3101 Johnson Rd, Petersburg VA 23805-2338. 804/861-7110.

Phoebus Senior High School
100 Ireland St, Hampton VA 23663-2150. 804/727-1000.

Potomac High School
16706 Jefferson Davis Hwy, Dumfries VA 22026-2115. 703/221-1134.

Preston High School
400 Preston Dr, Kingwood WV 26537-1553. 304/329-0400.

Princess Anne High School
4400 Virginia Beach Blvd, Virginia Beach VA 23462-3198. 804/473-5000.

Pulaski County High School
5414 Cougar Trail Rd, Dublin VA 24084-3841. 540/674-4605.

Robinson Secondary School
5035 Sideburn Rd, Fairfax VA 22032-2637. 703/323-7500.

Salem High School
1993 Sun Devil Dr, Virginia Beach VA 23464-8905. 804/474-8484.

South Lakes High School
11400 S Lakes Dr, Reston VA 22091-4199. 703/476-5270.

Stafford High School
33 Stafford Indians Ln, Fredericksbrg VA 22405-5803. 540/371-7200.

Stonewall Jackson High School
8820 Rixlew Ln, Manassas VA 22110-3799. 703/368-2106.

Stuart High School
3301 Peace Valley Ln, Falls Church VA 22044-1508. 703/820-1114.

Washington High School
701 Broad St, Danville VA 24541-2627. 804/799-6410.

Washington Senior High School
1111 Park Ave, Norfolk VA 23504-3619. 804/441-2443.

West Potomac High School
6500 Quander Rd, Alexandria VA 22307-1099. 703/768-2121.

Wheeling Park High School
RR 4, Wheeling WV 26003-9804. 304/243-0400.

Williams High School
3330 King St, Alexandria VA 22302-3001. 703/824-6800.

Woodbridge High School
3001 Old Bridge Rd, Woodbridge VA 22192-3221. 703/494-7135.

Woodson High School
9525 Main St, Fairfax VA 22031-4099. 703/323-1911.

Grafton School
407 Elm St, Winchester VA 22601-5925. 540/722-9172.

Clay County School District
PO Box 120, Clay WV 25043-0120. 304/587-4266.

Fredericksburg City School District
817 Princess Anne St, Fredericksbrg VA 22401-5819. 540/372-1130.

Gilmer County School District
201 N Court St, Glenville WV 26351-1216. 304/462-7386.

Grant County School District
204 Jefferson Ave, Petersburg WV 26847-1628. 304/257-1011.

Hardy County School District
510 Ashby St, Moorefield WV 26836-1001. 304/538-2348.

Lancaster County School District
PO Box 2000, Kilmarnock VA 22482-2000. 804/435-3183.

Morgan County School District
903 S Washington St, Berkeley Springs WV 25411-1031. 304/258-2430.

Pocahontas County School District
926 5th Ave, Marlinton WV 24954-1209. 304/799-4505.

Webster County School District
315 S Main St, Webster Spgs WV 26288-1123. 304/847-5638.

Bristol City School District
222 Oak St, Bristol VA 24201-4154. 540/669-8181.

Charlottesville City School District
1562 Dairy Rd, Charlottesvle VA 22903-1304. 804/979-9250.

Colonial Heights Public School District
512 Boulevard, Colonial Hgts VA 23834-3743. 804/526-0811.

Mineral County School District
1 Baker Pl, Keyser WV 26726-2824. 304/788-4200.

Randolph County School District
40 11th St, Elkins WV 26241-3512. 304/636-9150.

Upshur County School District
PO Box 580, Buckhannon WV 26201-0580. 304/472-5480.

Wetzel County School District
333 Foundry Street, North Martinsville WV 26155-1110. 304/455-2441.

Bedford County School District
PO Box 748, Bedford VA 24523-0748. 540/586-1045.

Buchanan County School District
PO Box 833, Grundy VA 24614-0833. 540/935-2331.

Mingo County School District
815 Alderson St, Williamson WV 25661-3215. 304/235-3333.

Nicholas County School District
400 Old Main Dr, Summersville WV 26651-1360. 304/872-3611.

Suffolk City School District
PO Box 1549, Suffolk VA 23439-1549. 804/925-5500.

COLLEGES, UNIVERSITIES, AND PROFESSIONAL SCHOOLS

Bluefield State College
219 Rock St, Bluefield WV 24701-2198. 304/327-4000.

CBN University
1000 Centerville Tpke, Virginia Beach VA 23464-5041. 804/424-7000.

College Of West Virginia
PO Box AG, Beckley WV 25802. 304/253-7351.

Eastern Mennonite College
1200 Park Rd, Harrisonburg VA 22801-2404. 540/432-4000.

Fairmont State College
Locust Ave, Fairmont WV 26554. 304/367-4000.

Glenville State College
200 High St, Glenville WV 26351-1200. 304/462-7361.

Hampden Sydney College
PO Box 667, Hampden Sydney VA 23943-0667. 804/223-6000.

Lynchburg College
1501 Lakeside Dr, Lynchburg VA 24501-3113. 804/522-8100.

Marymount University
2807 N Glebe Rd, Arlington VA 22207-4299. 703/522-5600.

National Business College
1813 E Main St, Salem VA 24153-4524. 703/986-1800.

Randolph Macon College
PO Box 5005, Ashland VA 23005-5505. 804/752-7200.

Randolph Macon Woman's College
2500 Rivermont Ave, Lynchburg VA 24503-1555. 804/947-8000.

Saint Paul's College
406 Windsor Ave, Lawrenceville VA 23868-1299. 804/848-3111.

Salem Teikyo University
PO Box 5, Salem WV 26426-0005. 304/782-5011.

Strayer College
3045 Columbia Pike, Arlington VA 22204-4338. 703/892-5100.

University Of Richmond
University Of Richmond, Richmond VA 23173. 804/289-8000.

Virginia Intermont College
1013 Moore St, Bristol VA 24201-4225. 540/669-6101.

Virginia Union University
1500 N Lombardy St, Richmond VA 23220-1711. 804/257-5600.

Virginia Wesleyan College
Wesleyan Drive, Norfolk VA 23502. 804/455-3200.

West Virginia State College
PO Box 1000, Institute WV 25112-1000. 304/766-3000.

West Virginia Wesleyan College
College Ave, Buckhannon WV 26201. 304/473-8000.

Wheeling Jesuit College
316 Washington Ave, Wheeling WV 26003-6295. 304/243-2000.

JUNIOR COLLEGES AND TECHNICAL INSTITUTES

Blue Ridge Community College
PO Box 80, Weyers Cave VA 24486. 540/234-9261.

Central Virginia Community College
3506 Wards Rd, Lynchburg VA 24502-2448. 804/386-4500.

Danville Community College
1008 S Main St, Danville VA 24541-4088. 804/797-2222.

Germanna Community College
PO Box 339, Locust Grove VA 22508-0339. 540/423-1333.

John Tyler Community College
PO Box T, Chester VA 23831-0437. 804/796-4000.

Lord Fairfax Community College
PO Box 47, Middletown VA 22645-0047. 540/869-1120.

Mountain Empire Community College
PO Box 700, Big Stone Gap VA 24219-0700. 540/523-2400.

New River Community College
1580 N Franklin St, Christiansbrg VA 24073-1412. 540/674-3600.

Patrick Henry Community College
PO Box 5311, Martinsville VA 24115-5311. 540/638-8777.

Piedmont Virginia Comm College
RR 6 Box 1, Charlottesvle VA 22902-9806. 804/977-3900.

Southern West Virginia CommunityCollege
PO Box 2900, Logan WV 25601-2900. 304/792-4300.

Southside Virginia CommunityCollege
RR 1 Box 60, Alberta VA 23821-9719. 804/949-1000.

Southwest Virginia Community College
Box S V C C, Richlands VA 24641. 703/964-2555.

Thomas Nelson Community College
PO Box 9407, Hampton VA 23670-0407. 804/825-2700.

Tidewater Community College Chesapeake
1428 Cedar Rd, Chesapeake VA 23320-7199. 804/547-9271.

Tidewater Communtiy College Virginia Beach
1700 College Crescent, Virginia Beach VA 23456-1918. 804/427-7100.

Tidewater Community College
State Route 135, Portsmouth VA 23703. 804/484-2121.

Virginia Highlands Community College
PO Box 828, Abingdon VA 24212-0828. 540/628-6094.

Virginia Western Community College
PO Box 14065, Roanoke VA 24038-4065. 540/857-7231.

West Virginia Northern CommunityCollege
College Square, Wheeling WV 26003. 304/233-5900.

Wytheville Community College
1000 E Main St, Wytheville VA 24382-3308. 540/228-5541.

BUSINESS, SECRETARIAL, AND DATA PROCESSING SCHOOLS

Becker CPA Review Course
3541 Chain Bridge Rd, Fairfax VA 22030-2793. 703/352-2530.

Dominion Business School
Roanoke Salem Plaza, Roanoke VA 24017. 540/362-7738.

MISC. SCHOOLS AND EDUCATIONAL SERVICES

Charleston Conservatory of Music
2300 MacCorkle Ave SE, Charleston WV 25304-1045. 304/357-4905.

CHILD DAYCARE SERVICES

Childtime Children's Center
6048 Providence Rd, Virginia Beach VA 23464-3807. 804/431-9353.

Early Works Day Care Center
2400 Strawberry Ln, Chesapeake VA 23324-3113. 804/543-4221.

Headstart Program
925 24th St, Parkersburg WV 26101-2618. 304/485-7404.

Kinder Care Learning Center
4900 Oakleys Ln, Richmond VA 23231-2920. 804/222-1103.

La Petite Academy
20110 Ashburn Village Blvd, Ashburn VA 22011-3346. 703/729-0500.

Montessori Center For Child
122 N Courthouse Rd, Richmond VA 23236-3128. 804/794-8661.

Rutherford A Child Development Center
3417 Bennett Dr NW, Roanoke VA 24017-4513. 540/342-5851.

YMCA Before & After School Program
310 Thole St, Norfolk VA 23505-4247. 804/622-9622.

YMCA Before & After School Program
1129 W Princess Anne Rd, Norfolk VA 23507-1205. 804/622-9622.

YMCA Before & After School Program
200 Shirley Ave, Norfolk VA 23517-2214. 804/622-9622.

Kanawha County Schools Head Start
200 Elizabeth St, Charleston WV 25311-2119. 304/348-7706.

For more information on career opportunities in educational services:

Associations

AMERICAN ASSOCIATION OF SCHOOL ADMINISTRATORS
1801 North Moore Street, Arlington VA 22209-9988. 703/528-0700. Fax: 703/841-1543. An organization of school system leaders. Membership includes a national conference on education; programs and seminars; *The School Administrator,* a monthly magazine; *Leadership News,* a bi-monthly newspaper; *The AASA Professor,* a quarterly publication; and a catalog of other publications and audiovisuals.

AMERICAN FEDERATION OF TEACHERS
555 New Jersey Avenue NW, Washington DC 20001. 202/879-4400.

COLLEGE AND UNIVERSITY PERSONNEL ASSOCIATION
1233 20th Street NW, Suite 301, Washington DC 20036. 202/429-0311. Membership required.

NATIONAL ASSOCIATION OF BIOLOGY TEACHERS
11250 Roger Bacon Drive, Suite 19, Reston VA 22090-5202. 703/471-1134. Toll-free number: 800/406-0775. Fax: 703/435-5582. A professional organization for biology and life science educators. E-mail address: nabter@aol.com.

NATIONAL ASSOCIATION OF COLLEGE ADMISSION COUNSELORS
1631 Prince Street, Alexandria VA 22314. 703/836-2222. An education association of secondary school counselors, college and university admission officers, and related individuals who work with students as they make the transition from high school to post-secondary education.

NATIONAL ASSOCIATION OF COLLEGE AND UNIVERSITY BUSINESS OFFICERS
1 DuPont Circle, Suite 500, Washington DC 20036. 202/861-2500. Association for those involved in the financial administration and management of higher education. Membership required.

NATIONAL SCIENCE TEACHERS ASSOCIATION
1840 Wilson Boulevard, Arlington VA 22201-3000. 703/243-7100. Organization committed to the improvement of science education at all levels, preschool through college. Publishes five journals, a newspaper, and a number of special publications. Also conducts national and regional conventions.

Books

ACADEMIC LABOR MARKETS
Falmer Press, Taylor & Francis, Inc., 1900 Frost Road, Suite 101, Bristol PA 19007. 800/821-8312.

HOW TO GET A JOB IN EDUCATION
Adams Media Corporation, 260 Center Street, Holbrook MA 02343. 617/767-8100.

Directories

WASHINGTON HIGHER EDUCATION ASSOCIATION DIRECTORY
Council for Advancement and Support of Education, 11 DuPont Circle NW, Suite 400, Washington DC 20036 202/328-5900.

ELECTRONIC/INDUSTRIAL ELECTRICAL EQUIPMENT

Heading into 1996, industry analysts expect productivity in the fast-paced electronics industry to continue to spiral downward, even as the number of production workers in the industry levels off. Intense competition from overseas has companies cutting costs by sending labor-intensive operations to low-wage regions like the Far East and Mexico. On the other hand, the increased computerization of the industry is fueling the demand for highly-trained, knowledgeable workers.

Semiconductor manufacturers, in particular, are growing steadily. Starting out the year, the Semiconductor Industry Association forecasted a growth rate of about 15 percent. The year actually came in at 26 percent. Factors spawning a high demand for semiconductors: a surging PC market, new information highway markets, and a stronger telecommunications and consumer electronics market.

ABB POWER T&D COMPANY, INC.
P.O. Box 38, Bland VA 24315. 540/688-3325. **Contact:** Human Resources. **Description:** ABB Power T&D Company, Inc. manufactures commercial, industrial, and seismic transformers.

ABB POWER T&D COMPANY, INC.
P.O. Box 831, Lewisburg WV 24901. 304/647-4358. **Contact:** Ms. Kay Holliday, Human Resources Director. **Description:** A manufacturer of analytical instruments for commercial and industrial use.

AMP INC.
1175 North Main Street, Harrisonburg VA 22801. 703/433-3200. **Contact:** Richard Myers, Human Resources Representative. **Description:** AMP Inc. manufactures and assembles electrical connectors.

AUTOMATA, INC.
1200 Severn Way, Sterling VA 20166. 703/450-2600. **Contact:** Human Resources. **Description:** Automata, Inc.'s primary business is manufacturing printed circuit boards. **Common positions include:** Accountant/Auditor; Blue-Collar Worker Supervisor; Buyer; Chemist; Computer Programmer; Customer Service Representative; Designer; Human Resources Specialist; Industrial Engineer; Manufacturer's/Wholesaler's Sales Rep.; Mechanical Engineer; Operations/Production Manager; Purchasing Agent and Manager; Quality Control Supervisor. **Educational backgrounds include:** Accounting; Chemistry; Engineering; Marketing. **Benefits:** Dental Insurance; Disability Coverage; Life Insurance; Medical Insurance; Profit Sharing; Tuition Assistance. **Corporate headquarters location:** This Location. **Operations at this facility include:** Administration; Manufacturing; Research and Development; Sales.

CUBIC CORPORATION
325 Burgh Westra Drive, Hampton VA 23669-1742. 804/850-4886. **Contact:** Human Resources. **Description:** Founded in 1951 as an electronics firm, Cubic Corporation today is the parent company of two major segments: the Cubic Automatic Revenue Collection Group and the Cubic Defense Group. The Cubic Automatic Revenue Collection Group designs and

manufactures automatic revenue collection systems throughout the world for public mass transit including rail, buses, bridges, tunnels, toll roads and parking lots. The Cubic Defense Group provides instrumented training systems for the U.S. Army, Air Force, and Navy, as well as avionics, data link, aerospace systems and product logistical support. This group also provides battle command training, radio communication systems, and provides field service operation and maintenance. **NOTE:** For employment information, contact the Personnel Director at the field office in San Diego CA at 619-277-6780.

DCS CORPORATION
1330 Braddock Place, Alexandria VA 22314. **Contact:** Human Resources. **Description:** A research and development firm providing services and products for the government and private industry in areas such as electro-optics, virtual reality, fiber optics, and defense weapons and tactics. **Common positions include:** Computer Systems Analyst; Electrical/Electronics Engineer; Software Engineer. **Educational backgrounds include:** Computer Science; Engineering; Physics. **Benefits:** 401K; Dental Insurance; Disability Coverage; Life Insurance; Medical Insurance; Pension Plan; Profit Sharing; Tuition Assistance. **Corporate headquarters location:** This Location. **Other U.S. locations:** Nationwide; CA; MD; MO. **Operations at this facility include:** Administration; Research and Development. **Listed on:** Privately held. **Number of employees at this location:** 150. **Number of employees nationwide:** 320.

DYNALECTRIC COMPANY
1420 Spring Hill Road, Suite 500, McLean VA 22102. 703/556-8000. **Contact:** Lynn Mauer, Human Resources. **Description:** An electronics company.

E-SYSTEMS, INC.
FALLS CHURCH DIVISION
7700 Arlington Boulevard, Falls Church VA 22046. 703/560-5000. **Fax:** 703/280-4267. **Contact:** Human Resources/Staffing Department. **Description:** A systems contractor in the areas of remotely-controlled reconnaissance, information processing and display, electronic combat operations, digitally-controlled communications, and intrusion detection. **Common positions include:** Computer Programmer; Draftsperson; Electrical/Electronics Engineer; Industrial Engineer; Mechanical Engineer; Physicist/Astronomer; Systems Analyst; Technical Writer/Editor. **Educational backgrounds include:** Computer Science; Engineering; Mathematics; Physics. **Benefits:** Credit Union; Dental Insurance; Disability Coverage; Employee Discounts; Life Insurance; Medical Insurance; Pension Plan; Savings Plan; Stock Option; Tuition Assistance. **Corporate headquarters location:** Dallas TX. **Operations at this facility include:** Divisional Headquarters; Manufacturing; Research and Development.

DAVIS H. ELLIOT CO. INC.
2751 Lee Highway South, Cloverdale VA 24077-2521. 540/992-2865. **Contact:** Mike Leech, Human Resources Director. **Description:** An electrical contracting company.

ENSCO INC.
5400 Port Royal Road, Springfield VA 22151. 703/321-9000. **Contact:** Bill Moore, Technical Recruiter. **Description:** A research, development, applied systems engineering, and professional services firm providing sensor- and computer-based systems in the areas of defense, transportation, and business applications. **Common positions include:** Computer Programmer; Computer Systems Analyst; Department Manager; Electrical/Electronics Engineer; Mechanical Engineer; Systems Analyst; Technical Writer/Editor. **Educational backgrounds include:** Computer Science; Engineering; Mathematics; Physics. **Benefits:** Dental Insurance; Disability Coverage; Employee Discounts; Life Insurance; Medical Insurance; Pension Plan; Tuition

headquarters location: This Location. **Other U.S. locations:** CA; FL; IN; NY. **Operations at this facility include:** Administration; Divisional Headquarters; Research and Development. **Listed on:** Privately held. **Number of employees at this location:** 140. **Number of employees nationwide:** 400.

GENERAL ELECTRIC COMPANY
DRIVE SYSTEMS OPERATIONS
1501 Roanoke Boulevard, Salem VA 24153. 703/387-7000. **Contact:** Attn: Room 18. **Description:** Manufactures AC/DC drivers and panels. Overall, General Electric operates in the following areas: aircraft engines (jet engines, replacement parts, and repair services for commercial, military, executive, and commuter aircraft); appliances; broadcasting (NBC); industrial (lighting products, electrical distribution and control equipment, transportation systems products, electric motors and related products, a broad range of electrical and electronic industrial automation products, and a network of electrical supply houses); materials (plastics, ABS resins, silicones, super abrasives, and laminates); power systems (products for the generation, transmission, and distribution of electricity); technical products and systems (medical systems and equipment, as well as a full range of computer-based information and data interchange services for both internal use and external commercial and industrial customers); and capital services (consumer services, financing, specialty insurance, and Kidder, Peabody investment bank and securities broker).

GENERAL ELECTRIC COMPANY
WINCHESTER LAMP PLANT
125 Apple Valley Road, Winchester VA 22602. 703/667-5990. **Contact:** Human Resources. **Description:** Manufactures light bulbs. Overall, General Electric operates in the following areas: aircraft engines (jet engines, replacement parts, and repair services for commercial, military, executive, and commuter aircraft); appliances; broadcasting (NBC); industrial (lighting products, electrical distribution and control equipment, transportation systems products, electric motors and related products, a broad range of electrical and electronic industrial automation products, and a network of electrical supply houses); materials (plastics, ABS resins, silicones, super abrasives, and laminates); power systems (products for the generation, transmission, and distribution of electricity); technical products and systems (medical systems and equipment, as well as a full range of computer-based information and data interchange services for both internal use and external commercial and industrial customers); and capital services (consumer services, financing, specialty insurance, and Kidder, Peabody investment bank and securities broker).

GENERAL KINETICS INC.
14130-C Sullyfield Circle, Chantilly VA 22021-1615. 703/802-9300. **Fax:** 703/818-3706. **Contact:** Mr. Chris Davis, Human Resources. **Description:** A leading designer, producer, and marketer of secure digital facsimile equipment and secure local area networks, principally to the U.S. and foreign governments, through its Secure Communications Division (formerly Cryptek, Inc.) which is also at this location. Secure facsimile equipment utilizes technological safeguards to prevent interception of sensitive communications by unauthorized parties. Through its Electronic Enclosure Division (Johnstown PA and Orlando FL), General Kinetics, founded in 1954, also designs and manufactures precision enclosures for electronic systems, principally for sale to the U.S. Department of Defense and U.S. Navy. Food Technology Corporation (also at this location), a subsidiary of the company, manufactures and distributes food testing equipment and machine vision equipment. **Benefits:** ESOP. **Corporate headquarters location:** This Location. **Listed on:** American Stock Exchange. **Number of employees nationwide:** 122.

HALIFAX CORPORATION
5250 Cherokee Avenue, P.O. Box 11904, Alexandria VA 22312. 703/750-2202. **Fax:** 703/658-2999. **Contact:** Claudette Wassell, Personnel Administration. **Description:** Halifax Corporation is an electronics and facilities support services company, serving U.S. government agencies, systems integrators, financial institutions, and the educational community worldwide since 1967. The company is engaged in the installation, operation, maintenance, and logistics support of equipment, systems, and facilities, ranging from common hardware to technically-sophisticated equipment, such as local area networks, computers, and communications systems. **Common positions include:** Accountant/Auditor; Aerospace Engineer; Buyer; Clerical Supervisor; Computer Programmer; Computer Systems Analyst; Customer Service Representative; Electrical/Electronics Engineer; Electrician; Payroll Clerk; Purchasing Agent and Manager; Quality Control Supervisor; Receptionist; Secretary; Services Sales Representative; Software Engineer; Stationary Engineer. **Educational backgrounds include:** Accounting; Business Administration; Computer Science; Marketing. **Benefits:** 401K; Dental Insurance; Disability Coverage; Employee Discounts; Life Insurance; Medical Insurance; Profit Sharing; Tuition Assistance. **Corporate headquarters location:** This Location. **Other U.S. locations:** Nationwide. **Operations at this facility include:** Administration; Regional Headquarters; Sales; Service. **Listed on:** American Stock Exchange. **Number of employees at this location:** 70. **Number of employees nationwide:** 490.

ITW/PAKTRON
P.O. Box 4539, Lynchburg VA 24502. 804/239-6941. **Contact:** Ms. Terri J. Brown, Human Resources Manager. **Description:** Manufactures film capacitors. **Common positions include:** Accountant/Auditor; Buyer; Computer Programmer; Customer Service Representative; Electrical/Electronics Engineer; Financial Analyst; General Manager; Human Resources Specialist; Industrial Engineer; Manufacturer's/Wholesaler's Sales Rep.; Mechanical Engineer; Operations/Production Manager; Quality Control Supervisor. **Educational backgrounds include:** Accounting; Business Administration; Electronics; Engineering; Marketing; Physics. **Benefits:** Dental Insurance; Disability Coverage; Life Insurance; Medical Insurance; Pension Plan; Savings Plan; Tuition Assistance. **Corporate headquarters location:** Chicago IL. **Operations at this facility include:** Divisional Headquarters; Manufacturing. **Listed on:** New York Stock Exchange.

ISOMET CORPORATION
5263 Port Royal Road, Springfield VA 22151. 703/321-8301. **Fax:** 703/321-8546. **Contact:** Ms. Vanda Gallagher, Controller. **Description:** Designs and manufactures acousto-optic laser control components and electronics for information handling and other applications. Isomet also produces high resolution digital color scanners, laser film recorders, and specialized interface software and electronics packages for color image reproduction markets. **Corporate headquarters location:** This Location. **Subsidiaries include:** Isomet, Ltd. (Wales UK), which markets and services graphic arts equipment in Europe; and Isomet Laser Systems, Ltd. (Wales UK), which markets and services laser control devices in Europe. **Listed on:** NASDAQ. **Number of employees worldwide:** 49.

KOLLMORGEN CORPORATION
INLAND MOTOR DIVISION
501 First Street, Radford VA 24141. 703/639-9045. **Contact:** Velma R. Nester, Human Resources Manager. **Description:** Manufactures DC torque motors, amplifiers, electromechanical actuators and controllers, and other advanced motion control products. **Common positions include:** Accountant/Auditor; Administrator; Aerospace Engineer; Assistant Manager; Blue-Collar Worker Supervisor; Buyer; Computer Programmer; Credit Manager; Customer Service Representative; Department Manager; Draftsperson; Financial Analyst; General Manager; Human Resources Specialist; Industrial Engineer; Industrial Production Manager; Management

Trainee; Manufacturer's/Wholesaler's Sales Rep.; Marketing Specialist; Mechanical Engineer; Operations/Production Manager; Purchasing Agent and Manager; Quality Control Supervisor; Technical Writer/Editor. **Educational backgrounds include:** Accounting; Business Administration; Communications; Computer Science; Engineering; Finance; Marketing; Mathematics. **Benefits:** Dental Insurance; Disability Coverage; Life Insurance; Medical Insurance; Pension Plan; Profit Sharing; Savings Plan; Tuition Assistance. **Corporate headquarters location:** Waltham MA. **Operations at this facility include:** Administration; Divisional Headquarters; Manufacturing; Sales; Service. **Listed on:** New York Stock Exchange. **Number of employees nationwide:** 1,888.

LORAL ADVANCED PROJECTS
P.O. Box 1339, Manassas VA 22110. 703/367-2371. **Contact:** Dr. Keith Higginbotham, Human Resources Director. **Description:** Loral develops advanced concepts for aircraft, maritime and land combat vehicle self-protection systems, precision guided weapons, reconnaissance and surveillance systems, and navigation law applications. Loral performs operations research in support of Loral Corporation product development and concentrates on applications which cut across multiple Loral divisions. The parent company, Loral Corporation, manufactures a wide array of defense electronics technologies which concentrate on six growth businesses: electronic combat, reconnaissance, training, tactical weapons, C3I, and space systems. The defense divisions serve all four branches of the U.S. military, while space systems support NASA, the National Oceanic and Atmospheric Administration, the U.S. Defense Department, and international telecommunication and broadcast companies. **Common positions include:** Electrical/Electronics Engineer; Physicist/Astronomer. **Educational backgrounds include:** Engineering; Physics. **Benefits:** 401K; Daycare Assistance; Dental Insurance; Disability Coverage; Employee Discounts; Life Insurance; Medical Insurance; Pension Plan; Savings Plan; Tuition Assistance. **Corporate headquarters location:** New York NY. **Other U.S. locations:** Nationwide. **Parent company:** Loral Corporation. **Operations at this facility include:** Research and Development. **Listed on:** New York Stock Exchange. **Number of employees at this location:** 10. **Number of employees nationwide:** 40,000.

M&G ELECTRONICS
P.O. Box 8187, Virginia Beach VA 23450. 804/468-6000. **Fax:** 804/468-5442. **Contact:** Margie Outten, Human Resource Manager. **Description:** Assembles wiring harnesses and installs gauges for boat dashboards. **Common positions include:** Accountant/Auditor; Customer Service Representative; Draftsperson; General Manager; Human Resources Specialist; Industrial Production Manager; Inventory Control Specialist; Mechanical Engineer; Operations/Production Manager; Quality Control Supervisor; Sales Representative. **Educational backgrounds include:** Accounting; Business Administration; Computer Science; Engineering. **Benefits:** 401K; Dental Insurance; Disability Coverage; Life Insurance; Medical Insurance. **Corporate headquarters location:** This Location. **Other U.S. locations:** NC; SC. **Operations at this facility include:** Administration; Customer Service; Divisional Headquarters; Manufacturing; Sales. **Listed on:** Privately held. **Number of employees at this location:** 400. **Number of employees nationwide:** 430.

nVIEW CORPORATION
860 Omni Boulevard, Newport News VA 23606. 804/873-1354. **Fax:** 804/873-2153. **Contact:** Marsha Loving, Human Resources Manager. **Description:** nVIEW manufactures and markets devices designed to project high-quality images from personal computers, VCRs, laser disc players, television receivers, and video cameras on standard overhead projectors and in proprietary self-contained projectors. nVIEW's products allow audiences to view computer generated and multimedia images interactively and in real

time for business, educational, entertainment, and other purposes. **Corporate headquarters location:** This Location. **Listed on:** NASDAQ.

POLY-SCIENTIFIC
1213 North Main Street, Blacksburg VA 24060. 540/552-3011. **Contact:** Davis Walker, Human Resource Manager. **Description:** Division of Litton Industries that designs, manufactures and sells electric relays and security devices. Poly-Scientific's relays are used in such objects as radar and helicopters. Their security devices are used in museums and airports. **Number of employees at this location:** 627.

Note: Because addresses and telephone numbers of smaller companies change rapidly, we recommend you call each company to verify the information below before inquiring about job opportunities. Mass mailings are not recommended.

Additional small employers:

TRANSFORMERS

Compact Fluorescent Ballast
245 Capitol Ln, Winchester VA 22602-2441. 540/678-1788.

Murray Electrical Products
Rt 660, Earlysville VA 22936. 804/974-5100.

SWITCHGEAR AND SWITCHBOARD APPARATUS

Pyott-Boone Electronics
PO Box 809, Tazewell VA 24651-0809. 540/988-5505.

ELECTRICAL INDUSTRIAL APPARATUS

Fanuc Automation G E
PO Box 8106, Charlottesvle VA 22906-8106. 804/978-5000.

SMC Electrical Products
PO Box 880, Barboursville WV 25504-0880. 304/736-8933.

ELECTRIC LIGHTING AND WIRING EQUIPMENT

Weidmuller Inc.
821 Southlake Blvd, Richmond VA 23236-3900. 804/794-2877.

Triangle Wire & Cable
1701 Wheeling Ave, Glen Dale WV 26038-1728. 304/845-4020.

Line Power Manufacturing Plant 2
1330 Jani Hammit Dr, Bristol VA 24201-4800. 540/645-8582.

ELECTRICAL EQUIPMENT, MACHINERY, AND SUPPLIES

Hughes Training Inc.
13775 McLearen Rd, Herndon VA 22071-3212. 703/481-4500.

AEROSPACE AND/OR NAUTICAL SYSTEMS AND INSTRUMENTS

Avionics Specialties Inc.
PO Box 6400, Charlottesvle VA 22906-6400. 804/973-3311.

Brunswick Composites
150 Johnston Rd, Marion VA 24354-4324. 540/783-3121.

Quintron Corp.
3901-L Centreville Dr, Chantilly VA 22021. 703/478-2830.

System Planning Corp.
1425 N Quincy St, Arlington VA 22207-3645. 703/351-8700.

ELECTRONIC COMPONENTS AND ACCESSORIES

Eurotherm Circuits Inc.
4230 Lafayette Center Dr, Chantilly VA 22021-1208. 703/968-4533.

Waytec Electronics Corp.
1104 McConville Rd, Lynchburg VA 24502-4534. 804/237-6391.

Federal Pacific Transformer
PO Box 8200, Bristol VA 24203-8200. 540/466-8200.

Barker Microfarads
Mill St, Hillsville VA 24343. 540/728-9121.

ITT Gallium Arsenide Tech
7670 Enon Dr, Roanoke VA 24019-3268. 540/563-8600.

ELECTRICAL EQUIPMENT WHOLESALE

Dominion Electric Supply Company
5053 Lee Hwy, Arlington VA 22207-2582. 703/536-4400.

ECK Supply Co.
1405 W Main St, Richmond VA 23220-4629. 804/359-5781.

Grumman Emergency Products Inc.
1723 Seibel Dr NE, Roanoke VA 24012-5623. 703/982-6666.

State Electric Supply Co.
210 20th St, Huntington WV 25703-1117. 304/523-7491.

Westinghouse Electrical Supply
100 Oakley Ave,

Lynchburg VA 24501-3237. 804/845-0948.

Falk Corporation
601 East Street, South Charleston WV 25303-1545. 304/744-7510.

Ferguson Enterprises Inc.
5268 Olde Towne Road, Williamsburg VA 23188-1924. 804/220-0200.

Moore Products Company
723 Kanawha Blvd E, Charleston WV 25301-2703. 304/343-0307.

Reliance Electric
2807 N Parham Rd, Richmond VA 23294-4410. 804/527-1157.

ELECTRONIC PARTS AND EQUIPMENT WHOLESALE

Communications Specialists
52 Le Way Dr, Fredericksbrg VA 22406-1030. 540/373-4178.

For more information on career opportunities in the electronic/industrial electrical equipment industry:

Associations

AMERICAN CERAMIC SOCIETY
735 Ceramic Place, Westerville OH 43081. 614/890-4700. 800/837-1804. Provides ceramics futures information. Membership required.

ELECTROCHEMICAL SOCIETY
10 South Main Street, Pennington NJ 08534-2896. 609/737-1902. Fax: 609/737-2743. An international society which holds bi-annual meetings internationally and periodic meetings through local sections. Publications include the monthly *Journal of the Electrochemical Society* and the quarterly *Interface.*

ELECTRONICS TECHNICIANS ASSOCIATION
602 North Jackson Street, Greencastle IN 46135. 317/653-8262. Offers published job-hunting advice from the organization's officers and members. Also offers educational material and certification programs.

INSTITUTE OF ELECTRICAL AND ELECTRONICS ENGINEERS (IEEE)
1828 Elm Street NW, Suite 1202, Washington DC 20036-5104. Professional activities line: 202/785-0017. National information line: 202/785-2180.

INSTITUTE OF ELECTRICAL AND ELECTRONICS ENGINEERS (IEEE)
345 East 47th Street, New York NY 10017. 212/705-7900. Toll-free customer service line: 800/678-4333.

ELECTRONIC INDUSTRIES ASSOCIATION
2500 Wilson Boulevard, Arlington VA 22201-3834. 703/907-7500.

INTERNATIONAL BROTHERHOOD OF ELECTRICAL WORKERS
1125 15th Street NW, Washington DC 20005. 202/833-7000. Has over 1,000 apprenticeship programs.

INTERNATIONAL SOCIETY OF CERTIFIED ELECTRONICS TECHNICIANS
2708 West Berry Street, Ft. Worth TX 76109. 817/921-9101.

NATIONAL ELECTRONICS SALES AND SERVICES ASSOCIATION
2708 West Berry, Ft. Worth TX 76109. 817/921-9061. Provides newsletters and directories to members.

SOCIETY OF MANUFACTURING ENGINEERS (SME)
One SME Drive, P.O. Box 930, Dearborn MI 48121. 313/271-1500. Offers a resume database for members.

ENVIRONMENTAL AND WASTE MANAGEMENT SERVICES

According to the Environmental Protection Agency, the increase in environmental awareness over recent decades is more than just a trend. State and national legislation, such as the 1990 amendments to the Clean Air Act, have generated a new range of opportunities in skilled administrative, professional, and technical areas. However, the most critical positions needing to be filled are for scientists and engineers. These two groups develop new solutions to old problems, and therefore are instrumental in the research and development stages.

On the other hand, the current climate in the Congress is significantly cooler towards environmental regulation than in years past. Many members of Congress argue that American business is already overburdened by the federal government, and some propose that the Environmental Protection Agency itself be disbanded.

BFI (BROWNING-FERRIS INDUSTRIES)
P.O. Box 2828, Fairmont WV 26555. 304/366-8900. **Contact:** Mark Osborne, Operations Manager. **Description:** Engaged primarily in the collection and disposal of solid wastes for commercial, industrial, and residential customers. Services provided by Browning-Ferris Industries, Inc. include: landfill services, waste-to-energy programs, hazardous waste removal, and liquid waste removal. The company has worldwide operations at more than 500 facilities.

CLEAN HARBORS ENVIRONMENTAL SERVICES
P.O. Box 1409, Colonial Heights VA 23834. 804/520-0466. **Contact:** Human Resources. **Description:** This location is a regional environmental service center. **Parent company:** Clean Harbors, Inc. through its subsidiaries, provides comprehensive environmental services in 35 states in the Northeast, Midwest, Central, and Mid-Atlantic regions. Clean Harbors provides a wide range of hazardous waste management and environmental support services to a diversified customer base from over 40 locations. The company's hazardous waste management services include treatment, storage, recycling, transportation, risk analysis, site assessment, laboratory analysis, site closure, and disposal of hazardous materials through environmentally sound methods, including incineration. Environmental remediation services include emergency response, surface remediation, ground water restoration, industrial maintenance, and facility decontamination. Customers include nearly 300 of the *Fortune* 500 companies; regional utilities; oil, pharmaceutical, and chemical companies; small businesses, and the high-tech and biotech industries. **Corporate headquarters location:** Quincy MA. **Other U.S. locations:** Nationwide. **Number of employees nationwide:** 1,400.

ETS INTERNATIONAL, INC.
1401 Municipal Road NW, Roanoke VA 24012-1309. 540/265-0004. **Fax:** 540/265-0082. **Contact:** Amy Fulton, Human Resources Coordinator. **Description:** A technology-based firm which provides environmental and infrastructure products and services. ETS International specializes in toxic emission measurement and control as well as infrastructure design,

construction, and maintenance. **Corporate headquarters location:** This Location. **Subsidiaries include:** ETS, Inc. (Roanoke VA, Philadelphia PA, and Taiwan); ETS Analytical Services, Inc. (Roanoke and Richmond VA); and ETS Water and Waste Management, Inc. (Richmond and Fairfax VA). ETS, Inc. offers training, contract research and development, engineering, consulting, regulatory assistance, and field testing. ETS Analytical Services, Inc. is an environmentally-oriented analytical lab serving both government and industry. ETS Water and Waste Management, Inc. is a construction and maintenance service firm providing storm and sewer line, water system and gas line construction, and the design and installation of septic and irrigation systems. **Listed on:** American Stock Exchange. **Number of employees nationwide:** 70.

ICF KAISER INTERNATIONAL, INC.
9300 Lee Highway, Fairfax VA 22031-1207. 703/934-3600. **Contact:** Marian Hyder, Employment Manager. **Description:** One of the nation's largest engineering, construction, and consulting services companies. ICF Kaiser provides fully integrated capabilities to clients worldwide in four related market areas: environment, infrastructure, industry, and energy. The majority of ICF Kaiser professionals study and resolve environmental problems. Projects address issues such as hazardous and radioactive waste cleanup, waste minimization and disposal, risk assessment, permitting, environmental compliance, global climate change and clean air, alternative fuels, ground water contamination, and pollution of harbors and waterways. ICF Kaiser also has extensive experience in the infrastructure and industrial fields. Projects include the design, construction, and management of rapid transit systems, highways, hydroelectric plants, and mining and manufacturing facilities. Foreign locations include: Perth; Taipei; Lisbon; London; Moscow; Paris; Mexico City. **Common positions include:** Biological Scientist/Biochemist; Chemist; Civil Engineer; Computer Programmer; Economist/Market Research Analyst; Electrical/Electronics Engineer; Financial Analyst; Geologist/Geophysicist; Industrial Engineer; Mechanical Engineer; Petroleum Engineer; Physicist/Astronomer; Statistician; Systems Analyst. **Educational backgrounds include:** Biology; Business Administration; Chemistry; Computer Science; Economics; Engineering; Geology; Liberal Arts; Mathematics; Physics. **Benefits:** Dental Insurance; Disability Coverage; Life Insurance; Medical Insurance; Pension Plan; Tuition Assistance. **Corporate headquarters location:** This Location. **Listed on:** New York Stock Exchange. **Number of employees worldwide:** 5,700.

VERSAR, INC.
6850 Versar Center, Springfield VA 22151. 703/750-3000. **Fax:** 703/642-6825. **Contact:** Human Resources. **Description:** Versar is an environmental risk management company that provides a full range of services geared toward the prevention, control and remediation of environmental health and safety problems caused by hazardous materials, toxic substances, or pollutants. Versar operates 14 offices throughout the United States. The company works with its industrial and governmental clients to ensure that they are in compliance with regulations, avoid and reduce liability, solve environmental problems, improve infrastructure, and prevent pollution. Since the company's founding in 1969, it has worked on thousands of commercial and government environmental projects. Versar's services are grouped into three main areas covering the spectrum of environmental services: pollution prevention, compliance management and remedial/corrective action. Management believes that Versar's total environmental risk management services give the company an advantage over its single-focus competitors. **Other U.S. locations:** Tempe AZ; Fair Oaks CA; Alameda CA; Northglenn CO; Hollywood FL; Oak Brook IL; Columbia MD; Eden Prairie MN; Cincinnati OH; Langhorne PA; American Fork UT.

Note: *Because addresses and telephone numbers of smaller companies change rapidly, we recommend you call each company to verify the information below before inquiring about job opportunities. Mass mailings are not recommended.*

Additional small employers:

SANITARY SERVICES

Waste Management VA Blue Ridge
134 Leake Ln, Charlottesville VA 22902-5476. 804/293-8020.

BFI Waste Systems
403 Lenoir Dr, Winchester VA 22603-4605. 540/667-7474.

Browning-Ferris Industries
2490 Charles City Road, Richmond VA 23231-4402. 804/222-7070.

For more information on career opportunities in environmental and waste management services:

__Associations__

AIR & WASTE MANAGEMENT ASSOCIATION
One Gateway Center, Third Floor, Pittsburgh PA 15222. 412/232-3444. A non-profit, technical and educational organization providing a neutral forum where all points of view of an environmental management issue can be addressed.

ASSOCIATION OF STATE & INTERSTATE WATER POLLUTION CONTROL ADMINISTRATORS
750 First Street NE, Suite 910, Washington DC 20002. 202/898-0905. Fax: 202/898-0929. A national, nonpartisan professional organization comprised of government officials. Members implement surface and groundwater protection programs throughout the nation.

INSTITUTE OF CLEAN AIR COMPANIES
1707 L Street NW, Suite 570, Washington DC 20036. 202/457-0911-4201. A national association of companies involved in stationary source air pollution control.

ENVIRONMENTAL INDUSTRY ASSOCIATION
4301 Connecticut Avenue NW, Suite 300, Washington DC 20008. 202/244-4700.

WATER ENVIRONMENT FEDERATION
601 Wythe Street, Alexandria VA 22314. 703/684-2400. Subscription to jobs newsletter required for career information.

__Magazines__

CAREERS AND THE ENGINEER
Adams Media Corporation, 260 Center Street, Holbrook MA 02343. 617/767-8100.

ENVIRONMENTAL CAREER OPPORTUNITIES
1776 I Street NW, Suite 710, Washington DC 20006. A publication that lists career opportunities in the environmental fields. $67 for 12 issues; $127 for 26 issues.

JOURNAL OF AIR AND WASTE MANAGEMENT ASSOCIATION
One Gateway Center, Third Floor, Pittsburgh PA 15222. 412/232-3444.

FABRICATED/PRIMARY METALS AND PRODUCTS

In 1995, the demand for steel dropped from 114 million to 110 million tons, and executives in the industry weren't expecting a turnaround in '96. While the price of structural beams rose, the price for flat-rolled steel -- used in automobiles, for example -- plummeted. Unfortunately, in early 1995, the industry was undergoing a boom in minimill-construction. These new mills may add more capacity to an already glutted market.

ABB POWER T&D COMPANY, INC.
P.O. Box 920, South Boston VA 24592. 804/575-7971. **Contact:** Human Resources. **Description:** A large manufacturing facility for steel fabrication.

ALLEN-MORRISON, INC.
P.O. Box 10245, Lynchburg VA 24506. 804/846-8461. **Contact:** Brown Holston, Director of Human Resources. **Description:** A metal fabricating company. Allen-Morrison uses metal to produce signs and other original equipment for consumers.

ATLAS MACHINE & IRON WORKS INC.
13951 Lee Highway, Gainesville VA 22065. 703/754-4171. **Contact:** Sandra Wince, Administrative Assistant. **Description:** Produces a wide range of fabricated steel plates.

CROWN CORK & SEAL CO.
P.O. Box 2820, Winchester VA 22604. 703/662-2591. **Contact:** Human Resources. **Description:** Manufactures ends of beverage cans.

INCO ALLOYS INTERNATIONAL INC.
3200 Riverside Drive, Huntington WV 25705. 304/526-5100. **Contact:** J.N. Houghton, Human Resources Director. **Description:** Develops, manufactures, and markets high-nickel alloy products in a variety of mill forms. Primary customers are in the following industries: aerospace, marine, petrol-chemical, environmental, and other high-temperature/corrosion applications. **Common positions include:** Accountant/Auditor; Buyer; Chemist; Computer Programmer; Credit Manager; Customer Service Representative; Electrical/Electronics Engineer; Human Resources Specialist; Industrial Production Manager; Manufacturer's/Wholesaler's Sales Rep.; Marketing Specialist; Mechanical Engineer; Metallurgical Engineer; Operations/Production Manager; Purchasing Agent and Manager; Systems Analyst. **Educational backgrounds include:** Accounting; Business Administration; Computer Science; Engineering; Marketing. **Benefits:** Dental Insurance; Disability Coverage; Life Insurance; Medical Insurance; Pension Plan; Profit Sharing; Savings Plan; Tuition Assistance. **Corporate headquarters location:** This Location.

NIBCO, INC.
RR 1, Box 236, Stuarts Draft VA 24477. 703/337-1213. **Contact:** Jimmy Craig, Personnel Manager. **Description:** Manufacturer and distributor of copper fittings. NIBCO, Inc. distributes to both national and international companies. **Number of employees at this location:** 300.

RAVENSWOOD ALUMINUM CORPORATION
Route 2, P.O. Box 98, Ravenswood WV 26164. 304/273-6308. **Fax:** 304/273-6560. **Contact:** Cindy Fairbanks, Human Resources Manager. **Description:** Fabricates aluminum ingots, sheets, and plates. Produces primary aluminum. Recycles used beverage cans. **Common positions include:** Accountant/Auditor; Chemical Engineer; Computer Systems Analyst; Credit Manager; Customer Service Representative; Designer; Draftsperson; Electrical/Electronics Engineer; Electrician; Emergency Medical Technician; Environmental Engineer; Human Resources Specialist; Industrial Engineer; Industrial Production Manager; Licensed Practical Nurse; Materials Engineer; Mechanical Engineer; Metallurgical Engineer; Operations/Production Manager; Purchasing Agent and Manager; Quality Control Supervisor; Registered Nurse; Secretary; Services Sales Representative; Software Engineer; Welder. **Educational backgrounds include:** Accounting; Business Administration; Computer Science; Engineering; Finance; Health Care; Liberal Arts; Marketing; Mathematics; Physics. **Benefits:** 401K; Dental Insurance; Disability Coverage; Employee Discounts; Life Insurance; Medical Insurance; Pension Plan; Profit Sharing; Savings Plan; Tuition Assistance. **Special Programs:** Internships. **Corporate headquarters location:** This Location. **Other U.S. locations:** Bedford IN. **Operations at this facility include:** Administration; Divisional Headquarters; Manufacturing; Regional Headquarters; Research and Development; Sales; Service. **Listed on:** American Stock Exchange. **Number of employees at this location:** 2,000.

REYNOLDS METALS COMPANY
Caverns Boulevard, Grottoes VA 24441. 703/249-5711. **Contact:** Keith Bauer, Human Resource Manager. **Description:** Reynolds Metals Company is a producer of metals and other materials through its worldwide operations. The company primarily functions as an integrated producer of a wide variety of added-value aluminum products. Reynolds Metals also produces certain plastic products to more fully serve key markets. This company's corporate headquarters is located in Richmond, VA. **Number of employees worldwide:** 29,000.

ROANOKE ELECTRIC STEEL CORPORATION
P.O. Box 13948, Roanoke VA 24038. 540/342-1831. **Contact:** Sam Miller, Director of Human Resources. **Description:** Rolling steel mill that distributes its products primarily to service centers which then redistribute the steel. Roanoke Electric Steel Corporation, established in 1955, has two subsidiaries: John W. Hancock in Salem, VA and SOCAR, Inc. with two locations, one in Continental, OH and the other in Florence, SC. Roanoke Electric Steel Corporation owns two companies in Virginia that help with their manufacturing: RESCO Steel, which fabricates the steel for particular industries and Shredded Products, Inc., which recycles scrap metal from automobiles. **Number of employees in this location:** 750.

STEEL OF WEST VIRGINIA
P.O. Box 2547, Huntington WV 25726. 304/696-8200. **Contact:** Larry Gue, Personnel Director. **Description:** Fabricates mine beams, rail, steel mine ties and other locomotive-related products.

STERLING PLUMBING GROUP, INC.
P.O. Box 798, Morgantown WV 26507-0798. 304/292-6391. **Contact:** Sid Devaul, Manager of Materials and Personnel. **Description:** Manufactures plumbing fixture fittings. **Common positions include:** Accountant/Auditor; Blue-Collar Worker Supervisor; Buyer; Computer Programmer; Department Manager; Draftsperson; General Manager; Human Resources Specialist; Industrial Engineer; Mechanical Engineer; Operations/Production Manager; Purchasing Agent and Manager; Quality Control Supervisor; Systems Analyst. **Educational backgrounds include:** Accounting; Business Administration; Computer Science; Engineering; Finance; Liberal Arts. **Benefits:** Dental Insurance; Disability Coverage; Employee Discounts; Life Insurance; Medical Insurance; Pension Plan; Savings Plan; Tuition

Assistance; Vision Insurance. **Special Programs:** Internships. **Corporate headquarters location:** Schaumburg IL. **Parent company:** Kohler. **Operations at this facility include:** Manufacturing.

WALKER SYSTEMS, INC.
A WIRE MOLD COMPANY
620 Depot Street, Parkersburg WV 26101. 304/485-1611. **Contact:** Don Beaver, Human Resources. **Description:** Manufactures metal products. **Number of employees at this location:** 300.

WEIRTON STEEL
400 Three Springs Drive, Weirton WV 26062. 304/797-2000. **Contact:** Jeff Robinson, Recruiting and Staffing Manager. **Description:** An integrated manufacturer of flat-rolled carbon steel and tin for the construction, automotive, food and beverage, electrical, container, appliance, service center, and commercial equipment markets. The company also sells its products to other steel milling companies. Weirton Steel's subsidiary, Crown Cork & Seal Company, is a major U.S. can producer. **Listed on:** New York Stock Exchange.

WHEELING MACHINE TOOL
98 Peninsula Street, Wheeling WV 26003. 304/234-9600. **Contact:** Director of Personnel. **Description:** A manufacturer of cast iron and steel rolls for use in steel mills. **Common positions include:** Accountant/Auditor; Advertising Clerk; Blue-Collar Worker Supervisor; Buyer; Computer Programmer; Draftsperson; Electrical/Electronics Engineer; Financial Analyst; Human Resources Specialist; Industrial Engineer; Manufacturer's/Wholesaler's Sales Rep.; Mechanical Engineer; Metallurgical Engineer; Purchasing Agent and Manager; Quality Control Supervisor; Systems Analyst; Transportation/Traffic Specialist. **Educational backgrounds include:** Accounting; Business Administration; Computer Science; Engineering; Finance; Marketing. **Benefits:** Dental Insurance; Disability Coverage; Employee Discounts; Life Insurance; Medical Insurance; Pension Plan; Tuition Assistance. **Operations at this facility include:** Manufacturing.

WHEELING-PITTSBURGH STEEL COMPANY
1134 Market Street, Wheeling WV 26003. 304/234-2526. **Contact:** James G. Bronchik, Director of Human Resources. **Description:** Integrated producer of flat rolled, tin coated, galvanized and corrugated steel products. **Common positions include:** Accountant/Auditor; Administrator; Attorney; Blue-Collar Worker Supervisor; Buyer; Chemical Engineer; Chemist; Civil Engineer; Claim Representative; Computer Programmer; Computer Systems Analyst; Credit Manager; Department Manager; Draftsperson; Electrical/Electronics Engineer; Financial Analyst; General Manager; Human Resources Specialist; Industrial Engineer; Industrial Production Manager; Management Trainee; Manufacturer's/Wholesaler's Sales Rep.; Marketing Specialist; Mechanical Engineer; Metallurgical Engineer; Operations/Production Manager; Public Relations Specialist; Purchasing Agent and Manager; Quality Control Supervisor; Systems Analyst. **Educational backgrounds include:** Accounting; Business Administration; Chemistry; Computer Science; Engineering; Finance; Marketing. **Benefits:** Dental Insurance; Disability Coverage; Life Insurance; Medical Insurance; Pension Plan. **Corporate headquarters location:** This Location. **Other U.S. locations:** AL; KS; NC; OH; PA; TX. **Parent company:** WHX Corporation. **Operations at this facility include:** Administration; Manufacturing; Sales; Service. **Listed on:** New York Stock Exchange. **Number of employees at this location:** 5,500.

Note: *Because addresses and telephone numbers of smaller companies change rapidly, we recommend you call each company to verify the information below before inquiring about job opportunities. Mass mailings are not recommended.*

Additional small employers:

WHOLESALE METALS SERVICE CENTERS AND OFFICES

NB Handy Co.
PO Box 11258, Lynchburg VA 24506-1258. 804/847-4495.

Steel Services Inc.
7231 Forest Ave, Ste 100, Richmond VA 23226-3793. 804/673-3810.

STEEL WORKS, BLAST FURNACES, AND ROLLING MILLS

American Longwall Face Conveyor
26161 Old Trail Rd, Abingdon VA 24210-7631. 540/628-4141.

Midwest Corp.
PO Box 271, Charleston WV 25321-0271. 304/343-8874.

ELECTROMETALLURGICAL PRODUCTS

American Alloys Inc.
PO Box 218, New Haven WV 25265-0218. 304/882-3248.

STEEL WIRE, NAILS, AND SPIKES

Teleflex Automotive Group
Rt 71, Lebanon VA 24266. 540/889-0041.

STEEL SHEET, STRIP, AND BARS

Follansbee Steel
State St, Follansbee WV 26037. 304/527-1260.

IRON AND STEEL FOUNDRIES

Bingham & Taylor Corp.
Nalle Pl, Culpeper VA 22701. 540/825-8334.

Dominion Metallurgical
310 5th St, Lynchburg VA 24504-1316. 804/847-8309.

Virginia Metalcrafters
1010 E Main St, Waynesboro VA 22980-5855. 540/949-9400.

Howmet Hampton Casting
1 Howmet Dr, Hampton VA 23661-1333. 804/825-6800.

Graham-White Manufacturing Co.
1242 S Colorado St, Salem VA 24153-6931. 540/387-5600.

ALUMINUM

Alcan Rolled Products
1800 Speedway St, Fairmont WV 26554-3350. 304/367-5000.

SMELTING AND REFINING OF NONFERROUS METALS

Elkem Metals Co.
Rt 60, Alloy WV 25002. 304/779-3200.

Peck Recycling Co.
3220 Deepwater Terminal Rd, Richmond VA 23234-1827. 804/232-5601.

NONFERROUS ROLLING AND DRAWING OF METALS

Howell Metal Co. Inc.
Rte 728, New Market VA 22844. 540/740-3111.

Westinghouse Electric Corp.
18259 Westinghouse Road, Abingdon VA 24210-7931. 540/676-9100.

Hapco Division Kearney National
26252 Hillman Hwy, Abingdon VA 24210-7616. 540/628-7171.

Reynolds Metals Co.
750 Old Abingdon Highway, Bristol VA 24201-1847. 540/466-2261.

Reynolds Metals Co.
1701 Reymet Rd, Richmond VA 23237-3727. 804/743-6700.

Keller Aluminum Products Of VA
Rt 640, Milford VA 22514. 804/633-5061.

Neuman USA Ltd
Laurel Hill Rd, Verona VA 24482. 540/248-2703.

DIE-CASTINGS

North American Die Casting
1104 Summit St, Fredericksbrg VA 22401-7033. 540/371-9220.

Reynolds Metals Co.
1711 Reymet Rd, Richmond VA 23237-3727. 804/743-6578.

ALUMINUM FOUNDRIES

Berkley Machine Works & Foundry
703 Pearl St, Norfolk VA 23523-1041. 804/545-3561.

NONFERROUS FOUNDRIES

Sheidow Bronze Corp.
125 Sisler St, Kingwood WV 26537-1026. 304/329-1105.

PRIMARY METAL PRODUCTS

Morton International Inc.
2460 N 4th St, Wytheville VA 24382-4418. 540/228-1500.

Sexton Can Co.
Fairfax Av, Martinsburg WV 25401. 304/267-8923.

METAL CONTAINERS

Ball Metal Beverage Container
8935 Pocahontas Trail, Williamsburg VA 23185-6249. 804/887-2061.

FABRICATED STRUCTURAL METAL PRODUCTS

Atlantic Industrial Constructors Inc.
4500 Oakleys Ln,

Richmond VA 23231-2912. 804/222-3400.

Globe Iron Construction
1401 Maltby Ave, Norfolk VA 23504-2997. 804/625-2542.

Hirschfeld Steel Co.
300 Rangoon Rd, Lynchburg VA 24502-3599. 804/239-6650.

John W. Hancock Jr. Inc.
2535 Diuguids Ln, Salem VA 24153-2272. 540/389-0211.

Jonathan Corp.
5898 Thurston Ave, Virginia Beach VA 23455-3307. 804/363-0880.

Raleigh Mine & Industrial Supplies
Mill Creek Rd, Mount Hope WV 25880. 304/877-5503.

Wheeling Corrugating Co.
Rte 2 Box 37, Beech Bottom WV 26030. 304/234-4275.

General Products Co. Inc.
3000 Mine Rd, Fredericksbrg VA 22408-0218. 540/898-5700.

Rusco Window Of Roanoke
3631 Aerial Way Dr SW, Roanoke VA 24018-1507. 540/345-4901.

Simonton Windows
1 Cochrane Dr, Pennsboro WV 26415-9404. 304/659-2851.

West Window Corp.
Martinsville Industrial Pk, Martinsville VA 24112. 540/638-2394.

Adamson Co. Inc.
13200 Ramblewood Dr, Chester VA 23831-5527. 804/748-6453.

Alfa Laval Thermal Inc.
5400 International Trade Dr, Richmond VA 23231-2927. 804/222-5300.

Huntington Piping Inc.
PO Box 1568, Huntington WV 25716-1568. 304/525-7868.

Manchester Tank & Equipment Co.
23209 Airpark Dr, Petersburg VA 23803-6931. 804/732-9157.

Reco Industries Inc.
PO Box 25189, Richmond VA 23260-5189. 804/644-2611.

Rockwell International
1745 Jefferson Davis Hwy, Arlington VA 22202-3402. 703/553-6600.

Wexco Corp.
1015 Dillard Dr, Lynchburg VA 24502. 804/385-6006.

Lofton Corp.
Rt 666 E, Greenville VA 24440. 540/377-3200.

Riddleberger Brothers Inc.
Rt 11 N, Mt Crawford VA 22841. 540/434-1731.

Parkline Inc.
Eleanor Industrial Pk, Eleanor WV 25070. 304/586-2113.

METAL FORGINGS

Cerro Metal Products Co.
300 Triangle Dr, Weyers Cave VA 24486. 540/234-9251.

METAL STAMPINGS

Litton Poly-Scientific
1213 N Main St, Blacksburg VA 24060-3100. 540/552-3011.

COATING, ENGRAVING, AND ALLIED SERVICES

Bontex
1 Bontex Dr, Buena Vista VA 24416-1500. 540/261-2181.

FABRICATED WIRE PRODUCTS

Rochester Corp.
751 Old Brandy Rd, Culpeper VA 22701-2866. 540/825-2111.

FABRICATED METAL PRODUCTS

Kanawha Manufacturing Co.
PO Box 1786, Charleston WV 25326-1786. 304/342-6127.

Tread Corp.
1764 Granby St NE, Roanoke VA 24012-5694. 703/982-6881.

For more information on career opportunities in the fabricated/primary metals and products industries:

Magazines

AMERICAN METAL MARKET
25 7th Avenue, New York NY 10019. 212/887-8580.

IRON AGE NEW STEEL
191 South Gary, Carol Stream IL 60188. 708/462-2285.

IRON & STEEL ENGINEER
Association of Iron and Steel Engineers, Three Gateway Center, Suite 2350, Pittsburgh PA 15222. 412/281-6323.

MODERN METALS
625 North Michigan Avenue, Suite 2500, Chicago IL 60611. 312/654-2300.

Associations

AMERICAN FOUNDRYMEN'S SOCIETY
505 State Street, Des Plaines IL 60016-847/824-0181.

AMERICAN WELDING SOCIETY
550 LeJeune Road NW, Miami FL 33126. 305/443-9353.

ASM INTERNATIONAL: THE MATERIALS INFORMATION SOCIETY
Materials Park OH 44073. 800/336-5152. Gathers, processes, and disseminates technical information to foster the understanding and application of engineered materials.

Directories

DIRECTORY OF STEEL FOUNDRIES IN THE UNITED STATES, CANADA, AND MEXICO
Steel Founder's Society of America, 455 State Street, Des Plaines IL 60016. 847/299-9160.

FINANCIAL SERVICES

You can't get much better than 1995. The stock market soared throughout the year, boosting business at brokerage houses. And, although the market isn't expected to be as hot in '96, it appears likely that the Federal Reserve will lower interest rates, putting the pieces into place for another solid year.

Jobseekers who have experience with mergers and acquisitions should benefit. At the same time, expect more consolidation among brokerage houses themselves. Analysts believe that the largest houses will get larger and the small boutique firms will continue to prosper, but the firms in the middle may get crunched.

CAPITAL ONE FINANCIAL CORPORATION
2980 Fairview Park Drive, Suite 1300, Falls Church VA 22042. 703/205-1000. **Contact:** Liza Wright, Management Recruiter. **Description:** A financial services company whose primary business is offering credit card products. With approximately 5 million accounts, Capital One is among the largest credit card issuers in the United States. The company was established as an independent corporation in late 1994, after 41 years as the credit card division of Signet Bank/Virginia. Capital One has begun to market nationally a customized array of secured cards, college student cards, joint account cards, and affinity offers. The company has also begun to explore opportunities outside of the credit card industry, including both lending and non-lending consumer financial services. **Benefits:** Pension Plan; Stock Option. **Corporate headquarters location:** This Location. **Other U.S. locations:** Fredericksburg VA; Richmond VA. **Subsidiaries include:** Capital One Bank. **Listed on:** New York Stock Exchange. **Number of employees nationwide:** 2,600.

FEDERAL HOME LOAN MORTGAGE CORPORATION
8250 Jones Branch Drive, McLean VA 22102. 703/903-2000. **Contact:** Candice Mendenhall, Senior Vice President of Human Resources. **Description:** In 1970, the U.S. government established the Federal Home Loan Mortgage Corporation, nicknamed Freddie Mac, to increase mortgage credit for housing. The company now provides secondary mortgages. **NOTE:** Ms. Mendenhall can be reached at 703/918-5390. **Listed on:** New York Stock Exchange.

THE FINANCE COMPANY
MID-ATLANTIC REGIONAL SERVICE CENTER
5425 Robin Hood Road, Suite 101A, Norfolk VA 23513. 804/858-1400. **Fax:** 804/858-6393. **Contact:** Nancy Hawkins, Human Resources Director. **Description:** Engaged primarily in buying and servicing installment contracts originated by used car dealers. Most of The Finance Company's income comes from interest charged on contracts and from the discounts at which it purchases contracts. The company also receives revenue from the commissions received on ancillary products, such as credit insurance, limited physical damage insurance, and product warranties offered by the company and underwritten by third-party vendors. **Corporate headquarters location:** This Location. **Parent company:** TFC Enterprises.

THE FINANCE COMPANY
7000 Infantry Ridge Road, Manassas VA 23110. 703/361-1699. **Fax:** 703/361-7023. **Contact:** Sandy Rabatin, Human Resources. **Description:** Engaged primarily in buying and servicing installment contracts originated by

used car dealers. Most of The Finance Company's income comes from interest charged on contracts and from the discounts at which it purchases contracts. The company also receives revenue from the commissions received on ancillary products, such as credit insurance, limited physical damage insurance, and product warranties offered by the company and underwritten by third-party vendors. **Corporate headquarters location:** Norfolk VA. **Other U.S. locations:** Jacksonville FL; Dallas TX. **Parent company:** TFC Enterprises.

LEGG MASON
P.O. Box 9700, McLean VA 22102. 703/821-9100. **Contact:** Dianna Rodgers, Office Manager. **Description:** Legg Mason is a holding company with subsidiaries engaged in securities brokerage and trading; investment management of mutual funds and individual and institutional accounts; underwriting of corporate and municipal securities and other investment banking activities; sales of annuity and banking; and the provision of other financial services. The company's principal units are Baltimore-based Legg Mason, Wood Walker, and New Orleans-based Howard, Weil, Labouisse, Friedrichs, Inc. The company serves its brokerage clients through 86 offices. As investment advisors, they manage more than $16 billion in assets for individual and institutional accounts and mutual funds. The company's mortgage banking subsidiaries have direct and master servicing responsibilities for $12 billion of commercial mortgages. **Number of employees nationwide:** 2,400.

NATIONAL RURAL UTILITIES COOPERATIVE FINANCE CORPORATION
Woodland Park, 2201 Cooperative Way, Herndon VA 22071-3025. 703/709-6700. **Contact:** Human Resources. **Description:** A not-for-profit financial institution owned by more than 1,000 rural electric systems and related organizations. National Rural Utilities Cooperative Finance Corporation offers its member-owners a variety of loan, investment, member service, and specialized financing options to supplement the loan programs of the Rural Utilities Service of the United States Department of Agriculture. The company operates through 11 regional representatives located throughout the United States. The company also has two controlled affiliates, Rural Telephone Finance Cooperative and Guaranty Funding Cooperative. **Corporate headquarters location:** This Location. **Number of employees nationwide:** 1,039.

SCOTT & STRINGFELLOW, INC.
909 East Main Street, Richmond VA 23219. 804/643-1811. **Toll-free phone:** 800/552-7757 in VA; 800/446-7075 out of state. **Contact:** Jordan Ball, Manager. **Description:** A full-service regional brokerage and investment banking firm. Services of Scott & Stringfellow include investment advice and brokerage for individual and institutional clients, investment banking and securities underwriting for corporations and municipalities, and a wide array of other investment-related financial services including investment advisory services through its affiliate, Scott & Stringfellow Capital Management, Inc. Scott & Stringfellow has 27 offices located in Virginia (19), North Carolina (7), and West Virginia (1). **Corporate headquarters location:** This Location. **Parent company:** Scott & Stringfellow Financial, Inc. (this location). **Listed on:** New York Stock Exchange. **Number of employees nationwide:** 475.

SCOTT & STRINGFELLOW, INC.
105 Law & Commerce Building, Bluefield WV 24701. 304/325-3631. **Toll-free phone:** 800/733-0850. **Contact:** John E. Biggs III, Manager. **Description:** A full-service regional brokerage and investment banking firm. Services of Scott & Stringfellow include investment advice and brokerage for individual and institutional clients, investment banking and securities underwriting for corporations and municipalities, and a wide array of other investment-related financial services including investment advisory services through its affiliate, Scott & Stringfellow Capital Management, Inc. Scott & Stringfellow has 27 offices located in Virginia (19), North Carolina (7), and West Virginia (this

location). **Corporate headquarters location:** Richmond VA. **Parent company:** Scott & Stringfellow Financial, Inc. (Richmond VA). **Listed on:** New York Stock Exchange. **Number of employees nationwide:** 475.

Note: *Because addresses and telephone numbers of smaller companies change rapidly, we recommend you call each company to verify the information below before inquiring about job opportunities. Mass mailings are not recommended.*

Additional small employers:

CREDIT AGENCIES AND INSTITUTIONS

Amsouth Mortgage Company Inc.
2809 S Lynnhaven Rd, Virginia Beach VA 23452-6700. 804/463-8100.

Associates Financial Services
1900 Rio Hill Ctr, Charlottesvle VA 22901-1142. 804/973-8388.

Auto Credit Of Virginia
603 J Clyde Morris Blvd, Ste 5, Newport News VA 23601-1826. 804/591-1022.

Beach Fed Mortgage Corp.
860 Greenbrier Cir, Chesapeake VA 23320-2640. 804/366-8900.

Blazer Financial Services
316 S Virginia Ave, Collinsville VA 24078-2302. 540/647-3865.

Chevy Chase Bank
5238 Valleypointe Pky, Roanoke VA 24019-3066. 540/265-5626.

Equity One
4411 Plank Rd, Fredericksbrg VA 22407-4809. 540/785-0074.

GM Credit Co.
6530 E Virginia Beach Blvd, Norfolk VA 23502-3012. 804/499-7520.

Household Finance Corporation
10780 Sudley Manor Dr, Manassas VA 22110-2833. 703/361-9191.

Public Finance Corp.
214 Broad St, Charleston WV 25301-2483. 304/343-7528.

Public Finance Corp.
316 7th Ave SW, S Charleston WV 25303-1248. 304/744-4576.

Household Finance Corporation
Plaza At Landmark, Annandale VA 22003. 703/658-4604.

Mercury Finance Company
8075 W Broad St, Richmond VA 23294-4219. 804/270-3336.

Mortgage Company Of Virginia
4 Commonwealth Blvd E, Martinsville VA 24112-1920. 540/632-9431.

FBO Funding
1446 Kempsville Rd, Ste 204A, Virginia Beach VA 23464-7300. 804/495-5968.

American General Finance
5 The Koger Ctr, Norfolk VA 23502. 804/461-5737.

American Home Funding Operating Office
2812 Emerywood Pky, Richmond VA 23294-3718. 804/756-6800.

Associates Financial Services
4300 Plank Rd Apt 210, Fredericksbrg VA 22407-0102. 540/786-0085.

Loan Offices
9030 Stony Point Parkway, Richmond VA 23235-1936. 804/323-0046.

Bank Card Center
11013 W Broad St, Glen Allen VA 23060-5937. 804/747-2000.

CIT Commercial Services
134 Wooding Ave, Danville VA 24541-3763. 804/791-6200.

MORTGAGE BANKERS

Atlantic Coast Mortgage Company
5041 Corporate Woods Dr, Ste 15, Virginia Beach VA 23462-4375. 804/497-1000.

Atlantic Coast Mortgage Company
12700 Fair Lakes Cir, Fairfax VA 22033-4905. 703/631-0098.

BA Mortgage
2810 N Parham Rd, Richmond VA 23294-4400. 804/762-5000.

Beach Fed Mortgage Corp.
9030 Stony Point Pky, Richmond VA 23235-1936. 804/330-8300.

Columbia First Mortgage
1950 Old Gallows Rd, Ste 100, Vienna VA 22182-3933. 703/506-1700.

Crestar Mortgage Corporation
7617 Little River Tpke, Annandale VA 22003-2603. 703/813-4000.

Developers Mortgage Corp.
11320 Random Hills Rd, Fairfax VA 22030-6001. 703/691-0222.

First Fidelity Mortgage
161 John Jefferson Rd,

Williamsburg VA 23185-5640. 804/221-8249.

First Home Mortgage Corp.
7231 Forest Ave, Ste 303, Richmond VA 23226-3793. 804/288-8400.

First Investment Company
1100 9th St, Vienna WV 26105-2176. 304/295-6612.

First Washington Mortgage Corp.
7611 Little River Tpke, Annandale VA 22003-2602. 703/642-2400.

Heritage Savings & Loan Association
10th & Main St, Richmond VA 23219. 804/643-0162.

ICM Mortgage Corp.
10600 Arrowhead Dr, Ste 250, Fairfax VA 22030-7306. 703/934-9350.

Inland Mortgage Corp.
1238 Holland Rd, Ste 111, Suffolk VA 23434-6313. 804/925-4900.

Mid-Atlantic Financial Group
717 N Courthouse Rd, Richmond VA 23236-4061. 804/794-7665.

Market Street Mortgage Corp.
7700 Little River Tpke, Annandale VA 22003-2406. 703/941-6600.

Saxon Mortgage Management Corp.
4101 Cox Rd, Glen Allen VA 23060-3320. 804/273-6700.

Southern National Mortgage Service
1520 Huguenot Rd, Midlothian VA 23113-2477. 804/378-5415.

The Mortgage Authority
12150 Monument Dr, Fairfax VA 22033-4051. 703/352-3133.

Town & Country Mortgage
3018 Javier Rd, Fairfax VA 22031-4609. 703/573-0770.

SECURITY BROKERS AND DEALERS

Derand Corp. Of America
2201 Wilson Blvd, Ste 300, Arlington VA 22201-3323. 703/247-2900.

Eagle Corp.
1020 Harris St, Charlottesvle VA 22903-5315. 804/971-2686.

Hannon Armstrong and Company
112 S Alfred St, Alexandria VA 22314-3061. 703/684-7776.

JC Bradford & Co.
202 S Jefferson St, Roanoke VA 24011-1702. 703/982-0017.

AG Edwards & Sons Inc.
208 W Main St, Tazewell VA 24651-1034. 540/988-3323.

AMI Marketing Inc.
8260 Greensboro Dr, McLean VA 22102-3806. 703/506-5059.

Davenport & Co. Of Virginia
161 John Jefferson Rd, Williamsburg VA 23185-5640. 804/220-3310.

Edward D. Jones & Co.
514 E Atlantic St, South Hill VA 23970-2704. 804/447-3399.

Edward D. Jones & Co.
107 Loudoun St SE, Leesburg VA 22075. 703/771-1931.

Edward D. Jones & Co.
617 Market St, Parkersburg WV 26101-5145. 304/422-3919.

Edward D. Jones & Co.
120 W Grayson St, Galax VA 24333-2810. 540/236-4191.

REAL ESTATE INVESTMENT TRUSTS

The Great Atlantic Companies
2 Eaton St, Ste 1100, Hampton VA 23669-4054. 804/722-5211.

For more information on career opportunities in financial services:

<u>**Associations**</u>

FINANCIAL EXECUTIVES INSTITUTE
P.O. Box 1938, Morristown NJ 07962-1938. 201/898-4600. Fee and membership required. Publishes biennial member directory. Provides member referral service.

INSTITUTE OF FINANCIAL EDUCATION
111 East Wacker Drive, Chicago IL 60601. 312/946-8800. Offers career development program.

NATIONAL ASSOCIATION OF BUSINESS ECONOMISTS
1233 20th Street NW, Suite 505, Washington DC 20036. 202/463-6223. Bulletin board number: 216/241-6254. Newsletter and electronic bulletin board list job openings. Members can upload resumes and listed positions desired to bulletin board.

NATIONAL ASSOCIATION OF CREDIT MANAGEMENT
8815 Centre Park Drive, Suite 200, Columbia MD 21045-2158. 410/740-5560. Contact: Delores Richman. Publishes a business credit magazine.

NATIONAL ASSOCIATION OF REAL ESTATE INVESTMENT TRUSTS
1129 20th Street NW, Suite 305, Washington DC 20036. 202/785-

8717. Contact: Donna Smith, Membership.

PUBLIC SECURITIES ASSOCIATION
40 Broad Street, 12th Floor, New York NY 10004. 212/809-7000. Contact: Caroline Binn x427. Publishes an annual report and several newsletters.

SECURITIES INDUSTRY ASSOCIATION
120 Broadway, 35th Floor New York NY 10271. 212/608-1500. Contact: Phil Williams/Membership. Publishes a security industry yearbook.

TREASURY MANAGEMENT ASSOCIATION
7315 Wisconsin Avenue, Suite 1250-W, Bethesda MD 20814. 301/907-2862.

Directories

DIRECTORY OF AMERICAN FINANCIAL INSTITUTIONS
Thomson Business Publications, 6195 Crooked Creek Road, Norcross GA 30092. 770/448-1011. Sales 800/321-3373.

MOODY'S BANK AND FINANCE MANUAL
Moody's Investor Service, 99 Church Street, New York NY 10007. 212/553-0300.

Magazines

BARRON'S: NATIONAL BUSINESS AND FINANCIAL WEEKLY
Dow Jones & Co., 200 Liberty Street, New York NY 10281. 212/416-2700.

FINANCIAL PLANNING
40 West 57th Street, 11th Floor, New York NY 10019. 212/765-5311.

FINANCIAL WORLD
Financial World Partners, 1328 Broadway, 3rd Floor, New York NY 10001. 212/594-5030.

FUTURES: THE MAGAZINE OF COMMODITIES AND OPTIONS
250 South Wacker Drive, Suite 1150, Chicago IL 60606. 312/977-0999.

INSTITUTIONAL INVESTOR
488 Madison Avenue, 12th Floor, New York NY 10022. 212/303-3300.

FOOD AND BEVERAGES/AGRICULTURE

Employment in food processing is expected to fall slightly through 2005. Although the industry's output should grow, increasing automation and productivity will mean food can be produced with fewer workers. However, some food processing industries are likely to remain fairly labor intensive. For example, meat packing and poultry processing are difficult to fully automate because each animal processed is different. Professional specialty occupations, although small in number, are also expected to grow. The growth of these occupations -- including engineers, systems analysts, and food scientists -- reflects the industry's emphasis on scientific research to improve food products and production processes. Demand for food scientists will also grow in response to expanding government inspection and regulation of food production.

Several factors may slow the decline in food processing employment. As consumers increasingly seek 'ready-to-heat' foods, the food processing industry has introduced many new products. Many of these new goods, which require more processing than the items they are replacing, will help maintain the demand for food processors in the future. In addition, the food processing industry is taking advantage of new technology to perform much of the processing formerly done by retailers. One other factor that may help stem employment decline is growing international trade in food products. Food processing firms expect growing trade to provide new markets for their products. The emerging field of biotechnology and other new food science technologies may also provide new jobs.

AMPRO FISHERIES, INC.
P.O. Box 319, Reedville VA 22539. 804/453-3808. **Contact:** Jeanette Cralle, Human Resources Representative. **Description:** Manufactures Manhaden fish meal, fish oil, and fish products.

ANHEUSER-BUSCH INC.
7801 Pocahontas Trail, Williamsburg VA 23185. 804/253-3600. **Contact:** Human Resources. **Description:** This location is a beer brewing facility. Anheuser-Busch is a diverse company which is involved in the entertainment, brewing, baking, and manufacturing industries. The company is one of the largest domestic brewers, operating 13 breweries throughout the U.S. and distributing through over 900 independent wholesalers. Beer brands include Budweiser, Michelob, Busch, King Cobra, and O'Doul's non-alcoholic beverages. Related businesses include can manufacturing, paper printing, and barley malting. Anheuser-Busch is also one of the largest operators of amusement parks in the U.S., with locations in Florida, Virginia, Texas, Ohio, and California. Through subsidiary Campbell Taggart Inc., Anheuser-Busch is also one of the largest commercial baking companies in the United States, producing foods under Eagle Snacks, Cape Cod, and Colonial brand names, among others. Anheuser-Busch also has real estate interests.

BIRDSONG CORPORATION
P.O. Box 1400, Suffolk VA 23439. 804/539-3456. **Contact:** Human Resources. **Description:** A wholesaler of raw peanuts.

BOAR'S HEAD PROVISION CO., INC.
P.O. Box 277, Jarratt VA 23867. 804/535-8581. **Contact:** Robin Patrick, Human Resources Manager. **Description:** This location is a primarily a production plant. Boar's Head Provision Co., Inc. produces a variety of deli products, including ham, beef, bologna, hot dogs, and salami.

COMMONWEALTH BROKERS INC.
Ten North Leadbetter Road, Ashland VA 23005-3295. 804/798-1428. **Contact:** Human Resources. **Description:** A food service brokerage firm, which acts as a middleman between food manufacturers and food distributors.

COORS BREWING COMPANY
P.O. Box 25, Elkton VA 22827. 703/289-8000. **Contact:** Human Resources. **Description:** A packaging facility. Coors Brewing Company, the only subsidiary of Adolph Coors Company, is the third-largest brewer in the United States. The company's largest selling brand, Coors Light, is the fourth best-selling beer nationwide. In addition, through its UniBev Limited division, Coors is the only major brewer currently producing and marketing a seasonal line of hand-crafted specialty beers. Other brands also include Zima Clearmalt, a clear, lightly carbonated alcohol beverage, and Killian's Irish Red, which has become the largest selling specialty beer in America. In total Coors now brews 16 quality malt beverages, up from just one in 1977. At the end of 1992, the company spun off a number of non-brewing activities that make up the operations of ACX Technologies, Inc. ACX operates through the following companies: Golden Aluminum Company, Graphic Packaging Corporation, Coors BioTech Inc., Coors Energy Company, Golden Technologies Company, Inc., and Coors Ceramics.

DIMON INC.
512 Bridge Street, P.O. Box 681, Danville VA 24543-0681. 804/792-7511. **Contact:** Norma Lutz, Human Resources Director. **Description:** Founded in 1995 upon the merger of Dibrell Brothers, Inc. of Danville, Virginia and Monk-Austin, Inc. of Farmville, North Carolina, DIMON is operates two international businesses -- purchasing, processing, packing and storing tobacco and importing and distributing fresh-cut flowers.

ESKIMO PIE CORPORATION
901 Moorefield Park Drive, P.O. Box 26906, Richmond VA 23261. 804/560-8400. **Fax:** 804/330-3537. **Contact:** Robert Staples, Director of Personnel. **Description:** Eskimo Pie Corporation markets a broad range of frozen novelty, frozen yogurt, and frozen dairy dessert products under the brand names Eskimo Pie, Sugar Creek, Welch's, Weight Watchers, and 7UP. The company has plans to develop and market products utilizing various Nabisco cookie brand trademarks. Eskimo Pie Corporation also manufactures and markets Sugar Creek and Eskimo Pie brand soft-serve frozen yogurt mix, and various ingredients and packaging for the dairy industry. **Benefits:** Retirement Plan; Stock Option. **Corporate headquarters location:** This Location. **Other U.S. locations:** Los Angeles CA; Bloomfield NJ; New Berlin WI. **Listed on:** NASDAQ. **Number of employees nationwide:** 182.

HERSHEY CHOCOLATE USA
P.O. Box 1028, Stuarts Draft VA 24477. 703/337-4700. **Contact:** Employee Relations. **Description:** Manufactures Hershey chocolates. Parent company Hershey Foods makes and sells a wide selection of confectionery, chocolate, and pasta products with over 50 brands marketed throughout the world. The company operates through the following primary segments: Hershey Chocolate USA, Hershey International, Hershey Pasta Group, and Hershey Canada Inc. Brands of confections include Kit Kat, Mr. Goodbar, Reese's, Rolo, Twizzlers, Skor, and Kisses. Pasta brands include Ronzoni, Skinner, P&R, Light 'n Fluffy, and American Beauty. **NOTE:** Please call for application procedure. **Parent company:** Hershey Foods.

HESTER INDUSTRIES INC.
104 South Main Street, Moorefield WV 26836. 304/538-2381. **Contact:** Greg Gaynor, Department of Human Resources. **Description:** Produces pre-cooked and frozen chicken products. **Corporate headquarters location:** This Location.

INTERBAKE FOODS, INC.
2821 Emerywood Parkway, Suite 210, Richmond VA 23294. 804/755-7107. **Contact:** Human Resources. **Description:** Produces cookies and crackers.

MARS, INC.
6885 Elm Street, McLean VA 22101. 703/821-4900. **Contact:** Human Resources. **Description:** A food processing company.

MAZO LERCH COMPANY, INC.
4720 Eisenhower Avenue, Alexander VA 22304. 703/370-5900. **Contact:** Human Resources. **Description:** A wholesale food distributor. Mazo Lerch Company, Inc. delivers their food to restaurants, nursing homes, and schools. They offer a non-food bar to assist the customer in the ordering of appliances, dishes, utensils and other kitchen supplies.

McKEE FOODS CORPORATION
P.O. Box 486, Stuarts Draft VA 24477. 540/943-7101. **Contact:** Personnel Department. **Description:** Manufacturer and distributor of Little Debbie Snacks. McKee Food Corporation offers positions in Production, Engineering, Maintenance, Shipping/Receiving and Quality Assurance. **Number of employees at this location:** 800

MOORE'S QUALITY SNACK FOODS
P.O. Box 1909, Bristol VA 24203. 540/669-6194. **Contact:** Kathy Myers, Personnel Manager. **Description:** This wholesale snack food manufacturer was established in 1924. Moore's Quality Snack Foods distributes its line of salty snack foods (i.e., potato chips, tortillas and popcorn) to various warehouses and grocery stores. The company buys and sells its own brand of crackers.

NATIONAL FRUIT PRODUCT COMPANY, INC.
P.O. Box 2040, Winchester VA 22604-1240. 703/662-3401. **Fax:** 703/665-4686. **Contact:** Herb Glass, Corporate Human Resources Manager. **Description:** A food processor. National Fruit primarily produces apple juice, apple sauce, vinegar, apple butter, apple slices, and pie fillings. **Common positions include:** Accountant/Auditor; Blue-Collar Worker Supervisor; Buyer; Computer Programmer; Computer Systems Analyst; Electrical/Electronics Engineer; Food Scientist/Technologist; General Manager; Human Resources Specialist; Industrial Production Manager; Mechanical Engineer; Operations/Production Manager; Purchasing Agent and Manager. **Educational backgrounds include:** Accounting; Business Administration; Chemistry; Computer Science; Engineering. **Benefits:** Disability Coverage; Employee Discounts; Life Insurance; Medical Insurance; Pension Plan; Profit Sharing; Tuition Assistance. **Corporate headquarters location:** This Location. **Operations at this facility include:** Administration; Manufacturing; Research and Development; Sales. **Listed on:** Privately held. **Number of employees at this location:** 500. **Number of employees nationwide:** 1,000.

NESTLE REFRIGERATED FOOD
201 Airside Drive, Danville VA 24540. 804/822-4000. **Contact:** Mickey Durmick, Human Resource Manager. **Description:** Manufactures Nestle refrigerated foods.

PARK 500
4100 Bermuda Hundred Road, Chester VA 23831. 804/751-2000. **Contact:** Charlie Martin, Human Resource Manager. **Description:** Manufacturing plant for tobacco. Park 500 is a division of Philip Morris USA.

PHILIP MORRIS USA
P.O. Box 26603, Richmond VA 23261. 804/274-2000. **Contact:** Deborah Cross, Manager of Placement and E.E.O. **Description:** In the tobacco industry, Philip Morris U.S.A. and Philip Morris International together form one of the largest international cigarette operations in the world. U.S. brand names include Marlboro, Parliament, Virginia Slims, Benson & Hedges, and Merit. Parent company, Philip Morris Companies, is a holding company whose principal wholly-owned subsidiaries are Philip Morris Inc. (Philip Morris U.S.A.), Philip Morris International Inc., Kraft Foods, Inc., Miller Brewing Company, and Philip Morris Capital Corporation. In the food industry, Kraft Foods, Inc. is one of the largest producers of packaged grocery products in North America. Major brands include Jell-O, Post, Kool-Aid, Crystal Light, Entenmann's, Miracle Whip, Stove Top, and Shake 'n' Bake. Kraft markets a number of products under the Kraft brand including natural and process cheeses and dry packaged dinners. The Oscar Mayer unit markets processed meats, poultry, lunch combinations, and pickles under the Oscar Mayer, Louis Rich, Lunchables, and Claussen brand names. Kraft is also one of the largest coffee companies with principal brands including Maxwell House, Sanka, Brim, and General Foods International Coffees. Kraft Foods Ingredients Corporation manufactures private-label and industrial food products for sale to other food processing companies. Miller Brewing Company brews brands names including Molsen Ice, Miller Genuine Draft, Miller High Life, Sharp's non-alcoholic, Red Dog, Miller Lite, Icehouse, Foster's Lager, and Lowenbrau. Philip Morris Capital Corporation is engaged in financial services and real estate. **Parent company:** Philip Morris Companies.

PINKERTON TOBACCO COMPANY
6600 West Broad Street, Richmond VA 23230. 804/287-3200. **Contact:** A.W. Stalnaker, Human Resource Director. **Description:** Manufactures smokeless tobacco and moist snuff. Pinkerton Tobacco Company distributes its products both nationally and internationally. Among its most popular smokeless tobaccos are Redman, Golden Blend, and Renegades. **Number of employees at this location:** 58.

RICHFOOD HOLDINGS, INC.
P.O. Box 26967, Richmond VA 23261-6967. 804/746-6000. **Contact:** Jennifer Dandridge, Personnel Manager. **Description:** One of the largest wholesale food distributors in the Mid-Atlantic. Richfood Holdings supplies national brand and private label grocery products, frozen foods, dairy products, fresh produce items, meats, delicatessen and bakery products, and non-food items to more than 1,500 retail grocery stores throughout the Mid-Atlantic region. Richfood Holdings serves its customers from New York to North Carolina from its distribution facilities in Mechanicsville, Virginia and West Point, Pennsylvania. **Corporate headquarters location:** This Location. **Listed on:** NASDAQ. **Number of employees nationwide:** 1,500.

ROCCO INC.
P.O. Box 549, Harrisonburg VA 22801. 703/568-1400. **Contact:** William Christian, Vice President of Human Resources. **Description:** A producer and marketer of poultry food products. **Common positions include:** Accountant/Auditor; Computer Programmer; Customer Service Representative; Department Manager; General Manager; Manufacturer's/Wholesaler's Sales Rep.; Quality Control Supervisor. **Educational backgrounds include:** Accounting; Marketing. **Corporate headquarters location:** This Location.

THE SMITHFIELD COMPANIES, INC.
311 County Street, Portsmouth VA 23704. 804/399-3100. **Contact:** Human Resources. **Description:** A diversified producer of branded food products, The Smithfield Companies, Inc. markets its products mostly to the retail grocery and food service industry throughout the United States with its primary market area being the Southeast. The company operates through the following businesses: The Smithfield Ham and Products Co., VW Joyner & Co., Bunker Hill Foods, Pruden Packing Co., Williamsburg Foods, Morton House Foods, Prudence Foods and The New Orleans School of Cooking.

SMITHFIELD FOODS, INC.
501 North Church Street, P.O. Box 447, Smithfield VA 23431. 804/357-4321. **Contact:** Michelle Ross, Vice President of Human Resources. **Description:** An integrated meat packing and processing company which also produces and markets pork products. The company's brand names include Smithfield, Esskay, Valleydale, Mash's, Luter's, Gwaltney, Hamilton, and Patrick Cudahy. The company's sales are primarily on the eastern seaboard states. **Corporate headquarters location:** This Location. **Subsidiaries include:** Smithfield Packing Co., Gwaltney of Smithfield Ltd., Patrick Cudahy, Inc., Brown's of Carolina, Inc., and Smith-Caroll's. **Listed on:** NASDAQ. **Number of employees nationwide:** 8,000.

SOUTHERN PROCESSORS, INC.
P.O. Box 1707, Danville VA 24543. 804/797-4414. **Contact:** Bryant Grabitte, Plant Manager. **Description:** Processors of tobacco. Southern Processors, Inc. is a subsidiary of Universal Leaf. They process tobacco for Philip Morris Companies.

UNIVERSAL CORPORATION
P.O. Box 25099, Richmond VA 23260. 804/359-9311. **Contact:** Mike Oberschmidt Jr., Human Resources Director. **Description:** An agricultural products holding company with interests primarily in tobacco through Universal Leaf Company. Other subsidiaries are involved in coffee, tea, rubber, sunflower seeds, lumber, and building materials. The company's tobacco operations consist of selecting, buying, shipping, processing, packing, storing, and financing tobacco for manufacture and distribution. Universal markets its products and has production facilities throughout the world. **Corporate headquarters location:** This Location. **Listed on:** New York Stock Exchange.

VIE DE FRANCE CORPORATION
85 South Bragg Street, Suite 600, Alexandria VA 22312. 703/750-9600. **Contact:** Betsy Powell, Accounting Manager. **Description:** A producer of prepared foods, Vie de France has developed its market through its development of 'sous vide' technology. The sous vide process is a prepared food system, originally developed by chefs in France for use in their own restaurants. Food is prepared for cooking, vacuum sealed in pouches, and then cooked using low temperature, slow cooking methods. Once cooked, the products are quickly frozen to maintain texture and taste. Since 1990, Vie de France has operated a 30,000 square foot plant in Alexandria, Virginia, specially designed for the sous vide process. The plant produces about 35,000 portions a day. Since 1994, the company has operated a second facility, located in Norway. **Common positions include:** Accountant/Auditor; Administrative Services Manager; Chef/Cook/Kitchen Worker; Computer Programmer; Electrical/Electronics Engineer; Food Scientist/Technologist; Industrial Production Manager; Manufacturer's/Wholesaler's Sales Rep.; Operations/Production Manager. **Educational backgrounds include:** Accounting; Computer Science; Cooking; Marketing. **Benefits:** 401K; Dental Insurance; Disability Coverage; Employee Discounts; Life Insurance; Medical Insurance. **Corporate headquarters location:** This Location. **Operations at this facility include:** Administration; Divisional Headquarters; Manufacturing; Sales. **Number of employees at this location:** 100.

WLR FOODS
P.O. Box 7000, Broadway VA 22815-7000. 540/896-7001. **Fax:** 540/896-0498. **Contact:** Human Resources. **Description:** A fully-integrated poultry and turkey processor, marketer, and distributor. WLR Foods offers over 250 brand name and private label poultry and related products, and operates seven processing plants and packaging facilities, and three further processing plants. **Corporate headquarters location:** This Location. **Subsidiaries include:** May Supply Company, Inc., a wholesale distributor of plumbing supplies and equipment; Cassco Ice & Cold Storage, Inc. makes and distributes ice and offers refrigerated warehouse storage services; and Rockingham Poultry, Inc., an export company. **Listed on:** NASDAQ. **Number of employees nationwide:** 9,000.

Note: *Because addresses and telephone numbers of smaller companies change rapidly, we recommend you call each company to verify the information below before inquiring about job opportunities. Mass mailings are not recommended.*

Additional small employers:

POULTRY AND EGGS

Cuddy Farms Inc.
1724 Country Club Rd, Harrisonburg VA 22801-8860. 540/433-0702.

Southern Poultry Farms Chicken Division
410 Stone Spring Rd, Harrisonburg VA 22801-9659. 540/433-4099.

MEAT AND POULTRY PROCESSING

Fiorucci Foods Inc.
1800 Ruffin Mill Rd, Colonial Hgts VA 23834-5936. 804/520-7775.

Gwaltney Of Smithfield Ltd
2175 Elmhurst Ln, Portsmouth VA 23701-2626. 804/465-0666.

VW Joyner & Co.
315 Main St, Smithfield VA 23430-1326. 804/357-2161.

White Packing Co. Inc.
RR 3 Box 245, King George VA 22485-9219. 540/775-7700.

Bunker Hill Foods
Rt 122 South, Bedford VA 24523. 540/586-8274.

Smithfield Companies
311 County St, Portsmouth VA 23704-3716. 804/399-3100.

Valleydale Foods Inc.
1013 Iowa St, Salem VA 24153-5223. 540/389-5473.

Advantage Food Products
PO Box 247, Petersburg WV 26847-0247. 304/257-2119.

Perdue Farms Inc.
Hwy 58 W, Emporia VA 23847. 804/348-5700.

Perdue Farms Inc.
22520 Lankford Hwy, Accomac VA 23301-1420. 804/787-2700.

Perdue Farms Inc.
100 Quality St, Bridgewater VA 22812-1618. 540/828-2581.

Rocco Further Processing
Coop Dr, Timberville VA 22853. 540/896-7041.

Rocco Turkeys Inc.
Rt 42 & Huffman Dr, Dayton VA 22821. 540/879-2521.

Tyson Foods Inc.
501 N Liberty St, Harrisonburg VA 22801-3917. 540/433-0720.

Tyson Foods Inc.
11224 Lankford Hwy, Temperancevle VA 23442-2445. 804/824-3471.

Tyson Foods Inc.
13264 Mountain Road, Glen Allen VA 23059-1737. 804/798-8357.

DAIRY PRODUCTS

Breyers Co.
3031 Norfolk St, Richmond VA 23230-4509. 804/342-5000.

Shenandoah's Pride Dairy Company
5325 Port Royal Road, Springfield VA 22151-2159. 703/321-9500.

Shenandoah's Pride Dairy Company
Rt 11, Mt Crawford VA 22841. 540/434-7328.

Flav-O-Rich Inc.
PO Box 1539, Bristol VA 24203-1539. 540/669-5161.

Marva Maid Dairy
5500 Chestnut Ave, Newport News VA 23605-2118. 804/245-3857.

Valley Rich Dairy
3621 Aerial Way Drive Southwest, Roanoke VA 24018-1507. 540/344-5143.

Virginia Milk Producers Cooperative
PO Box 218, Mt Crawford VA 22841-0218. 540/434-7328.

PRESERVED FRUITS AND VEGETABLES

Bowman Apple Products Co. Inc.
Route 11 North, Mount Jackson VA 22842. 540/477-3111.

Knouse Foods Co-Op Inc.
PO Drawer E, Inwood WV 25428. 304/229-5855.

Krisp-Pak Co. Inc.
835 Southampton Ave, Norfolk VA 23510-1015. 804/622-8440.

Maruchan VA Inc.
8101 Whitepine Rd, Richmond VA 23237-2288. 804/275-2800.

Zeropack Co.
560 N Loudoun St, Winchester VA 22601-4854. 540/662-3885.

Conagra Frozen Foods
RR 1 Box 24-A, Crozet VA 22932-9801. 804/823-3200.

Golden West Foods Inc.
940 Orange St, Bedford VA 24523-3303. 540/586-8284.

Culpeper Farmers Co-Op
819 James Madison Hwy, Culpeper VA 22701-2405. 540/825-2200.

PREPARED FEEDS AND INGREDIENTS FOR ANIMALS

Augusta Co-Op Farm Bureau Inc.
1205-B Richmond Rd, Staunton VA 24401. 540/885-1265.

Valley Proteins Inc.
1444 Indian Hollow Rd, Winchester VA 22603-3600. 540/877-2590.

Wampler-Longacre Feed Mill
PO Box 539, Moorefield WV 26836-0539. 304/538-2195.

BAKERY PRODUCTS

Continental Baking Co.
10 S Jefferson St, Richmond VA 23220-5618. 804/649-7511.

Flowers Baking Co. Of West VA
PO Box 308, Bluefield WV 24701-0308. 304/327-3561.

Flowers Baking Of Norfolk
1209 Corprew Ave, Norfolk VA 23504-3403. 804/622-6317.

Heiners Bakery Inc.
PO Box 9247, Huntington WV 25704-0247. 304/523-8411.

Kotarides Baking Co. Inc.
117 E 16th St, Norfolk VA 23510-2629. 804/625-0301.

McKee Foods Corp.
Rt 634 & 639 E County Rd, Stuarts Draft VA 24477. 540/943-7101.

Rainbo Bread Co. Inc.
2609 Plantation Rd Ne, Roanoke VA 24012-4459. 540/366-8881.

Rich Products Corp.
801 N Kent St, Winchester VA 22601-5415. 540/667-1955.

Schmidt Baking Co. Inc.
311 Cumberland Valley Pl, Martinsburg WV 25401-2667. 304/263-0961.

Storck Baking Co. Inc.
PO Box 389, Parkersburg WV 26102-0389. 304/485-5441.

Ukrop's Bakery
10911 Southlake Ct, Richmond VA 23236-3913. 804/794-1321.

Virga Pizza Crust Of VA
4005 Victory Blvd, Portsmouth VA 23701-2816. 804/488-4493.

FATS AND OILS

C&T Quincy Inc.
2000 W Broad St, Richmond VA 23220-2006. 804/359-5786.

Carolina By-Products
107 Kavnaugh Rd, Lynchburg VA 24505. 804/847-8895.

SUGAR AND CONFECTIONERY PRODUCTS

Russell Stover Candies
Hwy 722, Clarksville VA 23927. 804/374-2171.

BEVERAGES

Oakencroft Vineyards & Winery
RR 5, Box 429, Charlottesvle VA 22901-8856. 804/296-4188.

Bluefield Beverage Co.
RR 2, Box 173-I, Bluefield VA 24605-9802. 540/322-3411.

Central Coca-Cola Bottling Company
R R 2, Box 224-B, Staunton VA 24401. 540/886-3427.

General Foods USA
220 Park Centre Dr, Winchester VA 22603-5754. 540/678-0442.

Mid-Atlantic Coca-Cola
1310 Roseneath Rd, Richmond VA 23230-4624. 804/358-2351.

Pepsi Cola General Bottlers
730 Rogers St, Princeton WV 24740-3650. 304/425-9525.

Pepsi-Cola Bottlers Of VA
211 Washington Ave, Marion VA 24354-2364. 540/783-7232.

Pepsi-Cola Bottling Co.
100 Independent Ave, Nitro WV 25143-2511. 304/755-4393.

Pepsi-Cola Bottling Co.
1150 Pepsi Place, Charlottesvle VA 22901-2865. 804/978-2140.

Pepsi-Cola Co.
17200 Warwick Blvd, Newport News VA 23603-1312. 804/887-2310.

Pepsi-Cola Co.
RR 11, #N, Roanoke VA

24019-9803. 540/992-2661.

Pepsi-Cola East
1531 Monroe Ave, Huntington WV 25704-2335. 304/429-6767.

Pepsi-Cola Norton Inc.
12th & Park Ave, Norton VA 24273. 540/679-1122.

RC 7-Up Bottling Co.
5330 Port Royal Rd, Springfield VA 22151-2105. 703/321-7900.

Royal Crown Bottling Co. Of VA
711 W 24th St, Norfolk VA 23517-1102. 804/625-1668.

Valley Bell Division
508 Roane St, Charleston WV 25302-2091. 304/344-2511.

SEAFOOD

Consolidated Foodservice Companies
PO Box 61789, Virginia Beach VA 23466-1789. 804/456-2009.

Eastern Shore Seafood Products
13249 Lankford Hwy, Mappsville VA 23407. 804/824-5651.

Sandler Foods Inc.
1224 Diamond Springs Rd, Virginia Beach VA 23455-3701. 804/464-3551.

Bonums Oyster Co. Inc.
RR 1, Kinsale VA 22488-9801. 804/472-2667.

Drewer & Son Inc.
Saxis Rd, Saxis VA 23427. 804/824-3403.

Graham & Rollins Inc.
19 Rudd Ln, Hampton VA 23669-4029. 804/723-3831.

Martin & Richardson Seafood Co.
817 Jefferson Ave, Newport News VA 23607-6117. 804/245-6911.

Zapata Protein USA Inc.
U S Hwy 659, Reedville VA 22539. 804/453-4211.

CHIPS AND SNACKS

Terry's Inc.
1400 Newton St, Bristol VA 24201-3797. 540/669-8149.

MANUFACTURED ICE

Cassco Ice & Cold Storage
125 W Bruce St, Harrisonburg VA 22801-3615. 540/433-2751.

FOOD PREPARATIONS

Mrs Giles Country Kitchens
125 Oakley Ave, Lynchburg VA 24501-3203. 804/845-4577.

TOBACCO PRODUCTS

American Tobacco Company
13203 N Enon Church Rd, Chester VA 23831-3122. 804/751-2100.

Lorillard Tobacco
1811 Huguenot Rd, Midlothian VA 23113-5600. 804/379-4598.

Lorillard Tobacco Co.
1009 5th Ave, Rm 104, Huntington WV 25701-2202. 304/523-9706.

P Lorillard Co.
5021 Brook Rd, Richmond VA 23227-3416. 804/262-6023.

RJ Reynolds Tobacco Company
420 Porterfield Hwy SW, Abingdon VA 24210-2532. 540/628-3668.

Single Stick
7518 Whitepine Rd, Richmond VA 23237-2217. 804/271-0674.

Swisher International Inc.
4000 Water St, Wheeling WV 26003-4308. 304/232-4000.

American Tobacco Co.
13101 N Enon Church Rd, Chester VA 23831-3120. 804/751-7500.

Lorillard Tobacco Co.
200 Kentuck Rd, Danville VA 24540-5055. 804/792-0521.

Maclin-Zimmer McGill Tobacco
PO Box 550, Petersburg VA 23804-0550. 804/733-6095.

Maclin-Zimmer-McGill Tobacco
70520 Unico Rd, McKenney VA 23872. 804/478-4075.

Phillip Morris Inc.
4100 Bermuda Hundred Rd, Chester VA 23831-3244. 804/751-2009.

Swedish Tobacco Company
P.O. Box 6873, Richmond VA 23230. 804/673-8800.

ALCOHOL WHOLESALE

Associated Distributors Inc.
401 Woodlake Dr, Chesapeake VA 23320-8903. 804/424-6300.

Blue Ridge Beverage
PO Box 700, Salem VA 24153-0700. 540/380-2000.

Tri-Cities Beverage Corp.
612 Industrial Park Dr, Newport News VA 23608-1305. 804/874-6600.

Hoffman Beverage Co.
4105 S Military Hwy, Chesapeake VA 23321-2701. 804/487-4500.

Loveland Distributing Co.
2290 Dabney Rd, Richmond VA 23230-3344. 804/355-4943.

Broudy-Kantor Co. Inc.
8501 Princess Anne Dr, Norfolk VA 23502. 804/643-7830.

Forman Distributing Co.
7550 Accotink Park Rd, Springfield VA 22150-3644. 703/644-2425.

FARM SUPPLIES WHOLESALE

Piedmont Fertilizer
2453 Birchwood Creek Dr, King George VA 22485-6604. 540/775-2985.

Rockingham Cooperative Farm Bureau Inc.
101 W Grace St, Harrisonburg VA 22801-1806. 540/434-3856.

Wetsel Seed Company
PO Box 791, Harrisonburg VA 22801-0791. 540/434-6753.

TOBACCO AND TOBACCO PRODUCTS WHOLESALE

Charles M. Sledd Co.
100 E Cove Ave, Wheeling WV 26003-5027. 304/243-1820.

FOOD WHOLESALE

Bon Ton Foods Inc.
1031 44th St, Newport News VA 23607-2312. 804/245-6410.

Eli The Witt Company
RR 1, Ashland VA 23005-9801. 804/798-1336.

Herbert Halperin Distributing Corp.
404 S Leadbetter Rd, Ashland VA 23005-3200. 804/550-2274.

Industrial Commodities Inc.
163 Dow Gil Rd, Ashland VA 23005-9464. 804/752-2100.

McLane Distribution Center
PO Box 5339, Falmouth VA 22403-0339. 540/374-2000.

Mid-Mountain Foods Inc.
PO Box 129, Abingdon VA 24212-0129. 540/628-3105.

Nash Finch Co.
1400 Cavalier Blvd, Chesapeake VA 23323-1602. 804/487-2586.

Nash Finch/Bluefield
PO Box 949, Bluefield VA 24605-0949. 540/326-2654.

PYA-Monarch
1025 Electric Rd, Salem VA 24153-6437. 540/389-0255.

Roanoke Restaurant Service Inc.
122755 S Washington Hwy, Ashland VA 23005. 804/752-6650.

Schenck Foods Company
PO Box 2298, Winchester VA 22604-1498. 540/869-1870.

Snak Attack
2904 Barn Way, Chesapeake VA 23323-1831. 804/487-5131.

Supervalu Inc.
James River Trnpk, Barboursville WV 25504. 304/736-5251.

Supervalu Inc.-Milton Division
PO Box 386, Milton WV 25541-0386. 304/743-9087.

Sysco Food Service Of Virginia
RR 11 Box 20020, Harrisonburg VA 22801-9811. 540/434-0761.

UTZ Quality Foods Inc.
3832 Holland Blvd, Chesapeake VA 23323-1517. 804/487-0418.

Acosta Sales Co. Inc.
100 Timber Ridge Dr, Ashland VA 23005-9433. 804/550-2521.

Joe Dell Brokerage Inc.
341 Cleveland Place, Ste 109, Virginia Beach VA 23462-6547. 804/456-5348.

Edy's Grand Ice Cream
1600 Mactavish Ave, Richmond VA 23230-4416. 804/353-1252.

Tyson Foods
3301 US 33, Glen Allen VA 23060. 804/798-8357.

UTZ Quality Foods
8561 Virginia Meadows Dr, Manassas VA 22110-7824. 703/330-5232.

International Seafoods
PO Box 1150, Hayes VA 23072-1150. 804/642-6362.

Lawson Seafood Company
15 Rudd Ln, Hampton VA 23669-4029. 804/722-6211.

Ocean To Ocean Seafood Sales Co.
448 Viking Dr, Ste 200, Virginia Beach VA 23452-7331. 804/431-8500.

Blue Ridge Market
Rt 757, Ferrum VA 24088. 540/365-6313.

Tasty Kake
3030 Nicholas Ave NE, Roanoke VA 24012-5620. 540/345-4425.

Fredericksburg Livestock Exchange
1122 Summit St, Fredericksbrg VA 22401-7033. 540/373-6269.

For more information on career opportunities in the food, beverage, and agriculture industries:

<u>Associations</u>

AMERICAN ASSOCIATION OF CEREAL CHEMISTS (AACC)
3340 Pilot Knob Road, St. Paul MN 55121. 612/454-7250. Contact: Marla Meyers. Dedicated to the dissemination of technical information and continuing education in cereal science.

AMERICAN FROZEN FOOD INSTITUTE
1764 Old Meadow Lane, Suite 350. McLean VA 22102. 703/821-0770. A

national trade association representing the interests of the frozen food industry.

AMERICAN SOCIETY OF AGRICULTURAL ENGINEERS
2950 Niles Road, St. Joseph MI 49085. 616/429-0300. Contact: Julie Swim.

AMERICAN SOCIETY OF BREWING CHEMISTS ASSOCIATION
3340 Pilot Knob Road, St. Paul MN 55121. 612/454-7250. Founded in 1934 to improve and bring uniformity to the brewing industry on a technical level.

CIES - THE FOOD BUSINESS FORUM
3800 Moore Plaza, Alexandria VA 22305. 703/549-4525. A global food business network. Membership is on a company basis. Members learn how to manage their businesses more effectively and gain access to information and contacts.

DAIRY AND FOOD INDUSTRIES SUPPLY ASSOCIATION (DFISA)
1451 Dolly Madison Boulevard, McLean VA 22101-3850. 703/761-2600. Contact: Dorothy Brady. A trade association whose members are suppliers to the food, dairy, liquid processing, and related industries.

MASTER BREWERS ASSOCIATION OF THE AMERICAS (MBAA)
2421 North Mayfair Road, Suite 310, Wauwatosa, WI 53226. 414/774-8558. Promotes, advances, improves, and protects the professional interests of brew and malt house production and technical personnel. Disseminates technical and practical information.

NATIONAL AGRICULTURAL CHEMICALS ASSOCIATION
1156 15th Street NW, Suite 900, Washington DC 20005. 202/296-1585.

NATIONAL BEER WHOLESALERS' ASSOCIATION
1100 South Washington Street, Alexandria VA 22314-4494. 703/683-4300. Fax: 703/683-8965. Contact: Karen Craig.

NATIONAL FOOD PROCESSORS ASSOCIATION
1401 New York Avenue NW, Suite 400, Washington DC 20005. 202/639-5900. Contact: Ned Endler.

NATIONAL SOFT DRINK ASSOCIATION
1101 16th Street NW, Washington DC 20036. 202/463-6732.

UNITED DAIRY INDUSTRY ASSOCIATION (UDIA)
10255 West Higgins Road, Suite 900, Rosemont IL 60018. 847/803-2000. A federation of state and regional dairy promotion organizations that develop and execute effective programs to increase consumer demand for U.S.-produced milk and dairy products.

Directories

FOOD ENGINEERING'S DIRECTORY OF U.S. FOOD PLANTS
Chilton Book Company, Chilton Way, Radnor PA 19089. 800/695-1214.

THOMAS FOOD INDUSTRY REGISTER
Thomas Publishing Company, Five Penn Plaza, New York NY 10001. 212/695-0500.

Magazines

BEVERAGE WORLD
Keller International Publishing Corporation. 150 Great Neck Road, Great Neck NY 11021. 516/829-9210.

FOOD PROCESSING
301 East Erie Street, Chicago IL 60611. 312/644-2020.

FROZEN FOOD AGE
Maclean Hunter Media, #4 Stamford Forum, Stamford CT 06901. 203/325-3500.

PREPARED FOODS
Gorman Publishing Company, 8750 West Bryn Mawr, Chicago IL 60631. 312/693-3200.

GOVERNMENT

While the federal government is still the nation's largest employer, the number of federal jobs is rapidly on the decline. Adding to this instability was the federal government's shutdown on more than one occasion while the President and Congress were in budgetary deadlock. The decrease in Department of Defense employment that started with the collapse of the Soviet Union has only increased due to federal deficits. The Defense Department is expected to reduce its workforce through attrition over the next decade.

Employment in other executive agencies is also expected to fall. Many workers are being offered buyouts, early retirement, and other incentives to leave the federal government. Demand remains strong, however, for nurses and engineers.

The outlook for state and local government workers is somewhat better. While opportunities vary from one state to the next, the Bureau of Labor Statistics forecasts a 16 percent job rise through 2005. Adding to the demand is the rising need for services. Since the early '80s, the government has decentralized and states have assumed more responsibility for providing services. Many policy decisions have been shifted to individual state governments, which are increasingly dealing with transportation problems, health care issues, energy policies, and poverty.

Even so, future job growth may be slowed by budgetary constraints. Local governments are struggling to meet the demand for services because tax revenues and federal aid are declining. Many states have cut their workforces to reduce spending and keep budgets balanced.

THE DEFENSE SUPPLY CENTER RICHMOND
Office of Civilian Personnel, Richmond VA 23297-5000. 804/279-4600. **Contact:** Personnel. **Description:** A general supply center for the defense.

FARM CREDIT ADMINISTRATION
1501 Farm Credit Drive, McLean VA 22102-5090. 703/883-4135. **Contact:** Philip J. Shebest, Chief of Human Resources. **Description:** A government agency which regulates and examines the Farm Credit System. Eight field locations. **NOTE:** Applicants must submit the appropriate form (Government Form SF-171) following specific vacancy announcements; unsolicited resumes are disregarded. Farm Credit Administration provides benefits due to federal government employees. **Common positions include:** Accountant/Auditor; Attorney; Computer Engineer; Economist/Market Research Analyst; Financial Analyst. **Educational backgrounds include:** Accounting; Business Administration; Economics; Finance. **Corporate headquarters location:** This Location. **Operations at this facility include:** Administration.

FEDERAL BUREAU OF INVESTIGATION
CLARKSBURG RESIDENT AGENCY
P.O. Box 666, Clarksburg WV 26302. 304/624-6200. **Contact:** Human Resources. **Description:** This location is an FBI identification facility, engaged

primarily in fingerprint analysis. **NOTE:** For employment inquiries, call 304/625-2000.

INTERNATIONAL ASSOCIATION OF CHIEFS OF POLICE
515 North Washington Street, Alexandria VA 22314. 703/836-6767. **Contact:** Mr. Gene Cromartie, Human Resources Manager. **Description:** National headquarters for the trade association representing police chiefs and other ranking law enforcement officials. **Common positions include:** Accountant/Auditor; Administrator; Computer Programmer; Technical Writer/Editor. **Educational backgrounds include:** Accounting; Business Administration; Communications; Computer Science. **Benefits:** Medical Insurance.

U.S. DEPARTMENT OF VETERANS AFFAIRS DELEGATED EXAMINING UNIT
P.O. Box 24269, Richmond VA 23224-0269. 804/675-5000x4782. **Contact:** Personnel Office. **Description:** The Delegated Examining Unit (DEU) of the Department of Veterans Affairs provides employment information and application forms for all Department of Veterans Affairs positions. **NOTE:** The DEU can be contacted at 800/368-6008, or if calling within Virginia, at 800/552-3045. This firm does not accept unsolicited resumes. Please only respond to advertised openings.

U.S. NAVY CIVIL ENGINEER CORPS (CEC)
Naval Facilities Engineering Command, Code 12A1, 200 Stovall Street, Alexandria VA 22332-2300. 703/614-3635. **Contact:** LCDR David Stewart, Accessions Officer. **Description:** CEC officers are U.S. Naval officers who are responsible for the design, construction, maintenance, repair, and operation of the Navy's shore facilities. **NOTE:** If preferred, contact one of the regional Accessions Officers: Western U.S. - Lt. Gary Wick at 415/244-2005; Eastern U.S. - Lt. Paul Webb at 202/433-7285. Worldwide assignment possibilities. **Common positions include:** Architect; Chemical Engineer; Civil Engineer; Construction Contractor and Manager; Department Manager; Electrical/Electronics Engineer; Financial Manager; General Manager; Industrial Engineer; Landscape Architect; Mechanical Engineer; Petroleum Engineer; Structural Engineer; Surveyor. **Educational backgrounds include:** Architecture; Engineering. **Benefits:** Daycare Assistance; Dental Insurance; Disability Coverage; Life Insurance; Medical Insurance; Pension Plan; Tuition Assistance. **Number of employees nationwide:** 1,400.

U.S. PATENT AND TRADEMARK OFFICE
Office of Human Resources, 2011 Crystal Drive Suite 200, Arlington VA 22202. 703/305-8231. **Fax:** 703/305-8501. **Contact:** Dawn Dowell, Recruitment Coordinator. **Description:** Reviews applications for patents and makes legal determinations concerning the granting of patents. The U.S. Patent and Trademark Office employs more than 1,000 people, primarily scientists and engineers. **NOTE:** Send resumes to the chosen department: Recruitment/Patent, Kim Minnigh; Recruitment, Kim Clark; or Recruitment/Patent, Nancy Strother. **Common positions include:** Aerospace Engineer; Architect; Architectural Engineer; Biological Scientist/Biochemist; Biomedical Engineer; Chemical Engineer; Chemist; Civil Engineer; Computer Engineer; Electrical/Electronics Engineer; Food Scientist/Technologist; Industrial Designer; Industrial Engineer; Mechanical Engineer; Metallurgical Engineer; Mining Engineer; Petroleum Engineer; Physicist/Astronomer. **Educational backgrounds include:** Architecture; Art/Design; Chemistry; Communications; Computer Science; Engineering; Physics. **Benefits:** Dental Insurance; Disability Coverage; Life Insurance; Medical Insurance; Pension Plan; Profit Sharing; Sick Days; Tuition Assistance. **Corporate headquarters location:** This Location. **Other U.S. locations:** Washington DC. **Parent company:** Department of Commerce.

Note: Because addresses and telephone numbers of smaller companies change rapidly, we recommend you call each company to verify the information below before inquiring about job opportunities. Mass mailings are not recommended.

Additional small employers:

REGULATORY ADMINISTRATION OF TRANSPORTATION

Virginia Port Authority
600 World Trade Center, Norfolk VA 23510. 804/683-8000.

PUBLIC ORDER/SAFETY

Brunswick Correctional
RR 1 Box 207C, Lawrenceville VA 23868-9799. 804/848-4131.

UNITED STATES POSTAL SERVICE

United States Post Office/West Springfield Branch
6200 Rolling Road, Springfield VA 22152-2306. 703/451-6131.

ADMINISTRATION OF PUBLIC HEALTH PROGRAMS

Mental Health Services Division
7969 Ashton Avenue, Manassas VA 22110-2885. 703/792-7800.

For more information about career opportunities in the government:

<u>**Directories**</u>

ACCESS...FCO ON-LINE
Federal Research Service, Inc., P.O. Box 1059, 243 Church Street, Vienna VA 22183-1059. 703/281-0200. This is the online service of the *Federal Career Opportunities* publication. To join online, the cost is $25 for the set-up and $45 for one hour, payable by credit card over the phone.

HEALTH CARE: SERVICES, EQUIPMENT, AND PRODUCTS

With no time to worry about the failure of government-proposed health care reforms, the health care industry is surging ahead with its own solutions, pressured by a competitive marketplace to cut costs. HMOs and insurance providers are looking to nursing homes and home care companies as an alternative to long-term hospital stays, and shifting from inpatient to less expensive outpatient care. Hospitals are streamlining operations and consolidating, with cutback efforts targeting staff, as well as unnecessary tests and laboratory fees. Hospital cost-cutting has also hurt medical equipment suppliers, as many hospitals form networks to share expensive equipment.

Even so, from 1990 to 1995, the number of health care workers in the United States grew from 8.86 million 10.5 million. Despite pressure to cut back, the health care industry remains a growth area. As the elderly population continues to grow faster than the population as a whole and the survival rate of the severely ill continues to improve, the need for new workers will continue to increase, and the large employment base will create replacement needs.

ALEXANDRIA HOSPITAL
4320 Seminary Road, Alexandria VA 22304. 703/504-3000. **Contact:** David Tatro, Director of Human Resources. **Description:** A general medical and surgical hospital.

ALLEGHANY REGIONAL HOSPITAL
P.O. Box 7, Low Moor VA 24457. 540/862-6200. **Contact:** Mac Campbell, Human Resources Administrator. **Description:** A general acute care 196-bed hospital.

ARLINGTON HOSPITAL
1701 North George Mason Drive, Arlington VA 22205. 703/558-5000. **Contact:** Pat Pence, Employment Coordinator. **Description:** A full-service, non-profit, 350-bed hospital. Arlington Hospital offers outpatient clinics, a cancer center, and a cardiac unit. The hospital is JCAHO accredited with commendation.

BEDFORD COUNTY MEMORIAL HOSPITAL
P.O. Box 688, Bedford VA 24523-0688. 540/586-2441. **Contact:** Diane Bowyer, Human Resources Director. **Description:** A non-profit, JCAHO accredited medical facility. Bedford County Memorial Hospital serves as a 110-bed nursing home and a 55-bed hospital.

BLESSINGS CORPORATION
200 Enterprise Drive, Newport News VA 23603. 804/887-2100. **Fax:** 804/887-3787. **Contact:** Ken Hudson, Director of Human Resources. **Description:** A diversified manufacturer of products oriented principally toward the health care field. The Edison Plastics Film Division produces extruded polyethylene and polypropylene films for use in a variety of disposable hygiene products as well as in numerous other industrial and agricultural end uses. The Geri-Care Products Division manufactures and markets an expanding family of reusable and disposable products designed to

promote the health and comfort of those in need of incontinence care in nursing homes, hospitals, and at home. **Common positions include:** Accountant/Auditor; Chemical Engineer; Computer Programmer; Computer Systems Analyst; Financial Analyst; Quality Control Supervisor; Receptionist; Secretary. **Educational backgrounds include:** Accounting; Business Administration; Chemistry; Computer Science; Economics; Engineering; Finance. **Benefits:** 401K; Disability Coverage; Life Insurance; Medical Insurance; Pension Plan. **Corporate headquarters location:** This Location. **Other U.S. locations:** Washington GA; McAlester OK. **Operations at this facility include:** Administration; Divisional Headquarters; Manufacturing; Regional Headquarters; Research and Development; Sales. **Listed on:** American Stock Exchange. **Number of employees at this location:** 15. **Number of employees nationwide:** 1,440.

CATAWBA HOSPITAL
P.O. Box 200, Catawba VA 24070-0200. 703/375-4200. **Contact:** Human Resources. **Description:** A 195-bed state mental health facility. Catawba Hospital is a JCAHO accredited facility, which offers both a geriatric unit and an adult unit.

CENTRA HEALTH INC.
1920 Atherholt Road, Lynchburg VA 24501-1104. 804/947-4705. **Contact:** Mr. Glen McGrath, Vice President of Human Resources. **Description:** A health systems organization. Centra Health Inc. serves as the corporate office for Lynchburg General Hospital and Virginia Baptist Hospital.

CENTRAL VIRGINIA TRAINING CENTER
P.O. Box 1098, Lynchburg VA 24505. 804/947-6326. **Contact:** Will St. John, Human Resources Manager. **Description:** A state residential facility for the mentally retarded.

CHILDREN'S HOSPITAL OF THE KING'S DAUGHTERS
601 Children's Lane, Norfolk VA 23507-1910. 804/668-7000. **Contact:** Human Resources. **Description:** Virginia's only free-standing, full-service pediatric hospital. A not-for-profit institution, Children's Hospital of the King's Daughters is a 173-bed medical center, treating children from birth to age 21. This location also serves as a regional pediatric referral center.

CHILDREN'S NATIONAL MEDICAL CENTER
3022 Williams Drive, Fairfax VA 22031. 703/573-9383. **Contact:** Human Resources. **Description:** The Children's National Medical Center was established 125 years ago for the sole purpose of benefiting children. Over the years, the center has pioneered studies of antibiotic resistance and the causes of severe respiratory tract infection; developed a special form of Vitamin D to treat kidney failure; accomplished the first bone marrow and heart transplants; and identified three viruses that cause infant pneumonia, infant diarrhea, and croup. The center offers comprehensive home care programs and is the regional pediatric trauma center. A nonprofit health center, the Children's National Medical Center relies on donations and fundraising from corporations, foundations, clubs, and individuals to help support building projects, establish new programs, and provide care to children whose families cannot afford their services. **NOTE:** Interested jobseekers should contact human resources at the headquarters of Children's National Medical Center, 111 Michigan Avenue NW, Washington DC 20010-2970. **Corporate headquarters location:** Washington DC.

COMMUNITY MEMORIAL HEALTH CENTER
P.O. Box 90, South Hill VA 23970. 804/447-3151. **Contact:** Human Resources. **Description:** A full-service, general, acute care hospital. Community Memorial is a 125-bed hospital and nursing home, offering both emergency and skilled care.

DePAUL MEDICAL CENTER
150 Kingsley Lane, Norfolk VA 23505. 804/889-5000. **Contact:** Human Resources. **Description:** A 366-bed, not-for-profit, member of the Daughters of Charity National Health System. DePaul Medical Center is both an inpatient and outpatient acute care teaching hospital, offering residencies in medicine, obstetrics/gynecology, pediatrics, urology, radiology, surgery, and ENT. Specialized treatment centers include: The Cancer Center, The Center for Birth, The Laser Center, The Diabetes Center, and the Elise and Henry Clay Hofheimer II Gerontology Center. Its multi-disciplinary rehabilitation services department consists of physical, occupational, and speech therapists.

FAIRFAX HOSPITAL
3300 Gallows Road, Fairfax VA 22046. 703/698-1110. **Contact:** Human Resources. **Description:** A full-service, 656-bed, inpatient and outpatient care hospital. **NOTE:** For employment information, call Nova Health Systems at 703/205-2380.

FAUQUIER HOSPITAL
500 Hospital Drive, Warrenton VA 22186-3099. 703/347-2550. **Contact:** Benny Shepherd, Director of Personnel. **Description:** A 120-bed, not-for-profit hospital providing inpatient, outpatient, and emergency care. Its Radiology Department provides complete X-ray, MRI, CT, SPECT, nuclear medicine studies, and stereotactic breast biopsy. Rehabilitative services include, physical, occupational, and speech therapy, as well as cardiac and pulmonary rehabilitation. Fauquier's Home Health Department, providing Medicare-certified nursing and therapy services, makes over 10,000 home visits each year. Also affiliated with the hospital is Warrenton Overlook Health and Rehabilitation Center, a 115-bed nursing home/rehabilitation center. **Number of employees at this location:** 600.

FORUM GROUP, INC.
11320 Random Hills Road, Suite 400, Fairfax VA 22030. 703/277-7000. **Contact:** Lisa Peterson, Vice President, Human Resources. **Description:** The Forum Group provides acute and long-term health care services through the ownership and management of retirement living centers, nursing homes and facilities for the developmentally disabled.

HENRICO DOCTOR'S HOSPITAL
1602 Skipwith Road, Richmond VA 23229. 804/289-4500. **Contact:** Human Resources. **Description:** A hospital. One of Richmond's leading employers, Henrico Doctor's Hospital employs over 1,300 people.

MARY IMMACULATE HOSPITAL
2 Bernadine Drive, Newport News VA 23602. 804/886-6600. **Contact:** Human Resources. **Description:** Established in 1952, this 110-bed acute care general hospital believes in treating a person physically, emotionally, socially and spiritually. Mary Immaculate Hospital offers a Discovery Care Center (child care facility) and two MedCare centers (provide walk-in general care). This hospital has four centers to aid their community: St. Francis Nursing Center which provides ten beds for skilled care and 105 beds for intermediate care; Kiosk which provides free weekly blood pressure screenings and Family Focus which provides support for parents and families. Some of the hospital's services include: 24-hour Emergency; The Birthplace (maternity unit); Day Surgery; Laser Services; Intensive & Coronary Care Unit; Kidney Dialysis Unit; Arthroscopy; Home Health; Life Care (psychological, social, physical and spiritual support for the terminally ill); Cardiac Rehabilitation; 24-hour Laboratory, X-ray, Cardiopulmonary and Anesthesia; Physical and Occupational Therapy; Speech Pathology and Audiology; Radiology Neurology Services; Endoscopy; Nutrition Counseling; Cardiac Cath Lab; Occupational Medicine and the Get Well Card Program (quick registration, free screenings and other services). **Benefits:** Medical Insurance.

MENTAL HEALTH MANAGEMENT, INC.
7601 Lewinsville Road, Suite 200, McLean VA 22102. 703/749-4600. **Fax:** 703/749-4604. **Contact:** Human Resources. **Description:** Provides behavioral health services through its seven psychiatric and substance abuse facilities. Mental Health Management provides inpatient care and alternative care such as partial hospitalization and outpatient treatment. The company's Extended Care Services Division provides specialized medical and behavioral health services to more than 800 nursing homes and assisted living centers in 12 states. This division also serves the mental health needs of more than 2,000 Medicaid patients in nursing homes under a contract with the State of Georgia. Mental Health Management was formerly a wholly-owned subsidiary of MEDIQ Inc. **Corporate headquarters location:** This Location. **Subsidiaries include:** Pacific Shores Behavioral Health System (serving Southern California); Pinon Hills Behavioral Health System (serving the southwestern United States); Windsor Hospital (serving Cleveland); Aspen Hill Hospital (serving Arizona, Colorado, Nevada, and New Mexico); Oakview Treatment Center (serving Maryland and Washington DC); and Mountain Crest Hospital (serving Colorado). **Listed on:** American Stock Exchange. **Number of employees nationwide:** 510.

METROPOLITAN HOSPITAL
701 West Grace Street, Richmond VA 23220. 804/775-4100. **Contact:** Lisa Sluyk, Human Resource Manager. **Description:** Saint Elizabeth Hospital and Grace Hospital merged in 1978 to form Metropolitan Hospital. This 180-bed facility has three psychiatric units, an emergency room, an occupational medicine unit, an out-patient unit, an intensive care recovery room and a medical surgery unit. Psychiatry and occupational medicine are Metropolitan Hospital's most extensive fields.

MOUNT REGIS CENTER
405 Kimball Avenue, Salem VA 24153. 540/389-4761. **Contact:** Jeanette Webber, Human Resource Director. **Description:** Drug and alcohol treatment facility. The Mount Regis Center has a 25 inpatient bed capacity with day treatment and outpatient services available.

NEWPORT NEWS GENERAL HOSPITAL
5100 Marshall Avenue, Newport News VA 23605. 804/247-7200. **Contact:** Sharon Alexander, Human Resource Manager. **Description:** Established in 1908, the Newport News General Hospital has an 126-bed capacity. The various units include: Urgent Care, Psychiatric, Medical Surgery, Intensive Care and Cardiac Care. **Number of employees at this location:** 275.

NORTHERN VIRGINIA DOCTORS HOSPITAL
601 South Carlin Springs Road, Arlington VA 22204. 703/578-2045. **Contact:** Jerry Clipp, Director, Human Resources. **Description:** An adult medicine, surgery, and psychiatric acute health care facility. **Common positions include:** Licensed Practical Nurse; Pharmacist; Physical Therapist; Radiological Technologist; Registered Nurse; Respiratory Therapist. **Educational backgrounds include:** Nursing. **Benefits:** 401K; Daycare Assistance; Dental Insurance; Disability Coverage; Employee Discounts; Life Insurance; Medical Insurance; Profit Sharing; Tuition Assistance. **Corporate headquarters location:** Nashville TN. **Operations at this facility include:** Service. **Listed on:** New York Stock Exchange. **Number of employees at this location:** 500. **Number of employees nationwide:** 30,000.

OWENS & MINOR, INC.
4800 Cox Road, Glen Allen VA 23060. 804/747-9794. **Fax:** 804/273-0232. **Contact:** Richard Dean, Manager, Human Resources. **Description:** A wholesale distributor of national branded medical, surgical, and nontraditional supplies. The distribution centers of Owens & Minor serve hospitals, integrated health care systems, primary care facilities, and group purchasing organizations throughout the United States. The company also helps customer control health care costs and improve inventory management

through services in asset management, logistics, and electronic data interchange. **Common positions include:** Accountant/Auditor; Attorney; Budget Analyst; Computer Operator; Computer Programmer; Credit Manager; Customer Service Representative; Employment Interviewer; Financial Manager; Graphic Artist; Human Resources Specialist; Industrial Engineer; Management Analyst/Consultant; Management Trainee; Manufacturer's/Wholesaler's Sales Rep.; Operations Research Analyst; Payroll Clerk; Purchasing Agent and Manager; Receptionist; Typist/Word Processor. **Educational backgrounds include:** Accounting; Business Administration; Communications; Computer Science; Finance; Marketing. **Benefits:** Daycare Assistance; Dental Insurance; Disability Coverage; Employee Discounts; Life Insurance; Medical Insurance; Pension Plan; Savings Plan; Stock Option; Tuition Assistance. **Special Programs:** Internships. **Corporate headquarters location:** This Location. **Other U.S. locations:** AL; AZ; CA; FL; GA; IA; LA; MD; MI; NC; NE; NJ; OH; OR; TX. **Operations at this facility include:** Manufacturing; Regional Headquarters. **Listed on:** New York Stock Exchange. **Number of employees at this location:** 2,790.

PHP HEALTHCARE CORPORATION
11440 Commerce Park Drive, Reston VA 22091. 703/758-3600. **Contact:** Karen Bess, Human Resource Manager. **Description:** A managed care solutions company. PHP Healthcare delivers health care through physician practice management as an essential element of the company's Integrated Systems of Care (ISOC). An integrated system of care organizes and manages a network of physicians, hospitals, and other providers; manages the individual and group practices of physicians who participate in the ISOC network; operates the ISOC system through the use of managed care technologies, including information systems, to coordinate and integrate the services, outcomes, and financial result; and enters into contracts with various third party payers, such as HMOs, insurers, or employee health benefit plans. PHP Healthcare is the dominant provider of primary health care services to the Department of Defense and manages health care programs for a number of state governments. **Corporate headquarters location:** This Location. **Listed on:** New York Stock Exchange. **Number of employees nationwide:** 2,900.

PIEDMONT GERIATRIC HOSPITAL
Highways 360/460, Burkeville VA 23922. 804/767-4449. **Fax:** 804/767-4947. **Contact:** Caroline Williams, Employment Representative. **Description:** Provides inpatient treatment to mentally ill elderly. **Common positions include:** Human Service Worker; Licensed Practical Nurse; Medical Records Technician; Occupational Therapist; Physical Therapist; Physician; Psychologist; Recreational Therapist; Registered Nurse; Social Worker. **Educational backgrounds include:** Nursing. **Benefits:** Dental Insurance; Disability Coverage; Employee Discounts; Life Insurance; Medical Insurance; Pension Plan; Savings Plan; Tuition Assistance. **Special Programs:** Internships. **Corporate headquarters location:** Richmond VA. **Parent company:** Department of Mental Health. **Operations at this facility include:** Administration; Research and Development; Service. **Number of employees at this location:** 450.

PORTSMOUTH GENERAL HOSPITAL
850 Crawford Parkway, Portsmouth VA 23704. 804/398-4000. **Contact:** Theresa Parker, Human Resource Manager. **Description:** An 184-bed hospital that specializes in rehabilitation, dialysis, ophthalmology, gynecology, and urology. Tidewater Health Care is the parent company of Portsmouth General Hospital. **Number of employees at this location:** 800. **Parent company:** Tidewater Health Care.

POTOMAC HOSPITAL
2300 Opitz Blvd., Woodbridge VA 22191. 703/670-1313. **Contact:** Human Resources. **Description:** An 153-bed non-profit hospital. Potomac Hospital

offers the following Clinical Services: 24-hour Emergency Room, Critical Care, Progressive Care Unit, Maternal & Infant Care, Neonatology, LDRs, Pediatrics, Lamaze/Expectant Parent Classes, Operating Room, Amulatory Care Surgery, Post Anesthesia Care Unit, Surgery, Medicine/Oncology, Hospice Care, Mental Health-Adult/Adolescent, Cardiology Services, Physical Medicine and Rehabilitation Services, Radiation Oncology, Respiratory Services, Radiology/Angiography, Ultrasound, Nuclear Medicine, CT Scanner, MRI, Laboratory, Occupational Therapy and Inpatient/Retail Pharmacy Service. The hospital offers the following benefits: Health Insurance, Life Insurance, Dental Insurance, Disability Programs, Retirement Program, Paid Days Off, Tuition Assistance, Credit Union, Free Parking, Tax deferred annuity program and Cafeteria/Pharmacy Discount.

PRINCE WILLIAM HOSPITAL
8700 Sudley Road, Manassas VA 22110. 703/369-8000. **Contact:** Deborah Hagwood, Human Resource Manager. **Description:** Established in 1964, Prince William Hospital is a non-profit community hospital. This facility features a Birthing Center, Pediatric Unit, Center for Psychiatric Treatment, Oncology and a Critical Care Unit. The hospital owns a nursing home that is also located in Manassas, VA. **Number of employees at this location:** 900.

PULASKI COMMUNITY HOSPITAL
P.O. Box 759, Pulaski VA 24301. 703/980-6822. **Contact:** Katie Kirk, Human Resource Manager. **Description:** An acute care facility established in 1973. Pulaski Community Hospital has 153 licensed beds. The hospital has various services and units among them are: home health, cardiac rehabilitation, Family Birthing Center, Intensive Care Unit, Cardiac Care Unit, Progressive Care Unit, oncology, Emergency Center, physical therapy, orthopedic care and they are presently constructing an Outpatient Cancer Treatment Center. Pulaski Community Hospital is affiliated with the Columbia Health Care system in Nashville, Tennessee. **Number of employees at this location:** 400.

RADFORD COMMUNITY HOSPITAL
700 Randolph Street, Radford VA 24141. 703/731-2000. **Contact:** Deb Hedrick, Human Resources. **Description:** An acute care facility with 175 licensed beds. Radford Community hospital offers the following community services: Lifeline, a personal emergency response system; Meals on Wheels; Viva Club, health care club for people 55 and older; and Home Health Plus, a home health agency that provides nursing and other services in the home. The hospital also offers critical care, dietary services, emergency care, emergency medial services, extended care, endoscopic services, intravenous therapy, neurology, obstetrics, pediatric care, patient education, patient financial services, physical therapy, progressive care, radiology, respiratory care services, same day surgery and a Sleep Disorder Center.

RAPPAHANNOCK GENERAL HOSPITAL
P.O. Box 1449, Kilmarnock VA 22482. 804/435-8000. **Contact:** Emmerson Gravatt, Human Resource Manager. **Description:** Established around 1977, this acute care community-owned hospital is a 76-bed facility. Located in the Northern neck of Virginia on Chesapeake Bay, Rappahannock General Hospital offers an array of services which include: 24-hour Emergency, stationary MRI, Rappahannock Home Health Agency, Physical Therapy, Maternity Center, Diagnostic X-Ray, Mammography, Ultrasonography and they are in the process of building a new Oncology Center. **Number of employees at this location:** 425.

RETREAT HOSPITAL
2621 Grove Avenue, Richmond VA 23220. 804/254-5100. **Contact:** Debbie Slayden, Resource Manager Director. **Description:** General acute care facility with 230 licensed beds. Retreat Hospital offers the following units and services: Cardiac, Endoscopy, Cardiac/Pulmonary Rehabilitation, Physical

Therapy, Occupational Therapy, Home Health and a 24-hour Emergency Room. **Number of employees at this location:** 450.

RICHMOND MEMORIAL HOSPITAL
P.O. Box 26783, Richmond VA 23261. 804/254-6000. **Contact:** Don Anderson, Human Resource Manager. **Description:** A hospital.

RIVERSIDE HEALTH SYSTEM
606 Denbigh Boulevard, Suite 601, Newport News VA 23608. **Contact:** Larry Boyles, Human Resource Manager. **Description:** Integrated health care provider which encompasses hospitals, nursing homes, home health and wellness fitness centers. **Number of employees at this location:** 20.

ROCKINGHAM MEMORIAL HOSPITAL
235 Cantrell Avenue, Harrisonburg VA 22801. 703/433-4106. **Fax:** 703/564-5446. **Contact:** Diane R. Mullins, Recruitment/Employment Manager. **Description:** A 330-bed, non-profit community hospital located in the Shenandoah Valley. **Common positions include:** Accountant/Auditor; Clerical Supervisor; Computer Programmer; Computer Systems Analyst; Customer Service Representative; Dentist; EEG Technologist; EKG Technician; Electrician; Financial Analyst; Human Resources Specialist; Librarian; Licensed Practical Nurse; Mechanical Engineer; Medical Records Technician; Nuclear Medicine Technologist; Occupational Therapist; Pharmacist; Physical Therapist; Physician; Purchasing Agent and Manager; Recreational Therapist; Registered Nurse; Respiratory Therapist; Restaurant/Food Service Manager; Social Worker; Surgical Technician. **Educational backgrounds include:** Accounting; Business Administration; Engineering; Finance; Marketing. **Benefits:** Dental Insurance; Disability Coverage; Employee Discounts; Life Insurance; Medical Insurance; Pension Plan; Savings Plan; Tuition Assistance. **Corporate headquarters location:** This Location. **Operations at this facility include:** Service. **Number of employees at this location:** 1,500.

ST. JOSEPH HOSPITAL
P.O. Box 327, Parkersburg WV 26102-0327. 304/424-4793. **Fax:** 304/424-4648. **Contact:** Anthony Green, Manager of Employment & Compensation. **Description:** A hospital. **Common positions include:** Biomedical Engineer; Dietician/Nutritionist; EEG Technologist; EKG Technician; Electrical/Electronics Engineer; Emergency Medical Technician; Food Scientist/Technologist; Health Services Manager; Licensed Practical Nurse; Medical Records Technician; Nuclear Medicine Technologist; Occupational Therapist; Pharmacist; Physical Therapist; Radiological Technologist; Registered Nurse; Respiratory Therapist; Surgical Technician. **Educational backgrounds include:** Nursing. **Benefits:** Dental Insurance; Disability Coverage; Employee Discounts; Life Insurance; Medical Insurance; Pension Plan; Savings Plan; Tuition Assistance. **Corporate headquarters location:** This Location. **Operations at this facility include:** Administration. **Listed on:** Privately held. **Number of employees at this location:** 1,120.

SAINT MARY'S HOSPITAL
P.O. Box 620, Norton VA 24273. 703/679-9100. **Contact:** Kathleen Resnick, Human Resource Manager. **Description:** A health care facility.

ST. MARY'S HOSPITAL
5801 Bremo Road, Richmond VA 23226. 804/285-2011. **Contact:** Human Resources. **Description:** A hospital. **NOTE:** For employment information, contact the Human Resources Department at 804/342-1650. **Number of employees at this location:** 1,723.

SENTARA HAMPTON GENERAL HOSPITAL
3120 Victoria Boulevard, Hampton VA 23661. 804/727-7000. **Contact:** Joanne Wilton, Human Resource Manager. **Description:** Acute care facility

that houses 369 beds. Sentara Hampton General Hospital offers a same day surgery wing, an outpatient wing and a skilled nursing facility wing.

SENTARA HEALTH SYSTEM
6015 Poplar Hall Drive, Norfolk VA 23502. 804/455-7150. **Contact:** Robert Pindall, Human Resource Manager. **Description:** Established in 1888, this non-profit regional health management organization is directed by 15 community leaders who serve on a volunteer basis as the Board of Directors. The Sentara Health System has more than 50 care giving sites which encompass four hospitals, nine skilled nursing and assisted living centers, 23 health care centers, an integrated outpatient health care campus, home health care service, ground and air medical transport services, mobile diagnostic vans, fitness facility and community health education programs. Presently there are more than 213,000 people covered by Sentara. The system is comprised of a regional tertiary hospital and three acute care hospitals containing a total of 1,421 beds. They have the region's only air ambulance, Level 1 trauma center and transplant program. Among the services offered by Sentara are: a health and fitness center, outpatient diagnostic testing and surgical facilities, six nursing centers and three assisted-living centers, mobile meals for the elderly, an adult day health care program, an Alzheimer's center, a mobile diagnostic and mammography services and a women's health information center which provides resources on health-related issues affecting women.

SENTARA LEIGH HOSPITAL
830 Kempsville, Norfolk VA 23502. 804/666-6000. **Contact:** Human Resources Department. **Description:** A hospital.

SENTARA NORFOLK GENERAL HOSPITAL
600 Gresham Drive, Norfolk VA 23507. 804/628-3000. **Contact:** Joyce Overton, Human Resources. **Description:** This 644-bed tertiary care facility is the leader in bringing new services, techniques, and equipment to southeastern Virginia and northeastern North Carolina. Sentara Norfolk General Hospital is the nation's first in vitro birth and is known for its world-renowned expertise in high-risk pregnancy. The hospital has the region's first and highest rated Shock Trauma Center. It is home to the region's only comprehensive Cancer Institute, offering research, diagnosis, surgery, chemotherapy, and radiation therapy. It houses the first Burn Center in the region. Sentara Norfolk General Hospital has an international reputation in reconstructive and plastic surgery. Among other services, the hospital is home to Nightingale, the region's only helicopter ambulance service, which transports critically ill patients throughout southeastern Virginia and northeastern North Carolina. **Number of employees at this location:** 3,300+.

SHELTERING ARMS
PHYSICAL REHABILITATION HOSPITAL
1311 Palmyra Avenue, Richmond VA 23227. 804/342-4350. **Fax:** 804/342-4310. **Contact:** Human Resources Department. **Description:** A nonprofit organization providing comprehensive services to those challenged with physical and cognitive disabilities. **Common positions include:** Licensed Practical Nurse; Occupational Therapist; Physical Therapist; Psychologist; Recreational Therapist; Registered Nurse; Social Worker; Speech-Language Pathologist. **Benefits:** 403B; Dental Insurance; Disability Coverage; Employee Discounts; Life Insurance; Medical Insurance; Pension Plan; Tuition Assistance. **Corporate headquarters location:** This Location. **Operations at this facility include:** Administration. **Number of employees at this location:** 350.

SOUTHAMPTON MEMORIAL HOSPITAL
100 Fairview Drive, Franklin VA 23851. 804/569-6390. **Contact:** Paul Slagenweit, Human Resource Manager. **Description:** This is a hospital.

SOUTHSIDE COMMUNITY HOSPITAL
800 Oak Street, Farmville VA 23901. 804/392-8811. **Contact:** Judy Black, Director of Human Resources. **Description:** Established in 1927, this locally governed community hospital strives to provide quality and affordable health care to all residents of Southside Virginia regardless of their ability to pay. Joining the Medical College of Virginia's Massey Cancer Center, the hospital now offers an Oncology Clinic to area cancer patients. The level III trauma center Allows the Emergency Department to handle the most critical cases. The newly renovated Intensive Care Unit is designed to patients required intensive nursing care and complex medical equipment. Southside Community Hospital offers the following services: dialysis, pharmacy, respiratory therapy, Home Health, Lifeline (personal emergency response system), social services, Anatomical & Clinical Laboratory, radiology, nuclear medicine, Cardiac Diagnostic Unit, surgery, out-patient surgery, anesthesiology, Mobile Lithostar System (state-of-the-art technology to remove kidney stones), physical therapy, patient teaching, speech therapy, pain management, obstetrics, nursery, pediatrics, Residency Program, organ donation, Mobile Health Fair Program (free medical screening to area businesses and their employees) and a speakers bureau.

SOUTHSIDE REGIONAL MEDICAL CENTER
801 South Adams, Petersburg VA 23803. 804/862-5000. **Contact:** Elke Jones, Employment Management. **Description:** This is a health care facility.

SOUTHWESTERN VIRGINIA MENTAL HEALTH INSTITUTE
502 East Main Street, Marion VA 24354. 540/783-1204. **Fax:** 540/783-9712. **Contact:** Human Resource Office. **Description:** A 266-bed, JCAHO-accredited state psychiatric hospital. Southwestern Virginia Mental Health Institute employs 500 health care professionals, paraprofessionals, and support staff. **Common positions include:** Occupational Therapist; Psychologist; Registered Nurse; Social Worker. **Educational backgrounds include:** Health Care. **Benefits:** Dental Insurance; Life Insurance; Medical Insurance; Pension Plan; Savings Plan. **Corporate headquarters location:** Richmond VA. **Parent company:** Virginia Department of Mental Health. **Number of employees at this location:** 500.

STERILE CONCEPTS, INC.
5100 Commerce Road, Richmond VA 22323-4223. 804/275-0592. **Fax:** 804/271-3761. **Contact:** Elissa M. Ecker, Director of Human Resources. **Description:** Sterile Concepts, Inc. is the second largest maker of customized clinical and surgical procedure trays in the U.S. A customized procedure tray is a kit that contains sterile, disposable items used in a surgical or other medical procedure. The company assembles, packages and sterilizes ready-to-use custom procedure trays for hospitals, outpatient surgery centers and medical clinics. Sterile Concepts sells custom procedure trays to about 1,300 individual accounts. Customers consist of mainly hospitals and outpatient surgery centers. The company's custom procedure trays are designed to meet individual customer needs. The company can produce simple basin sets, or even complex trays for open heart surgery. All of the items included in the company's trays are disposable. Typical items include drapes and gowns, endoscopic and other instruments such as sutures, needles, gloves, tubing, sponges, towels and gauze. **Common positions include:** Accountant/Auditor; Computer Programmer; Computer Systems Analyst; Human Resources Specialist. **Educational backgrounds include:** Accounting; Business Administration; Computer Science. **Benefits:** Dental Insurance; Disability Coverage; Life Insurance; Medical Insurance; Pension Plan; Tuition Assistance. **Corporate headquarters location:** This Location. **Operations at this facility include:** Administration; Manufacturing; Sales; Service. **Listed on:** New York Stock Exchange. **Number of employees at this location:** 650.

VALUEMARK WEST END BEHAVIORAL HEALTH CARE SYSTEM
12800 West Creek Parkway, Richmond VA 23238. 804/784-2200. **Contact:** Ellen Melser, Human Resource Manager. **Description:** Formerly known as Psychiatric Institute Richmond, ValueMark West End Behavioral Health Care System was founded in 1964. This is an acute care psychiatric facility and houses 84 beds that service children, adolescents, adults and geriatrics. They offer residence for children and adolescents.

MARY WASHINGTON HOSPITAL
1991 Sam Perry Boulevard, Fredricksburg VA 22401. 703/899-1100. **Contact:** Human Resources. **Description:** An acute care hospital established in 1899. Mary Washington Hospital is a 308-bed facility. They offer such services as Neurology and Cardiology. Mary Washington Hospital also has various centers, such as a nursing home, Assisted Living Center, Retirement Center, Free-standing Psychiatric Hospital, Same-Day Surgery Center and an Urgent Care Center throughout the Fredricksburg region to aide and support the community throughout their life. This hospital has strived to modernize the old community health care technique by adding such facilities. Mary Washington Hospital is an entity of MWH MediCorp.

Note: *Because addresses and telephone numbers of smaller companies change rapidly, we recommend you call each company to verify the information below before inquiring about job opportunities. Mass mailings are not recommended.*

Additional small employers:

MEDICAL EQUIPMENT AND SUPPLIES WHOLESALE

KCI Concepts
1453 Miller Store Rd, Ste 100, Virginia Beach VA 23455-3324. 804/464-2286.

Owens And Minor Inc.
PO Box 27626, Richmond VA 23261-7626. 804/747-9794.

Gambro Co.
5000 Chestnut Ave, Newport News VA 23605-2108. 804/247-0105.

Biomedical Equipment Rental & Sales Inc.
3923 Deep Rock Rd, Richmond VA 23233-1416. 804/270-7090.

Colonial Pharmacy
8907 Three Chopt Rd, Richmond VA 23229-4614. 804/288-1882.

Hologic Inc.
5905 Sir Cambridge Way, Alexandria VA 22315-4722. 703/922-8234.

Medi Home Care
RR 1, Palestine WV 26160-9801. 304/275-0913.

Medsurg Industries
3007 Pacific Ave, Virginia Beach VA 23451-3026. 804/428-2011.

Patterson Dental Company
2852 E Parham Rd, Richmond VA 23228-2918. 804/262-4070.

AJ Buck & Son Inc.
7516 Whitepine Rd, Richmond VA 23237-2217. 804/743-9141.

DOCTORS' OFFICES AND CLINICS

Capitalcare Inc.
1921 Gallows Rd, Ste 900, Vienna VA 22182-3900. 703/761-5400.

Cigna Healthcare
4050 Innslake Dr, Ste 300, Glen Allen VA 23060-3327. 804/273-1100.

Peninsula Health Care
2220 Edward Holland Dr, Richmond VA 23230-2519. 804/354-3954.

Select Med Of West Virginia
1 Hillcrest Dr E, Charleston WV 25311-1622. 304/346-0611.

OFFICES AND CLINICS OF HEALTH PRACTITIONERS

Braxton County Memorial Hospital
100 Hoylman Dr, Gassaway WV 26624-9321. 304/364-5156.

Health & Rehabilitation Center
313 MacCorkle Ave SW, S Charleston WV 25303-1263. 304/744-2300.

Carilion Community Care
3130 Chaparral Dr, #B-209, Roanoke VA 24018-4369. 540/772-4211.

Visiting Nurse Association Northern VA Inc.
11150 Sunset Hills Rd, Reston VA 22090-5321. 703/709-7820.

NURSING AND PERSONAL CARE FACILITIES

Berger's Home For Adults
416 Richardson St, Danville VA 24540-4323. 804/799-1625.

Caring & Sharing Adult Home
2214 Marshall Ave, Newport News VA 23607-4618. 804/245-7822.

Convalescent Care Inc.
7204 Glen Forest Dr, Ste 101, Richmond VA 23226-3778. 804/285-7600.

Highland House
RR 1, Box 56A, Clifton Forge VA 24422-9711. 540/862-4271.

Accomack County Nursing Home
26181 Parksley Rd, Parksley VA 23421-3723. 804/665-5133.

Amelia Nursing Center
8830 Virginia Street, Amelia Ct House VA 23002-4826. 804/561-5611.

Americare Arlington Nurse
1716 Gihon Rd, Parkersburg WV 26101-9655. 304/485-5511.

Americare Dunbar Nursing & Rehabilitation
501 Caldwell Ln, Dunbar WV 25064-2026. 304/744-4761.

Americare Putnam Nursing & Rehabilitation
300 Seville Rd, Hurricane WV 25526-9206. 304/757-6805.

Annaburg Manor Nursing Home
9201 Maple St, Manassas VA 22110-5134. 703/631-0444.

Ansted Health Care Center
Old Route 60, Ansted WV 25812. 304/658-5271.

Arbors At Fairmont Nursing Center
130 Kaufman Dr, Fairmont WV 26554-2179. 304/363-5633.

Arthur B. Hodges Center
500 Morris St, Charleston WV 25301-1331. 304/345-6560.

Asbury Center At Birdmont
990 Holston Rd, Wytheville VA 24382-4105. 540/228-5595.

Ashland Convalescent Center Inc.
Rt 54 W, Ashland VA 23005. 804/798-3291.

Autumn Care Of Altavista
1317 Lola Ave, Altavista VA 24517-1352. 804/369-6651.

Autumn Care Of Great Bridge
821 Cedar Rd, Chesapeake VA 23320-7025. 804/547-4528.

Autumn Care Of Portsmouth
3610 Winchester Dr, Portsmouth VA 23707-4330. 804/397-0725.

Autumn Care Of Suffolk
2580 Pruden Blvd, Suffolk VA 23434-4229. 804/934-2363.

Avante At Roanoke Health Care
324 King George Ave SW, Roanoke VA 24016-5213. 540/345-8139.

Avante's At Lynchburg
2081 Langhorne Rd, Lynchburg VA 24501-1443. 804/846-8437.

Susan B. Miller Nursing Homes Inc.
118 N Muhlenberg St, Woodstock VA 22664-1462. 540/459-2118.

Barbour County Good Samaritan
RR 3, Box 15C, Belington WV 26250-9422. 304/823-2555.

Bayside Convalescent Center
1 Vantage Dr, Poquoson VA 23662-1400. 804/868-9960.

Bayside Health Care Center
1004 Independence Blvd, Virginia Beach VA 23455-5503. 804/464-4058.

Berkshire Health Care Center
705 Clearview Dr, Vinton VA 24179-3699. 703/982-6691.

Berry Hill Nursing Home
621 Berry Hill Rd, South Boston VA 24592-2299. 804/572-8901.

Beverly Manor Of Portsmouth
900 London Blvd, Portsmouth VA 23704-2236. 804/393-6864.

Blue Ridge Highlands Nursing Home
836 Glendale Rd, Galax VA 24333-2311. 540/236-9991.

Blue Ridge Nursing Center
Commerce St, Stuart VA 24171. 540/694-7161.

Bon Secours Maryview Nursing
4775 Bridge Rd, Suffolk VA 23435-2045. 804/686-0488.

Boone Health Care
Lick Creek Rd, Danville WV 25053. 304/369-0986.

Brandon Oaks
3804 Brandon Ave SW, Roanoke VA 24018. 540/776-2600.

Brent-Lox Hall Nursing Center
1017 George Washington Hwy N, Chesapeake VA 23323-3598. 804/485-5500.

Brian Center Nursing Care Alleghany
Alleghany Regional Hospital Ln, Low Moor

VA 24457. 540/862-3610.

Brightwood Nursing Home
840 Lee Rd, Follansbee WV 26037-1783. 304/527-1100.

Burke Health Care Center
9640 Burke Lake Rd, Burke VA 22015-3022. 703/425-9765.

Burrell Nursing Center
611 McDowell Ave NW, Roanoke VA 24016-1225. 540/224-3800.

Camelot Hall Nursing Home
1945 Roanoke Blvd, Salem VA 24153-6408. 540/345-3894.

Camelot Hall Of Lynchburg
5615 Seminole Ave, Lynchburg VA 24502-2201. 804/239-2657.

Cameron Glen Care Center
1800 Cameron Glen Dr, Reston VA 22090-3312. 703/834-5800.

Canterbury Of Shepherdstown
Rt 45, Shepherdstown WV 25443. 304/876-9422.

Capital City Nursing Home
1301 Virginia St E, Charleston WV 25301-3089. 304/346-5725.

Care Haven Of Sistersville
201 Wood St, Sistersville WV 26175-1523. 304/652-1032.

Cedar Lawn Convalescent Home
600 Waldon Rd NE, Abingdon VA 24210-2328. 540/628-2111.

Cedar Ridge Nursing & Rehabilitation Center
302 Cedar Ridge Rd, Sissonville WV 25320-9502. 304/984-0046.

Cherrydale Healthcare Center
3710 Lee Hwy, Arlington VA 22207-3721. 703/243-7640.

Chesapeake Healthcare
688 Kingsborough Sq, Chesapeake VA 23320-4908. 804/547-9111.

Clarksburg Continuous Care Center
Davisson Run Rd, Clarksburg WV 26301. 304/624-6500.

Coliseum Park Nursing Home
305 Marcella Rd, Hampton VA 23666-2466. 804/827-8953.

Colonial Heights Convalescent Center
831 E Ellerslie Ave, Colonial Hgts VA 23834-1720. 804/526-6851.

Colonnades At Marriott Sr Living
2600 Barracks Rd, Charlottesvle VA 22901-2100. 804/971-1892.

Convalescent Care Inc.
7300 Forest Ave, Richmond VA 23226-3735. 804/288-3152.

Convalescent Care Inc.
905 Cousins Ave, Hopewell VA 23860-6507. 804/748-8794.

Crystal City Nurse & Rehab Center
1785 S Hayes St, Arlington VA 22202-2714. 703/920-5700.

Cumberland Care Center
Rogers, Bluefield WV 24701. 304/325-5448.

Eldercare Gardens
1150 Northwest Dr, Charlottesvle VA 22901-2309. 804/973-7933.

Eldercare Of Farmville
Scott Rd, Farmville VA 23901. 804/392-8806.

Eldercare Of Franklin County
500 Hatcher St, Rocky Mount VA 24151-1255. 540/483-9261.

Eldercare Of Hillsville
222 Fulcher St, Hillsville VA 24343-1633. 540/728-2486.

Elkins Regional Convalescent Center
Beverly Pike, Elkins WV 26241. 304/636-1391.

Evergreene Nursing Center
Rt 33, Stanardsville VA 22973. 804/985-4434.

Fairfax Nursing Center
10701 Main St, Fairfax VA 22030-6995. 703/273-7705.

Fairhaven Rest Home
302 Adams Ave, Huntington WV 25701-1197. 304/522-0032.

Friendship Manor
327 Hershberger Rd Nw, Roanoke VA 24012-1961. 540/265-2100.

GB Kegley Manor
RR 1, Bastian VA 24314-9801. 540/688-4141.

Good Shepherd Nursing Home
159 Edgington Ln, Wheeling WV 26003-1542. 304/242-1093.

Grace Lodge
1503 Grace St, Lynchburg VA 24504-3211. 804/528-0969.

Grant County Nursing Home
27 Early Ave, Petersburg WV 26847-9403. 304/257-4233.

Gretna Health Care Center
Rt 40-W, Gretna VA 24557. 804/656-1206.

Guggenheimer Nursing Home
1902 Grace St, Lynchburg VA 24504-3524. 804/947-5100.

Hairston Home For Adults
601 Armstead Ave, Martinsville VA 24112-2598. 540/638-5121.

Hampshire Health Care Center
Sunrise Blvd, Romney WV 26757. 304/822-7527.

Harper Home For Aged
2156 N Main St, Danville VA 24540-2729. 804/793-9118.

Heart & Soul Home For Adults
1147 27th St, Newport News VA 23607-4231. 804/245-0011.

Heartland Of Beckley
300 Dry Hill Rd, Beckley WV 25801-2602. 304/256-1650.

Heartland Of Charleston
3819 Chesterfield Ave, Charleston WV 25304-2647. 304/925-4771.

Heartland Of Clarksburg
100 Parkway Dr, Clarksburg WV 26301-4357. 304/624-6401.

Heartland Of Martinsburg
210 Clover St, Martinsburg WV 25401-3804. 304/263-8921.

Heartland Of Preston County
300 Miller Rd, Kingwood WV 26537-1335. 304/329-3195.

Heartland Of Rainelle
606 Pennsylvania Ave, Rainelle WV 25962-1522. 304/438-6127.

Henrico County Of
Elizabeth Adam Crump Manor Nur, Glen Allen VA 23060. 804/672-8725.

Heritage Hall
205 Houston St, Lexington VA 24450-2415. 540/464-8181.

Heritage Hall
5580 Daniel Smith Rd, Virginia Beach VA 23462-1104. 804/499-7029.

Heritage Hall
633 Cook Av, Brookneal VA 24528. 804/376-3774.

Heritage Hall
College Road, Wise VA 24293. 540/328-2721.

Heritage Hall
9468 Hospital Ave, Nassawadox VA 23413-1818. 804/442-5600.

Heritage Hall
121 Ben Bolt Ave, Tazewell VA 24651-9799. 540/988-2515.

Heritage Hall
3610 S Main St, Blacksburg VA 24060-7082. 540/951-7000.

Heritage Hall
800 S Main St, Blackstone VA 23824-2608. 804/292-5301.

Heritage Hall
2045 Valley View Dr E, Big Stone Gap VA 24219-3319. 540/523-3000.

Heritage Hall
122 Morven Park Rd, Leesburg VA 22075. 703/777-8700.

Hidden Valley Health Care
422 23rd St, Oak Hill WV 25901-2830. 304/465-1903.

Highland Manor
Hanks St, Dublin VA 24084. 540/674-4193.

Hillhaven Nansemond Rehab
200 W Constance Rd, Suffolk VA 23434-4413. 804/539-8744.

Hilton Plaza Inc.
311 Main St, Newport News VA 23601-3809. 804/596-6010.

Holbrook Nursing Home Inc.
346 S Florida St, Buckhannon WV 26201-2452. 304/472-3280.

Holly Manor Nursing Home
Cobb, Farmville VA 23901. 804/392-6106.

Jefferson A. Marriott Senior Living
900 N Taylor St, Arlington VA 22203-1858. 703/351-0011.

Kings Grant Retirement Community
1 Kings Way Rd, Martinsville VA 24112-6600. 540/634-1000.

Lafayette Villa Health Care
3900 Llewellyn Ave, Norfolk VA 23504-1298. 804/625-5363.

Laurel Meadows Home
RR 1, Laurel Fork VA 24352-9801. 540/398-2117.

Leewood Nursing Home
7120 Braddock Rd, Annandale VA 22003-6086. 703/256-9770.

Libbie Rehabilitation Center
1901 Libbie Ave, Richmond VA 23226-1808. 804/282-9767.

Liberty House Nursing
RR 60 E, Clifton Forge VA 24422. 540/862-5791.

Life Care Center Of New Market
315 East Lee Highway, New Market VA 22844-3103. 540/740-8041.

Little Sisters Of The Poor
1503 Michael Rd, Richmond VA 23229-4822. 804/288-6245.

Logan Park Nursing Home
1000 W Park Ave, Logan WV 25601-3155. 304/752-8723.

Lovingston Health Care Center
Route 29, Lovingston VA 22949. 804/263-4823.

Lynn Shores Manor
340 Lynn Shores Dr, Virginia Beach VA 23452-2400. 804/340-6611.

Malin Health Care Center
100 Edgemont Rd, Wytheville VA 24382-4337. 540/228-7380.

Manor Care Imperial
1719 Bellevue Ave, Richmond VA 23227-3901. 804/262-7364.

Manor Care Nurse & Rehab Centers
12475 Lee Jackson

Memorial Hwy, Fairfax VA 22033-2803. 703/352-7172.

Manor Care Nurse & Rehab Centers
550 S Carlin Springs Rd, Arlington VA 22204-1022. 703/379-7200.

Mariner Health Care Huntington
1720 17th St, Huntington WV 25701-4235. 304/529-6031.

Marmet Health Care Center
1 Sutphin Dr, Marmet WV 25315-1999. 304/949-1580.

Meadowbrook Acres Nursing Center
Meadowbrook Plaza, Charleston WV 25311. 304/344-4268.

Meadowview Manor Health Care Center
Crestview Terrace, Bridgeport WV 26330. 304/842-7101.

Medical Care Center
2200 Landover Place, Lynchburg VA 24501-2199. 804/846-4626.

Medical Facilities Of America
2917 Penn Forest Blvd, Ste 30, Roanoke VA 24018-4374. 540/989-3618.

Miletree Health Care Center
825 Summit St, Spencer WV 25276-1099. 304/927-1007.

Mingo Manor Nursing Home
100 Hillcrest Dr, Williamson WV 25661-3948. 304/235-7005.

Monpointe Continuing Care Center
995 Maple Dr, Morgantown WV 26505-2812. 304/285-2720.

Montview Nursing Home
30 Montview Dr, Luray VA 22835-1673. 540/743-4571.

Morgan Manor Nurse & Rehab Center
1379 Van Voorhis Rd, Morgantown WV 26505-2499. 304/599-9480.

Morris Memorial Convalescent & Nurse
Milton Nitro, Milton WV 25541. 304/755-0427.

Mountain View Nursing Home Inc.
HCR 5, Box 186, Aroda VA 22709-9709. 540/948-6831.

Nella's Nursing Home Inc.
301 Central St, Elkins WV 26241-3199. 304/636-2033.

New Horizons Hospice
804 Oak St, Farmville VA 23901-1122. 804/392-3042.

New Martinsville Health Care Center
225 Russell Ave, N Martinsville WV 26155-1572. 304/455-2600.

Nicholas County Health Care Center
18 4th St, Richwood WV 26261-1203. 304/846-2668.

Northampton Convalescent Center
1028 Toppings Ln, Hampton VA 23666-1922. 804/826-4922.

Oak Hill Health Care Center
512 Houston St, Staunton VA 24401-3525. 540/886-2335.

Oak Meadow Nursing Center
1510 Collingwood Rd, Alexandria VA 22308-1698. 703/765-6107.

Oak Spr Warrenton Comprehensive
Hastings Ln, Warrenton VA 22186. 540/347-4770.

Onika House
1229 28th St, Newport News VA 23607-4215. 804/244-2538.

Orange County Nursing Home
120 Dogwood Ln, Orange VA 22960-1058. 540/672-2611.

Our Lady Of Peace
751 Hillsdale Dr, Charlottesvle VA 22901-3300. 804/973-1155.

Parkview Healthcare Center
1600 27th St, Parkersburg WV 26101-2815. 304/485-6476.

Pavilion At Williamsburg
5700 Williamsburg Landing Dr, Williamsburg VA 23185-3775. 804/253-0303.

Pendleton Nursing Home
Rt 33 E, Franklin WV 26807. 304/358-2322.

Pine View Continuous Care
400 McKinley Ave, Harrisville WV 26362-1150. 304/643-2712.

Piney Forest Health Care Center
450 Piney Forest Rd, Danville VA 24540-4011. 804/799-1565.

Pleasant Valley Nurse Care Center
Sand Hill Rd, Pt Pleasant WV 25550. 304/675-5236.

Presbyterian Manor
101 13th St, Huntington WV 25701-1654. 304/525-7622.

Princeton Health Care Center
315 Courthouse Rd, Princeton WV 24740-2421. 304/487-3458.

Raleigh Court Health Care Center
1527 Grandin Road Southwest, Roanoke VA 24015-2300. 540/342-9525.

Raleigh Nursing & Rehab Center
Rt 19 & 4H Lake Rd, Daniels WV 25832-9709. 304/763-3051.

Ravenswood Village Health Center
200 S Ritchie Ave, Ravenswood WV 26164-1721. 304/273-9385.

Regency Health Care Center
112 N Constitution Dr, Grafton VA 23692-2792. 804/890-0675.

Regency Manor
1776 Cambridge Dr, Richmond VA 23233-3203. 804/740-6174.

Reverside Convalescent Centers
414 Algonquin Rd, Hampton VA 23661-1698. 804/722-9881.

Richardson Adult Care
419 W 28th St, Norfolk VA 23508-3303. 804/622-4363.

Richfield Nursing Center
3615 W Main St, Salem VA 24153-1961. 540/380-4500.

Richmond Nursing Home
1900 Cool Ln, Richmond VA 23223-3997. 804/343-6100.

Riverside Convalescent Center West Point
2960 Chelsea Rd, West Point VA 23181-9793. 804/843-4323.

Riverside Convalescent Centers
200 Lou Mac Court, Newport News VA 23602-6817. 804/244-7008.

Riverside Convalescent Centers
1000 Old Denbigh Blvd, Newport News VA 23602-2078. 804/875-2000.

Roman Eagle Memorial Home
2526 N Main St, Danville VA 24540-2395. 804/836-9510.

Rose Hill Nursing Home Inc.
110 Chalmers Court, Berryville VA 22611-1397. 540/955-9995.

Rosewood Health Care Center
Rose St, #8, Grafton WV 26354-1678. 304/265-0095.

Ryan Nursing Center
Hwy 60 E, Amherst VA 24521. 804/847-6221.

Saint Francis Nursing Center
2 Ridgewood Pky, Newport News VA 23608-1969. 804/886-6500.

Sentara Nursing Center-Hampton
2230 Executive Dr, Hampton VA 23666-2430. 804/826-3100.

Sentara Nursing Centers
4201 Greenwood Dr, Portsmouth VA 23701-3250. 804/488-4400.

Sentara Nursing Centers
776 Oak Grove Rd, Chesapeake VA 23320-3728. 804/547-5156.

Shawnee Springs Nursing Home
380 Millwood Ave, Winchester VA 22601-4498. 540/667-7010.

Shenandoah Manor Adult Care
601 Granville Ave, Clifton Forge VA 24422-1815. 540/862-1614.

Shenandoah Manor Nursing Home
1000 Fairview Ave, Clifton Forge VA 24422-1873. 540/863-4096.

Shenandoah Manor Of Ronceverte
608 Greenbrier Avenue, Ronceverte WV 24970-1208. 304/645-7270.

Shenandoah Nursing Home
803 Westminister Drive, Fishersville VA 22939-9773. 540/949-8665.

Shenandoah Valley Health Care Center
3737 Catalpa Ave, Buena Vista VA 24416-9620. 540/261-7444.

Sleepy Hollow Manor Nurse
6700 Columbia Pike, Annandale VA 22003-3498. 703/256-7000.

Snyder Nursing Home
11 N Broad St, Salem VA 24153-3799. 540/389-6305.

South Roanoke Nursing Home
3823 Franklin Rd Sw, Roanoke VA 24014-3043. 540/344-4325.

Stanleytown Health Care Center
Rt 57 A, Stanleytown VA 24168. 540/629-1772.

Staunton Manor Nurse Home Inc.
1734 Churchville Ave, Staunton VA 24401-1724. 540/885-3611.

Summers Continuous Care Center
John Cook Rd, Hinton WV 25951. 304/466-0332.

Sundale Nursing Home
800 J D Anderson Dr, Morgantown WV 26505-3474. 304/599-0497.

The Madison
445 Van Voorhis Rd, Morgantown WV 26505. 304/598-2900.

The Maples
1600 Bland St, Bluefield WV 24701-3763. 304/327-2485.

The Newport
11141 Warwick Blvd, Newport News VA 23601-2347. 804/595-3733.

The Pines Convalescent Center
1235 S Mount Vernon Ave, Williamsburg VA 23185-2835. 804/229-4121.

The Woodview
103 Rosehill Dr, South Boston VA 24592-4843. 804/572-4906.

Thornton Hall
827 Norview Ave,

Norfolk VA 23509-1540. 804/853-6281.

Twin Oaks Convalescent Home
406 Oak Ln, South Boston VA 24592-1696. 804/572-2925.

VA Beach Healthcare & Rehab Center
1801 Camelot Dr, Virginia Beach VA 23454-2401. 804/481-3500.

Valley Health Care Center
940 W Lee Hwy, Chilhowie VA 24319-4615. 540/646-8911.

Valley Health Village
1000 Lincoln Dr, S Charleston WV 25309-2398. 304/768-4400.

Vernon Mount Nursing Center
8111 Tis Well Dr, Alexandria VA 22306-3297. 703/360-4000.

Virginia Health Services
540 Aberthaw Ave, Newport News VA 23601-4103. 804/595-2273.

Waddell Nursing Home
202 Painter St, Galax VA 24333-3800. 540/236-5164.

Warrenton Overlook Care Center
360 Hospital Dr, Warrenton VA 22186-3006. 540/349-1919.

Washington House
5100 Fillmore Ave, Alexandria VA 22311-5035. 703/845-5100.

Waverly Healthcare Center
456 E Main St, Waverly VA 23890. 804/834-3975.

Webster Continuous Care Center
Erbacon Rd, Cowen WV 26206. 304/226-5301.

Weirton Geriatric Center
2525 Pennsylvania Ave, Weirton WV 26062-3634. 304/723-4300.

Westwood Health Care Center
Westwood Medical Prk, Bluefield VA 24605. 703/322-5439.

Windermere At Virginia Beach
1604 Old Donation Pky, Virginia Beach VA 23454-3063. 804/496-3939.

Windsor Health Care
3600 Grove Ave, Richmond VA 23221-2202. 804/353-3881.

Wishing Well
1539 Country Club Rd, Fairmont WV 26554-1306. 304/366-9100.

Woodbine Rehab & Healthcare
2729 King St, Alexandria VA 22302-4008. 703/836-8838.

Woodbridge Nursing Center
14906 Jefferson Davis Hwy, Woodbridge VA 22191-3902. 703/550-9692.

Wyoming Continuous Care Center
Twin Pine Est, New Richmond WV 24867. 304/294-7584.

York Convalescent Center
113 Battle Rd, Yorktown VA 23692-4140. 804/898-1491.

Brookwood Nursing Home
140 Andrew Chapel Rd, Stafford VA 22554-5520. 540/659-4670.

Culpeper Baptist Retirement Community
12425 Village Loop, Culpeper VA 22701-4375. 540/825-2411.

Marion Health Care
401 Guffey St, Fairmont WV 26554-4099. 304/363-2500.

Shenandoah Home
131 E 3rd Ave, Ranson WV 25438-1688. 304/725-3404.

United Hospital-TCC
3 Hospital Plz, Clarksburg WV 26301-9316. 304/624-2782.

Arcadia Nursing Center
PO Box 97, Nelsonia VA 23414-0097. 804/665-5555.

Bedford County Nursing Home
RR 7 Box 70, Bedford VA 24523-9474. 540/586-7658.

Bowling Green Health Care Center
120 Anderson Ave, Bowling Green VA 22427-9401. 804/633-4839.

Brian Center Nurse Care Fincastle
PO Box 559, Fincastle VA 24090-0559. 540/473-2288.

Care Haven Of Point Pleasant
RR 1, Box 326, Point Pleasant WV 25550-9724. 304/675-3005.

Carriage Hill Nursing Home
5040 Plank Rd, Fredericksbrg VA 22407-6647. 540/786-4549.

Carter Hall Nursing Home
PO Box 59, Dryden VA 24243-0059. 703/546-4114.

Cortland Acres Nursing Home
Hc 60 Box 98, Thomas WV 26292-9704. 304/463-4181.

Courtland Health Care Center
23020 Main St, Courtland VA 23837-1133. 804/653-0908.

Davis Medical Center-SNF
PO Box 4030, Petersburg VA 23803-0030. 804/524-7344.

Fox Nursing Home
RR 1, Box 2, Chester WV 26034. 304/387-0101.

Golden Harvest Unit
454 McDowell St, Welch

WV 24801-2029. 304/436-8461.

Goodwyn House
4800 Fillmore Ave, Alexandria VA 22311-5075. 703/578-1000.

Goodwyn House Health Care Unit
3440 S Jefferson St, Falls Church VA 22041. 703/820-1488.

Heritage Hall-Dillwyn
PO Box 580, Dillwyn VA 23936-0580. 804/983-2058.

Hillcrest Nursing Home
110 Lauck Dr, Winchester VA 22603-4218. 540/667-7830.

Lynchburg Nursing Home
701 Hollins St, Lynchburg VA 24504-2244. 804/847-1493.

Newport News Baptist Retirement Community
955 Harpersville Rd, Newport News VA 23601-1045. 804/599-4376.

Pocahontas Continuous Care Center
RR 1, Box 500, Marlinton WV 24954-9754. 304/799-7375.

Rappahannock Westminster
10 Lancaster Dr, Irvington VA 22480-9740. 804/438-4000.

Riverside Convalescent Center
200 Lumar Rd, Smithfield VA 23430-1521. 804/357-3282.

Riverside Convalescent Center Matthews
Rt 14 & Hwy 611, Mathews VA 23109. 804/725-9443.

Riverside Convalescent Center Saluda
PO Box 303, Saluda VA 23149-0303. 804/758-2363.

Riverside Nursing Home
6500 MacCorkle Ave, Saint Albans WV 25177-2398. 304/768-0002.

Riverview Nursing Home
120 Virginia Ave, Rich Creek VA 24147-9656. 540/726-2328.

Roanoke City Nursing Home
4365 Coyner Springs Rd, Roanoke VA 24012-8821. 703/977-1018.

Skyline Terrace Convalescent Home
US Rt 11 S & Lakeview Rd, Woodstock VA 22664-0191. 540/459-3738.

Springs Nursing Center
PO Box I, Hot Springs VA 24445-1003. 540/839-2299.

Village Nursing Center
Rte 15, Fork Union VA 23055. 804/842-2916.

Wayne Continuous Care Center
RR 1 Box 1372, Wayne WV 25570-9724. 304/697-7007.

Avante At Harrisonburg
94 South Ave, Harrisonburg VA 22801-2327. 540/433-2791.

Adams Christian Convalescent Center
200 Weaver Ave, Emporia VA 23847-1230. 804/634-6581.

Birmingham Green Health Care Center
8605 Centreville Rd, Manassas VA 22110-5265. 703/257-0935.

Hodges Continuous Care Center
600 Medical Park, Wheeling WV 26003-7601. 304/243-3800.

Bridgewater Retirement Community
302 N 2nd St, Bridgewater VA 22812-1712. 540/828-2531.

Culpeper Health Care Center
602 Madison Rd, Culpeper VA 22701-3324. 540/825-2884.

District Home
1400 District Home Dr, Waynesboro VA 22980-9304. 540/942-5237.

Glenwood Park Retirement Village
RR 1 Box 464, Princeton WV 24740-9244. 304/425-8128.

Heartland Of Keyser
135 Southern Dr, Keyser WV 26726-2010. 304/788-3415.

Heritage Hall-Grundy
RR 5 Box 104, Grundy VA 24614-9504. 540/935-8144.

Heritage Hall-King George
PO Box 495, King George VA 22485-0495. 540/775-4000.

Hilltop Nursing & Rehab Center
PO Box 125, Hilltop WV 25855-0125. 304/469-2966.

IHS Of West Virginia At Charlestown
1 Jeffersonian Mnr, Charlestown WV 25414-9346. 304/725-6575.

Lakin Hospital-SNF
1 Bateman Cir, West Columbia WV 25287-9784. 304/675-0860.

Lancashire Nursing Home
PO Box 1509, Kilmarnock VA 22482-1509. 804/435-1684.

Martinsville Convalescent Center
PO Box 3191, Martinsville VA 24115-3191. 540/632-7146.

Nella's Nursing Home
PO Box 1639, Elkins WV 26241-1639. 304/636-1008.

Oak Lea Nursing Home
1475 Virginia Ave, Harrisonburg VA 22801-2433. 540/564-3500.

Pinecrest Hospital-ICF
105 S Eisenhower Dr, Beckley WV 25801-4999. 304/256-6600.

St. Francis Nursing Center
4 Ridgewood Pky,

Newport News VA 23608-1969. 804/886-6500.

Sunnyside Presbyterian Home
100 Sunnyside Dr, Ste A, Harrisonburg VA 22801-8438. 540/568-8200.

Virginia Veteran Care Center
4550 Shenandoah Ave NW, Roanoke VA 24017-4749. 703/982-2860.

Walnut Hill Convalescent Center
287 E South Blvd, Petersburg VA 23805-2765. 804/733-1190.

Walter Reed Convalescent Center
Route 17 & Meredith Dr, Gloucester VA 23061. 804/693-6503.

Warsaw Health Care Center
PO Box 39, Warsaw VA 22572-0039. 804/333-3616.

Westminister Lk Rdg Retirement
12191 Clipper Dr, Woodbridge VA 22192-2237. 703/643-9711.

Woodmont Health Care Center
PO Box 419, Fredericksbrg VA 22404-0419. 540/371-9414.

Worthington Manor
36th & Core Rd, Parkersburg WV 26104-4010. 304/485-7447.

Blue Ridge Rehab Center
PO Box 4904, Martinsville VA 24115-4904. 540/638-8701.

Hancock Geriatric Treatment Center
PO Box 8791, Williamsburg VA 23187-8791. 804/253-5326.

Dignity Hospice
PO Box 4455, Chapmanville WV 25508. 304/855-7104.

Familycare Home Care & Hospice
610 Laurel St, Culpeper VA 22701-3910. 540/829-4140.

Hospice Of The Panhandle
306 W Burke St, Martinsburg WV 25401-3324. 304/264-0406.

Camelot Health & Rehabilitation Center
1225 Reservoir St, Harrisonburg VA 22801-4415. 540/433-2623.

Grace Home
401 W Grace St, Richmond VA 23220-4909. 804/644-4011.

Harbor Manor Inc.
1003 28th St, Newport News VA 23607-4233. 804/928-0875.

Milam's Home For Adults
1111 N Main St, Danville VA 24540-4433. 804/799-9482.

Old Dominion Home
3003 Parkwood Ave, Richmond VA 23221-3534. 804/353-5431.

HOSPITALS AND MEDICAL CENTERS

Broaddus Hospital
College Hill, Philippi WV 26416. 304/457-1760.

Dickenson County Medical Center
PO Box 1390, Clintwood VA 24228-1390. 540/926-0300.

Maryview Medical Center
3640 High St, Ste 2A, Portsmouth VA 23707-3236. 804/398-2130.

Montgomery Regional Hospital
PO Box 90004, Blacksburg VA 24062-9004. 540/953-5101.

National Hospital For Orthopaedics
2455 Army Navy Dr, Arlington VA 22206-2905. 703/920-6700.

Northern VA Mental Health Institute
3302 Gallows Rd, Falls Church VA 22042-3307. 703/207-7111.

Peninsula Psychiatric Hospital
2244 Executive Dr, Hampton VA 23666-2430. 804/827-1001.

Putnam General Hospital
PO Box 900, Hurricane WV 25526-0900. 304/757-1700.

Southern VA Mental Health Institute
382 Taylor Dr, Danville VA 24541-4023. 804/799-6220.

St. Luke's Hospital
PO Box 1190, Bluefield WV 24701-1190. 304/327-2900.

State Hospital
1530 Norway Ave, Huntington WV 25705-1336. 304/525-7801.

Tidewater Psychiatric Inst Norfolk
860 Kempsville Rd, Norfolk VA 23502-3920. 804/461-4565.

Warren Memorial Hospital
1000 N Shenandoah Ave, Front Royal VA 22630-3598. 540/636-0300.

Tidewater Psychiatric Institute
1700 Will O Wisp Dr, Virginia Beach VA 23454-3164. 804/481-1211.

Alcohol Rehabilitation Center
2097 S Military Hwy, Chesapeake VA 23320-4424. 804/543-6888.

Cancer Helplink
500 J Clyde Morris Blvd, Newport News VA 23601-1929. 804/594-3181.

Women & Children's Hospital
800 Pennsylvania Ave, Charleston WV 25302-3392. 304/348-2724.

HOME HEALTH CARE SERVICES

Absolute Nursing Care Of Virginia
2823 Duke St,

Alexandria VA 22314-4512. 703/461-8202.

Bristol Homecare
245 North St, Bristol VA 24201-3275. 540/669-4711.

Care Tenders Of Richmond
Imperial Plaza, Richmond VA 23227. 804/264-9614.

Central VA Home Theraputics Inc.
312 Progress St, Fredericksbrg VA 22401-3356. 540/372-1493.

First American Home Care
1700 Bayberry Court, Ste 105, Richmond VA 23226-3791. 804/282-0014.

First American Home Care
2401 Godwin Blvd, Suffolk VA 23434-8031. 804/925-4941.

Homecare USA Medical Equipment Co.
8441 Glazebrook Ave, Richmond VA 23228-2804. 804/288-6444.

Lee County Community Hospital Home Health
PO Box 70, Pennington Gap VA 24277-0070. 703/546-1440.

McDowell Continuous Care Center
PO Box 220, Gary WV 24836-0220. 304/448-2121.

Medshares Home Care Of Central VA
1001 Boulders Pky, Richmond VA 23225-5522. 804/320-0135.

Nurse's House Call
1503 Santa Rosa Rd, #234, Richmond VA 23229-5105. 804/648-3636.

PWH Home Health Services
8650 Sudley Rd, Manassas VA 22110-4416. 703/631-0895.

Riverside Tappahannock Home
HC 2, Box 612, Tappahannock VA 22560-9323. 804/443-6276.

Tazewell Community Hospital Home Health
141 Ben Bolt Ave, Tazewell VA 24651-9700. 540/988-2506.

Twin County Regional Home Health
111 S Main St, Galax VA 24333-3909. 540/236-7935.

Westminster Canterbury Home
1600 Westbrook Ave, Richmond VA 23227. 804/264-6000.

SPECIALTY OUTPATIENT FACILITIES

Parc Place
625 4th Ave, Huntington WV 25701-1320. 304/525-1522.

Substance Abuse Service New River Valley
10 E Main St, Christiansbrg VA 24073-3028. 540/382-5050.

Tucker Pavilion
Chippenham Pkwy & Jahnke Rd, Richmond VA 23225. 804/323-8695.

Institute For Supported Living
119 W Washington St, Lewisburg WV 24901-1326. 304/645-1282.

HEALTH AND ALLIED SERVICES

Brookside Health Care
550E Oyster Point Rd, Newport News VA 23602-6920. 804/249-8231.

Healthtronic Solutions
3940 Cogbill Rd, Richmond VA 23234-4839. 804/275-5289.

Virginia Blood Services
4040 Cox Rd, Glen Allen VA 23060-6705. 804/270-0156.

First Hospital Corporation
240 Corporate Blvd, Norfolk VA 23502-4948. 804/459-5100.

Inova Health System
8001 Braddock Rd, Springfield VA 22151-2110. 703/321-4213.

RESIDENTIAL CARE

Beth Sholom Woods
2027 Lauderdale Dr, Richmond VA 23233-3913. 804/741-4691.

Heritage Oaks Retirement Residence
1100 German School Rd, Richmond VA 23225-4275. 804/323-3800.

Hermitage On The Eastern Shore
23610 North St, Onancock VA 23417-2024. 804/787-4343.

Kelly Assisted Living
4118 W Broad St, #A, Richmond VA 23230-3302. 804/353-8501.

Kelly Assisted Living
1018 Kanawha Blvd E, Ste 103, Charleston WV 25301-2827. 304/346-8650.

Sentara Village At Chesapeake
778 Oak Grove Rd, Chesapeake VA 23320-3728. 804/547-5666.

The Madison Home
3212 Chamberlayne Ave, Richmond VA 23227-4807. 804/358-9300.

Westminster-Canterbury
300 Westminster Canterbury Dr, Winchester VA 22603-4252. 540/665-0156.

MEDICAL EQUIPMENT

Microaire Surgical Instruments
1000 Allview Dr, Crozet VA 22932. 804/975-8000.

Hollister Inc.
Rt 608, Stuarts Draft VA 24477. 540/337-3310.

Med-Surg Industries Inc.
251 Exchange Pl,
Herndon VA 22070-4822. 703/742-9700.

Alcon Surgical Cilco
6065 Kyle Ln,
Huntington WV 25702-9795. 304/736-5230.

Chiron Vision Corp.
100 Industrial Ln,
Huntington WV 25702.
304/528-2000.

For more information on career opportunities in the health care industry:

Associations

ACCREDITING COMMISSION ON EDUCATION FOR HEALTH SERVICES ADMINISTRATION
1911 North Fort Myer Drive, Suite 503, Arlington VA 22209. 703/524-0511.

AMERICAN ACADEMY OF FAMILY PHYSICIANS
8880 Ward Parkway, Kansas City MO 64114. 816/333-9700. Promotes continuing education for family physicians.

AMERICAN ACADEMY OF PHYSICIAN ASSISTANTS
950 North Washington Street, Alexandria VA 22314. 703/836-2272. Promotes the use of physician assistants.

AMERICAN ASSOCIATION FOR CLINICAL CHEMISTRY
2101 Lovely Street NW, Suite 202, Washington, DC 20037-1526. 202/857-0717. A non-profit association for clinical, chemical, medical, and technical doctors.

AMERICAN ASSOCIATION FOR RESPIRATORY CARE
11030 Ables Lane, Dallas TX 75229-4593. 214/243-2272. Promotes the art and science of respiratory care, while focusing on the needs of the patients.

AMERICAN ASSOCIATION OF COLLEGES OF OSTEOPATHIC MEDICINE
6110 Executive Boulevard, Suite 405, Rockville MD 20852. 301/468-2037. Provides applications processing services for colleges of osteopathic medicine.

AMERICAN ASSOCIATION OF COLLEGES OF PODIATRIC MEDICINE
1350 Piccard Drive, Suite 322, Rockville MD 20850. 301/990-7400. Provides applications processing services for colleges of podiatric medicine.

AMERICAN ASSOCIATION OF DENTAL SCHOOLS
1625 Massachusetts Avenue NW, Washington DC 20036-2212. 202/667-9433. Fax: 202/667-0642. E-mail address: aads@aads.jhu.edu. Represents all 54 of the dental schools in the U.S., as well as individual members. Goals of the organization include the expansion of postdoctoral training and increasing the number of women and minorities in the dental field.

AMERICAN ASSOCIATION OF HEALTHCARE CONSULTANTS
11208 Waples Mill Road, Suite 109, Fairfax VA 22030. 703/691-2242.

AMERICAN ASSOCIATION OF HOMES AND SERVICES FOR THE AGING
901 E Street NW, Suite 500, Washington DC 20004-2037. 202/783-2242.

AMERICAN ASSOCIATION OF MEDICAL ASSISTANTS
20 North Wacker Drive, Suite 1575, Chicago IL 60606. 312/899-1500.

AMERICAN ASSOCIATION OF NURSE ANESTHETISTS
222 South Prospect Avenue, Park Ridge IL 60068-4001. 847/692-7050.

AMERICAN CHIROPRACTIC ASSOCIATION
1701 Clarendon Boulevard, Arlington VA 22209. 703/276-8800. A national, non-profit professional membership organization. Provides educational services (through films, booklets, texts, and kits), regional seminars and workshops, and major health and education activities to provide information on public health, safety, physical fitness, and disease prevention.

AMERICAN COLLEGE OF HEALTHCARE ADMINISTRATORS
325 South Patrick Street, Alexandria VA 22314. 703/549-5822. A professional membership society for individual long-term care professionals. Sponsors educational programs, supports research, and produces a number of publications, including the *Journal of Long-Term Care Administration* and *The Long-Term Care Administrator.*

AMERICAN COLLEGE OF HEALTHCARE EXECUTIVES
One North Franklin, Suite 1700, Chicago IL 60606-3491. 312/424-2800. Offers credentialing and

educational programs. Publishes *Hospital & Health Services Administration* (a journal), and *Healthcare Executive* (a magazine).

AMERICAN COLLEGE OF MEDICAL PRACTICE EXECUTIVES
104 Inverness Terrace, East Englewood CO 80112-5306. 303/397-7869.

AMERICAN COLLEGE OF PHYSICIAN EXECUTIVES
4890 West Kennedy Boulevard, Suite 200, Tampa FL 33609-2575. 813/287-2000.

AMERICAN DENTAL ASSOCIATION
211 East Chicago Avenue, Chicago IL 60611. 312/440-2500.

AMERICAN DENTAL HYGIENISTS ASSOCIATION
Division of Professional Development, 444 North Michigan Avenue, Suite 3400, Chicago IL 60611. 312/440-8900.

AMERICAN DIETETIC ASSOCIATION
216 West Jackson Boulevard, Chicago IL 60606-6995. 312/899-0040 or 800/877-1600. Promotes optimal nutrition to improve public health and well-being.

AMERICAN HEALTH INFORMATION MANAGEMENT ASSOCIATION
919 North Michigan Avenue, Suite 1400, Chicago IL 60611. 312/787-2672.

AMERICAN HOSPITAL ASSOCIATION
One North Franklin Street, Suite 2700, Chicago IL 60606. 312/422-3000.

AMERICAN MEDICAL ASSOCIATION
515 North State Street, Chicago IL 60610. 312/464-5000. An organization for medical doctors.

AMERICAN MEDICAL TECHNOLOGISTS
710 Higgins Road, Park Ridge IL 60068. 847/823-5169.

AMERICAN NURSES ASSOCIATION
600 Maryland Avenue SW, Suite 100W, Washington DC 20024-2571. 202/554-4444.

AMERICAN OCCUPATIONAL THERAPY ASSOCIATION
4720 Montgomery Lane, Bethesda MD 20824-1220. 301/652-2682. 800/377-8555. Fax: 301/652-7711.

AMERICAN OPTOMETRIC ASSOCIATION
243 North Lindbergh Boulevard, St. Louis MO 63141. 314/991-4100. Offers publications, discounts, and insurance programs for members.

AMERICAN ORGANIZATION OF NURSE EXECUTIVES
One North Franklin Street, Suite 3400, Chicago IL 60606. 312/422-2800.

AMERICAN PHYSICAL THERAPY ASSOCIATION
1111 North Fairfax Street, Alexandria VA 22314. 703/684-2782. Small fee required for information.

AMERICAN PUBLIC HEALTH ASSOCIATION
1015 15th Street NW, Suite 300, Washington DC 20005. 202/789-5600.

AMERICAN VETERINARY MEDICAL ASSOCIATION
1931 North Meacham Road, Suite 100, Schaumburg IL 60173-4360. 847/925-8070. Provides a forum for the discussion of issues of importance to the veterinary profession, and for the development of official positions.

ASSOCIATION OF MENTAL HEALTH ADMINISTRATORS
60 Revere Drive, Suite 500, Northbrook IL 60062. 847/480-9626.

ASSOCIATION OF UNIVERSITY PROGRAMS IN HEALTH ADMINISTRATION
1911 North Fort Myer Drive, Suite 503, Arlington VA 22209. 703/524-5500.

GROUP HEALTH ASSOCIATION OF AMERICA, INC.
1129 20th Street NW, Suite 600, Washington DC 20036. 202/778-3200.

HEALTHCARE FINANCIAL MANAGEMENT ASSOCIATION
Two Westbrook Corporate Center, Suite 700, Westchester IL 60154. 708/531-9600.

NATIONAL MEDICAL ASSOCIATION
1012 Tenth Street NW, Washington DC 20001. 202/347-1895.

Magazines

AMERICAN JOURNAL OF NURSING
555 West 57th Street, New York NY 10019. Publishes five editions: Hospital, Critical Care, Continuing Care, Regular, and Nurse Practitioner. Accredited as a provider of continuing education in nursing by the American Nurses Credentialing Center.

AMERICAN MEDICAL NEWS
American Medical Association, 515 North State Street, Chicago IL 60605. 312/464-5000.

CHANGING MEDICAL MARKETS
Theta Corporation, Theta Building, Middlefield CT 06455. 860/349-1054.

HEALTH CARE EXECUTIVE
American College of Health Care Executives, One North Franklin, Suite 1700, Chicago IL 60606. 312/424-2800.

MODERN HEALTHCARE
Crain Communications, 740 North Rush Street, Chicago IL 60611. 312/649-5374.

NURSEFAX
Springhouse Corporation, 1111 Bethlehem Pike, P.O. Box 908, Springhouse PA 19477. 215/646-8700. This is a jobline service designed to be used in conjunction with *Nursing* magazine. Please call to obtain a copy of a magazine or the Nursing directory.

HOTELS AND RESTAURANTS

Job opportunities in the restaurant industry are plentiful. A number of trends will boost job growth, including population growth, rising incomes, and more dual-income families. Some demand will be met through labor saving innovations like salad bars, untended meal stations, automated beverage stations, and central kitchens that serve a number of establishments in the same restaurant chain. In the fast-food sector, use of labor-saving technology is essential to remain competitive. Since the most time-consuming transaction at drive-in windows is making change, some restaurants are experimenting with debit and credit cards to reduce transaction time. However, despite labor-saving innovations, the increased demand for services will increase the need for workers.

Jobs in hotels, motels, and other lodging places will be plentiful throughout the next decade. Driving the growth will be many of the same trends affecting the restaurant industry, as well as low-cost airfares and foreign tourism in the U.S. Another hot trend: legalized gambling. The hotel and motel industry invests heavily in the gaming industry, and that has further fueled job growth. This growth will continue as hotels increasingly attract families by offering relatively inexpensive casino vacation packages.

The greatest growth is in all-suite properties and budget motels. Since they don't have restaurants, dining rooms, lounges, or kitchens, these properties offer few jobs for food and beverage workers, but jobs should be available for managers and assistant managers. The trend toward chain-affiliated lodging places should provide managers with opportunities for advancement into general manager positions and corporate administrative jobs.

CHESAPEAKE RESTAURANT GROUP
8027 Leesburg Pike, Suite 506, Vienna VA 22182. 703/827-0320. **Contact:** Becky Wedemeyer, Director of Human Resources. **Description:** Corporate offices for a restaurant chain, Chesapeake Bay Seafood House. The company currently operates 20 restaurants and will continue to expand in the Washington, DC market. **Common positions include:** Assistant Manager; Management Trainee. **Educational backgrounds include:** Business Administration; Hotel Administration. **Benefits:** Dental Insurance; Disability Coverage; Employee Discounts; Life Insurance; Medical Insurance; Pension Plan. **Special Programs:** Internships. **Corporate headquarters location:** This Location. **Operations at this facility include:** Administration; Research and Development.

DOMINO'S TEAM WASHINGTON, INC.
817B Slaters Lane, Alexandria VA 22314. 703/684-5000. **Contact:** Human Resources. **Description:** Owns a number of Domino's Pizza franchises.

THE GREENBRIAR HOTEL
West Main Street, White Sulpher Spring WV 24986. 304/536-1110. **Contact:** Human Resources. **Description:** A hotel.

GUEST SERVICES
3055 Prosperity Avenue, Fairfax VA 22031. 703/849-9300. **Contact:** Personnel. **Description:** Manages a variety of contract food and hospitality services. **Common positions include:** Accountant/Auditor; Administrator; Claim Representative; Computer Programmer; Customer Service Representative; Dietician/Nutritionist; Electrical/Electronics Engineer; Hotel Manager/Assistant Manager; Human Resources Specialist; Industrial Engineer; Management Trainee; Manufacturer's/Wholesaler's Sales Rep.; Marketing Specialist; Mechanical Engineer; Operations/Production Manager; Public Relations Specialist. **Benefits:** Dental Insurance; Disability Coverage; Employee Discounts; Life Insurance; Medical Insurance; Pension Plan; Savings Plan; Tuition Assistance. **Corporate headquarters location:** This Location. **Operations at this facility include:** Regional Headquarters. **Number of employees at this location:** 80. **Number of employees nationwide:** 3,500.

McDONALD'S CORPORATION
3015 Williams Drive, Fairfax VA 22031. 703/698-4000. **Contact:** Paul Van Sickle, Personnel Director. **Description:** Regional offices for the worldwide developer, operator, and franchiser. Company services a system of restaurants which process, package, and sell a limited menu of fast food items. Overall, the company is one of the largest restaurant chain and food service organizations in the world, operating 6,000 McDonald's restaurants in all 50 states and 26 foreign countries. **Corporate headquarters location:** Oak Brook IL. **Listed on:** New York Stock Exchange.

RWS ENTERPRISE COUNTRY COOKING
4335 Brambleton Avenue, Roanoke VA 24018. 703/774-0613. **Contact:** Human Resources. **Description:** The corporate office for the restaurant chain Country Cooking. Currently there are 14 restaurants located throughout Virginia. This family style restaurant offers inexpensive, large portions of various home-cooked food.

UPTOWNER INNS, INC.
1415 4th Avenue, Huntington WV 25701. 304/525-7741. **Contact:** Human Resources. **Description:** Operates a group of Holiday Inn franchises, as well as apartment buildings and other rental properties.

***Note:** Because addresses and telephone numbers of smaller companies change rapidly, we recommend you call each company to verify the information below before inquiring about job opportunities. Mass mailings are not recommended.*

Additional small employers:

EATING PLACES

Annabelle's
2733 Park Ave, Petersburg VA 23805-2421. 804/732-0997.

Applebees Neighborhood Grill & Bar
808 Lynnhaven Pky, Virginia Beach VA 23452-7202. 804/468-4245.

Arby's Roast Beef Restaurant
5220 Williamsburg Rd, Richmond VA 23231. 804/222-7438.

Arby's Roast Beef Restaurant
1132 Hermitage Rd, Richmond VA 23220-1301. 804/358-2148.

Artie's
3260 Old Lee Hwy, Fairfax VA 22030-1502. 703/273-7600.

Bamboo Hut Chinese Restaurant
1801 Pleasure House Rd, Virginia Beach VA 23455-2864. 804/460-6490.

Bennigan's
11778 Fair Oaks Mall, Fairfax VA 22033. 703/691-2208.

Bennigan's
6632 Springfield Mall, Springfield VA 22150-1712. 703/922-6004.

Bill's Barbecue
927 Myers St, Richmond VA 23230-4812. 804/353-2757.

Bob Evans Restaurant
8700 Midlothian Tpke, Richmond VA 23235-5024. 804/330-2628.

Bob Evans Restaurant
6309 MacCorkle Ave SE,

Charleston WV 25304-2917. 304/925-2223.

Boston Market
6198 Arlington Blvd, Falls Church VA 22044-2902. 703/237-7300.

Broughton's Ice Cream Store
3411 Emerson Ave, Parkersburg WV 26104-1807. 304/428-4111.

Burger King
5705 MacCorkle Ave SE, Charleston WV 25304-2803. 304/925-2184.

Burger King
223 E City Hall Ave, #200, Norfolk VA 23510-1728. 804/623-6490.

Captain D's Seafood Restaurant
330 Old Riverside Dr, Danville VA 24541-3454. 804/799-0770.

Captain D's Seafood Restaurant
4617 Jefferson Davis Hwy, Richmond VA 23234-3150. 804/271-5530.

Carlos O'Kelly's Mexican Cafe
2306 Plank Rd, Fredericksbrg VA 22401-4902. 540/373-5436.

Chanello's Pizza
5300 Kemps River Dr, Ste 118, Virginia Beach VA 23464-5369. 804/523-1000.

Chanello's Pizza
6657 Indian River Rd, Virginia Beach VA 23464. 804/366-9600.

Chi Chi's Mexican Restaurante
403 Grand Central Ave, Parkersburg WV 26105-2138. 304/428-4594.

Chi-Chi's Mexican Restaurante
5515 MacCorkle Ave SE, Charleston WV 25304-2319. 304/925-2138.

Chi-Chi's Mexican Restaurante
8701 Midlothian Tpke, Richmond VA 23235-5023. 804/330-7575.

Chick-Fil-A
7201 Midlothian Tpke, Richmond VA 23225-6603. 804/276-0037.

Chili's Southwest Grill & Bar
14432 Gideon Dr, Woodbridge VA 22192-4600. 703/490-3118.

Coffee Pot Barbeque And Grill
2902 Brambleton Ave SW, Roanoke VA 24015-4402. 540/774-8256.

Crystal Dinery
1664 Crystal City Arcade, Arlington VA 22202. 703/920-3930.

Damon's Franconia
7027 Manchester Blvd, Franconia VA 22310-3227. 703/719-0670.

Darryl's Restaurant & Bar
1400 Starling Dr, Richmond VA 23229-5531. 804/741-1861.

Denny's Restaurant
803 E Parham Rd, Richmond VA 23227-1107. 804/261-3687.

Dogs Etc.
Martinsburg Mall, Martinsburg WV 25401. 304/267-9359.

Dwight's Corporate Office
730 9th Ave, Huntington WV 25701-2719. 304/697-2181.

East Coast Foods Inc.
1147 Independence Blvd, Ste 5, Virginia Beach VA 23455-5596. 804/464-1951.

Eat'N Park Restaurant
226 Three Springs Dr, Weirton WV 26062-3815. 304/723-5179.

Eat'N Park Restaurant
100 Tolley Dr, Bridgeport WV 26330-1668. 304/842-7668.

Fifth Quarter Restaurant
Quarrier & Clendenin Streets, Charleston WV 25301. 304/345-2726.

Fran-Mar Corp.
1895-B Billingsgate Cl, Richmond VA 23233. 804/740-3005.

Friday's
2070 Chain Bridge Rd, Vienna VA 22182-2500. 703/556-6173.

Fritzbe's
7050 Columbia Pike, Annandale VA 22003-3104. 703/354-4560.

Golden Corral
11 S Providence Rd, Richmond VA 23236-3351. 804/320-5078.

Golden Corral
Southgate Shopping Ctr, Farmville VA 23901. 804/392-9567.

HI Ribster's
7243 Little River Tpke, Annandale VA 22003-3309. 703/750-2751.

Happy Eatery
17483 Jefferson Davis Hwy, Dumfries VA 22026-2244. 703/221-8889.

Hard Times Cafe
3028 Wilson Blvd, Arlington VA 22201-3810. 703/528-2233.

Hardee's
Suffolk West Shopping Ctr, Suffolk VA 23435. 804/539-0484.

Hardee's
9705 MacCorkle Ave, Marmet WV 25315-1847. 304/949-4077.

House Of Lions
11180 Main St, Fairfax VA 22030-5009. 703/273-3998.

Long John Silver's Seafood Shop
2001 Plank Rd, Fredericksbrg VA 22401-5103. 540/371-4536.

Long John Silver's Seafood Shop
Roanoke Rd, Christiansbrg VA 24073. 540/382-7024.

Long John Silver's Seafood Shop
1202 S Main St, Blacksburg VA 24060-5546. 540/552-7188.

Long John Silver's Seafood Shop
3013 Town Center Mall, Charleston WV 25314. 304/344-5071.

Jose Fitzgerald's
812 Kanawha Blvd E, Charleston WV 25301-2807. 304/345-0053.

Kelly's Carry Out
2354 N Main St, Danville VA 24540-2408. 804/799-5718.

KFC
762 Piney Forest Rd, Danville VA 24540-2859. 804/797-2623.

KFC
4821 Williamsburg Rd, Richmond VA 23231-2825. 804/226-2143.

L&N Seafood
1100 S Hayes St, Arlington VA 22202-4907. 703/415-2055.

Libby Hill Seafood Restaurant
2843 Orange Ave NE Roanoke VA 24012-6252. 540/342-0826.

Little Caesar's Pizza
108 N Virginia Ave, Collinsville VA 24078-2218. 540/647-8811.

Little Caesar's Pizza
213 Nor Dan Dr, Danville VA 24540-1611. 804/836-6666.

Lone Star Steakhouse & Saloon
460 Elden St, Herndon VA 22070-4513. 703/904-0064.

Lone Star Steakhouse & Saloon
6515 MacCorkle Ave SE, Charleston WV 25304-2921. 304/926-8459.

Macado's
922 University City Blvd, Blacksburg VA 24060-2710. 540/953-2700.

McDonald's
2135 Wards Rd, Lynchburg VA 24502-5311. 804/239-7852.

Mike's American Grill
6210 Backlick Rd, Springfield VA 22150-2629. 703/644-7100.

Morrison's Fresh Cooking
701 Lynnhaven Pky, Virginia Beach VA 23452-7304. 804/631-0861.

NM Cafe-Neiman Marcus
2255 International Dr, McLean VA 22102-3911. 703/761-1600.

Olive Garden Italian Restaurant
7113 W Broad St, Richmond VA 23294-3703. 804/672-6220.

Olive Garden Italian Restaurant
9750 Midlothian Tpke, Richmond VA 23235-4973. 804/330-7391.

Olive Garden Italian Restaurant
4117 Chesapeake Square Blvd, Chesapeake VA 23321-2200. 804/465-2139.

Olive Garden Italian Restaurant
Greenbriar Mall Pkwy, Chesapeake VA 23320. 804/424-4758.

Olive Garden Italian Restaurant
7501 Broken Branch Ln, Manassas VA 22110-2657. 703/369-3635.

Omelet Shoppe
3712 E 7th St, Parkersburg WV 26101-3879. 304/485-3161.

Open House Diner
5191 Shore Dr, Virginia Beach VA 23455-2502. 804/460-0555.

Outback Steakhouse
150 Elden St, Herndon VA 22070-4831. 703/318-0999.

Outback Steakhouse
5702 Union Mill Rd, Clifton VA 22024-1088. 703/818-0804.

Pargo's Restaurant
4330 Franklin Rd SW, Roanoke VA 24014-5233. 540/989-3189.

Pargo's Restaurant
334 Patteson Dr, Morgantown WV 26505-3232. 304/598-0700.

Picadilly Cafeteria
500 Gate City Hwy, Ste 110, Bristol VA 24201-2352. 540/466-9342.

Pizza Hut
5281 Princess Anne Rd, Virginia Beach VA 23462-6307. 804/490-9369.

Pizza Hut
4225 MacCorkle Ave SE, Charleston WV 25304-2501. 304/925-6604.

Pizza Hut
2345 National Rd, Wheeling WV 26003-5362. 304/242-0880.

Pizza Hut
7153 Staples Mill Rd, Richmond VA 23228-4104. 804/262-1300.

Pizza Hut
551 E Laburnum Ave, Richmond VA 23222-2122. 804/321-3000.

Pizza Hut
2905 Patterson Ave, Richmond VA 23221-1710. 804/358-3333.

Ragazzi's
424 S Witchduck Rd, Virginia Beach VA 23462-3617. 804/557-0517.

Rally's Hamburgers
1667 3rd Ave, Charleston WV 25312-2528. 304/345-2808.

Rock-Ola Cafe
140 Crown Dr, Danville VA 24540-5932. 804/793-1848.

Roy Rogers Family Restaurants
9911 Georgetown Pike, Great Falls VA 22066-2826. 703/759-5797.

Seasons Cafe
110 S Henry St, Williamsburg VA 23185-4105. 804/259-0018.

Shakers Restaurant Corp.
2095 Langhorne Rd, Ste C, Lynchburg VA 24501-1403. 804/847-0234.

Spinnaker's Restaurant
Valley View Mall, Roanoke VA 24012. 540/362-4086.

Subway Sandwiches & Salads
3021 Charleston Town Ctr, Charleston WV 25389-3021. 304/346-8193.

Subway Sandwiches & Salads
Ceredo Plaza, Ceredo WV 25507. 304/453-3731.

Subway Sandwiches & Salads
665 Newtown Rd, Ste 106, Virginia Beach VA 23462-1683. 804/456-5012.

Susi's Nashville East
1724 Potters Rd, Virginia Beach VA 23454-4447. 804/491-9950.

TC Bishop Enterprise
6419 Mechanicsville Tpke, Mechanicsville VA 23111-3695. 804/746-3345.

Taco Bell
2500 Market St, Christiansbrg VA 24073-6515. 540/381-0641.

Taco Bell
5709 MacCorkle Ave SE, Charleston WV 25304-2803. 304/925-6034.

Taco Bell
543 Jefferson Davis Hwy, Fredericksbrg VA 22401-4420. 540/371-2577.

Texas Steakhouse & Saloon
5025 Valley View Blvd NW, Roanoke VA 24012-2037. 540/265-1809.

Texas Steakhouse & Saloon
140 Harper Park Dr, Beckley WV 25801-2660. 304/253-1436.

TGI Friday's
13071 Worldgate Dr, Herndon VA 22070-4374. 703/787-9630.

The Lobster House
1402 Richmond Rd # B, Williamsburg VA 23185-2803. 804/229-7771.

The Olive Garden-Norfolk
5920 E Va Beach Blvd, Norfolk VA 23502. 804/455-5875.

Thompson Hospitality
11911 Freedom Dr, Reston VA 22090-5602. 703/709-0145.

Tidewater Grill
1060 Charleston Town Ctr, Charleston WV 25389-1060. 304/345-2620.

Waffle House
5105 Plaza Dr, Hopewell VA 23860-7324. 804/452-0386.

Wendy's Old Fashioned Hamburgers
901 E Cary St, Richmond VA 23219-4057. 804/648-6947.

Wendy's Old Fashioned Hamburgers
4026 Glenside Dr, Richmond VA 23228-4102. 804/264-3696.

Wendy's Old Fashioned Hamburgers
2301 Plank Rd, #A, Fredericksbrg VA 22401-4901. 540/373-8886.

Wendy's Old Fashioned Hamburgers
Pidgeon Hill Dr, Sterling VA 22170. 703/450-6976.

Wendy's Old Fashioned Hamburgers
7111 Williamson Rd, Roanoke VA 24019-4232. 540/366-6889.

Wendy's Old Fashioned Hamburgers
3934 Electric Rd, Roanoke VA 24018-4513. 540/774-9521.

Wendy's Old Fashioned Hamburgers
2201 Grand Central Ave, Vienna WV 26105-1344. 304/295-8642.

Western Sizzlin Steak House
5902 Richmond Hwy, Alexandria VA 22303-1805. 703/329-1555.

Western Sizzlin Steak House
12540 Jefferson Davis Hwy, Chester VA 23831-5317. 804/748-2202.

Rax Restaurants
4007 MacCorkle Ave SW, Charleston WV 25309-1510. 304/744-0664.

Rax Restaurants
223 MacCorkle Ave, Saint Albans WV 25177-1825. 304/727-4593.

McDonald's
3102-A Plank Road, Fredericksbrg VA 22401. 540/786-6533.

McDonald's
316 Butler Rd, Fredericksbrg VA 22405-2514. 540/373-3743.

Gino's Pizza & Spaghetti House
3405 Kanawha Blvd E, Malden WV 25306-6626. 304/925-0103.

Little Caesar's Pizza
10613 Courthouse Rd, Fredericksbrg VA 22407-1665. 540/898-8100.

Plus One Pizza
101 E Brockway Ave, Morgantown WV 26505-6205. 304/296-4000.

Ukrop's Hand-Tossed Pizza
Oxbridge Square, Richmond VA 23236. 804/745-4920.

Villa Pizza
New River Valley Mall, Christiansbrg VA 24073. 540/381-0864.

Hyatt Hotels & Resorts
12777 Fair Lakes Cir, Fairfax VA 22033-4922. 703/818-1234.

Japanese Gourmet Catering
212 N 23rd St, Richmond VA 23223-7139. 804/644-1430.

Ogden Allied Food Service Corp.
201 W Brambleton Ave, Norfolk VA 23510-1530. 804/640-0328.

HOTELS AND MOTELS

Best Western Arlington
2480 S Glebe Rd, Arlington VA 22206-2576. 703/979-4400.

Desco Corp.
12205 S Crater Rd, Petersburg VA 23805-7442. 804/733-0600.

Guest Quarters
100 South Reynolds Street, Alexandria VA 22304-3199. 703/370-9600.

Hyatt Arlington
1325 Wilson Boulevard, Arlington VA 22209-2301. 703/525-1234.

John Smiley's Motel Inc.
6210 MacCorkle Ave, Saint Albans WV 25177-2331. 304/766-6231.

Marriott Dulles Hotel
333 W Service Road, Chantilly VA 22021. 703/471-9500.

Ramada Renaissance Hotel
950 North Stafford Street, Arlington VA 22203-1813. 703/528-6000.

Sheraton Crystal City Hotel
1800 Jefferson Davis Hwy, Arlington VA 22202-3506. 703/486-1111.

Sheraton Inn Fredericksburg
2801 Plank Rd, Fredericksbrg VA 22401-4947. 540/786-8321.

Snowshoe Mountain Resort
PO Box 10, Snowshoe WV 26209-0010. 304/572-1000.

The Founders Inn
5641 Indian River Rd, Virginia Beach VA 23464-5247. 804/424-5511.

The Rosslyn Westpark Hotel
1900 Fort Myer Dr, Arlington VA 22209-1602. 703/527-4814.

Williamsburg Center Hotel
600 Bypass Rd, Williamsburg VA 23185-2929. 804/220-2800.

Comfort Inn Herndon-Dulles
200 Elden St, Herndon VA 22070-4811. 703/437-7555.

Comfort Inn Of Tysons Corners
1587 Spring Hill Rd, Vienna VA 22182-2200. 703/448-8020.

Fairfield Inn By Marriott
7300 W Broad St, Richmond VA 23294-3604. 804/672-8621.

Howard Johnson
Rt 29 N, Lynchburg VA 24501. 804/845-7041.

Howard Johnson
7135 Pocahontas Trail, Williamsburg VA 23185-4768. 804/229-6900.

Howard Johnson
5327 Jefferson Davis Hwy, Fredericksbrg VA 22408-2607. 540/898-1800.

Massad House Hotel
11 N 4th St, Richmond VA 23219-2215. 804/648-2893.

Quality Inn Executive
6111 Arlington Blvd, Falls Church VA 22044-2708. 703/534-9100.

Red Roof Inns
Chippenham Pkwy & Midlothian T, Richmond VA 23225. 804/745-0600.

Sheraton Hotels
Sheraton National Hotel Columb, Arlington VA 22204. 703/521-1900.

Super 8 Motel
8260 Midlothian Tpke, Richmond VA 23235-5118. 804/320-2823.

Dulles Renaissance Hotel
1091 McCue Court, Great Falls VA 22066-1543. 703/478-2900.

Holiday Inn Chester
Rt 10 & Interstate 95, Chester VA 23831. 804/748-6321.

Hyatt Hotels & Resorts
2799 Jefferson Davis Hwy, Arlington VA 22202. 703/418-1234.

Ramada Inn Airport At Newtown
6360 Newtown Rd, Norfolk VA 23502-4801. 804/461-1081.

For more information on career opportunities in hotels and restaurants:

Magazines

CORNELL HOTEL AND RESTAURANT ADMINISTRATION QUARTERLY
Cornell University School of Hotel Administration, Statler Hall, Ithaca NY 14853-6902. 607/255-9393.

HOTEL AND MOTEL MANAGEMENT
120 West 2nd Street, Duluth MN 55802. 218.

INNKEEPING WORLD
Box 84108, Seattle WA 98124. 206/362-7125.

NATION'S RESTAURANT NEWS
Lebhar-Friedman, Inc., 3922 Coconut Palm Drive, Tampa, FL 33619. 813/664-6700.

Associations

AMERICAN HOTEL AND MOTEL ASSOCIATION
1201 New York Avenue NW, Suite 600, Washington DC 20005-3931. 202/289-3100. Provides lobbying services and educational programs, maintains and disseminates industry data, and produces a variety of publications.

THE EDUCATIONAL FOUNDATION OF THE NATIONAL RESTAURANT ASSOCIATION
250 South Wacker Drive, 14th Floor, Chicago IL 60606. 312/715-1010. Offers educational products, including textbooks, manuals, instruction guides, manager and employee training programs, videos, and certification programs.

NATIONAL RESTAURANT ASSOCIATION
1200 17th Street NW, Washington DC 20036. 202/331-5900. Provides a number of services, including government lobbying, communications, research, and information, and operates the Educational Foundation (see separate address).

Directories

DIRECTORY OF CHAIN RESTAURANT OPERATORS
Business Guides, Inc., Lebhar-Friedman, Inc., 3922 Coconut Palm Drive, Tampa FL 33619-8321. 813/664-6700.

DIRECTORY OF HIGH-VOLUME INDEPENDENT RESTAURANTS
Lebhar-Friedman, Inc., 3922 Coconut Palm Drive, Tampa FL 33619-8321. 813/664-6700.

INSURANCE

What's the job outlook in insurance? That depends on which industry segment you're looking at. Health insurers, who have avoided any Washington-based reforms, are reaping record profits, while property-casualty and life insurers are still struggling. The industry has been consolidating with major mergers, and that's likely to continue in 1996. Under pressure from low returns, and a growing number of environmental claims, the property-casualty industry needs to cut overhead. In many cases, that also means jobs.

The picture in health insurance is much brighter. By moving more and more consumers into managed care, insurers are benefiting from the economies of scale. Many of the biggest players in the insurance industry have moved into managed care.

ALLSTATE INSURANCE COMPANY
12150 East Monument Drive, Suite 600, Fairfax VA 22033. **Fax:** 703/218-0097. **Recorded Jobline:** 800/999-6693. **Contact:** Adrienne Snider, Human Resources. **Description:** As one of the nation's largest insurance companies, Allstate Insurance provides a full circle of property, liability, life, reinsurance, and commercial lines of insurance. A member of the Sears Financial Network. **Common positions include:** Claim Representative; Education Administrator; Human Resources Specialist; Insurance Agent/Broker; Underwriter/Assistant Underwriter. **Benefits:** 401K; Dental Insurance; Disability Coverage; Life Insurance; Medical Insurance; Pension Plan; Profit Sharing; Tuition Assistance. **Corporate headquarters location:** Northbrook IL. **Other U.S. locations:** Nationwide. **Operations at this facility include:** Regional Headquarters. **Number of employees at this location:** 2,000.

FIRST COLONY CORPORATION
Riverfront Plaza, West Tower, 901 East Byrd Street, Suite 1350, Richmond VA 23219. 804/775-0300. **Contact:** Human Resources. **Description:** First Colony Corporation provides individual life and annuity products to independent general agents and agents throughout the country. With over 100,000 licensed agents, its distribution network is one of the largest in the industry. The company also sells its products through financial institutions, stock brokerage firms, employee plan specialists, and other financial services marketing outlets. **Benefits:** 401K; Pension Plan; Retirement Plan; Stock Option. **Corporate headquarters location:** This Location. **Subsidiaries include:** First Colony Life Insurance Company (Lynchburg, VA); and American Mayflower Life Insurance Company (New York). **Listed on:** New York Stock Exchange.

GUARANTY NATIONAL CORPORATION
7204 Glen Forest, Suite 305, Richmond VA 23226. 804/288-9265. **Contact:** Human Resources. **Description:** Guaranty National Corporation has five insurance company subsidiaries: Guaranty National Insurance Company; Landmark American Insurance Company; Colorado Casualty Insurance Company; Peak Property and Casualty Insurance Company; and Guaranty National Insurance Company of California. The company offers standard and specialty property and casualty insurance, and is a leading writer of nonstandard personal automobile insurance through independent agents. Its coverages are sold throughout most of the United States. Guaranty National

has approximately $600 million in assets, and $145 million of capital. **Corporate headquarters location:** Englewood CO.

HILB, ROGAL AND HAMILTON COMPANY
4235 Innslake Drive, P.O. Box 1220, Glen Allen VA 23060-1220. 804/747-6500. **Fax:** 804/747-6046. **Contact:** Ann Davis, Vice President, Human Resources. **Description:** Performs retail insurance services. Hilb, Rogal and Hamilton Company serves as an intermediary between its clients, traditionally mid-size businesses, and insurance companies which underwrite clients' risks. The company has agencies in more than 50 U.S. cities in 17 states and the District of Columbia. Hilb, Rogal and Hamilton assist clients in transferring their risks in areas such as property, casualty, life, and health insurance, and employee benefits. **Benefits:** Profit Sharing; Retirement Plan. **Corporate headquarters location:** This Location. **Listed on:** New York Stock Exchange. **Number of employees nationwide:** 1,630.

HOME BENEFICIAL CORPORATION
3901 West Broad Street, P.O. Box 27572, Richmond VA 23230. 804/358-8431. **Contact:** Billy T. Boyd, Vice President, Human Resources. **Description:** Home Beneficial Corporation is a holding company with one subsidiary, Home Beneficial Life Insurance Company. Home Beneficial Life Insurance Company is engaged in the life, accident, and health insurance business. The company sells group life insurance, including universal life, whole life, term, and annuities, together with accidental death and disability riders. The business of Home Beneficial Life Insurance Company is concentrated in six Mid-Atlantic states and the District of Columbia, and its policies are marketed through its own sales force. **Benefits:** Pension Plan; Retirement Plan. **Corporate headquarters location:** This Location. **Listed on:** NASDAQ. **Number of employees nationwide:** 1,386.

LAWYERS TITLE INSURANCE CORPORATION
6630 West Broad Street, Richmond VA 23230. 804/281-6700. **Contact:** Robert Martin, Vice President. **Description:** Provides title insurance and other real estate-related services on commercial and residential transactions in the United States, Canada, the Bahamas, Puerto Rico, and the U.S. Virgin Islands. Lawyers Title Insurance Corporation also provides search and examination services and closing services for a broad-based customer group that includes lenders, developers, real estate brokers, attorneys, and home buyers. This location covers Delaware, Washington DC, Maryland, North Carolina, South Carolina, Virginia, and West Virginia.**Corporate headquarters location:** This Location. **Other U.S. locations:** Pasadena CA; Tampa FL; Chicago IL; Boston MA; Troy MI; White Plains NY; Westerville OH; Memphis TN; Dallas TX. **Subsidiaries include:** Datatrace Information Services Company, Inc. (Richmond VA), which markets automated public record information for public and private use; Genesis Data Systems, Inc. (Englewood CO), which develops and markets computer software tailored specifically to the title industry; and Lawyers Title Exchange Company, which operates out of 10 of Lawyers Title Insurance Corporation's regional offices, and functions as an intermediary for individual and corporate investors interested in pursuing tax-free property exchanges under Section 1031 of the Internal Revenue Code. **Parent company:** Lawyers Title Corporation. **Listed on:** NASDAQ.

LIFE INSURANCE COMPANY OF VIRGINIA
6610 West Broad Street, Richmond VA 23230. 804/281-6000. **Contact:** Nancy Spence, Director of Human Resources. **Description:** A life insurance company.

LOUDOUN MUTUAL INSURANCE COMPANY
15609 High Street, P.O. Box 58, Waterford VA 22190. 540/882-3232. **Contact:** Human Resources. **Description:** A property and casualty insurance company operating exclusively in the state of Virginia. **Number of employees at this location:** 15.

MARKEL CORPORATION
4551 Cox Road, P.O. Box 2009, Glen Allen VA 23058-2009. 804/747-0136. **Toll-free phone:** 800/446-6671. **Fax:** 804/965-1600. **Contact:** Ms. Gita Ward, Employment Administrator. **Description:** Markets and underwrites specialty insurance products and programs to a variety of niche markets. Markel Corporation's significant areas of underwriting include professional and products liability, excess and surplus lines, specialty programs, and specialty personal lines. Professional liability coverage is offered to physicians and health professionals, insurance companies, directors and officers, attorneys, architects, and engineers. Products liability is provided to manufacturers and distributors. Property/casualty insurance for non-standard and hard-to-place risks is underwritten on an excess and surplus line basis. Specialty program insurance includes coverages for camps, youth and recreation, health and fitness and agribusiness organizations, as well as accident and health insurance for colleges. The company also underwrites personal lines insurance for water crafts and motorcycles, and maintains wholesale and retail brokerage operations that produce business primarily for its insurance subsidiaries. Markel's operating units include: Essex Insurance Company (Glen Allen VA); Shade/Evanston Group (Evanston IL); Markel Underwriters & Brokers (Glen Allen VA); American Underwriting Managers (Glen Allen VA); and Markel Service, Inc. (Glen Allen VA). **Common positions include:** Accountant/Auditor; Actuary; Computer Programmer; Computer Systems Analyst; Insurance Agent/Broker. **Educational backgrounds include:** Accounting; Business Administration; Finance; Liberal Arts. **Benefits:** 401K; Daycare Assistance; Dental Insurance; Disability Coverage; Life Insurance; Medical Insurance; Profit Sharing; Tuition Assistance. **Special Programs:** Internships. **Corporate headquarters location:** This Location. **Other U.S. locations:** Evanston IL. **Listed on:** NASDAQ. **Number of employees at this location:** 470.

MOUNTAIN STATE BLUE CROSS AND BLUE SHIELD
P.O. Box 1948, Parkersburg WV 26102. 304/424-7700. **Contact:** Connie Knollinger, Team Leader. **Description:** A health insurance provider. Every state in the country has a Blue Cross & Blue Shield (BC/BS) office, each operating as a separate entity. **Corporate headquarters location:** Boston MA.

TRIGON BLUE CROSS AND BLUE SHIELD
2221 Edward Holland Drive, Maildrop 41A, Richmond VA 23230. 804/354-2800. **Contact:** Human Resources Department. **Description:** A health insurance company. **Common positions include:** Actuary; Claim Representative; Computer Systems Analyst; Underwriter/Assistant Underwriter. **Educational backgrounds include:** Business Administration; Health Care. **Benefits:** 401K; Daycare Assistance; Dental Insurance; Disability Coverage; Employee Discounts; Life Insurance; Medical Insurance; Pension Plan; Savings Plan; Tuition Assistance. **Corporate headquarters location:** This Location. **Other U.S. locations:** Roanoke VA. **Operations at this facility include:** Administration; Divisional Headquarters; Regional Headquarters; Sales; Service. **Listed on:** Privately held. **Number of employees at this location:** 3,200. **Number of employees nationwide:** 4,000.

Note: *Because addresses and telephone numbers of smaller companies change rapidly, we recommend you call each company to verify the information below before inquiring about job opportunities. Mass mailings are not recommended.*

Additional small employers:

INSURANCE COMPANIES

Monticello Life Insurance
PO Box 85055, Richmond VA 23285-5055. 804/673-5977.

Old Dominion Life Insurance
2301 Brambleton Ave SW, Roanoke VA 24015-4701. 703/985-4400.

Settlers Life Insurance Co.
PO Box 8600, Bristol VA 24203-8600. 540/645-4307.

Blue Cross and Blue Shield of Virginia
2015 Staples Mill Rd, Richmond VA 23230-3108. 804/354-7000.

Building Trades Welfare Fund
21 Armory Dr, Wheeling WV 26003-6370. 304/242-8836.

Home Warranty Corp.
1110 N Glebe Rd, Arlington VA 22201-4795. 703/516-4110.

Virginia Mutual Insurance
7501 Boulder View Dr, Ste 300, Richmond VA 23225-4047. 804/272-1992.

INSURANCE AGENTS, BROKERS, AND SERVICES

First Health Services
4300 Cox Rd, Glen Allen VA 23060-3358. 804/965-7400.

CCN Inc.
11400 Commerce Park Dr, Reston VA 22091-1549. 703/758-9700.

Alexander & Alexander Virginia Inc.
701 E Byrd St, Ste 1800, Richmond VA 23219-4528. 804/788-4490.

Rockingham Mutual Insurance Co.
633 E Market St, Harrisonburg VA 22801-4229. 540/434-5344.

The Travelers Companies
8230 Boone Blvd, Vienna VA 22182-2621. 703/902-2100.

National Council On Compensation Insurance
1313 E Main St, Richmond VA 23219-3600. 804/643-3266.

For more information on career opportunities in insurance:

Associations

ALLIANCE OF AMERICAN INSURERS
1501 Woodfield Road, Suite 400 West, Schaumburg IL 60173-4980. 847/330-8500.

HEALTH INSURANCE ASSOCIATION OF AMERICA
555 13th Street North, Suite 600E, Washington DC 20004. 202/824-1600.

INSURANCE INFORMATION INSTITUTE
110 William Street, 24th Floor, New York NY 10038. 212/669-9200. Provides informational products on property/casualty insurance.

SOCIETY OF ACTUARIES
475 North Martingale Road, Suite 800, Schaumburg IL 60173-2226. 847/706-3500.

Directories

INSURANCE ALMANAC
Underwriter Printing and Publishing Company, 50 East Palisade Avenue, Englewood NJ 07631. 201/569-8808. Hardcover annual, 639 pages, $115. Available at libraries.

INSURANCE MARKET PLACE
Rough Notes Company, Inc., P.O. Box 564, Indianapolis IN 46206. 317/634-1541.

INSURANCE PHONE BOOK AND DIRECTORY
Reed Reference Publishing, 121 Chanlon Road, New Providence NJ 07974. 800/521-8110. $89.95, new editions available every other year. Also available at libraries.

NATIONAL DIRECTORY OF HEALTH MAINTENANCE ORGANIZATIONS
Group Health Association of America, 1129 20th Street NW, Suite 600, Washington DC 20036. 202/778-3200.

Magazines

BEST'S REVIEW
A.M. Best Company, A.M. Best Road, Oldwick NJ 08858-9988. 908/439-2200. Monthly.

INSURANCE JOURNAL
Wells Publishing, 9191 Towne Centre Drive, Suite 550, San Diego, CA 92122-1231 619/455-7717. A biweekly magazine covering the insurance industry. Subscription: $78 per year, $3 for a single issue.

INSURANCE TIMES
M & S Communications, 20 Park Plaza, Suite 1101, Boston MA 02116. 617/292-7117. A regional biweekly insurance newspaper for insurance professionals.

LEGAL SERVICES

The number of people working in the legal services field has exploded since the early '70s. According to a 1969 survey by the Bureau of Labor Statistics (BLS), there were 387,000 workers in legal services. Today, that number is well over 1 million. The glut of lawyers has led to tremendous competition in the legal profession. Law firms are laying off associates and firing unproductive partners. Graduates of prestigious law schools face tough competition for jobs, but for the top graduates, the offers will be there. According to Jon Sargent, an economist for the Office of Economic Growth at the BLS, some jobseekers looking to break into this industry may need to look outside the mainstream legal services industry: nonprofit companies, government positions, or law firms in smaller communities.

Paralegals have carved out a niche for themselves and continue to be the fastest-growing profession in legal services. "Paralegals have become a cost-effective way to provide legal services in many cases," says Sargent, referring to the realization by many employers that paralegals can do many of the same jobs as associates, at a much lower cost.

BOWLES, RICE, McDAVID, GRAFF & LO
P.O. Box 1386, Charleston WV 25325. 304/347-1100. **Contact:** Kim Snodgrass, Human Resources Director. **Description:** A law firm engaged in a variety of legal services, but specializing in corporate law.

OBLON, SPIVAK & McLELLAND
1755 Jefferson Davis Highway, Arlington VA 22202. 703/521-5940. **Contact:** Kristine Wood, Recruiting Coordinator. **Description:** A legal services firm specializing in intellectual property.

SPOTTS, SMITH, FAIN & RAWLS PC
411 East Franklin Street, Suite 601, Richmond VA 23219. 804/788-1190. **Contact:** Sandy Schubert, Office Manager. **Description:** A full-service law firm, specializing in bankruptcies and collections.

Note: *Because addresses and telephone numbers of smaller companies change rapidly, we recommend you call each company to verify the information below before inquiring about job opportunities. Mass mailings are not recommended.*

Additional small employers:

LEGAL SERVICES

Burns Doane Swecker & Mathis
699 Prince St, Alexandria VA 22314-3117. 703/836-6620.

National Legal Research Group
2421 Ivy Rd, Charlottesvle VA 22903-4971. 804/977-5690.

Vandeventer Black Meredith
World Trade Center, Norfolk VA 23510. 804/446-8600.

Christian Barton Epps Et Al
12th Floor Mutual Building, Richmond VA 23219. 804/644-7851.

Williams Mullen Christian & Dobbins
PO Box 1320, Richmond VA 23210-1320. 804/643-1991.

Herge Sparks & Christopher
8201 Greensboro Dr, Ste

200, Mc Lean VA 22102. 703/848-4700.

Kaufman & Canoles PC
PO Box 3037, Norfolk VA 23514-3037. 804/624-3000.

Willcox & Savage PC
1800 Nationsbank Center, Norfolk VA 23510. 804/628-5500.

Kay Casto Chaney Love & Wise
PO Box 2031, Charleston WV 25327-2031. 304/345-8900.

Shutler and Low PC
14500 Avion Pky, Ste 300, Chantilly VA 22021-1108. 703/818-1320.

Jackson & Kelly
PO Box 553, Charleston WV 25322-0553. 304/340-1000.

Steptoe & Johnson
PO Box 2190, Clarksburg WV 26302-2190. 304/624-8000.

Spilman Thomas & Battle
PO Box 273, Charleston WV 25321-0273. 304/340-3800.

Robinson & McElwee
PO Box 1791, Charleston WV 25326-1791. 304/344-5800.

Mezzullo & McCandlish PC
PO Box 796, Richmond VA 23206-0796. 804/775-3100.

Mays & Valentine
PO Box 1122, Richmond VA 23208-1122. 804/697-1200.

McGuire Woods Battle & Boothe
901 E Cary St, Richmond VA 23219-4057. 804/775-1000.

Woods Rogers & Hazlegrove
PO Box 14125, Roanoke VA 24038-4125. 703/983-7600.

For more information on career opportunities in legal services:

Associations

AMERICAN BAR ASSOCIATION
750 North Lake Shore Drive, Chicago IL 60611. 312/988-5000.

FEDERAL BAR ASSOCIATION
1815 H. Street NW, Suite 408, Washington DC 20006-3697. 202/638-0252.

NATIONAL ASSOCIATION OF LEGAL ASSISTANTS
1516 South Boston, Suite 200, Tulsa OK 74119-4013. 918/587-6828. An educational association. Offers the National Voluntary Association Exam. Memberships are available.

NATIONAL FEDERATION OF PARALEGAL ASSOCIATIONS
P.O. Box 33108, Kansas City MO 64114-0108. 816/941-4000. World Wide Web address: http://www.paralegals.org. Offers magazines, seminars, and Internet job listings.

NATIONAL PARALEGAL ASSOCIATION
P.O. Box 629, 6186 Honey Hollow Road, Doylestown PA 18901. 215/297-8333.

MANUFACTURING: MISCELLANEOUS CONSUMER

The consumer goods manufacturing industry is more than just one industry. To generally forecast about the entire range of companies that make products for consumers is risky, since so much can differ from one segment to the next. In fact, many consumer manufacturers are listed under more specific categories in this book.

With that said, some general statements can be made about the outlook for this gigantic field. Over the long term, many analysts are optimistic. An improved economy, as well as an aging baby boom generation with growing disposable income, should provide stimulus for increases in personal durables. Continued growth in international trade should also point to a favorable long-term outlook for household consumer durables.

U.S. exports of household durables should also expand as trade barriers drop. The North American Free Trade Agreement (NAFTA), passed in early 1994, will give U.S. manufacturers even greater access to what is already the second-largest export market for U.S. household durables. Other trade agreements may follow with several Latin American countries. Potential markets in Eastern Europe and independent states of the former Soviet Union may also open.

AMERICAN SAFETY RAZOR COMPANY
P.O. Box 500, Staunton VA 24402-0500. 703/248-8000. **Fax:** 703/248-0522. **Contact:** Jerry Sams, Personnel Administrator. **Description:** American Safety Razor Company is divided into three industry segments, consisting of razors and blades, custom bar soap, and cotton products, which are designed, manufactured, and marketed by the company. The razors and blades segment includes private-brand and branded shaving blades and razors, branded disposable and cartridge razors, bladed hand tools and blades, and specialty industrial and medical blades. The custom bar soap segment includes cosmetic, skin care, bath, pharmaceutical, and specialty custom bar soaps. The cotton products segment includes cotton swabs, cotton balls and puffs, and foot care products. Foreign locations include: Nottingham, England; San Juan, Puerto Rico; Obegon, Mexico, and Toronto, Canada. **Common positions include:** Accountant/Auditor; Design Engineer; Manufacturing Engineer; Plastics Engineer; Sales Representative. **Benefits:** Life Insurance; Pension Plan; Retirement Plan. **Corporate headquarters location:** This Location. **Other U.S. locations:** Maplewood NJ; Union NJ; Cleveland OH; Dayton OH. **Operations at this facility include:** Distribution; Manufacturing; Sales. **Listed on:** NASDAQ. **Number of employees nationwide:** 1,630.

AMERICAN WOODMARK CORPORATION
3102 Shawnee Drive, P.O. Box 1980, Winchester VA 22604. 703/665-9100. **Contact:** Laura Ivins/Maria Jerke, Human Resources. **Description:** American Woodmark manufactures and distributes kitchen cabinets and vanities for the remodeling and new home construction markets. The company offers almost 100 cabinet lines in a wide variety of designs, materials, and finishes. Its products are sold on a national basis through a

network of independent distributors and directly to home centers, major builders, and home manufacturers. **Benefits:** 401K; ESOP; Pension Plan. **Corporate headquarters location:** This Location. **Other U.S. locations:** AZ; GA; WV. **Listed on:** NASDAQ. **Number of employees nationwide:** 2,170.

AMES COMPANY
P.O. Box 1774, Parkersburg WV 26102. 304/424-3211. **Fax:** 304/424-3234. **Contact:** Tom Davies, Director of Industrial Relations. **Description:** Manufactures hand tools. **Common positions include:** Accountant/Auditor; Electrician; Industrial Engineer; Materials Engineer; Mechanical Engineer. **Educational backgrounds include:** Engineering. **Benefits:** 401K; Dental Insurance; Disability Coverage; Employee Discounts; Life Insurance; Medical Insurance; Pension Plan; Profit Sharing; Savings Plan; Tuition Assistance. **Corporate headquarters location:** This Location. **Other U.S. locations:** Nationwide. **Parent company:** USI. **Operations at this facility include:** Administration; Divisional Headquarters; Manufacturing; Regional Headquarters; Research and Development; Sales; Service. **Listed on:** New York Stock Exchange. **Number of employees at this location:** 1,500.

ARMSTRONG FURNITURE
P.O. Box 848, Appomattox VA 24522. 804/352-7181. **Contact:** Human Resources. **Description:** Armstrong is primarily a manufacturer and marketer of interior furnishings. Its products include floor coverings (resilient flooring and all ceramic tile), building products, and furniture. Armstrong also manufactures and markets a variety of specialty products for the building, automotive, textile, and other industries. **Subsidiaries include:** Thomasville Furniture Industries manufactures and markets wood and upholstered furniture under its own brand name. The company also manufactures furniture under the Armstrong Furniture brand name and produces contract furniture for the nonresidential market. Armstrong Furniture is marketed through large furniture and mass merchandiser chains in North America. Thomasville Furniture is sold by independent furniture retailers worldwide.

BASSETT FURNITURE INDUSTRIES, INC.
P.O. Box 626, Bassett VA 24055. 703/629-6000. **Contact:** James Philpott, Director of Human Resources. **Description:** Manufactures and sells a full line of furniture for the home, such as bedroom and dining suites, accent pieces, occasional tables, wall and entertainment units, upholstered sofas, chairs and love seats, recliners, and mattresses and box springs. **Corporate headquarters location:** This Location. **Other U.S. locations:** Dumas AR; Phoenix AZ; Stockton CA; Los Angeles CA; Lake Wales FL; West Plam Beach FL; Dublin GA; Macon GA; Newnan GA; Tipton MO; Saltillo MS; Booneville MS; Newton NC; Taylorsville NC; Statesville NC; Hickory NC; Mount Airy NC; Ramseur NC; High Point NC; Amherst NH; Columbus OH; Pottstown PA; Austin TX; Martinsville VA; Christiansburg VA; Burkeville VA; Fredericksburg VA; Chehalis WA; Walworth WI. **Number of employees nationwide:** 7,800.

BASSETT MIRROR CO.
P.O. Box 627, Bassett VA 24055. 540/629-3341. **Contact:** Rick Mullins, Human Resources Director. **Description:** A manufacturer of mirrors.

COOPER WOOD PRODUCTS
P.O. Box 489, Rocky Mount VA 24151. 703/483-9201. **Contact:** Sue Chitwood, Human Resources Manager. **Description:** A manufacturer of household wood furniture, including mirrors, tables, and clocks.

DAYSTROM FURNITURE
P.O. Box 130, Highway 654, South Boston VA 24592. 804/572-3981. **Contact:** Human Resources. **Description:** Manufactures dining room furniture for sale to retail stores.

ELECTROLUX
1887 Euclid Avenue, Bristol VA 24201-3605. 540/466-2942. **Contact:** Human Resources. **Description:** A manufacturer and retailer of vacuums. This location is a corporate office. **NOTE:** For information about manufacturing positions, call 540/466-2251.

ELIZABETH ARDEN
4411 Plantation Road NE, Roanoke VA 24012-7410. 703/563-3000. **Contact:** Human Resources. **Description:** An international manufacturer and distributor of a wide range of cosmetics and toiletries.

HAMILTON BEACH PROCTOR SILEX
4421 Waterfront Drive, Glen Allen VA 23060. 804/273-9777. **Contact:** Susan Wall, Personnel Director. **Description:** Corporate headquarters for the company. Hamilton Beach Proctor Silex manufactures electronic products.

HOMER LAUGHLIN CHINA COMPANY
Harrison Street, Newell WV 26050-1299. 304/387-1300. **Contact:** Eric Furbee, Personnel Director. **Description:** Manufactures dinnerware. **Common positions include:** Blue-Collar Worker Supervisor; Ceramics Engineer; Industrial Engineer. **Benefits:** Disability Coverage; Employee Discounts; Life Insurance; Medical Insurance; Pension Plan; Profit Sharing; Savings Plan. **Corporate headquarters location:** This Location. **Number of employees nationwide:** 900.

KENFAIR MANUFACTURING COMPANY
840 South Pickett Street, Alexandria VA 22304. 703/751-5900. **Contact:** Brenda Morgan, Human Resources. **Description:** A drapery hardware and window blinds manufacturer.

LANE COMPANY, INC.
East Franklin Avenue, P.O. Box 151, Altavista VA 24517. 804/369-5641. **Contact:** Leonard Brown, Director of Human Resources. **Description:** A furniture manufacturer.

MERILLAT INDUSTRIES, INC.
1325 Industrial Park, P.O. Box 719, Mount Jackson VA 22842. 540/477-2961. **Fax:** 540/477-2838. **Contact:** Personnel Manager. **Description:** A kitchen and bath cabinet manufacturer. **Common positions include:** Accountant/Auditor; Computer Programmer; Human Resources Specialist; Industrial Engineer; Industrial Production Manager; Mechanical Engineer; Quality Control Supervisor. **Educational backgrounds include:** Accounting; Business Administration. **Benefits:** 401K; Dental Insurance; Disability Coverage; Employee Discounts; Life Insurance; Medical Insurance; Pension Plan; Tuition Assistance. **Corporate headquarters location:** Adrian MI. **Parent company:** MASCO. **Operations at this facility include:** Administration; Manufacturing. **Listed on:** New York Stock Exchange. **Number of employees at this location:** 320. **Number of employees nationwide:** 2,200.

NAUTILUS ACQUISITION CORPORATION
709 Powerhouse Road, Independence VA 24348. 703/773-2881. **Contact:** Margie Stewart, Human Resource Manager. **Description:** Nautilus Acquisition Corporation manufactures a variety of exercise equipment, including the Nautilus Time Machine, Personal Circuit, the Next Generation line, and Nautilus Aerobics. The company distributes its products both nationally and internationally. Established in 1974.

C.M. OFFRAY & SON
255 Stinson Drive, Danville VA 24540-5066. 804/799-7839. **Contact:** William Marlowe, Human Resources Director. **Description:** Manufactures decorative and craft ribbons.

PULASKI FURNITURE CORPORATION
One Pulaski Square, P.O. Box 1371, Pulaski VA 24301. 703/980-7330. **Contact:** Diane Hall, Human Resources Director. **Description:** A furniture manufacturer. **Corporate headquarters location:** This Location. **Listed on:** NASDAQ. **Number of employees nationwide:** 2,287.

REHRIG INTERNATIONAL
901 North Lombardy Street, Richmond VA 23220. 804/355-7864. **Contact:** Susan Gregory-Stokes, Human Resource Manager. **Description:** Manufactures plastic shopping carts, hand baskets, etc.

ROWE FURNITURE
239 Rowan Street, Salem VA 24153. 703/389-8671. **Contact:** John Clark, Corporate Director of Human Resources. **Description:** A leading designer and manufacturer of upholstered furniture. Products include sofas, sleeper sofas, love seats, chairs and motion furniture. The company primarily markets its products in the middle and upper-middle price range, with sofas usually selling for between $600 and $900. Rowe sells its furniture nationwide through its own commissioned sales force to over 1,200 national, regional, and local retailers. These retailers include furniture chains, independent furniture retailers, warehouse showrooms, as well as 93 Rowe ShowPlace locations. Seven of the Rowe ShowPlace showrooms are operated by the company. A Rowe ShowPlace is either an area within a retail furniture store or a separate store where Rowe's products are displayed exclusively. Rowe's manufacturing facilities include four manufacturing plants, two in Missouri and two in Virginia. In addition to manufacturing its own line of furniture, the company manufactures furniture frames and kiln-dries hardwood and pine lumber for outside customers.

SINGER FURNITURE COMPANY
3322 Hollins Road Northeast, Roanoke VA 24012. 703/366-0361. **Contact:** Kim Carte, Personnel Director. **Description:** Manufacturers and distributors of furniture (mainly bedroom, dining room and tables). Singer Furniture nationally sells their product to retail chains, such as Heilig Meyers, Levitz, and Sears. **Corporate headquarters location:** High Point NC. **Number of employees at this location:** 425.

STANLEY ACQUISITION CORPORATION
STANLEY INTERIORS
P.O. Box 30, Stanleytown VA 24168. 703/629-7561. **Contact:** Rick Minichcauer, Human Resources Director. **Description:** A furniture manufacturer.

STANLEY FURNITURE COMPANY, INC.
P.O. Box 30, Highway 57 West, Stanleytown VA 24168. 540/629-7561. **Contact:** Nola Turner, Personnel Director. **Description:** Manufactures dining room and bedroom furniture. Stanley Furniture Company, Inc. has one upholstery plant in North Carolina and three other manufacturing plants in North Carolina. **Number of employees at this location:** 3,000.

STIHL INC.
536 Viking Drive, P.O. Box 2015, Virginia Beach VA 23450-2015. 804/486-8444. **Contact:** Carole G. Cowling, Specialist/Employment. **Description:** A manufacturer of portable outdoor power equipment. **Common positions include:** Accountant/Auditor; Advertising Clerk; Blue-Collar Worker Supervisor; Buyer; Ceramics Engineer; Computer Systems Analyst; Credit Manager; Draftsperson; Electrician; Human Resources Specialist; Industrial Engineer; Management Trainee; Materials Engineer; Mechanical Engineer; Metallurgical Engineer. **Educational backgrounds include:** Accounting; Business Administration; Computer Science; Engineering; Finance; Marketing. **Benefits:** 401K; Dental Insurance; Disability Coverage; Employee Discounts; Life Insurance; Medical Insurance; Pension Plan; Profit Sharing; Tuition Assistance. **Other U.S. locations:** CT; WA. **Parent company:** Andreas

Stihl. **Operations at this facility include:** Administration; Manufacturing; Sales. **Listed on:** Privately held. **Number of employees at this location:** 600.

Note: *Because addresses and telephone numbers of smaller companies change rapidly, we recommend you call each company to verify the information below before inquiring about job opportunities. Mass mailings are not recommended.*

Additional small employers:

WOOD KITCHEN CABINETS

Custom Wood Products
3304 Aerial Way Dr SW, Roanoke VA 24018-1502. 540/345-8821.

Merillat Industries Inc.
641 Maddox Rd, Culpeper VA 22701-4100. 540/825-5884.

HOUSEHOLD FURNITURE

American Furniture Company Inc.
128 E Church St, Martinsville VA 24112-2846. 540/632-2061.

Butler Lumber Co.
239 W B St, Chase City VA 23924-1921. 804/372-4151.

Frank Chervan Inc.
412 Jackson St, Bedford VA 24523-3414. 540/586-5600.

Hooker Furniture Corp.
PO Box 4708, Martinsville VA 24115-4708. 540/632-2133.

Hooker Furniture Corp.
2005 Greenbrier Ave SE, Roanoke VA 24013-2628. 540/344-4328.

Keller Manufacturing Company
RR 3, Culpeper VA 22701-9803. 540/825-1201.

Lane Co. Inc.
129 Pell Ave, Rocky Mount VA 24151-1113. 540/483-5258.

Pine Factory Ltd
100 Haley Rd, Ashland VA 23005-2448. 804/798-9156.

Ridgeway Clock Company
1 Pulaski Sq, Pulaski VA 24301. 703/980-8990.

Seely Pine Furniture Inc.
PO Box 70, Berkeley Springs WV 25411-0070. 304/258-2343.

Charter Of Lynchburg
Winebarger Cir, Lynchburg VA 24502. 804/239-2671.

Jackson Furniture Co. Of VA
239 E 6th St, Front Royal VA 22630-3409. 540/635-3187.

Lea Industries
355 Industrial Park Rd, Chilhowie VA 24319-3901. 540/646-8901.

MHS Holdings Corp.
4401 Fair Lakes Ct, Fairfax VA 22033-3848. 703/968-8015.

Sam Moore Furniture Industries Inc.
1556 Dawn Dr, Bedford VA 24523-2217. 540/586-8253.

Schweiger Industries
1131 Court St, Victoria VA 23974-9477. 804/696-2152.

Virginia House Furniture Corp.
PO Box 138, Atkins VA 24311-0138. 540/783-7217.

Thomasville Furniture Industries Inc.
U S Hwy 501 N, Brookneal VA 24528. 804/376-2301.

This End Up Furniture
1309 Exchange Alley, Richmond VA 23219-4130. 804/644-1248.

MISC. FURNITURE AND FIXTURES

Collier Industries Inc.
Colliers Way, Colliers WV 26035. 304/748-1600.

Associated Furniture
2501 Guyan Ave, Huntington WV 25703-1236. 304/526-4545.

Design Horizons
1500 Industrial Rd, Marion VA 24354-3916. 540/783-8173.

Hopeman Brothers Inc.
435 Essex Ave, Waynesboro VA 22980-4046. 540/949-9200.

WATCHES, CLOCKS, AND RELATED PARTS

Ridgeway Clocks
S R 902, Ridgeway VA 24148. 540/956-3111.

JEWELRY, SILVERWARE, AND PLATED WARE

Hoover & Strong Inc.
10700 Trade Rd, Richmond VA 23236-3000. 804/794-3700.

TOYS/SPORTING GOODS

Baby World Co. Inc.
One Pike Street, Grafton WV 26354. 304/265-2120.

Ben Hogan Co.
8000 Villa Park Dr, Richmond VA 23228-6500. 804/262-3000.

Lasco Bathware
Hwy 931 W, South Boston VA 24592. 804/572-1200.

BURIAL CASKETS

Clarksburg Casket Co.
PO Box 66, Clarksburg

WV 26302-0066.
304/624-6471.

COSMETICS AND RELATED PRODUCTS

CB Fleet Co. Inc.
4615 Murray Place,
Lynchburg VA 24502-
2235. 804/528-4000.

Tri Tech Laboratories
1000 Robins Road,
Lynchburg VA 24506.
804/845-7073.

Wella Corporation
4650 Oakleys Lane,
Richmond VA 23231-
2914. 804/236-0078.

OFFICE AND ART SUPPLIES

West Point Products, Inc.
PO Box 50, Valley Grove
WV 26060-0050.
304/547-1360.

For more information on career opportunities in consumer manufacturing:

Associations

ASSOCIATION FOR MANUFACTURING TECHNOLOGY
7901 Westpark Drive, McLean VA 22102. 703/893-2900. Offers research services.

ASSOCIATION OF HOME APPLIANCE MANUFACTURERS
20 North Wacker Drive, Chicago IL 60606. 312/984-5800.

NATIONAL ASSOCIATION OF MANUFACTURERS
1331 Pennsylvania Avenue NW, Suite 1500, Washington DC 20004. 202/637-3000. A lobbying association for manufacturers.

NATIONAL HOUSEWARES MANUFACTURERS ASSOCIATION
6400 Schafer Court, Suite 650, Rosemont IL 60018. 847/292-4200. Offers shipping discounts and other services.

SOCIETY OF MANUFACTURING ENGINEERS
P.O. Box 930, One SME Drive, Dearborn MI 48121. 313/271-1500. Offers educational events and educational materials on manufacturing.

Directories

APPLIANCE MANUFACTURER ANNUAL DIRECTORY
Appliance Manufacturer, 5900 Harper Road, Suite 105, Solon OH 44139. 216/349-3060. $25.00.

HOUSEHOLD AND PERSONAL PRODUCTS INDUSTRY BUYERS GUIDE
Rodman Publishing Group, 17 South Franklin Turnpike, Ramsey NJ 07446. 201/825-2552. $12.00.

Magazines

APPLIANCE
1110 Jorie Boulevard, Oak Brook IL 60522-9019. 708/990-3484. Monthly. $70.00 for a one-year subscription.

COSMETICS INSIDERS REPORT
Advanstar Communications, 131 West 1st Street, Duluth MN 55802. Toll-free phone: 800/346-0085. $189.00 for a one year subscription; 24 issues annually. Features timely articles on cosmetics marketing and research.

MANUFACTURING: MISCELLANEOUS INDUSTRIAL

New investments by American businesses have generated much of the U.S. economy's expansion in recent years. That's good news for machinery manufacturers, who have been very busy. Through October 1995, the manufacturing of machinery and equipment was up about 12 percent over the previous year.

AMF BAKERY SYSTEMS, INC.
2115 West Laburnum Avenue, Richmond VA 23227. 804/355-7961. **Contact:** Human Resources. **Description:** Manufactures baking equipment for bakeries.

AMF REECE
P.O. Box 15778, Richmond VA 23227. 804/559-5000. **Contact:** Barbara Melton, Personnel Director. **Description:** A manufacturer of industrial machinery, including conveyor pressing machines. **Common positions include:** Accountant/Auditor; Department Manager; Financial Analyst. **Educational backgrounds include:** Accounting; Business Administration; Finance; Marketing. **Benefits:** Dental Insurance; Disability Coverage; Life Insurance; Medical Insurance; Salary Continuation; Tuition Assistance. **Corporate headquarters location:** This Location.

AIR-A-PLANE CORPORATION
Virginia Beach Boulevard, Norfolk VA 23504. 804/622-5761. **Contact:** Kim King, Personnel Director. **Description:** Manufactures air conditioning and heating equipment. **Common positions include:** Electrical/Electronics Engineer; Heating/AC/Refrigeration Technician; Mechanical Engineer; Production Engineer.

ALCO CONTROLS
555 Peppers Ferry Road, Wytheville VA 24382. 540/228-8131. **Contact:** Mr. Gale Orr, Human Resources. **Description:** A manufacturer of valves for coolant and heating systems.

ALLIED RESEARCH CORPORATION
ARC SERVICES, INC.
8000 Towers Crescent Drive, Suite 750, Vienna VA 22182. 703/847-5268. **Fax:** 703/847-5334. **Contact:** Mr. Yarborough, Corporate Vice President. **Description:** Allied Research Corporation is a holding company which provides management and marketing services to its subsidiaries, which include MECAR S.A. (Belgium); Barnes & Reinecke, Inc. (Illinois and Michigan); Allied Research Corporation Limited (United Kingdom); and ARC Services, Inc. (this location). MECAR develops, designs, manufactures, and sells ammunition and weapon systems. Barnes & Reinecke is an engineering and manufacturing firm that specializes in design, prototype fabrication, production, test, and inspection documentation for government and industry. Allied Research Corporation Limited is a systems integrator in the ammunition industry. ARC Services provides demilitarization and environmental services to governments and private corporations. **Corporate headquarters location:** This Location. **Listed on:** American Stock Exchange. **Number of employees worldwide:** 492.

AMERICAN FILTRONA COMPANY
8401 Jefferson Davis Highway, Richmond VA 23237-1337. 804/275-2631. **Fax:** 804/743-0321. **Contact:** Personnel Supervisor. **Description:** Manufactures bonded fibers. **Common positions include:** Buyer; Clerical Supervisor; Draftsperson; Electrical/Electronics Engineer; Electrician; Human Resources Specialist; Industrial Engineer; Industrial Production Manager; Mechanical Engineer; Purchasing Agent and Manager; Quality Control Supervisor. **Educational backgrounds include:** Business Administration; Engineering; Marketing. **Parent company:** American Filtrona Corporation (Richmond VA) was founded in 1954 to manufacture cigarette filters The company has since diversified, also manufacturing and selling fiber and plastic products. The company develops and produces fiber filters for cigarettes and cigars, fiber ink reservoirs and tips for writing instruments, and other bonded fiber specialties. American Filtrona Corporation also converts plastic resins and films into a variety of products used in food packaging, lighting fixtures, signs and displays, and many other applications. **Number of employees at this location:** 350.

AMERICAN FILTRONA CORPORATION
3951 Westerre Parkway, Suite 300, Richmond VA 23233. 804/346-2400. **Fax:** 804/346-0164. **Contact:** Mr. Bragg, Personnel Manager. **Description:** Founded in 1954 to manufacture cigarette filters, American Filtrona Corporation has become a diversified company manufacturing and selling fiber and plastic products. The company develops and produces fiber filters for cigarettes and cigars, fiber ink reservoirs and tips for writing instruments, and other bonded fiber specialties. American Filtrona Corporation converts plastic resins and films into a variety of products used in food packaging, lighting fixtures, signs and displays, and many other applications. **Corporate headquarters location:** This Location. **Subsidiaries include:** American Filtrona Company (Richmond, VA); A&B Plastics, Inc. (Yakima, WA); A&B Plastics Southwest, Inc. (Phoenix, AZ); Duall Plastics, Inc. (Athol, MA); Filpac Inc. (Terrebonne, Quebec); Porth Plastic Company (Des Plaines, IL); Southern Plastics Company (Columbia, SC); Tri-Lite Plastics, Inc. (Fallsington, PA); and Tri-Lite Plastics South, Inc. (Pell City, AL). **Listed on:** NASDAQ. **Number of employees nationwide:** 1,000.

AMERICAN OF MARTINSVILLE
128 East Church Street, Martinsville VA 24115. 703/632-2061. **Contact:** Mr. Guy Stanley, Director of Human Resources. **Description:** Manufactures contract furniture primarily for hotels and motels. **Parent company:** LADD Furniture (High Point, NC).

BRENCO, INC.
One Park West Circle, Suite 201, Midlothian VA 23113. 804/378-2095. **Contact:** Human Resources. **Description:** Brenco, Inc. manufactures tapered roller bearings and component parts for railroad cars. The company sells tapered roller bearings to most major railroads and railroad car builders worldwide. Automotive forgings are sold principally to the automobile manufacturers. Sales are made through both a company sales force and independent manufacturer's representative. Quality Bearing Service, a wholly-owned subsidiary, is devoted to bearing reconditioning and the sale of replacement bearings. Rail Link, Inc., another wholly-owned subsidiary, provides third-party contract switching services to large industrial rail users. **NOTE:** Human resources can be contacted at Petersburg Industrial Park, P.O. Box 389, Petersburg VA. 804/794-1436. **Corporate headquarters location:** This Location.

BRENCO, INC.
P.O. Box 389, Petersburg VA 23804-0389. 804/732-0202. **Contact:** Human Resources. **Description:** Brenco, Inc. manufactures tapered roller bearings and component parts for railroad cars. It sells tapered roller bearings to most major railroads and railroad car builders worldwide. Automotive forgings are sold principally to the automobile manufacturers. Sales are made through

both a company sales force and independent manufacturer's representative. Quality Bearing Service, a wholly-owned subsidiary, is devoted to bearing reconditioning and the sale of replacement bearings. Rail Link, Inc., another wholly-owned subsidiary, provides third-party contract switching services to large industrial rail users.

BRISTOL COMPRESSORS
15185 Industrial Park Road, Bristol VA 24202. 540/466-4121. **Contact:** Louise Anderson, Human Resources Director. **Description:** Manufactures compressors used primarily in air conditioning units.

CAMCAR TEXTRON/AMSCO PRODUCTS
345 East Marshall Street, Wytheville VA 24382. 540/228-8141. **Contact:** Linda Batchelor, Human Resources Director. **Description:** Manufactures fasteners. Camcar Textron/Amsco Products manufactures screws used primarily in automobiles and appliances.

CANON VIRGINIA, INC.
12000 Canon Boulevard, Newport News VA 23606. 804/881-6000. **Contact:** Dave Herring, Manager, Human Resources. **Description:** Manufactures office machines.

COLUMBUS McKINNON CORPORATION
22364 Jeb Stuart Highway, Damascus VA 24236-2504. 540/475-3124. **Contact:** Robert Myers, Human Resources Manager. **Description:** A manufacturer of hoists used primarily in theatrics. Hoists are designed to facilitate the lifting of heavy objects, including stage curtains, sets, and props.

CONNEX PIPE SYSTEMS, INC.
One Connex Way, P.O. Box 275, Troutville VA 24175. 540/992-1600. **Contact:** Corrinna Durham, Human Resources Administrator. **Description:** A fabricator of piping assemblies for use in nuclear-fueled power plants, petrochemical plants, refineries, and chemical plants. **Common positions include:** Accountant/Auditor; Administrator; Buyer; Cost Estimator; Draftsperson; Engineer; General Manager; Human Resources Specialist; Inspector/Tester/Grader; Operations/Production Manager; Purchasing Agent and Manager; Quality Control Supervisor; Sales Manager; Scheduler; Systems Analyst. **Educational backgrounds include:** Accounting; Drafting; Engineering. **Benefits:** Dental Insurance; Disability Coverage; Life Insurance; Medical Insurance; Savings Plan; Tuition Assistance. **Operations at this facility include:** Manufacturing.

COURTALDS PERFORMANCE FILM
P.O. Box 5068, Martinsville VA 24115. 703/629-1711. **Contact:** Human Resources. **Description:** Processes high-performance film. The company specializes in dyed, coated, laminated, and metalized films for solar control.

DUNHAM-BUSH INC.
101 Burgess Road, Harrisonburg VA 22801-9754. 703/434-0711. **Contact:** Personnel Department. **Description:** A manufacturer of heating, ventilation, and air conditioning components for commercial and industrial use.

E.I. DuPONT deNEMOURS & CO.
One DuPont Road, Martinsville VA 24112. 703/666-5000. **Contact:** Human Resources. **Description:** Manufactures nylon. E.I. DuPont de Nemours & Company is a corporation whose diverse activities include the manufacturing of biomedical, industrial, and consumer products (such as photographic, data-recording, and video devices); the production of man-made fiber products (with applications in a variety of consumer and commercial industries); polymer products (such as plastic resins, elastomers, and films); agricultural and industrial chemicals (such as herbicides and insecticides, pigments, fluorochemicals, petroleum additives, and mineral acids); the

exploration and production of crude oil and natural gas; the refining, marketing, and downstream transportation of petroleum; and the mining and distribution of steam and metallurgical coals. Industries served range from aerospace, agriculture, and apparel to transportation, health care, and printing and publishing.

E.I. DuPONT deNEMOURS & CO.
P.O. Box 27001, Richmond VA 23261. 804/383-2000. **Contact:** Human Resources. **Description:** A fibers plant. Manufactures teflon, kevlar, tyvex, and nomex. E.I. DuPont de Nemours & Company is a corporation whose diverse activities include the manufacturing of biomedical, industrial, and consumer products (such as photographic, data-recording, and video devices); the production of man-made fiber products (with applications in a variety of consumer and commercial industries); polymer products (such as plastic resins, elastomers, and films); agricultural and industrial chemicals (such as herbicides and insecticides, pigments, fluorochemicals, petroleum additives, and mineral acids); the exploration and production of crude oil and natural gas; the refining, marketing, and downstream transportation of petroleum; and the mining and distribution of steam and metallurgical coals. Industries served range from aerospace, agriculture, and apparel to transportation, health care, and printing and publishing.

THE FAIRCHILD CORPORATION
300 West Service Road, P.O. Box 10803, Chantilly VA 22021. 703/478-5800. **Fax:** 703/478-5767. **Contact:** Personnel. **Description:** The Fairchild Corporation operates in many different divisions: Fairchild Communications Services Company, which provides comprehensive centralized telecommunications services for tenants in commercial office buildings (also at this location); Fairchild Fasteners-U.S., which manufactures and supplies precision fastening systems and components and latching devices for aerospace and industrial applications (Torrance CA); D-M-E Company, which manufactures and supplies tooling and electronic control systems for the plastics injection molding industry (Madison Heights MI); Fairchild Convac U.S., which manufactures and supplies process equipment and systems for the semiconductor and related industries (Fremont CA); and Fairchild Data Corporation, which manufactures and supplies satellite modems and related high-speed products providing transmission of RF signals (Scottsdale AZ). **Common positions include:** Accountant/Auditor; Administrator; Attorney. **Educational backgrounds include:** Accounting; Business Administration; Liberal Arts. **Benefits:** Dental Insurance; Disability Coverage; Medical Insurance; Pension Plan; Savings Plan; Tuition Assistance. **Corporate headquarters location:** This Location. **Subsidiaries include:** Fairchild Fasteners - Europe: Camloc GmbH (Germany); Voi-Shan/Diessel GmbH (Germany); Fairchild Technologies: Fairchild Convac GmbH (Germany); Gas Springs Division (England); and Fairchild Scandinavian Bellyloading Company AB (Sweden). **Listed on:** New York Stock Exchange. **Number of employees worldwide:** 3,500.

FEDERAL MOGUL INC.
300 Industrial Park Road SE, Blacksburg VA 24060-6608. 703/951-1211. **Contact:** Dennis Young, Human Resources Manager. **Description:** Federal Mogul Inc. is an international company that manufactures bearings for automobile, tractor, truck, and heavy equipment engines.

HOPPMANN CORPORATION
14560 Lee Road, P.O. Box 601, Chantilly VA 22021. 703/631-2700. **Contact:** Barbara O. Egnor, Director of Human Resources. **Description:** Produces automated parts-handling systems. **Common positions include:** Administrator; Customer Service Representative; Designer; Draftsperson; Electrical/Electronics Engineer; Electrician; Mechanic; Mechanical Engineer; Purchasing Agent and Manager; Technical Writer/Editor. **Educational backgrounds include:** Business Administration; Drafting; Engineering; Liberal Arts. **Benefits:** 401K; Daycare Assistance; Dental Insurance; Disability

Coverage; Leave Time; Life Insurance; Medical Insurance; Profit Sharing; Tuition Assistance. **Corporate headquarters location:** This Location. **Other U.S. locations:** Madison Heights VA. **Operations at this facility include:** Administration; Divisional Headquarters; Manufacturing; Research and Development; Sales; Service. **Number of employees at this location:** 150.

INGERSOLL-RAND CO.
7500 Shadwell Drive, Roanoke VA 24019. 703/362-3321. **Contact:** Human Resources. **Description:** A rock drill manufacturer. Overall, Ingersoll-Rand manufactures compressors, pumps, and other non-electrical industrial equipment and machinery. Other products of the company include air compression systems, anti-friction systems, construction equipment, air tools, bearings, locks, tools, and pumps. Ingersoll-Rand operates 93 production facilities throughout the world.

MEDECO SECURITY LOCKS, INC.
P.O. Box 3075, Salem VA 24153. 703/380-1611. **Fax:** 703/380-1715. **Contact:** Dennis Taggart, Vice President, Human Resources. **Description:** A manufacturer of high-security lock cylinders. **Common positions include:** Electrical/Electronics Engineer; Mechanical Engineer; Software Engineer.

MOLINS MACHINE COMPANY, INC.
3900 Carolina Avenue, Richmond VA 23222. 804/329-9081. **Contact:** Judy King, Human Resource Director. **Description:** Manufacturer of machines that pack cigarettes, established in 1931. Molins Machine Company, Inc. distributes its machines internationally. Its office consists of 50 percent production workers and 50 percent office workers (including design engineers). **Number of employees at this location:** 133.

PITNEY BOWES INC.
6100 Lincolnia Road, Alexandria VA 22312-2764. **Toll-free phone:** 800/322-8000. **Contact:** Sue Frazier, District Sales Manager. **Description:** Commercial sales and service facility for the world's largest producer of postage meters and other office products. Pitney Bowes Inc. is a *Fortune* 150 company. The mailing division manufactures and markets postage meters, mail processing and shipping systems, addressing systems, manifesting systems, folding and inserting systems, and mailing software throughout the United States and internationally. **NOTE:** Please address resumes to the following: Pitney Bowes, Northeastern Division, P.O. Box 7011, Bridgeport CT 06011-7011, to the attention of the Human Resources Department.

PRECIPTECH, INC.
11864 Canon Boulevard, Suite 105, Newport News VA 23606. 804/595-7982. **Contact:** Keith Frigo, Human Resources Director. **Description:** PrecipTech provides the U.S. electrostatic precipitator markets with replacement parts, control systems, and services. Electrostatic precipitators are a type of air pollution control equipment. As a fully integrated company, PrecipTech manufactures mechanical and electrical products and have a full range of engineering and service capabilities. Production operations include a 105,000 square foot facility in Folkston, Georgia and a 21,000 square foot facility in Newport News, Virginia. PrecipTech is a subsidiary of the BHA Group, which designs, manufactures and sells replacement parts and accessories for electrostatic precipitators and for another type of industrial air pollution control equipment known as bag houses, and provides rehabilitation and conversion services for the types of industrial air pollution control equipment it produces. **Parent company:** BHA Group.

RADFORD ARMY AMMUNITION PIT
P.O. Box 1, Radford VA 24141. 703/639-7631. **Contact:** Charles Lee, Human Resource Manager. **Description:** Manufactures alliant tech systems.

RUBATEX CORPORATION
906 Adams Street, Bedford VA 24523. 540/586-2611. **Toll-free phone:** 800/782-2839. **Contact:** Michael Haydek, Personnel Director. **Description:** Manufactures rubber products.

XEROX CORPORATION
1700 Bayberry Court, Suite 200, Richmond VA 23226. 703/527-6400. **Contact:** Human Resources. **Description:** An office machine manufacturing company. **NOTE:** Send resumes to Human Resources, P.O. Box 660512, Dallas TX 75266. 800/428-2203.

***Note:** Because addresses and telephone numbers of smaller companies change rapidly, we recommend you call each company to verify the information below before inquiring about job opportunities. Mass mailings are not recommended.*

Additional small employers:

COMMERCIAL FURNITURE AND FIXTURES

Ethan Allen Inc.
Chesapeake Ave, Bridgewater VA 22812. 540/828-2546.

The Hon Co.
11200 Old Stage Rd, Chester VA 23831-2445. 804/796-3100.

Virginia Manufacturing
PO Box 340, Pennington Gap VA 24277-0340. 703/546-3328.

Virginia Metal Industries
12314 Old Gordonsville Rd, Orange VA 22960. 540/672-2800.

PACKAGING PAPER AND PLASTICS FILM

Kern's Bakeries Inc.
PO Box 549, Bristol VA 24203-0549. 540/669-2167.

Piedmont Label Co. Inc.
311 W Depot St, Bedford VA 24523-1937. 540/586-2311.

GASKETS, PACKING, AND SEALING DEVICES

ARS Manufacturing Inc.
1619 Diamond Springs Rd, Virginia Beach VA 23455-3009. 804/363-8101.

Kingston-Warren Corp.
1150 S 3rd St, Wytheville VA 24382-3925. 540/228-6150.

Southland Industries Inc.
PO Box 868, Norfolk VA 23501-0868. 804/543-5701.

METAL HARDWARE

ASAA Technologies Inc.
600 Regional Park Rd, Lebanon VA 24266-3700. 540/889-7000.

Dile Manufacturing Inc.
Rte 5, PO Box 220, Grantsville WV 26147. 304/354-7318.

HEATING EQUIPMENT

Modine Manufacturing
1221 Magnolia Ave, Buena Vista VA 24416-3317. 540/261-2166.

MISC. PIPE FITTINGS AND/OR VALVES

Limitorque Corp.
5114 Woodall Rd, Lynchburg VA 24502-2248. 804/528-4400.

FABRICATED PIPE AND PIPE FITTINGS

Griffin Pipe Products Co.
10 Adams St, Lynchburg VA 24504-4402. 804/845-8021.

Victor Tube Corporation
810 North Main St, Harrisonburg VA 22801-4625. 540/434-4411.

FARM MACHINERY AND EQUIPMENT

Amadas Industries Inc.
1100 Holland Rd, Suffolk VA 23434-6311. 804/539-0231.

MacTavish Machine Manufacturing Co.
9001 Hermitage Road, Richmond VA 23228-2808. 804/264-6109.

Monoflo International Inc.
882 Baker Ln, Winchester VA 22603-5722. 540/665-1691.

Shenandoah Manufacturing Company
1070 Virginia Ave, Harrisonburg VA 22801-2533. 540/434-3838.

CONSTRUCTION MACHINERY AND EQUIPMENT

Franklin Equipment Company
33551 Carver Rd, Franklin VA 23851. 804/562-6111.

CONVEYORS AND CONVEYING EQUIPMENT

Automated Conveyor Systems Inc.
800 Kemper St, Lynchburg VA 24501-1328. 804/528-3822.

Sentry Equipment Erectors
RR 1, Forest VA 24551-9801. 804/525-0769.

Simplimatic Engineering
PO Box 11709, Lynchburg VA 24506-1709. 804/582-1200.

METAL CUTTING OR FORMING TOOLS

Kennametal Inc.
450 New Market Rd, New Market VA 22844. 540/740-3128.

PRINTING MACHINERY AND EQUIPMENT

3M Company
PO Box 947, Charles Town WV 25414-0947. 304/725-2031.

SPECIAL INDUSTRIAL MACHINERY

Environmental Products Corp.
11240 Waples Mill Rd, Fairfax VA 22030-6078. 703/591-1001.

The Cardwell Machine Company
2831 Cardwell Rd, Richmond VA 23234-3875. 804/275-1471.

PUMPS AND PUMPING EQUIPMENT

Ingersoll-Dresser Pump Company
3900 Cook Blvd, Chesapeake VA 23323-1626. 804/485-8000.

Strum Engineered Products
PO Box 277, Barboursville WV 25504-0277. 304/763-3476.

BALL AND ROLLER BEARINGS

Rail Link Inc.
1 Park West Cir, Ste 201, Chesterfield VA 23832. 804/794-1436.

Timken Co.
Dearing Ford Rd, Altavista VA 24517. 804/369-1300.

COMPRESSORS

Bauer Compressors Inc.
1328 Azalea Garden Rd, Norfolk VA 23502-1904. 804/855-6006.

Long-Airdox Co.
227 Maple Ave, Oak Hill WV 25901-3475. 304/469-3301.

FANS, BLOWERS, AND AIR PURIFICATION EQUIPMENT

Buffalo Air Handling
Zane Snead Dr, Amherst VA 24521. 804/946-7455.

Tri-Dim Filter Corp.
Louisa County Industrial Air Pk, Louisa VA 23093. 540/967-2600.

PACKAGING MACHINERY

Acma USA Inc.
501 Southlake Blvd, Richmond VA 23236-3042. 804/794-6688.

Stone Container Corp. Corrugated Container
PO Box 25, Richmond VA 23218-0025. 804/222-5433.

POWER TRANSMISSION EQUIPMENT

Valeo Clutches & Transmissions
310 E St, Hampton VA 23661-1210. 804/827-0310.

MISC. INDUSTRIAL MACHINERY AND EQUIPMENT

Controls Corp. Of America
1501 Harpers Rd, Virginia Beach VA 23454-5303. 804/422-8330.

Des Champs Laboratories
PO Box 220, Natural Bridge Station VA 24579. 540/291-1111.

Figgie Fire Protection Systems
W 2nd Ave, Ranson WV 25438. 304/725-9721.

VENDING MACHINES

Royal Vendors Inc.
201 Industrial Blvd, Kearneysville WV 25430-9628. 304/728-7056.

AIR-CONDITIONING, HEATING, AND REFRIGERATION EQUIPMENT

B&B Service Company
806 Balthrope Rd, Newport News VA 23608-1907. 804/874-6985.

Leigh Hall Mechanical
222 Windsor Castle Dr, Newport News VA 23608-1827. 804/877-4509.

Marine Development Corp.
8433 Erle Rd, Mechanicsville VA 23111-1507. 804/746-1313.

McQuay International
Rt 612, Verona VA 24482. 540/248-0711.

SERVICE INDUSTRY MACHINERY

Infilco Degremont Inc.
2924 Emerywood Pky, Richmond VA 23294-3746. 804/756-7600.

ENGINE PARTS

Zenith Fuel Systems
14570 Industrial Park Rd, Bristol VA 24202-3706. 540/669-5555.

INDUSTRIAL AND COMMERCIAL MACHINERY AND EQUIPMENT

Dreadnought Marine Inc.
3200 E Princess Anne Rd, Norfolk VA 23504-3119. 804/533-5466.

Xaloy Incorporated
102 Xaloy Way, Pulaski VA 24301. 703/980-7560.

York Machinery Service Center
1715 Merrimac Trail, Williamsburg VA 23185-5904. 804/220-6900.

MOTORS AND GENERATORS

Electro-Tec Corporation
1501 North Main Street, Blacksburg VA

24060-2523. 540/552-2111.

Magnetek/Altavista
201 Ogden Road, Altavista VA 24517-1040. 804/369-4794.

Smith Services Inc.
Rte 290-1, Bluefield WV 24701. 304/325-2446.

Thiokol Government Relations
1735 Jefferson Davis Hwy, Arlington VA 22202-3401. 703/413-6300.

MEASURING AND CONTROLLING EQUIPMENT

Telenex Corp/AR Test Systems
7425 Boston Blvd, Springfield VA 22153-3122. 703/644-9190.

D Star Instruments Inc.
8424 Quarry Rd, Ste 203, Manassas VA 22110-5326. 703/335-0770.

Tele-Path Industries Inc.
3602 Melrose Ave NW, Roanoke VA 24017-2741. 703/982-8844.

VDO-Yazaki Corp.
188 Brooke Rd, Winchester VA 22603-5762. 540/665-0100.

Virginia Panel Corp.
1400 New Hope Rd, Waynesboro VA 22980-2647. 540/949-8376.

Miles Inc.
S Rt 11, Middletown VA 22645. 540/869-3200.

For more information on career opportunities in industrial manufacturing:

Associations

INSTITUTE OF INDUSTRIAL ENGINEERS
25 Technology Park, Norcross GA 30092. 770/449-0460. A non-profit organization with 27,000 members. Conducts seminars and offers reduced rates on its books and publications.

NATIONAL ASSOCIATION OF MANUFACTURERS
1331 Pennsylvania Avenue NW, Suite 1500, Washington DC 20004. 202/637-3000. A lobbying association.

NATIONAL SCREW MACHINE PRODUCTS ASSOCIATION
6700 West Snowville Road, Brecksville OH 44141. 216/526-0300. Provides resource information.

NATIONAL TOOLING AND MACHINING ASSOCIATION
9300 Livingston Road, Fort Washington MD 20744. 301/248-1250. Reports on wages and operating expenses. Produces monthly newsletters. Offers legal advice.

SOCIETY OF MANUFACTURING ENGINEERS
P.O. Box 930, One SME Drive, Dearborn MI 48121. 313/271-1500. Offers educational events and educational materials on manufacturing.

Directories

DIRECTORY OF TEXAS MANUFACTURERS
University of Texas at Austin, Bureau of Business Research, Box 7459, Austin TX 78713. 512/471-1616.

TEXAS MANUFACTURERS REGISTER
Manufacturer's News, Inc., 1633 Central Street, Evanston IL 60201. 847/864-7000.

Special Programs

BUREAU OF APPRENTICESHIP AND TRAINING
U.S. Department of Labor, 200 Constitution Avenue NW, Washington, DC 20210. 202/219-6540.

MINING/GAS/PETROLEUM/ENERGY RELATED

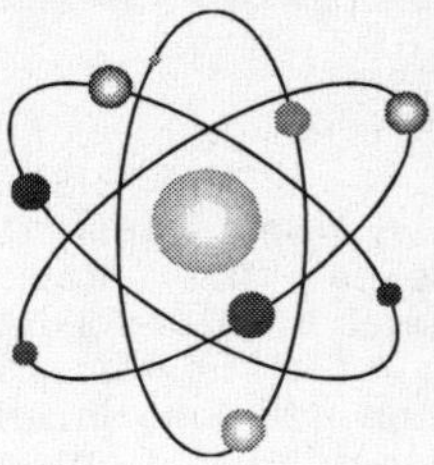

The energy industry just isn't what it used to be. In recent years, energy companies have been restructuring their operations in order to insure solid cash flows even in an era of low prices. Smaller, independent companies are now able to finance new production and land purchases with cash generated from stock sales.

Even so, jobseekers can't expect increased production to lead to much employment growth. Layoffs are expected to continue, but advanced technologies used by the energy industry continue to crop up, and jobseekers with engineering backgrounds should watch for energy-related, high-tech jobs.

In mining, earnings are much higher than average, but technological innovations, international competition, and environmental regulation will reduce employment. Best bets in the mining industry are for scientific technicians, professional specialty workers (such as geologists), and truck drivers.

ALAMCO INC.
200 West Main Street, Clarksburg WV 26301. 304/623-6671. **Contact:** Human Resources. **Description:** A developer and seller of gas and oil reserves, Alamco also serves as an energy service company by maintaining gas and oil wells for other companies.

AMEX COAL/CANNELTON, INC.
101 Washington Street East, Charleston WV 25301. 304/348-0500. **Contact:** Christy Fitzpatrick, Human Resources Director. **Description:** A mining company.

AMVEST CORPORATION
P.O. Box 5347, Charlottesville VA 22905-5347. 804/977-3350. **Contact:** Kelly Tracey, Human Resources Assistant. **Description:** The home office of a coal mining corporation.

ARCH OF WEST VIRGINIA
P.O. Box 156, Yolyn WV 25654. 304/792-8200. **Contact:** Alan Gleason, Human Resources Manager. **Description:** A mining company.

ASHLAND COAL, INC.
2205 Fifth Street Road, Huntington WV 25701. 304/526-3333. **Contact:** Human Resources. **Description:** Ashland Coal mines, processes, markets, and distributes low-sulfur bituminous coal, which it markets mostly in the eastern United States and in Europe. Headquartered in Huntington, West Virginia, the company also has sales offices in St. Clairsville, Ohio, and in Paris, France. Ashland has about 688 million tons of proven and probable low-sulfur coal reserves located in southern West Virginia and eastern Kentucky. **Subsidiaries include:** Coal-Mac, Inc.; Dal-Tex Coal Corporation; Hobet Mining, Inc.; Mingo Logan Coal Company; and Tri-State Testing Company, Inc. **Number of employees at this location:** 1,660.

BABCOCK & WILCOX CO. (NAVAL NUCLEAR FUEL DIVISION)
P.O. Box 785, Lynchburg VA 24505. 804/385-2000. **Contact:** Human Resources. **Description:** Babcock & Wilcox is engaged in the design,

manufacture, and service of steam generating and associated equipment for industrial and commercial power plants. The company also designs and manufactures process control systems and produces nuclear fuel and equipment for the Naval Nuclear Shipbuilding Program. **Parent company:** McDermott International, Inc. (New Orleans LA).

CNG TRANSMISSION CORPORATION
P.O. Box 2450, Clarksburg WV 26302. 304/623-8174. **Fax:** 304/623-8048. **Recorded Jobline:** 304/623-8177. **Contact:** Janice Tyler, Human Resources Consultants. **Description:** An interstate gas pipeline that provides transportation and storage services to other subsidiaries of Consolidated Natural Gas, non-affiliated utilities, and other customers in the Midwest, Mid-Atlantic, and Northeast regions of the country. **Common positions include:** Accountant/Auditor; Chemical Engineer; Computer Programmer; Computer Systems Analyst; Electrical/Electronics Engineer; Mechanical Engineer; Software Engineer. **Educational backgrounds include:** Accounting; Computer Science; Engineering. **Benefits:** 401K; Dental Insurance; Disability Coverage; Medical Insurance; Pension Plan; Savings Plan. **Parent company:** Consolidated Natural Gas Company (Pittsburgh PA). **Operations at this facility include:** Administration; Divisional Headquarters; Sales. **Number of employees at this location:** 800. **Number of employees nationwide:** 2,000.

CLINCHFIELD COAL COMPANY
P.O. Box 5100, Lebanon VA 24266. 703/889-6000. **Contact:** Judy Edwards, Human Resources Director. **Description:** A coal mining company.

EASTERN AMERICAN ENERGY
501 56th Street SE, Charleston WV 25304-2393. 304/925-6100. **Contact:** Human Resources. **Description:** Purchases, distributes, and supplies natural gas, conducts developmental natural gas drilling and production operations, markets natural gas, and operates exploratory and developmental oil drilling and production operations.

EASTERN ASSOCIATED COAL CORPORATION
P.O. Box 1233, Charleston WV 25324. 304/344-0300. **Contact:** Elizabeth Wills, Human Resources Director. **Description:** A coal mining company.

ELK RUN COAL COMPANY, INC.
State Route 3, P.O. Box 497, Sylvester WV 25193. 304/854-1890. **Contact:** Butch Brown, Human Resources Director. **Description:** A coal mining company.

ETHYL CORPORATION
330 South Fourth Street, P.O. Box 2189, Richmond VA 23218. 804/788-5000. **Recorded Jobline:** 804/788-5588. **Contact:** Human Resources. **Description:** Manufactures fuel and lubricant additives including products for gas and diesel fuels, engine oils, automatic transmission fluids, gear oils, hydraulic fluids, and industrial oils. Through its subsidiary Whitby, Inc., Ethyl Corporation markets ethical and over-the-counter drugs such as analgesics, bronchodilators, and nutritional supplements. **Common positions include:** Accountant/Auditor; Buyer; Chemical Engineer; Chemist; Computer Programmer; Electrical/Electronics Engineer; Financial Analyst; Human Resources Specialist; Manufacturer's/Wholesaler's Sales Rep.; Mechanical Engineer; Operations/Production Manager; Petroleum Engineer; Purchasing Agent and Manager; Quality Control Supervisor. **Educational backgrounds include:** Accounting; Chemistry; Computer Science; Engineering; Finance. **Benefits:** Dental Insurance; Disability Coverage; Life Insurance; Medical Insurance; Pension Plan; Savings Plan; Tuition Assistance. **Corporate headquarters location:** This Location. **Listed on:** New York Stock Exchange. **Number of employees at this location:** 300. **Number of employees nationwide:** 1,500.

JAMES RIVER COAL COMPANY
701 East Byrd Street, Richmond VA 23219-4528. 804/780-3003. **Contact:** Deborah Waters, Human Resources Representative. **Description:** The sales office for a coal company. **Operations at this facility include:** Accounting/Auditing; Administration; Sales.

MARROWBONE DEVELOPMENT COMPANY
P.O. Box 119, Naugatuck WV 25685. 304/235-7650. **Contact:** Mike Hymes, Human Resources Director. **Description:** A mining company.

A.T. MASSEY COAL COMPANY, INC.
P.O. Box 2676, Richmond VA 23261. 804/788-1800. **Contact:** Pauline Donato, Human Resources Director. **Description:** A coal mining company.

MILLER OIL COMPANY
P.O. Box 1858, Norfolk VA 23501. 804/623-6600. **Contact:** Charlotte Surdousky, Personnel Director. **Description:** An oil supplier.

MOBIL CORPORATION
3225 Gallows Road, Fairfax VA 22037-0001. 703/846-3000. **Contact:** Staffing and Training. **Description:** An integrated oil company engaged in petroleum and chemical products marketing, refining, manufacturing, exploration, production, transportation, and research and development in more than 100 countries. Exploration is conducted in 34 countries. The company has interests in 21 refineries in 12 countries, owns 28 oil tankers, and has interests in over 36,000 miles of pipeline worldwide. Mobil markets its products through more than 19,000 company-owned retail outlets in over 90 countries. Other products include fabricated plastics, films, food bags, houseware, garbage bags, and building materials. The company also has subsidiaries involved in real estate development and mining operations. **Corporate headquarters location:** This Location. **Listed on:** New York Stock Exchange. **Number of employees worldwide:** 58,500.

MOBIL MINING AND MINERALS COMPANY
10329 Stoney Run Lane, Ashland VA 23005. 804/550-2636. **Contact:** Robert Nastanovich, Employee Relations Manager. **Description:** A mining company.

MOUNTAINEER GAS COMPANY
P.O. Box 3152, 414 Summer Street, Charleston WV 25332. 304/347-0566. **Fax:** 304/365-1569. **Contact:** Moses Skaff, Human Resources Manager. **Description:** A natural gas utility. **Common positions include:** Account Manager; Attorney; Blue-Collar Worker Supervisor; Civil Engineer; Electrical/Electronics Engineer; Human Resources Specialist; Industrial Engineer; Mechanical Engineer; Metallurgical Engineer. **Educational backgrounds include:** Accounting; Business Administration; Engineering; Finance; Marketing. **Benefits:** 401K; Dental Insurance; Disability Coverage; Life Insurance; Medical Insurance; Pension Plan; Tuition Assistance. **Special Programs:** Internships. **Parent company:** Allegheny & Western Energy. **Operations at this facility include:** Administration; Divisional Headquarters. **Listed on:** American Stock Exchange. **Number of employees at this location:** 560.

PETROLEUM DEVELOPMENT CORPORATION
P.O. Box 26, 103 East Main Street, Bridgeport WV 26330. 304/842-6256. **Contact:** Human Resources. **Description:** Involved in oil and gas exploration, production, and development as well as related property management. The company grants credit to purchasers of oil and gas and the owners of managed properties, almost all of whom are located in the Basin area of West Virginia, Tennessee, Pennsylvania, and Ohio.

Note: *Because addresses and telephone numbers of smaller companies change rapidly, we recommend you call each company to verify the information below before inquiring about job opportunities. Mass mailings are not recommended.*

Additional small employers:

WHOLESALE COAL, MINERALS, AND ORES

Blue Crystal Coal Sales Company
701 E Byrd St, Richmond VA 23219-4528. 804/780-3003.

Coastal Coal Sales Inc.
PO Box 1871, Roanoke VA 24008-1871. 703/983-0222.

Eastern Associated Coal Corp. Fed No
Miracle Run, Fairview WV 26570. 304/449-1911.

PETROLEUM AND PETROLEUM PRODUCTS WHOLESALE

Sussex Oil Company Inc.
PO Box 400, Wakefield VA 23888-0400. 804/899-3791.

Matthews Brothers Wholesale
PO Box 1186, Clarksburg WV 26302-1186. 304/624-7601.

Parker Oil Company Inc.
PO Box 120, South Hill VA 23970-0120. 804/447-3146.

Commonwealth Propane
2014-C Lafayette Blvd, Fredericksbrg VA 22401. 540/898-0357.

COAL MINING

A&G Coal Corp.
106 Spring Ave N E, Wise VA 24293. 540/328-3421.

Buffalo Coal Co. Inc.
Front St, Bayard WV 26707. 304/693-7642.

Consolidation Coal Co.
Portal, Mannington WV 26582. 304/795-4421.

Heritage Mining Co.
McClure Ave, Clintwood VA 24228. 540/926-4380.

Humphreys Enterprises
Dorchester Rd Rt 610, Norton VA 24273. 540/679-1400.

Jewell Coal & Coke Co.
Rt 460, Vansant VA 24656. 540/935-8810.

Mingo Logan Coal Co.
1000 Mingo Logan Ave, Wharncliffe WV 25651. 304/664-3873.

Old Ben Coal Co.
S R 49, Thacker WV 25694. 304/426-4020.

Old Hickory Coal Co. Inc.
Rt 17, Sharples WV 25183. 304/369-2359.

Paramont Coal Corp.
5345 Esserville Rd, Wise VA 24293. 540/679-8600.

Pittston Coal Group Inc.
Hwy 19, Lebanon VA 24266. 540/889-6000.

Powell Mountain Coal Co.
Bonnie Blue Section, Saint Charles VA 24282. 540/383-4412.

Vandalia Resources Inc.
512 3rd Ave, Montgomery WV 25136-2102. 304/442-5448.

Beth Energy Mines Inc.
Jerry Fork Rd, Drennen WV 26667. 304/872-4425.

Betty B. Coal Co. Inc.
Guest River Rd, Norton VA 24273. 540/679-0806.

Cannelton Industries Inc.
Rt 60 E, Cannelton WV 25036. 304/442-9575.

Carter-Roag Coal Co. Inc.
Rte 250, Elkins WV 26241. 304/636-8320.

Consolidation Coal Co.
RR 4 Box 425, Moundsville WV 26041-9804. 304/843-3500.

Eagle Nest Inc.
C R 28, Van WV 25206. 304/245-8236.

LK Mining Co.
Rt 10, Lyburn WV 25632. 304/792-6213.

Martinka Coal Co.
750 Levels Rd, Fairmont WV 26554-8330. 304/366-5515.

Peabody Coal Co.
50 School House Rd, Seth WV 25181-9416. 304/837-3313.

Powell Mountain Coal
2537 4th Ave E, Big Stone Gap VA 24219-3601. 540/523-4932.

Rauer Coal
Rt 20 N, Buckhannon WV 26201. 304/472-8493.

Terry Eagle Coal Co.
RR 2 Box 900, Summersville WV 26651-9648. 304/872-6100.

Virginia Iron Coal & Coke Company
1014 Laurel Ave, Coeburn VA 24230-3827. 540/395-3316.

PETROLEUM AND NATURAL GAS

Eastern American Energy Corp.
501 56th St Se, Charleston WV 25304-2341. 304/925-6100.

Wiser Oil Co.
210 Charles St, Sistersville WV 26175-1202. 304/652-3861.

PETROLEUM REFINING

Amoco Oil Co.
2201 Goodwin Neck Rd,

Grafton VA 23692-4451. 804/898-9700.

Congo Refinery
PO Box 336, Newell WV 26050-0336. 304/387-3530.

Pennzoil Products Co.
Rt 50 & Flinderation Rd, Bristol WV 26332. 304/782-3591.

Pennzoil Products Co.
601 Grand Central Ave, Vienna WV 26105-2141. 304/422-6565.

PETROLEUM AND COAL PRODUCTS

Big Mountain Complex
General Delivery, Seth WV 25181-9999. 304/837-3313.

Cannelton Industries Inc.
Rte 60 E, Montgomery WV 25136. 304/442-9575.

Colony Bay Coal Co.
PO Box 151, Wharton WV 25208-0151. 304/247-6272.

Cub Branch Mining Inc.
PO Box 191, Dunlow WV 25511-0191. 304/385-4932.

Cyprus Kanawha Coal
Hc 61 Box 30, Powellton WV 25161-9701. 304/442-4572.

Hobet Mining Inc.
PO Box 305, Madison WV 25130-0305. 304/369-6780.

Island Creek Coal
Star Rte Box 425, Mount Storm WV 26739. 304/259-5800.

Leckie Smokeless Coal
PO Box A, Rupert WV 25984-0198. 304/392-6394.

Maple Meadow Mining
Rte 99, Fairdale WV 25839. 304/934-5301.

Virginia Crews Coal Co.
PO Box 727, Iaeger WV 24844-0727. 304/938-5700.

Windsor Power House Coal
PO Box 39, West Liberty WV 26074-0039. 304/336-7203.

MINING MACHINERY AND EQUIPMENT

American LaFrance
600 Mountain Lane Ave S, Bluefield VA 24605-9600. 540/326-1121.

American Mine Research
Rt 61 & I-77, Rocky Gap VA 24366. 540/928-1712.

American Mine Tool
1027 Kendall Rd, Chilhowie VA 24319. 540/646-8990.

Appalachian Electrical Instruments Inc.
PO Box 518, Ronceverte WV 24970-0518. 304/647-5855.

EIMCO
2101 Pleasant Valley Road, Fairmont WV 26554-8554. 304/363-1048.

JH Fletcher & Co.
PO Box 2187, Huntington WV 25722-2187. 304/525-7811.

Long-Airdox Co.
South Route 611, Pulaski VA 24301. 703/980-4530.

Rock Drill Division
7500 Shadwell Dr, Roanoke VA 24019-5106. 540/362-3321.

For more information on career opportunities in the mining, gas, petroleum, and energy industries:

Associations

AMERICAN ASSOCIATION OF PETROLEUM GEOLOGISTS
P.O. Box 979, Tulsa OK 7410-0979. 918/584-2555. International headquarters for petroleum geologists.

AMERICAN GEOLOGICAL INSTITUTE
4220 King Street, Alexandria VA 22302-1507. 703/379-2480. Scholarships available. Publishes monthly *Geotimes*. Offers job listings.

AMERICAN NUCLEAR SOCIETY
555 North Kensington Avenue, La Grange Park IL 60525. 708/352-6611. Offers educational services.

AMERICAN PETROLEUM INSTITUTE
1220 L Street NW, Suite 900, Washington DC 20005. 202/682-8000. A trade association.

GEOLOGICAL SOCIETY OF AMERICA
3300 Penrose Place, P.O. Box 9140, Boulder CO 80301. 303/447-2020. Membership of over 17,000. Offers sales items and publications. Also conducts society meetings.

SOCIETY OF EXPLORATION GEOPHYSICISTS
P.O. Box 702740, Tulsa OK 74170-2740. 918/493-3516. A membership association. Offers publications.

Directories

BROWN'S DIRECTORY OF NORTH AMERICAN AND INTERNATIONAL GAS COMPANIES
Advanstar Communications, 7500 Old Oak Boulevard, Cleveland OH 44130. 800/225-4569.

NATIONAL PETROLEUM NEWS FACT BOOK
Adams/Hunter Publishing Company, 2101 South Arlington Heights Road, Suite 150, Arlington Heights IL 60005-4142. 847/427-9512.

OIL AND GAS DIRECTORY
Geophysical Directory, Inc., P.O. Box 130508, Houston TX 77219. 713/529-8789.

Magazines

AMERICAN GAS MONTHLY
1515 Wilson Boulevard, Arlington VA 22209. 703/841-8686.

GAS INDUSTRIES
Gas Industries News, Inc., 6300 North River Road, Suite 505, Rosemont IL 60018. 312/693-3682.

NATIONAL PETROLEUM NEWS
Adams/Hunter Publishing Company, 2101 South Arlington Heights Road, Suite 150, Arlington Heights IL 60005-4142. 847/427-9512.

OIL AND GAS JOURNAL
PennWell Publishing Company, 1421 South Sheridan Road, P.O. Box 1260. Tulsa OK 74101. 918/835-3161.

MISCELLANEOUS WHOLESALING

Employment in the wholesale trade sector is closely tied to the growth of the economy. However, industry trends will change a good portion of the composition and nature of wholesale trade employment. Consolidation of the industry into fewer firms and the spread of new technology should slow growth in some occupations, but many new jobs will be created in others as firms provide a growing array of support services. In addition, these trends will change the role of many other workers.

Heightened competition and pressure to lower operating costs should continue to force distributors to merge with or acquire other firms. The resulting consolidation of wholesale trade among fewer, larger firms will reduce the demands for some workers as merged companies eliminate duplicated staff. Consolidation and greater competition among wholesale trade firms, however, will lead more firms to expand customer service, increasing the demand for these types of workers. Clerks or sales workers will advance to many of these new customer service or marketing jobs, and new workers may be needed for financial, logistical, technical, or advertising positions.

CHAMPION INDUSTRIES
2450 First Avenue, P.O. Box 2968, Huntington WV 25729-2968. 304/528-2791. **Contact:** Human Resources. **Description:** A diversified holding company with two lines of business, Champion Industries is engaged in both the distribution of office furniture and supplies and commercial printing.

McJUNKIN CORPORATION
P.O. Box 513, Charleston WV 25322. 304/348-5263. **Contact:** William Board, Personnel Director. **Description:** A distributor of industrial supplies, including pipes, valves, and fittings. **Common positions include:** Accountant/Auditor; Branch Manager; Computer Programmer; Credit Manager; Department Manager; Draftsperson; Financial Analyst; General Manager; Manufacturer's/Wholesaler's Sales Rep.; Systems Analyst. **Educational backgrounds include:** Accounting; Business Administration; Computer Science; Marketing. **Benefits:** Dental Insurance; Disability Coverage; Employee Discounts; Life Insurance; Medical Insurance; Pension Plan; Profit Sharing; Tuition Assistance. **Corporate headquarters location:** This Location. **Operations at this facility include:** Administration; Manufacturing; Research and Development; Sales; Service.

NOLAND COMPANY
2700 Warwick Boulevard, Newport News VA 23607. 804/928-9000. **Contact:** William Smith, Human Resources Manager. **Description:** An independent wholesaler, with 99 branches in 15 states. Noland Company sells a wide variety of mechanical equipment and supplies to contractors, industrial plants, and others, drawing on more than 6,000 vendor sources. Products are categorized under plumbing/heating, electrical, industrial, and air conditioning/refrigeration. These products are sold to all major areas of manufacturing, domestic water systems, the maintenance/repair/modernization market, and construction, including residential; nonresidential (commercial, institutional, industrial); and non-building (highways, sewer, water, utilities). Noland Properties, Inc., a wholly-owned subsidiary, holds and manages the real estate holdings of the company and acquires sites and provides facilities to house the company's various branches as required. **Corporate headquarters location:** This Location. **Listed on:** NASDAQ.

CECIL I. WALKER MACHINERY COMPANY
P.O. Box 2427, Charleston WV 25329. 304/949-6400. **Contact:** Mr. A.S.J. Southworth III, Vice President of Finance. **Description:** Engaged in the sale and service of industrial machinery and equipment. **Common positions include:** Branch Manager; Computer Programmer; Computer Systems Analyst; Credit Manager; Mechanic. **Educational backgrounds include:** Accounting; Business Administration; Computer Science; Marketing. **Benefits:** 401K; Dental Insurance; Disability Coverage; Life Insurance; Medical Insurance; Pension Plan. **Operations at this facility include:** Administration; Sales; Service. **Listed on:** Privately held. **Number of employees at this location:** 264. **Number of employees nationwide:** 481.

Note: *Because addresses and telephone numbers of smaller companies change rapidly, we recommend you call each company to verify the information below before inquiring about job opportunities. Mass mailings are not recommended.*

Additional small employers:

WHOLESALE FURNITURE AND HOME FURNISHINGS

Budget Office Furniture
8811 Forest Hill Ave, Richmond VA 23235-2433. 804/320-5138.

Ginns Office Products
12th & Main Sts, Richmond VA 23219. 804/643-2000.

Restaurant Equipment International
210 The Strand, Alexandria VA 22314-3320. 703/370-1301.

HARDWARE WHOLESALE

Nelson-Roanoke Corporation
PO Box 13046, Roanoke VA 24030-3046. 703/982-7575.

Armstrong's Lock & Supply
1333 Azalea Garden Rd, Norfolk VA 23502-1933. 804/853-0611.

INDUSTRIAL MACHINERY AND EQUIPMENT WHOLESALE

Gardner Denver
1700 Blue Hills Dr NE, Roanoke VA 24012-8601. 703/983-1200.

Rish Equipment Co.
PO Box 330, Bluefield WV 24701-0330. 304/327-5124.

Shelton-Witt Equipment Corp.
4112 Holland Blvd, Chesapeake VA 23323-1523. 804/485-3314.

Con-Link Equipment Co.
212 Freedom Court, Fredericksbrg VA 22408-2461. 540/891-7774.

Mitchell Distributing Company
1410 W Hundred Rd, Chester VA 23831-2529. 804/748-6411.

Tarmac Mid-Atlantic Inc.
1151 Azalea Garden Rd, Norfolk VA 23502-5601. 804/858-6500.

James McGraw Inc.
2900 Deepwater Terminal Rd, Richmond VA 23234-1824. 804/233-3071.

Salem Tools Of Eastern VA
2948 Bells Rd, Richmond VA 23234-1606. 804/271-7247.

McIntyre Equipment Co.
1301 Mountain Rd, Glen Allen VA 23060-4054. 804/266-4911.

Fork Lift Service
5013 Morgan Dr, Cross Lanes WV 25313-2109. 304/776-3191.

Duriron Co. Inc.
7445 Whitepine Rd, Richmond VA 23237-2261. 804/271-4031.

Cummins-Wagner Co.
430 S Leadbetter Rd, Ashland VA 23005-3200. 804/798-6177.

BFI Waste Systems
2813 Juniper St, Fairfax VA 22031-4401. 703/560-8866.

Young-Phillips Sales Co.
3031 Frontier Rd NW, Roanoke VA 24012-2856. 540/362-8152.

Industrial Rubber Products Company
815 Court St, Charleston WV 25301-1048. 304/344-1791.

Industrial Rubber Products Company
1910 12th Ave, Parkersburg WV 26101-6175. 304/485-6491.

Eastern Belt Maintenance
713 Johnston Willis Dr, Richmond VA 23236-3953. 804/379-8070.

Automatic Switch Co.
1503 Santa Rosa Rd, Richmond VA 23229-5105. 804/282-3521.

Georgia-Pacific Corporation
Dabney & Bethlehem Rds, Richmond VA 23230. 804/355-9187.

Motion Industries
9203 Burge Ave, Richmond VA 23237-3044. 804/743-8000.

Frenzelit North America
43990 Maiden Creek Ct, Ashburn VA 22011-3923. 703/318-9444.

BOC Gases
4323 Bainbridge Blvd, Chesapeake VA 23324-1407. 804/545-2485.

Chesapeake Sprinkler Co.
44642 Guilford Dr, Ste 108, Ashburn VA 22011-6005. 703/478-8811.

OFFICE EQUIPMENT WHOLESALE

Electronic Systems
361 Southport Cir, Virginia Beach VA 23452-1144. 804/497-8000.

SCRAP AND WASTE MATERIALS WHOLESALE

Cycle Systems Inc.
2580 Broadway Ave SW, Roanoke VA 24014-1620. 703/981-1211.

PAPER AND OFFICE SUPPLIES WHOLESALE

Office America Inc.
PO Box 2430, Glen Allen VA 23058-2430. 804/747-9964.

Standard Register Co.
2965 Colonnade Dr, Ste 310, Roanoke VA 24018-3541. 540/989-8808.

Tab Products
1749 Old Meadow Rd, Ste 210, McLean VA 22102-4310. 703/506-0099.

McBee Systems
1606 Santa Rosa Rd, Ste 121, Richmond VA 23229-5014. 804/673-1040.

Reynolds and Reynolds
10340 Democracy Ln, Ste 101, Fairfax VA 22030-2518. 703/691-4899.

DRUGS, DRUG PROPRIETARIES, AND DRUGGISTS' SUNDRIES

Ohio Valley-Clarksburg
71 Mil Acres Dr, Wheeling WV 26003-5089. 304/242-9526.

For more information on career opportunities in wholesaling:

<u>Associations</u>

APPLIANCE PARTS DISTRIBUTORS ASSOCIATION
228 East Baltimore Street, Detroit MI 48202. 313/875-8455. An association for wholesale distributors of appliance parts.

PAPER AND WOOD PRODUCTS

The year 1995 was a dramatic one for the paper industry. Prices jumped higher and faster than they had at any time since World War II. According to Dean Witter, profits were up an astounding 180 percent during the year at the nation's 19 largest paper and paperboard companies.

By mid-1995, however, customers had begun to hoard paper, forcing prices back down. Luckily, even as profits soared in the early part of the year, the industry played its hand conservatively by resisting the impulse to expand capacity. Analysts expect prices to continue to stay down during 1996. That means that jobseekers shouldn't anticipate a major increase in industry hiring.

One hot trend, however, may provide opportunity. Environmental concerns should give the paper packaging segment an advantage over plastics, as companies move to become "green." The industry hopes to recycle at least half of the paper it produces by the turn of the century. Minimills, which convert cardboard into pulp, are springing up nationwide. Among the industry's recycling leaders: Weyerhaeuser and Boise Cascade.

CHESAPEAKE CORPORATION
P.O. Box 2350, Richmond VA 23218-2350. 804/697-1000. **Contact:** Tom Smith, Vice President of Human Resources. **Description:** An integrated forest products company for the construction, institutional, health care, restaurant, hotel, and commercial industries. Products include paper, tissue, towels, placemats, pulp, paperboard, corrugated containers, and wood products. Chesapeake Corporation operates four sawmills in Virginia for Kraft products and seven corrugated container plants. The company also provides graphic packaging services. **Corporate headquarters location:** This Location. **Listed on:** New York Stock Exchange. **Number of employees nationwide:** 5,200.

DOUBLE ENVELOPE COMPANY
7702 Plantation Road, Roanoke VA 24019-3225. 703/362-3311. **Contact:** Human Resources. **Description:** Manufactures a variety of paper products, including labels, order forms, and envelopes.

GEORGIA-PACIFIC CORPORATION
634 Davis Street, Emporia VA 23847. 804/634-5123. **Contact:** Denise Montgomery, Personnel Director. **Description:** A plywood plant. Georgia-Pacific Corporation is a manufacturer, wholesaler, and distributor of building products, industrial wood products, pulp, paper, packaging, and related chemicals. The company is one of the world's largest manufacturers of forest products, with facilities in 48 states and overseas. Georgia-Pacific Corporation owns 6 million acres of forest land in North America.

JAMES RIVER CORPORATION OF VIRGINIA
120 Tredegar Street, Richmond VA 23219. 804/644-5411. **Contact:** Larry Olszewski, Director of Human Resources. **Description:** A manufacturer of a variety of paper products, plastic tableware, and retail packaging products like cartons, bags, and wraps. Paper products include tissues, towels, business and correspondence paper, coated papers for catalogs, and premium printing papers. Brand names include Brawny, Quilted Northern, Vanity Fair, Nice 'n Soft, and Dixie. James River markets its paper products to consumers as well as restaurants, hotels, offices, factories, schools, and other institutional and commercial markets. **Corporate headquarters location:** This Location. **Listed on:** New York Stock Exchange.

STONE CONTAINER CORPORATION
2333 Commerce Street, Wellsburg WV 26070. 304/737-3311. **Contact:** Dave Bertoia, Human Resources Representative. **Description:** A paper bag manufacturing facility. Overall, Stone Container Corporation is a multinational paper and packaging company with annual sales of approximately $5 million. Its primary businesses are paperboard and paper packaging, and white paper and pulp operations. The paperboard and paper packaging segment is composed primarily of facilities which produce and sell containerboard and corrugated containers for manufacturers of consumable and durable goods and other manufacturers of corrugated containers; boxboard, folding cartons, and other products for manufacturers of consumable goods including food, beverage, and tobacco products, and for other box manufacturers; and kraft paper and bags for supermarket chains and other retailers of consumable products, as well as for the food, agricultural, chemical, and cement industries. The white paper and pulp segment produces and sells newsprint for newspaper publishers and commercial printers; uncoated groundwood paper for producers of advertising materials, magazines, directories, and computer papers; and market pulp for manufacturers of paper products including fine papers, photographic papers, tissue, and newsprint. Other operations consist primarily of wood products operations which produce and sell lumber, plywood, and veneer for the construction and furniture industries. Including its subsidiaries and affiliates, Stone Container Corporation maintains nearly 200 manufacturing facilities and sales offices in North America, Latin America, Europe, and the Far East.

UNION CAMP CORPORATION
P.O. Box 178, Franklin VA 23851. 804/569-4705. **Contact:** Howard N. Soucek, Personnel Manager. **Description:** This facility manufactures pulp, particleboard, fine paper, and related products. Union Camp Corporation receives raw materials here. Other fields of operation include minerals, land development, chemicals, school supplies, retail building supplies, printing machinery, packaging machinery and systems, plastic products, and cartons and containers. The company has operations in the United States and abroad. United States facilities include pulp and paper mills, lumber mills, plywood and particleboard plants, and chemical plants. Union Camp Corporation's research and development activities are centered in Princeton NJ. **Common positions include:** Accountant/Auditor; Attorney; Blue-Collar Worker Supervisor; Buyer; Chemical Engineer; Chemist; Civil Engineer; Computer Programmer; Customer Service Representative; Department Manager; Draftsperson; Electrical/Electronics Engineer; Forester/Conservation Scientist; General Manager; Human Resources Specialist; Industrial Engineer; Manufacturer's/Wholesaler's Sales Rep.; Marketing Specialist; Mechanical Engineer; Public Relations Specialist; Purchasing Agent and Manager; Quality Control Supervisor; Systems Analyst; Transportation/Traffic Specialist. **Educational backgrounds include:** Accounting; Business Administration; Chemistry; Computer Science; Engineering. **Benefits:** Disability Coverage; Life Insurance; Medical Insurance; Pension Plan; Savings Plan; Stock Option; Tuition Assistance. **Corporate headquarters location:** Wayne NJ. **Operations at this facility include:** Divisional Headquarters; Manufacturing; Sales; Service. **Listed on:** New York Stock Exchange.

WESTVACO CORPORATION
Corporate Center, 1011 Boulder Springs Drive, Richmond VA 23225. **Contact:** Kelley R. McNamara, Manager of College Relations and Employment. **Description:** A producer of paper packaging and specialty chemicals. Worldwide, Westvaco operates 50 facilities. These facilities include paper and paperboard mills, converting plants, chemical plants, lumber mills, research and development laboratories, and real estate operations. **Common positions include:** Accountant/Auditor; Financial Analyst; Manufacturer's/Wholesaler's Sales Rep. **Educational backgrounds include:** Business Administration; Engineering; Liberal Arts; Marketing. **Benefits:** Dental Insurance; Disability Coverage; Life Insurance; Medical

Insurance; Savings Plan; Tuition Assistance. **Corporate headquarters location:** New York NY. **Listed on:** New York Stock Exchange. **Number of employees nationwide:** 14,000.

Note: Because addresses and telephone numbers of smaller companies change rapidly, we recommend you call each company to verify the information below before inquiring about job opportunities. Mass mailings are not recommended.

Additional small employers:

LUMBER AND WOOD WHOLESALE

Burruss
103 Maddox St, Brookneal VA 24528-2907. 804/376-2666.

Dean Co.
PO Box 1239, Princeton WV 24740-1239. 304/425-8701.

Diamond Hill Plywood
3000 Cofer Rd, Richmond VA 23224-7106. 804/232-6726.

Dejarnette Lumber Corp.
17186 Alliance Dr, Milford VA 22514. 804/633-9821.

Rex Lumber Company
1405 Valley Rd, Richmond VA 23222-5404. 804/329-7391.

INDUSTRIAL PAPER AND RELATED PRODUCTS WHOLESALE

Mead Packaging
3105 W Marshall St, Richmond VA 23230-4729. 804/320-7085.

TIMBER TRACTS

Chesapeake Forest Products Co.
King St, Keysville VA 23947. 804/736-8505.

LOGGING

Virginia Log Co. Inc.
320 Dupont St, West Point VA 23181-9519. 804/843-2900.

WOOD MILLS

Burke-Parsons-Bowlby Corp.
Rt 39, Goshen VA 24439. 540/997-9251.

Century Stair Co. Inc.
15175 Washington St, Haymarket VA 22069-2951. 703/385-0078.

Coastal Lumber Co.
316 Moore Ave, Suffolk VA 23434-3820. 804/934-3281.

Fairfax Lumber & Millwork Company
PO Box 5500, Springfield VA 22150-5500. 703/644-4045.

Inter-State Hardwoods
Rte 250 PO Box 7, Bartow WV 24920. 304/456-4597.

Mullican Lumber & Manufacturing Co.
PO Box 279, Ronceverte WV 24970-0279. 304/647-5150.

Taylor-Ramsey Corp.
PO Box 11888, Lynchburg VA 24506-1888. 804/929-7443.

Elkins Hardwood Dimension
PO Box 927, Elkins WV 26241-0927. 304/636-5615.

Mongold Lumber Enterprises Inc.
RR 1 Box 6, Elkins WV 26241-9801. 304/636-2081.

PW Plumly Lumber Corp.
600 N Kent St, Winchester VA 22601-5313. 540/662-3891.

Rosewood Lumber Co.
Cleveland Mountain, Rt 20 S, Kanawha Head WV 26228. 304/924-5669.

Ruffin & Payne Inc.
PO Box 27286, Richmond VA 23261-7286. 804/329-2691.

Salem Frame Co. Inc.
1972 Salem Industrial Dr, Salem VA 24153-3148. 540/389-8661.

Stuart Flooring Corp.
Dobyns Rd, Stuart VA 24171. 540/694-4547.

The Burruss Company
2301 Mayflower Dr, #2657, Lynchburg VA 24501-6611. 804/845-1207.

MILLWORK, PLYWOOD, AND STRUCTURAL MEMBERS

Annandale Millwork Corp.
PO Box 387, Haymarket VA 22069-0387. 703/754-7177.

Foreign & Domestic Woods
PO Box 449, Bowling Green VA 22427-0449. 804/633-5001.

MW Manufacturers Inc.
130 Franklin St, Rocky Mount VA 24151-1328. 540/483-0211.

Marmac Corp.
1000 Grand Central Ave, Parkersburg WV 26105-1047. 304/485-4494.

Premdor
Donovan Rd, Stanley VA 22851. 540/778-2211.

Visador Co. Inc.
1000 Industrial Rd, Marion VA 24354-3906. 540/783-7251.

Chesapeake Hardwood Products
201 Dexter St W, Chesapeake VA 23324-3023. 804/543-1601.

Columbia Forest Products
100 Paul Rd S W, Chatham VA 24531. 804/432-2591.

Columbia West Virginia Corp.
PO Box 160, Craigsville WV 26205-0160. 304/742-5317.

Georgia-Pacific Corp.
79 N Pax Ave, Mount Hope WV 25880-1004. 304/877-5656.

Henry County Plywood
Phospho Springs Rd, Ridgeway VA 24148. 540/956-3121.

Woodtech Inc.
RR 3 Box 338, Bluefield VA 24605-9658. 540/326-1100.

Louisiana-Pacific Corp.
Hwy 65 S, Dungannon VA 24245. 540/467-2812.

WOOD BOXES AND SHOOK

Gatewood Products Inc.
PO Box 766, Parkersburg WV 26102-0766. 304/422-3103.

Smalley Package Co. Inc.
210 1st St, Berryville VA 22611-1601. 540/955-2550.

Tinker Mountain Industries
Rt 11, Troutville VA 24175. 540/992-3614.

WOOD PRODUCTS

International Paper Co.
Rt 40, Waverly VA 23890. 804/834-2201.

Georgia-Pacific Corp.
234 Forest Rd, Skippers VA 23879. 804/634-6133.

Georgia-Pacific Corp.
116 Allen Rd, Jarratt VA 23867-9056. 804/535-8541.

Ivy Industries Inc.
111 Monticello Ave, Charlottesvle VA 22902-5670. 804/979-0715.

Lester Properties/Forestlands
14 Liberty Street Ext, Martinsville VA 24112-1828. 540/632-2195.

Wood Fiber Industries
Masonite Dr, Danville VA 24541. 804/797-1321.

PAPER MILLS

Chesapeake Paper Products Co.
19th St, West Point VA 23181. 804/843-5000.

Custom Papers Group
110 Tredegar St, Richmond VA 23219-4306. 804/649-4216.

The Paper Factory
6401 Richmond Rd, Williamsburg VA 23188-7202. 804/565-2174.

Halltown Paperboard Co.
PO Box 10, Halltown WV 25423-0010. 304/725-2076.

Stone Container Corp.
910 Industrial St, Hopewell VA 23860. 804/541-9600.

WOOD PRESERVING

Burke Parsons Bowlby Corp.
PO Box 231, Ripley WV 25271-0231. 304/372-2211.

Potomac Supply Corp.
U S Hwy 203 N, Kinsale VA 22488. 804/472-2527.

Trus Joist MacMillan
RR 5 Box 50, Buckhannon WV 26201-9105. 304/472-2436.

PAPERBOARD CONTAINERS AND BOXES

Westvaco Corporation
2828 Cofer Rd, Richmond VA 23224-7102. 804/232-6746.

Chesapeake Packaging
802 Kyle Ave NE, Roanoke VA 24012-5340. 540/344-3224.

Corrugated Container Corp.
6405 Commonwealth Dr, Roanoke VA 24018-5159. 540/774-0500.

Corrugated Container Division Martinsville
PO Box 5231, Martinsville VA 24115-5231. 540/632-2176.

Corrugated Container Division-Richmond
2900 Sprouse Dr, Richmond VA 23231-6041. 804/222-6380.

Inland Container Corp.
2333 Wells Rd, Petersburg VA 23805-8925. 804/861-8164.

Interstate Resources Inc.
1800 N Kent St, Ste 1200, Arlington VA 22209-2145. 703/243-3355.

Packaging Corp. Of America
400 Pleasant Valley Rd, Harrisonburg VA 22801-9743. 540/434-0785.

St. Joe Container Co.
723 Fenway Ave, Chesapeake VA 23323-3330. 804/487-2506.

Stone Container Corp/North Plant
5700 Lewis Rd, Sandston VA 23150-2406. 804/222-5433.

Weyerhaeuser Paper Co.
3491 Mayflower Dr, Lynchburg VA 24501-5018. 804/845-6071.

Star Paper Tube Inc.
Rt 29 N, Danville VA 24540. 804/836-0321.

Gravure Packaging Inc.
4500 Sarellen Rd, Richmond VA 23231-4435. 804/222-1016.

COATED AND LAMINATED PAPER

Richmond Converting Division
4700 Deepwater Terminal Rd, Richmond VA 23234-2209. 804/271-3700.

PAPER BAGS

Vanguard Plastics Inc.
2800 Sprouse Dr, Richmond VA 23231-6039. 804/222-2012.

CONVERTED PAPER AND PAPERBOARD PRODUCTS

Brown Products Inc.
S R 620, Axton VA 24054. 540/650-3121.

Creative Label Co.
1100 Hoult Rd, Fairmont WV 26554-5700. 304/366-8755.

Mundet-Hermelite Inc.
21st Buena Vista, Buena Vista VA 24416. 540/261-7435.

Westvaco Corp.
300 Westvaco Rd, Low Moor VA 24457. 540/969-5339.

PAPER PRODUCTS

American Paper Envelopes
3801 Carolina Ave, Richmond VA 23222-2203. 804/359-5500.

Colortree Inc. Of VA
2519 Britton Hill Rd, Richmond VA 23230-2503. 804/358-4245.

Union Envelope Co.
1607 Sherwood Ave, Richmond VA 23220-1008. 804/358-5555.

Plymouth Inc.
10 Corporate Dr, Radford VA 24141-5100. 540/633-3333.

For more information on career opportunities in the paper and wood products industries:

Associations

AMERICAN FOREST AND PAPER ASSOCIATION
1111 19th Street NW, Suite 700, Washington DC 20036. 202/463-2700. A lobbying group that conducts informational gatherings.

AMERICAN FOREST AND PAPER ASSOCIATION
260 Madison Avenue, New York NY 10016. 212/340-0600. Headquartered in Washington DC. A lobbying group that conducts informational gatherings.

FOREST PRODUCTS SOCIETY
2801 Marshall Court, Madison WI 53705-2295. 608/231-1361. An international, non-profit, educational association that provides an information network for all segments of the forest products industry. Offers employment referral service.

NATIONAL PAPER TRADE ASSOCIATION
111 Great Neck Road, Great Neck NY 11021. 516/829-3070. Offers management services to wholesalers. Offers books, seminars, and research services.

TECHNICAL ASSOCIATION OF THE PULP AND PAPER INDUSTRY
P.O. Box 105113, Atlanta GA 30348. 404/446-1400. Non-profit. Offers conferences and education.

PAPERBOARD PACKAGING COUNCIL
888 17th Street NW, Suite 900, Washington DC 20006. 202/289-4100. Offers statistical and lobbying services.

Directories

DIRECTORY OF THE FOREST PRODUCTS INDUSTRY
Miller Freeman Publications, Inc., 600 Harrison Street, San Francisco CA 94107. 415/905-2200.

LOCKWOOD-POST'S DIRECTORY OF THE PAPER AND ALLIED TRADES
Miller Freeman Publications, Inc., 600 Harrison Street, San Francisco CA 94107. 415/905-2200.

POST'S PULP AND PAPER DIRECTORY
Miller Freeman Publications, Inc., 600 Harrison Street, San Francisco CA 94107. 415/905-2200.

Magazines

PAPERBOARD PACKAGING
Advanstar Communications, 131 West First Street, Duluth MN 55802. 218/723-9200.

PULP AND PAPER WEEK
Miller Freeman Publications, Inc., 600 Harrison Street, San Francisco CA 94107. 415/905-2200.

WOOD TECHNOLOGIES
Miller Freeman Publications, Inc., 600 Harrison Street, San Francisco CA 94107. 415/905-2200.

PRINTING AND PUBLISHING

The big news in publishing in 1995 was the paper shortage. Paper costs account for 30 to 40 percent of the manufacturing costs of a book. Many companies compensated for the rising costs by stockpiling paper, designing books more tightly, lowering paper grades, and increasing book prices. The paper pinch also affected the magazine and newspaper industries. Newsprint prices rose more than 30 percent from early 1994 to early 1995. Magazines became noticeably shorter. One good sign for newspapers and magazines: As the economy improves, companies will increase their print advertising budgets. And, with a presidential election and a Summer Olympics on the calendar in '96, spending for advertising will increase.

Another way some publishers are balancing their books against the paper crunch is by looking to electronic media, a competitive and rapidly expanding medium. Many book publishers are offering CD-ROM versions of popular books, especially educational, reference, and children's books. Also, books-on-tape are growing in popularity. Magazines and newspapers also are joining the electronic bandwagon -- many periodicals and newspapers are now available online.

Book printing and distribution are also evolving. Traditionally, long print runs were necessary to keep costs down. But thanks to new digital presses that don't use plates, books can now be printed and distributed in small batches according to demand. Instead of printing and then distributing, publishers can now distribute and then print. Publishers will be able to use many small presses across the country, instead of one or two strategically placed large presses. The result: increased demand for computer-savvy printing professionals and dramatic cuts in shipping and warehousing.

AMERICAN PRESS, INC.
One American Place, Gordonsville VA 22942. 540/832-2253. **Fax:** 540/832-7253. **Contact:** Jerry Bortner, Human Resources Manager. **Description:** America Press, Inc. is a printer of high-quality magazines and catalogs that utilize web offset processes. **Common positions include:** Accountant/Auditor; Advertising Clerk; Blue-Collar Worker Supervisor; Buyer; Computer Programmer; Computer Systems Analyst; Cost Estimator; Credit Manager; Customer Service Representative; Electrical/Electronics Engineer; Electrician; Financial Analyst; General Manager; Human Resources Specialist; Industrial Engineer; Industrial Production Manager; Mechanical Engineer; Operations/Production Manager; Purchasing Agent and Manager; Quality Control Supervisor. **Educational backgrounds include:** Accounting; Art/Design; Business Administration; Communications; Computer Science; Engineering; Finance; Liberal Arts; Marketing. **Benefits:** Disability Coverage; Life Insurance; Medical Insurance; Pension Plan; Savings Plan; Tuition Assistance. **Operations at this facility include:** Administration; Divisional Headquarters; Manufacturing; Sales. **Listed on:** Privately held. **Number of employees at this location:** 250.

ATLANTIC PUBLICATIONS INC.
P.O. Box 288, Tasley VA 23441. 804/787-1111. **Contact:** Human Resources. **Description:** Publishes weekly and biweekly newspapers, and

resort publications in Delaware, Maryland, and Virginia. **Common positions include:** Advertising Clerk; Editor; General Manager; Manufacturer's/ Wholesaler's Sales Rep.; Reporter. **Benefits:** Medical Insurance. **Corporate headquarters location:** This Location. **Operations at this facility include:** Administration.

BALMAR PRINTING AND GRAPHICS, INC.
5130 Wilson Boulevard, Arlington VA 22205. 703/528-9000. **Contact:** Ms. Cam Griewe, Human Resources Manager. **Description:** Balmar Printing and Graphics, Inc. is a commercial lithographic printer. **Number of employees at this location:** 100.

WILLIAM BYRD PRESS, INC.
2901 Byrdhill Road, Richmond VA 23228. 804/264-2711. **Contact:** Ralph Giannola, Director of Human Resources. **Description:** The William Byrd Press, Inc. specializes in the printing of longer-run annual reports, promotional printing, and specialty magazines, along with a number of other product lines. **Parent company:** Cadmus Communications Corporation (Richmond VA) is a graphic communications company offering specialized products and services in three broad areas: printing, marketing, and publishing. Cadmus is one of the largest graphic communications companies in North America. Product lines include annual reports, catalogs, direct marketing, financial printing, point-of-sale marketing, promotional printing, publishing, research journals, specialty magazines, and specialty packaging. Other subsidiaries of Cadmus Communications include: American Graphics, Inc. (Atlanta GA); Cadmus Color Center, Inc. (Sandston VA); Cadmus Consumer Publishing (Richmond VA); Cadmus Direct Marketing, Inc. (Charlotte NC); Cadmus Interactive (Tucker GA); Cadmus Journal Services (Linthicum MD, and Easton MD); Central Florida Press, L.C. (Orlando FL); Expert Brown (Sandston VA); Garamond, Inc. (Baltimore MD); Graphtech Corporation (Charlotte NC); Marblehead Communications, Inc. (Boston MA); Three Score, Inc. (Tucker GA); and Washburn Graphics, Inc. (Charlotte NC).

CADMUS COLOR CENTER, INC.
5301 Louis Road, Sandston VA 23150. 804/236-4500. **Contact:** Nino Sofia, Human Resources Manager. **Description:** Cadmus Color Center is a color printer. The company recently installed a state-of-the-art color prepress system, which has increased production capabilities in Cadmus' specialty publication and commercial product lines. **Parent company:** Cadmus Communications Corporation (Richmond VA) is a graphic communications company offering specialized products and services in three broad areas: printing, marketing, and publishing. Cadmus is one of the largest graphic communications companies in North America. Product lines include annual reports, catalogs, direct marketing, financial printing, point-of-sale marketing, promotional printing, publishing, research journals, specialty magazines, and specialty packaging. Subsidiaries of Cadmus Communications Corporation include: American Graphics, Inc. (Atlanta GA); Cadmus Consumer Publishing (Richmond VA); Cadmus Direct Marketing, Inc. (Charlotte NC); Cadmus Interactive (Tucker GA); Cadmus Journal Services (Linthicum MD, Easton MD, and Richmond, VA); Central Florida Press, L.C. (Orlando FL); Expert Brown (also at this location); Garamond, Inc. (Baltimore MD); Graphtech Corporation (Charlotte NC); Marblehead Communications, Inc. (Boston MA); Three Score, Inc. (Tucker GA); Washburn Graphics, Inc. (Charlotte NC); and The William Byrd Press (Richmond VA).

CADMUS COMMUNICATIONS CORPORATION
P.O. Box 27367, Richmond VA 23261-7367. 804/287-5680. **Fax:** 804/287-6267. **Contact:** Laura Farley, Director of Human Resources and Quality. **Description:** Cadmus Communications Corporation is a graphic communications company offering specialized products and services in three broad areas: printing, marketing, and publishing. Cadmus is one of the largest graphic communications companies in North America. Product lines include annual reports, catalogs, direct marketing, financial printing, point-of-

sale marketing, promotional printing, publishing, research journals, specialty magazines, and specialty packaging. **Corporate headquarters location:** This Location. **Other U.S. locations:** GA; MA; MD; NC. **Subsidiaries include:** American Graphics, Inc. (Atlanta GA); Cadmus Color Center, Inc. (Sandston VA); Cadmus Consumer Publishing (Richmond VA); Cadmus Direct Marketing, Inc. (Charlotte NC); Cadmus Interactive (Tucker GA); Cadmus Journal Services (Linthicum MD, Easton MD, and Richmond VA); Central Florida Press, L.C. (Orlando FL); Expert Brown (Sandston VA); Garamond, Inc. (Baltimore MD); Graphtech Corporation (Charlotte NC); Marblehead Communications, Inc. (Boston MA); Three Score, Inc. (Tucker GA); Washburn Graphics, Inc. (Charlotte NC); and The William Byrd Press (Richmond VA). **Listed on:** NASDAQ. **Number of employees nationwide:** 2,500.

CADMUS CONSUMER PUBLISHING
1934 East Parham Road, Richmond VA 23228. 804/266-0140. **Contact:** Traci Elliott, Human Resources Manager. **Description:** Cadmus Consumer Publishing is the publisher of *Tuff Stuff*, a monthly magazine directed to trading card collectors, and *Collect!,* a monthly magazine directed to non-sport collectors and hobbyists. **Parent company:** Cadmus Communications Corporation (Richmond VA) is a graphic communications company offering specialized products and services in three broad areas: printing, marketing, and publishing. Cadmus is one of the largest graphic communications companies in North America. Product lines include annual reports, catalogs, direct marketing, financial printing, point-of-sale marketing, promotional printing, publishing, research journals, specialty magazines, and specialty packaging. Other subsidiaries of Cadmus Communications Corporation include: American Graphics, Inc. (Atlanta GA); Cadmus Color Center, Inc. (Sandston VA); Cadmus Direct Marketing, Inc. (Charlotte NC); Cadmus Interactive (Tucker GA); Cadmus Journal Services (Linthicum MD, Easton MD, and Richmond VA); Central Florida Press, L.C. (Orlando FL); Expert Brown (Stanson VA); Garamond, Inc. (Baltimore MD); Graphtech Corporation (Charlotte NC); Marblehead Communications, Inc. (Boston MA); Three Score, Inc. (Tucker GA); Washburn Graphics, Inc. (Charlotte NC); and The William Byrd Press (Richmond VA).

CADMUS JOURNAL SERVICES, INC.
2901 Byrdhill Road, Richmond VA 23228-5867. 804/261-3000. **Contact:** Human Resources. **Description:** Cadmus Communications Corporation partners with its customers to advance science, medicine, technology, and education by integrating, packaging, and distributing breakthrough information to the world. Formed by the combination of the Byrd Press Journal Division and the acquisition of Waverly Press, Cadmus Journal Services is an international leader in the production of research journals. This product line serves four distinct markets: medical and biomedical; technical and scientific; learned and scholarly; and mathematics. **Benefits:** 401K; Computer Loans; Dental Insurance; Disability Coverage; Employee Discounts; Life Insurance; Medical Insurance; Pension Plan; Profit Sharing; Savings Plan; Tuition Assistance. **Special Programs:** Internships. **Parent company:** Cadmus Communications Corporation (Richmond VA) is a graphic communications company offering specialized products and services in three broad areas: printing, marketing, and publishing. Cadmus is one of the largest graphic communications companies in North America. Product lines include annual reports, catalogs, direct marketing, financial printing, point-of-sale marketing, promotional printing, publishing, research journals, specialty magazines, and specialty packaging. Other subsidiaries of Cadmus Communications Corporation include: American Graphics, Inc. (Atlanta GA); Cadmus Color Center, Inc. (Sandston VA); Cadmus Consumer Publishing (Richmond VA); Cadmus Direct Marketing, Inc. (Charlotte NC); Cadmus Interactive (Tucker GA); Central Florida Press, L.C. (Orlando FL); Expert Brown (Sandston VA); Garamond, Inc. (Baltimore MD); Graphtech Corporation (Charlotte NC); Marblehead Communications, Inc. (Boston MA); Three Score, Inc. (Tucker

GA); Washburn Graphics, Inc. (Charlotte NC); and The William Byrd Press (also at this location).

CHAMPION INDUSTRIES
2450 First Avenue, P.O. Box 2968, Huntington WV 25729-2968. 304/528-2791. **Contact:** Human Resources. **Description:** A diversified holding company with two lines of business, Champion Industries is engaged in both commercial printing and the distribution of office furniture and supplies.

R.R. DONNELLEY & SONS COMPANY
4201 Murray Place, Lynchburg VA 24501. 804/522-7400. **Contact:** Dexter Stulz, Human Resource Manager. **Description:** A commercial printer. R.R. Donnelley & Sons is a world leader in managing, reproducing, and distributing print and digital information for publishing, merchandising, and information technology customers. The company is one of the largest commercial printers in the world, producing catalogs, inserts, magazines, books, directories, computer documentation, and financial printing. R.R. Donnelley has more than 180 strategically located sales offices and production facilities and 35,000 employees worldwide. Principal services offered by the company are conventional and digital prepress operations, computerized printing and binding, and sophisticated pool shipping and distribution services for printed products; information repackaging into multiple formats (print, magnetic, and optical media); database management, list rental, list enhancement, and direct mail production services; turnkey computer documentation services (outsourcing, translation, printing, binding, diskette replication, kitting, licensing, republishing, and fulfillment); reprographics and facilities management; creative design and communication services; and digital and conventional map creation and related services. Founded in 1864.

R.R. DONNELLEY & SONS COMPANY
1400 Kratzer Road, Harrisonburg VA 22801. 703/434-8833. **Contact:** Dave Purdy, Human Resource Manager. **Description:** Book printing and binding plant. R.R. Donnelley & Sons is a world leader in managing, reproducing, and distributing print and digital information for publishing, merchandising, and information technology customers. The company is one of the largest commercial printers in the world, producing catalogs, inserts, magazines, books, directories, computer documentation, and financial printing. R.R. Donnelley has more than 180 strategically located sales offices and production facilities and 35,000 employees worldwide. Principal services offered by the company are conventional and digital prepress operations, computerized printing and binding, and sophisticated pool shipping and distribution services for printed products; information repackaging into multiple formats (print, magnetic, and optical media); database management, list rental, list enhancement, and direct mail production services; turnkey computer documentation services (outsourcing, translation, printing, binding, diskette replication, kitting, licensing, republishing, and fulfillment); reprographics and facilities management; creative design and communication services; and digital and conventional map creation and related services. Founded in 1864.

EXPERT BROWN
5301 Louis Road, Sandston VA 23150. 804/236-4400. **Contact:** Human Resources. **Description:** Expert Brown is a sheet fed printing company whose products include annual reports, and promotional and financial printing. **Parent company:** Cadmus Communications Corporation (Richmond VA) is a graphic communications company offering specialized products and services in three broad areas: printing, marketing, and publishing. Cadmus is one of the largest graphic communications companies in North America. Product lines include annual reports, catalogs, direct marketing financial printing, point-of-sale marketing, promotional printing, publishing, research journals, specialty magazines, and specialty packaging. Other subsidiaries of Cadmus Communications Corporation include: American Graphics, Inc. (Atlanta GA);

Cadmus Color Center, Inc. (also at this location); Cadmus Consumer Publishing (Richmond VA); Cadmus Direct Marketing, Inc. (Charlotte NC); Cadmus Interactive (Tucker GA); Cadmus Journal Services (Linthicum MD, Easton MD, and Richmond VA); Central Florida Press, L.C. (Orlando FL); Garamond, Inc. (Baltimore MD); Graphtech Corporation (Charlotte NC); Marblehead Communications, Inc. (Boston MA); Three Score, Inc. (Tucker GA); Washburn Graphics, Inc. (Charlotte NC); and The William Byrd Press (Richmond VA).

GANNETT COMPANY, INC.
1100 Wilson Boulevard, Arlington VA 22234. 703/284-6226. **Contact:** Cyndi Makowski, Recruiter. **Description:** Gannett, a nationwide news and information company, publishes 81 newspapers including *USA Today* and *Gannett News Service*, and is the largest outdoor advertising company in North America. Gannett is also involved in marketing, television news and program production, research satellite information systems, and owns a national group of commercial printing facilities. Gannett has operations in 41 states, the District of Columbia, Guam, the Virgin Islands, Canada, Great Britain, Hong Kong, Singapore, and Switzerland. **Common positions include:** Accountant/Auditor; Attorney; Buyer; Computer Programmer; Financial Analyst; Human Resources Specialist; Operations/Production Manager; Paralegal; Purchasing Agent and Manager; Secretary. **Benefits:** 401K; Adoption Assistance; Dental Insurance; Disability Coverage; Employee Discounts; Life Insurance; Medical Insurance; Pension Plan; Profit Sharing; Stock Option; Tuition Assistance. **Special Programs:** Internships. **Corporate headquarters location:** This Location. **Number of employees nationwide:** 36,000.

JUDD'S INC.
One Shenandoah Valley Drive, Strasburg VA 22657. 540/465-6606. **Fax:** 540/465-6610. **Contact:** Carl Dysart, Personnel Manager. **Description:** Provides commercial printing services, primarily of magazines and catalogs. **Common positions include:** Accountant/Auditor; Administrative Services Manager; Buyer; Computer Programmer; Computer Systems Analyst; Cost Estimator; Customer Service Representative; Electrical/Electronics Engineer; Electrician; Mechanical Engineer; Purchasing Agent and Manager. **Educational backgrounds include:** Business Administration. **Benefits:** 401K; Dental Insurance; Disability Coverage; Life Insurance; Medical Insurance; Pension Plan; Profit Sharing; Savings Plan; Tuition Assistance. **Corporate headquarters location:** Washington DC. **Other U.S. locations:** Baltimore MD. **Operations at this facility include:** Administration; Manufacturing. **Listed on:** Privately held. **Number of employees at this location:** 735. **Number of employees nationwide:** 1,200.

THE MICHIE COMPANY
P.O. Box 7587, Charlottesville VA 22906. 804/972-7600. **Contact:** Human Resources. **Description:** A publisher of legal materials. Formats include hard copy and CD-ROM.

NEWSPAPER ASSOCIATION OF AMERICA
Newspaper Center, 11600 Sunrise Valley Drive, Reston VA 22091-1412. 703/648-1000. **Contact:** Sandy Weatley, Personnel Director. **Description:** A professional association dedicated to servicing the needs and interests of the newspaper publishing industry.

PROGRESS PRINTING COMPANY
3523 Waterlick Road, Lynchburg VA 24502. 804/239-9213. **Contact:** Barbara Wilder, Human Resource Manager. **Description:** Established in 1962, the Progress Printing Company prints annual reports, direct mailings, college brochures, and pocket folders in four, six and eight color presses. **Number of employees in this location:** 300.

QUEBECOR PRINTING MARTINSBURG
1989 Arcata Boulevard, P.O. Box 11, Martinsburg WV 25401. 304/267-3600. **Fax:** 304/267-9625. **Contact:** Frank Diehl, Human Resource Manager. **Description:** One- and two-color printer and binder of trade, lifestyle, computer, and college text books. **Common positions include:** Accountant/Auditor; Blue-Collar Worker Supervisor; Buyer; Civil Engineer; Customer Service Representative; Electrician; General Manager; Industrial Engineer; Industrial Production Manager; Management Trainee; Mechanical Engineer; Operations/Production Manager; Quality Control Supervisor. **Educational backgrounds include:** Accounting; Business Administration; Engineering; Liberal Arts. **Benefits:** 401K; Dental Insurance; Disability Coverage; Life Insurance; Medical Insurance; Pension Plan; Tuition Assistance. **Special Programs:** Internships. **Corporate headquarters location:** Boston MA. **Parent company:** Quebcor Printing (USA) Inc. **Operations at this facility include:** Administration; Manufacturing; Service. **Listed on:** American Stock Exchange. **Number of employees at this location:** 400. **Number of employees nationwide:** 30,000.

RICHMOND TIMES-DISPATCH
P.O. Box 85333, Richmond VA 23293. 804/649-6000. **Contact:** Assistant Managing Editor. **Description:** A daily newspaper with a circulation of approximately 220,000 during the week and 260,000 on Sundays.

TIME-LIFE INC.
777 Duke Street, Alexandria VA 22314. 703/838-7000. **Contact:** Thomas Swiger, Human Resources Director. **Description:** A publishing company.

USA TODAY
1000 Wilson Boulevard, Arlington VA 22229. 703/276-3400. **Contact:** Ms. Terry Sullivan, Human Resources Director. **Description:** A national newspaper. **Parent company:** Gannett Company, Inc.

WASHINGTON BUSINESS JOURNAL
2000 14th Street North, Suite 500, Arlington VA 22201. 703/875-2200. **Fax:** 703/875-2231. **Contact:** Ellen Duhamel, Business Manager. **Description:** Publishers of a weekly business newspaper. **Common positions include:** Advertising Account Executive; Advertising Clerk; Credit Manager; Customer Service Representative; Department Manager; Editor; General Manager; Marketing Specialist; Operations/Production Manager; Radio/TV Announcer/Broadcaster; Reporter; Services Sales Representative; Technical Writer/Editor. **Educational backgrounds include:** Accounting; Art History; Communications; Liberal Arts; Marketing. **Benefits:** 401K; Dental Insurance; Disability Coverage; Life Insurance; Medical Insurance; Savings Plan; Stock Option. **Special Programs:** Internships. **Corporate headquarters location:** Charlotte NC. **Parent company:** American City Business Journals. **Operations at this facility include:** Administration; Publishing; Sales; Service. **Listed on:** NASDAQ. **Number of employees at this location:** 45.

WHEELING NEWS REGISTER
OGDEN NEWSPAPERS, INC.
1500 Main Street, Wheeling WV 26003. 304/233-0100. **Contact:** Bob Nuttey, Human Resources Manager. **Description:** A newspaper publisher.

Note: *Because addresses and telephone numbers of smaller companies change rapidly, we recommend you call each company to verify the information below before inquiring about job opportunities. Mass mailings are not recommended.*

Additional small employers:

NEWSPAPERS: PUBLISHING AND/OR PRINTING

Beckley Newspapers Inc.
801 N Kanawha St, Beckley WV 25801-3899. 304/255-4400.

Washington Post
7171 Wimsatt Rd, Springfield VA 22151-4081. 703/916-2230.

Bristol Newspapers Inc.
320 Bob Morrison Blvd, Bristol VA 24201-3812. 540/669-2181.

Charleston Newspapers
1001 Virginia St E, Charleston WV 25301-2895. 304/348-5140.

Clarksburg Publishing Co.
324 Hewes Ave # 326, Clarksburg WV 26301-2744. 304/624-6411.

DCI Publishing Inc.
7670 Old Springhouse Rd, McLean VA 22102-3403. 703/821-5050.

Donrey News Bureau
912 N Liberty St, Arlington VA 22205-1417. 703/533-8188.

Free Lance-Star Publishing Company
616 Amelia St, Fredericksbrg VA 22401-3887. 540/374-5000.

Jack Kent Cooke Inc.
PO Box 2110, Middleburg VA 22117-2110. 540/687-4000.

Journal Newspapers
2720 Prosperity Ave, Fairfax VA 22034. 703/560-4000.

Leader Publishing Co.
PO Box 59, Staunton VA 24402-0059. 540/885-7281.

London Times Mirror Inc.
9 E Market St, Leesburg VA 22075-3013. 703/777-1111.

Louisville Courier Journal
1000 Wilson Blvd, Arlington VA 22209-3901. 703/276-5423.

News & Advance
101 Wyndale Dr, Lynchburg VA 24501-6710. 804/385-5440.

Portland Press Herald
2716 N Wyoming St, Arlington VA 22213-1722. 703/237-0560.

Potomac Newspaper Inc.
14010 Smoketown Rd, Woodbridge VA 22192-4704. 703/878-8000.

Progress Index
3740 W Hundred Rd, Chester VA 23831-1928. 804/796-9709.

Roanoke Times & World-News
Rt 114, Christiansbrg VA 24073. 540/674-5325.

SLN Service Co.
2411 Dulles Corner Park, Herndon VA 22071-3430. 703/713-1920.

Scripps League Newspaper
HCR 1, Box 38, Charlottesvle VA 22901-9812. 804/973-3345.

Bluefield Daily Telegraph
928 Bluefield Ave, Bluefield WV 24701-2744. 304/327-6171.

The Daily Press Inc.
7505 Warwick Blvd, Newport News VA 23607-1517. 804/247-4600.

The Times West Virginian
PO Box 2530, Fairmont WV 26555-2530. 304/367-2500.

Virginia Gazette
216 Ironbound Rd, Williamsburg VA 23188-2618. 804/220-1736.

Virginian Pilot & Ledger Star
1001 E Broad St, Ste 340, Richmond VA 23219-1928. 804/697-1560.

Virginian Pilot & Ledger Star
5429 Greenwich Rd, Virginia Beach VA 23462-6511. 804/446-2800.

Washington Post
1001 E Broad St, Ste 420, Richmond VA 23219-1928. 804/649-7575.

Washington Times
910 Capitol St, Richmond VA 23219-3400. 804/788-4261.

Winchester Star
2 North Kent St, Winchester VA 22601-5098. 540/667-3200.

Worrell Enterprises Inc.
685 W Rio Rd, Charlottesville VA 22901-1413. 804/978-7200.

PERIODICALS: PUBLISHING AND/OR PRINTING

Viguerie Communications Corp.
7777 Leesburg Pike, Falls Church VA 22043-2403. 703/893-2568.

BOOKS: PUBLISHING AND/OR PRINTING

EPM Publications Inc.
1003 Turkey Run Road, McLean VA 22101-1707. 703/442-7810.

St. Anthony Publishing
500 Montgomery Street, Alexandria VA 22314-1560. 703/549-0100.

Berryville Graphics
25 Springsbury Road, Berryville VA 22611. 540/955-2750.

Bookcrafters Inc.
3591 Lee Hill Industrial Park, Fredericksbrg VA 22408. 540/371-3800.

MISCELLANEOUS PUBLISHING

Airline Tariff Publishing
400 West Service Road,

Chantilly VA 22021. 703/471-7510.

Treasure Chest Advertising
7619 Doane Dr, Manassas VA 22110-2430. 703/369-7600.

Datanational
3800 Concorde Pky, Ste 500, Chantilly VA 22021-1119. 703/818-0120.

BLANK BOOKS AND BOOKBINDING

General Binding Corp.
15401 Goodesbridge Rd, Amelia Ct House VA 23002. 804/561-2531.

COMMERCIAL PRINTING

Banta Co.
3330 Willow Springs Rd, Harrisonburg VA 22801-9729. 540/564-3900.

Carter Printing Co.
2007 North Hamilton Street, Richmond VA 23230-4103. 804/359-9206.

Copac Inc.
1905 Huguenot Rd, Richmond VA 23235-4312. 804/378-9073.

Ennis Eastern Division
PO Box 490, Chatham VA 24531-0490. 804/432-2121.

Goodway Graphics Of VA
6628 Electronic Dr, Springfield VA 22151-4301. 703/941-1160.

JW Fergusson & Sons
4107 Castlewood Rd, Richmond VA 23234-2700. 804/275-2611.

Perlmuter Printing Co.
2828 W Broad St, Richmond VA 23230-5101. 804/359-1153.

Stephenson Printing
5731 General Washington Dr, Alexandria VA 22312-2418. 703/642-9000.

United Lithographic Services Inc.
2818 Fallfax Drive, Falls Church VA 22042-2804. 703/560-5700.

Quebecor Printing Richmond
7400 Impala Dr, Richmond VA 23228-3741. 804/264-3800.

Richmond Gravure
3400 Deepwater Terminal Rd, Richmond VA 23234-1829. 804/232-1201.

Southern Graphic Systems
2891 Sprouse Dr, Richmond VA 23231-6040. 804/226-2490.

Transprint USA
1000 Pleasant Valley Rd, Harrisonburg VA 22801-9790. 540/433-9101.

Century Graphics Corp.
160 Century Ln, Winchester VA 22603-4601. 540/722-6000.

Deluxe Check Printers
3405 Commerce Rd, Richmond VA 23234-1843. 804/231-9728.

Globe Envelope Co.
3106 Lanvale Ave, Richmond VA 23230-4217. 804/359-9286.

Journal Publishing Co.
207 W King St, Martinsburg WV 25401-3211. 304/263-3381.

Master Print Inc.
8401 Terminal Rd, Newington VA 22122. 703/550-9555.

Printpack Inc.
3551 Lee Hill Dr, Fredericksbrg VA 22408-7323. 540/373-7251.

BUSINESS FORMS

Moore Business Forms & Systems
1 Moore Ave, Buckhannon WV 26201. 304/472-3100.

Standard Register Co.
Indl Ave, Rocky Mount VA 24151. 540/483-9281.

PRINTING TRADE SERVICES

Graphic Data Services
5407 Port Royal Rd, #A, Springfield VA 22151-2302. 703/321-8770.

Rototype
6817 Hopewell Ave, Springfield VA 22151-3841. 703/642-1919.

IR International Inc.
PO Box 38130, Richmond VA 23231-0930. 804/222-2821.

Graphic Art Service
6010-C N Crestwood Av, Richmond VA 23230. 804/282-5606.

Wire Colortech
5624 Eastport Blvd, Richmond VA 23231-4443. 804/236-0902.

PHOTO FINISHING LABORATORIES

Nashua Photo Inc.
400 Rayon Dr, Parkersburg WV 26101-6668. 304/422-6418.

Qualex Inc.
622 Huntington Blvd NE, Roanoke VA 24012-3547. 540/366-0300.

Fox Photo
Silk Greenhouse Turnpike, Richmond VA 23235. 804/330-0707.

For more information on career opportunities in printing and publishing:

Associations

ASSOCIATION OF GRAPHIC ARTS
330 7th Avenue, 9th Floor, New York NY 10001-5010. 212/279-2100. Offers educational classes and seminars.

BINDING INDUSTRIES OF AMERICA
70 East Lake Street, Suite 300,

Chicago IL 60601. 312/372-7606. Offers credit collection, government affairs, and educational services.

AMERICAN BOOKSELLERS ASSOCIATION
828 South Broadway, Tarrytown NY 10591. 914/591-2665.

AMERICAN INSTITUTE OF GRAPHIC ARTS
919 3rd Avenue, 22nd Floor, New York NY 10003-3004. 212/807-1990. A 36-chapter, nationwide organization sponsoring programs and events for graphic designers and related professionals.

AMERICAN SOCIETY OF NEWSPAPER EDITORS
P.O. Box 4090, Reston VA 22090-1700. 703/648-1144.

THE DOW JONES NEWSPAPER FUND
P.O. Box 300, Princeton NJ 08543-0300. 609/520-4000.

GRAPHIC ARTISTS GUILD
11 West 20th Street, 8th Floor, New York NY 10011. 212/463-7730. A union for artists.

INTERNATIONAL GRAPHIC ARTS EDUCATION ASSOCIATION
4615 Forbes Avenue, Pittsburgh PA 15213. 412/682-5170.

MAGAZINE PUBLISHERS ASSOCIATION
919 Third Avenue, 22nd Floor, New York NY 10022. 212/752-0055. A membership association.

NATIONAL ASSOCIATION OF PRINTERS AND LITHOGRAPHERS
780 Pallisade Avenue, Teaneck NJ 07666. 201/342-0700. Membership. Offers consulting services and a publication.

NATIONAL NEWSPAPER ASSOCIATION
1525 Wilson Boulevard, Arlington VA 22209. 703/907-7900.

NATIONAL PRESS CLUB
529 14th St. NW, 13th Floor, Washington DC 20045. 202/662-7500. Offers professional seminars, career services, and conference facilities, as well as members-only restaurants and a health club.

NEWSPAPER ASSOCIATION OF AMERICA
Newspaper Center, 11600 Sunrise Valley Drive, Reston VA 22091. 703/648-1000. The technology department publishes marketing research.

THE NEWSPAPER GUILD
Research and Information Department, 8611 2nd Avenue, Silver Spring MD 20910. 301/585-2990. A trade union.

PRINTING INDUSTRIES OF AMERICA
100 Dangerfield Road, Alexandria VA 22314. 703/519-8100. Members are offered publications, insurance, and political action.

TECHNICAL ASSOCIATION OF THE GRAPHIC ARTS
68 Lomb Memorial Drive, Rochester NY 14623. 716/475-7470. Conducts an annual conference and offers newsletters.

WRITERS GUILD OF AMERICA WEST
8955 Beverly Boulevard, West Hollywood CA 90048. 310/550-1000. A membership association which registers scripts.

Directories

EDITOR & PUBLISHER INTERNATIONAL YEARBOOK
Editor & Publisher Company Inc., 11 West 19th Street, New York NY 10011. 212/675-4380. $100.00. Offers newspapers to editors in both the United States and foreign countries.

GRAPHIC ARTS BLUE BOOK
A.F. Lewis & Company, 245 Fifth Avenue, New York NY 10016. 212/679-0770. $80.00. Manufacturers and dealers.

JOURNALISM CAREER AND SCHOLARSHIP GUIDE
The Dow Jones Newspaper Fund, P.O. Box 300, Princeton NJ 08543-0300. 609/520-4000.

Magazines

AIGA JOURNAL
American Institute of Graphic Arts, 164 Third Avenue, New York NY 10010. 212/807-1990. $21.50. A 56-page quarterly magazine dealing with contemporary issues.

EDITOR & PUBLISHER
Editor & Publisher Company Inc., 11 West 19th Street, New York NY 10011. 212/675-4380.

GRAPHIC ARTS MONTHLY
249 West 49th Street, New York NY 10011. 212/463-6836.

GRAPHIS
141 Lexington Avenue, New York NY 10016. 212/532-9387. $89.00.

Magazine covers portfolios, articles, designers, advertising, and photos.

PRINT
104 Fifth Avenue, 19th Floor New York NY 10011. 212/463-0600. Offers a graphic design magazine. $55.00 for subscription.

PUBLISHER'S WEEKLY
249 West 17th Street, New York NY 10011. Weekly publication for book publishers and sellers.

Special Book and Magazine Programs

THE NEW YORK UNIVERSITY SUMMER PUBLISHING PROGRAM
48 Cooper Square, Room 108, New York NY 10003. 212/998-7219.

THE RADCLIFFE PUBLISHING COURSE
77 Brattle Street, Cambridge MA 02138. 617/495-8678.

RICE UNIVERSITY PUBLISHING PROGRAM
Office of Continuing Studies, P.O. Box 1892, Houston TX 77251-1892. 713/520-6022.

UNIVERSITY OF DENVER PUBLISHING INSTITUTE
2075 South University Boulevard, #D-114, Denver CO 80208. 303/871-4868.

REAL ESTATE

Rising interest rates in early 1995 caused housing starts to drop and sales of existing single-family homes to moderately decline. However, by mid-summer, rates began falling once more. Solid opportunities for jobseekers are available for those looking to enter the real estate field. Occupancy will go up in the office sector, as few new office properties are being built. Apartment construction, on the other hand, is on the rise. Commercial property sales will help maintain employment opportunities for real estate agents, brokers, and appraisers. The number of job openings in these occupations is expected to match the number of openings for most other careers nationwide. The majority of these openings, however, will be replacement positions, as agents return or leave the field, rather than new positions.

Property and real estate managers will have even greater opportunities to find employment, as more openings appear for these positions than for other occupations. The people with the most qualified backgrounds for these jobs will be those with college degrees in business administration and other related studies.

AVALON PROPERTIES, INC.
5904 Richmond Highway, Suite 300, Alexandria VA 22303-1864. 703/329-6300. **Fax:** 703/329-9130. **Contact:** Laura Novak, Director of Human Resources. **Description:** Avalon is a self-administered and self-managed equity real estate investment trust that specializes in development, construction, acquisition, and management of apartment communities in the Mid-Atlantic and Northeastern U.S. Avalon's real estate consists of 10,005 apartment homes in 33 communities located in six states and Washington DC. **Corporate headquarters location:** New Canaan CT. **Other U.S. locations:** Braintree MA; Princeton NJ; Richmond VA.

McARTHUR/GLEN REALTY CORPORATION
8400 Westpark Drive, Suite 500, McLean VA 22102. 703/556-6444. **Fax:** 703/556-9151. **Contact:** Human Resources. **Description:** McArthur/Glen Realty Corporation owns and operates 19 manufacturer's outlet shopping centers in 15 states. Together, the centers contain a total of about 3.5 million square feet of gross leasable area. The company is the sole general partner, owning a 60.6 percent interest, in McG Outlet Centers Limited Partnership. All of the company's operations are conducted through the limited partnership.

RESOURCE MORTGAGE CAPITAL, INC.
4880 Cox Road, Glen Allen VA 23060. 804/967-5800. **Contact:** Linda Conley, Vice President of Human Resources. **Description:** A self-managed real estate investment trust that originates, services, securitizes and invests in residential mortgage loans and securities. According to management, the company's strategy is to grow its net margin income and use its mortgage operations to create investments for its portfolio.

SMITHY BRAEDON COMPANY
3040 Williams Drive, Suite 300, Fairfax VA 22031. 703/641-8000. **Contact:** Human Resources Department. **Description:** A full-service commercial real estate firm covering Maryland, Virginia, and the District of Columbia.

UNITED DOMINION REALTY TRUST, INC.
10 South Sixth Street, Suite 203, Richmond VA 23219-3802. 804/780-2691. **Fax:** 804/343-1912. **Contact:** Human Resources. **Description:** United Dominion Realty Trust, Inc., founded in 1972, is the largest real estate investment trust specializing in residential apartment communities in the Southeast. United Dominion is a fully integrated real estate company, handling acquisition, construction and property management. The trust owns 138 properties, including 29,282 apartments in 120 communities, 14 neighborhood shopping centers and four other commercial properties. It is United Dominion's policy to focus on two types of apartments: newer properties that can be acquired at discounts from replacement cost and properties that can be upgraded and repositioned by capital improvements and intensive management.

UPTOWNER INNS, INC.
1415 4th Avenue, Huntington WV 25701. 304/525-7741. **Contact:** Human Resources. **Description:** Operates a group of Holiday Inn franchises, as well as apartment buildings and other rental properties.

VIRGINIA BAPTIST HOMES INC.
P.O. Box 191, Culpeper VA 22701. 703/825-1569. **Contact:** Human Resources. **Description:** A retirement community.

Note: *Because addresses and telephone numbers of smaller companies change rapidly, we recommend you call each company to verify the information below before inquiring about job opportunities. Mass mailings are not recommended.*

Additional small employers:

REAL ESTATE OPERATORS

Ashley Park Apartments
6901 Marlowe Rd, Richmond VA 23225-4282. 804/272-4499.

Beth Sholom Sands
6405 Auburn Dr, Virginia Beach VA 23464-3612. 804/420-0891.

Bethany Springs
2412 S Kenmore Rd, Richmond VA 23225-1941. 804/323-6169.

Bluffs Apartments
600 Victoria St, Hopewell VA 23860-2168. 804/748-9416.

Breckenridge Apartments
9951 Racquet Club Ln, Glen Allen VA 23060-4346. 804/270-7182.

Charter Oak Apartments
11637 Charter Oak Ct, Reston VA 22090-4522. 703/471-5335.

Chelsea Square Apartments
5734 Backlick Rd, Springfield VA 22150-3205. 703/451-8550.

Condominium Management Company
1903 Key Blvd, Arlington VA 22201-3227. 703/525-5557.

Conway Gardens Apartments
3203 Lake Powell Rd, Williamsburg VA 23185-3700. 804/229-4432.

Copper Croft Apartments
4333 Electric Rd, Roanoke VA 24014-4139. 540/774-7027.

Crater Woods Apartments
121 Crater Woods Ct, Petersburg VA 23805-9143. 804/732-0220.

Crystal House II Apartments
2000 S Eads St, Arlington VA 22202-3136. 703/521-4200.

Dominion Plaza
1200 S Court House Rd, Arlington VA 22204-4654. 703/920-2000.

Foxcroft Village Apartments
600 Foxcroft Ave, Martinsburg WV 25401-5301. 304/263-3323.

Kingley Ones
1903 Hopkins Rd, Richmond VA 23224-6328. 804/231-9191.

Lafayette Towers Apartments
4601 Mayflower Rd, Norfolk VA 23508-2749. 804/622-5451.

Langley Square
130 Doolittle Rd, Ste 12, Hampton VA 23669-2639. 804/722-4894.

Lee Square Apartments
126 Chanel Ter, Falls Church VA 22046-4108. 703/533-8860.

Manchester Lake Townhouse Apartments
2100 Mandalay Dr, Richmond VA 23224-2600. 804/276-5474.

Pepperwood Associates II
3790 Pepperwood Ct,

Portsmouth VA 23703-2776. 804/483-6390.

Pipers Landing-Laurel Court
401 River Post Ct, Virginia Beach VA 23454-4911. 804/422-4042.

Springfield West Apartments
9500 Brightway Ct, Richmond VA 23294-5557. 804/270-2028.

The Brittany
4500 S Four Mile Run Dr, Arlington VA 22204-3558. 703/671-2646.

The Dolphin Inn
1705 Atlantic Ave, Virginia Beach VA 23451-3424. 804/491-1420.

The Manor At England Run
101 Knights Ct, Fredericksbrg VA 22406-6413. 540/372-3793.

Thousand Oaks
1020 Thousand Oaks Dr, Virginia Beach VA 23454-3526. 804/481-2748.

Timberlake Village Apartments
Doswell St, Farmville VA 23901. 804/392-9207.

University Heights Apartments
20300 River Ridge Terrace, Ashburn VA 22011-2655. 703/478-8388.

Vantage Apartments
2212 Vantage Pt, Virginia Beach VA 23455-2145. 804/464-5422.

Weston Arbors
401 John St, Weston WV 26452-2174. 304/269-7344.

Westwood Village Apartments
748 Westwood Blvd NW, Roanoke VA 24017-6618. 540/343-8356.

Windsor Apartments
2506 Atwell Dr, Richmond VA 23234-1001. 804/231-9368.

Woodlake Village Apartments
6500 Woodlake Village Ct, Midlothian VA 23112-2208. 804/739-4528.

REAL ESTATE AGENTS AND MANAGERS

Coldwell Banker Residential Real Estate
1953 Gallows Rd, Ste 650, Vienna VA 22182-3934. 703/556-6100.

General Services Corporation
2922 Hathaway Rd, Ste 100, Richmond VA 23225-1733. 804/320-7101.

Legum and Norman Inc.
1430 Spring Hill Rd, Ste 300, Mc Lean VA 22102-3000. 703/848-4321.

Long & Foster Real Estate
11351 Random Hills Rd, Fairfax VA 22030-6081. 703/359-1500.

Snyder-Hunt Corp.
800 Hethwood Blvd, Blacksburg VA 24060-4299. 540/552-3515.

CB Commercial
8260 Greensboro Dr, McLean VA 22102-3806. 703/790-3333.

H&H Grandis Property
4401 Waterfront Dr, Ste 220, Glen Allen VA 23060-6745. 804/270-3500.

Lawson Residential Realty
373 Edwin Dr, Virginia Beach VA 23462-4522. 804/499-6161.

Long & Foster Realtors
5511 Princess Anne Rd, Virginia Beach VA 23462-3312. 804/497-1800.

Long & Foster Realtors
205 Laskin Rd, Virginia Beach VA 23451-3017. 804/428-4600.

Long & Foster Realtors
5739 Burke Centre Pky, Burke VA 22015-2296. 703/425-8000.

Long & Foster Realtors
7010 Little River Tpke, Annandale VA 22003-3241. 703/750-2800.

Long & Foster Realtors
4421 Dale Blvd, Dale City VA 22193-2550. 703/680-5001.

Old Colony Co. Better Homes & Gardens
1210 Kanawha Blvd E, Charleston WV 25301-2901. 304/344-2581.

Prentiss Properties Ltd Inc.
3112 Fairview Park Dr, Falls Church VA 22042-4509. 703/560-4700.

Pulte Homes Corp.
703 Catoctin Cir NE, Leesburg VA 22075-4949. 703/689-1316.

Rose & Krueth Realty Corp.
300 Cedar Lakes Dr, Chesapeake VA 23320-8344. 804/436-3636.

Town & Country Properties
4701 Old Dominion Dr, Arlington VA 22207-3596. 703/522-7474.

William E. Wood & Associates Realtors
222 Mustang Trail, Virginia Beach VA 23452-7513. 804/486-2410.

William E. Wood & Associates Realtors
1208 E Little Creek Rd, Norfolk VA 23518-3902. 804/588-0213.

William E. Wood & Associates Realtors
13750 Warwick Blvd, Newport News VA 23602-5423. 804/874-8300.

Harman Enterprises
1790 Dealton Ave, Harrisonburg VA 22801-2723. 540/434-1367.

Beacon Management Co.
2531 Jefferson Davis Hwy, Arlington VA 22202-3905. 703/418-1453.

Childress Klein Properties
300 Arboretum Pl, Ste 260, Richmond VA 23236-3465. 804/330-3900.

The Galbreath Company
2101 Wilson Blvd, Arlington VA 22201-3062. 703/527-9444.

Chestnut Grove Condominiums
11252 Chestnut Grove Sq, Reston VA 22090-5145. 703/471-1700.

Mt. Vernon-Wiechert Realty
2 Cardinal Park Dr SE, Ste 101C, Leesburg VA 22075-4447. 703/777-3977.

LAND SUBDIVIDERS AND DEVELOPERS

Potomac Partners
1201 E Abingdon Dr, Alexandria VA 22314-1420. 703/549-9000.

The Van Metre Companies
5252 Lyngate Ct, Burke VA 22015-1688. 703/425-2600.

West Group
1600 Anderson Rd, McLean VA 22102-1609. 703/356-2400.

William A. Hazel Company
4305 Hazel Park Ct, Chantilly VA 22021-2925. 703/378-8300.

CEMETERY SUBDIVIDERS AND DEVELOPERS

Grandview Memory Gardens
Blfd Taze Rd, Bluefield VA 24605. 540/322-5479.

For more information on career opportunities in real estate:

Associations

INSTITUTE OF REAL ESTATE MANAGEMENT
430 North Michigan Avenue, P.O. Box 109025, Chicago IL 60610-9025. 312/661-1930. Dedicated to educating and identifying real estate managers who are committed to meeting the needs of real estate owners and investors.

INTERNATIONAL ASSOCIATION OF CORPORATE REAL ESTATE EXECUTIVES
440 Columbia Drive, Suite 100, West Palm Beach FL 33409. 407/683-8111. An international association of real estate brokers.

Magazines

JOURNAL OF PROPERTY MANAGEMENT
Institute of Real Estate Management, 430 North Michigan Avenue, Chicago IL 60610. 312/661-1930.

NATIONAL REAL ESTATE INVESTOR
6151 Powers Ferry Road, Atlanta GA 30339. 404/955-2500.

RETAIL

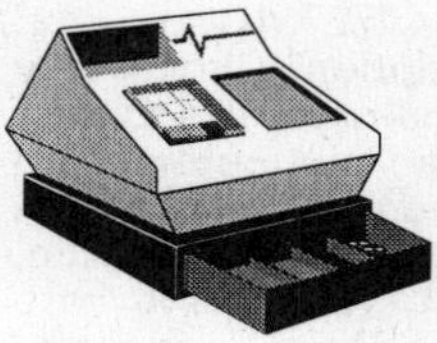

The '90s have been turbulent times for the retail industry. During the early years of the decade, the industry struggled as the national economy remained mired in recession. Now that the recession has technically been over for several years, one would think that shoppers would be flocking back to stores. Think again.

During 1995, sales rose by only 4.5 percent, and analysts expected about the same for '96. During 1995 alone, 15,000 retailers filed for Chapter 11 bankruptcy. Many of them, according to Business Week, *were regional chains with outdated stores and merchandise.*

The problem is simple: Consumers just aren't spending like they used to, and when customers insist on cut-rate bargains, only the giants, like Wal-Mart and Target, can survive. And not even all of them are safe from the threat of red ink. Kmart, the nation's third-largest chain, is closing 70 stores; while Bradlees and Ames are both having financial problems of their own.

ACME MARKETS OF VIRGINIA, INC.
P.O. Box 246, North Tazewell VA 24630. 540/988-2561. **Contact:** Danny Meadows, Human Resources. **Description:** Acme Markets is a supermarket chain of ten stores in Virginia and West Virginia. **Corporate headquarters location:** This Location.

ADVANCE STORES COMPANY, INC.
P.O. Box 2710, Roanoke VA 24001. 703/345-4911. **Contact:** Darrel Porter, Director of Human Resources. **Description:** This is the home office of a chain of auto part stores. Store locations cover the entire east coast.

BEST PRODUCTS COMPANY
P.O. Box 26303, Richmond VA 23260. 804/261-2000. **Contact:** Wayne Tennent, Vice President of Human Resources. **Description:** A retail chain of general merchandise stores. The stores sell jewelry, diamonds, and consumer goods including housewares, small appliances, silverware, luggage, cameras, radios, televisions, and electronic equipment. Best Products operates 163 stores in 22 states. **Corporate headquarters location:** This Location. **Number of employees nationwide:** 16,300.

BEST PRODUCTS COMPANY
2800 South Randolph Street, Arlington VA 22206. 703/578-4600. **Contact:** Jack Jackson, Manager, Personnel. **Description:** A retail chain of general merchandise stores. The stores sell jewelry, diamonds, and consumer goods including housewares, small appliances, silverware, luggage, cameras, radios, televisions, and electronic equipment. Best Products operates 163 stores in 22 states. **Common positions include:** Department Manager; Retail Sales Worker; Warehouse/Distribution Worker. **Educational backgrounds include:** Accounting; Business Administration. **Benefits:** Dental Insurance; Disability Coverage; Employee Discounts; Life Insurance; Medical Insurance; Pension Plan; Savings Plan; Tuition Assistance. **Corporate headquarters location:** Richmond VA. **Other U.S. locations:** Nationwide. **Listed on:** NASDAQ. **Number of employees nationwide:** 16,300.

BONNIE BE-LO MARKETS, INC.
1157 Production Road, Norfolk VA 23513-3903. 804/855-3371. **Contact:** Steve Rosa, Human Resources Manager. **Description:** Corporate headquarters

for a chain of grocery stores. Bonnie Be-Lo Markets, Inc. has 28 stores in Virginia and North Carolina.

CIRCUIT CITY STORES, INC.
9950 Mayland Drive, Richmond VA 23233-1464. 804/527-4000. **Fax:** 804/527-4086. **Contact:** Trina Crawford, Recruiter. **Description:** Circuit City Stores, Inc. is one of the largest U.S. retailers of brand-name consumer electronics and major appliances, as well as personal computers and software. In 1993, the company also began selling used cars at CarMax Auto Superstores. Circuit City has over 300 stores in operation nationwide, including locations of Circuit City Express, with plans to expand into untapped areas of the country. **Common positions include:** Accountant/Auditor; Advertising Clerk; Budget Analyst; Buyer; Computer Programmer; Computer Systems Analyst; Construction Contractor and Manager; Customer Service Representative; Economist/Market Research Analyst; Electrical/Electronics Engineer; Financial Analyst; General Manager; Human Resources Specialist; Industrial Engineer; Operations/Production Manager; Property and Real Estate Manager; Purchasing Agent and Manager; Real Estate Agent; Software Engineer; Wholesale and Retail Buyer. **Educational backgrounds include:** Accounting; Art/Design; Business Administration; Communications; Computer Science; Economics; Engineering; Finance; Liberal Arts; Marketing; Mathematics. **Benefits:** Dental Insurance; Disability Coverage; Employee Discounts; Life Insurance; Medical Insurance; Savings Plan; Tuition Assistance. **Special Programs:** Internships. **Corporate headquarters location:** This Location. **Operations at this facility include:** Administration; Divisional Headquarters; Regional Headquarters; Sales; Service. **Listed on:** New York Stock Exchange. **Number of employees nationwide:** 31,183.

DOLLAR TREE STORES, INC.
2555 Ellsmere Avenue, P.O. Box 2500, Norfolk VA 23501-2500. 804/857-4600. **Contact:** Len Intrieri, Vice President of Human Resources. **Description:** Dollar Tree Stores is a leading operator of discount variety stores offering merchandise at the $1.00 price point. The company's stores offer a wide assortment of everyday general merchandise in many traditional variety store categories, including housewares, toys, seasonal goods, gifts, food, stationery, health and beauty aids, books, party goods, and hardware. **Benefits:** 401K; Incentive Plan; Profit Sharing; Stock Option. **Corporate headquarters location:** This Location. **Subsidiaries include:** Dollar Tree Management, Inc.; and Dollar Tree Distribution, Inc. **Operations at this facility include:** Administration; Warehouse/Distribution. **Listed on:** NASDAQ. **Number of employees nationwide:** 4,500.

FINE'S MEN'S SHOPS INC.
1164 Azalea Garden Road, Norfolk VA 23502-5612. 804/857-6013. **Contact:** Mitchell Fine, Human Resources Director. **Description:** Corporate headquarters of a chain of men's clothing stores with 48 locations on the East Coast.

THE HECHT COMPANY
685 North Glebe Road, Arlington VA 22203-2199. 703/558-1200. **Contact:** Bruce Kelso, Senior Vice President, Human Resources. **Description:** A general merchandise retailer.

HEILIG-MEYERS
2235 Staples Mill Road, Richmond VA 23230. 804/359-9171. **Contact:** Ronald M. Raglund, Vice President of Human Resources and Training. **Description:** Heilig-Meyers is primarily engaged in the retail sale of home furnishings, including electronics, large and small appliances, bicycles, outdoor furniture, jewelry, floor coverings, and bedding. Stores are located throughout the United States and in Puerto Rico. Subsidiary Berrios Enterprises of Caguas, Puerto Rico, operates the 17 stores located there. Heilig-Meyers has plans to continue its nationwide expansion. **Corporate**

headquarters location: This Location. **Listed on:** New York Stock Exchange; Pacific Exchange. **Number of employees at this location:** 7,850. **Number of employees nationwide:** 12,510.

LILLIAN VERNON CORPORATION
2600 International Parkway, Virginia Beach VA 23452. 804/427-7700. **Contact:** William Sharkey, Vice President of Human Resources. **Description:** Lillian Vernon is a specialty catalog company that markets gift, household, gardening, decorative, Christmas, and children's products. Lily's Kids offers a broad assortment of toys, room decor, and fashion accessories for all age groups, from infants through pre-teens. Welcome is a specialty catalog dedicated to the needs of people who have recently moved and are often in need of organizers, accessories, and room decor. Christmas Memories offers a wide assortment of unique and festive Christmas decorations, trim, and accessories. Private Sale catalogs sells overstocked and discontinued products. This location is the company's national distribution center. **Corporate headquarters location:** New Rochelle NY. **Operations at this facility include:** Distribution.

LORD & TAYLOR
Tyson Corner, 7950 Tyson Corner Center, McLean VA 22102. 703/506-1156. **Contact:** Personnel Director. **Description:** A full-line department store carrying high-quality clothing, accessories, home furnishings, and many other retail items. Stores are located in many major United States metropolitan areas. **Corporate headquarters location:** New York NY. **Parent company:** May Department Stores Company.

NATIONAL AUTO DEALERS ASSOCIATION
8400 Westpark Drive, McLean VA 22102. 703/821-7000. **Contact:** Cathy Lester, Human Resources Director. **Description:** An association representing 19,500 new car and truck dealerships.

PEEBLES INC.
One Peebles Street, South Hill VA 23970. 804/447-5297. **Contact:** Tim Moyer, Training and Recruitment Director. **Description:** Operates a department store chain, selling moderate to better merchandise. **Common positions include:** Accountant/Auditor; Advertising Clerk; Buyer; Credit Manager; Customer Service Representative; Department Manager; Human Resources Specialist; Instructor/Trainer; Management Trainee; Teacher; Transportation/Traffic Specialist. **Educational backgrounds include:** Accounting; Business Administration; Liberal Arts; Marketing. **Benefits:** Dental Insurance; Disability Coverage; Employee Discounts; Life Insurance; Medical Insurance; Pension Plan. **Special Programs:** Internships. **Corporate headquarters location:** This Location. **Other U.S. locations:** DE; KY; MD; NC; SC; TN; VA. **Number of employees at this location:** 2,200. **Number of employees nationwide:** 2,341.

PETSMART INC.
13850 Metro Tech Drive, #448, Chantilly VA 22021. 703/222-0992. **Contact:** George Morvan, Marketing Consultant. **Description:** A retail company which sells pet food and supplies.

PLUMA, INC.
RR 1 Box 10B, Chatham VA 24531. 804/432-3830. **Contact:** Claire Mihalski, Personnel Manager. **Description:** Retail seller of fleece apparel and T-shirts that was established in 1987. Pluma, Inc. has two divisions in Virginia and the corporate office is located in North Carolina. **Number of employees at this location:** 387.

PLUMA, INC.
RR 2 Box 10, Martinsville VA 24112. 703/666-2126. **Contact:** Claire Mihalski, Personnel Manager. **Description:** Retail seller of fleece apparel and T-shirts that was established in 1987. Pluma, Inc. has two divisions in

Virginia and the corporate office is located in North Carolina. This division does distribution, operation and warehouse work.

S&K FAMOUS BRANDS, INC.
P.O. Box 31800, Richmond VA 23294-1800. 804/346-2500. **Contact:** Gray Rawlings, Human Resource Manager. **Description:** Engaged in the retail sale of men's clothing, furnishings, sportswear, and accessories. As of January 1995, S&K Famous Brands operated 172 stores in 27 states, predominantly east of the Mississippi River. **Corporate headquarters location:** This Location. **Operations at this facility include:** Administration; Distribution. **Listed on:** NASDAQ. **Number of employees nationwide:** 1,575.

SOUTHLAND CORPORATION
7-ELEVEN CONVENIENCE STORES
5300 Shawnee Road, Alexandria VA 22312. 703/642-0711. **Fax:** 703/354-0492. **Recorded Jobline:** 800/JOB-0711. **Contact:** Janine Mohl, Division Recruiter. **Description:** The Southland Corporation, 7-Eleven Convenience Stores, is one of the largest store chains in the world. Founded in 1927 in Dallas, Southland operates and franchises more than 6,000 7-Eleven and other convenience units in the United States and Canada. **NOTE:** Applications for management positions should be addressed to Division Recruiter, 814 Baker Road, Virginia Beach, VA 23462. **Common positions include:** Assistant Manager; Field Consultant Trainee; Management Trainee; Store Manager. **Educational backgrounds include:** Business Administration; Liberal Arts; Marketing. **Benefits:** 401K; Credit Union; Dental Insurance; Disability Coverage; Life Insurance; Medical Insurance; Profit Sharing; Savings Plan. **Special Programs:** Internships. **Corporate headquarters location:** Dallas TX. **Operations at this facility include:** Divisional Headquarters; Sales; Service. **Listed on:** New York Stock Exchange. **Number of employees at this location:** 8,000. **Number of employees nationwide:** 40,000.

STONE & THOMAS
1030 Main Street, Wheeling WV 26003. 304/232-3344. **Contact:** Human Resources. **Description:** A department store featuring appliances, carpeting, clothing, dishware, furniture, and housewares.

Note: *Because addresses and telephone numbers of smaller companies change rapidly, we recommend you call each company to verify the information below before inquiring about job opportunities. Mass mailings are not recommended.*

Additional small employers:

VIDEO TAPE RENTAL

Blockbuster Video
835 J Clyde Morris Blvd, Newport News VA 23601-1307. 804/591-2449.

Blockbuster Video
4014 Electric Rd, Roanoke VA 24014-2813. 540/989-1286.

Blockbuster Video
3200 Academy Ave, Portsmouth VA 23703-3203. 804/483-4500.

Errol's Video Midlothian
8200 Midlothian Tpke, Richmond VA 23235-5118. 804/320-0317.

RETAIL LUMBER AND BUILDING MATERIALS

Home Depot
2815 Merrilee Dr, Fairfax VA 22031-4409. 703/205-1245.

HQ Home Quarters Warehouse
2211 W Mercury Blvd, Hampton VA 23666-3112. 804/838-8210.

Lowe's
1048 N Eisenhower Dr, Beckley WV 25801-3116. 304/253-6000.

Lowe's
Rt 100 S, Dublin VA 24084. 540/674-8821.

Lowe's
2501 Garfield Ave, Parkersburg WV 26101-1916. 304/422-7200.

Lowe's
Rt 19, Summersville WV 26651. 304/872-5700.

Lowe's
199 Woodland Dr SW, Wise VA 24293-4623. 540/328-1400.

Lowe's
1130 Winchester Ave, Martinsburg WV 25401-5035. 304/264-1400.

Roper Bros Lumber Co. Inc.
PO Box 488, Colonial Hgts VA 23834-0488. 804/732-9321.

Builders Supply & Lumber Company
13234 Airpark Dr, Culpeper VA 22701. 540/825-0200.

AAPCO Of Richmond
6710 Jefferson Davis Hwy, Richmond VA 23237-1219. 804/748-4842.

Windows & Doors Of Southwest VA
5130 Carriage Dr, Roanoke VA 24018-2212. 540/776-2858.

Zacks Industries Inc.
403 Fort Hill Dr, Charleston WV 25314-1018. 304/343-5353.

PAINT, GLASS, AND WALLPAPER STORES

Chesterfield Glass Shop
2007 Chamberlayne Ave, Richmond VA 23222-4813. 804/321-4000.

Guardian Auto Glass
320 North St, Bluefield WV 24701-4038. 304/325-2511.

Glass Odyssey
1120 Radford St, Christiansbrg VA 24073-2832. 540/381-6956.

Duron Paints & Wallcoverings
620 S Military Hwy, Virginia Beach VA 23464-1820. 804/420-9563.

HARDWARE STORES

Fastenal Co.
43rd St & Jacob St, Wheeling WV 26003. 304/232-0365.

Fuel Feed Plaza Home Center Inc.
601 Nevan Rd, Virginia Beach VA 23451-6115. 804/340-4911.

The Disston Co.
Rt 29 N PO Box 3000, Danville VA 24543. 804/836-5322.

Home Quarters Warehouse
575 Lynnhaven Pky, Virginia Beach VA 23452-7311. 804/498-7100.

MOBILE HOME DEALERS

Larry's Homes Of VA Inc.
9720 Jefferson Davis Hwy, Fredericksbrg VA 22407-9406. 540/898-4554.

DEPARTMENT STORES

Nordstrom
1400 S Hayes St, Arlington VA 22202-5007. 703/415-1121.

SH Heironimus Co. Inc.
405 S Jefferson St, Roanoke VA 24011-2005. 540/343-6941.

Woodward & Lothrop Inc.
2800 Eisenhower Ave, Alexandria VA 22314-4578. 703/329-5000.

JCPenney Co. Inc.
7704 Richmond Hwy, Alexandria VA 22306-2844. 703/799-0902.

JCPenney Co. Inc.
2700 Potomac Mills Cir, Woodbridge VA 22192-4625. 703/494-0089.

JCPenney Co. Inc.
4200 Portsmouth Blvd, Ste 200, Chesapeake VA 23321-2100. 804/465-0569.

Kmart Stores
13412 Jefferson Davis Hwy, Woodbridge VA 22191-1211. 703/491-7089.

Kmart Stores
1150 Winchester Ave, Martinsburg WV 25401-5035. 304/264-9004.

Kmart Stores
101 Great Teays Blvd, Scott Depot WV 25560-9548. 304/342-6333.

Kmart Stores
5636 US Route 60 E, Barboursville WV 25504. 304/736-2844.

Kmart Stores
312 Constitution Dr, Virginia Beach VA 23462-3102. 804/497-0389.

Montgomery Ward & Co.
Mountaineer Mall, Morgantown WV 26505. 304/292-6321.

Wal-Mart Discount Cities
721 Beverly Pike, Elkins WV 26241-9729. 304/636-2138.

Wal-Mart Discount Cities
640 Highway 58 E, Norton VA 24273-3002. 540/679-7327.

Wal-Mart Discount Cities
240 Commonwealth Bld, Martinsville VA 24112. 540/638-5100.

Wal-Mart Discount Cities
4210 Franklin Rd SW, Roanoke VA 24014-5267. 540/772-3892.

Wal-Mart Discount Cities
950 Edwards Ferry Road Northeast, Leesburg VA 22075-3324. 703/779-0102.

Wal-Mart Discount Cities
14000 Worth Ave, Woodbridge VA 22192-4121. 703/497-2590.

Wal-Mart Discount Cities
3900 Wards Rd, Lynchburg VA 24502-2942. 804/832-0304.

Wal-Mart Discount Cities
1111 Bell Creek Rd S, Mechanicsville VA 23111-3405. 804/730-8877.

Wal-Mart Discount Cities
Hwy 17, Gloucester VA 23061. 804/694-0110.

Belk-Leggett Co.
Piedmont Mall, Danville VA 24540. 804/792-6211.

Big Lots
2000 Plank Rd, Fredericksbrg VA 22401-5104. 540/374-1639.

Hill's Department Store
Int 64 & Rt 34, Hurricane WV 25526. 304/757-0941.

Hill's Department Store
20 By Pass Plaza Shpg Ctr, Beckley WV 25801-2209. 304/252-6546.

Hill's Department Stores
1200 N State Route 2, N Martinsville WV 26155-2523. 304/455-6550.

Hill's Department Store
Mercer Mall, Bluefield WV 24701. 304/327-6103.

Rose's Stores Inc.
Washington Square Shopping Ctr, Grafton VA 23692. 804/898-6797.

PM Mill Outlet
Rock Branch Industrial Pk, Poca WV 25159. 304/755-7666.

Villeroy & Boch Factory Outlet
3044 Richmond Rd, Williamsburg VA 23185-2013. 804/565-3820.

Hecht's
701 Lynnhaven Pky, Virginia Beach VA 23452-7304. 804/463-4910.

Hecht's
River Ridge Shopping Ctr, Lynchburg VA 24502. 804/239-5611.

Lazarus Department Store
Huntington Mall, Barboursville WV 25504. 304/733-0244.

Leggett Department Store
PO Box 11764, Lynchburg VA 24506-1764. 804/237-6611.

Leggett Department Store
Patrick Henry Mall 12300 Jeffe, Newport News VA 23602. 804/249-1963.

Leggett Department Store
Chesterfield Towne Center, Richmond VA 23235. 804/379-1333.

Leggett Department Store
1601 Willow Lawn Dr, Richmond VA 23230-3427. 804/282-1652.

Leggett Department Store
8300 Sudley Rd, Manassas VA 22110-3458. 703/361-4181.

Pharmhouse Department Store
5099 Jefferson Davis Hwy, Fredericksbrg VA 22408-4263. 540/898-4680.

Value City Department Store
Virginia Beach & Witchduck Rd, Virginia Beach VA 23462. 804/490-5889.

Woodward & Lothrop
5801 Duke St, Alexandria VA 22304-3208. 703/354-1700.

VARIETY STORES

Dollar Bills Discount Sales Variety
3563 Plank Rd, Fredericksbrg VA 22407-6800. 540/786-9342.

Eagles Store
Clarksville Crossing Ctr, Clarksville VA 23927. 804/374-2084.

Only One Dollar Inc.
2555 Ellsmere Ave, Norfolk VA 23513-2417. 804/857-4600.

Sternheimer Bros Inc.
5501 Ferncroft Rd, Sandston VA 23150-1911. 804/226-1324.

MISC. GENERAL MERCHANDISE STORES

Capital Sales
2705 Peters Creek Rd NW, Roanoke VA 24019-3509. 540/562-0525.

Service Merchandise
13856 Metro Tech Dr, Chantilly VA 22021-3241. 703/803-3105.

GROCERY AND CONVENIENCE STORES

7-Eleven
1st & Pepper Sts, Christiansbrg VA 24073. 540/382-0737.

7-Eleven
13830 Lee Hwy, Centreville VA 22020-2441. 703/818-8657.

7-Eleven
5141 Hull Street Rd, Richmond VA 23224-2421. 804/233-3838.

7-Eleven
343 2nd Ave SW, S Charleston WV 25303-1213. 304/744-4632.

7-Eleven
701 S Crater Rd, Petersburg VA 23803-5212. 804/861-1628.

Camellia Foods Stores
PO Box 2320, Norfolk VA 23501-2320. 804/855-3371.

Community Pride Food Stores
1911 W Main St, Richmond VA 23220-4521. 804/359-0842.

County Market
800 Grand Central Mall, Parkersburg WV 26101-1131. 304/485-9350.

Deskins Super Market Inc.
276 Tazewell Ave, Tazewell VA 24651-1334. 540/988-4210.

E-Z-N Food Mart
4040 Electric Rd, Roanoke VA 24014-2813. 540/989-3888.

Farm Fresh
737 Independence Blvd, Virginia Beach VA 23455-6205. 804/473-9240.

Farm Fresh
US Hwy 17, Hayes VA 23072. 804/642-6101.

Farm Fresh Inc.
7530 Tidewater Dr,

Norfolk VA 23505-3703. 804/480-6700.

Fas Mart Convenience Stores Inc.
624 Garrisonville Rd, Stafford VA 22554-3774. 540/659-4025.

Fas Mart Convenience Stores Inc.
6021 Belmont Rd, Richmond VA 23234-4007. 804/276-3781.

Fas Mart Convenience Stores Inc.
840 Warrenton Rd, Fredericksbrg VA 22406-1072. 540/372-6716.

Food City
210 US Highway 23 N, Weber City VA 24290-6825. 703/386-9041.

Food Lion Stores Inc.
588 Cummings St, Abingdon VA 24210-3240. 540/628-8196.

Food Lion Stores Inc.
275 Battlefield Plaza, Petersburg VA 23801. 804/732-1142.

Food Lion Stores Inc.
1061 Old Abingdon Hwy, Bristol VA 24201-1878. 540/669-7341.

Food Lion Stores Inc.
13100 Midlothian Tpke, Midlothian VA 23113-4206. 804/379-8988.

Food Lion Stores Inc.
315 College Ave, Bluefield VA 24701-4644. 540/322-2911.

Food Lion Stores Inc.
4221 Pleasant Valley Rd, Virginia Beach VA 23464-8519. 804/495-9624.

Food Lion Stores Inc.
1077 Virginia Beach Blvd, Virginia Beach VA 23451-5670. 804/425-6376.

Fresh Fields Markets
6548 Little River Tpke, Alexandria VA 22312-1443. 703/914-0040.

Giant Food Store
220 Zan Rd, Charlottesvle VA 22901-2859. 804/973-7860.

Go-Mart Inc.
1502 Greenbrier St, Charleston WV 25311-1008. 304/344-4350.

Goodsons Super Markets
PO Box 858, Welch WV 24801-0858. 304/436-8481.

Harris Teeter Inc.
6619 Williamson Rd, Roanoke VA 24019-4631. 540/362-1267.

Jet Store
Sprice & US 60, Saint Albans WV 25177. 304/727-1761.

Junior Market
412A Newtown Rd, Virginia Beach VA 23462-5619. 804/499-1128.

Kroger Co.
2840 Linkhorne Dr, Lynchburg VA 24503-3322. 804/384-0642.

Kroger Co.
Ashton Place, Charleston WV 25302. 304/342-8807.

Lem Markets Inc.
1523 Wilborn Ave, #813, South Boston VA 24592-2425. 804/575-7886.

Lowe's Food Store
Rt 8 S, Stuart VA 24171. 540/694-5656.

Lucky Convenience Stores
405 E Laburnum Ave, Richmond VA 23222-2120. 804/329-9370.

Magruder's Grocery
6936 Braddock Rd, Annandale VA 22003-6036. 703/750-1266.

Meadowood IGA
5118 Richmond Henrico Tpke, Richmond VA 23227-3627. 804/321-2191.

Miller Mart
13797 Warwick Blvd, Newport News VA 23602-5422. 804/874-5806.

Mr. Bulky's
Charleston Town Center, Charleston WV 25389. 304/342-7871.

Neighbors Convenience Store
1001 E Market St, Harrisonburg VA 22801-4332. 540/434-0759.

Nick's Markets
9520 Woodman Rd, Richmond VA 23228-1324. 804/264-5357.

Papco Food Mart
1407 Kempsville Rd, Virginia Beach VA 23464-7301. 804/467-9422.

Pennzoil Shop & Go
1500 Washington St E, Charleston WV 25311-2506. 304/343-8924.

Safeway Supermarkets
3713 Lee Hwy, Arlington VA 22207-3720. 703/841-1155.

Safeway Supermarkets
5061 Jefferson Davis Hwy, Fredericksbrg VA 22408-4263. 540/898-1213.

Southern Food Store
600 E Washington St, Suffolk VA 23434-4009. 804/925-0765.

Store Stop
US Rt 13, Onley VA 23418. 804/787-7371.

Super Fresh
10320 Festival Ln, Manassas VA 22110-3548. 703/335-1343.

Super Fresh Food Markets VA Inc.
Meadowbrook Plaza, Richmond VA 23234. 804/275-1092.

The Grocery Store
11400 W Huguenot Rd, Midlothian VA 23113-1119. 804/379-1395.

The Marketplace
730 W 21st St, Norfolk VA 23517-1921. 804/625-2705.

The Pantry Store
214 W Main St, Salem WV 26426-1220. 304/782-3039.

Ukrop's Super Markets
60 West Shopping Center, Richmond VA 23235. 804/272-5812.

Ukrop's Super Markets
4717 Walmsley Blvd, Richmond VA 23234-2348. 804/275-7861.

Uni-Marts Inc.
5700 W Broad St, Richmond VA 23230-2616. 804/288-0637.

Uni-Marts Inc.
3842 Shenandoah Ave Nw, Roanoke VA 24017-6516. 540/345-1541.

Wade's Supermarkets
510 Roanoke St, Christiansbrg VA 24073-3141. 540/382-4995.

Weis Markets
13866 Metro Tech Dr, Chantilly VA 22021-3242. 703/266-0401.

Wilco Food Mart
3601 Airline Blvd, Portsmouth VA 23701-2601. 804/488-1754.

Wilco Food Mart
4877 Haygood Rd, Virginia Beach VA 23455-5319. 804/490-5788.

Winn Dixie
Seminole Shopping Center, Madison Hts VA 24572. 804/929-8706.

Winn Dixie
6569 Market Dr, Gloucester VA 23061. 804/693-3488.

Winn-Dixie
Rt 57 & 57 A, Stanleytown VA 24168. 540/629-7232.

Zooms
2605 Kecoughtan Rd, Hampton VA 23661-3322. 804/728-0010.

High's Dairy Store
10501 Courthouse Rd, Fredericksbrg VA 22407-1611. 540/898-1687.

Hunter Mill Deli
11213 Lee Hwy, #A, Fairfax VA 22030-5608. 703/352-9193.

MISC. FOOD STORES

Doughtie's Foods Inc.
2410 Wesley St, Portsmouth VA 23707-1717. 804/393-6007.

Virginia Fish Market Inc.
100 N Union St, Alexandria VA 22314-3244. 703/836-5676.

Godiva Chocolatier
1100 S Hayes St, Arlington VA 22202-4907. 703/415-3811.

Broughton Foods Company
1931 Washington St W, Charleston WV 25312-1406. 304/342-4131.

Dairy Mart
1205 Dorsey Ave, Morgantown WV 26505-7037. 304/292-9246.

Farm Fresh Stores Inc.
RR 2, #S, Ravenswood WV 26164-9802. 304/273-5882.

Highs Dairy Products Corp.
846 E Moler Ave, Martinsburg WV 25401-4730. 304/263-8598.

Nature Food Centres Inc.
7728 Midlothian Tpke, Richmond VA 23235-5226. 804/330-5774.

RETAIL BAKERIES

Arnold Bakery Thrift Store
10834 Warwick Blvd, Newport News VA 23601-3741. 804/595-5795.

Ukrop's Bakery
60 West Shopping Center, Richmond VA 23235. 804/320-5912.

Ukrop's Bakery
Crossroads Shopping Center, Richmond VA 23230. 804/379-1422.

Weis Markets
Colonial Bake Shop, Manassas VA 22110. 703/590-0408.

AUTO DEALERS

Casey Auto Group Inc.
813 Diligence Dr, Ste 116, Newport News VA 23606-4237. 804/591-1000.

Farrish Oldsmobile/Jeep/Subaru
9610 Lee Hwy, Fairfax VA 22031-2376. 703/273-0200.

JKJ Chevrolet
2000 Chain Bridge Rd, Vienna VA 22182-2599. 703/356-0400.

Koons Of Manassas
7105 Sudley Rd, Manassas VA 22110-2636. 703/631-9500.

Lantzsch-Andreas Enterprises
8545 Leesburg Pike, Vienna VA 22182-2203. 703/448-2222.

Love Lexus Toyota Dealership
1433 MacCorkle Ave, Saint Albans WV 25177-1826. 304/727-7777.

Mid-Atlantic Cars Inc.
10287 Lee Hwy, Fairfax VA 22030-2202. 703/352-5555.

Rosenthal Jaguar
1592 Spring Hill Rd, Vienna VA 22182-2275. 703/893-1700.

Casey Honda/Casey BMW
783 J Clyde Morris Blvd, Newport News VA 23601-1513. 804/591-1300.

Haywood-Clarke Buick
7837 Carousel Ln, Richmond VA 23294-4209. 804/747-6060.

Jerry's Chevrolet Geo and Oldsmobile
325 E Market St, Leesburg VA 22075-4102. 703/771-8300.

Radley Honda-Chevrolet
3670 Jefferson Davis Hwy, Fredericksbrg VA

22408-4160. 540/898-4000.

Wilkins Epperly Chrysler Plymouth
US 19 S, Oak Hill WV 25901. 304/469-2956.

Sheehy Ford Of Springfield
6727 Loisdale Rd, Springfield VA 22150-1994. 703/491-8269.

Rosenthal AMC Jeep Eagle
1100 S Glebe Rd, Arlington VA 22204-4309. 703/553-6585.

Purvis Ford Inc.
3660 Jefferson Davis Hwy, Fredericksbrg VA 22408-4163. 540/898-3000.

Ted Britt Nissan-Mitsubishi
9010 Liberia Ave, Manassas VA 22110-5322. 703/361-8758.

Brown's Fairfax Nissan
11000 Main St, Fairfax VA 22030-5007. 703/591-8009.

Hondas By Radley
3670 Jefferson Davis Hwy, Fredericksbrg VA 22408-4160. 703/273-2811.

S&S Auto Sales
1722 7th St, Parkersburg WV 26101-5008. 304/424-5111.

CONSUMER SUPPLY STORES

All Parts
254 W Lee Hwy, Warrenton VA 22186-2501. 540/349-9450.

Tire America
1 Bryan Dr, Wheeling WV 26003-6121. 304/233-5760.

Advance Auto Parts
980 J Clyde Morris Blvd, Ste 11, Newport News VA 23601-1078. 804/595-3536.

Advance Auto Parts
1522 N Main St, Suffolk VA 23434-4327. 804/539-2911.

Advance Auto Parts
3103 Western Branch Blvd, Chesapeake VA 23321-5513. 804/686-1276.

Advance Auto Parts
172 S Plaza Trail, Virginia Beach VA 23452-5553. 804/498-8707.

Advance Auto Parts
Waterlick Plaza, Lynchburg VA 24502. 804/239-0193.

Advance Auto Parts
435 E Nelson St, Lexington VA 24450-2725. 540/463-2191.

Advance Auto Parts
106 W Stuart Dr, Galax VA 24333-2114. 540/236-9973.

Advance Auto Parts
2170 Roanoke St, Christiansbrg VA 24073-2512. 540/382-1111.

Advance Auto Parts
406 W Atlantic St, Emporia VA 23847-1208. 804/634-9019.

Advance Auto Parts
1452 Seminole Trl, Charlottesvle VA 22901-1436. 804/974-6165.

Advance Auto Parts
7051 Brook Rd, Richmond VA 23227-2247. 804/264-3433.

Advance Auto Parts
425 N State Route 2, N Martinsville WV 26155-2711. 304/455-3656.

Carquest Auto Parts
2201 Perl Rd, Richmond VA 23230-2007. 804/288-0364.

Hi-Gear Discount Auto Parts
Gunston Plaza Shopping Center, Lorton VA 22079. 703/550-1447.

Hi-Gear Discount Auto Parts
1281 Jefferson Davis Hwy, Fredericksbrg VA 22401-4415. 540/373-2277.

JEC
2913 Plantation Rd NE, #A, Roanoke VA 24012-4465. 540/366-7345.

Napa Auto Parts
800 Southlake Blvd, Richmond VA 23236-3918. 804/794-7626.

SPR Shops Automtive Performance Centers
6445 Midlothian Tpke, Richmond VA 23225-5607. 804/276-8544.

Trak Auto
1060 Elden St, Herndon VA 22070-3803. 703/437-9439.

Trak-Auto
4000 Mechanicsville Pike, Richmond VA 23223-1137. 804/321-2447.

Tread Quarters Inc.
340 2nd St, Williamsburg VA 23185-4528. 804/874-7035.

Tread Quarters Inc.
5003 George Washington Hwy, Portsmouth VA 23702-2601. 804/487-3400.

Twin B Auto Parts
4105 George Washington Hwy, Portsmouth VA 23702-2001. 804/397-2751.

Twin B Auto Parts
4865 Shore Dr, Virginia Beach VA 23455-2714. 804/460-3961.

Twin B Auto Parts Inc.
528 S Military Hwy, Virginia Beach VA 23464-1818. 804/420-3342.

Twin B Auto Parts
4608 Pembroke Blvd, Virginia Beach VA 23455-6400. 804/490-3233.

Twin B Auto Parts
756 First Colonial Rd, Virginia Beach VA 23451-6124. 804/422-8430.

Tire Station
5002 Airport Rd NW, Ste 49, Roanoke VA 24012-1607. 540/362-3355.

NTW-National Tire Warehouse
14501 Telegraph Rd, Woodbridge VA 22192-4621. 703/491-7141.

Goodyear Auto Service Centers
4511 Williamsburg Rd, Richmond VA 23231-2737. 804/236-8867.

Kramer Tire Co.-Goodyear
3300 Holland Rd, Virginia Beach VA 23452-4819. 804/427-3009.

Rosson & Troilo Motor Co.
18327 Brandy Rd, Brandy Station VA 22714-2215. 540/825-3722.

Merchant's Tire & Auto Centers
6609 Backlick Rd, Springfield VA 22150-2702. 703/644-4377.

Merchant's Tire & Auto Centers
737 Independence Blvd, Virginia Beach VA 23455-6205. 804/497-2100.

American Tire & Service
202 Williamson Rd SE, Roanoke VA 24011-1804. 703/982-0173.

Anderson Tire Center
1600 Tidewater Trail, Spotsylvania VA 22553. 540/373-0005.

Pay-Less Tire & Auto Repair
13177 Warwick Blvd, Newport News VA 23602-8345. 804/988-0311.

APPAREL AND ACCESSORY STORES

Casual Male Big & Tall
7335 Midlothian Tpke, Richmond VA 23225-6702. 804/745-9828.

S&K Famous Brands Inc.
11100 W Broad St, Glen Allen VA 23060-5813. 804/346-2500.

Steven-Windsor
2762 Duke St, Alexandria VA 22314-4511. 703/751-8844.

Annie Sez
5195 Leesburg Pike, Falls Church VA 22041-3207. 703/931-6544.

Canned Heat
Beach Mall, Virginia Beach VA 23451. 804/425-0610.

Capezio
Regency Square, Richmond VA 23229. 804/740-9051.

Carroll Reed Inc.
Berkeley Commons, Williamsburg VA 23188. 804/565-6306.

Casual Corner
Regency Square, Richmond VA 23229. 804/740-1391.

Catherine's
2312 W Mercury Blvd, Hampton VA 23666-3115. 804/826-8062.

Cato
271 Wadsworth Dr, Richmond VA 23236-4525. 804/320-1626.

Cato
517 Commerce Dr, Bluefield VA 24605-9697. 540/322-2546.

Deb
701 Lynnhaven Pky, Virginia Beach VA 23452-7304. 804/340-9406.

Dress Barns
1239 Jefferson Davis Hwy, Fredericksbrg VA 22401-4415. 540/899-0593.

English's Clothing
Hunting Hills Shopping Center, Roanoke VA 24018. 540/989-3240.

Fashion Cents
Suffolk Shopping Center, Suffolk VA 23434. 804/934-0431.

Laura Ashley
1404 N Parham Rd, Richmond VA 23229-5533. 804/740-1406.

Laura Ashley
Merchants Square Shopping Cent, Williamsburg VA 23185. 804/229-0353.

Leggett Department Store
Hwy 15 S, Farmville VA 23901. 804/392-8843.

Limited Express
11929 Market St, Reston VA 22090-5615. 703/904-9245.

Loehmann's Inc.
8904E W Broad St, Richmond VA 23294-5803. 804/270-1257.

Maurice's
776 New River Rd, Christiansbrg VA 24073-6503. 540/381-1718.

Maurice's
Mercer Mall, Bluefield WV 24701. 304/327-7581.

Proffitts
11500 Midlothian Tpke, Richmond VA 23235-4761. 804/379-5000.

Sassafras
9043 W Broad St, Richmond VA 23294-5810. 804/747-9933.

Sassafras
Best Square Shopping Ctr, Norfolk VA 23502. 804/461-9355.

Schwabe-May
Charleston Town Center, Charleston WV 25389. 304/357-4500.

The Answer
Loehmanns Plaza Shopping Cente, Falls Church VA 22042. 703/573-0485.

The Talbots Inc.
6223 River Rd, Richmond VA 23229-8522. 804/288-0020.

Thelma's Boutique
108 Salem Ave SE,

Roanoke VA 24011-1410. 540/342-0132.

Mother Care Stores Inc.
Valley View Mall, Roanoke VA 24012. 540/366-1596.

Cacique
Tysons Corner Center, McLean VA 22102. 703/893-1130.

The Gap Kids
11920 Market St, Reston VA 22090-5614. 703/709-7994.

Gabriel Brothers Inc.
55 Scott Ave, Morgantown WV 26505-8853. 304/292-6965.

Turtles In A Carte
2700 Potomac Mills Cir, Woodbridge VA 22192-4625. 703/490-6988.

County Seat Stores
Charleston Town Center, Charleston WV 25389. 304/346-8129.

Life Uniform & Shoe Shops
Chesterfield Towne Center, Richmond VA 23235. 804/379-2432.

Chic Wig Salon
Coliseum Mall, Hampton VA 23666. 804/838-2259.

Banana Republic
11910 Market St, Reston VA 22090-5614. 703/709-7992.

SHOE STORES

Bootlegger Shoes
7439 Midlothian Tpke, Richmond VA 23225-6411. 804/276-4630.

Bootlegger Shoes
4300 Portsmouth Blvd, Ste 210, Chesapeake VA 23321-2138. 804/488-8935.

Bootlegger Shoes
5720 Brook Rd, Richmond VA 23227-2276. 804/264-5906.

Shore Enterprises Inc.
804 Greenbrier Cir, Chesapeake VA 23320-2624. 804/366-0199.

Lady Foot Locker
Coliseum Mall, Hampton VA 23666. 804/827-9482.

Hofheimers Stride Rite Bootery
12300 Jefferson Ave, Newport News VA 23602-6900. 804/249-1239.

Hofheimers Stride Rite Bootery
Pembroke Mall Shopping Center, Virginia Beach VA 23462. 804/499-7732.

Banister Manufacturers Outlet
Blue Ridge Outlet Mall, Martinsburg WV 25401. 304/263-6808.

Burlington Shoes
2060 Plank Rd, Fredericksbrg VA 22401-5104. 540/373-9157.

Foot Action Inc.
Valley View Mall, Roanoke VA 24012. 540/366-9128.

Foot Action Inc.
River Ridge Mall, Lynchburg VA 24502. 804/832-0887.

Hofheimer's Shoe Stores
Tower Mall, Portsmouth VA 23701. 804/488-8764.

Jarman Shoe Store
Tysons Corner Shopping Center, Mc Lean VA 22102. 703/893-5587.

Naturalizer Shoes
7201 Midlothian Tpke, Richmond VA 23225-6603. 804/674-8902.

Pic 'N Pay Shoes Inc.
707 E Broad St, Richmond VA 23219-1835. 804/644-2711.

Shoe Show
Tower Mall, Portsmouth VA 23701. 804/488-7526.

Shoe Show
1008 Memorial Dr, Pulaski VA 24301-2920. 703/980-5788.

FURNITURE STORES

Brass Beds Of Virginia-Levin's
12300 Jefferson Ave, Newport News VA 23602-6900. 804/249-2222.

Cargo Furniture
4302 Electric Rd, Roanoke VA 24014-2920. 540/774-1633.

Grand Piano and Furniture Company
4235 Electric Rd, #100, Roanoke VA 24014-4145. 540/343-1707.

Grand Discount Furniture Stores Retail Sales
1301 Baker Rd, Virginia Beach VA 23455-3317. 804/460-3391.

Haverty's Fine Furniture Co.
2501 Glen Center St, Richmond VA 23223-2341. 804/643-0181.

Haynes Furniture Co.
5324 Virginia Beach Blvd, Virginia Beach VA 23462-1828. 804/497-5833.

Hub Furniture Centers
12097 Jefferson Ave, Newport News VA 23606-4325. 804/249-5336.

Mario Furniture Company
5650 General, Alexandria VA 22312. 703/941-0800.

Schewel Furniture Co.
1031 Main St, Lynchburg VA 24504-1800. 804/522-0200.

The Bombay Company
8300 Sudley Rd, Manassas VA 22110-3458. 703/335-5542.

United Consumers Club
14101 Sullyfield Cir, Chantilly VA 22021-1625. 703/817-0220.

Mattress Discounters
6832 Midlothian Tpke,

Richmond VA 23225-5615. 804/745-2512.

Mattress Discounters
1508 N Parham Rd, Richmond VA 23229-4621. 804/965-0680.

Mattress Discounters
4914 W Broad St, Richmond VA 23230-3123. 804/353-3817.

Mattress Discounters
1998 William St, Fredericksbrg VA 22401-5128. 540/373-3200.

Mattress Discounters
11001 Midlothian Tpke, Richmond VA 23235-4709. 804/379-0101.

Mattress Discounters
9011 W Broad St, Richmond VA 23294-5809. 804/965-0540.

Mattress Discounters
1865 Southpark Blvd, Colonial Hgts VA 23834-3607. 804/526-7773.

Hechinger
7665 Sudley Rd, Manassas VA 22110-2811. 703/369-7755.

MISC. HOME FURNISHINGS STORES

L Fishman & Son Inc.
2243 Tomlyn St, Richmond VA 23230-3334. 804/358-8400.

New York Carpet World
4207 Portsmouth Blvd, Portsmouth VA 23701-2530. 804/488-1136.

Blue Grass Electric Co.
348 N Monroe Ave, Covington VA 24426-1223. 703/965-5200.

Ferguson Enterprises Inc.
711 Research Rd, Richmond VA 23236-3927. 804/379-2275.

HOUSEHOLD APPLIANCE STORES

Holdren's Inc.
2309 Franklin Road Southwest, Roanoke VA 24014-1111. 540/345-1584.

CONSUMER ELECTRONICS STORES

Southern Autotronics Inc.
1701 Williamson Rd NE, Roanoke VA 24012-5225. 703/982-8100.

COMPUTER AND SOFTWARE STORES

Games & Gadgets
1800 West Mercury Blvd, #12A, Hampton VA 23666-3211. 804/827-0877.

International Computer Networks
8394 Terminal Road, Lorton VA 22079-1422. 703/550-0500.

Software Etc.
Galleria At Tysons II, McLean VA 22102. 703/821-2043.

RECORD AND PRERECORDED TAPE STORES

Saturday Matinee
Valley View Mall, Roanoke VA 24012. 540/563-1195.

Suncoast Motion Picture
Military Circle Mall, Norfolk VA 23502. 804/461-7805.

Suncoast Motion Picture
Chesterfield Towne Center, Richmond VA 23235. 804/794-0356.

Camelot Music
Military Circle Shopping Ctr, Norfolk VA 23502. 804/461-0895.

Disc Jockey Records
Liberty Fair Mall, Martinsville VA 24112. 540/666-6790.

Disc Jockey Records
Martinsburg Mall, Martinsburg WV 25401. 304/267-9405.

Mother's Records
754 New River Rd, Christiansbrg VA 24073-6503. 540/381-0910.

Sam Goody
Cloverleaf Mall Shopping Ctr, Richmond VA 23225. 804/276-6304.

Wall To Wall Sound & Video
800 Foxcroft Ave, Ste 201, Martinsburg WV 25401-1829. 304/267-4906.

DRUG STORES

Discount Emporium Inc.
1603 Kanawha Blvd W, Charleston WV 25312-2535. 304/345-5921.

Fruth Pharmacy Inc.
RR 1, Pt Pleasant WV 25550-9801. 304/675-1612.

Nelson's Drug Store
2107 Pike St, Parkersburg WV 26101-6973. 304/485-5517.

Revco Discount Drug Center
783 E Main St, Abingdon VA 24210-2353. 540/628-8119.

CVS Pharmacy
9030 W Broad St, Richmond VA 23294-5804. 804/747-9531.

CVS Pharmacy
133 Junction Dr, Ashland VA 23005-2200. 804/752-2092.

Super X Drugs
Ceredo Plaza, Ceredo WV 25507. 304/453-3503.

Rite Aid Pharmacies
500 Main St, Logan WV 25601-3814. 304/752-2910.

Rite Aid Pharmacies
Harmon Shopping Plz, Grafton WV 26354. 304/265-0758.

Rite Aid Pharmacies
435 N Ridge Rd, Richmond VA 23229-7403. 804/282-4219.

Rite Aid Pharmacies
Cape Henry Shopping Center, Virginia Beach VA 23451. 804/496-9636.

Farmco Pharmacies
4717 Jefferson Davis

Hwy, Richmond VA 23234-3152. 804/271-5203.

Rural Acres Pharmacy
252 Rural Acres Dr, Beckley WV 25801-3503. 304/255-6800.

Southeast Pharmacy
801 E Franklin St, Richmond VA 23219-2315. 804/775-0839.

Standard Drug Co.
10681 Courthouse Rd, Fredericksbrg VA 22407-7743. 540/898-2116.

Standard Drug Co.
PO Box 27561, Richmond VA 23261-7561. 804/355-7426.

LIQUOR STORES

Liquor Plus
2054 3rd Ave, Huntington WV 25703-1109. 304/522-7630.

SPORTING GOODS STORES

A&N Store
The Plaza, Lynchburg VA 24501. 804/845-5544.

Athletic Attic
Spotsylvania Mall, Fredericksbrg VA 22407. 540/786-8444.

Britches Of Georgetowne
Arlington Fashion Center, Arlington VA 22202. 703/415-2300.

CMT Sporting Goods
3441 Brandon Ave SW, Roanoke VA 24018-1521. 540/343-5533.

CP Dean & Co. Inc.
3015 Cutshaw Ave, Richmond VA 23230-5108. 804/355-5796.

Champ's Sports
132 Southpark Cir, Colonial Hgts VA 23834-2963. 804/526-0660.

Champ's Sports
11500 Midlothian Trpk, Richmond VA 23235. 804/794-4992.

Famous Footwear
9774 Midlothian Tpke, Richmond VA 23235-4974. 804/330-0414.

Famous Footwear
5116 Southpoint Pky, Fredericksbrg VA 22407-2661. 540/891-7758.

Hermans World Of Sporting Goods
6787 Springfield Mall, Springfield VA 22150-1704. 703/971-8303.

Koenig Sports
290 Spotsylvania Mall, Fredericksbrg VA 22407-1125. 540/786-9555.

Score Sportswear
New River Valley Mall, Christiansbrg VA 24073. 540/382-0991.

Score Sportswear
4802 Valley View Blvd NW, Roanoke VA 24012-2019. 540/366-3737.

The Nike Factory Store
5707 Richmond Rd, Williamsburg VA 23188-1929. 804/565-2963.

Dr. Golf Inc.
3534 Electric Rd, Roanoke VA 24018-4453. 540/774-6867.

BOOKSTORES

Family Bookstores
11500 Midlothian Tpke, Richmond VA 23235-4761. 804/794-8716.

Razzoli International Bookstore
423 W Duke Of Gloucester St, Williamsburg VA 23185-3602. 804/229-9821.

Tech Bookstore
118 S Main St, Blacksburg VA 24060-4898. 540/552-6444.

STATIONERY AND OFFICE SUPPLY STORES

Staples Inc.
9470 Arlington Blvd, Fairfax VA 22031-2402. 703/591-7287.

OfficeMax
1372 Towne Square Blvd NW, Roanoke VA 24012-1619. 540/265-0644.

OfficeMax
749 Hilltop North Shopping Ctr, Virginia Beach VA 23451-6198. 804/428-1200.

Joyce Office Products Centers
1101 E Laburnum Ave, Richmond VA 23222-2212. 804/329-3561.

Lucas Virginia
1600 Roseneath Rd, Richmond VA 23230-4449. 804/354-0796.

Office City
Gateway Village, Fredericksbrg VA 22401. 540/899-2088.

Office Depot Inc.
1991 Chain Bridge Rd, McLean VA 22102-4407. 703/821-8371.

JEWELRY STORES

Charge Jewelers
Military Circle Shopping Center, Norfolk VA 23502. 804/455-8244.

Claire's Boutique
Newmarket Fair, Newport News VA 23605. 804/826-7496.

Fink's Jewelers
1404 E Parham Rd, Richmond VA 23228-2300. 804/741-3131.

Gemstone Jewelers
10101 Brook Rd, Ste 1012, Glen Allen VA 23060-6523. 804/261-0242.

Gold N Gifts
Valley Mall, Harrisonburg VA 22801. 540/564-0613.

Henebrys Jewelers
Martinsburg Mall, Martinsburg WV 25401. 304/264-8717.

Impostors
1100 S Hayes St, Arlington VA 22202-4907. 703/415-2460.

Morton's Jewelers
Chesterfield Mall, Richmond VA 23235. 804/794-4669.

Morton's Jewelers
1060 Temple Ave, Colonial Hgts VA 23834-2981. 804/520-9809.

Piercing Pagoda
Military Circle Shopping Center, Norfolk VA 23502. 804/461-6052.

Piercing Pagoda Inc.
Charleston Town Ctr, Charleston WV 25389. 304/344-8375.

Schwarzschild Jewelers
3124 W Cary St, Richmond VA 23221-3504. 804/355-2136.

Shaw's Jewelers
895 Huntington Mall, Barboursville WV 25504-1832. 304/733-0727.

Silver & Gold Connection
Chesterfield Towne Center, Richmond VA 23235. 804/379-4346.

HOBBY, TOY, AND GAME SHOPS

Toy Liquidators
6401 Richmond Rd, Williamsburg VA 23188-7202. 804/565-0528.

Frank's Nursery & Crafts
1257 Jefferson Davis Hwy, Fredericksbrg VA 22401-4415. 540/371-3232.

Michaels-Arts & Crafts
4300 Portsmouth Blvd, Chesapeake VA 23321-2137. 804/465-8800.

CAMERA AND PHOTOGRAPHIC SUPPLY STORES

Ritz Camera Center
8300 Sudley Rd, Manassas VA 22110-3458. 703/368-7676.

Ritz Camera Center
1069 Charleston Town Ctr, Charleston WV 25389-1069. 304/345-3787.

Ritz Camera Center
722 Hilltop North Shopping Ctr, Virginia Beach VA 23451-6198. 804/422-2750.

Ritz Camera Center
1401 Greenbrier Pky, Chesapeake VA 23320-2830. 804/424-3904.

Ritz Camera Center
600 King St, Alexandria VA 22314-3106. 703/683-1194.

Ritz Camera Center
Ballston Common Malls, Arlington VA 22203. 703/243-6877.

Ritz Camera Center
Clover Leaf Mall, Richmond VA 23225. 804/276-9072.

Ritz Camera Center
Fountain Square Shoppers World, Richmond VA 23229. 804/747-9535.

GIFT, NOVELTY, AND SOUVENIR SHOPS

Scribbles
2045 Charleston Town Ctr, Charleston WV 25389. 304/342-5756.

The Pampered Party
Gateway Village Shopping Center, Fredericksbrg VA 22401. 540/373-2806.

Elm Tree Cards & Gifts
1925 E Market St, Harrisonburg VA 22801-3432. 540/433-0831.

Heidi's Hallmark Cards & Gifts
406 Grand Central Mall, Parkersburg WV 26101-1112. 304/485-3405.

Kirkland's
Valley View Mall, Roanoke VA 24012. 540/366-4188.

Lenox Factory Outlet
3032 Richmond Rd, Williamsburg VA 23185-2001. 804/565-0800.

San Francisco Music Box Company
640 Huntington Mall, Barboursville WV 25504-1830. 304/736-1126.

Spencer Gifts
Greenbrier Mall, Chesapeake VA 23320. 804/424-2984.

The Disney Store
Regency Square, Richmond VA 23229. 804/740-8034.

Welcome Home
5709 Richmond Rd, Williamsburg VA 23188-1929. 804/565-0030.

If It's Paper
5760 Northampton Blvd, Ste 116, Virginia Beach VA 23455-3728. 804/460-2354.

Rainbow Bay Craft
Seminole Square Shopping Ctr, Charlottesvle VA 22901. 804/974-6800.

Card Cage
Fashion Sq Mall, Charlottesvle VA 22901. 804/973-7768.

LUGGAGE AND LEATHER GOODS STORES

Hamilton Luggage & Handbags
2700 Potomac Mills Cir, Ste 755, Woodbridge VA 22192-4625. 703/491-8241.

SEWING SUPPLIES STORES

Cloth World
227 Wadsworth Dr, Richmond VA 23236-4510. 804/330-0396.

Jo-Ann Fabrics & Crafts
Battlefield Shopping Center, Leesburg VA 22075. 703/771-7850.

Jo-Ann Fabrics & Crafts
Riverview Shopping Center, N Martinsville WV 26155. 304/455-1928.

Piece Goods Shop
9051 W Broad St, Richmond VA 23294-5839. 804/270-9701.

Piece Goods Shop
360 West Shopping Center, Richmond VA 23235. 804/745-9830.

Piece Goods Shop
3330 S Crater Rd, Petersburg VA 23805-9277. 804/732-9487.

Total Crafts Stores
13653-B Lee Jackson Hwy, Chantilly VA 22021. 703/817-0770.

Yarns Etcetera
215 King St, Alexandria VA 22314-3209. 703/548-3508.

CATALOG AND MAIL-ORDER HOUSES

Crutchfield Corp.
1 Crutchfield Park, Charlottesvle VA 22911-9097. 804/973-1811.

Evans Distributors & Jewelers Inc.
13055 Lee Jackson Memorial Hwy, Fairfax VA 22033-2001. 703/817-1700.

Total Fulfillment Services
3342 Melrose Ave Nw, Roanoke VA 24017-5910. 540/345-7640.

OPTICAL GOODS STORES

For Eyes Optical Co.
509 N Military Hwy, Norfolk VA 23502-3622. 804/466-1116.

FUEL DEALERS

Commonwealth Propane
800 Moorefield Park Drive, Richmond VA 23236-3659. 804/323-5300.

Massey Coal Services
300 Kanawha Blvd E, Ste 400, Charleston WV 25301. 304/345-3556.

FLORISTS

Farm Fresh-House Of Flowers
2110 W Great Neck Rd, Virginia Beach VA 23451-1504. 804/481-6298.

MISC. RETAIL STORES

Books-A-Million
2700 Potomac Mills Cir, Woodbridge VA 22192-4625. 703/490-3809.

Cracker Barrel Old Country Store
200 Bypass Rd, Williamsburg VA 23185-2921. 804/220-3384.

Crate & Barrel
Tysons Corner Center, McLean VA 22102. 703/847-8555.

Crystal & China
3044 Richmond Rd, Williamsburg VA 23185-2013. 804/565-3476.

Anne Klein Outlet
5699 Richmond Rd, Ste 14, Williamsburg VA 23188-1941. 804/565-0250.

Top Of The Line Cosmetics
5699 Richmond Rd, Ste 20, Williamsburg VA 23188-1941. 804/564-9452.

Electrahome
400 S Washington St, Winchester VA 22601-4033. 540/678-1200.

H&R Office Products
3607 Saunders Ave, Richmond VA 23227-4354. 804/796-6292.

Northern Handyman Headquarters
116 S Independence Blvd, Virginia Beach VA 23462-3803. 804/552-0726.

Hearx Ltd
5701 Midlothian Tpke, Richmond VA 23225-6115. 804/232-1146.

Ferguson Enterprises
2903 Commerce St, Blacksburg VA 24060-6602. 540/953-1258.

Hajoca Corp.
701 Washington St W, Charleston WV 25302-1803. 304/344-2556.

Moores Lumber and Building Supply
1502 Grand Central Ave, Vienna WV 26105-1057. 304/295-8571.

Rigorno Sunglass Elegance
Tysons Cornor Center, McLean VA 22101. 703/556-0216.

Sun Gear
7201 Midlothian Tpke, Richmond VA 23225-6603. 804/276-8575.

For more information on career opportunities in retail:

Directories

AUTOMOTIVE NEWS MARKET DATA BOOK
Automotive News, Crain Communication, 1400 Woodbridge Avenue, Detroit MI 48207-3187. 313/446-6000.

Associations

NATIONAL INDEPENDENT AUTOMOTIVE DEALERS ASSOCIATION
2521 Brown Boulevard, Suite 100, Arlington TX 76006. 817/640-3838.

INTERNATIONAL COUNCIL OF SHOPPING CENTERS
665 Fifth Avenue, New York NY 10022. 212/421-8181. Offers conventions, research, education, a variety of publications, and awards programs.

INTERNATIONAL ASSOCIATION OF CHAIN STORES
3800 Moor Place, Alexandria VA 22305. 703/549-4525.

NATIONAL RETAIL FEDERATION
325 7th Street NW, Suite 1000, Washington DC 20004. 202/783-7971. Provides information services, industry outlooks, and a variety of educational opportunities and publications pertaining to the retail industry.

STONE, CLAY, GLASS, AND CONCRETE PRODUCTS

Growth in stone, clay, glass, concrete, and related materials is closely tied to the success of the construction industry. On the one hand, analysts believe that the fortunes of the construction industry should remain solid in the short term, despite the added pressure of an economy that has cooled from its torrid pace of growth in 1994 and early 1995. On the other hand, the longer-term forecast is for much slower growth, since infrastructure construction is dependent on declining local government budgets. In general, the stone, clay, glass, and concrete industry should see revenue growth of about 1 to 2 percent annually over the next few years.

AFG INDUSTRIES, INC.
Route 3, Box 151N, Bridgeport WV 26330. 304/739-4355. **Contact:** Michael Morris, Human Resources Manager. **Description:** AFG Industries, Inc. is a nationwide flat glass manufacturer. **Common positions include:** Accountant/Auditor; Blue-Collar Worker Supervisor; Ceramics Engineer; Civil Engineer; Electrical/Electronics Engineer; Human Resources Specialist; Mechanical Engineer; Operations/Production Manager. **Educational backgrounds include:** Accounting; Engineering. **Benefits:** Disability Coverage; Life Insurance; Medical Insurance; Pension Plan; Profit Sharing; Savings Plan; Tuition Assistance. **Corporate headquarters location:** Kingsport TN.

AMERICAN FLAT GLASS DISTRIBUTORS, INC. (AFGD)
6200 Gorman Road, Richmond VA 23231. 804/222-0120. **Fax:** 804/226-1859. **Contact:** Don Armstrong, Branch Manager. **Description:** American Flat Glass Distributors specializes in architectural insulated units and custom tempering. The firm manufactures a complete line of insulated units for commercial and residential applications. The product line includes clear, tint, and reflective float glass; laminated, low-emissivity, tempered, acrylic, mirror, obscure, insulated, and polished wire glass; as well as a complete line of glass handling, storage, and transportation equipment. Since 1983, when Southern Wholesale Glass was purchased by AFG and renamed American Flat Glass Distributors, the company has grown from nine locations and 400 employees into today's 19 locations with 1,000 workers. The company has a computerized order entry systems which allows almost immediate production on orders, and stock orders are turned around in roughly 24 hours. **Common positions include:** Blue-Collar Worker Supervisor; Branch Manager; Ceramics Engineer; Clerical Supervisor; Credit Manager; Customer Service Representative; Industrial Engineer; Industrial Production Manager; Management Trainee; Manufacturer's/Wholesaler's Sales Rep.; Materials Engineer; Mechanical Engineer; Metallurgical Engineer; Operations/Production Manager. **Educational backgrounds include:** Business Administration; Engineering; Finance; Marketing; Sales. **Benefits:** 401K; Disability Coverage; Life Insurance; Medical Insurance; Profit Sharing; Savings Plan; Tuition Assistance. **Corporate headquarters location:** Atlanta GA. **Other U.S. locations:** Nationwide. **Parent company:** AFG Industries. **Operations at this facility include:** Manufacturing; Sales. **Listed on:** Privately held. **Number of employees at this location:** 75. **Number of employees nationwide:** 1,000.

BGF INDUSTRIES INC.
401 Amherst Avenue, Altavista VA 24517-1513. 804/369-4751. **Contact:** Bob Childress, Human Resources Manager. **Description:** A manufacturer of industrial fiberglass cloths.

CORNING INC.
265 Corning Drive, Danville VA 24541-6262. 804/793-9511. **Contact:** Personnel. **Description:** This location is a manufacturing plant. Corning Inc. is a diverse manufacturer of specialty glass and glass ceramic products in specialty materials, consumer products, and fiber optic cable. Brand names include Corning and Pyrex kitchenware. The company produces over 60,000 products through 45 plants in eight countries. Corning also offers medical laboratory services through 62 facilities in 10 countries.

LAFARGE CORPORATION
11130 Sunrise Valley Drive, Suite 300, Reston VA 22091. 703/264-3600. **Contact:** Human Resources. **Description:** Lafarge Corporation produces cement, concrete, aggregates, and related products in the United States and in Canada through its subsidiary, Lafarge Canada Inc. The company operates 15 full-production cement plants and 420 construction materials facilities. Subsidiary Systech Environmental Corporation is a processor and recycler of industrial waste products into fuel for the cement kilns. **NOTE:** Lafarge Corporation does not hire at this location, except for local administrative positions. **Corporate headquarters location:** This Location. **Listed on:** New York Stock Exchange. **Number of employees nationwide:** 6,470.

LOUIE GLASS
Route 3, Box 5D, Weston WV 26452. 304/269-4700. **Contact:** Karen Carson, Human Resources Office. **Description:** Produces hand-blown crystal glassware. **Corporate headquarters location:** This Location.

SCHULLER INTERNATIONAL
2905 3rd Avenue, P.O. Box 5130, Vienna WV 26105. 304/295-9361. **Contact:** John Privitera, Manager/Employee Relations. **Description:** Schuller International manufactures glass and fiberglass for automotive and commercial industries. **Common positions include:** Accountant/Auditor; Ceramics Engineer; Computer Programmer; Customer Service Representative; Department Manager; Draftsperson; Electrical/Electronics Engineer; Industrial Engineer; Mechanical Engineer; Operations/Production Manager. **Educational backgrounds include:** Accounting; Business Administration; Engineering; Finance; Industrial Relations; Personnel Relations. **Benefits:** Accident Insurance; Dental Insurance; Disability Coverage; Employee Discounts; Life Insurance; Medical Insurance; Pension Plan; Prescription Drugs; Savings Plan; Tuition Assistance. **Operations at this facility include:** Manufacturing.

VULCAN MATERIALS COMPANY
P.O. Box 509, Manassas VA 22110. 703/368-3135. **Contact:** Ms. Robin Hollyfield, Plant Clerk. **Description:** Produces crushed stone for construction applications. **Listed on:** New York Stock Exchange.

Note: *Because addresses and telephone numbers of smaller companies change rapidly, we recommend you call each company to verify the information below before inquiring about job opportunities. Mass mailings are not recommended.*

Additional small employers:

CRUSHED AND BROKEN STONE

Blue Ridge Stone Corp.
PO Box 13527, Roanoke VA 24035-3527. 540/344-6601.

E. Dillon and Co.
PO Box 160, Swords Creek VA 24649-0160. 540/873-6816.

Eastern Ridge Lime Co.
PO Box 34, Ripplemead

VA 24150-0034. 540/626-7186.

Chantilly Crushed Stone Inc.
RR 50, Fairfax VA 22033-9850. 703/471-4461.

ASPHALT

APAC-Virginia Inc.
239 Eastwood Dr, Danville VA 24540-4940. 804/792-4211.

APAC-Virginia Inc.
3600 Warboro Rd, Midlothian VA 23112-3900. 804/744-1135.

APAC-Virginia Inc.
8738 Vulcan Ln, Manassas VA 22110-3951. 703/968-6370.

Adams Construction Co.
523 Rutherford Ave NE, Roanoke VA 24016-2117. 703/982-2366.

Rea Construction Co.
3425 Westminster Ave, Norfolk VA 23504-4618. 804/622-4200.

The United Co.
PO Box 1280, Bristol VA 24203-1280. 540/466-3322.

GLASS AND GLASS PRODUCTS

Blenko Glass Co. Inc.
PO Box 67, Milton WV 25541-0067. 304/743-9081.

Fourco Glass Co.
RR 3 Box 151N, Bridgeport WV 26330-9411. 304/739-4355.

Anchor Glass Container
PO Box 968, Keyser WV 26726-0968. 304/788-4055.

Fenton Art Glass Co.
700 Elizabeth St, Williamstown WV 26187-1050. 304/375-6122.

Mid Atlantic Of West VA
PO Box 279, Ellenboro WV 26346-0279. 304/869-3351.

Pilgrim Glass Corp.
Airport Rd, Ceredo WV 25507. 304/453-3553.

Schott Scientific Glass Inc.
1624 Staunton Ave, Parkersburg WV 26101-5044. 304/422-6531.

American Mirror Company
PO Box 1277, Galax VA 24333-1277. 540/236-5111.

Consolidated Glass & Mirror
110 Jack Guynn Dr, Galax VA 24333-2534. 540/236-5196.

Eagle Convex Glass Co.
PO Box 1340, Clarksburg WV 26302-1340. 304/624-7461.

Opton Inc.
251 Enterprise Dr, Newport News VA 23603-1335. 804/888-0700.

Virginia Mirror Company
PO Box 5431, Martinsville VA 24115-5431. 540/632-9816.

CEMENT

Capitol Cement Corp.
South Queen St, Martinsburg WV 25401. 304/267-8966.

Riverton Investment Corp.
158 Front Royal Pike, Ste 305, Winchester VA 22602-4371. 540/722-4333.

Roanoke Cement Co.
S R 779, Cloverdale VA 24077. 540/992-1501.

TILE

Brick and Tile Corp.
PO Box 45, Lawrenceville VA 23868-0045. 804/848-3151.

General Shale Brick
RR 4 Box 127, Marion VA 24354-9400. 540/783-3159.

Glen-Gery Corp.
9905 Godwin Dr, Manassas VA 22111-4920. 703/368-3178.

CONCRETE, GYPSUM, AND PLASTER PRODUCTS

Betco Block & Products Inc.
5291 Wellington Rd, Gainesville VA 22065-1616. 703/754-9009.

Concrete Structures Inc.
1650 Darbytown Rd, Richmond VA 23231-4021. 804/222-8111.

Alcon
PO Box 49, Clarksburg WV 26302-0049. 304/622-5351.

American Marietta
22 Industrial Blvd, Parkersburg WV 26101-9732. 304/464-4888.

Arban & Carosi Inc.
13800 Dawson Beach Rd, Woodbridge VA 22191-1497. 703/491-5121.

Bayshore Concrete Products Corp.
PO Box 230, Cape Charles VA 23310-0230. 804/331-2300.

Concrete Pipe & Products
2900 Terminal Ave, Richmond VA 23234-1632. 804/233-5471.

Exposaic Industries Inc.
4717 Massaponax Church Rd, Fredericksbrg VA 22408-8751. 540/898-1221.

Reservco Inc.
2010 Corporate Rdg, Mc Lean VA 22102-7838. 703/821-1175.

Tindall Concrete VA Inc.
5400 Olgers Rd, Petersburg VA 23803-6884. 804/861-8447.

Valley Blox Inc.
210 Stone Spring Rd, Harrisonburg VA 22801-9651. 540/434-6725.

Alcon
U S 33 W, Elkins WV 26241. 304/622-5351.

Cardinal Concrete Co.
6860 Commercial Dr, Springfield VA 22151-4201. 703/354-6322.

Falcon Concrete Corp.
8115 Mims St, Lorton VA 22079-2412. 703/550-6163.

JF Allen Co.
Davisson Run Rd, Clarksburg WV 26301. 304/623-3336.

Tarmac America Inc.
13873 Park Center Rd, Herndon VA 22071-3223. 703/481-3104.

Tidewater Materials
2100 Deepwater Terminal Rd, Richmond VA 23234-1816. 804/232-1200.

Virginia Concrete Co.
6860 Commercial Dr, Springfield VA 22151-4201. 703/354-7100.

APG Lime Corp.
S R 635, Ripplemead VA 24150. 540/626-7163.

Chemstone Corporation
1696 Oranda Rd, Strasburg VA 22657. 540/465-5161.

United States Gypsum Company
1001 Buchanan St, Norfolk VA 23523. 804/545-2461.

United States Gypsum Company
RR 1 Box 7, Saltville VA 24370-9602. 540/496-7733.

CUT STONE AND STONE PRODUCTS

Virginia Marble Manufacturers
Hwy 138, Kenbridge VA 23944. 804/676-3204.

POTTERY PRODUCTS

Williamsburg Pottery Factory
U S Route 60, Lightfoot VA 23090. 804/564-3326.

For more information on career opportunities in stone, clay, glass, and concrete products:

Associations

THE AMERICAN CERAMIC SOCIETY
735 Ceramic Place, Westerville OH 43081. 614/890-4700. Offers a variety of publications, meetings, information, and educational services. Also operates Ceramic Futures, an employment service with a resume database.

NATIONAL GLASS ASSOCIATION
8200 Greensboro Drive, Suite 802, McLean VA 22102. 703/442-4890.

Magazines

GLASS MAGAZINE
National Glass Association, 8200 Greensboro Drive, McLean VA 22102. 703/442-4890.

ROCK PRODUCTS
MacLean Hunter Publishing Company, 29 North Wacker Drive, Chicago IL 60606. 312/726-2805.

TRANSPORTATION

According to Labor Department estimates the number of jobs in the air transportation industry will increase faster than average. Passenger and cargo traffic should increase in response to a rise in population, incomes and business activity. Employment in other air transport activities will also increase as more aircraft are purchased for business, agriculture, and recreation. Despite this expected growth, jobseekers should expect strong competition as the number of applicants for airline jobs exceeds the number of jobs available. Not only are airline jobs highly sought after, but the industry has been going through a period of consolidation, and today more and more of the business is concentrated with a handful of the major carriers, such as American, Delta, and USAir.

In the trucking and warehousing industry, the number of jobs created is very closely related to the health of the national economy. Competition in the industry is intense, both among truckers and with the railroads. Trucking companies compete by slashing rates or offering more customized service. Motor carriers must quote rates high enough to cover costs but low enough to remain competitive. Still, job opportunities for truckers are expected to be good. In some areas, companies have had trouble recruiting well-trained drivers. Although some routes have switched to intermodal transportation and recent downturns in the economy have eased some driver shortages, turnover is relatively high. That should ensure a steady supply of jobs.

On the railroads, the use of both freight and passenger rail will climb. And according to the U.S. Commerce Department, increased trade and stronger freight rates should help the performance of U.S. flag liner companies operating in the Asian markets. Domestic use of water transportation should also increase, especially between Alaska and the lower 48 states.

AMERICAN TRUCKING ASSOCIATIONS
2200 Mill Road, Alexandria VA 22314. 703/838-1726. **Fax:** 703/836-5880. **Recorded Jobline:** 703/838-1726. **Contact:** Kay Pulchine, Director of Human Resources. **Description:** This national federation of the trucking industry represents all types of trucking companies. It is affiliated with 51 independent state trucking associations and 10 national conferences, which represent particular segments of the trucking industry. The American Trucking Associations (ATA) consist of the Executive Office, the Foundation, and five divisions: Communications, Federation Relations, Law and Finance, Government Affairs, and Membership and Marketing. Included in this structure are seven councils allowing experts in particular aspects of trucking operations to join and interact with their peers. ATA publishes a weekly trade newspaper titled Transport Topics. **Common positions include:** Customer Service Representative; Marketing Specialist; Transportation/Traffic Specialist; Writer. **Educational backgrounds include:** Accounting; Business Administration; Communications; Economics; Finance; Marketing; Public Policy; Transportation/Logistics. **Benefits:** Dental Insurance; Disability Coverage; Employee Discounts; Life Insurance; Medical Insurance; Pension Plan; Tuition Assistance. **Corporate headquarters location:** This Location. **Operations at this facility include:** Administration;

Communications; Legal/Legal Research; Marketing; Publishing; Sales; Service. **Number of employees nationwide:** 302.

ATLANTIC COAST AIRLINES, INC.
One Export Drive, Sterling VA 20164. 703/406-6500. **Fax:** 703/406-6599. **Contact:** Cheryl Morrow, Director of Human Resources. **Description:** Atlantic Coast Airlines, Inc. is the holding company of Atlantic Coast Airlines, one of the largest regional airlines operating in the United States, serving 41 destinations in 16 states with approximately 430 scheduled departures each weekday. Atlantic Coast Airlines, operating as United Express, serves the eastern United States in the areas between Maine, Ohio, and South Carolina, from its hub at Dulles International Airport. The company has 55 aircraft and is growing. **Corporate headquarters location:** This Location. **Listed on:** NASDAQ. **Number of employees nationwide:** 1,240.

CI TRAVEL
CRUISE INTERNATIONAL
501 Front Street, Norfolk VA 23510. 804/627-8000. **Contact:** Ms. Micki Hawks, Vice President, Retail Travel. **Description:** An ocean cruise line.

CSX CORPORATION
901 East Cary Street, P.O. Box 85629, Richmond VA 23285-5629. 804/782-1400. **Contact:** Linda Amato, Manager. **Description:** An operator of container ship lines, railcars, and barges, CSX also provides intermodal and logistics services, operates two resorts, and conducts real estate activities. The company's rail systems consists of 18,779 miles of track in 20 states and Ontario, Canada. **Corporate headquarters location:** This Location. **Subsidiaries include:** Sea-Land Service, which conducts operations in 100 ports in 70 countries with 83 vessels and over 160,000 containers; CSX Intermodal, Inc.; Customized Transportation Inc.; and American Commercial Lines, with a fleet of 3,353 barges and 123 tug boats. **Listed on:** New York Stock Exchange.

DYNAIR SERVICES INC.
2000 Edmund Halley Drive, Reston VA 22091. 703/264-9500. **Contact:** William Rodriguez, Vice President of Human Resources. **Description:** Provides a wide range of ground services for airlines and airports. **Corporate headquarters location:** Jamaica NY. **Parent company:** Dynalectron Corporation.

GENERAL DYNAMICS CORPORATION
3190 Fairview Park Drive, Falls Church VA 22042-4523. 703/876-3000. **Contact:** Mr. Wylie, Corporate Vice President, Human Resources. **Description:** A producer of nuclear submarines and land systems. General Dynamics has two main divisions. The Electric Boat Division designs and builds nuclear submarines, including the Seawolf class attack submarine and the New Attack submarine due to go into production in 1998. The Land Systems Division designs and builds armored vehicles, such as the M1 series of battle tanks, for the U.S. Army, the U.S. Marine Corps, and a number of international customers. The company has submarine manufacturing facilities in New Jersey, Connecticut, South Carolina, and Rhode Island and tank production facilities in Ohio and Michigan. The company also has coal mining operations located primarily in central Illinois, provides ship management services for the U.S. government on propositioning and ready reserve ships, and leases liquefied natural gas tankers. **Common positions include:** Accountant/Auditor; Secretary. **Educational backgrounds include:** Accounting; Business Administration; Finance. **Benefits:** Dental Insurance; Disability Coverage; Life Insurance; Medical Insurance; Pension Plan; Profit Sharing; Savings Plan. **Corporate headquarters location:** This Location. **Listed on:** New York Stock Exchange. **Number of employees at this location:** 60. **Number of employees nationwide:** 24,200.

LANDSTAR SYSTEM, INC.
6225 Brandon Avenue, Suite 320, Springfield VA 22150. 703/912-6808. **Toll-free phone:** 800/443-6808. **Contact:** Human Resources. **Description:** The government transportation services office of one of the largest multi-modal transportation service companies in North America. The company is divided into specialized freight transportation segments. Its business is a mix of regular accounts and spot hauls, with the top 100 clients generating more than one-third of the revenue. Landstar is the only publicly traded trucking company relying on independent owner-operators rather than salaried company drivers, with the company owns just 10 percent of the trucks in its fleet. Landstar buys many trucking supplies co-op, so its drivers receive large discounts on trucks, tires, gas and lodging, in addition to getting 75 percent of the gross revenue from a load. **NOTE:** Interested jobseekers should direct inquiries to the corporate headquarters location: Landstar System, Inc., First Shelton Place, 1000 Bridgeport Avenue, P.O. Box 898, Shelton CT 06484. **Corporate headquarters location:** Shelton CT. **Other U.S. locations:** Jacksonville FL; Madisonville KY; Romulus MI. **Subsidiaries include:** Landstar Expedited, Inc., Landstar Express America, Inc., Landstar Gemini, Inc., Landstar Inway, Inc., Landstar ITCO, Inc., Landstar Ligion, Inc., Landstar Poole, Inc., Landstar Ranger, Inc., Landstar T.L.C., Inc., Landstar Transportation Service, Inc. **Number of employees nationwide:** 2,500.

LINDEN MOTOR FREIGHT INC.
506 29th Street, Parkersburg WV 26101. 304/485-0611. **Contact:** Human Resources. **Description:** A trucking company.

METRO MACHINE CORPORATION
P.O. Box 1860, Norfolk VA 23501. 804/543-6801. **Contact:** Don Fisher, Personnel Director. **Description:** A shipyard.

NEWPORT NEWS SHIPBUILDING
Employment, 4101 Washington Avenue, Newport News VA 23607. 804/380-4878. **Fax:** 804/380-3114. **Recorded Jobline:** 804/380-2142. **Contact:** Jay Dunn, Human Resources. **Description:** Engaged in the design, construction, repair, overhaul, and refueling of conventional and nuclear-powered merchant and naval surface ships and submarines. **Common positions include:** Accountant/Auditor; Budget Analyst; Buyer; Civil Engineer; Computer Programmer; Computer Systems Analyst; Cost Estimator; Designer; Draftsperson; Electrical/Electronics Engineer; Environmental Engineer; Financial Analyst; Human Resources Specialist; Industrial Engineer; Materials Engineer; Mechanical Engineer; Medical Records Technician; Metallurgical Engineer; Naval Architect; Nuclear Engineer; Physician; Public Relations Specialist; Registered Nurse; Software Engineer; Structural Engineer; Technical Writer/Editor. **Educational backgrounds include:** Engineering. **Benefits:** 401K; Daycare Assistance; Dental Insurance; Disability Coverage; Employee Discounts; Life Insurance; Medical Insurance; Pension Plan; Tuition Assistance. **Corporate headquarters location:** This Location. **Parent company:** Tenneco, Inc. **Operations at this facility include:** Administration; Divisional Headquarters; Manufacturing; Research and Development. **Listed on:** New York Stock Exchange. **Number of employees at this location:** 20,000.

NORFOLK SHIPBUILDING AND DRYDOCK CORPORATION
P.O. Box 2100, Norfolk VA 23501. 804/494-4000. **Contact:** Mary Sharp, Human Resource Manager. **Description:** Involved in the building, wrecking, and repairing of commercial ships. Norfolk Shipbuilding and Drydock Corporation houses three docks. **Number of employees at this location:** 2,500.

NORFOLK SOUTHERN CORPORATION
223 East City Hall Avenue, Suite 208, Norfolk VA 23510. **Fax:** 804/533-4318. **Contact:** Eric Garrison, Senior Employment Officer. **Description:** A *Fortune* 100 transportation company, Norfolk Southern is a holding company

that controls Norfolk Southern Railway, North American Van Lines, and Pocahontas Land Corporation. Rail lines extend through 20 states primarily in the southeast and midwest United States, and Ontario, Canada. **Common positions include:** Accountant/Auditor; Civil Engineer; Computer Programmer; Computer Systems Analyst; Electrical/Electronics Engineer; Mechanical Engineer; Transportation/Traffic Specialist. **Educational backgrounds include:** Accounting; Engineering; Marketing. **Benefits:** 401K; Dental Insurance; Disability Coverage; Life Insurance; Medical Insurance; Tuition Assistance. **Corporate headquarters location:** This Location. **Listed on:** New York Stock Exchange. **Number of employees nationwide:** 27,168.

OVERNITE TRANSPORTATION, INC.
P.O. Box 1216, Richmond VA 23209. 804/231-8000. **Contact:** John Enright, Vice President of Human Resources. **Description:** A trucking company.

QED SYSTEMS, INC.
4646 North Witchduck Road, Virginia Beach VA 23455. 804/490-5000. **Contact:** James Lyons, Human Resource Manager. **Description:** A government contracting facility that was established in 1970. QED Systems, Inc. handles marine engineering, manufactures technical manuals and performs shipboard inspections.

USAIR, INC.
Crystal Park 4, 2345 Crystal Drive, Arlington VA 22227. 703/418-7000. **Contact:** John P. Frestel, Jr., Senior Vice President of Human Resources. **Description:** USAir provides air transportation of passengers, property, and mail; reservations and ground support services to commuter carriers; aircraft remarketing; aircraft appraisal services; general aviation and spare parts sales; fixed-based operations; fuel services; and other aviation-related activities. USAir offers service to 155 cities in the U.S., Canada, the Bahamas, Bermuda, Puerto Rico, the Virgin Islands, France, and Germany. Primary hubs are in Charlotte, Pittsburgh, Baltimore/Washington, and Philadelphia. **Parent company:** USAir Group, Inc. is a transportation holding company with regional, national, and international scheduled air services and express cargo operations. **Corporate headquarters location:** This Location. **Subsidiaries include:** USAir Express, USAir Florida Shuttle, and regional carriers Allegheny Commuter Airlines, Piedmont Airlines, and Jetstream International. **Listed on:** New York Stock Exchange.

VINNELL CORPORATION
12150 East Monument Drive, Suite 800, Fairfax VA 22033-4053. 703/385-4544. **Contact:** William Cobb, Corporate Director, Human Resources. **Description:** An arranger of transportation of freight and cargo. **Number of employees at this location:** 1,000.

WORLDCORP
13873 Park Center Road, Suite 490, Herndon VA 22071. 703/834-9200. **Contact:** Barbara Zeiller, Director of Human Resources. **Description:** WorldCorp is the parent company of World Airways, an airline.

Note: *Because addresses and telephone numbers of smaller companies change rapidly, we recommend you call each company to verify the information below before inquiring about job opportunities. Mass mailings are not recommended.*

Additional small employers:

SHIP/BOAT BUILDING AND REPAIRING

Blohm & Voss
5828 Glen Forest Dr, Falls Church VA 22041-2513. 703/845-5679.

Colonna's Shipyard Inc.
400 E Indian River Rd, Norfolk VA 23523-1756. 804/545-2414.

Jonathan Corp.
10205 Colvin Run Rd,

Great Falls VA 22066-1833. 703/759-6400.

Litton
Ingalls Shipbuilding, Arlington VA 22202. 703/418-0300.

Lyon Shipyard Inc.
1818 Brown Ave, Norfolk VA 23504-4458. 804/622-4661.

Marine Hydraulics International Inc.
543 E Indian River Rd, Norfolk VA 23523-1797. 804/545-6400.

Marine Services International Inc.
117 E Princess Anne Rd, Norfolk VA 23510-2621. 804/625-5071.

National Steel & Shipbuilding Co.
2301 Jefferson Davis Hwy, Arlington VA 22202-3820. 703/418-1195.

Pacord Inc.
2117 Springfield Ave, Norfolk VA 23523-2436. 804/461-5900.

Tidewater Equipment Corp.
Rt 104, Chesapeake VA 23320. 804/547-2181.

Xenotechnix Inc.
313 S Main St, Norfolk VA 23523-1131. 804/494-1088.

Associated Naval Architects
3400 Shipwright St, Portsmouth VA 23703-2496. 804/484-5320.

LOCAL AND INTERURBAN PASSENGER TRANSIT

Pentran
3400 Victoria Blvd, Hampton VA 23661-1509. 804/722-2837.

Carolina Trailways
2910 N Boulevard, Richmond VA 23230-4317. 804/355-6178.

Beach Limousine
750 Lord Dunmore Dr, Virginia Beach VA 23464-2662. 804/481-6597.

TRUCKING

Burlington Motor Carriers
1700 Willis Rd, Richmond VA 23237-2911. 804/271-7814.

Carolina Freight Carriers Corp.
6810 Hull Street Rd, Richmond VA 23224-2534. 804/745-0612.

Carpet Transport Inc.
1801 Willis Rd, Ste D, Richmond VA 23237-2968. 804/743-0738.

Estes Express Lines
221 Bollingbrook St, Petersburg VA 23803-3368. 804/733-3923.

Highway Express Inc.
5600 Midlothian Tpke, Richmond VA 23225-6114. 804/232-5600.

Lee Sartin Trucking Co.
Route 52, Naugatuck WV 25685. 304/235-2870.

PGT Trucking Inc.
Rt 89, Proctor WV 26055. 304/455-1033.

Putnam Transfer & Storage Company
504 29th St, Parkersburg WV 26101-1904. 304/428-8135.

Sundown Express Inc.
PO Box 20976, Roanoke VA 24018-0098. 703/450-4133.

Wilson Trucking Corporation
8550 Terminal Rd, Newington VA 22122. 703/550-9622.

Wilson Trucking Corporation
2501 60th Street, Hampton VA 23661-1303. 804/827-8700.

Brooks Transfer & Storage Company
14200 Ustice Rd, Midlothian VA 23113. 804/358-5501.

Grayson Mitchell Inc.
PO Box 128, Emporia VA 23847-0128. 804/634-9159.

Lawrence Transportation Systems
PO Box 13126, Roanoke VA 24031-3126. 540/366-8844.

Liquid Transport Corp.
2209 6th Ave, Charleston WV 25312-1962. 304/346-8300.

Wilson Trucking Corp.
PO Box 200, Fishersville VA 22939-0200. 540/949-3200.

Yeatts Transfer Co.
PO Box 687, Altavista VA 24517-0687. 804/369-5695.

Dunmar Moving Systems
2602 Deepwater Terminal Rd, Richmond VA 23234-1841. 804/233-9235.

Colonial Storage Co.
4500 Southgate Pl, Chantilly VA 22021-1714. 703/802-3416.

DD Jones Transfer & Warehouse Co.
630 22nd St, Chesapeake VA 23324-2612. 804/494-0200.

Graebel Movers International Inc.
7426 Alban Station Blvd, Springfield VA 22150-2323. 703/644-3524.

Paxton Van Lines Inc.
5300 Port Royal Rd, Springfield VA 22151-2112. 703/321-7600.

RAILROAD EQUIPMENT

Plasser American Corp.
2001 Myers Rd, Chesapeake VA 23324-3231. 804/543-3526.

Shippers Car Division/ACF Industries
155 Silver St, Poca WV 25159-9725. 304/755-4611.

WAREHOUSING AND STORAGE

Allied Warehousing
20 26th St, Huntington

WV 25703-1233. 304/523-2131.

Continental Terminal Inc.
3440 Trant Ave, Norfolk VA 23502-3117. 804/487-5354.

Lambert's Point Docks Inc.
PO Box 89, Norfolk VA 23501-0089. 804/446-1200.

Storaway Self Storage
636 N Witchduck Rd, Virginia Beach VA 23462-1917. 804/499-5779.

MAINTENANCE FACILITIES FOR MOTOR FREIGHT TRANSPORTATION

Conoco Inc.
5517 Midland Dr, Charleston WV 25306-6138. 304/925-6233.

WATER TRANSPORTATION OF FREIGHT

DSR-Senator Agency
201 E City Hall Ave, Norfolk VA 23510-1724. 804/625-7725.

United Arab Shipping Company
1 Greenbrier Point 1401 Greenb, Chesapeake VA 23320. 804/523-2775.

Port Amherst Ltd
2 Port Amherst Dr, Charleston WV 25306-6637. 304/926-1100.

MARINE CARGO HANDLING

Cooper-Smith Stevedoring
2400 Wesley St, Portsmouth VA 23707-1717. 804/393-6970.

ITO Corporation Of Virginia
7737 Hampton Blvd, Rm 214, Norfolk VA 23505-1200. 804/489-7327.

TOWING AND TUGBOAT SERVICES

Allied Towing Corp.
500 E Indian River Rd, Norfolk VA 23523-1718. 804/545-7301.

Kanawha River Towing
State Rt 2, Pt Pleasant WV 25550. 304/675-4545.

AIR TRANSPORTATION AND SERVICES

Continental Airlines
16th & K St NW, Alexandria VA 22314. 703/478-9700.

Worldwide Airline Services
1443 Emerson Ave, McLean VA 22101-5706. 703/356-5515.

PASSENGER TRANSPORTATION ARRANGEMENT SERVICES

Carlson Wagonlit Travel
600 Army Navy Dr, Arlington VA 22202-4208. 703/418-1095.

Land'Or International
7814 Carousel Ln, Ste 200, Richmond VA 23294-4213. 804/346-8200.

Scheduled Airline Traffic Office
1005 N Glebe Rd, Arlington VA 22201-4751. 703/358-1200.

Travel Services Group
1500 King St, Ste 200, Alexandria VA 22314-2730. 703/684-2777.

US Travel
4200 Wilson Blvd, Arlington VA 22203-1800. 703/524-5900.

VIP Travel Agency
450 W Broad St, Ste 117, Falls Church VA 22046-3318. 703/534-3377.

Spirit Cruises
501 Front St, Norfolk VA 23510-1009. 804/627-2900.

Business Destinations
1011 Boulder Springs Dr, Richmond VA 23225-4950. 804/323-6848.

PACKING AND CRATING

Transus Freight
801 Broad St, #105, Portsmouth VA 23707-2000. 804/398-9331.

MISC. TRANSPORTATION SERVICES

Port Services Company
999 Wagner Rd, Petersburg VA 23805. 804/732-5119.

WHOLESALE OF TRANSPORTATION EQUIPMENT AND SUPPLIES

Airbus Industries Of North America
593 Herndon Pky, Herndon VA 22070-5242. 703/834-3400.

For more information on career opportunities in transportation:

__Associations__

AIR TRANSPORT ASSOCIATION OF AMERICA
1301 Pennsylvania Avenue NW, Suite 1100, Washington DC 20004. 202/626-4000.

AMERICAN BUREAU OF SHIPPING
2 World Trade Center, 106th Floor, New York NY 10048. 212/839-5000.

AMERICAN MARITIME ASSOCIATION
380 Madison Avenue, 17th Floor, New York NY 10017. 212/557-9520. A trade association which offers collection and bargaining services.

AMERICAN SOCIETY OF TRAVEL AGENTS
1101 King Street, Suite 200, Alexandria VA 22314. 703/739-2782. For information, send a SASE

with $.75 postage to the attention of the Fulfillment Department.

AMERICAN TRUCKING ASSOCIATION
2200 Mill Road, Alexandria VA 22314-4677. 703/838-1700.

ASSOCIATION OF AMERICAN RAILROADS
50 F Street NW, Washington DC 20001. 202/639-2100.

FUTURE AVIATION PROFESSIONALS OF AMERICA
4959 Massachusetts Boulevard, Atlanta GA 30337. 404/997-8097. Publishes monthly newsletter which monitors the job market for flying jobs; a pilot employment guide, outlining what is required to become a pilot; and a directory of aviation employers.

INSTITUTE OF TRANSPORTATION ENGINEERS
525 School Street SW, Suite 410, Washington DC 20024-2797. 202/554-8050. Scientific and educational association, providing for professional development of members and others.

MARINE TECHNOLOGY SOCIETY
1828 L Street NW, Suite 906, Washington DC 20036. 202/775-5966.

NATIONAL MARINE MANUFACTURERS ASSOCIATION
401 North Michigan Avenue, Suite 1150, Chicago IL 60611. 312/836-4747. A partnership of three manufacturer groups: The National Association of Boat Manufacturers; The Association of Marine Engine Manufacturers; and The National Association of Marine Products & Services. Subscription to job listing publication is available for a fee.

NATIONAL MOTOR FREIGHT TRAFFIC ASSOCIATION
2200 Mill Road, Alexandria VA 22314-4654. 703/838-1810. Works towards the improvement and advancement of the interests and welfare of motor common carriers.

NATIONAL TANK TRUCK CARRIERS
2200 Mill Road, Alexandria VA 22314. 703/838-1700. A trade association representing and promoting the interests of the highway bulk transportation community.

Directories

MOODY'S TRANSPORTATION MANUAL
Moody's Investors Service, Inc., 99 Church Street, New York NY 10007. 212/553-0300. $12.95 per year with weekly updates.

NATIONAL TANK TRUCK CARRIER DIRECTORY
2200 Mill Road, Alexandria VA 22314. 703/838-1700.

OFFICIAL MOTOR FREIGHT GUIDE
1700 West Courtland Street, Chicago IL 60622. 312/278-2454.

Magazines

AMERICAN SHIPPER
P.O. Box 4728, Jacksonville FL 32201. 904/355-2601. Monthly.

FLEET OWNER
707 Westchester Avenue, White Plains NY 10604-3102. 914/949-8500.

HEAVY DUTY TRUCKING
Newport Communications, P.O. Box W, Newport Beach CA 92658. 714/261-1636.

ITE JOURNAL
Institute of Transportation Engineers, 525 School Street SW, Suite 410, Washington DC 20024-2797. 202/554-8050. One year subscription (12 issues): $50.

MARINE DIGEST AND TRANSPORTATION NEWS
P.O. Box 3905, Seattle WA 98124. 206/682-3607.

SHIPPING DIGEST
51 Madison Avenue, New York NY 10010. 212/689-4411.

TRAFFIC WORLD MAGAZINE
741 National Press Building, Washington DC 20045. 202/383-6140.

TRANSPORT TOPICS
2200 Mill Road, Alexandria VA 22314. 703/838-1772.

UTILITIES: ELECTRIC/GAS/WATER

With deregulation looming closer and closer, utilities are adjusting by cutting costs and providing better service. This is a good sign for the industry but a bad sign for jobseekers, as employment should remain just about flat. Job prospects in the utilities industry are probably best with large electric utilities, water supply facilities, and sanitary services right now. The most common positions with public utilities are precision production workers and operators, fabricators, and laborers.

MOUNTAINEER GAS COMPANY
1205 Sixth Avenue, Huntington WV 25713. 304/528-2555. **Contact:** Nancy Shelton, Human Resources Director. **Description:** A distributor of natural gas.

NORTHERN VIRGINIA ELECTRIC COOPERATIVE
5399 Wellington Road, Gainesville VA 22065. 703/754-6700. **Contact:** Human Resources. **Description:** An electric utility company. **NOTE:** All employment inquiries should be directed to the Director of Human Resources, Northern Virginia Electric Cooperative, P.O. Box 2710, Manassas VA 22110. 703/631-9873.

SHENANDOAH VALLEY ELECTRIC COOPERATIVE
P.O. Box 236, Mount Crawford VA. 540/434-2200. **Contact:** M.O. Brown, Human Resources Manager. **Description:** An electric utility company.

Note: *Because addresses and telephone numbers of smaller companies change rapidly, we recommend you call each company to verify the information below before inquiring about job opportunities. Mass mailings are not recommended.*

Additional small employers:

ELECTRIC SERVICES

Appalachian Power Company
181 E Jackson St, Gate City VA 24251-3418. 540/386-3851.

Appalachian Power Company
704 Bland St, Bluefield WV 24701-3504. 304/327-3511.

Appalachian Power Company
Rt 35, Saint Albans WV 25177. 304/755-5301.

Central Operating Co.
PO Box 389, New Haven WV 25265-0389. 304/882-3213.

Franklin Municipal Light
1050 Pretlow St, Franklin VA 23851-2067. 804/562-8568.

Liberty Electric Service
10720 Main St, Fairfax VA 22030-3712. 703/273-3427.

Mecklenburg Electric Co-Op
Hwy 92 W, Chase City VA 23924. 804/372-4161.

Monongahela Power Company
1803 Murdoch Ave, Parkersburg WV 26101-3229. 304/422-6421.

Northern VA Electric Cooperative
349 E Market St, Leesburg VA 22075-4102. 703/777-2041.

Northern VA Electric Cooperative
14500 Minnieville Rd, Dale City VA 22193-3216. 703/878-6100.

Northern VA Electric Cooperative
PO Box 2710, Manassas VA 22110-0875. 703631-9873.

Potomac Edison Company
Berkeley County, Martinsburg WV 25401. 304/263-3700.

Potomac Edison Company
RR 11, Winchester VA 22603-9846. 540/665-0115.

Rappahannock Electric
PO Box 7388,

Fredericksbrg VA 22404-7388. 540/898-8500.

Shenandoah Valley Electric Cooperative
PO Box 236, Mt Crawford VA 22841-0236. 540/434-2200.

Southside Electric Cooperative
PO Box 7, Crewe VA 23930-0007. 804/645-7721.

Virginia Power Co.
1719 Hydraulic Rd, Charlottesvle VA 22901-2835. 804/980-6910.

Virginia Power Co.
1199 5th St SW, Charlottesvle VA 22902-6466. 804/980-6918.

Virginia Power Co.
1600 Hamilton Ave, Portsmouth VA 23707-3528. 804/393-3890.

Wheeling Power Co.
51 16th St, #751, Wheeling WV 26003-3672. 304/234-3000.

Chesapeake Energy
2701 Vepco St, Chesapeake VA 23323-6119. 804/485-6700.

Doswell Ltd. Partnership
1051 Technology Park Dr, Glen Allen VA 23060-4500. 804/266-9066.

Possum Point Power Station
19000 Possum Point Rd, Dumfries VA 22026-2802. 703/221-3181.

Potomac River Generating Station
1400 N Royal St, Alexandria VA 22314-1111. 703/838-3721.

Richmond Power Plant
5001 Commerce Rd, Richmond VA 23234-2288. 804/743-9710.

SE Public Service Authority Power Plant
3809 Elm Ave, Portsmouth VA 23704-7101. 804/396-7168.

Willow Island Generating Station
2 Power Station Blvd, Willow Island WV 26134-9726. 304/665-3100.

GAS UTILITY SERVICES

Commonwealth Propane
210 Main, Kenbridge VA 23944. 804/676-8217.

Hope Gas Inc.
1000 Dupont Rd, Morgantown WV 26505-9624. 304/296-8581.

United Cities Gas Company
112 Country Club Dr, Blacksburg VA 24060. 540/951-9184.

Virginia Natural Gas Company
750 Diligence Dr, Newport News VA 23606-4290. 804/873-1322.

Virginia Natural Gas Inc.
5100 East Virginia Boulevard, Norfolk VA 23502. 804/466-5400.

Commonwealth Propane
3323 S Crater Rd, Petersburg VA 23805-9214. 804/732-9223.

For more information on career opportunities in the utilities industry:

Associations

AMERICAN PUBLIC GAS ASSOCIATION
Lee Highway, Suite 102, Fairfax VA 22030. 703/352-3890. Publishes a weekly newsletter.

AMERICAN PUBLIC POWER ASSOCIATION (APPA)
2301 M Street NW, Washington DC 20037. 202/467-2970. Represents publicly-owned utilities. Provides many services including: government relations, educational programs, and industry-related information publications.

AMERICAN WATER WORKS ASSOCIATION
6666 West Quincy Drive, Denver CO 80235. 303/794-7711.

NATIONAL RURAL ELECTRIC COOPERATIVE ASSOCIATION
1800 Massachusetts Avenue NW, Washington DC 20036. 202/857-9500.

Directories

MOODY'S PUBLIC UTILITY MANUAL
Moody's Investors Service, Inc., 99 Church Street, New York NY 10007. 212/553-0300. Annually available at libraries.

Magazines

PUBLIC POWER
2301 M Street NW, Washington DC 20037. 202/467-2900.

EMPLOYMENT SERVICES

NOTE: *While every effort is made to keep the addresses and phone numbers of these companies up-to-date, employment services often move or change hands and are therefore more difficult to track. Please notify the publisher if you find any discrepancies.*

TEMPORARY EMPLOYMENT AGENCIES

ACCOUNTEMPS
1100 Wilson Boulevard, Suite 900, Arlington VA 22209. 703/243-3600. **Contact:** Amy Long, Administrative Staff. **Description:** Temporary agency. **Specializes in the areas of:** Accounting/Auditing.

ADIA TEMPORARY SERVICES
45 West Boscawen, Winchester VA 22601. 540/667-1916. **Contact:** C. Lynn Weakley, Jr., Owner/Manager. **Description:** Temporary agency. **Specializes in the areas of:** Non-Specialized. **Positions commonly filled include:** Administrative Assistant; Advertising Clerk; Bookkeeper; Clerk; Computer Operator; Computer Programmer; Construction Trade Worker; Customer Service Representative; Data Entry Clerk; Draftsperson; EDP Specialist; Factory Worker; Human Resources Specialist; Laboratory Technician; Legal Secretary; Light Industrial Worker; Medical Secretary; Nurse; Quality Assurance Engineer; Receptionist; Secretary; Technician; Typist/Word Processor. Company pays fee. **Number of placements per year:** 200 - 499.

EDP/TEMPS OF VIRGINIA
2095 Chain Bridge Road, Vienna VA 22182. 703/893-2400. **Contact:** Manager. **Description:** Temporary agency. **Specializes in the areas of:** Accounting/Auditing; Administration/MIS/EDP; Banking; Computer Hardware/Software; Engineering; Finance; Insurance; Manufacturing; Non-Profit; Personnel/Labor Relations; Printing/Publishing; Technical and Scientific. **Positions commonly filled include:** Computer Operator; Computer Programmer; EDP Specialist; MIS Specialist; Systems Analyst; Technical Writer/Editor. Company pays fee. **Number of placements per year:** 1000+.

EXPRESS PERSONNEL SERVICES
2155 Electric Road, Suite B, Roanoke VA 24018. 540/776-8729. **Fax:** 540/776-5437. **Contact:** Hartley R. Gaston, Owner. **Description:** Founded in 1995, this is a worldwide temporary agency franchise. **Specializes in the areas of:** Administration/MIS/EDP; Computer Science/Software; Manufacturing; Non-Specialized; Personnel/Labor Relations; Secretarial. **Positions commonly filled include:** Accountant/Auditor; Administrative Services Manager; Blue-Collar Worker Supervisor; Branch Manager; Claim Representative; Clerical Supervisor; Computer Programmer; Computer Systems Analyst; Credit Manager; Customer Service Representative; Draftsperson; General Manager; Human Resources Specialist; Human Service Worker; Industrial Engineer; Industrial Production Manager; Management Analyst/Consultant; Management Trainee; Market Research Analyst; Operations/Production Manager; Paralegal; Property and Real Estate Manager; Public Relations Specialist; Purchasing Agent and Manager; Quality Control Supervisor; Restaurant/Food Service Manager; Software Engineer; Typist/Word Processor; Underwriter/Assistant Underwriter. **Benefits available to temporary workers:** Health; Vacation; Scholarships. **Corporate headquarters location:** Oklahoma City OK. **Average salary range of placements:** $20,000 - $29,999.

EXTRAS SUPPORT STAFFING
1217A Garfield Avenue, Parkersburg WV 26101. 304/485-5200. **Fax:** 304/485-5212. **Contact:** Charlotte King, Manager. **Description:** A temporary and permanent placement agency. **Specializes in the areas of:** Accounting; Banking; Finance; General Management; Industrial; Manufacturing; Personnel/Human Resources; Sales and Marketing; Secretarial; Light Industrial. **Positions commonly filled include:** Accountant/Auditor; Administrative Services Manager; Advertising Clerk; Blue-Collar Worker Supervisor; Branch Manager; Human Resources Specialist; Paralegal; Teacher; Typist/Word Processor. **Benefits available to temporary workers:** Paid Vacation; Paid Holidays. **Number of placements per year:** 1000+. **Average salary range of placements:** less than $20,000.

KELLY TEMPORARY SERVICES
3232 Riverside Drive, Danville VA 24541. 804/791-1597. **Contact:** A. Fulcher, Supervisor. **Description:** Temporary agency. **Specializes in the areas of:** Computer Science/Software; Secretarial. **Positions commonly filled include:** Administrative Assistant; Marketing Specialist; Secretary; Typist/Word Processor. Company pays fee. **Benefits available to temporary workers:** Holiday; Medical; Vacation. **Corporate headquarters location:** Troy MI. **Other U.S. locations:** 1,100 offices worldwide. **Number of placements per year:** 200 - 499. **Average salary range of placements:** less than $20,000.

MANPOWER TEMPORARY SERVICES
605 Jefferson Davis Highway, Fredericksburg VA 22401-4436. 540/373-7801. **Fax:** 540/373-8106. **Contact:** Darla Burton, Branch Manager. **Description:** A full-service temporary agency with many available positions, including temporary to permanent as well as short-term assignments. **Specializes in the areas of:** Industrial; Insurance; Manufacturing; Non-Specialized; Sales and Marketing; Secretarial. **Positions commonly filled include:** Claim Representative; Clerical Supervisor; Customer Service Representative; Industrial Engineer; Insurance Agent/Broker. **Benefits available to temporary workers:** Health Insurance; Life Insurance; Paid Holidays; Paid Vacations. **Corporate headquarters location:** Milwaukee WI. **Other U.S. locations:** Worldwide. **Average salary of placements:** $20,000-$29,999. **Number of placements per year:** 1000+.

MANPOWER TEMPORARY SERVICES
6564 Loisdale Court, #400, Springfield VA 22150. 703/451-8822. **Fax:** 703/451-8910. **Contact:** Kathy Kapsak, Branch Manager. **Description:** Temporary agency. Founded in 1947. **Specializes in the areas of:** Secretarial. **Positions commonly filled include:** Accountant/Auditor; Claim Representative; Clerical Supervisor. **Benefits available to temporary workers:** Medical Insurance; Vacation; Holiday; Recognition Awards. **Corporate headquarters location:** Milwaukee WI. **Other U.S. locations:** 1,000 U.S. offices nationwide. **Number of placements per year:** 1000+. **Average salary range of placements:** $20,000-$29,999.

MANPOWER TEMPORARY SERVICES
8280 Greensboro Drive, Suite 450, McLean VA 22102. 703/821-0101. **Contact:** Recruitment. **Description:** Temporary agency. **Specializes in the areas of:** Clerical; Personnel/Labor Relations; Word Processing. **Positions commonly filled include:** Administrative Assistant; Bookkeeper; Clerk; Customer Service Representative; Data Entry Clerk; Legal Secretary; Secretary; Stenographer; Technical Writer/Editor; Typist/Word Processor. Company pays fee. **Number of placements per year:** 1000+.

TAC/TEMPS INC. OF THE DISTRICT OF COLUMBIA
1700 North Moore Street, Suite 1225, Arlington VA 22209. 703/522-4988. **Contact:** Manager. **Description:** Temporary agency. **Specializes in the areas of:** Accounting/Auditing; Advertising; Banking; Clerical; Education; Finance; Health/Medical; Insurance; Legal; Manufacturing; Non-Profit; Personnel/Labor Relations; Printing/Publishing; Sales and Marketing; Transportation. **Positions**

commonly filled include: Bookkeeper; Clerk; Data Entry Clerk; Driver; Factory Worker; Legal Secretary; Light Industrial Worker; Medical Secretary; Receptionist; Secretary; Typist/Word Processor. Company pays fee. **Number of placements per year:** 1000+.

TAC/TEMPS, INC. OF VIRGINIA
2095 Chain Bridge Road, Vienna VA 22182. 703/893-5260. **Contact:** Manager. **Description:** Temporary agency. **Specializes in the areas of:** Accounting/Auditing; Advertising; Banking; Clerical; Education; Finance; Health/Medical; Insurance; Legal; Manufacturing; Non-Profit; Personnel/Labor Relations; Printing/Publishing; Sales and Marketing; Transportation. **Positions commonly filled include:** Bookkeeper; Clerk; Data Entry Clerk; Driver; Factory Worker; Legal Secretary; Light Industrial Worker; Medical Secretary; Receptionist; Secretary; Typist/Word Processor. Company pays fee. **Number of placements per year:** 1000+.

TECH/AID OF VIRGINIA
2095 Chain Bridge Road, Suite 300, Vienna VA 22182. 703/893-6444. **Contact:** Manager. **Description:** Temporary agency. **Specializes in the areas of:** Architecture/Construction/Real Estate; Cable TV; Computer Hardware/Software; Engineering; Manufacturing; Technical and Scientific. **Positions commonly filled include:** Aerospace Engineer; Architect; Buyer; Ceramics Engineer; Chemical Engineer; Civil Engineer; Draftsperson; Electrical/Electronics Engineer; Estimator; Industrial Designer; Industrial Engineer; Manufacturing Engineer; Mechanical Engineer; Metallurgical Engineer; Mining Engineer; Operations/Production Manager; Petroleum Engineer; Purchasing Agent and Manager; Quality Control Supervisor; Technical Writer/Editor; Technician. Company pays fee. **Number of placements per year:** 1000+.

TELESEC TEMPORARY PERSONNEL OF FALLS CHURCH
6245 Leesburg Pike, Suite 305, Falls Church VA 22044. 703/237-8001. **Contact:** Manager. **Description:** Temporary agency. **Specializes in the areas of:** Non-Specialized. **Positions commonly filled include:** Administrative Assistant; Bookkeeper; Claim Representative; Customer Service Representative; Legal Secretary; Librarian; Library Technician; Light Industrial Worker; Medical Secretary; Receptionist; Secretary; Stenographer; Typist/Word Processor.

PERMANENT EMPLOYMENT AGENCIES

ACTS
10108 Hollingsworth Court, Richmond VA 23235. 804/560-9546. **Contact:** Laurie Sandberg, Administrative Assistant. **Description:** Employment agency. **Specializes in the areas of:** Child Care, In-Home; Eldercare, In-Home. **Positions commonly filled include:** Licensed Practical Nurse; Preschool Worker. Company pays fee. **Number of placements per year:** 50 - 99.

AMERICAN TECHNICAL RESOURCES
1651 Old Meadow Road, Sixth Floor, McLean VA 22102-4308. 703/917-7800. **Contact:** Jim Hollister, Manager of Technical Recruiting. **Description:** Employment agency. **Specializes in the areas of:** Administration/MIS/EDP; Computer Hardware/Software; Defense Industry; Engineering; Military; Technical and Scientific. **Positions commonly filled include:** Account Executive; Computer Operator; Computer Programmer; Computer Scientist; Customer Service Representative; Database Management Specialist; Electrical/Electronics Engineer; MIS Specialist; Operations/Production Manager; Software Engineer; Systems Analyst; Technical Writer/Editor. Company pays fee. **Number of placements per year:** 200 - 499.

CORE PERSONNEL
8201 Greensborough Drive, Suite 100, McLean VA 22102. 703/556-9610. **Contact:** Harvey Silver, President. **Description:** Employment agency. **Specializes in the areas of:** Computer Hardware/Software. **Positions commonly filled include:** Administrative Assistant; Clerk; Computer Programmer; Customer Service Representative; EDP Specialist; Legal Secretary; Medical Secretary; Receptionist; Sales Representative; Secretary; Stenographer; Systems Analyst; Typist/Word Processor. Company pays fee.

H.R. DIRECTIONS
P.O. Box 712, Wytheville VA 24382. 540/228-8337. **Contact:** Faye Sutherland, President. **Description:** Employment agency. **Specializes in the areas of:** Accounting/Auditing; Engineering; Industrial; Manufacturing; Personnel/Labor Relations. **Positions commonly filled include:** Accountant/Auditor; Architect; Blue-Collar Worker Supervisor; Civil Engineer; Clerical Supervisor; Computer Programmer; Customer Service Representative; Draftsperson; Electrical/Electronics Engineer; General Manager; Industrial Engineer; Industrial Production Manager; Insurance Agent/Broker; Mechanical Engineer; Operations/Production Manager; Purchasing Agent and Manager; Quality Control Supervisor; Sales Representative. Company pays fee. **Number of placements per year:** 100 - 199.

HALBRECHT & COMPANY, INC.
10195 Main Street, Suite L, Fairfax VA 22031. 703/359-2880. **Contact:** Thomas Maltby, Vice President. **Description:** Employment agency. **Specializes in the areas of:** Administration/MIS/EDP; Computer Hardware/Software; Technical and Scientific. **Positions commonly filled include:** Actuary; Computer Programmer; EDP Specialist; Electrical/Electronics Engineer; Financial Analyst; Management Analyst/Consultant; Petroleum Engineer; Statistician; Systems Analyst. Company pays fee.

ROBERT HALF INTERNATIONAL
1100 Wilson Boulevard, Suite 900, Arlington VA 22209. 703/243-3600. **Contact:** Manager. **Description:** Employment agency. **Specializes in the areas of:** Accounting/Auditing. **Positions commonly filled include:** Accountant/Auditor; Bookkeeper; Data Entry Clerk; EDP Specialist; Financial Analyst. Company pays fee. **Number of placements per year:** 200 - 499.

KEY PERSONNEL
1124 Fourth Avenue, Suite 300, Huntington WV 25701. 304/529-3377. **Contact:** Office Manager. **Description:** A full-service employment agency specializing in professional placements. Key Personnel usually focuses on placements within a 200-mile radius. **Specializes in the areas of:** Accounting/Auditing; Banking; Computer Science/Software; Engineering; Finance; Food Industry; General Management; Health/Medical; Industrial; Manufacturing; Personnel/Human Resources; Sales and Marketing; Technical and Scientific; Transportation. **Positions commonly filled include:** Accountant/Auditor; Adjuster; Bank Officer/Manager; Branch Manager; Chemical Engineer; Claim Representative; Computer Systems Analyst; Cost Estimator; Credit Manager; Customer Service Representative; Health Services Manager; Human Resources Specialist; Industrial Engineer; Management Trainee; Manufacturer's/Wholesaler's Sales Rep.; Mechanical Engineer; Mining Engineer; MIS Specialist; Purchasing Agent and Manager; Quality Control Supervisor; Restaurant/Food Service Manager; Services Sales Representative; Transportation/Traffic Specialist; Underwriter/Assistant Underwriter. **Number of placements per year:** 50 - 99. **Average salary range of placements:** $30,000 - $50,999.

CAROL McNEW EMPLOYMENT SERVICES
300 Moore Street, Suite C, Bristol VA 24201. 540/466-3318. **Contact:** Carol McNew, Owner. **Description:** Employment agency. **Positions commonly**

filled include: Accountant/Auditor; Administrative Assistant; Bank Officer/Manager; Bookkeeper; Clerk; Computer Operator; Computer Programmer; Credit Manager; Customer Service Representative; Data Entry Clerk; Factory Worker; General Manager; Insurance Agent/Broker; Medical Secretary; Nurse; Purchasing Agent and Manager; Quality Control Supervisor; Receptionist; Sales Representative; Secretary; Stenographer; Typist/Word Processor. Company pays fee. **Number of placements per year:** 100 - 199.

PAT MURPHY ASSOCIATES
2009 North 14th Street, Suite 301, Arlington VA 22201. 703/522-4441. **Fax:** 703/522-4456. **Contact:** Pat Murphy, Owner. **Description:** Employment agency. **Specializes in the areas of:** Accounting/Auditing; Administration/MIS/EDP; Legal; Non-Profit; Personnel/Labor Relations; Retail; Sales and Marketing; Secretarial. **Positions commonly filled include:** Accountant/Auditor; Administrative Services Manager; Advertising Clerk; Biological Scientist/Biochemist; Buyer; Chemist; Clerical Supervisor; Customer Service Representative; Services Sales Representative.

PAE PLACEMENT
1601 North Kent Street, Suite 900, Arlington VA 22209. 703/243-6464. **Fax:** 703/243-5607. **Contact:** Manager. **Description:** Employment agency. **Specializes in the areas of:** Bilingual; International Executives.

PAUL-TITTLE ASSOCIATES, INC.
1485 Chain Bridge Road, Suite 304, McLean VA 22101-4501. 703/442-0500. **Fax:** 703/893-3871. **Contact:** Manager. **Description:** Employment agency. **Specializes in the areas of:** Computer Science/Software; Electronics; Engineering; Sales and Marketing; Telecommunications.

POTOMAC PERSONNEL
1640 King Street, Suite A, Alexandria VA 22314. 703/549-5055. **Contact:** Chandra Pappas, Branch Manager. **Description:** Employment agency. **Specializes in the areas of:** Clerical; Personnel/Labor Relations. **Positions commonly filled include:** Administrative Assistant; Bookkeeper; Clerk; Computer Operator; Data Entry Clerk; Legal Secretary; Medical Secretary; Receptionist; Secretary; Stenographer; Typist/Word Processor. Company pays fee.

PROFESSIONAL CAREER CONSULTANTS
319 William Street, Fredericksburg VA 22401. 703/371-8608. **Fax:** 703/371-0764. **Contact:** Christine Garber, Manager. **Description:** Employment agency. **Specializes in the areas of:** Insurance.

SNELLING PERSONNEL SERVICES
45 West Boscawen Street, Winchester VA 22601-4750. 703/667-1911. **Fax:** 703/667-0505. **Contact:** C. Lynn Weakley, Jr., Owner/Manager. **Description:** Employment agency. **Specializes in the areas of:** Accounting/Auditing; Administration/MIS/EDP; Art/Design; Banking; Education; Engineering; Food Industry; Health/Medical; Legal; Manufacturing; Personnel/Labor Relations; Printing/Publishing; Retail; Sales and Marketing; Secretarial; Technical and Scientific. **Positions commonly filled include:** Accountant/Auditor; Administrative Services Manager; Aerospace Engineer; Attorney; Bank Officer/Manager; Branch Manager; Buyer; Ceramics Engineer; Chemical Engineer; Civil Engineer; Electrical/Electronics Engineer; Health Services Manager; Hotel Manager/Assistant Manager; Human Resources Specialist; Industrial Engineer; Industrial Production Manager; Library Technician; Management Trainee; Manufacturer's/Wholesaler's Sales Rep.; Materials Engineer; Mechanical Engineer; Metallurgical Engineer; Occupational Therapist; Paralegal; Purchasing Agent and Manager; Registered Nurse; Respiratory Therapist; Services Sales Representative; Teacher; Wholesale and Retail Buyer. **Number of placements per year:** 100 - 199.

TEAM PLACEMENT SERVICE, INC.
5113 Leesburg Pike, Suite 510, Falls Church VA 22041. 703/820-8618. **Contact:** Betty Peebles, Manager. **Description:** Employment agency. **Specializes in the areas of:** Health/Medical.

TECHNICAL SEARCH CORPORATION
7400 Beaufont Springs Drive, Suite 425, Richmond VA 23225. 804/323-3000. **Fax:** 804/330-9378. **Contact:** Mr. W.J. Kymmell, President. **Description:** Employment agency. **Specializes in the areas of:** Computer Science/Software. **Positions commonly filled include:** Computer Programmer; Computer Systems Analyst; Software Engineer. **Number of placements per year:** 50 - 99.

VANTAGE PERSONNEL, INC.
2300 Clarendon Boulevard, Suite 1109, Arlington VA 22201. 703/247-4100. **Fax:** 703/247-4102. **Contact:** Mary Ann Wilkinson, CPC, President. **Description:** Employment agency. **Specializes in the areas of:** Administration/MIS/EDP; Computer Science/Software; Office Support; Telecommunications. **Positions commonly filled include:** Administrator; Management; Secretary; Typist/Word Processor.

WANNAMAKER ASSOCIATES INC.
P.O. Box 5699, Richmond VA 23220. 804/358-0091. **Contact:** Bill Wannamaker, President. **Description:** Employment agency. **Specializes in the areas of:** Engineering; Manufacturing; Personnel/Labor Relations; Technical and Scientific. **Positions commonly filled include:** Aerospace Engineer; Ceramics Engineer; Chemical Engineer; Draftsperson; Electrical Engineer; Electronics Engineer; Industrial Designer; Industrial Engineer; Machinist; Manufacturing Engineer; Mechanical Engineer; Metallurgical Engineer; Operations/Production Manager; Packaging Engineer; Quality Control Supervisor; Software Engineer. Company pays fee. **Number of placements per year:** 50 - 99.

BILL YOUNG & ASSOCIATES
8550 Arlington Boulevard, Suite 202, Fairfax VA 22031. 703/573-0200. **Fax:** 703/573-3612. **Contact:** Bill Young, Owner. **Description:** Employment agency. **Specializes in the areas of:** Administration/MIS/EDP; Computer Science/Software; Electronics; Engineering; Manufacturing; Packaging; Telecommunications.

EXECUTIVE SEARCH FIRMS

ABILITY RESOURCES, INC.
716 Church Street, Alexandria VA 22314. 703/548-6400. **Contact:** Noel L. Ruppert, President. **Description:** Executive search firm. **Specializes in the areas of:** Administration/MIS/EDP; Computer Science/Software; Defense Industry; Economics; Engineering; Finance; General Management; Non-Profit; Personnel/Labor Relations; Sales and Marketing; Technical and Scientific. **Positions commonly filled include:** Accountant/Auditor; Administrative Services Manager; Computer Programmer; Computer Systems Analyst; Economist/Market Research Analyst; Engineer; Financial Analyst; General Manager; Management Analyst/Consultant; Mathematician; Operations/Production Manager; Public Relations Specialist; Statistician; Technical Writer; Technical Editor. Company pays fee. **Number of placements per year:** 1 - 49.

THE BEST AGENCY
2905 Lamkin Way, Charlottesville VA 22901. 804/978-7748. **Fax:** 804/978-7387. **Contact:** James N. Best, President. **Description:** Executive search firm.

Places senior management people in the hotel industry. The Best Agency was founded in 1985. **Positions commonly filled include:** Accountant/Auditor; Hotel Manager/ Assistant Manager. Company pays fee. **Corporate headquarters location:** This Location. **Other U.S. locations:** Worldwide. **Number of placements per year:** 1 - 49. **Average salary of placements:** More than $50,000.

CAREER REGISTRY
1600 East Little Creek Road, Norfolk VA 23518-4136. **Contact:** Office Manager. **Description:** Executive search firm. Career Registry is an employment agency that works on both a contingency and retainer basis. **Specializes in the areas of:** Engineering; Manufacturing. **Positions commonly filled include:** Accountant/Auditor; Biomedical Engineer; Chemical Engineer; Computer Programmer; Computer Systems Analyst; Electrical/Electronics Engineer; Electrician; Environmental Engineer; Industrial Engineer; Manufacturer's/Wholesaler's Sales Rep.; Mechanical Engineer; Software Engineer.

CASE GROUP EXECUTIVE SEARCH
10260 Epsilon Road, Richmond VA 23235. 804/272-8272. **Contact:** Richard J. Velzy, Managing Partner. **Description:** Executive search firm. **Specializes in the areas of:** Accounting/Auditing; Architecture/Construction/Real Estate; Economics; Engineering; Manufacturing; Sales and Marketing. **Positions commonly filled include:** Attorney; Civil Engineer; Electrical/Electronics Engineer; Food Scientist/Technologist; General Manager; Industrial Engineer; Mechanical Engineer; Metallurgical Engineer; Purchasing Agent and Manager; Software Developer. Company pays fee. **Number of placements per year:** 1 - 49.

CORPORATE CONNECTION LTD.
7204 Glen Forest Drive, Richmond VA 23226-3778. 804/288-8844. **Contact:** Marshall W. Rotella, Jr., President. **Description:** Executive search firm. Founded in 1980, Corporate Connection is a full-service recruiting firm. **Specializes in the areas of:** Accounting/Auditing; Administration/MIS/EDP; Banking; Computer Science/Software; Engineering; Finance; General Management; Industrial; Insurance; Legal; Manufacturing; Non-Profit; Personnel/Labor Relations; Printing/Publishing; Retail; Sales and Marketing; Secretarial; Technical and Scientific. **Positions commonly filled include:** Accountant/Auditor; Adjuster; Administrative Services Manager; Advertising Clerk; Aerospace Engineer; Agricultural Engineer; Aircraft Mechanic/Engine Specialist; Bank Officer/Manager; Biological Scientist/Biochemist; Biomedical Engineer; Blue-Collar Worker Supervisor; Branch Manager; Brokerage Clerk; Budget Analyst; Buyer; Chemical Engineer; Chemist; Civil Engineer; Claim Representative; Clerical Supervisor; Clinical Lab Technician; Computer Programmer; Computer Systems Analyst; Construction Contractor and Manager; Cost Estimator; Credit Manager; Customer Service Representative; Design Engineer; Designer; Draftsperson; Electrical/Electronics Engineer; Environmental Engineer; Financial Analyst; General Manager; Human Resources Specialist; Industrial Engineer; Industrial Production Manager; Insurance Agent/Broker; Librarian; Library Technician; Management Analyst/Consultant; Management Trainee; Manufacturer's/Wholesaler's Sales Rep.; Market Research Analyst; Mechanical Engineer; Medical Records Technician; Metallurgical Engineer; Mining Engineer; Property and Real Estate Manager; Public Relations Specialist; Purchasing Agent and Manager; Quality Control Supervisor; Restaurant/Food Service Manager; Securities Sales Rep.; Services Sales Representative; Software Engineer; Strategic Relations Manager; Structural Engineer; Transportation/Traffic Specialist; Travel Agent; Typist/Word Processor; Underwriter/Assistant Underwriter; Urban/Regional Planner. **Corporate headquarters location:** This Location **Number of placements per year:** 200 - 499. **Average salary range of placements:** $20,000 - $50,000.

CAROL DAY AND ASSOCIATES
2105 Electric Road Southwest, Roanoke VA 24018. 540/989-2831. **Fax:** 540/989-5910. **Contact:** Carol Day, Owner. **Description:** Established in 1989, this is both an executive search firm and a permanent professional placement agency. **Specializes in the areas of:** Accounting/ Auditing; Administration/MIS/EDP; Computer Science/Software; Engineering; Health/Medical; Manufacturing; Retail; Sales and Marketing; Secretarial. **Positions commonly filled include:** Accountant/Auditor; Buyer; Chemical Engineer; Civil Engineer; Clerical Supervisor; Computer Programmer; Customer Service Representative; Electrical/Electronics Engineer; Hotel Manager/Assistant Manager; Industrial Engineer; Management Trainee; Mechanical Engineer; MIS Specialist; Paralegal; Quality Control Supervisor; Software Engineer. Company pays fee. **Number of placements per year:** 200 - 499. **Corporate headquarters location:** This Location. **Average salary range of placements:** $20,000 - $29,999.

DONMAC ASSOCIATES
P.O. Box 2541, Reston VA 22090. 703/620-2866. **Fax:** 703/620-2867. **Contact:** Connie Andersen, President. **Description:** Executive search firm. **Specializes in the areas of:** Computer Science/Software. **Positions commonly filled include:** Computer Programmer; Computer Systems Analyst; Electrical/Electronics Engineer; Software Engineer. Company pays fee. **Number of placements per year:** 50 - 99.

DUNHILL PROFESSIONAL SEARCH
8100 Three Chopt Road, Suite 133, Richmond VA 23229-4833. 804/282-2216. **Contact:** P. Frank Lassiter, President. **Description:** Executive search firm. Founded in 1974. Dunhill Professional Search operates on both a retainer and contingency basis. **Specializes in the areas of:** Banking; Engineering. **Positions commonly filled include:** Bank Officer/Manager; Chemical Engineer; Design Engineer; Industrial Engineer; Mechanical Engineer; Securities Sales Rep.; Trust Officer. Company pays fee. **Number of placements per year:** 1 - 49. **Average salary range of placements:** $30,000-$50,000.

EXECUTIVE RECRUITERS
1907 Clarks Glen Place, Vienna VA 22182. 703/556-9580. **Contact:** Joe Segal, President. **Description:** Executive search firm. **Specializes in the areas of:** Food Industry; Hotel/Restaurant. **Positions commonly filled include:** Hotel Manager/Assistant Manager; Restaurant/Food Service Manager. Company pays fee. **Number of placements per year:** 50 - 99.

EXECUTIVE SALES SEARCH
8232 Ammonett Drive, Richmond VA 23235. 804/560-7327. **Fax:** 804/560-7564. **Contact:** David W. Bell, President. **Description:** Executive Sales Search is an independent recruiting firm with 20 years' experience in placing professionals. The company recruits nationally for positions in sales and marketing, including senior level officers, and is committed to providing companies with experienced professional candidates at all levels. Additionally, Executive Sales Search is a member of one of the nation's largest, most prestigious networking organizations for independent recruiters and is able to access and input to the resources of over 600 of its affiliate offices nationwide. The company operates on a contingency basis and also acts as a contract services firm. **Specializes in the areas of:** Sales and Marketing. **Positions commonly filled include:** Branch Manager; General Manager; Manufacturer's/Wholesaler's Sales Rep. Company pays fee. **Corporate headquarters location:** This Location. **Other U.S. locations:** Nationwide. **Number of placements per year:** 100 - 199. **Average salary range of placements:** more than $50,000.

INFORMATION SPECIALISTS, INC.
5 South Hampton Road, Suite 6, Virginia Beach VA 23452-7513. 804/340-0022. **Fax:** 804/340-1505. **Contact:** Hugo E. Schluter, CPC, Senior Vice

President. **Description:** Executive search firm. **Specializes in the areas of:** Computer Science/Software; Engineering; Industrial; Manufacturing; Technical and Scientific. **Positions commonly filled include:** Aerospace Engineer; Biomedical Engineer; Chemical Engineer; Civil Engineer; Computer Systems Analyst; Construction and Building Inspector; Electrical/Electronics Engineer; Geologist/Geophysicist; Industrial Engineer; Mechanical Engineer; Metallurgical Engineer; Nuclear Engineer; Quality Control Supervisor; Science Technologist; Software Engineer; Stationary Engineer; Structural Engineer; Technical Writer/Editor. Company pays fee. **Number of placements per year:** 1 - 49.

KOGEN PERSONNEL
127 Danville Avenue, Colonial Heights VA 23805. 804/526-0870. **Fax:** 804/526-0869. **Contact:** A.B. Porter, Management. **Description:** Established in 1967, this is a nationwide temporary and executive search firm. **Specializes in the areas of:** Computer Science/Software; Engineering; Food Industry; General Management; Retail; Sales and Marketing; Technical and Scientific. **Positions commonly filled include:** Accountant/Auditor; Administrative Services Manager; Attorney; Bank Officer/Manager; Biological Scientist/Biochemist; Blue-Collar Worker Supervisor; Branch Manager; Buyer; Chemist; Claim Representative; Clerical Supervisor; Computer Programmer; Computer Systems Analyst; Construction and Building Inspector; Counselor; Credit Manager; Customer Service Representative; Draftsperson; Economist/Market Research Analyst; Education Administrator; Electrical/Electronics Engineer; Electrician; Financial Analyst; Food Scientist/Technologist; General Manager; Health Services Manager; Hotel Manager/Assistant Manager; Human Resources Specialist; Industrial Engineer; Industrial Production Manager; Insurance Agent/Broker; Landscape Architect; Librarian; Library Technician; Licensed Practical Nurse; Management Analyst/Consultant; Management Trainee; Manufacturer's/Wholesaler's Sales Rep.; Mechanical Engineer; Medical Records Technician; Paralegal; Pharmacist; Physical Therapist; Physician; Property and Real Estate Manager; Public Relations Specialist; Purchasing Agent and Manager; Quality Control Supervisor; Radio/TV Announcer/Broadcaster; Radiological Technologist; Real Estate Agent; Recreational Therapist; Registered Nurse; Reporter; Respiratory Therapist; Restaurant/Food Service Manager; Science Technologist; Securities Sales Rep.; Services Sales Representative; Social Worker; Sociologist; Software Engineer; Surveyor; Teacher; Technical Writer/Editor; Telecommunications Manager; Transportation/Traffic Specialist; Travel Agent; Typist/Word Processor; Underwriter/Assistant Underwriter; Veterinarian. **Corporate headquarters location:** This Location. **Number of placements per year:** 100 - 199. **Average salary range of placements:** $20,000 - $29,999.

MANAGEMENT RECRUITERS OF LEESBURG
44084 Riverside Parkway, Suite 170, Leesburg VA 22075-5102. 703/729-5600. **Contact:** Account Executive. **Description:** Executive search firm. **Specializes in the areas of:** Engineering; Health/Medical. **Positions commonly filled include:** Chemical Engineer.

MANAGEMENT RECRUITERS OF MANASSAS
8807 Sudley Road, Suite 208, Manassas VA 22110-4719. 703/330-1830. **Contact:** Professional Placement. **Description:** Executive search firm. **Specializes in the areas of:** Accounting/Auditing; Administration/MIS/EDP; Advertising; Architecture/Construction/Real Estate; Banking; Communications; Computer Hardware/Software; Design; Electrical; Engineering; Finance; Food Industry; General Management; Health/Medical; Insurance; Legal; Manufacturing; Operations Management; Personnel/Labor Relations; Printing/Publishing; Procurement; Retail; Sales and Marketing; Technical and Scientific; Textiles; Transportation.

MANAGEMENT RECRUITERS OF McLEAN
6849 Old Dominion Drive, Suite 225, McLean VA 22101. 703/442-4842. **Contact:** Howard Reitkopp, Manager. **Description:** Executive search firm. **Specializes in the areas of:** Accounting/Auditing; Administration/MIS/EDP; Advertising; Architecture/Construction/Real Estate; Banking; Communications; Computer Hardware/Software; Design; Electrical; Engineering; Finance; Food Industry; General Management; Health/Medical; Insurance; Legal; Manufacturing; Operations Management; Personnel/Labor Relations; Printing/Publishing; Procurement; Retail; Sales and Marketing; Technical and Scientific; Textiles; Transportation.

MANAGEMENT RECRUITERS OF ROANOKE
1960 Electric Road, Suite B, Roanoke VA 24018. 703/989-1676. **Contact:** Paul Sharp, Manager. **Description:** Executive search firm. **Specializes in the areas of:** Accounting/Auditing; Administration/MIS/EDP; Advertising; Architecture/Construction/ Real Estate; Banking; Communications; Computer Hardware/Software; Design; Electrical; Engineering; Finance; Food Industry; General Management; Health/Medical; Insurance; Legal; Manufacturing; Operations Management; Personnel/Labor Relations; Printing/Publishing; Procurement; Retail; Sales and Marketing; Technical and Scientific; Textiles; Transportation.

MID-ATLANTIC SEARCH
P.O. Box 62162, Virginia Beach VA 23466. 804/456-2244. **Fax:** 804/456-0220. **Contact:** Jerry Kiehne, President. **Description:** Executive search firm. **Specializes in the areas of:** Engineering; Manufacturing. **Positions commonly filled include:** Chemical Engineer; Chemist; Civil Engineer; Electrical/Electronics Engineer; Industrial Engineer; Materials Engineer; Mechanical Engineer; Nuclear Engineer; Structural Engineer. Company pays fee. **Number of placements per year:** 1 - 49.

NORRELL SERVICES
9011 Arboretum Parkway, Richmond VA 23236. 804/272-5000. **Fax:** 804/272-7882. **Contact:** Meike Smith, Area Services Manager. **Description:** Founded in 1961, Norrell Services is a nationwide temporary, executive search, and contract services agency. The company has 350 locations throughout North America. **Specializes in the areas of:** Accounting/Auditing; Administration/MIS/EDP; Advertising; Banking; Computer Hardware/ Software; Engineering; Finance; Food Industry; General Management; Manufacturing; Personnel/Labor Relations; Sales and Marketing; Secretarial; Technical and Scientific. **Positions commonly filled include:** Accountant/Auditor; Administrative Services Manager; Architect; Biological Scientist/Biochemist; Biomedical Engineer; Blue-Collar Worker Supervisor; Branch Manager; Budget Analyst; Buyer; Chemical Engineer; Chemist; Civil Engineer; Claim Representative; Clerical Supervisor; Clinical Lab Technician; Computer Programmer; Computer Systems Analyst; Cost Estimator; Customer Service Representative; Design Engineer; Designer; Draftsperson; Editor; Electrical/Electronics Engineer; Electrician; Environmental Engineer; Financial Analyst; General Manager; Human Resources Specialist; Human Service Worker; Industrial Engineer; Industrial Production Manager; Internet Services Manager; Management Trainee; Mechanical Engineer; Medical Records Technician; Metallurgical Engineer; MIS Specialist; Multimedia Designer; Operations/Production Manager; Paralegal; Purchasing Agent and Manager; Quality Control Supervisor; Restaurant/Food Service Manager; Services Sales Representative; Software Engineer; Statistician; Structural Engineer; Typist/Word Processor. Company pays fee. **Benefits available for contract workers:** 401K; Health insurance; Dental Insurance; Vacation; Holidays. **Corporate headquarters location:** Atlanta GA. **Number of placements per year:** 1000+. **Average salary range of placements:** $20,000 - $29,999.

OERTH ASSOCIATES, INC.
601 King Street, Suite 400, Alexandria VA 22314. 703/739-1348. **Fax:** 703/739-1349. **Contact:** Lorraine C. Oerth, President. **Description:** Executive search firm. **Specializes in the areas of:** Construction; Real Estate. **Positions commonly filled include:** Construction Contractor and Manager; Estimator; Property and Real Estate Manager; Superintendent. Company pays fee. **Number of placements per year:** 50 - 99.

PLACEMENT PROFESSIONALS INC.
P.O. Box 29772, Richmond VA 23242. 804/741-1246. **Contact:** Manager. **Description:** Executive search firm. **Specializes in the areas of:** Accounting/Auditing; Advertising; Banking; Computer Hardware/Software; Economics; Engineering; Finance; Health/Medical; Insurance; Legal; Manufacturing; Personnel/Labor Relations; Sales and Marketing; Technical and Scientific. **Positions commonly filled include:** Accountant/Auditor; Aerospace Engineer; Agricultural Engineer; Attorney; Bank Officer/Manager; Biological Scientist/Biochemist; Biomedical Engineer; Budget Analyst; Buyer; Chemical Engineer; Civil Engineer; Computer Programmer; Computer Systems Analyst; Controller; Credit Manager; Economist/Market Research Analyst; Electrical/Electronics Engineer; Financial Analyst; Human Resources Specialist; Industrial Engineer; Mechanical Engineer; Metallurgical Engineer; Nuclear Engineer; Occupational Therapist; Petroleum Engineer; Pharmacist; Physical Therapist; Public Relations Specialist; Purchasing Agent and Manager; Registered Nurse; Software Engineer; Speech-Language Pathologist; Stationary Engineer; Structural Engineer; Technical Writer/Editor; Underwriter/Assistant Underwriter; Wholesale and Retail Buyer. Company pays fee.

PROFESSIONAL SEARCH PERSONNEL
4900 Leesburg Pike, Suite 402, Alexandria VA 22302-1103. **Contact:** Chuck Cherel, Owner/Manager. **Description:** Founded in 1974, this executive search firm works on both a retainer and contingency basis and only handles permanent positions. **Specializes in the areas of:** Accounting/Auditing; Administration/MIS/EDP; Architecture/Construction/Real Estate; Banking; Biology; Computer Hardware/Software; Engineering; Finance; Health/Medical; Industrial; Personnel/Labor Relations; Technical and Scientific. **Positions commonly filled include:** Accountant/Auditor; Actuary; Aerospace Engineer; Architect; Bank Officer/Manager; Biological Scientist/Biochemist; Biomedical Engineer; Buyer; Chemical Engineer; Chemist; Computer Programmer; Computer Systems Analyst; Cost Estimator; Credit Manager; Design Engineer; Designer; Draftsperson; Electrical/Electronics Engineer; Environmental Engineer; Financial Analyst; Geologist/Geophysicist; Human Resources Specialist; Industrial Engineer; Internet Services Manager; Manufacturer's/Wholesaler's Sales Rep.; Mechanical Engineer; Metallurgical Engineer; MIS Specialist; Nuclear Engineer; Occupational Therapist; Petroleum Engineer; Physical Therapist; Quality Control Supervisor; Respiratory Therapist; Securities Sales Rep.; Software Engineer. Company pays fee. **Corporate headquarters location:** This Location. **Number of placements per year:** 50 - 99. **Average salary range of placements:** $50,000+.

DON RICHARD ASSOCIATES OF RICHMOND
7275 Glen Forest Drive, Suite 200, Richmond VA 23226-3772. 804/282-6300. **Fax:** 804/282-6792. **Jobline:** 804/282-1177. **Contact:** Mike Beck, MIS Director. **E-mail address:** dranet@i2020.net. **World Wide Web address:** http://donrichard.com. **Description:** Executive search firm. Established in 1978, this is the third of twelve nationwide offices to open along the East Coast. The company specializes in permanent and temporary placement of accounting and information systems professionals. **Specializes in the areas of:** Accounting/Auditing; Administration/MIS/EDP; Computer Science/

Software; Finance; Secretarial. **Positions commonly filled include:** Accountant/Auditor; Administrative Services Manager; Budget Analyst; Clerical Supervisor; Computer Programmer; Computer Systems Analyst; Credit Manager; Design Engineer; Financial Analyst; Internet Services Manager; Management Analyst/Consultant; MIS Specialist; Multimedia Designer; Operations/Production Manager; Quality Control Supervisor; Services Sales Representative; Software Engineer; Technical Writer/Editor; Telecommunications Manager; Typist/Word Processor. Company pays fee. **Corporate headquarters location:** This Location. **Other U.S. locations:** Atlanta GA; Charlotte NC; Norfolk VA; Tampa FL; Washington DC. **Number of placements per year:** 50 - 99. **Average salary range of placements:** $30,000 - $50,000.

SOURCE SERVICES
8614 Westwood Center Drive, Suite 750, Vienna VA 22182. 703/790-5610. **Contact:** Manager. **Description:** Executive search firm. **Specializes in the areas of:** Computer Science/Software.

VIRGINIA EMPLOYMENT REFERRAL
6767 Forest Hill Avenue, Richmond VA 23225-1856. 804/560-9242. **Fax:** 804/560-7108. **Contact:** Bill Auchmoody, Vice President. **E-mail address:** varefr19@mail.us.net. **Description:** Executive search firm. Virginia Employment Referral is also a full-service employment agency, with operations based in Richmond. **Specializes in the areas of:** Accounting/Auditing; Administration/MIS/EDP; Advertising; Banking; Engineering; Food Industry; General Management; Manufacturing; Personnel/Labor Relations; Sales and Marketing; Secretarial; Technical and Scientific. **Positions commonly filled include:** Accountant/Auditor; Bank Officer/Manager; Blue-Collar Worker Supervisor; Branch Manager; Civil Engineer; Computer Programmer; Electrical/Electronics Engineer; Financial Analyst; General Manager; Industrial Engineer; Management Trainee; Manufacturer's/Wholesaler's Sales Rep.; Mechanical Engineer; MIS Specialist; Operations/Production Manager; Purchasing Agent and Manager; Restaurant/Food Service Manager; Services Sales Representative; Telecommunications Manager. Company pays fee. **Corporate headquarters location:** This Location. **Number of placements per year:** 100 - 199. **Average salary range of placements:** $30,000 - $50,000.

WISDOM & WILLIAMS ASSOCIATES, INC.
205 South Whiting Street, Suite 204, Alexandria VA 22304. 202/457-0617. **Fax:** 202/463-0350. **Contact:** Deborah Williams, President. **Description:** Executive search firm. **Specializes in the areas of:** Health/Medical; Legal; Non-Profit. **Positions commonly filled include:** Administrative Assistant; Clerk; Receptionist; Secretary; Typist/Word Processor. Company pays fee. **Number of placements per year:** 50 - 99.

RESUME/CAREER COUNSELING SERVICES

ACTION RESUMES
RUTKALS RESUMES
218 Light Road, Winchester VA 22603-2028. 703/888-3790. **Contact:** Mike Rutkals, Owner. **Description:** Action Resumes provides career/outplacement counseling services

IMAGE ARCHITECTURE
1600 South Joyce Street, Suite 1600, Arlington VA 22202. 703/979-9001. **Contact:** Eric Lazar, Owner. **Description:** Image Architecture is a

career/outplacement counseling agency. **Specializes in the areas of:** Non-Specialized. **Number of placements per year:** 100 - 199.

ERICH NORD ASSOCIATES
6801 Whittier Avenue, McLean VA 22101. 703/556-9505. **Contact:** Joan Wikstrom, Principal. **Description:** Firm specializes in Career/Outplacement Counseling.

INDEX OF PRIMARY EMPLOYERS

NOTE: *Below is an alphabetical index of primary employer listings included in this book. Those employers in each industry that fall under the headings "Additional employers" are not indexed here.*

A

B

N

O

P

Q, R

V

W

X, Y, Z

Your Job Hunt
Your Feedback

Comments, questions, or suggestions? We want to hear from you. Please complete this questionnaire and mail it to:

The JobBank Staff
Adams Media Corporation
260 Center Street
Holbrook, MA 02343

Did this book provide helpful advice and valuable information which you used in your job search? Was the information easy to access?

Recommendations for improvements. How could we improve this book to help in your job search? No suggestion is too small or too large.

Would you recommend this book to a friend beginning a job hunt?

Name: ______________________________

Occupation: ______________________________

Which JobBank did you use? ______________________________

Address: ______________________________

Daytime phone: ______________________________

Other Adams Media Books

The Adams Jobs Almanac

Updated annually, *The Adams Jobs Almanac* includes names and addresses of over 7,000 leading employers; information on which jobs each company commonly fills; industry forecasts; geographical cross-references; a look at over 90 popular professions; a detailed forecast of 21st-century careers; and advice on preparing resumes and standing out at interviews. $5^1/_2$" x $8^1/_2$", 916 pages, paperback, $15.95.

The JobBank Series

There are 30 local *JobBank* books, each providing extensive, up-to-date employment information on hundreds of the largest employers in each job market. The #1 best-selling series of employment directories, the *JobBank* series has been recommended as an excellent place to begin your job search by the *New York Times*, the *Los Angeles Times*, the *Boston Globe*, and the *Chicago Tribune*. *JobBank* books have been used by millions of people to find jobs. Titles available:

The Atlanta JobBank • *The Austin/San Antonio JobBank* • *The Boston JobBank* • *The Carolina JobBank* • *The Chicago JobBank* • *The Cincinnati JobBank* • *The Cleveland JobBank* • *The Dallas-Fort Worth JobBank* • *The Denver JobBank* • *The Detroit JobBank* • *The Florida JobBank* • *The Houston JobBank* • *The Indianapolis JobBank* • *The Las Vegas JobBank* • *The Los Angeles JobBank* • *The Minneapolis-St. Paul JobBank* • *The Missouri JobBank* • *The Northern New England JobBank* • *The New Mexico JobBank* • *The Metropolitan New York JobBank* • *The Upstate New York JobBank* • *The Greater Philadelphia JobBank* • *The Phoenix JobBank* • *The Pittsburgh JobBank* • *The Portland JobBank* • *The San Francisco Bay Area JobBank* • *The Seattle JobBank* • *The Tennessee JobBank* • *The Virginia JobBank* • *The Metropolitan Washington, DC JobBank*

Each JobBank book is 6" x $9^1/_4$", at least 320 pages, paperback, $16.95.

Available Wherever Books Are Sold

If you cannot find these titles at your favorite retail outlet, you may order them directly from the publisher. BY PHONE: Call 1-800-872-5627 (in Massachusetts 617-767-8100). We accept Visa, Mastercard, and American Express. $4.50 will be added to your total order for shipping and handling. BY MAIL: Write out the full titles of the books you'd like to order and send payment, including $4.50 for shipping and handling, to: Adams Media Corporation, 260 Center Street, Holbrook, MA 02343. 30-day money-back guarantee.

Visit our exciting career and employment site at http://www.adamsjobbank.com

Other Adams Media Books

The Adams Cover Letter Almanac

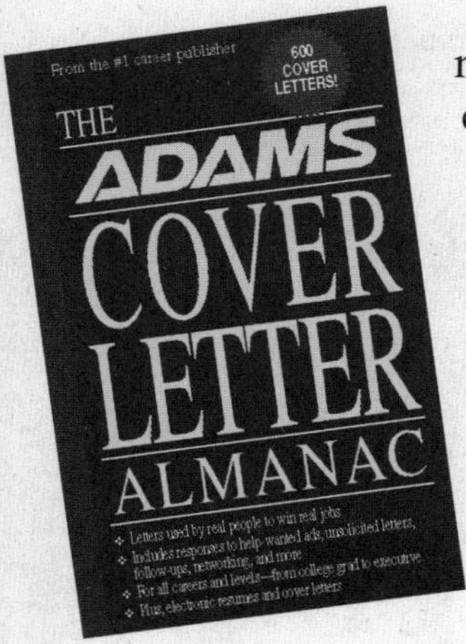

The Adams Cover Letter Almanac is the most detailed cover letter resource in print, containing 600 cover letters used by real people to win real jobs. It features complete information on all types of letters, including networking, "cold," broadcast, and follow-up. In addition to advice on how to avoid fatal cover letter mistakes, the book includes strategies for people changing careers, relocating, recovering from layoff, and more. 5½" x 8½", 736 pages, paperback, $10.95.

The Adams Resume Almanac

This almanac features detailed information on resume development and layout, a review of the pros and cons of various formats, an exhaustive look at the strategies that will definitely get a resume noticed, and 600 sample resumes in dozens of career categories. *The Adams Resume Almanac* is the most comprehensive, thoroughly researched resume guide ever published. 5½" x 8½", 768 pages, paperback, $10.95.

Available Wherever Books Are Sold

If you cannot find these titles at your favorite retail outlet, you may order them directly from the publisher. BY PHONE: Call 1-800-872-5627 (in Massachusetts 617-767-8100). We accept Visa, Mastercard, and American Express. $4.50 will be added to your total order for shipping and handling. BY MAIL: Write out the full titles of the books you'd like to order and send payment, including $4.50 for shipping and handling, to: Adams Media Corporation, 260 Center Street, Holbrook, MA 02343. 30-day money-back guarantee.

Visit our exciting career and employment site at http://www.adamsjobbank.com